# Portfolio of Business Forms, Agreements, and Contracts

# Portfolio of Business Forms, Agreements, and Contracts

Valera Grapp
J.D., LL.M.

Prentice-Hall, Inc.
Englewood Cliffs, New Jersey

Prentice-Hall International, Inc., *London*
Prentice-Hall of Australia, Pty. Ltd., *Sydney*
Prentice-Hall Canada, Inc., *Toronto*
Prentice-Hall of India Private Ltd., *New Delhi*
Prentice-Hall of Japan, Inc., *Tokyo*
Prentice-Hall of Southeast Asia Pte. Ltd., *Singapore*
Whitehall Books, Ltd., *Wellington, New Zealand*
Editora Prentice-Hall do Brasil Ltda., *Rio de Janeiro*


© 1985 by
Prentice-Hall, Inc.
Englewood Cliffs, N.J.

Second Printing . . . . . November 1987

This publication is designed to provide accurate and authoritative information in regard to the subject matter covered. It is sold with the understanding that the publisher is not engaged in rendering legal, accounting, or other professional service. If legal advice or other expert assistance is required, the services of a competent professional person should be sought.

*. . . From the Declaration of Principles jointly adopted by a Committee of the American Bar Association and a Committee of Publishers and Associations.*

**Library of Congress Cataloging in Publication Data**

Grapp, Valera
  Portfolio of business forms, agreements, and contracts.

  Includes index.
  1. Contracts—United States—Forms.  2. Corporation law—United States—Forms.  I. Title.
  KF801.A65G68    1984      346.73′02′0269      84-11647
                            347.30620269

ISBN 0-13-686791-X

Printed in the United States of America

# About the Author

Valera Grapp's distinguished career spans four decades of law practice and practical business experience. Ms. Grapp received her law degree from the University of Pittsburgh in 1941 and was admitted to the Pennsylvania bar in 1942. In the following year she was admitted to practice before the federal courts and, in 1945, to the Supreme Court of the United States. She earned her master of laws degree in trade regulation from New York University in 1959.

Her business experience is equally comprehensive. In the 1960s she was president of the J. M. Hoffmann Company, a Pittsburgh-based, family-owned corporation. In addition, she has served as contract negotiator for the United States Air Force Air Materiel Command and as trust administrator for a major Pittsburgh bank. For 15 years Ms. Grapp served as general counsel and secretary of an expanding interstate business corporation, where her responsibilities included contract drafting, negotiation, and corporate mergers and consolidations.

Ms. Grapp is a member of the American Bar Association and now lives in Florida, where she does consulting and legal research for other attorneys. Her work focuses on new developments in all phases of contract law and its modern administrative regulation. She is the author of two books previously published by Prentice-Hall: the *Paralegal's Encyclopedic Dictionary* and the *Law Office Desk Book*.

DEDICATED IN MEMORY OF
my father and mother
EDWARD HOFFMANN GRAPP and SARAH KEPLER GRAPP

# Special Thanks for Contributions

# What This Book Will Do for You

The *Portfolio of Business Forms, Agreements, and Contracts* is a comprehensive collection of legal forms that cover all key aspects of business operations. This easy-to-use, single-volume *Portfolio* has been carefully designed to save you hours of research and drafting time by putting literally hundreds of forms and agreements at your fingertips, all clearly identified and indexed for ready reference. Not only will the *Portfolio* streamline and simplify document drafting, it will also help you prepare sound contracts that clearly express the intent and purpose of the parties involved, thereby avoiding future litigation.

Here are just a few of the reasons why you'll find this *Portfolio* an invaluable aid in your work with business clients:

- It covers the entire spectrum of business operations, from forming, financing, and operating a modern business entity through drawing up employment contracts, service contracts, and leases to dissolving or terminating a business. The forms can be used as written or with minor adaptation in all states.
- It contains dozens of alternative clauses to help you tailor forms, agreements, and contracts to your business clients' particular needs.
- It is fully up to date on current trends in law and legal writing. Simplicity and clear legal language are the hallmark of these forms, and they are written to comply with new statutory, regulatory, and public policy requirements for business forms and agreements.
- It is fully cited to *American Jurisprudence 2d* and to recent federal statutes and regulations as well as the Uniform Commercial Code and other uniform acts adopted by the various states. In the Appendix you'll also find citations to ERISA and consumer practice legislation.

Perhaps best of all, this *Portfolio* makes it easier for you to delegate to your secretary or legal assistant the routine tasks involved in document drafting, leaving you more time to concentrate on the job you're trained to do: practice law. Here's how the *Portfolio* can help:

- Its quick-reference Index and Table of Contents make it easy for your staff to locate the right document fast and prepare a preliminary draft for your review.
- It includes forms, agreements, and contracts that are fully illustrated using sample names and data. These sample entries make it easy for your staff to understand and use the forms. Of course, you supply the actual terms after your investigation of the facts and legal issues involved in each case.

- It comes complete with easy-to-use client questionnaires to help you and your staff get the facts necessary to prepare each document. These questionnaires will help save legal and support staff time, enable you to get all necessary information during the initial client interview, and help make sure that nothing is overlooked.

The forms, agreements, and contracts included in this *Portfolio* have been prepared by attorneys and have been time-tested in legal and business practice. You'll refer to the *Portfolio* again and again for authoritative guidance whenever you draft business documents.

# How to Use This Book

The *Portfolio of Business Forms, Agreements, and Contracts* is divided into eight major areas, which are designated Parts: (Part I) contracts and forms concerning the ownership, powers, and liabilities of corporations; (Part II) contracts and forms concerning the ownership, powers, and liabilities of partnerships and joint ventures; (Part III) registration of sole proprietorships; (Part IV) contracts and forms involving employment; (Part V) contracts and forms for creating independent service and agency relationships; (Part VI) contracts and forms involving business personal property, including sales; (Part VII) contracts and forms concerning the ownership and use of business real estate, including modern mortgages, long-term lease agreements, condominium and cooperative documents; and (Part VIII) a miscellaneous Part that contains general and supplementary contracts and forms used in all areas of the law, such as acknowledgments, affidavits, escrow agreements, guaranties, options, releases, and satisfactions, among others. The miscellaneous Part also includes complete contract forms that involve combinations of areas of law, such as aircraft and airport contracts, loans and creditor compositions, options, and sales of businesses.

The Parts of the book are further divided into lettered Sections. For example, Part VII, Business Real Property Contracts, is divided into Subsections A through F. Subsection A of Part VII deals with Leases, Subsection B with Licenses and Easements, Subsection C with Sale or Purchase, Subsection D with Mortgages, Subsection E with Building Construction, and Subsection F with Condominiums and Cooperatives. The number of each form reflects the Part and Section in which it can be found, as Form VIIA 1.03 Lease for furniture store. That form appears as the third form in Section A of Part VII.

The Parts, Sections, and specific forms under each section are described in the detailed chapter Table of Contents. In addition to the detailed chapter Table of Contents, there is an alphabetical Index to the book.

The specific citations throughout the book to *American Jurisprudence 2d* and to federal and uniform laws are supplemented by the general subject citations to those laws which appear in the Appendixes to the book.

The Client Questionnaires throughout the book are designed to get the facts that are necessary to draft an accurate and appropriate contract on the particular subject of the questionnaire.

To get the most from the *Portfolio*, the following procedure is recommended:

1. Determine the general area of the legal problem.
2. Check the detailed chapter Table of Contents for that area to find the Introduction and Client Questionnaire applicable to the problem.

3. Read the Client Questionnaire and get that factual information from the client.

4. Check citations to *Am. Jur. 2d* contained in the Introduction and the Client Questionnaire to refresh memory as to the niceties of the general law affecting the problem, *if necessary.*

5. Check citations to statutes and government regulations to ensure applicable compliance, *if necessary.* For a quick citation to a uniform law that has been adopted by your state, check the Appendix listing state citations to the appropriate uniform law.

6. Check the detailed chapter Table of Contents for applicable form and alternative clauses or forms to suit the factual and legal situation that is now apparent.

If one will scan the *Portfolio* from cover to cover before using it, the above procedure will be easier to follow and one will find many other uses for the book.

# Contents

# PART I
# CORPORATIONS

# PART I

# Corporations

## INTRODUCTION

The documents in Part I are used to form, operate, or liquidate a business[1] or a not-for-profit[2] corporation.

Forms for use in forming partnerships, limited partnerships, and joint ventures instead of incorporating a business or profession are given in Part II.

Before drafting any document, read the Introduction and the Client Questionnaire for the appropriate Section of this book. A review of the Table of Contents for the Part of the book on the general subject will lead you to the appropriate Section.

Using the applicable Client Questionnaire will provide the *facts* that are to be considered before drafting the instrument.

The footnotes to the Introduction, Client Questionnaire, and the forms will alert you to possible problems and give you an overview of the *law* that affects the particular form.

For example, the following considerations may influence the choice of incorporating or forming some other legal relationship for the operating of a business or profession: requirement for filing annual corporation reports and tax returns, state income or franchise tax on corporations, the burden of keeping proper corporate action records to retain corporate limited liability and tax benefits, and possible double taxation for a closely held corporation. Consider whether a Subchapter S[3] corporation or Section 1244 stock[4] may make a corporation desirable. On the other hand, a limited partnership[5] may create a legitimate tax shelter for an individual above the 49 percent bracket. IRA[6] and Keogh[7] plans may be preferable to corporate retirement plans for the small-business owner.

The ownership, powers, rights, and liabilities of stockholders or shareholders are governed by the Articles of Incorporation (Charter) and by the bylaws of the corporation in conjunction with the corporation law of the state[8] in which the corporation is formed. It is important to check the business or nonprofit corporation law for the state of proposed incorporation before drafting the articles or charter and the bylaws. The sample forms in this book are appropriate for use in most states.

---

[1] *18 Am. Jur. 2d Corporations*, para. 21.
[2] *18 Am. Jur. 2d Corporations*, para. 10.
[3] 26 U.S.C.A. 1372.
[4] 26 U.S.C.A. 1244.
[5] Part IIB.
[6] Part IVA.
[7] Part IVA.
[8] *18 Am. Jur. 2d Corporations*, paras. 481–493.

Even though stock of the corporation is not offered for "public" sale, its ownership and transfer is regulated by the various state commercial codes, which generally follow Article 8 of the Uniform Commercial Code.[9]

The forms in this Part have been prepared for use by close corporations that do not offer stock for interstate or intrastate "public sale."

If a business corporation will offer stock for "public" sale, state "blue-sky laws" and federal securities statutes[10] and regulations must be consulted and be complied with before the stock is offered for sale.

Section 2 of Part I contains forms for use in acquiring or maintaining control of a corporation after it is formed. The section includes shareholders' agreements, mandatory buy-sell agreement, stock redemption and sale agreements. The Client Questionnaire Form IA 2.00 will get the facts necessary to choose the form desired for the transfer of stock or control of a business corporation.

Some states now have statutes allowing the creation of a hybrid corporation called Limited Liability Company. The Articles of Organization for the hybrid corporation follow the format of the sample Articles of Incorporation given in Part I Section A. The substance of the Articles of Organization must follow the state statute allowing the creation of the limited-liability company. The name must include the initials L.C. to distinguish it from an ordinary corporation or partnership.

## SECTION A          BUSINESS CORPORATIONS

The forms in Section A are for use in forming business corporations, regulating their stock ownership and dissolving them. The business corporation is distinguished from the relatively new professional corporation and the not-for-profit corporation which is used for charitable, educational and similar purposes. Section B covers professional corporations and Section C not-for-profit corporations.

The Subchapter S Revision Act of 1982 simplifies the eligibility requirements and operation of Subchapter S business corporations, making them a more useful form of ownership for some businesses. Forms IA 1.06, 1.07 and 1.08 are used to create a Subchapter S corporation.

### FORM IA 1.00

### CLIENT QUESTIONNAIRE FOR FORMING A CORPORATION[1]

1. Name and address of client(s)
2. Business *and* home telephone numbers of client(s)
3. Has client considered the pros and cons of operation of the business as a sole proprietorship, partnership, or corporation? Ref. Chapters II and III; Chapter VIIIN and Chapter VIIIQ
4. Is there a written agreement to form a business corporation? Ref. Form IA 1.01
5. What is the purpose of the corporation?
   a. Business
   b. Professional
   c. Not-for-profit (charitable, educational, or other tax-exempt purpose)
   d. Should purpose clause be broad or narrow? Ref. Form IA 1.03 for broad and Form IA 1.03(a) for narrow
6. Is there an existing partnership or sole proprietorship?
   a. If so, how will its assets and liabilities be treated in relation to the corporation to be formed? Ref. Chapter II and Form IA 1.01 and Form IA 1.02

---

[9] *15A Am. Jur. 2d Commercial Code,* paras. 73–76 and Appendix VI.
[10] 15 U.S.C.A. 77b.

7. Is there an existing corporation to be merged, consolidated, or dissolved? Ref. Form IA 2.00
8. Corporate name desired
    a. Desired name and one or two alternate names
    b. Check availability of name with state division or bureau of corporations
    c. Reserve name before proceeding
9. Duration of corporation
    a. Perpetual or specified time
    b. If for specified time, is there a federal income tax problem?[2]
10. Type of stock and number of shares
    a. Common or preferred
    b. Voting or nonvoting
    c. Par or no par—if par, get dollar amount per share
11. Are preemptive rights desired?
    a. If so, are they limited? Ref. Form IA 1.03
    b. If so, are they general? Ref. Form IA 1.03(c)
12. Is cumulative voting for directors or one-for-one share voting desired?
    a. Cumulative voting. Ref. Form IA 1.03(b)
    b. One-for-one voting. Ref. Form IA 1.03(e)
13. Does client desire a requirement of more than a majority vote of shareholders for any of the following: Ref. Form IA 1.03(d)
    a. Amendment of articles of incorporation
    b. Amendment of the bylaws of the corporation
    c. Increase of the capital stock of the corporation
    d. Voluntary bankruptcy of the corporation
    e. Dissolution of the corporation
    f. Change in preemptive rights in the corporate stock
    g. Abolition of cumulative voting for directors
    h. Other
14. Does client desire any limitations or restrictions on the issuance or transfer of the stock of the corporation?
    a. If so, include the limitation or restriction in the articles of incorporation and the bylaws, *or*
    b. Prepare shareholders' buy-sell agreement and include appropriate legend thereof on the stock certificates. Ref. Chapter IA 2.00
15. Street address of the corporation's initial registered office
16. Name(s) and residence address(es) of each incorporator. In some cases, it may be the attorney who is the incorporator
17. Name and address of the corporation's initial registered agent and/or resident agent for acceptance of service of process on the corporation, as required by the law of the state of incorporation
18. Name(s) and residence address(es) of the initial board of directors, if known or required by law of the state of incorporation
19. Does the client want you to purchase a corporate minute book, stock certificates, and corporate seal (corporation kit)?
    a. If so, discuss type of kit and price and order it
20. Does the client want you to maintain the corporate action records after the incorporation?[3]
21. Is stock subscription agreement or assignment of stock subscription rights to be prepared before or after incorporation? Ref. Form IA 1.02, Form IA 1.04, and Form IA 1.05
22. Should the corporation be a Subchapter S corporation[4] or should its common stock be Section 1244 stock[5]? Ref. Form IA 1.06, Form IA 1.07, Form IA 1.08, and Form IA 1.09
23. Does client want you to draft the bylaws for the corporation? If so, obtain the following information in addition to the above information and adapt the bylaws form in the corporate kit or draft original bylaws to reflect the appropriate information
    a. Date on which fiscal year of the corporation will begin (January 1, date of incorporation, or other)
    b. Date on which annual shareholders' meetings will be held
    c. Place where annual shareholders' meetings will be held
    d. Will annual directors' meetings be held immediately after such annual shareholders' meeting?
    e. Number of directors and the time and manner of their election

f. Who shall call special meetings of shareholders and directors and by what method?

g. List titles of all officers of the corporation

(1) Will officers be appointed or elected by the board of directors? Appointment is customary in closed corporations

(2) Will officers have the customary duties of their offices? If not, specify different duties

h. Are there any special voting requirements for voting stock?[6] Ref. Form IA 1.03(d) and (13), above

[1]Office procedure for incorporating. *Law Office Desk Book* by Grapp, Prentice-Hall, Inc., Page 107.
[2]26 U.S.C.A. 341 et seq. Collapsible Corporations.
[3]Office procedure for maintaining corporate action records. *Law Office Desk Book,* supra, Page 109.
[4]26 U.S.C.A. 1371–1374, Subchapter S corporation.
[5]26 U.S.C.A. 1244, Section 1244 stock.
[6]*19 Am. Jur. 2d Corporations* 627.

**FORM IA 1.01**

**AGREEMENT TO FORM A BUSINESS CORPORATION[1]**

AGREEMENT made January 15, 1982, between GEORGE PINE, doing business under the trade name of Evergreen Nursery and Landscaping (herein called "Pine"), and JOHN DOE (herein called "Doe").

WHEREAS, Pine and Doe have agreed to organize a corporation to which Pine will assign and transfer his nursery and landscaping business, and in which Doe will subscribe for shares in an amount equal to the net worth of Pine's nursery and landscaping business, on the following terms:

IT IS AGREED:

1. *Formation of corporation.* Pine and Doe shall organize a corporation under the laws of the State of Pennsylvania to be known as Evergreen Nursery and Landscaping, Inc. (hereinafter called the "Corporation"), which shall begin business on March 1, 1983.

2. *Certificate of incorporation.* The Corporation shall be organized so as to provide for the following:

(a) The duration of the Corporation shall be perpetual.

(b) The number of directors shall be two.

(c) The aggregate number of shares that the Corporation shall have authority to issue shall be 100 shares without par value common stock.

(d) The purposes of the Corporation shall include the growing and research development of plants, shrubs, flowers, and trees and the development and manufacture of fertilizers and pest-control formulas and the purchase and sale thereof, wholesale and retail, and the operation of a landscaping business, and all other purposes necessary for the continued and expanded operation of the business now conducted by Pine and the development of new business.

(e) The principal place of business of the Corporation shall be in the County of Allegheny, and State of Pennsylvania.

(f) A copy of the proposed Articles of Incorporation is attached hereto as Exhibit A.

3. *Distribution of shares.* Upon incorporation, the shares of the Corporation shall be issued as follows:

(a) To Pine—50 common no-par shares, fully paid and nonassessable, for which Pine shall transfer to the Corporation, on March 1, 1983, all the assets of his business, subject to all its liabilities. Upon such transfer, the Corporation shall assume all such liabilities. No other consideration shall be paid to Pine for such transfer, and he shall accept the 50 common no-par shares in full payment.

(b) To Doe—50 common no-par shares, fully paid and nonassessable, for which Doe shall pay to the Corporation, on March 1, 1983, an amount in cash equivalent to the net worth of the assets transferred by Pine to the Corporation, as shown by a balance sheet to be prepared by Herbert Rich & Associates, certified public accountants. In the preparation of this balance sheet, the value of all assets shall be taken as shown on the books of Evergreen Nursery and Landscaping on February 28, 1983, and all liabilities shall be similarly taken, except that no liability of Pine for income taxes shall be recorded on the books of the Corporation. No other consideration shall be paid to Doe for such payment, and he shall accept the 50 common no-par shares in full satisfaction of the payment so made to the Corporation.

4. *Control.* Pine and Doe shall vote their shares whenever appropriate so as to provide for the following:

(a) The directors shall be: Pine and Doe.

(b) The officers shall be: President—Pine; Secretary-Treasurer—Doe.

(c) All corporate checks shall be signed by the President and countersigned by the Treasurer.

(d) Pine shall be employed by the Corporation as general manager at an annual salary of $30,000, payable in equal semimonthly installments. Pine shall devote his entire time and efforts to the affairs of the Corporation. Such employment and compensation shall end, however, upon the death or disability of Pine. No other compensation shall be paid to Pine for services rendered as an officer or director of the Corporation.

(e) Doe shall be employed by the Corporation as sales manager at an annual salary of $25,000, payable in equal semimonthly installments. Doe shall devote his entire time and effort to the affairs of the Corporation. Such employment and compensation shall end, however, upon the death or disability of Doe. No other compensation shall be paid to Doe for services rendered as an officer or director of the Corporation.

5. *Representations.* To induce Doe to enter into this Agreement, Pine represents the following:

(a) He is not a party to any litigation, nor is the business now operated by him involved in any legal controversy that could reasonably be foreseen to lead to litigation.

(b) The books of the business do not reflect any values for goodwill, trade names, trademarks, patents, or any similar intangibles.

(c) The various trade names and labels for plants and products now in use by him have been used in the past without interference or adverse claim, and all rights of ownership that he may have in these trade names and labels shall be included in the proposed transfer to the Corporation together with all other intangible assets of the business.

(d) Until transferred to the Corporation, the business shall be operated only in the manner heretofore conducted. No purchase or disbursement shall be made and no expense or liability shall be incurred except in accordance with prior practice.

(e) He has procured the consent of the landlord to the assignment of the lease covering the premises now occupied by his business in Little Township, Allegheny County, Pennsylvania.

(f) He will warrant and defend the title of all assets transferred by him to the Corporation against all claims and all persons, except as to the liabilities as shown on the balance sheet to be prepared by Herbert Rich & Associates.

6. *Legal services.* All legal services required in connection with the organization of the Corporation and with the performance of the various provisions of this agreement shall be performed by Robert Smith, Esq., and his charge for such services, plus all necessary disbursements incurred by him in the performance of the services, shall be paid by the Corporation.

7. *Implementation of this agreement.* Pine and Doe shall promptly execute all documents required to carry out the terms of this Agreement.

IN WITNESS WHEREOF, the parties have signed this Agreement.

GEORGE PINE

JOHN DOE

[1]*18 Am. Jur. 2d Corporations*, paras. 18 and 19.

**FORM IA 1.02**

(Prior to incorporation)

**SUBSCRIPTION TO STOCK OF DEVELOP-CONSTRUCTION CO., INC.**[1]

For value received, and in further consideration of the subscription of the other parties to this Agreement, the undersigned subscribers severally agree and subscribe for the purchase of shares of stock in DEVELOP-CONSTRUCTION CO., INC., a proposed corporation to be incorporated under the laws of the State of Florida by David F. Jones, in accordance with proposed articles of incorporation a copy of which is attached hereto and made part hereof.

The terms and conditions of these subscriptions are:

1. The subscriptions shall become absolute only when:

   (a) The articles of incorporation have been accepted for filing by the Secretary of State for the State of Florida; and if said acceptance for filing occurs within ninety (90) days of the date of this subscription agreement; and

   (b) When subscriptions, including those agreed to herein, have been entered into totaling Four Thousand Dollars ($4,000) for delivery of 400 of the 500 shares of the Ten-Dollar ($10) par value common stock of the corporation to all subscribers, including the undersigned.

2. Upon the happening of the above conditions, the undersigned agree to pay to the incorporator, David F. Jones as Trustee for the Corporation, the amounts set opposite their names for the number of shares indicated, within ten (10) days of his written demand for same:

John Doe                              $1,000                            100 shares
10 First Street
Middletown, Florida 32600

Richard Roe                           $2,000                            200 shares
20 Second Street
Boomtown, Florida 32622

3. The Trustee shall deliver all moneys paid under this agreement to the treasurer of DEVELOP-CONSTRUCTION CO., INC., immediately after the appointment of corporate officers for the Corporation, provided the treasurer delivers to the Trustee proper and sufficient certificates of the capital stock of the Corporation appropriately issued to the stock subscribers described herein in accordance with the terms hereof.

4. This Subscription Agreement is made for the use and benefit of the proposed Corporation, and, upon its coming into being, this Agreement shall continue and run in its favor, and its proper officers may maintain any proper proceedings, at law or in equity, to enforce the terms of this Agreement against the subscribers or the Trustee.

5. In the event that any legal action, in law or equity, is brought to enforce this Subscription Agreement by any of the undersigned, the Trustee or the Corporation, the prevailing party in such action shall be entitled to recover a reasonable attorney's fee from the nonprevailing party or parties. It is further understood that none of the undersigned, nor the Trustee, nor the Corporation shall be responsible for any act or omission of each other.

6. This Subscription Agreement cannot be modified except by a writing signed by the party to whose prejudice or disadvantage the modification(s) would operate.

Dated this 17th day of June, 1982, at Middletown, Florida.

_____
JOHN DOE

_____
RICHARD DOE

Agreed to:

_____
David F. Jones, as Trustee

[1]18 Am. Jur. 2d Corporations, paras. 288–298, 339, 360–371, 466, and 467. Ref. Form IA 1.04 and footnotes for subscription *after* incorporation.

## FORM IA 1.03

### (Broad business purpose for land development and building business)

### ARTICLES OF INCORPORATION[1]
### of
### DEVELOP-CONSTRUCTION CO., INC.

ARTICLE I

*NAME*

The name of the Corporation is DEVELOP-CONSTRUCTION CO., INC.

ARTICLE II

*DURATION*

The Corporation shall have perpetual existence.

ARTICLE III

*PURPOSE*[2]

The Corporation is organized for the following purposes:

1. To purchase, improve, develop, hold, and own real estate, and to lease, mortgage, and sell the same in such parts or parcels improved or unimproved, an on such terms as from time to time and manner of payment as the Corporation may, by its Board of Directors, agree.

2. To maintain and keep places for storage and warehouses for the storage and deposit of goods and merchandise of all kinds and descriptions, and conduct all business appertaining thereto, including the making of advances on goods stored or deposited with it, and to have and to receive all the rights and emoluments thereto belonging.

3. To carry on business, in the United States or elsewhere, as factors, agents, commission merchants, or merchants to buy, sell, and deal in, at wholesale or retail, merchandise, goods, wares, and commodities of every sort, kind, or description, and to carry on any other business whether manufacturing or otherwise that can be conveniently carried on within any of the corporation's objectives; to open stores, offices, or agencies throughout the United States or elsewhere, or to allow or cause the legal estate and interest in any properties or business acquired, established, or carried on by the Corporation to remain or be vested in the name of or carried on by any other company formed or to be formed, and either upon trust for or as agents or nominees of the Corporation, and to manage the affairs or take over and carry on the business of any such other company formed or to be formed, and to exercise all or any of the powers of such company, or of holders of shares of stock or securities thereof, and to receive and distribute as profits the dividends and interest on such shares of stock and securities; to purchase or otherwise acquire and undertake all or any part of the business, property, and liabilities of any persons or company, carrying on any kind of business that the Corporation is authorized to carry on; to enter into partnership or into any arrangement for sharing profits, union of interest, reciprocal concessions, joint venture, or cooperate with any person with which the Corporation is authorized to carry on; or any business or transaction capable of being conducted, so as, directly or indirectly, to benefit the Corporation.

4. To lend money, either with or without security, and generally to such persons and upon such terms and conditions as the corporation may think fit, and in particular for the purpose of undertaking to build or improve any property in which the Corporation is interested as tenant, builder, or contractor.

5. To conduct a general brokerage agency and commission business for others in the purchase, sale, and management of real estate or personal property for others to negotiate loans thereon.

6. To purchase and sell for others personal property, stocks, bonds, and notes and to negotiate loans thereon for others.

7. To manufacture, purchase, or otherwise acquire, own, mortgage, pledge, sell, assign, and transfer or otherwise dispose of, to invest, trade, deal in, and deal with goods, wares and merchandise, and real and personal property of every class and description.

8. To acquire and pay for, in cash or otherwise, stocks and bonds of the Corporation, the good-

will, rights, assets, and property, and to undertake or assume the whole or any part of the obligation or liabilities of any person, firm, association, or corporation.

9. To acquire, hold, use, sell, assign, lease, grant licenses and privileges, inventions, improvements, and processes, copyrights, trademarks, and trade names, relating to or useful in connection with any business of the Corporation.

10. To guarantee, purchase, hold, vote, sell, assign, transfer, mortgage, pledge or otherwise dispose of shares of the capital stock of or any bonds, securities, or evidence of indebtedness created by any other corporation or corporations organized under the laws of this state or any other state, country, nation, or government, and while the owner thereof to exercise all the rights, powers, and privileges of ownership.

11. To issue bonds, debentures, or obligations of the Corporation from time to time, for any of the objects or purposes of the Corporation, and to secure the same by mortgage, pledge, deed of trust, or otherwise.

12. To purchase, hold, sell, and transfer the shares of its own capital stocks; PROVIDED, it shall not use its funds or property for the purchase of its own shares of capital stock when such use would cause any impairment of its capital; and, PROVIDED FURTHER, that shares of its own capital stock belonging to it shall not be voted upon, directly or indirectly.

13. To have one or more offices to carry on all or any of its operations and business, and without restrictions or limit as to amount, to purchase or otherwise acquire, hold, own, mortgage, sell, convey, or otherwise dispose of real and personal property of every class and description in any of the states, districts, territories, or colonies of the United States or other country.

14. To act as a general contractor and subcontractor and to engage in the business or construction of commercial buildings or residences, and improvements and additions to same; and generally to perform or do any act customarily performed by a construction company.

15. In general, to carry on any other business in connection with the foregoing, whether manufacturing or otherwise, and to have and exercise all the powers conferred by the laws of Florida upon corporations, and to do any or all of the things above set forth to the same extent as natural persons might or could do.

16. To transact any or all lawful business.

17. The foregoing clauses shall be construed both as objects and powers, and it is hereby expressly provided that the foregoing enumeration of specific powers shall not be held to limit or restrict in any manner the powers of the Corporation.

18. The above and foregoing businesses enumerated are intended as illustrative and not restrictive, and the Corporation shall have the power to handle such other business or businesses, either in its own behalf or as agent or broker for others, and shall further engage in any or all like or kindred businesses that may be necessary or profitable in conjunction with the businesses above enumerated; and generally shall have and exercise all powers, privileges, and immunities of businesses of like kind and nature incorporated under the laws of the State of Florida, and shall enjoy the privileges and immunities pertaining to incorporators under the laws of the State of Florida.

## ARTICLE IV

### *CAPITAL STOCK*

The Corporation is authorized to issue Five Hundred (500) shares of Ten-Dollar ($10) par value common stock, which shall be designated "Common Shares."

## ARTICLE V

### *PREEMPTIVE RIGHTS*

Every shareholder, upon the sale for cash of any additional stock of the Corporation of the same kind, class, or series as that which he already holds, shall have the right to purchase his pro rata share thereof (as nearly as may be done without issuance of fractional shares) at the price at which it is offered to others.

## ARTICLE VI

### *INITIAL REGISTERED OFFICE AND AGENT*

The street address of the initial registered office of the Corporation is 200 East Street, Middletown, Florida, and the name of the initial registered agent of this Corporation at that address is DAVID F. JONES.

## ARTICLE VII

### *INITIAL BOARD OF DIRECTORS*

The Corporation shall have one (1) director initially. The number of directors may be either increased or diminished from time to time by the Bylaws, but shall never be fewer than one (1). The names and addresses of the initial directors of the Corporation are:

*NAME*
Richard Roe

*ADDRESS*
100 West Street
Middletown, Florida 32600

## ARTICLE VIII

### *INCORPORATOR*

The name and address of the person signing these Articles is:

David F. Jones
200 East Street
Middletown, Florida 32600

## ARTICLE IX

### *BYLAWS*

The power to adopt, alter, amend, or repeal Bylaws not inconsistent with these Articles of Incorporation is vested in the Board of Directors of the Corporation.

## ARTICLE X

### *AMENDMENT*

The Corporation reserves the right to amend or repeal any provisions contained in these Articles of Incorporation, or any amendment hereto, by a majority vote of the shareholders of the Corporation.

IN WITNESS WHEREOF, the undersigned subscriber has executed these Articles of Incorporation this 1st day of July, 1983.

_____
David F. Jones

STATE OF FLORIDA
COUNTY OF CITRUS

BEFORE ME, a notary public in and for said county and state, personally appeared DAVID F. JONES, known to me and known by me to be the person who executed the foregoing Articles of Incorporation, and he acknowledged before me that he executed those Articles of Incorporation for the purposes set forth therein.

IN WITNESS WHEREOF, I have hereunto set my hand and affixed my official seal, in the state and county aforesaid, this 1st day of July, 1983.

_____
Notary Public
My commission expires:

[1] *18 Am. Jur. 2d Corporations*, paras. 36–42.
[2] Ultra vires acts, *19 Am. Jur. 2d Corporations*, paras. 968–972.

## FORM IA 1.03(a)

### (Narrow business purpose)[1]

### ALTERNATIVE CLAUSE

#### ARTICLE ___

##### *PURPOSE*

1. To engage in the furniture business to manufacture, distribute, and deal in furniture, and allied and incidental products, retail and wholesale, and to perform services in connection therewith.

2. To buy, hold, mortgage, sell, convey, lease, or otherwise dispose of real and personal property.

3. To do everything necessary, proper, or convenient for the accomplishment of the foregoing purposes, and to do all other things incidental to them or connected with them that are not forbidden by the Florida Business Corporation Act, by other law, or by these Articles of Incorporation.

[1] *18 Am. Jur. 2d Corporations, paras. 31–34 and 37.*

## FORM IA 1.03(b)

### (Cumulative voting)[1]

### ALTERNATIVE CLAUSE

ARTICLE ___

### *CUMULATIVE VOTING*

At each election for directors, every holder of the capital stock (or voting stock, if there is more than one class and one class is nonvoting) shall have the right to vote, in person or by proxy, the number of shares registered in his name for as many persons as there are directors to be elected and for whose election he has a right to vote, or to cumulate his votes by giving one candidate as many votes as the number of such directors multiplied by the number of his shares shall equal, or by distributing such votes on the same principle among any number of such candidates.

[1] *19 Am. Jur. 2d Corporations, paras. 662–668.*

## FORM IA 1.03(c)

### (Broad preemptive rights without restrictions)[1]

### ALTERNATIVE CLAUSE

ARTICLE ___

### *PREEMPTIVE RIGHTS*

The registered holders of the shares of the capital stock of the Corporation shall have the preemptive right to purchase additional stock on such equitable terms, prices, and conditions as shall be fixed by the Board of Directors for the issuance of any stock in the Corporation from time to time. Such preemptive right shall be exercised in the ratio that the number of shares held by each stockholder bears to the total number of shares outstanding.

[1] *18 Am. Jur. 2d Corporations, paras. 275–281.*

## FORM IA 1.03(d)

### (Special vote requirements)[1]

### ALTERNATIVE CLAUSE

ARTICLE ___

### *SPECIAL VOTE REQUIREMENTS*

1. The following acts of the Corporation shall not be performed without the written consent or affirmative vote of two-thirds (2/3) of the issued and outstanding common stock of the Corporation:
    (1) amendment of the Articles of Incorporation
    (2) amendment of the Bylaws of the Corporation
    (3) increase of the capital stock of the Corporation
    (4) voluntary bankruptcy of the Corporation

(5) dissolution of the Corporation

(6) change in preemptive rights in the corporate stock

(7) abolition of cumulative voting

[1]*19 Am. Jur. 2d Corporations,* para. 627.

## FORM IA 1.03(e)

### (One-for-one share voting)[1]

### ALTERNATIVE CLAUSE

ARTICLE ___

*ONE-FOR-ONE VOTING*

At each election for directors, each holder of the capital stock (or voting stock, if there is more than one class and one class is nonvoting) shall be entitled to one vote for each share of stock owned by such shareholder. Upon demand of any shareholder, the vote for directors shall be by ballot.

[1]*19 Am. Jur. 2d Corporations,* paras. 635 and 636.

## FORM IA 1.04

### (After incorporation)[1]

### SUBSCRIPTION OF STOCK TO CORPORATION

I, John Jones, of Boomtown, Florida, do hereby subscribe for One Hundred (100) shares of the capital stock of DEVELOP-CONSTRUCTION CO., INC., a Florida corporation, at the par value of Ten Dollars ($10) per share, for which I agree to pay the total sum of One Thousand Dollars ($1,000) in two (2) installments as follows: Five Hundred Dollars ($500) in cash at the time of signing this subscription agreement, and the balance of Five Hundred Dollars ($500) in six (6) months from the date hereof.

Dated: October 1, 1983

_____

JOHN JONES
10 East Street
Boomtown, Florida 32622

[1]*18 Am. Jur. 2d Corporations,* para. 288. Ref. Form IA 1.02 and footnotes for subscription *before* incorporation.

## FORM IA 1.05

### ASSIGNMENT OF STOCK SUBSCRIPTION RIGHTS[1]

KNOW ALL MEN BY THESE PRESENTS, that the undersigned, in consideration of the sum of One Dollar ($1) and other good and valuable consideration, receipt of which is hereby acknowledged, hereby sells, transfers, and assigns unto Frank Investor of Miami, Florida, all his right, title, and interest in and to the subscription for stock in DEVELOP-CONSTRUCTION CO., INC., a Florida corporation, and hereby authorizes, requests, and directs said corporation to issue a certificate or certificates for my subscribed shares to Frank Investor or such other person as he may order, upon payment by him of the amounts due on the said stock subscription and compliance with the other terms and conditions of said subscription.

Dated this 2nd day of July, 1983, at Middletown, Florida.

WITNESS:

_____          _____

JOHN DOE
10 First Street
Middletown, Florida

[1]*18 Am. Jur. 2d Corporations,* para. 290.

## FORM IA 1.06

### SUBCHAPTER S CORPORATION RESOLUTION[1]

RESOLVED, that the Treasurer of this Corporation be and is hereby authorized to take any and all action necessary to comply with the requirements of the Internal Revenue Service for making an election pursuant to Subchapter S of the Internal Revenue Code, Section 1372.[2]

[1]26 U.S.C.A. 1372 and *33 Am. Jur. 2d Federal Taxation*, paras. 2025–2066.
[2]26 U.S.C.A. 1371–1379 and 26 U.S.C.A. 6037; ref. Form IA 1.07 and 1.08; compare Form IA 1.09.

## FORM IA 1.07

### (To be attached to Treasury Department Form 2553)

### CONSENT TO ELECTION AS SUBCHAPTER S CORPORATION[1]

In accordance with the provisions of Section 1372, Internal Revenue Code, and the regulations issued thereunder, the undersigned, all the shareholders of DEVELOP-CONSTRUCTION CO., INC., a corporation formed under the laws of the State of Florida, do hereby consent to the election made by that Corporation on Treasury Department Form 2553 to which this Statement is attached, and do hereby submit the following information:

a. The name and address of the Corporation is:
DEVELOP-CONSTRUCTION CO., INC.
200 East Street
Middletown, Florida 32600

b. The name and address of each shareholder of the Corporation, the number of shares of stock owned by him, and the date or dates on which such stock was acquired, are as follows:

| NAME & ADDRESS OF SHAREHOLDER | NO. OF SHARES | DATE ACQUIRED |
|---|---|---|
| John Doe<br>10 First Street<br>Middletown, Florida 32600 | 100 | June 17, 1982 |
| Richard Roe<br>20 Second Street<br>Boomtown, Florida 32622 | 200 | June 17, 1982 |

DATED this 10th day of July, 1983.

_____

_____

[1]Ref. Form IA 1.06 and 1.08. Compare Form IA 1.09.

FORM IA 1.08

## SUBCHAPTER S CORPORATION

Form **2553**
(Rev. May 1983)
Department of the Treasury
Internal Revenue Service

# Election by a Small Business Corporation

(Under section 1362 of the Internal Revenue Code)
▶ For Paperwork Reduction Act Notice, see page 1 of instructions.
▶ See separate instructions.

OMB No. 1545–0146

**Note:** *This election to be treated as an "S corporation" can be approved only if all the tests in Instruction B are met.*

## Part I

| Name of corporation (see instructions) | Employer identification number (see instructions) | Principal business activity and principal product or service (see instructions) |
|---|---|---|
| Number and street | | Election is to be effective for tax year beginning (month, day, year) |
| City or town, State and ZIP code | | Number of shares issued and outstanding (see instructions) |

Is the corporation the outgrowth or continuation of any form of predecessor? . . . . . ☐ Yes ☐ No

Date and place of incorporation

If "Yes," state name of predecessor, type of organization, and period of its existence ▶ ..............................................

**A** If this election takes effect for the first tax year the corporation exists, enter the earliest of the following: (1) date the corporation first had shareholders, (2) date the corporation first had assets, or (3) date the corporation began doing business. ▶

**B** Selected tax year: Annual return will be filed for tax year ending (month and day) ▶ ...........................................
See Instructions before entering your tax year. If the tax year ends any date other than December 31, you must complete Part II or Part IV on back. You may want to complete Part III to make a back-up request.

| C Name of each shareholder, person having a community property interest in the corporation's stock, and each tenant in common, joint tenant, and tenant by the entirety. (A husband and wife (and their estates) are counted as one shareholder in determining the number of shareholders without regard to the manner in which the stock is owned.) | D Shareholders' Consent Statement. We the undersigned shareholders, consent to the corporation's election to be treated as an "S corporation" under section 1362(a). *(Shareholders sign and date below.) | E Stock owned | | F Social security number (employer identification number for estate or trust) | G Tax year ends (Month and day) |
|---|---|---|---|---|---|
| | | Number of shares | Dates acquired | | |
| | | | | | |
| | | | | | |
| | | | | | |
| | | | | | |
| | | | | | |
| | | | | | |
| | | | | | |
| | | | | | |
| | | | | | |
| | | | | | |

*For this election to be valid, the consent of each shareholder, person having a community property interest in the corporation's stock, and each tenant in common, joint tenant, and tenant by the entirety must either appear above or be attached to this form. (See instructions for column D, if continuation sheet or a separate consent statement is needed.)

Under penalties of perjury, I declare that I have examined this election, including accompanying schedules, and statements, and to the best of my knowledge and belief it is true, correct, and complete.

Signature and Title of Officer ▶

Date ▶

See Parts II, III, and IV on back.

**Part II—Selection of Tax Year Under Revenue Procedure 83–25**

I  Check the applicable box below to indicate whether the corporation is:
- ☐ Adopting the tax year entered in item B, Part I.
- ☐ Retaining the tax year entered in item B, Part I.
- ☐ Changing to the tax year entered in item B, Part I.

J  Check the applicable box below to indicate the representation statement the corporation is making as required under section 7.01 (item 4) of Revenue Procedure 83–25, 1983 Internal Revenue Bulletin No. 15, at page 13.

- ☐ Under penalties of perjury, I represent that shareholders holding more than half of the shares of the stock (as of the first day of the tax year to which the request relates) of the corporation have the same tax year or are concurrently changing to the tax year that the corporation adopts, retains or changes to per item B, Part I.

- ☐ Under penalties of perjury, I represent that shareholders holding more than half of the shares of the stock (as of the first day of the tax year to which the request relates) of the corporation have a tax year or are concurrently changing to a tax year that, although is different from the tax year the corporation is adopting, retaining, or changing to per item B, Part I, results in a deferment of income to each of these shareholders of three months or less.

- ☐ Under penalties of perjury, I represent that the corporation is adopting, retaining or changing to a tax year that coincides with its natural business year as verified by its satisfaction of the requirements of section 4.042(a), (b), (c), and (d) of Revenue Procedure 83–25.

K  Check here ☐ if the tax year entered in item B, Part I, is requested under the provisions of section 8 of Revenue Procedure 83–25.

   Attach to Form 2553 a statement and other necessary information pursuant to the ruling request requirements of Revenue Procedure 83–1, 1983 Internal Revenue Bulletin No. 1, at page 16. The statement must include the business purpose for the desired tax year. See instructions.

**Part III—Back-Up Request by Certain Corporations Initially Selecting a Fiscal Year (See Instructions.)**

Check here ☐ if the corporation agrees to adopt or to change to a tax year ending December 31 if necessary for IRS to accept this election for S corporation status (temporary regulations section 18.1378–1(b)(2)(ii)(A)). This back-up request does not apply if the fiscal tax year request is approved by IRS or if the election to be an S corporation is not accepted.

**Part IV—Request by Corporation for Tax Year Determination By IRS (See Instructions.)**

Check here ☐ if the corporation requests the IRS to determine the permitted tax year for the corporation based on information submitted in Part I (and attached schedules). This request is made under provisions of temporary regulations section 18.1378–1(d).

☆U.S. Government Printing Office: 1983–381-108/141

## FORM IA 1.09

### SECTION 1244 STOCK RESOLUTION[1]

RESOLVED, that the President and Treasurer of this Corporation are authorized and directed to sell and issue the common stock of this Corporation in the total amount of $50,000 in accordance with the following plan:

PLAN TO OFFER COMMON STOCK FOR SALE

The Corporation is a small-business corporation as defined in Internal Revenue Code, Section 1244 (c) 2.

There is no outstanding prior offering of the Corporation to sell or issue any of its common stock.

The Corporation shall sell and issue as many shares of the common stock of the Corporation at such price, payable in cash or other property (other than investment securities) as from time to time it deems to be in the best interests of the Corporation, for a total amount not to exceed $50,000.

The offer to sell pursuant to this plan shall remain in full force and effect until all of said shares are sold, or until the Corporation shall make a subsequent offering of common stock, or for a period of two years from the date of adoption of this plan by the Board of Directors this day, whichever occurs first.

All officers of the Corporation shall interpret and construe this plan and take such further steps as will enable this plan to qualify under Section 1244 of the Internal Revenue Code as will enable the shares of common stock issued pursuant to this plan to qualify as Section 1244 stock as defined in said section in the Code.

[1] 26 U.S.C.A. 1244 and *34 Am. Jur. 2d Federal Taxation*, paras. 4300–4332.

**FORM IA 2.00**

**CLIENT QUESTIONNAIRE FOR TRANSFER OF STOCK OR CONTROL OF BUSINESS
CORPORATION[1]**

1. Name and address of the individual client(s) or the individual(s) representing the corporate client, including corporate title of the individual(s)
2. Business *and* home telephone numbers of the individual(s)
3. Does client want a transfer of stock ownership *or* a delegation of voting rights?
   a. If ownership, see (4) through (11) below
   b. If delegation of voting rights only, see Form IA 2.01, Form IA 2.01(a) and (b), Form IA 2.02, and Form IA 2.03
4. In regard to *each* corporation involved in the proposed transfer of stock, obtain the following information:
   a. *Exact* registered name of each corporation and the general nature of its business
   b. State of incorporation and date of incorporation
   c. Copy of Articles of Incorporation (Charter) and all amendments
   d. Copy of bylaws of the corporation, as amended to date
   e. Type(s) of stock authorized and number of shares issued and outstanding
   f. *Exact* names and addresses of stockholders as they appear in the corporate records, and number of shares owned by each
   g. Are any of the shares owned by a trust, a decedent's estate, an incompetent, or a minor, or is there a voting trust in existence? If any of these, get the name and address of the trustee, personal representation of the decedent's estate, guardian of the minor or incompetent, or voting trustee
   h. Number of directors and names and addresses of all directors
   i. Titles, names, and addresses of all present officers
   j. Name and address of the present registered agent and/or the resident agent for service of process of the corporation(s)
   k. Are there any present restrictions on the sale or transfer of the stock?[2] If so, get copies of any written agreements restricting transfer if the restrictions do not appear in the Articles of Incorporation[3] or bylaws. Check available stock certificates for legend giving notice of any restrictions.[4] Get waivers, releases, or consents from the appropriate parties and/or prepare appropriate corporate resolutions for the proposed sale or purchase or other transfer
5. If there are no formal or legal restrictions on the proposed transfer of the stock, is there any known objection to the proposed transfer of stock or change in control of the corporation? If so, get names and corporate title(s) or status of the objector(s) and number of corporate shares he (they) own or control. See (4 k), above
6. What is the purpose of the transfer?
   a. Is the purchase or exchange for investment purposes only?
   b. Does the transferee intend to operate the business of the corporation?
   c. Will the transfer give the transferee the controlling or majority interest in the stock of the corporation?
   d. Is there to be a tax-free organization?[5]
7. What are the terms of the transfer?
   a. Sale or exchange for stock in another corporation
   b. Cash sale or installment cash sale and/or exchange
   c. If exchange, is it a tax-free exchange under the Internal Revenue Code and regulations?[6]
      (1) Is the client concerned about the tax liability, if any?
   d. Total purchase price and manner and time of paying it. *Must be stated specifically and clearly*
   e. If installment sale, who has voting rights during the installment period?
   f. If installment sale, who is entitled to any dividends declared during the installment period?
   g. Should there be any restrictions on operation of the business or declaration of dividends during the installment period if the purchaser or transferee does not have voting rights during the installment period? If so, should they be specific as not to raise management salaries or make specific long-term commitments, buy real estate, etc.? Should the written consent of the purchaser or transferee be required to do those things?
8. Should any warranties be required in addition to those set forth in Article 8 of the Uniform Commercial Code, or should any of those warranties be limited?
   a. As to present financial condition of the corporation(s)

b. As to the number of shares issued and outstanding

c. As to litigation or litigation reasonably foreseeable

d. As to major executory contracts not appearing as liability on the financial records of the corporation(s)

e. Other

9. Should any covenants by the transferrer or seller be included in the agreement to assure that the corporation(s) will be in the same financial condition at the time of closing as it is at the time of agreement to purchase or exchange?

a. Continue business in its ordinary course

b. Keep present management

c. No executory contracts over a certain amount, or other criteria

d. No major purchases of land or equipment over a certain amount, or other criteria

e. Other

10. Do co-purchasers of stock want an additional agreement drafted to control or dispose of their joint interest in case of death of an individual co-purchaser or dissolution or bankruptcy of a corporate co-purchaser in the stock to be purchased? Ref. Form IA 2.06

11. What state law should apply to the interpretation of the contract if the corporation is incorporated in one state and registered to do business in another state? Ref. Form IA 2.13(h)

12. In addition to drafting the stock purchase or transfer agreement, does client want you to:

a. Handle any state corporate formalities required to implement the agreement if it involves amendment to articles or change in resident agent for service of process, etc., or will the attorney for the other party handle this?

b. Handle IRS formalities, if any, or will the attorney for the other party handle this, or will an accountant for either party do it?

[1] *19 Am. Jur. 2d Corporation*, paras. 669 and 672.
[2] *18 Am. Jur. 2d Corporations*, para. 381 et seq.
[3] Ref. Form IA 1.03.
[4] *18 Am. Jur. 2d Corporations*, para. 386.
[5] *26 U.S.C.A. 351–368.*
[6] *26 U.S.C.A.*

## FORM IA 2.01

### (General proxy to vote stock at any future meeting until revoked)

### SHAREHOLDER'S GENERAL PROXY[1]

I, the undersigned, do hereby constitute and appoint John Doe of Middletown, Florida, my lawful proxy and attorney-in-fact for me and in my name to vote One Hundred (100) shares of the stock of XYZ COMPANY, INC., owned by me and standing in my name on the books of the Corporation, at any general, annual, or special meeting of the shareholders thereof pursuant to law until this authority shall be revoked by me, hereby ratifying and confirming whatsoever the said John Doe may have lawfully done by virtue hereof; and I hereby revoke and annul any and all authority heretofore given by me authorizing any person for me, or in my name, to vote my stock in the Corporation.

Dated:

_____

RICHARD ROE, Shareholder in XYZ Company, Inc.

[1] *18 Am. Jur. 2d Corporations*, paras. 673 and 675.

## FORM IA 2.01(a)

### (General proxy to vote stock at a particular meeting)[1]

### ALTERNATIVE FORM

I, the undersigned, do hereby constitute and appoint John Doe of Middletown, Florida, my lawful proxy and attorney-in-fact for me and in my name to vote One Hundred (100) shares of the stock of XYZ COMPANY, INC., owned by me and standing in my name on the books of the Corporation, at a special meeting of the Corporation's shareholders to be held in Middletown, Florida, at the offices of the Corporation on the 15th day of May, 1983, and at any and all adjournments thereof, and to do and perform all and any act or thing in my name and stead that I could do as a stockholder at such meeting or adjournment.

Dated:

WITNESSES:

_____                    _____
                                                     RICHARD ROE

_____

¹Compare Form IA 2.01 and Form IA 2.01(b).

## FORM IA 2.01(b)

### (Specific proxy solicited by management for a particular meeting)¹

#### ALTERNATIVE FORM

#### STOCKHOLDER PROXY FOR ANNUAL MEETING
#### of
#### WESTERN MANUFACTURING CORPORATION²

KNOW ALL MEN BY THESE PRESENTS that I, the undersigned shareholder of WESTERN MANUFACTURING CORPORATION, a Pennsylvania corporation, do hereby nominate, constitute, and appoint JOHN DOE or RICHARD ROE or either of them (with full power to act alone) my true and lawful attorney with full power of substitution, for and in my name, place, and stead to vote all of the Common Stock of said corporation standing in my name on its books as of January 31, 1983, at the annual meeting of its shareholders to be held at the general offices of the Corporation at 500 Wood Street, Pittsburgh, Pennsylvania, on February 15, 1983, at 10:00 A.M. or any adjournments thereof, with all the powers the undersigned would possess if personally present as follows:
1. The election of the nine (9) persons listed in the Proxy Statement³ dated January 31, 1983, accompanying the notice of said meeting.
                    FOR _____ AGAINST _____
2. Voting on 5 percent stock dividend.
                    FOR _____ AGAINST _____
3. Whatever other business may be brought before the meeting or any adjournment thereof. Management at present knows of no other business to be presented by or on behalf of the Corporation or its management at the meeting.

    This proxy confers authority to vote "FOR" each proposition listed above unless "AGAINST" is indicated. If any other business is properly presented at said meeting, this Proxy shall be voted in my name and stead in any manner that I could vote as a stockholder at the meeting or adjournment thereof.

    The management of the Corporation recommends a vote "FOR" each of the listed propositions. This proxy is solicited on behalf of management, and this proxy may be revoked by the undersigned prior to its exercise.

Dated: _____

                              _____ (L.S.)
                              ARTHUR RICH

Number of Shares
    250

¹19 Am. Jur. 2d Corporations, para. 678.
²Compare Form IA 2.01 and 2.01(a).
³See Form IA 2.02 for Proxy Statement.

**FORM IA 2.02**

**(To accompany solicited proxy and notice of shareholders' meeting)**

**PROXY STATEMENT[1]**

Annual Meeting of Shareholders of
WESTERN MANUFACTURING CORPORATION
to be held
10:00 A.M. Tuesday, February 15, 1983, at the general
office of the Corporation

The number of shares of common stock outstanding and entitled to vote at the Annual Share-holders' Meeting is 50,000 as of this date. Only those shareholders of record at the close of business on January 31, 1983, shall be entitled to vote at this annual meeting or any adjournment thereof.

*Election of Directors*

The Articles of Incorporation of the Corporation provide that there shall be nine (9) Directors of the Corporation to be elected at the annual Shareholders' Meeting.

The nine (9) persons named below will be nominated for election. It is the intention of the persons named in the proxy to vote for the election of the following nominees:

| *NAME* | *ADDRESS* |
| --- | --- |
| Charles Boe | 100 First Street, Pittsburgh, Pennsylvania |
| John Careful | 300 Main Street, Bradford, Pennsylvania |
| Alfred Doe | 200 North Street, McKeesport, Pennsylvania |
| James Jones | 500 Overstreet, Pittsburgh, Pennsylvania |
| Perry Mart | 100 East Street, Blawnox, Pennsylvania |
| Able Smith | 300 North Avenue, Pittsburgh, Pennsylvania |
| Roger Tom | 100 Main Street, Erie, Pennsylvania |
| Edward Trueheart | 400 West Street, Pittsburgh, Pennsylvania |
| John Zealous | 100 Second Street, Erie, Pennsylvania |

*Dividend*

In the opinion of the management of the Corporation, a dividend of 5 percent would be economically feasible and proper.

*Other Business*

At the present time, the management of the Corporation knows of no other business to be presented by or on behalf of the Corporation or its management at the meeting.

WESTERN MANUFACTURING CORPORATION

Edward Trueheart
President

ET/dp

[1]Ref. Form IA 2.01(b) for specific proxy.

**FORM IA 2.03**

**(For use in states where voting trusts are permissible)**

**VOTING TRUST AGREEMENT[1]**

THIS AGREEMENT, made in New York, New York, on January 3, 1983, between holders of stock in ABLE MANUFACTURING, INC., a New York corporation, who shall become parties to this agreement by signing the same (herein called "Subscribers"), and RICHARD ABLE, JOHN DOE, and RICHARD ROE, who reside in Hartford, Connecticut, and their successors (herein called "Voting Trustees"), witnesseth:

WHEREAS, each Subscriber represents that he is the owner of the number of fully paid and nonassessable shares of common no-par stock in Able Manufacturing, Inc., set opposite his signature; and

WHEREAS, the Subscribers deem it to be to the interests of Able Manufacturing, Inc., and of all the stockholders in the Corporation that this agreement should be made:

IT IS AGREED:

1. *Deposit of stock certificate(s)*. Each subscriber agrees to deposit with the Voting Trustees the certificate or certificates for his shares in the Corporation, together with a proper and sufficient separate instrument,[1] duly executed, for the transfer thereof to the Voting Trustees with all necessary transfer tax stamps affixed.

2. *Form, delivery, and transfer of voting trust certificate(s)*.

    a. Upon deposit, the Voting Trustees shall deliver to each Subscriber his voting trust certificate or certificates, for the same number of shares of common no-par stock of Able Manufacturing, Inc., as is represented by the stock certificate or certificates deposited, which voting trust certificates shall be in the following form:

Number of Voting Certificate(s) _____ Shares of stock deposited _____

ABLE MANUFACTURING, INC.
COMMON NO-PAR STOCK VOTING TRUST CERTIFICATE

    This certifies that on January 3, 1988, _____ will be entitled to receive a certificate or certificates expressed to be fully paid and nonassessable, for _____ shares of the common no-par stock of Able Manufacturing, Inc., a New York corporation, and, in the meantime, to receive payments from the Voting Trustees equal to the dividends, if any, collected by the Voting Trustees upon that number of shares of stock. Until the actual delivery of such stock certificates, the Voting Trustees shall, in respect of any and all such stock, possess and be entitled to exercise, except as otherwise expressly provided in the voting trust agreement hereafter mentioned, all stockholders' rights of every kind, including the right to vote and to take part in, or to consent to, any corporate stockholders' action.

    This certificate is issued under and pursuant to, and the rights of the holders are subject to and limited by, the terms and conditions of a voting trust agreement dated January 3, 1983, between the holders of common no-par stock of Able Manufacturing, Inc., and Richard Able, John Doe, and Richard Roe and successors as Voting Trustees, copies of which agreement are filed with the Voting Trustees and with Able Manufacturing, Inc.

    No stock certificate of Able Manufacturing, Inc., shall be due or deliverable to a holder of this voting trust certificate by the Voting Trustees before January 3, 1988, but the Voting Trustees, in their discretion, may make earlier delivery as provided in the voting trust agreement.

    This certificate is transferable only on the books of the Voting Trustees by the registered holder in person or by attorney, according to the rules established for that purpose by the Voting Trustee, and on surrender of this voting trust certificate. Until so transferred, the Voting Trustees may treat the registered holder of this voting trust certificate as the owner hereof for all purposes whatsoever.

    This certificate is not valid unless signed by all the Voting Trustees.

Dated: _____ , New York, New York

_____
RICHARD ABLE

_____
JOHN DOE

_____
RICHARD ROE

    b. The voting trust certificate shall be transferred as provided therein, and not otherwise. Transfer, as provided, of any voting trust certificate shall vest in the transferee all rights and interests of the transferrer in and under the certificate; and, upon such transfer, the Voting Trustees will deliver a voting trust certificate or certificates to the transferee for the same number of shares as the transferred voting trust certificate represents. Until such transfer, the Voting Trustees may treat the registered holder of the voting trust certificate as its owner for all purposes whatsoever.

    3. *Dividends payable to holder*. The holder of each voting trust certificate shall receive from the Voting Trustees payments equal to the dividends, if any, collected by the Voting Trustees upon the like number of shares of stock of Able Manufacturing, Inc., as is specified in such voting trust certificate. All dividends received by the Voting Trustees shall be remitted to the holder by the

Voting Trustees, or their agent or depositary, within twenty (20) days of the receipt thereof by the Voting Trustees.

4. *Termination of this Agreement.* On January 3, 1988, or on such earlier date as the Voting Trustees jointly shall in their discretion determine, the Voting Trustees shall distribute the specified number of shares of stock of Able Manufacturing, Inc., to the holders of the voting trust certificates upon presentation and surrender of voting trust certificates on or after that date. The voting trust certificates shall be accompanied by properly executed transfers thereof to the Voting Trustees. Any and all necessary transfer tax stamps to effect the exchange provided in this paragraph shall be paid by the holders of the voting trust certificates.

5. *Powers and duties of Voting Trustees and successors.*

a. The Voting Trustees may adopt their own rules of procedure. The action of a majority of the Voting Trustees expressed at a meeting or by a writing with or without a meeting shall constitute the action of the Voting Trustees and shall have the same effect as though assented to by all.

b. Any Voting Trustee may be an officer or director of Able Manufacturing, Inc.

c. In voting upon the shares of stock or doing any act with respect to the control or management of Able Manufacturing, Inc., or its affairs, as holders of the stock deposited hereunder, the Voting Trustees shall exercise their best judgment in the interests of Able Manufacturing, Inc., and to the end that its affairs shall be properly managed.

d. No Voting Trustee shall be liable for any error of judgment or mistake of law or other mistake or for anything except his own willful misconduct or gross negligence.

e. The Voting Trustees may vote the stock represented by the voting trust certificates in person or by such person or persons as they shall select as their proxy.

f. Any of the Voting Trustees may resign at any time by delivering to the other Voting Trustees his resignation in writing; and , in case of death or resignation, in vacancy so occurring shall be filled by the appointment in writing of a successor by the remaining Voting Trustees or Trustee. Notice of the appointment of the successor shall be mailed by United States mail to each voting trust certificate holder within five (5) days of the appointment.

g. Each successor appointed pursuant to Paragraph 5f shall, from the time of such appointment, be deemed a Voting Trustee and shall have all the estate, title, rights, and powers of a Voting Trustee hereunder.

6. *Additional subscribers.* Any holder of any of the common no-par stock of Able Manufacturing, Inc., may, at any time, become a Subscriber hereto with respect to any such stock, by subscribing this Agreement and depositing the certificate(s) of his stock as provided herein, and shall thereupon and thereafter be deemed a Subscriber hereunder.

7. *One agreement.* This Agreement may be executed in several parts of like form simultaneously or at different times, each of which part when executed shall be deemed to be an original; and such parts shall together constitute one and the same instrument.

8. *Governing law.* This Agreement shall be interpreted and governed by the laws of the State of New York.

Dated:

_____
RICHARD ABLE, Voting Trustee

_____
JOHN DOE, Voting Trustee

_____
RICHARD ROE, Voting Trustee

| *Subscriber/Stockholder* | *Address* | *Number of Shares* |
|---|---|---|
| _____ <br> HENRY RICH | 400 Main Street <br> Scranton, Pennsylvania 18519 | 100 |
| _____ <br> GEORGE WEALTHY | 100 Circle Drive <br> Hartford, Connecticut 06105 | 500 |

**FORM IA 2.04**

(Purchase price to be partly in cash and partly in stock)

### OPTION TO BUY STOCK[1]

AGREEMENT made January _____ , 1983, between JOHN DOE, RICHARD ROE, and HENRY KOE, all residents of Middle County, Florida (herein collectively called "Optionors"); and XYZ DISTRIBUTION CORPORATION, a Florida corporation (herein called the "Optionee").

WHEREAS, the Optionee desires to purchase certain issued and outstanding stock of Allied Products, Inc., a Florida corporation; and

WHEREAS, as part of the arrangement between the Optionors and the Optionee, it is agreed that the Optionee is granted an option to purchase 400 of the 500 issued and outstanding common One-Dollar ($1) par value shares of Allied Products, Inc., owned by Optionors as follows:

| | |
|---|---|
| John Doe | 200 shares |
| Richard Roe | 100 shares |
| Henry Koe | 100 shares |

and

WHEREAS, the Optionors and the Optionee have agreed upon all the terms and conditions of this option, and the execution and delivery of this Agreement has been duly authorized by the Board of Directors of the Optionee,

Now, therefore, in consideration of the foregoing, and of the mutual covenants herein contained, and of the payment of $10 per share, being a total of $4,000, the receipt whereof is hereby acknowledged, the parties hereto, intending to be legally bound, agree as follows:

1. *Grant of option.* The Optionors hereby grant to the Optionee an option to purchase from the Optionors, upon the terms and conditions hereinafter set forth, 400 shares of One-Dollar ($1) par value common stock of Allied Products, Inc.

2. *Disposition of option money paid.*

   a. The Four Thousand Dollars ($4,000) paid for this option shall be forfeited by the Optionee to the Optionors in the event that the option is not exercised by the Optionee under the terms and conditions of this Agreement.

   b. The Four Thousand Dollars ($4,000) paid for this option shall be applied to the purchase price set forth in paragraph 3, if the option is exercised by the Optionee under the terms and conditions of this Agreement.

3. *Price of shares.* The price of the shares to be purchased pursuant to the exercise of this option shall be One Hundred Dollars ($100) per share, to be paid partly in cash and partly in stock of the Optionee corporation to the Optionors as follows:

| | |
|---|---|
| John Doe | $8,000 cash and 1,200 shares of no-par common stock of XYZ DISTRIBUTION CORPORATION for 200 shares of Allied Products, Inc. |
| Richard Roe | $4,000 cash and 600 shares of no-par common stock of XYZ DISTRIBUTION CORPORATION for 100 shares of Allied Products, Inc. |
| Henry Koe | $4,000 cash and 600 shares of no-par common stock of XYZ DISTRIBUTION CORPORATION for 100 shares of Allied Products, Inc. |

4. *Time for payment for shares.* The option price of the shares to be purchased pursuant to the exercise of the option hereinbefore granted shall be paid in full at the time of the exercise of the option.

5. *Time of exercise of option.* The option hereinbefore granted may be exercised by the Optionee in whole, but not in part, on or before six (6) months from the date of this option Agreement.

6. *Method of exercising option.* At least five (5) days prior to the date upon which the option hereinbefore granted is to be exercised, the Optionee shall deliver to the Optionors written notice of its election to exercise the option, which notice shall specify the date, place, and time for the exercise of the option and the number of shares in respect of which the option is to be exercised.

The written notice shall be by U.S. mail addressed to the Optionors at the following addresses:

> John Doe
> 100 East Street
> Middletown, Florida 32612
>
> Richard Roe
> 500 Main Street
> Middletown, Florida 32612
>
> Henry Koe
> Star Route 1, Box 27G1
> Middletown, Florida 32612

7. *Payment and delivery of shares.* The Optionee shall, at the date and time specified in such notice, deliver a bank cashier's or treasurer's check in the amount of the cash price for each Optionor's shares less Ten Dollars ($10) per share paid for this option, and shall deliver to the Optionors certificates of the stock in the Optionee corporation required by Paragraph 3, duly endorsed and in proper form for transfer to the Optionors. Contemporaneously with such payments, the Optionors shall deliver to the Optionee, duly endorsed and in proper form for transfer to the Optionee, certificates representing their common shares of Allied Products, Inc., for which the option is being exercised.

8. *Optionors' representations and warranties.* The Optionors represent and warrant as follows:

a. Allied Products, Inc., is a duly organized and existing Florida corporation.

b. Allied Products, Inc., is duly licensed and qualified under the laws of the State of Florida to conduct its manufacturing business.

c. Allied Products, Inc., has no subsidiaries.

d. All of the issued and outstanding shares of Allied Products, Inc., are 500 shares of One-Dollar ($1) par value common stock, which include the 400 shares that are subject to this option.

e. Each Optionor represents and warrants that he is the owner, free and clear of any encumbrances, of the number of the shares in Allied Products, Inc., set opposite his name in Paragraph 3 of this Agreement.

f. An operating statement and balance sheet dated December 31, 1982, were submitted to the Optionee before the signing of this option Agreement, which are true and complete and have been prepared in accordance with generally accepted accounting principles consistently followed through the period indicated.

g. Except for suits of a character incident to the normal conduct of the business of Allied Products, Inc., and involving not more than $1,000 in the aggregate, there is no litigation or proceeding pending, or to the Optionors' knowledge threatened against or relating to, Allied Products, Inc., its properties or business, nor do the Optionors know or have any reasonable grounds to know of any basis for any such action, or of any governmental investigation relative to Allied Products, Inc., its properties or business.

h. The foregoing representations and warranties shall be true at the time of the exercise of the option as though such representations and warranties were made at the time of such exercise of the option.

9. *Optionors' covenants pending exercise of option.* The Optionors covenant that pending the exercise of this option and its closing, they will cause the following conduct of the business of Allied Products, Inc.:

a. The manufacturing business of Allied Products will be conducted only in the ordinary course.

b. No change will be made in the Corporation's Certificate of Incorporation or Bylaws, except as may be first approved in writing by the Optionee.

c. No change will be made in the Corporation's authorized or issued corporate shares.

d. No dividend or other distribution or payment will be declared or made in respect of the corporate shares.

e. No increase will be made in the compensation payable or to become payable by the Corporation to any officer, employee, or agent, nor will any bonus payment or arrangement be made by the Corporation to or with any officer, employee, or agent thereof.

f. No contract or commitment will be entered into by or on behalf of the Corporation extending beyond six (6) months from the date of this option, except normal commitments for the operation of the business, which in any single case will not involve payment by the Corporation of more than $1,000.

g. Use of their best efforts to preserve the Corporation's business organization and production and sales volume intact; to keep available to the Corporation the services of its present officers and employees; and to preserve for the Corporation the goodwill of its suppliers, customers, and others having business relations with the Corporation.

10. *Optionee's representations and warranties.* The Optionee represents and warrants as follows:

a. The book value of its common no-par common stock is Six Dollars ($6) per share at the time of the execution of this option Agreement.

b. The book value of Six Dollars ($6) per share was determined in accordance with generally accepted accounting principles.

11. *Modification.* This Agreement shall become effective as of the date hereof and, unless sooner terminated, shall remain in effect until six (6) months from the date hereof. No modification or amendment of this Agreement shall be effective unless such modification or amendment shall be in writing and signed by the parties hereto.

12. *Construction.* This Agreement shall be deemed to be made under and shall be construed in accordance with the laws of the State of Florida, which is the state of incorporation of the Optionee and of the corporate stock to be purchased.

13. *Binding and benefit.* This Agreement shall be binding upon and inure to the benefit of the Optionors, their successors and assigns, and the Optionee and its successors and assigns.

IN WITNESS WHEREOF, the individual parties have hereto set their hands and seals, and the corporate party has caused this Agreement to be executed under its respective corporate seal in Middle County, Florida.

 

JOHN DOE
_____

RICHARD ROE
_____

HENRY KOE

XYZ DISTRIBUTION CORPORATION

BY:_____
                                   President

(Corporate Seal)

Attest:

_____

Secretary of the Corporation

[1]*18 Am. Jur. 2d Corporations,* para. 376; and *15A Am. Jur. 2d Commercial Code,* paras. 73, 74, 76, 113, and 114.

## FORM IA 2.05

### (Stock purchase of a majority stock interest in closed corporation— payable in installments—insurance funding optional)

### STOCK PURCHASE AGREEMENT[1]

THIS AGREEMENT, made and entered into this 20th day of July, 1982, in the City of Pittsburgh, County of Allegheny and Commonwealth of Pennsylvania, by and between JOHN DOE of Pittsburgh, Pennsylvania (herein called "Seller"); and RICHARD ROE of Pittsburgh, County of Allegheny and Commonwealth of Pennsylvania, and GEORGE POE, of Pittsburgh, County of Allegheny, and Commonwealth of Pennsylvania (herein called "Buyers"), WITNESSETH THAT

WHEREAS, the Seller is presently the owner of at least 801 shares of the common stock of Doe Agency, Inc., a Pennsylvania corporation having its principal place of business located at 100 West Street, Pittsburgh, Pennsylvania, and Seller is the President of said corporation; and

WHEREAS, the Seller desires to sell his shares of stock to the Buyers and the Buyers desire to purchase said stock under certain terms and conditions, hereinafter defined:

NOW THEREFORE, the parties hereto mutually agree as follows:

(1) This Agreement shall become operative, effective, and binding between the parties hereto on October 1, 1982, or prior thereto upon the death or retirement of the Seller.

(2) Seller agrees to sell and Buyers agree to purchase 801 shares of Doe Agency, Inc., common stock for the total consideration of One Hundred Thousand Dollars ($100,000); One Thousand Dollars ($1,000) of which is to be paid at the signing of this Agreement, receipt of which is hereby acknowledged, and the balance of Ninety-nine Thousand Dollars ($99,000) shall be paid in monthly installments of Six Hundred Fifty Dollars ($650), beginning one month from the time this Agreement becomes effective and continuing for a term of 152 months, except that the final payment due upon maturity is Eight Hundred Fifty Dollars ($850).

(3) Seller convenants and warrants to Buyers that 801 shares of common stock of Doe Agency, Inc., represents more than 50 percent of the issued and outstanding stock of Doe Agency, Inc., and also represents more than 50 percent of the authorized capital stock of Doe Agency, Inc.

(4) The monthly payments as provided herein shall be paid directly to Seller, or in the event of his death, to his executors and/or trustees under his Last Will and Testament and Revocable Life Insurance Trust Agreement, as their interests appear.

(5) Seller grants permission to Buyers to purchase, at their own expense, insurance on his life and agrees to cooperate to the fullest extent in securing such insurance, if Buyers so desire, so that at the death of Seller, life insurance proceeds are available toward purchase price of the stock.

(6) It is understood and agreed that in addition to the regular monthly payments provided in Paragraph 2, Buyers may, at their option, make additional prepayments under the terms of this Agreement. However, the amount of credit to be given for such additional payments shall be subject to negotiation between the parties, their heirs, executors, and/or trustees.

(7) Seller covenants and agrees that upon the operative date of this Agreement, to wit, October 1, 1982, or prior thereto upon his death or retirement, he or his executors will execute in blank an assignment of the 801 shares of common stock of Doe Agency, Inc., and deliver same to the Pennsylvania National Bank, Pittsburgh, Pennsylvania, under an Agreement with said Bank, to hold said stock in escrow pending performance under this Agreement by Buyers. A copy of said Escrow Agreement is appended hereto and made part hereof.

(8) It is understood and agreed that the Escrow Agent, to wit, the Pennsylvania National Bank, shall hold such stock until the full amount of the purchase price under this Agreement has been fully paid, at which time the said Escrow Agent shall have authority to write in the names of the Buyers on said assignment so as to designate Buyers as the transferees and assignees of said stock, and immediately thereafter said Escrow Agent shall deliver said stock to Buyers with legal and equitable title to said stock passing to Buyers upon delivery.

(9) Seller, during his lifetime, shall vote the shares of common stock of Doe Agency, Inc., being transferred in escrow as mentioned aforesaid, until such time as Fifty Thousand Dollars ($50,000) of the principal sum due under this Agreement has been fully paid, at which time Seller warrants, covenants, and agrees that he shall execute and deliver proxies to Buyers, who shall thereafter vote said stock so long as Buyers are in compliance with this Agreement. In the event Seller dies prior to the time the amount of Fifty Thousand Dollars ($50,000) of the principal sum due under this Agreement has been fully paid, the Seller's Executors and/or Trustees shall execute proxies to Buyers, who shall thereafter vote said stock so long as Buyers are in compliance with this Agreement.

(10) In the event Buyers default in any payment due under the terms of this Agreement for a period of three consecutive monthly payments or ten cumulative payments during the life of this Agreement, Seller may, at his option, or his executors and/or trustees may at their option, declare this Agreement null and void, and in such event all moneys paid hereunder shall be retained as liquidated damages, and further, in such event, the Escrow Agent shall return the aforesaid shares of stock to Seller, his executors, and/or trustees freed and discharged from any liability whatsoever.

(11) All dividends declared by Doe Agency, Inc., on the aforesaid 801 shares of common stock shall be paid to Buyers as long as Buyers are in compliance with this Agreement.

(12) Seller agrees, as part of the consideration of this Agreement, that upon request of any duly authorized officer of Doe Agency, Inc., or upon request of the Board of Directors or the Executive Committee of said Corporation, he will be available as a consultant to said Corporation and shall render advice based on his experience and judgment, and will further render additional service to said Corporation in any circumstance wherein it is deemed by the Corporation as necessary, during any emergency or crisis; provided however, that Seller shall be paid any expense in-

curred while rendering such service and provided further that his health does not prevent the rendering of such service.

The parties hereto intend to be legally bound by this Agreement.

IN WITNESS WHEREOF, we have hereunto set our hands and seals this 20th day of July, 1982.

WITNESS:                                               _____ (SEAL)

_____                      _____ (SEAL)

_____                      _____ (SEAL)

[1] 15A Am. Jur. 2d Commercial Code, para. 112; and U.C.C. 8-107(2) for seller's action for price of stock. See also Forms IA 2.05(a) and (b).

## FORM IA 2.05(a)

### (Escrow agreement for sale of stock)

### ESCROW AGREEMENT[1]

The PENNSYLVANIA NATIONAL BANK hereby covenants and agrees with JOHN DOE, RICHARD ROE, and GEORGE POE to act as Escrow Agent, and in accordance with the terms and conditions of an Agreement between JOHN DOE, RICHARD ROE, and GEORGE POE, said Agreement being dated 20th day of July, 1982, attached hereto and made a part hereof, except that the PENNSYLVANIA NATIONAL BANK shall have no responsibility whatsoever, as Escrow Agent, to ascertain when payments under said Agreement have been made, or to determine when the total payments under said agreement have been made, or further, to determine if and when there is any default in payments under said Agreement, and PENNSYLVANIA NATIONAL BANK, as Escrow Agent, shall turn over the stock as provided in the Agreement attached hereto, only upon written instructions from the parties, their heirs, executors, assigns, or upon Order of an appropriate court of law.

Duly executed at Pittsburgh, Pennsylvania, this 20th day of July, 1982.

ATTEST:                                               PENNSYLVANIA NATIONAL BANK

_____                      BY_____
                                                                  Trust Officer

WITNESS:

_____                      _____

_____                      JOHN DOE

_____                      _____
                                                       RICHARD ROE

                                                      _____
                                                       GEORGE POE

[1] 28 Am. Jur. 2d Escrow, paras. 2 and 10. For other escrow agreements, see Chapter VI I.

## FORM IA 2.05(b)

### (Waiver agreement by wife of seller of stock)

### AGREEMENT

I, MARY DOE, wife of JOHN DOE, of Pittsburgh, County of Allegheny and Commonwealth of Pennsylvania, hereby approve and join in the Agreement attached hereto and dated July 20, 1982, by and between my husband, JOHN DOE, and RICHARD DOE and GEORGE ROE. I specifically approve and join in said Agreement, wherein my husband, JOHN DOE, is selling his 801 shares of Doe Agency, Inc., stock to Richard Roe and George Poe, together with all the terms, conditions, and restrictions contained in said Agreement, and I further agree to be bound by said

Agreement, its terms and conditions, and waive any and all intestate rights that I may have in said stock under the laws of the Commonwealth of Pennsylvania.

I intend to be legally bound by this Agreement.

WITNESS my hand and seal this 20th day of July, 1982.

WITNESS:

_____          _____ (SEAL)

## FORM IA 2.06

### (Buy-sell agreement between co-purchasers of stock under an installment stock purchase agreement)

### AGREEMENT

THIS AGREEMENT, made and entered into this 20th day of July, 1982, in Pittsburgh, County of Allegheny and Commonwealth of Pennsylvania, by and between RICHARD ROE, of Pittsburgh, County of Allegheny and Commonwealth of Pennsylvania (herein called "party of the first part"), and GEORGE ROE, of Pittsburgh, County of Allegheny and Commonwealth of Pennsylvania (herein called "party of the second part"), WITNESSETH THAT:

WHEREAS, the parties hereto are Co-Purchasers and Buyers under an Agreement dated July 20, 1982, and effective October 1, 1982, by and between Joe Doe, Seller, and themselves, for the installment purchase of 801 shares of Common Stock of Doe Agency, Inc., which Agreement is incorporated by reference thereto and made a part hereof, and herein referred to as the Installment Stock Purchase Contract; and

WHEREAS, the parties hereto believe it to be for the best interest of Doe Agency, Inc., and of the parties hereto, that all interest in the Installment Stock Purchase Contract or stock of a deceased party hereto be acquired by the surviving party; and

WHEREAS, it is the desire and intention of the parties hereto to provide for the disposition of said interest in the Installment Stock Purchase Contract, or stock, as the case may be, in the event of the death of either of them.

NOW, THEREFORE, the parties hereto mutually covenant and agree for themselves, their heirs, executors, administrators, and assigns as follows:

1. That in the event of the death of either party hereto on or before October 1, 1992, said date being ten (10) years from the operative date of the aforementioned Installment Stock Purchase Contract, the surviving party shall purchase and the legal representative or representatives of the deceased party shall sell and transfer to the surviving party all the rights and interest of the deceased party in the aforementioned Installment Stock Purchase Contract for the price of Fifteen Thousand Dollars ($15,000). Said purchase price of $15,000 shall be paid by the surviving party within ninety (90) days from the date of the death of the deceased party, unless there is no legal representative of the decedent's estate appointed within that time. If no legal representative of the decedent's estate shall have qualified within said ninety days, then said purchase price shall be paid within thirty (30) days of the appointment of said representative.

2. That in the event of the death of either party hereto, after October 1, 1992, but before the expiration of said Installment Stock Purchase Contract and transfer of the stock certificates by the Escrow Agent, Pennylvania National Bank, the surviving party shall purchase and the legal representative of the deceased party shall sell to the surviving party all the rights and interest of the deceased party in the aforementioned Installment Stock Purchase Contract for the price of Twenty Thousand Dollars ($20,000). Said purchase price of $20,000 shall be paid as follows: Seventy-five Hundred Dollars ($7,500) shall be paid within ninety (90) days from the date of the death of the deceased party unless there is no legal representative of the decedent's estate appointed within that time. If no legal representative of the decedent's estate shall have qualified within said ninety (90) days, then said $7,500 shall be paid within thirty (30) days of the appointment of said representative. Transfer of the decedent's interest shall be made upon payment of the said $7,500. The additional sum of Twelve Thousand Five Hundred Dollars ($12,500) shall be paid in equal monthly installments for a period not exceeding sixty (60) months after the death of the deceased party.

3. That in the event of the death of either party hereto on or after the expiration of said Installment Stock Purchase Contract and before or after the transfer of the stock certificates by the

Escrow Agent, Pennsylvania National Bank, the surviving party shall purchase and the legal representative of the deceased party shall sell to the surviving party all the rights and interest of the deceased party in the aforementioned Installment Stock Purchase Contract, or as the case may be, transfer to the surviving party all stock issued to the deceased party pursuant to said Installment Stock Purchase Contract, for the price of Fifty Thousand Dollars ($50,000). Said purchase price of $50,000 shall be paid as follows: The sum of Fifteen Thousand Dollars ($15,000) shall be paid within ninety (90) days from the date of death of the deceased party, unless there is no legal representative of the decedent's estate appointed within that time. If no legal representative of the decedent's estate shall have qualified within said ninety (90) days, then said $15,000 shall be paid within thirty (30) days of the appointment of said representative. Transfer of the decedent's interest, or stock, as the case may be, shall be made upon payment of the said $15,000 and the surviving party shall have the stock voting rights thereunder, subject to the provisions of Paragraph 6. However, the personal representative of the deceased party may retain physical possession of the stock certificates as a secured interest until the full $50,000 is paid. The additional sum of Thirty-Five Thousand Dollars ($35,000) shall be paid in equal monthly installments for a period not exceeding sixty (60) months after the death of the deceased party.

4. It is understood and agreed that under Paragraphs 2 and 3 of this Agreement, calling for installment payments, the surviving party shall have the option to pay at any time the entire amount due to the legal representative of the deceased party.

5. In the event the surviving party defaults in any installment payment due under the terms of this Agreement for a period of three (3) successive monthly payments or ten (10) cumulative payments during the life of this Agreement, the legal representative of the deceased party may at his option declare this Agreement null and void, and in such event all moneys paid hereunder shall be retained as liquidated damages.

6. That in the event of the death of either party hereto, the surviving party shall at the time the legal representative of the deceased party sells and transfers all the rights and interest of the deceased party in the aforementioned Installment Stock Purchase Agreement or sells and transfers the stock to the surviving party, as the case may be, execute proxies to the legal representative of the deceased party, and said legal representative of the deceased party shall have the right to vote said stock of the surviving party in the event the surviving party defaults in any of the installment payments due under this Agreement as provided in Paragraph 5 hereof.

7. In the event the parties hereto die within sixty (60) days of each other, this Agreement shall be deemed null and void and the heirs, executors or administrators of the parties hereto shall have no right or obligation hereunder, but their legal representative shall have the rights and obligations under the Installment Stock Purchase Contract, dated July 20, 1982, and effective October 1, 1982, with John Doe.

8. It is understood and agreed that each of the parties hereto, their heirs, executors, administrators, or assigns shall execute any and all documents required to effectuate the terms and conditions of this Agreement.

The parties hereto intend to be legally bound by this Agreement.

IN WITNESS WHEREOF, we have hereunto set our hands and seals this 20th day of July, 1982.

Witness:

_____    _____ (SEAL)

_____    _____ (SEAL)


### FORM IA 2.06(a)

(Waiver agreement by wife of a co-purchaser of stock under
Installment Stock Purchase Agreement)

### AGREEMENT

I, RUTH POE, of Pittsburgh, County of Allegheny and Commonwealth of Pennsylvania, hereby approve and join in the buy and sell Agreement, attached hereto and dated the 20th day of July, 1982, by and between my husband, GEORGE POE, and RICHARD ROE.

I especially approve and join in said buy and sell Agreement, wherein my husband, GEORGE POE, and RICHARD ROE have agreed, in the event of death of either of them, to the terms and conditions in the disposition of their rights and interest under the Installment Stock Purchase

Agreement with John Doe dated July 20, 1982, and/or the disposition of Doe Agency, Inc., stock of the deceased party as the case may be, and I further agree to be bound by the attached buy and sell Agreement, its terms and conditions, and waive any and all intestate rights that I may have in said stock under the laws of the Commonwealth of Pennsylvania.

I intend to be legally bound by this Agreement.

WITNESS my hand and seal this 20th day of July, 1982.

Witness:

_____     _____ (SEAL)

RUTH POE

## FORM IA 2.07

### (Stock purchase by a corporation for cash)

### STOCK PURCHASE AGREEMENT[1]

THIS AGREEMENT made December 30, 1982, by and between BUCKEYE INVESTMENT COR-PORATION, an Ohio corporation (herein called "Buyer"), and RICHARD ROE and MARY ROE, his wife, of Middleville, Ohio (herein called "Sellers"), sole stockholders in RM COMPUTER CENTER, INC., an Ohio corporation.

WITNESSETH:

WHEREAS, the Sellers own all of the issued and outstanding shares of all classes of capital stock of RM Computer Center, Inc. (herein called the "Corporation"); and

WHEREAS, the Corporation sells computer services to businesses in the Elk County, Ohio, area; and

WHEREAS, the Buyer desires to purchase the stock of the Corporation and the Sellers desire to sell to the Buyer;

NOW, THEREFORE, in consideration of the mutual promises, covenants, and warranties herein contained, and subject to the terms and conditions hereof, the parties agree as follows:

1. *Sale of stock*. Subject to the terms and conditions hereof, Sellers hereby agree to sell and Buyer hereby agrees to buy One Hundred (100) shares of the common stock of RM Computer Center, Inc., which shares are all of the issued and outstanding shares of all classes of the capital stock of RM Computer Center, Inc. (said shares of stock herein called the "Purchased Shares").

2. *Closing*. Closing shall occur March 20, 1982, at 2:00 P.M. in the Law Office of John Just, P.A., 100 Main Street, Dayton, Ohio.

3. *Purchase price*. The purchase price of the Purchased Shares of stock shall be the sum of $50,000 and other valuable consideration. The sum of $50,000 shall be paid in cash on closing.

4. *Instruments of conveyance*. At the closing, Sellers shall deliver to Buyer stock certificates for the Purchased Shares duly endorsed, with documentary stamps affixed, free of all encumbrances, rights, and interests of others.

5. *Indemnification*. Sellers shall indemnify and hold the Buyer harmless from any losses incurred as a direct result of any default by the Sellers under this Agreement.

6. *Representations and warranties of Sellers*. The Sellers, as officers of the Corporation, make the following representations and warranties, which Sellers, as officers of the Corporation, agree are true now, shall be true at closing as if made that date, and which shall survive the closing and the delivery of all instruments and documents contemplated herein and any investigation made at any time, for the benefit of the Buyer.

(a) *Organization; good standing*. The Corporation is a corporation duly organized, validly existing, and in good standing under the laws of the State of Ohio.

(b) *Capitalization*. The authorized capital stock of the Corporation consists of Two Hundred Fifty (250) shares of no-par value common stock, of which One Hundred (100) shares are validly issued and now outstanding, fully paid, nonassessable, free of liens, encumbrances, restrictions, and rights of others not a party to this Agreement, and the Sellers own the Purchased Shares without encumbrances and have a right to sell their shares upon the terms and conditions of this Agreement.

(c) *Company assets*. The above-mentioned purchase price shall include all Corporation assets as shown on the attached balance sheet and inventory of tangible assets, *except* accounts receivable and all cash on hand. The Sellers agree that at the time of closing, all tangible assets of the Corporation shall be in good operating condition and repair, subject only to ordinary wear and tear. This warranty is subject, however, to the inspection of Buyer prior to closing and shall not survive closing.

(d) *Title to stock.* At closing, the Sellers, as sole stockholders and as officers of the Corporation, shall have authority and ability to convey to the Buyer good and indefeasible title to the stock, free and clear of all covenants, restrictions, reversions, remainders, or interests of others, and all liens, pledges, charges, or encumbrances of any nature whatsoever.

(e) *Tax returns and payments.* The Corporation has duly filed all federal, state, and local tax returns and reports required to be filed and has duly paid or established adequate reserves for the proper payment of all taxes and other governmental charges upon it or its properties, assets, income, licenses, or sales. All moneys required to be withheld by the Corporation from employees for income taxes, Social Security, and unemployment insurance taxes have been collected or withheld, and either paid to the respective governmental agencies or set aside in accounts for such purposes, or accrued, reserved against, and entered upon the books of the Corporation.

(f) *Financial statements.* A year-end balance sheet and income statement for the Corporation showing earnings and liabilities shall be prepared in accordance with generally accepted accounting principles for the period ending December 30, 1982, and shall be delivered at closing to the Buyer. Said year-end statements shall be prepared, without audit, by Able Rich, P.A., independent certified public accountants for the Corporation.

(g) *Absence of undisclosed liabilities.* The Sellers, as officers of the Corporation, do not know or have reasonable grounds to know of any basis for assertion against the Corporation as of the date hereof of any material claim or liability of any nature in any amount not fully reflected or reserved against in the books and records of the Corporation.

(h) *Litigation, etc.* There is no suit, action or litigation, administrative arbitration, or other proceeding, or governmental investigation or inquiry of any kind regarding the Sellers or the Corporation or its business or properties, nor is there any suit, action, litigation, administrative arbitration, or other proceeding, or governmental investigation or inquiry threatened that might, severally or in the aggregate, materially and adversely affect the financial condition, business, property, assets, or prospects of the Corporation. To the best of Sellers' knowledge and belief, the Corporation has materially complied with and is not in default in any material respect with any law, ordinance, requirement, regulation, or order applicable to its business and properties, and the Corporation has not received notice of any claimed default with respect to any of the foregoing.

(i) *Adverse agreements.* To the best of Sellers' knowledge and belief, neither the Sellers nor the Corporation is a party to any agreement or instrument or subject to any charter or other corporate restriction or any judgment, order, writ, injunction, decree, rule, or regulation that materially and adversely affects or, as far as the Seller can now foresee, may in the future materially and adversely affect the business operations, prospects, properties, assets, or financial condition or otherwise of the Corporation.

7. *Covenants of the Sellers.* The Sellers agree that prior to the closing and upon execution hereof:

(a) *Cooperation.* The Sellers, acting as sole stockholders or as officers of the Corporation, shall use their best efforts to cause the sale contemplated by this Agreement to be consummated. The Sellers, acting as sole stockholders or as officers of the Corporation, will use their best efforts to preserve the Corporation's business organization intact and to keep available the services of its employees and representatives and to preserve the goodwill of its employees, customers, suppliers, and others having business relations with it and to cause the Corporation's business to be conducted so that the covenants, representations, warranties, and provisions hereof are true at closing. The Sellers, acting as sole stockholders or as officers of the Corporation, grant the Buyer the right as of the date of the execution of this agreement to disclose to all Corporation employees the sale of all Corporation stock to the Buyer with the right of the Buyer to retain those employees that meet the terms and conditions of employment that shall be set by the Buyer.

(b) *Transaction out of ordinary course of business.* Except with the prior written consent of the Buyer, the Sellers, acting as sole stockholders or as officers of the Corporation, will not enter into any transaction out of the ordinary course of business from the date hereof to the date of closing.

(c) *Maintenance of properties, etc.* The Sellers, acting as sole stockholders or as officers of the Corporation, will maintain all of the Corporation's properties in customary repair, order, and condition, reasonable wear and tear excepted, and will maintain insurance upon all of its properties and, with respect to the conduct of its business, in such amounts and of such kinds comparable to that in effect on the date of this Agreement.

(d) *Leases.* The Sellers, acting as sole stockholders or as officers of the Corporation, shall ratify and continue to pay those certain lease transactions entered into by the Corporation and its present management with XYZ Corporation for the lease of certain types of computer hardware.

(e) *Access to properties, etc.* The Sellers, acting as sole stockholders or as officers of the Corporation, will give to the Buyer and to Buyer's counsel, accountants, investment advisers, and other representatives full access during normal business hours to all of the properties, books, tax records, contracts, commitments, and records of the Corporation and will furnish to the Buyer all such documents and information with respect to the Corporation's affairs as the Buyer may from time to time reasonably request up to the closing of this transaction.

(f) *Maintenance of books, etc.* The Corporation will maintain its books, accounts, and records in the usual manner on a basis consistent with prior years. The Sellers, as officers of the Corporation, and the Corporation will duly comply in all material respects with all laws and decrees applicable to the Corporation and to the conduct of its business.

(g) *Certain prohibited transactions.* Except with the prior written consent of the Buyer, neither the Corporation nor the Sellers, as officers of the Corporation, shall enter into any contract to cause the Corporation to merge or consolidate with or sell its assets, except in the ordinary course of business, or change the nature or character of its business, or amend its charter or bylaws or enter into any employment agreement, lease, or other agreements not approved by Buyer in writing, nor shall Sellers, acting as officers of the Corporation, or the Corporation grant any stock option, pledge, gift, sell, or otherwise encumber or dispose of any shares of stock that are the subject hereof.

(h) *Limitation of debt.* Except with the prior written consent of the Buyer, the Corporation will not issue or contract to issue indebtedness for borrowed money or guarantees of debt except such accounts payable that may be associated with the purchase of supplies in the ordinary course of business.

(i) *Limitations upon dividends, etc.* No dividends or distributions or payments will be declared paid or made by the Corporation in respect to shares of its capital stock except with the written consent of Buyer. No issuance, purchase, redemption or other acquisition will be made, directly or indirectly, by the Corporation of any shares of its capital stock. No option shall be granted in regard to any of the capital stock of the Corporation by the Sellers, as officers of the corporation, or by the Corporation.

(j) *Other limitations.* No bonuses, salary increases, or extraordinary incentive compensation shall be paid to any agent or employee of the Corporation unless the Buyer has approved the same in writing.

8. *Covenant of Buyer.* The Buyer shall retain the services of Richard Roe, the chief operating officer of RM Computer Center, Inc., as vice-president and chief operating officer of RM Comuter Center, Inc., after the purchase of the Purchased Shares for a period of three (3) years at an annual salary of $25,000 and on such other terms and conditions as are mutually agreed by the parties.

9. *Performance of obligations and agreements.* The Sellers, acting as sole stockholders and as officers of the Corporation, shall cause the Corporation to perform all obligations, agreements, covenants, and conditions contained in this Agreement that require action of the Corporation.

10. *Time of essence.* Time is of the essence in this agreement. If the closing does not take place on or before March 20, 1982, this agreement is terminated. In the event of such termination, unless there shall have been breaches of the agreements or covenants contained in this Agreement, there shall be no liability on the part of the Sellers or the Buyer or their respective shareholders, officers, and directors.

11. *Waivers and notices.* Any failure by any party to this Agreement to comply with any of its obligations, agreements, or covenants hereunder may be waived in writing by the Sellers, acting as sole stockholders or as officers of the Corporation, in the case of a default by the Buyer, and by the Buyer in the case of a default by the Sellers.

12. *Miscellaneous.* This Agreement cannot be amended or terminated orally but only by a writing approved by the Sellers and Buyer.

13. *Survival.* The representations, warranties, promises, covenants, agreements, indemnities, and undertakings of the parties contained in this Agreement shall survive the closing and delivery of documents hereunder.

14. *Litigation costs.* If any legal proceeding is brought to enforce this Agreement, or any provision hereof, or because of a default in any representation, warranty, covenant, or other provision hereof, the successful or prevailing party shall be paid all costs including attorney's fees through all proceedings, trials, or appeals.

15. *Cooperation in lawsuits.* Each Seller agrees that from and after the day of the closing, they will cooperate with the Buyer, and each person who is an officer or director of the Buyer, in regard to any lawsuits against the Corporation that are pending at the time of this Agreement, and to facilitate and assist the Corporation and/or the Buyer and their insurance agents in the settlement and satisfactory resolution of such lawsuits, including, but not limited to, the giving of depositions, testimony, production of books and records, and other such matters that may be required.

IN WITNESS WHEREOF, the parties have executed this Agreement as of the date first above written.

WITNESSES:                                   BUCKEYE INVESTMENT CORPORATION

_____       BY: _____
                                                           President

WITNESSES:

_____

                                        _____
                                        RICHARD ROE

_____

                                        _____
                                        MARY ROE

[1]*15A Am. Jur. 2d Commercial Code*, para. 95. Compare Form VID 1.05 for sale of assets of a close corporation.

## FORM IA 2.07(a)

### (Conditions precedent)

### ALTERNATIVE CLAUSE

*Conditions precedent.* All obligations of the Buyer under this Agreement are subject to the fulfillment, prior to or at the closing, of each of the following conditions:

(a) *Representations and warranties true at closing.* The Sellers' representations and warranties contained in this Agreement shall be true at the time of closing as though such representations and warranties were made at such time.

(b) *Performance.* The Sellers shall have performed and complied with all agreements and conditions required by this Agreement to be performed or complied with by them prior to or at the closing.

(c) *Officers' certificate.* The Sellers shall have delivered to the Buyer a certificate of the Company's president and treasurer, dated the closing date, certifying in such detail as the Buyer may specify that the representations, warranties, and performance specified in this Paragraph have been fulfilled.

[1]*41 Am. Jr. 2d Indemnity*, paras. 1, 2 and 6. See also Chapter VIIIL for other indemnity agreements

## FORM IA 2.07(b)

### (Indemnification of buyer by seller of stock)[1]

### ALTERNATIVE CLAUSE

*Indemnification.* The Seller shall indemnify and hold harmless the Corporation and the Buyer, at all times after the date of this agreement, against and in respect of: (a) all liabilities of the Corporation of any nature, including, but not limited to, any brokerage fees or other commissions relative to this agreement, whether accrued, absolute, contingent, or otherwise, existing on March 1, 1982, to the extent not reflected or reserved against in full in the Corporation's balance sheet of that date, including, without limitation, any tax liabilities to the extent not so reflected or reserved against, accrued in respect of, or measured by the Corporation's income for, any period prior to March 1, 1982, or arising out of transactions entered into, or any state of facts existing, prior to such date; (b) all liabilities of, or claims against, the Corporation arising out of the conduct of the Corporation's business between March 1, 1982, and the closing, otherwise than in ordinary course or permitted under the terms of this Agreement.

[1] *41 Am. Jr. 2d Indemnity*, paras. 1, 2 and 6. See also Chapter VIIIL for other indemnity agreements

## FORM IA 2.08

### (Profit and loss statement)[1]

CLIENT #008                                     ABC COMPANY                                          DIV
FOR THE 7 MONTHS ENDED 06/30/82                                                                     PAGE 1

### STATEMENT OF INCOME AND EXPENSE[2]

|  | CURRENT MONTH | % | YEAR TO DATE | % |
|---|---|---|---|---|
| INCOME |  |  |  |  |
| SALES—REGULAR | .00 | .00 | 33,478.73 | 99.88 |
| SALES TAX COMMISSION | .00 | .00 | 40.85 | .12 |
| TOTAL INCOME | .00 | .00 | 33,519.58 | 100.00 |
| COST OF SALES |  |  |  |  |
| PURCHASES—REGULAR | .00 | .00 | 21,339.80 | 63.66 |
| TOTAL COST OF SALES | .00 | .00 | 21,339.80 | 63.66 |
| GROSS PROFIT | .00 | .00 | 12,179.78 | 36.34 |
| GENERAL EXPENSES |  |  |  |  |
| ACCOUNTING & LEGAL | .00 | .00 | 425.00 | 1.27 |
| ADVERTISING | .00 | .00 | 68.64 | .20 |
| BANK CHARGES | .00 | .00 | 30.19 | .09 |
| FUEL | .00 | .00 | 687.33 | 2.05 |
| HOSPITALIZATION INSURANCE | .00 | .00 | 473.52 | 1.41 |
| INSURANCE EXPENSE | .00 | .00 | 354.12 | 1.06 |
| LICENSES & TAXES | .00 | .00 | 86.71 | .26 |
| LIGHT, POWER, ETC. | .00 | .00 | 495.12 | 1.48 |
| RENT | .00 | .00 | 3,756.00 | 11.21 |
| TELEPHONE | .00 | .00 | 402.31 | 1.20 |
| TOTAL GENERAL EXPENSES | .00 | .00 | 6,778.94 | 20.22 |
| NET PROFIT OR LOSS | .00 | .00 | 5,400.84 | 16.11 |

[1] *1 AM. Jr. 2d Accountants*, para. 16. Compare Form IA 2.09.
[2] Contributed by James E. Patton, Accountant, Inverness, Florida.

## FORM IA 2.09

### (Balance sheet)[1]

CLIENT #008                                     ABC COMPANY                                          PAGE 1
DATE 06/30/82

### STATEMENT OF FINANCIAL CONDITION[2]

| ASSETS |  |  |
|---|---|---|
| CURRENT ASSETS |  |  |
| CASH ON HAND | 172.00 |  |
| PETTY CASH | 75.00 |  |
| CITIZENS BANK | 137.56 |  |
| ACCOUNT RECEIVABLES—TRADE | 151.97 |  |
| UTILITY DEPOSITS | 599.18 |  |
| INVENTORIES | 27,190.33 |  |
| TOTAL CURRENT ASSETS |  | 28,326.04 |
| PROPERTY, PLANT, & EQUIPMENT |  |  |
| TRUCKS & AUTO | 2,403.00 |  |
| FURNITURE, FIXTURES & EQUIP. | 16,272.15 |  |
| ACCUMULATED DEPRECIATION TRUCK | (1,722.24) |  |

| | | |
|---|---|---|
| ACCUMULATED DEPRECIATION FEE | (14,880.15) | |
| TOTAL P,P, & E | | 2,072.76 |
| TOTAL ASSETS | | | 30,398.80 |
| LIABILITIES & NET WORTH | | |
| CURRENT LIABILITIES | | |
| SALES TAX PAYABLES | 228.58 | |
| TOTAL CURRENT LIABILITY | | 228.58 |
| LONG-TERM DEBT | | |
| NOTES PAYABLE | 22,637.52 | |
| TOTAL LONG-TERM DEBT | | 22,637.52 |
| NET WORTH | | |
| CAPITAL | 6,381.86 | |
| DRAW | (4,250.00) | |
| NET PROFIT & LOSS | 5,400.84 | |
| TOTAL NET WORTH | | 7,532.70 |
| TOTAL NET WORTH & LIABILITY | | | 30,398.80 |

[1] *1 Am. Jur. 2d Accountants,* para. 16. Compare Form IA 2.08.
[2] Contributed by James E. Patton, Accountant, Inverness, Florida.

## FORM IA 2.10

### (Present redemption of entire stock of stockholder for cash)

#### STOCK REDEMPTION AGREEMENT[1]

AGREEMENT made May 1, 1983, between RIVER IRON PRODUCTS, INC., a Pennsylvania corporation (herein called the "Corporation"), and John Doe of Pittsburgh, Pennsylvania (herein called the "Retiring Stockholder").

WHEREAS, the authorized capital stock of the Corporation is 5,000 shares of no-par common stock, of which 3,500 shares are issued and outstanding; and

WHEREAS, the Retiring Stockholder is the owner of 2,000 shares of the stock of the Corporation and he desires to retire for reasons of health and has offered to sell all of his shares to the Corporation at a price of One Hundred Dollars ($100) per share; and

WHEREAS, the Board of Directors of the Corporation has duly determined that the price of $100 per share is fair and that the offer of the Retiring Stockholder should be accepted;

IT IS THEREFORE AGREED:

1. *Resignation of Retiring Shareholder.* Upon the signing of this Agreement, the Retiring Stockholder shall submit his resignation as a director and president of the Corporation, which resignations shall take effect immediately.

2. *Surrender of shares.* Upon the signing of this Agreement, the Retiring Stockholder shall surrender to the Corporation the certificates representing the 2,000 shares owned by him, each certificate duly endorsed in blank for transfer.

3. *Warranties and representations by Retiring Shareholder.* The Retiring Stockholder represents and warrants that he is the sole owner of the 2,000 shares of stock of the Corporation, and that all of the shares are free and clear of liens or encumbrances of any kind, including any third-party legal or beneficial interest of any kind.

4. *Warranties and representations by the Corporation.* The Corporation represents that its earned surplus immediately prior to the execution of this Agreement was in excess of the amount required to be paid to the Retiring Stockholder hereunder, and that the redemption of its shares pursuant to this Agreement is not in violation of any Corporation law or other laws to which the Corporation is subject.

5. *Mutual general releases.* Upon the signing of this Agreement, the Corporation and the Retiring Stockholder shall exchange general releases that shall except only their respective obligations under this agreement.

6. *Payment of redemption price.* Upon the signing of this Agreement, the Corporation shall forthwith accept from the Retiring Stockholder the surrender of the certificates for his 2,000 shares of the no-par common stock of the Corporation and his resignations and general release required hereunder, and the Corporation shall deliver forthwith to the Retiring Shareholder its

certified check for Two Hundred Thousand Dollars ($200,000) and its general release required hereunder.

ATTEST:                                        RIVER IRON PRODUCTS, INC.

_____   BY _____
Secretary of the Corporation                          President

                                        _____
                                                  JOHN DOE

[1] *18 Am. Jur. 2d Corporations,* paras. 282–287; and 26 U.S.C.A. 301 and 302 together, and 318. Compare Form IA 2.11 for alternative clauses where price is paid in installments.

## FORM IA 2.11

### (Stock redemption agreement—FUTURE insurance optional, cash or installment)

### STOCK REDEMPTION AGREEMENT[1]

THIS AGREEMENT made March 10, 1982, at Chicago, Illinois, by and between Roe Packing Co., Inc., an Illinois corporation (herein called the "Corporation"), and Richard Roe, John Doe, and George Poe, herein individually called "Stockholder" and collectively called "Stockholders."

WHEREAS, the Stockholders presently own all of the issued and outstanding capital stock of the Corporation; and

WHEREAS, the parties hereto desire to promote their mutual interests by imposing certain restrictions and obligations on their stock ownership in the Corporation and believe it is in the best interest of the Corporation to do so;

NOW, THEREFORE, in consideration of the mutual promises herein contained, it is agreed as follows:

1. *Future purchase and sale of stock.* Upon the termination of employment by the Corporation of one of the Stockholders for any reason whatever (including, without limitation, the death or disability of any such Stockholder), the Corporation shall purchase and the terminated employee, his estate, or his successor or successors in interest shall sell all the Corporation's stock owned by such person at the time of a termination or death at the price provided in Paragraph 2. All stock owned by the terminated or deceased Stockholder shall be purchased within sixty (60) days after the termination of his employment with the Corporation, or if such termination is occasioned by the death of such person, the sales hereunder shall be made within sixty (60) days after the appointment of a legal representative for his estate. Within such period of time, the respective seller or sellers shall endorse and deliver to the Corporation the stock certificate or certificates representing the share of stock required to be purchased and sold under this Agreement, and the purchase price shall be paid in accordance with Paragraphs 2 and 3.

2. *Determination of purchase price by book value.* The purchase price of the stock required to be purchased and sold hereunder shall be the book value thereof as of the close of business on the last day of the month in which the termination of employment occurs. Said book value shall be determined by the certified public accountant who is then servicing the account of the Corporation, and shall be made in accordance with sound and accepted accounting principles and practices consistently applied; provided, however, that the following directions shall be applied in arriving at the book value, unless the parties have agreed to a purchase price pursuant to Paragraph 3:

   (1) If a Stockholder's employment is terminated by reason of his death, all life insurance proceeds payable to the Corporation on account of the Stockholder's death shall be taken into account in determining the book value, whether or not such proceeds have been paid to the Corporation as of the valuation date.

   (2) Write-ups and write-downs in book value made by the directors or shareholders shall be disregarded.

   (3) Readily marketable securities owned by the Corporation as of the valuation date shall be taken into account at their fair market value.

   (4) If the Corporation owns, on the valuation date, stock possessing more than one-half of the voting power in another corporation, such stock shall be taken into account for this purpose at its book value pursuant to the books and records of such other corporation as of the

valuation date, and in determining such other corporation's book value for this purpose the directions contained in Paragraph 2 shall be followed.

3. *Determination of purchase price by agreement of parties.* There may from time to time be attached hereto one or more pages of paper designating a price agreed to by the parties as follows:

(1) The Corporation and the Stockholders may, from time to time after the execution of this Agreement, by mutual assent, designate a price to be paid by the Corporation for the shares presently owned by each of them.

(2) Each such designation of a price shall be dated as of the date it is added to this Agreement by the written attachment to the Agreement and shall be signed by the Corporation and the Stockholders.

(3) Notwithstanding the provisions of Paragraph 2(a), if a price has been designated after the execution of this Agreement, within the two-year period ending on the date of a Stockholder's termination of employment, then the price that was last added to this Agreement within such period shall be the price to be paid for the stock of the Corporation.

4. *Manner of payment.* Upon delivery of the stock certificate or certificates to the Corporation, the Corporation shall pay to each seller the Stockholder's proportionate part of the purchase price; provided, however, that if the termination of employment shall be for a reason other than the death of a Stockholder, or if such termination shall be occasioned by the death of a Stockholder but the insurance proceeds payable to the Corporation as a result of his death are insufficient in amount to pay each seller such Stockholder's proportionate part of the purchase price payable with respect to the stock purchased and sold hereunder on account of his death, then the Corporation shall pay to each such seller Thirty Percent (30%) of the purchase price payable to such Stockholder concurrently with the delivery of the stock certificate or stock certificates to the Corporation, and shall pay the balance of said purchase price in five (5) equal annual payments commencing one year from the date of such sale; together with interest at the rate of Nine Percent (9%) per annum, payable with each installment of principal. Upon default of any payment of principal or interest required to be made, which default is not cured within thirty (30) days after notice of default is given by the Stockholder or his successor or successors in interest to the Corporation, the entire unpaid balance owing to any and all persons by the Corporation on account of the purchase of stock shall become due and payable on the expiration of 30 days from the date of the notice of default.

5. *Prepayment.* The Corporation shall have the right to prepay after the calendar year in which the first payment is made, in whole or in part, the balance of the purchase price; provided, however, that if the Corporation shall make a prepayment at a time when such Corporation owes an amount pursuant to this agreement to two or more Stockholders, such prepayment shall be made to all such Stockholders in the proportion that the balance owing to each Stockholder bears to the aggregate balance owing hereunder pursuant to this Agreement; provided further that any such prepayment shall be applied to the installments due under Paragraph 4 hereinabove in reverse chronological order of their due dates.

6. *Cooperation of stockholders.* Each Stockholder agrees, for himself and his successor or successors in interest, to take appropriate action as a Stockholder of the Corporation to reduce the stated capital of the Corporation and/or to cause the Corporation to write up to fair market value any or all of its physical assets, if either or both of such actions are necessary or desirable to make lawful the purchase by the Corporation of its own shares pursuant to the provisions of this Agreement; provided, however, that no such write-up shall increase the book value that may be made pursuant to the provisions of Paragraph 2.

7. *Restrictions.* Each of the Stockholders agrees not to dispose of or encumber the stock presently owned by him in the Corporation except subject to the terms of this Agreement, and it is hereby agreed by and between the parties hereto that any such disposition or encumbrance shall at all times be subject to the terms of this Agreement, to the end that upon the termination of employment with the Corporation of a Stockholder, any person who then owns some or all of the stock presently owned by the Stockholder shall be obligated to sell his stock upon the terms and conditions set forth in this Agreement.

8. *Endorsement of restriction or stock certificate.* Upon the execution of this Agreement, the certificates of stock subject hereto shall be surrendered to the Corporation and endorsed as follows:

"The shares represented by this certificate are subject to a certain Agreement entered into on the 10th day of March, 1982, be and between Roe Packing Co., Inc., Richard Roe, John Doe, and George Poe, restricting the free transferability of said shares. The Corporation will mail to the holder of this certificate, without charge, a copy of such Agreement within five (5) days after receiving a written request therefor."

After endorsement, the certificates shall be returned to the Stockholders, who shall, subject to the terms of this Agreement, be entitled to exercise all rights of ownership of such stock. The Corporation agrees that it will cause a similar endorsement to be placed on all certificates hereafter issued by it, and which are subject to the provisions of this agreement.

9. *Necessary acts.* Each of the parties hereto agrees that he will do any act or thing and will execute any and all instruments necessary and/or proper to make effective the provisions of this Agreement.

10. *Agreement binding.* This Agreement shall inure to the benefit of and be binding upon the parties hereto and their respective next of kin, legatees, administrators, executors, legal representatives, successors, and assigns (including remote, as well as immediate, successors to and assignees of said parties).

IN WITNESS WHEREOF, the parties hereto have executed this Agreement in quadruplicate on the day and year first above written.

ATTEST:

ROE PACKING CO., INC.

BY _____
                     President

_____
Secretary of the Corporation

_____
RICHARD ROE

_____
JOHN DOE

_____
GEORGE POE

[1] *18 Am. Jur. 2d Corporations,* para. 286; and 26 U.S.C.A. 301 and 302 together, and 303; and 26 U.S.C.A. 1001 for installment method of reporting gain or election not to use installment method.

## FORM IA 2.11(a)

### (Life insurance proceeds to be *excluded* from book value in determining redemption price of stock)

### ALTERNATIVE CLAUSE

*Determination of purchase price by book value.* The purchase price of the stock required to be purchased and sold hereunder shall be the book value thereof as of the close of business on the last day of the month in which termination of employment occurs or, in the case of termination by the death of a Stockholder, on the last day of the month immediately preceding the Stockholder's death. Said book value shall be determined by the certified public accountant who is then servicing the account of the Corporation, and shall be made in accordance with sound and accepted accounting principles and practices consistently applied; provided, however, that the following directions shall be applied in arriving at the book value, unless the parties have agreed to a purchase price pursuant to this Agreement.

(1) If a Stockholder's employment is terminated by reason of his death, all life insurance proceeds payable to the Corporation on account of the Stockholder's death shall be excluded from the determination of book value; but such insurance proceeds shall be used to pay the purchase price for the deceased Stockholder's stock as provided in this Agreement.

(2) In the event that the insurance proceeds are insufficient to pay the full amount of the purchase price for the deceased Stockholder's stock as provided in this Agreement, the amount of the insurance proceeds shall be paid in full to his personal representative within ten (10) days of the personal representative's appointment. The balance of the purchase price shall be paid in accordance with the provisions for payment of balance of purchase price provided in Paragraph 4 of this Agreement.

**FORM IA 2.12**

(Agreement of majority stockholders with minority stockholder for
purchase of minority stock by majority stockholders and for the
cross-purchase of each majority stockholder's stock by the other—
with an option)

### CROSS-PURCHASE AGREEMENT AND OPTION[1]

THIS AGREEMENT made 5th day of November, 1982, by and between:
JOHN DOE and RICHARD ROE (herein called "Majority Shareholders") and GEORGE POE (herein called "Minority Shareholder"); WITNESSETH,

WHEREAS, the Majority Shareholders own Ninety-eight Percent (98%) of the entire capital stock and the Minority Shareholder owns Two Percent (2%) of the entire capital stock of Right Manufacturing, Inc., a corporation with its principal place of business in Atlanta, DeKalb County, Georgia (herein called "Corporation"); and

WHEREAS, the Shareholders wish to provide for the continuity and harmony in management of the Corporation in the event of the death or the withdrawal of any of them; and

WHEREAS, the Majority Shareholders wish to provide for the purchase by the remaining Majority Share of the other Majority Shareholder's stock in the event of his death, or in the event he wishes to dispose of any of his stock during his lifetime, and to provide the formula to establish a fair and justifiable price therefor; and

WHEREAS, the Shareholders wish to provide for the orderly and proper purchase or disposal of the shares held by the Minority Shareholder in the event of his death or in the event he wishes to dispose of his stock during his lifetime, and to provide a fair and equitable formula for maintenance of the balance of control between the Majority Shareholders.

NOW, THEREFORE, in consideration of the mutual promises herein contained and other good and valuable consideration, receipt of which is hereby acknowledged, the Shareholders mutually agree as follows:

1. RESTRICTION ON STOCK

A. *Majority Shareholders.* During the joint lives of John Doe and Richard Roe, neither of them shall, without the written consent of the other, encumber or dispose of the shares of stock of the Corporation now owned or hereafter acquired by him, unless he shall first offer to encumber or dispose of his shares of stock to the other upon the same terms and conditions offered by a bona fide prospective lender or purchaser. If there is no bona fide prospective lender or purchaser, then upon an offer by one of the Majority Shareholders to the other to sell his shares, the purchase price shall be determined by the book value of each such share as shown on the balance sheet of the Corporation at the end of its last preceding fiscal year, prepared and certified by the firm of accountants then servicing the Corporation; provided however, that the book value carried thereon of the real property and personal property owned by the Corporation shall be adjusted by using the fair market value of that property instead of the book value at the time of such offer. Fair market value is to be determined by the following formulas:

(1) Real Property. Fair market value of buildings and real property and personal property not described in Paragraph 2 below shall be determined by the use of outside professional appraisers. One appraiser shall be hired by the Corporation, and one shall be hired by the withdrawing Shareholder at his own expense. The two appraisers shall agree to hire a third appraiser. The cost of the third appraiser shall be shared equally between the Corporation and the withdrawing Shareholder. Each of the three appraisers shall arrive at his evaluation of the aforesaid property independently. The three evaluations shall be submitted to the Corporation and to the withdrawing Shareholder. The fair market value of the property in question shall be the sum of the three evaluations divided by three.

(2) Personal Property.

a) Manufacturing Equipment. Fair market value of manufacturing equipment is hereby agreed by and between the Corporation and any future withdrawing Shareholder to be that sum established by the manufacturing equipment distributor for that equipment who services the DeKalb County, Georgia, area, or who provided the bulk of the manufacturing equipment utilized by the Corporation, whichever is available, and that this portion of the total assets shall be arbitrarily determined by this single aforesaid appraisal.

b) Accounts Receivable. Fair market value of accounts receivable shall be by audit. The audit shall be performed by the accountant or accounting firm retained by the Corporation at the time the notice of withdrawal is received by the Corporation. The total amount of accounts receivable shall be reduced by the percentage of uncollectable accounts experienced by the Corporation during the two fiscal years prior to receipt of the notice of withdrawal by the Corporation. The first preceding fiscal year shall be arbitrarily determined to be the fiscal year in which said notice is received. The total amount of accounts receivable less uncollectables shall be divided by the number of active Shareholders at the time of the said notice of withdrawal to determine the withdrawing Shareholder's share. The withdrawing Shareholder may, at his own expense, retain an accounting firm of his own choice, and the Corporation agrees to make available the Corporation books and records or copies of same to that accountant. In the event of disagreement between the two auditing firms, the final determination of the value of the accounts receivable shall be a sum equal to one-half the difference between the two independent audits, plus the amount of the lesser audit.

B. *Minority Shareholder.* During the life of George Poe, he shall not, without the written consent of the Majority Shareholders, encumber or dispose of the shares of stock of the Corporation now owned or hereafter acquired by him, unless he shall first offer to encumber or dispose of his share of stock in equal shares to the Majority Shareholders upon the same terms and conditions offered by a bona fide prospective lender or purchaser.

2. OPTION TO PURCHASE STOCK ON DEATH

A. *Majority Shareholders.* Upon the death of either John Doe or Richard Roe, the survivor shall have the option to purchase all the shares of stock of the Corporation owned by the other upon the following terms:

(1) Exercise Option. The option to purchase the stock of the decedent shall be exercised by the survivor by serving written notice on the personal representative of the decedent's estate within thirty (30) days after the qualification of said personal representative.

(2) Purchase Price. The purchase price for each share of stock shall be the book value of each such share as shown on the balance sheet of the Corporation at the end of its last preceding fiscal year, prepared and certified by the firm of accountants then servicing the Company. No adjustment in the book value of such shares of stock shall be made for operations of the Corporation from the end of its last preceding fiscal year to the date of death.

(3) Payment of Purchase Price. Within ten (10) days after the exercise of this option, the survivor shall pay to the estate of the decedent not less than one-fourth of the total purchase price to be paid, and shall deliver to the estate of the decedent promissory notes for the balance of the purchase price providing for equal annual payments of the principal over a period not to exceed three years from the date of the decedent's death, the first annual payment to be made one year after the date of the decedent's death. The survivor shall have the right to prepay the entire unpaid principal and accrued interest on thirty (30) days' written notice to the decedent's estate. Such promissory notes shall bear interest at the rate of Eight Percent (8%) per annum, payable annually, and shall provide for the acceleration of the maturity of the unpaid principal and interest of all promissory notes upon default in the payment of any installment of principal or interest.

(4) Security for Payment. The entire stock of the decedent shall be pledged with the decedent's estate or an escrow agent mutually agreed upon to secure the full payment of the purchase price. So long as the survivor is not in default, he shall have all voting and dividend rights in the stock of the decedent. Upon full payment of the purchase price, the decedent's estate or the authorized escrow agent shall transfer such stock to the survivor. In the event of a default by the survivor, all the rights of the survivor in the decedent's stock shall automatically terminate, and the portion of the purchase price theretofore paid by the survivor shall be retained by the decedent's estate in full satisfaction of all damages caused by the survivor's default.

B. *Minority Shareholder.* Upon the death of George Poe, the Majority Shareholders shall have the option to purchase all the shares of stock of the Corporation owned by the decedent upon the following terms:

(1) Maintenance of Parity. If the Majority Shareholders elect to purchase the Minority Shareholder's stock, then each Majority Shareholder shall be allowed to acquire only that amount of shares equal to those acquired by the other Majority Shareholder, so that each Majority Shareholder shall not own more than the other Majority Shareholder.

(2) Purchase Price. The purchase price for each share of stock shall be the book value of each such share as shown on the balance sheet of the Corporation, at the end of its last preceding fiscal year, as prepared and certified by the firm of accountants then servicing the Corporation. No adjustment in the book value of such shares of stock shall be made for

operations of the Corporation from the end of its last preceding fiscal year to the date of death or for the market value of real and personal property provided in Paragraph 1A.

(3) Payment of Purchase Price. If the Majority Shareholders elect to purchase the Minority Shareholder's interest as defined in Paragraphs 2B(1) and 2B(2), the purchase offer shall be served in writing on the personal representative of the decedent within thirty (30) days after the qualification of said personal representative, and the purchase price shall be in cash, paid not more than sixty (60) days after service of the written notice of exercising the option to purchase.

(4) Election by Majority Shareholders Not to Purchase Minority Shareholder's Interest. If the Majority Shareholders elect not to purchase the deceased Minority Shareholder's interest, then any sale by the Estate of this asset shall be only to prospective purchasers of said asset whose approval has been gained by the Majority Shareholders, said approval to be in writing and executed in advance of any sale.

3. ENDORSEMENT ON STOCK CERTIFICATES

The certificates of stock of the Corporation now owned by John Doe, Richard Roe, and George Poe have been endorsed as follows:

"The shares of stock represented by this certificate are subject to an outstanding and unexercised purchase option and to all the terms of an agreement made November 5, 1982, between John Doe and Richard Roe, and George Poe, a copy of which is on file at the office of the Corporation."

Upon the purchase of any additional shares of common stock of the Corporation from the Corporation by John Doe, Richard Roe, or George Poe, the purchaser shall notify the Corporation of this agreement and the new stock certificate issued by the Corporation shall be similarly endorsed.

4. FAILURE TO EXERCISE OPTION

Upon the failure of the survivor(s) to exercise the option to purchase all the shares of stock of the Company owned by a decedent pursuant to Paragraph 2A or B, the restrictions imposed by this Agreement on the decedent's certificate shall automatically terminate and all the decedent's certificates for such shares of stock may be delivered to the Corporation, which shall thereupon issue new certificates without the endorsement of the legend provided for in Paragraph 3.

5. TERM

Notwithstanding anything herein contained to the contrary, this Agreement shall terminate and all rights and obligations thereunder shall cease upon the happening of any of the following events:

A. The adjudication of the Corporation as a bankrupt, the execution of it by any assignment for the benefit of creditors, or the appointment of a receiver for the Corporation.

B. The voluntary or involuntary dissolution of the Corporation.

C. The death of John Doe and Richard Roe in a common accident, or the death of one within thirty (30) days after the death of the other.

6. NECESSARY DOCUMENTS

Upon exercise of an option under Paragraph 2A or B, the personal representative of the decedent shall execute and deliver all necessary documents required to carry out the terms of this Agreement.

7. BENEFIT

This Agreement shall be binding upon, and inure to the benefit of all the parties hereto and their personal representative(s).

IN WITNESS WHEREOF, the parties have signed this Agreement in Atlanta, Georgia, on the above date.

WITNESS:

_____     _____
                                     JOHN DOE

_____     _____
                                     RICHARD ROE

_____     _____
                                     GEORGE POE

[1]*18 Am. Jur. 2d Corporations,* paras. 390–393.

## FORM IA 2.13

### (Mandatory buy-sell agreement between shareholders and the corporation funded by insurance)

### BUY-SELL AGREEMENT[1]

AGREEMENT made 5th day of December, 1982, between John Doe, Richard Roe, and George Poe, individuals (herein separately called "Stockholder" and collectively called "Stockholders"), and by them with Success Corporation, a Florida corporation (herein called "Corporation").

WITNESSETH:

WHEREAS, the Stockholders own all the authorized and outstanding stock in the Corporation, owning 333⅓ shares each of the authorized 1,000 shares of One-Dollar ($1) par value common stock of the Corporation; and

WHEREAS, there is not now nor is there likely in the future to be a substantial market for the shares of the Corporation; and the parties believe that it is in the best interest of the Corporation and the Stockholders to provide for the future disposition of the shares of the Corporation, and to provide that such shares shall be transferable only upon compliance with the terms of this Agreement; and

WHEREAS, for the foregoing reasons, the parties desire to provide (1) for the purchase of the stock of any party desiring to sell the same by the Corporation or the remaining parties, and (2) for the purchase of the stock of a deceased party by the Corporation or the surviving parties.

IT IS MUTUALLY AGREED, as follows:

1. *Consideration.* The consideration for this Agreement is Ten Dollars ($10) and the premises and the mutual promises herein contained.

2. *Stock transfer restricted.* No stockholder shall transfer, pledge, assign, encumber or otherwise dispose of all or any part of his stockholdings in the Corporation except as provided in this Agreement.

3. *Legend on shares.* The secretary of the Corporation shall endorse the following legend on each share certificate prior to its delivery to a stockholder:

"The shares of stock evidenced by this certificate may not be transferred, pledged, assigned, encumbered, or otherwise disposed of except in accordance with the terms of a buy-sell agreement dated December 5, 1982, a copy of which is inserted in the record book of the Corporation."

4. *Purchase during life of Stockholder.* In the event any Stockholder party to this Agreement desires to sell, transfer, encumber or otherwise dispose of all or any part of his shares in the Corporation, he shall deliver written notice of such desire to the Corporation and to each Stockholder member of this Agreement, specifying the number of shares he desires to dispose of. On receipt of such notice, the Corporation shall to the extent it is permitted to do so by the Florida General Corporation Act or any successor statute buy, and the Stockholder shall sell to the Corporation, the number of shares set forth in the notice at the place and on the terms set forth in Paragraphs 7 and 8 hereof.

5. *Purchase on death of Stockholder.* On the death of any Stockholder party to this Agreement, the Corporation shall, if not prohibited by the Florida General Corporation Act or any successor statute from doing so, buy, and the executor, administrator, or personal representative of the Stockholder shall sell to the Corporation, all of the shares owned by the Stockholder at the time of his death at the price and on the terms set forth in Paragraphs 6, 7, and 8 hereof.

6. *Remaining Stockholders' option to purchase on death of a Stockholder.* If the Corporation is prohibited by the Florida General Corporation Act or any successor statute from buying any of the shares offered for sale pursuant to this Agreement, or if the Corporation elects not to buy any of the shares offered for sale to it, then each of the other Stockholders shall have the option to buy, and the offering Stockholder(s) shall be obligated to sell to each, a proportion of such stock equal to the ratio of the number of shares owned by such Stockholders to the total shares owned by the remaining Stockholders excluding the seller, and if a Stockholder is unable or unwilling to buy the proportion of stock allotted to him, the other Stockholders shall have the right to buy the balance in a similar ratio. The purchase price for such stock and the terms of sale shall be as set forth in Paragraphs 7 and 8 hereof.

7. *Price and terms of sale.* The purchase price hereunder shall be the net book value per share multiplied by the number of shares to be purchased, such value to be determined in the case of inter vivos transfers on the date of delivery to the Corporation of the notice specified in Paragraph 3 hereof, and in the case of transfers occasioned by the death of a Stockholder, on the

date of such death. As used herein, the term "net book value per share" shall mean the aggregate book value of the shares of the corporation divided by the number of shares then issued and outstanding. The term "aggregate book value of the shares" shall mean the excess of the cost of all of the assets of the Corporation over the sum of (1) reserves for depreciation maintained on the books of the Corporation; (2) treasury stock, if any; (3) all determinable liabilities; and (4) the amount of any dividends paid or payable to stockholders of record on a date prior to the valuation date but not reflected in the books of the Corporation as of the valuation date.

In the event of any disagreement among the parties, their executors, administrators, personal representatives, or any of them with respect to the determination of the book value of any of the shares to be purchased hereunder, such book value shall be computed in accordance with this Paragraph by an independent certified public accountant selected by the Corporation, and such computation shall be final and binding on the Corporation and on each of the Stockholder(s) and their executors, administrators, and personal representatives. The cost of such accounting shall be borne equally by the parties unable to reach agreement hereunder.

It is understood that the purchase price, determined as set forth above, shall be the value of the purchase shares for all tax purposes. In the event such value is later increased by any federal or state taxing authority, any tax liability resulting from such increase shall be borne by the selling Stockholder or his executor, administrator, or personal representative, as the case may be.

The purchase price hereunder shall be payable at the option of the Corporation or purchasing Stockholder either in a lump sum within sixty (60) days following the valuation date as set forth above, or in three equal annual installments of principal beginning thirty (30) days after the valuation date, with interest on the unpaid balance at the rate of Eight Percent (8%) per annum, such interest to be payable with the final installment of principal. Any party electing to pay in installments shall have the right at any time to prepay without penalty all or any portion of the unpaid principal balance plus interest accrued to the date of payment.

8. *Delivery of certificates.* Certificates for all shares sold hereunder, properly endorsed to the Corporation or purchasing Stockholder, as the case may be, shall be delivered to the purchasing party by the seller not later than the date of the lump sum purchase price payment or first installment payment, whichever first occurs. Thereafter, the selling Stockholder, or his estate, shall cease to be a Stockholder of the Corporation with respect to such shares.

9. *Corporation to maintain insurance.* To insure or partially insure its obligation under this Agreement to purchase from the estate of a deceased Stockholder the shares owned by such Stockholder prior to his death, the Corporation shall purchase, and shall continue in force by timely payment of premiums, policies of insurance covering the lives of each of the Stockholders in amounts sufficient to pay the purchase price reasonably foreseeable under Paragraph 7 hereof. In the event any Stockholder ceases to be a Stockholder of the Corporation or reduces his holdings of the shares of the Corporation, by voluntary transfer or otherwise, the Corporation shall, as appropriate, terminate or procure a proportionate reduction in the face amount of insurance outstanding on the life of such Stockholder, and in the event any Stockholder increases his holdings of the shares of the Corporation, the Corporation shall procure and maintain additional insurance on the life of such stockholder proportionate to the increase in the holdings of such Stockholder.

10. *Purchase of insurance policies by stockholders.* If, pursuant to the provisions hereof, any insured Stockholder during his lifetime ceases to be a party to this Agreement, such Stockholder shall have the right to purchase from the Corporation the policies of insurance on his life held by the Corporation under this Agreement, at a price equal to the cash surrender value plus the unearned premiums, and accumulated dividends and accrued interest thereon, determined at the date of such cessation. Such right of purchase shall be exercised by notice given to the Corporation within ten (10) days after such cessation, and the payment of the purchase price shall be made in cash within such period of time. On receipt of the purchase price, the Corporation will deliver the policies of insurance and will execute all necessary instruments of transfer. All policies of insurance held by the Corporation under this Agreement not so purchased by the insured Stockholder shall be released from the terms of this Agreement.

11. *Obligation of corporation as to transfer of shares.* In no event shall the Corporation sell, transfer, or otherwise dispose of any of the shares of the Corporation, including any share repurchased by it pursuant to this Agreement, to any person or entity until such person or entity has become a party to this Agreement and is bound by its provisions.

12. *Amendments; waiver of agreement.* This Agreement may be amended, altered, or any of its provisions waived by execution of a written agreement duly authorized by a resolution of the Board of Directors of the Corporation and signed by all the parties hereto, or any of the shares

subject to this Agreement may be disposed of by any Stockholder to the Corporation or to any other person without regard to the terms of this Agreement on the written consent of each of the Stockholders and a resolution of the Board of Directors of the Corporation consenting thereto.

13. *Notices.* Any notice required to be given pursuant to this Agreement shall be sent, and shall be considered to have been delivered on the date when sent by prepaid United States registered or certified mail, return receipt requested, properly addressed to the party to receive it, as follows:

a. Notices to be sent to the Corporation shall be addressed to the Corporation at 100 East Street, Middletown, Florida, to the attention of the President.

b. Notices to be sent to a Stockholder shall be sent to him at his address as shown on the Corporation's stock records unless a different address has been designated in writing addressed to the Secretary of the Corporation.

14. *Successors and assigns.* This Agreement shall be binding on and inure to the benefit of the parties and their respective heirs, legal representatives, successors, and assigns.

15. *Prior agreements.* This Agreement supersedes all prior agreements made between the Stockholders and the Corporation affecting the stock of the Corporation, and all such prior agreements are hereby terminated.

IN WITNESS WHEREOF, the parties have duly executed this Agreement on the day and year first above written.

_____
JOHN DOE

_____
RICHARD ROE

_____
GEORGE POE

ATTEST:                                        SUCCESS CORPORATION

_____       BY _____
Secretary of the Corporation                        President

[1]*18 Am. Jur. 2d Corporations, paras. 387–393.*

## FORM IA 2.13(a)

### (Employment agreement[s] with stockholder[s] part of the consideration for a buy-sell agreement)[1]

### ALTERNATIVE CLAUSE

IT IS MUTUALLY AGREED as follows:

1. The consideration for this Agreement is the mutual promises herein and the employment contract(s) herewith simultaneously made between the Corporation and the Stockholder(s).

[1]*18 Am. Jur. 2d Corporations, para. 316.*

## FORM IA 2.13(b)

### (Insurance to fund buy-sell agreement may be purchased by the Corporation—excess proceeds to be paid to deceased stockholder's estate)

### ALTERNATIVE CLAUSE

*Option of Corporation to fund Agreement by insurance.* Stockholders each grant permission to the Corporation, at its sole option, to purchase, at the Corporation's expense, insurance on his life and agrees to cooperate to the fullest extent in securing such insurance if desired by the Corporation, so that at the death of a Stockholder, the life insurance proceeds are available toward the purchase price of his stock by the Corporation pursuant to this Agreement. Any excess of the insurance proceeds on the life of the deceased Shareholder shall be payable by the Corporation to his estate.

In the event that the Corporation does not insure the Stockholder's life or a balance on the purchase price remains after payment of any insurance proceeds on the life of the Stockholder received by the Corporation, that balance of purchase price shall be payable by the Corporation in thirty-six (36) equal monthly installments, the first installment payable one (1) month from the date of closing under Paragraph 6 hereof, and the remaining installments successively monthly thereafter. This indebtedness of the Corporation shall be represented by a promissory note of the Corporation, endorsed and guaranteed by the remaining Shareholder parties to this Agreement, delivered to the deceased Stockholder's personal representative. The note shall bear interest at a rate not to exceed Ten Percent (10%) per annum. The rate of interest shall be mutually determined on the date of closing, and if there is no agreement, then the rate shall be Eight Percent (8%) per annum. The promissory note shall provide that the maker shall have the privilege of repaying all or any part thereof after one year from date of the execution of the note without penalty, with interest to date of prepayment. The note shall provide for acceleration of the full amount due in the event of default in payment and shall provide for the maker to pay all costs and expenses of collection, including a reasonable attorney's fee.

## FORM IA 2.13(c)

### (Death of all shareholders within 60 days of each other where shareholders have obligation to purchase if the Corporation fails to elect to purchase)

### ALTERNATIVE CLAUSE

*Death of all shareholders within 60 days.* The provisions of this Agreement requiring the remaining Stockholders to purchase a deceased Stockholder's stock in any event shall be void and of no effect if all of the Stockholders shall die within sixty (60) days of each other.

## FORM IA 2.13(d)

### (Purchase of stockholder's stock on termination of employment by the Corporation or resignation)

### ALTERNATIVE CLAUSE

*Purchase on termination of employment.* Upon the termination of employment of a Stockholder by the Corporation, or upon a Stockholder resigning as a director and officer of the Corporation, all of the shares of the capital stock of the Corporation owned by that Stockholder (herein called "Retiring Stockholder") shall be sold by the Retiring Stockholder and purchased as provided in Paragraph 4 of this Agreement.

## FORM IA 2.13(e)

### (Certificates to be delivered to selling stockholder as collateral security for payment of the unpaid purchase price but purchasing stockholder can vote the stock if not in default)[1]

### ALTERNATIVE CLAUSE

*Purchase by Stockholder.* If any Stockholder purchases shares of stock under this Agreement, that purchaser (unless he shall have paid the entire purchase price in cash) shall within five (5) days after delivery of the purchased stock to him, endorse the new certificate of stock issued to him and deliver the same to the seller Stockholder as collateral security for the payment of the unpaid purchase price; and the stock shall be held by the seller Stockholder until the entire purchase price is paid. The purchasing Stockholder shall have the right to vote the stock held by the seller as collateral security so long as the purchaser is not in default. The selling Stockholder shall execute and deliver necessary proxies to the purchasing Stockholder on demand.

[1]See also Form VIIIN 1.01.


## FORM IA 2.13(f)

### (Modification of agreement to be in writing signed by all parties)

#### ALTERNATIVE CLAUSE

*Modification of Agreement.* No change, amendment, alteration, or waiver of this Agreement shall be valid unless the same be in writing, dated and signed by all the parties hereto.


## FORM IA 2.13(g)

### (Termination of agreement upon the happening of certain events)

#### ALTERNATIVE CLAUSE

*Termination.* This Agreement shall terminate upon the occurrence of any of the following events:

(a) Bankruptcy, receivership, or voluntary or involuntary dissolution of the Corporation.

(b) The purchase by the Corporation of all the stock of any two (2) Stockholders on their death, disability, termination of employment, or resignation from employment and the payment in full of the purchase price therefor.

(c) The voluntary agreement of all Stockholders.

(d) Upon termination of this Agreement, the Secretary of the Corporation shall, upon tender of the certificates of stock, delete the legend endorsed thereon pursuant to Paragraph 8 of this Agreement.


## FORM IA 2.13(h)

### (Governing law where corporation is incorporated in one state and registered in another state)[1]

#### ALTERNATIVE CLAUSE

*Governing law.* The parties agree that it is their intention and covenant that this Agreement shall be governed by the laws of the State of Florida.

[1]U.C.C. 1-105(1) and *15A Am. Jur. 2d Commercial Code*, paras. 12 and 13.


## FORM IA 2.13(i)

### (Arbitration)[1]

#### ALTERNATIVE CLAUSE

*Arbitration.* In the event of any dispute under this Agreement, such dispute shall be settled by arbitration in New York, New York, in accordance with the rules then obtaining of the American Arbitration Association, and judgment upon the award may be entered in any court having jurisdiction thereof.

[1]*5 Am. Jur. 2d Arbitration and Award*, para. 27. See also Chapter VIC for other arbitration clauses.

## FORM IA 2.13(j)

### (Price of stock to be determined annually)[1]

#### ALTERNATIVE CLAUSE

*PURCHASE PRICE OF STOCK.* The market value of the stock per share that shall be the purchase price hereunder shall be determined annually by the mutual written consent of the Board of Directors of the Corporation. As the value of the stock is determined from time to time, the price shall be inserted in the place indicated in Schedule B, and each director shall sign Schedule B to indicate his consent.

[1]See Form IA 2.13(k) for Schedule B to implement this form.

## FORM IA 2.13(k)

### (Sample Schedule B to implement Form IA 2.13(j)—provide price and signature lines for 10 years from date of Agreement)

#### ALTERNATIVE CLAUSE

SCHEDULE B
SUCCESS CORPORATION

1984 $_____per share      By: _____
                                         President

                                      _____
                                         Director

                                      _____
                                         Director

                                      _____
                                         Director

                                      SUCCESS CORPORATION

1985 $_____per share      By: _____
                                         President

                                      _____
                                         Director

                                      _____
                                         Director

                                      _____
                                         Director

(etc. for 10 years)

## FORM IA 2.14

### (Plan of reorganization and merger agreement—for implementing I.R.C. Class "A" reorganization)

#### REORGANIZATION PLAN AND MERGER AGREEMENT[1]

AGREEMENT made February 15, 1982, between Everbest Company, Inc., a New York corporation (herein called "Everbest"), and XYZ Corporation, a New York corporation (herein called "XYZ").

WHEREAS, the respective Boards of Directors of Everbest and XYZ have determined that it is advisable and in the best interests of the corporations and their respective shareholders that XYZ be merged into Everbest, which shall be the surviving corporation in the merger,

IT IS AGREED AS FOLLOWS:

1. *Approval of merger.* Everbest and XYZ will cause special meetings of their respective shareholders to be called and held on or before December 30, 1982, or such later date as the Boards of Directors of Everbest and XYZ shall approve, to consider and vote upon the merger of XYZ into Everbest on the terms and conditions hereinafter set forth. If the merger is approved by a two-thirds (2/3) vote of the shareholders of both corporations in accordance with the laws of New York, subject to the conditions set forth in Paragraph 6, a Certificate of Merger shall be executed and filed in the Department of State of the State of New York. The Certificate of Merger shall be substantially in the form of Exhibit A hereto, with such changes therein as the Boards of Directors of both corporations shall approve. The date on which such Certificate of Merger is filed by the Department of State shall be the "effective date of the merger."

2. *Identity and operation of surviving corporation.* Everbest shall be the surviving corporation, operating as follows:

(a) *Name of surviving corporation.* The name Everbest and its identity, existence, purposes, powers, objects, franchises, rights, and immunities shall be unaffected and unimpaired by the merger. On the effective date of the merger, the separate existence and corporate organization of XYZ, except as it may be continued by statute, shall cease.

(b) *Certificate of incorporation.* The certificate of incorporation of Everbest, as originally filed and recorded on July 16, 1972, and as thereafter from time to time amended, shall, on the effective date of the merger, be the certificate of incorporation by the surviving corporation until further altered, amended, or repealed by the surviving corporation as provided by law.

(c) *Bylaws.* The bylaws of Everbest in effect on the effective date of the merger shall be the bylaws of the surviving corporation until amended, rescinded, or repealed as provided therein or by law.

(d) *Directors of surviving corporation.* The directors of Everbest on the effective date of the merger shall continue to be directors of the surviving corporation for the terms for which they were elected, and until their successors are elected and qualified as provided by law and the bylaws of the surviving corporation.

(e) *Officers of surviving corporation.* The officers of Everbest on the effective date of the merger shall continue to be the officers of the surviving corporation, and shall hold office until their respective successors are chosen and qualified, as provided by law and the bylaws of the surviving corporation.

3. *Treatment of shares of constituent corporations.* The terms and conditions of the merger, the mode of carrying the same into effect, and the manner of converting the shares of XYZ into shares of Everbest are as follows:

(a) The outstanding shares of common stock of Everbest of the par value of $10 each shall not be affected by the merger.

(b) On the effective date of the merger, each common share of the par value of $1 of XYZ that shall be issued and outstanding and not owned by Everbest or by XYZ shall be converted into two-thirds of a common share of Everbest of the par value of $10. Everbest shall not be required to issue any fraction of a share of its common shares, but shall issue and deliver scrip certificates representing such fractional shares or provide such other substitute for the issuance of fractional shares as the Board of Directors of Everbest may determine.

After the effective date of the merger, each holder of an outstanding certificate or certificates theretofore representing common shares of XYZ may surrender the same to Everbest and such holder shall then be entitled to receive a certificate or certificates representing the number of full common shares of Everbest to which he is entitled under the terms of this agreement. Until XYZ shares are surrendered, the shares shall be deemed for all corporate purposes, other than payment of dividends, to evidence ownership of the common shares of Everbest into which such shares may have been converted. No dividend payable to the holders of record of common shares of Everbest as of any date subsequent to the effective date of the merger shall be paid to the holder of any outstanding certificate representing common shares of XYZ until such certificate shall be surrendered. Upon subsequent surrender pursuant to this agreement, all dividends withheld to the time of surrender shall be paid.

(c) On the effective date of the merger, each common share of the par value of $1 of XYZ, if any, that shall be owned by Everbest shall be canceled and all rights in respect thereof shall cease.

4. *Transfer of assets upon merger.* On the effective date of the merger, all of the estate, property, rights, privileges, powers, franchises, and interests of each of the constituent corporations and all of their property, real, personal, and mixed, and all the debts due on whatever account of either of them, as well as all share subscriptions and other choses in action belonging to either of them, shall be vested in Everbest as the surviving corporation, without further act or deed; and all claims, demands, property, and every other interest shall be as effectually the property of Everbest as the surviving corporation as they were of the constituent corporations, and the title to all real estate vested in either of the constituent corporations shall not be deemed to revert or to be in any way impaired by reason of the merger but shall be vested in Everbest as the surviving corporation.

5. *Covenants of parties.* At or prior to the effective date of the merger:

(a) As of January 31, 1982, XYZ had gross assets with a book value of $750,000 and a net worth of $500,000. Net sales during the year 1980 were $1,000,000, and net earnings were $75,000. A copy of XYZ's Balance Sheet and Income Statement is attached as Exhibit A.

(b) As of January 31, 1982, Everbest had gross assets with a book value of $5,000,000 and a net worth of $4,500,000. A copy of Everbest's Balance Sheet and Income Statement is attached as Exhibit C.

(c) Everbest and XYZ each represent that there is no substantial litigation pending or threatened against its corporation or its assets.

(d) XYZ will not (1) engage in any activity or transaction other than in the ordinary course of business without first obtaining the approval of Everbest; (2) make any change in its authroized shares; or (3) issue or sell, or issue options to purchase or rights to subscribe to, any of its shares; and XYZ will not declare any dividend on any of its shares other than a dividend of 25¢ per share on its common shares payable on or before December 31, 1981, and in the event the effective date of the merger is on or after December 31, 1982, an additional dividend of not more than 25¢ per share on its common shares.

(e) Everbest will not make any change in its authorized shares; and

(f) Everbest will not declare any dividend on any of its common shares that is payable in common shares.

6. *Conditions to merger.* Anything herein or elsewhere to the contrary notwithstanding, the merger shall not be made effective if prior to the effective date of the merger:

(a) *Election to abandon merger.* The Boards of Directors of Everbest and XYZ elect that it shall not be made effective, or

(b) The holders of a sufficiently large number of common shares of XYZ shall have objected to the merger and demanded payment for their shares pursuant to Section 623 of the Business Corporation Law of the State of New York so as to render it inadvisable, in the opinion of the Board of Directors of Everbest, to proceed with the merger, or

(c) Any covenant of either party as represented in Paragraph 5 is untrue or inaccurate in any substantial and material respect.

(d) If the Board of Directors of either Everbest or XYZ elects that the merger shall not be made effective as provided in this Paragraph 6, notice shall be given to the other, and thereupon, or upon the election of both such Boards of Directors that the merger shall not be made effective as provided in Subparagraph (a) of this Paragraph 6, this Agreement shall become wholly void and of no effect and there shall be no liability on the part of either Everbest or XYZ or their respective Boards of Directors or shareholders. Each party shall be liable for its own expense in negotiating and entering into this Agreement, in the event of abandonment of the merger pursuant to this Paragraph 6.

7. *Distribution of new shares.* If the merger becomes effective, XYZ authorizes Everbest to take or cause to be taken such steps as Everbest may deem necessary or advisable in order to effect the distribution, on the basis and terms specified herein of the Everbest share certificates that holders of XYZ shares shall be entitled to receive under the terms of the merger.

8. *Further documents to effectuate merger.* To the extent permitted by law, from time to time, as and when requested by Everbest or by its successors or assigns, XYZ shall execute and deliver, or cause to be executed and delivered, all such deeds and instruments, and to take or cause to be taken, such further or other action as Everbest may deem necessary or desirable, in order to vest in and confirm to Everbest title to, and possession of, any property of XYZ required by reason of or as a result of the merger, and the proper officers and directors of XYZ and the proper officers and directors of Everbest are fully authorized, in the name of XYZ or otherwise, to take any and all such action.

IN WITNESS WHEREOF, Everbest and XYZ have caused this Agreement to be executed by their duly authorized officers.

(Seal)                         EVERBEST COMPANY, INC.

Attest:

_____    by _____
Secretary of the Corporation                           President

(Seal)                         XYZ CORPORATION

Attest:

_____    by _____
Secretary of the Corporation                           President

[1] *19 Am. Jur. 2d Corporations,* paras. 1490–1493, 1515–1519, and *33 Am. Jur. 2d Federal Taxation,* paras. 2280–2349, 2295; and see 2407 for new rules for corporation loss carryovers; and see 2346(2), 2347, 2348 for treatment of "Section 306 stock." For definitions, see 26 U.S.C.A. 368, which is unchanged by ERTA of 1981 except as to "thrift institutions." See also 26 U.S.C.A. 351 et seq., and 381–383. Ref. Forms IA 2.15 and 2.16. See also Form VIIIB 1.06.

## FORM IA 2.15

(Certificate of merger of two corporations pursuant to I.R.C. Class "A" reorganization in State of New York)

## CERTIFICATE OF MERGER[1]
### of
### EVERBEST COMPANY, INC.
### and
### XYZ CORPORATION
### into
### EVERBEST COMPANY, INC.

Pursuant to the provisions of Section 904 of the Business Corporation Law of the State of New York, the undersigned hereby certify:

1. *Corporate parties.* The names of the constituent corporations are Everbest Company, Inc., a New York corporation, (herein called "Everbest"), and XYZ Corporation, a New York corporation (herein called "XYZ"). Everbest is the surviving corporation in the merger and its name as the surviving corporation is Everbest Company, Inc.

2. *Capitalization of constituent corporations.* The respective designations and numbers of shares of each class and series of capital stock of the constituent corporations outstanding on the date of the Reorganization Plan and Merger Agreement were as follows:

| Name of Corporation | Designation of Shares | Number of Shares Outstanding |
|---|---|---|
| Everbest | Common Stock | 10,000 |
| XYZ | Common Stock | 1,000 |

The number of outstanding shares of capital stock of the corporations may not be changed prior to the effective time of the merger. The holders of the outstanding shares of Common Stock of XYZ and the holders of the outstanding shares of Common Stock of Everbest are entitled to vote upon the merger. In order to adopt the Reorganization Plan and Merger Agreement, the affirmative vote of the holders of at least two-thirds of the outstanding shares of the Common Stock of both corporations was required.

3. *Effective date.* The merger provided for herein shall become effective at the close of business on the date it is filed by the Secretary of State.

4. *Termination or abandonment.* The Reorganization Plan and Merger Agreement may be terminated and abandoned at any time prior to the filing of this Certificate of Merger by the Department of State of the State of New York on the happening of any of the following:

(a) *Mutual consent.* By mutual consent of the Boards of Directors of Everbest and XYZ.

(b) *Conditions of merger not met.* By the Board of Directors of either corporation if any of the conditions set forth in Paragraph 5 of the Reorganization Plan and Merger Agreement shall not have been met.

5. *Filing dates.* The date of the filing of the Certificate of Incorporation of Everbest by the Department of State of the State of New York was July 16, 1972. The date of the filing of the Certificate of Incorporation of XYZ by the Secretary of State of the State of New York was February 10, 1976.

6. *Stockholder ratification of merger.* The merger was authorized:

(a) By the vote of the holders of at least two-thirds of the outstanding shares of Common Stock of Everbest at a meeting of shareholders of Everbest duly called and held on March 16, 1982, upon notice to each shareholder of record, all shareholders of record being entitled to vote thereon; and

(b) By the written consent, dated March 10, 1982, of the holders of all outstanding shares of Common Stock of XYZ, in accordance with Section 615 of the Business Corporation Law.

IN WITNESS WHEREOF, this Certificate has been signed this April 10, 1982.

ATTEST:                                          Everbest Company, Inc.

by _____          by _____
    Secretary of the Corporation                              President

ATTEST:                                          XYZ Corporation

by _____          by _____
    Secretary of the Corporation                              President

[1] *19 Am. Jur. 2d Corporations,* paras. 1494–1497. Check state corporation statute for merger procedure and required contents of certificate. Ref. Forms IA 2.14 and 2.16.

## FORM IA 2.16

(Articles of merger of two corporations pursuant to I.R.C. Class "A" reorganization in State of Florida)

**ARTICLES OF MERGER[1]
of
EVERBEST COMPANY, INC.
and
XYZ CORPORATION
into
EVERBEST COMPANY, INC.**

Pursuant to Section 214 Florida Statutes:

### ARTICLE I

The corporation parties to the merger are Everbest Company, Inc., a Florida corporation, and XYZ Corporation, a Florida corporation.

### ARTICLE II

The Plan of Merger is set forth in the Reorganization Plan and Merger Agreement attached hereto, made part hereof and marked Exhibit A.

### ARTICLE III

The plan of Merger attached hereto was adopted, pursuant to Section 607.221 Florida Statutes, by a two-thirds vote of the shareholders of the corporations entitled to vote at a meeting of the shareholders of Everbest Company, Inc., held on January 15, 1983, and a meeting of the shareholders of XYZ Corporation held on January 10, 1983.

### ARTICLE IV

The plan for exchange and cancellation of issued shares of the corporation is set forth in the Reorganization Plan and Merger Agreement attached hereto and made part hereof.

IN WITNESS WHEREOF, the undersigned subscribers have executed these Articles of Merger this 2nd day of February, 1983.

ATTEST:                        EVERBEST COMPANY, INC.

_____      _____

Secretary of Everbest              John Doe, President
Company, Inc.

ATTEST:                        XYZ CORPORATION

_____      _____

Secretary of XYZ Corporation          Richard Roe, President

STATE OF FLORIDA
COUNTY OF ORANGE

BEFORE ME, a notary public in and for said county and state, personally appeared JOHN DOE, President of Everbest Company, Inc., known to me and known by me to be one of the persons who executed the foregoing Articles of Merger, and he acknowledged before me that he executed those Articles of Merger for the purposes set forth therein.

IN WITNESS WHEREOF, I have hereunto set my hand and affixed my official seal, in the state and county aforesaid, this 2nd day of February, 1983.

_____

Notary Public

My commission expires:

[1] *19 Am. Jur. 2d Corporations,* paras. 1494–1497. Check state corporation statute for merger procedure and required contents of certificate and/or articles of merger. Ref. Forms IA 2.14 and 2.15.

## FORM IA 2.17

**(Articles of amendment changing corporate stock structure after issuance of shares)**

### ARTICLES OF AMENDMENT[1]
### for
### ABLE MANUFACTURING CORPORATION

Pursuant to Section 607.177 Florida Statutes:

### ARTICLE I

The name of the corporation is ABLE MANUFACTURING CORPORATION.

### ARTICLE II

Article IV of the Articles of Incorporation of the corporation is hereby amended to authorize an increase in the capital stock of the corporation as follows:

The corporation is authorized to issue One Thousand (1,000) shares of Ten-Dollar ($10.00) par value common stock, which shall be designated "Common Shares."

### ARTICLE III

The amendment set forth in Article II hereof was adopted by the affirmative vote of the holders of a majority of the shares of the corporation entitled to vote at a meeting of the shareholders held on January 10, 1983, which was duly called for the purpose of considering said amendment in accordance with Section 607.181 Florida Statutes.

### ARTICLE IV

The amendment does not provide for an exchange, reclassification, or cancellation of issued shares.

IN WITNESS WHEREOF, the undersigned subscribers have executed these Articles of Amendment in their respective corporation capacities this 15th day of January, 1983.

ATTEST:                                          ABLE MANUFACTURING CORPORATION

_____          _____
Secretary of the Corporation                     John Doe, President

STATE OF FLORIDA
COUNTY OF ORANGE

BEFORE ME, a notary public in and for said county and state, personally appeared JOHN DOE, President of Able Manufacturing Corporation, known to me and known by me to be one of the persons who executed the foregoing Articles of Amendment, and he acknowledged before me that he executed those Articles of Amendment for the purposes set forth therein.

IN WITNESS WHEREOF, I have hereunto set my hand and affixed my official seal, in the state and county aforesaid, this 15th day of January, 1983.

_____
Notary Public

My commission expires:

[1]*18 Am. Jur. 2d Corporations*, para. 105. Check state corporation statute for procedure and contents of articles of amendment.

## FORM IA 2.18

### ASSIGNMENT SEPARATE FROM CERTIFICATE[1]

FOR VALUE RECEIVED, I, JOHN DOE, hereby sell, assign, and transfer unto RICHARD ROE, One Hundred (100) shares of the common capital stock of the XYZ CORPORATION standing in my name on the books of said corporation represented by Certificate No. 401 herewith and do hereby irrevocably constitute and appoint the secretary of the corporation attorney to transfer the said stock on the books of the within-named corporation with full powers of substitution in the premises.

Dated _____

_____
JOHN DOE

[1]*15A Am. Jur. 2d Commercial Code*, para. 98.

## FORM IA 2.18(a)

### (Signature guarantee per U.C.C. 8-312(1) )

### ASSIGNMENT SEPARATE FROM CERTIFICATE[1]

FOR VALUE RECEIVED, I, JOHN DOE, hereby sell, assign, and transfer unto RICHARD ROE, One Hundred (100) shares of the common capital stock of the XYZ CORPORATION standing in my name on the books of said corporation represented by Certificate No. 401 herewith and do hereby irrevocably constitute and appoint the secretary of the corporation attorney to transfer the said stock on the books of the within-named corporation with full powers of substitution in the premises.

Dated _____

_____
JOHN DOE

SIGNATURE GUARANTEED BY:
J. Best Stock Brokers, Inc.

By _____
Frank Jones, Vice-President

[1]*15A Am. Jur. 2d Commercial Code*, para. 103.

## FORM IA 2.19

### (Election to voluntarily dissolve a corporation)

## PLAN OF COMPLETE LIQUIDATION[1]
### for
## GOOD MANUFACTURING COMPANY, INC.

1. *Consent to plan.* The undersigned being all the members of the Board of Directors of Good Manufacturing Company, Inc., a Pennsylvania corporation, hereby consent to the following plan for the complete liquidation of the corporation for cash.

2. *Plan of liquidation.* Good Manufacturing Company, Inc. (hereinafter called "Good"), shall be completely liquidated in the manner stated in this plan.

3. *Approval and ratification.* This plan is hereby adopted by Good's Board of Directors. The Board's action in adopting this plan shall be submitted to the shareholders of Good for ratification by the vote of the holders of record of two-thirds of the outstanding shares of Good entitled to vote thereon, at a shareholders' meeting duly called within sixty (60) days of the signing hereof.

4. *Sale of assets.* After this plan has been ratified by the shareholders, Good shall accomplish its liquidation by a sale of all of its properties and assets of every description, real and personal, for such consideration and upon such terms and conditions as may be determined to be in the best interests of Good and its shareholders. The proposed terms and conditions of any sale of assets having a book value of over One Thousand Dollars ($1,000) shall be submitted to a vote of Good's shareholders, and no agreement for such sale shall be final or binding on Good unless and until authorized and approved by the affirmative vote of the holders of record of two-thirds of the outstanding shares of Good entitled to vote thereon, at a shareholders' meeting duly called.

5. *Cessation of business.* Upon the sale of the plant located on State Route 14, Good shall cease doing business immediately, except to the extent required to wind up its affairs, and as soon thereafter as practicable shall make one or more substantial partial distributions of the proceeds of the sale of the plant pro rata to or for the account of its shareholders.

6. *Dissolution.* Within ninety (90) days after the closing of the sale of substantially all the assets of the corporation, Good shall be dissolved and its corporate existence terminated in accordance with the laws of the Commonwealth of Pennsylvania, and the balance of the proceeds of the sale and all of Good's other assets, if any, after the payment of Good's liabilities, and less any amounts reasonably required to meet claims or contingent liabilities, shall be distributed pro rata to or for the account of Good's shareholders forthwith.

7. *Authorization of necessary acts.* The officers of Good and its Board of Directors, both as directors and as trustees in dissolution for Good, and hereby authorized to do and perform such acts, execute and deliver such documents, and do all other things as may be reasonably necessary or advisable to accomplish this plan of liquidation.

Dated this 21st day of September, 1982.

_____
John Doe, as Director of Good Manufacturing Company, Inc.

_____
Richard Roe, as Director of Good Manufacturing Company, Inc.

_____
Peter Poe, as Director of Good Manufacturing Company, Inc.

[1] *19 Am. Jur. 2d Corporations,* para. 1586 and 1594; and *33 Am. Jur. 2d Federal Taxation,* paras. 2350–2389; and 26 U.S.C.A. 331 et seq. Ref. Forms IA 2.19(a), (b), and (c); and Forms IA 2.20 and 2.21; and Form IVD 1.05 to implement the liquidation.

**Form 966**
(Rev. Feb. 1978)
Department of the Treasury
Internal Revenue Service

# Corporate Dissolution or Liquidation

(Required under Section 6043(a) of the Internal Revenue Code)

**Please type or print**

| Name of corporation | Employer identification number |
|---|---|

Address (Number and street)

City or town, State and ZIP code

Check type of return ☐ 1120
☐ 1120 DISC   ☐ 1120L
☐ 1120M   ☐ 1120S
☐ Other ▶

| 1 Date incorporated | 2 Place incorporated | 3 Type of liquidation  ☐ Complete   ☐ Partial |
|---|---|---|

| 4 Internal Revenue Service Center where last income tax return was filed and taxable year covered thereby | Service Center | Taxable year ending |
|---|---|---|
| | | Month | Year |

5 Date of adoption of resolution or plan of dissolution, or complete or partial liquidation

6 Taxable year of final return . . . . . . . . . . . . .
Was final return filed with a parent corporation (consolidated return)? . . . . . . . . . . . . ☐ Yes   ☐ No
If "Yes," enter:
Name of parent corporation ▶ ----------------------------------------
Employer identification number ▶ ----------------------------------------
IRS Center where consolidated return was filed ▶

| | Common | Preferred |
|---|---|---|
| 7 Total number of shares outstanding at time of adoption of plan or liquidation . . . . . . . . . . | | |

| 8 Dates of any amendments to plan of dissolution | 9 Section of the Code under which the corporation is to be dissolved or liquidated | 10 If this return is in respect of an amendment of or supplement to a resolution or plan previously adopted and return has previously been filed in respect of such resolution or plan, give the date such return was filed |
|---|---|---|

**11. Liquidation Within One Calendar Month.**—If the corporation is a domestic corporation, and the plan of liquidation provides for a distribution in complete cancellation or redemption of all the capital stock of the corporation and for the transfer of all the property of the corporation under the liquidation entirely within one calendar month pursuant to section 333, and any shareholder claims the benefit of such section, then the corporation must also submit:
(a) A description of the voting power of each class of stock;
(b) A list of all the shareholders owning stock at the time of the adoption of the plan of liquidation, together with the number of shares of each class of stock owned by each shareholder, the certificate numbers thereof, and the total number of votes to which entitled on the adoption of the plan of liquidation;

(c) A list of all corporate shareholders as of January 1, 1954, together with the number of shares of each class of stock owned by each shareholder, the certificate numbers thereof, the total number of votes to which entitled on the adoption of the plan of liquidation, and a statement of all changes in ownership of stock by corporate shareholders between January 1, 1954, and the date of the adoption of the plan of liquidation, both dates inclusive; and

(d) A computation as described in section 1.6043–2(b) (following the format in Revenue Procedure 75–17, 1975–1 C.B. 677) of accumulated earnings and profits including all items of income and expense accrued up to the date on which the transfer of all property is completed.

**Attach a certified copy of the resolution or plan, together with all amendments or supplements not previously filed.**

Under penalties of perjury, I declare that I have examined this return, including accompanying schedules and statements, and to the best of my knowledge and belief it is true, correct, and complete.

| Date | Signature of officer | Title |
|---|---|---|

# Instructions

**1. Who must file.**—This form must be filed by every corporation that is to be dissolved or whose stock is to be liquidated in whole or in part. Exempt organizations are not required to file Form 966. These organizations should see the instructions for Form 990 or 990–PF.

Shareholders electing to be covered under section 333 of the Code must also file Form 964 within 30 days after the date of adoption of the plan of liquidation.

**2. When to file.**—This form must be filed within 30 days after the adoption of the resolution or plan for or in respect of the dissolution of a corporation or the liquidation in whole or in part of its capital stock. If after the filing of a Form 966 there is an amendment or supplement to the resolution or plan, an additional Form 966 based on the resolution or plan as amended or supplemented must be filed within 30 days after the adoption of such

amendment or supplement. A return in respect of an amendment or supplement will be deemed sufficient if it gives the date the prior return was filed and contains a certified copy of such amendment or supplement and all other information required by this form which was not given in such prior return.

**3. Where to file.**—This form must be filed with the Internal Revenue Service Center with which the corporation is required to file its income tax return.

**4. Signature.**—The return must be signed either by the president, vice president, treasurer, assistant treasurer or chief accounting officer, or by any other corporate officer (such as tax officer) who is authorized to sign. A receiver, trustee, or assignee must sign any return which is required to be filed on behalf of a corporation.

## FORM IA 2.19(b)

| For Official Use Only | |
|---|---|

**Form 1096**
Department of the Treasury
Internal Revenue Service

**Annual Summary and Transmittal of U.S. Information Returns**      **1981**

Place an "X" in the proper box to identify type of document being transmitted

| PAYER'S Federal identifying number | Enter number of documents | 1099 BCD 87 | 1099 DIV 91 | 1099 F 90 | 1099 INT 92 | 1099 L 93 | 1099 MED 94 | 1099 MISC 95 | 1099 NEC 83 | 1099 OID 96 | 1099 PATR 97 | 1099 R 98 | 1099 UC 81 | 1087 DIV 71 | 1087 INT 72 | 1087 MED 75 | 1087 MISC 77 | 1087 OID 78 |
|---|---|---|---|---|---|---|---|---|---|---|---|---|---|---|---|---|---|---|

69 ☐

Type or print PAYER'S name, address, and ZIP code below (Name must aline with arrow).

Name ▶

All documents are: (Place an "X" in the proper box. See instructions.)

| Original | Corrected |
|---|---|

All documents are: (Place an "X" in the proper box. See instructions.)

| With taxpayer identifying no. | Without taxpayer identifying no. |
|---|---|

(Magnetic tape filers: See the applicable Revenue Procedures regarding transmittal of returns on magnetic tape.)

Under penalties of perjury, I declare that I have examined this return, including accompanying documents and to the best of my knowledge and belief, it is true, correct, and complete. In the case of documents without recipients' identifying numbers I have complied with the requirements of the law by requesting such numbers from the recipients, but did not receive them.

Signature _____ Title _____ Date _____

☆ U.S. GOVERNMENT PRINTING OFFICE : 1980—O-313-104   23-0916750

## FORM IA 2.19(c)

| For Official Use Only | |
|---|---|

For instructions, see back of form

Type or print Corporation's name, address, ZIP code, and Federal identifying number.

OMB No. 1545-0113

**U.S. Information Return For**  **1981**

**Distributions in Liquidation During Calendar Year**

93 ☐

| Recipient's identifying number | 1 Cash | 2 Fair market value of property on date distributed | 3 Property (description) |
|---|---|---|---|

Name ▶

Type or print Shareholder's name, address, and ZIP code below (Name must align with arrow).

| 4 Number of shares owned | 5 Class of shares owned |
|---|---|

If account is for multiple payees, place an asterisk (*) by the name of the person or entity to whom the identifying number belongs.

**See Back of This Copy for Reporting Instructions**

**Form 1099L**   For Paperwork Reduction Act Notice see back of form.   Department of the Treasury—Internal Revenue Service
23-188-5979

Form **964**
(Rev. July 1972)
Department of the Treasury
Internal Revenue Service

# Election of Shareholder under Section 333 Liquidation

(To be filed in duplicate within 30 days after the adoption of the plan of liquidation. See Instructions on page 4.)

| Name of shareholder | Identifying Number (See instruction F.) |
|---|---|

Address of shareholder (Number, street, city, State, and ZIP code)

| Name of corporation | Employer Identification Number |
|---|---|

Address of corporation (Number, street, city, State, and ZIP code)

| Time and date of adoption of plan of liquidation | Calendar month of transfer of all property |
|---|---|

The above named shareholder hereby elects to have recognized and taxed in accordance with section 333 of the Internal Revenue Code the gain on each and every share of the capital stock of the above named corporation owned by him at the time of the adoption of the plan of complete liquidation providing for a distribution in complete cancellation or redemption of all corporate stock and for the transfer of all corporate property under the liquidation entirely within the above stated calendar month of transfer of all property.

## SCHEDULE A
### Statement of Shares of Stock Owned at the Time and Date of Adoption of Plan of Liquidation

| Class of stock | Certificate numbers | Number of shares | Total number of votes to which entitled on adoption of plan of liquidation |
|---|---|---|---|
| | | | |

## SCHEDULE B
### Statement of Shares of Stock Owned on Date of Execution of Election

| Class of stock | Certificate numbers | Number of shares | Total number of votes to which entitled on adoption of plan of liquidation |
|---|---|---|---|
| | | | |

## SCHEDULE C
### Statement of Shares of Stock Owned on January 1, 1954
### (To be filled in only by corporate shareholders)

| Class of stock | Certificate numbers | Number of shares | Total number of votes to which entitled on adoption of plan of liquidation |
|---|---|---|---|
| | | | |

Attach a statement showing all shares acquired or disposed of between January 1, 1954, and the time and date of adoption of plan of liquidation, both dates inclusive, giving date on which any share was acquired or disposed of, class of stock, the certificate numbers thereof, the number of shares involved in each transaction, the total number of votes to which entitled on adoption of plan of liquidation, and the name of the person from whom acquired or to whom transferred.

## SCHEDULE D

If any of the shares listed in any of the above schedules are not registered in the name of the person by whom this election is made, list below the name of the person in whose name such stock is registered giving the class of stock, the certificate numbers thereof, the number of shares, the total number of votes to which entitled on adoption of plan of liquidation, and all facts pertinent to the claim of ownership.

*(Use additional sheets if necessary)*

Under penalties of perjury, I declare that I have examined this return, including accompanying schedules and statements, and to the best of my knowledge and belief it is true, correct, and complete.

-----------------------------     --------------------------------------------------------
     (Date)                                        (Electing shareholder)

| The Internal Revenue Service does not require a seal on this form, but if one is used, please place it here. |
| --- |

**If a corporation**

-----------------------------     ---------------------------------------------------------     -----------------------------
     (Date)                     (Signature of officer)                      (Title)

# Instructions

*(References are to the Internal Revenue Code.)*

**A. Who Must File.**—This form is to be used by qualified electing shareholders who elect the benefits of section 333. A separate form, in duplicate, shall be executed by each electing shareholder. See instruction D, Consolidated Election.

**B. Qualified Electing Shareholder.**—No corporate shareholder may be a qualified electing shareholder if at any time between January 1, 1954, and the date of the adoption of the plan of liquidation, both dates inclusive, it was the owner of stock of the liquidating corporation possessing 50 percent or more of the total combined voting power of all classes of stock entitled to vote upon the adoption of the plan of liquidation. All other shareholders are divided into two groups for the purpose of determining whether they are qualified electing shareholders: (1) shareholders other than corporations, and (2) corporate shareholders.

Any shareholder of either of the two groups, whether or not the stock he owns is entitled to vote on the adoption of the plan of liquidation, is a qualified electing shareholder if—

(1) His written election to be governed by the provisions of section 333 has been made and filed as prescribed by the regulations; and

(2) Like elections have been made and filed by owners of stock possessing at least 80 percent of the total combined voting power of all classes of stock owned by shareholders of the same group at the time of, and entitled to vote upon, the adoption of the plan of liquidation, whether or not the shareholders making the elections actually realize gain upon the cancellation or redemption of the stock upon the liquidation.

**C. Election.**—An election to be governed by the provisions of section 333 can be made only by or on behalf of the person by whom gains, if any, will be realized. Thus, the shareholder who may make the election must be the actual owner of stock and not a mere record holder, such as a nominee.

A shareholder is entitled to make an election relative to the gain only on stock owned by him at the time of the adoption of the plan of liquidation. The election is personal to the shareholder making it and does not follow the stock into the hands of the transferee.

**D. Consolidated Election.**—Two or more electing shareholders may specifically authorize an attorney or agent, by power of attorney, to execute and file a consolidated election on Form 964 on their behalf. Within the 30-day period after the adoption of the plan of liquidation, the attorney or agent must file the Form 964 in duplicate, together with the power of attorney and a list of those shareholders who consent to be qualified electing shareholders, with the Internal Revenue Service Center where the corporation will file its final income tax return.

A shareholder may, however, individually file his own Form 964. In either case, a copy of the election must be attached to the shareholder's income tax return for his taxable year in which the transfer of all the property under the liquidation occurs.

**E. Time and Place for Filing.**—The original and one copy must be filed by the shareholder with the Internal Revenue Service Center where the final income tax return of the corporation will be filed. The elections must be filed within 30 days after the adoption of the plan of liquidation.

Under no circumstances shall section 333 be applicable to any shareholders who fail to file their elections within the 30-day period prescribed. Another copy of the election shall be attached to the shareholder's income tax return for his taxable year in which the transfer of all property under the liquidation occurs.

**F. Identifying Number.**—Individuals must enter their social security number; all others must enter their employer identification number.

**G. Calendar Month of Transfer of All Property.**—If the calendar month of transfer of all property under the liquidation is unknown when this election is filed, enter "unknown" and state the month on the copy of the election required to be attached to the shareholder's income tax return for his taxable year in which the transfer of all property under the liquidation occurs.

**H. Supplemental Statement.**—Each qualifying electing shareholder receiving distributions is required to file with his income tax return for the taxable year in which the liquidation occurs a supplemental statement that must include the following information:

(1) A statement of the stockholder's stock ownership in the liquidating corporation as of the record date of the distribution, showing the number of shares of each class owned on such date, the cost or other basis of each such share, and the date of acquisition of each share;

(2) A list of all the property, including money, received upon the distribution, showing the fair market value of each item of such property other than money on the date distributed and stating what items, if any, consist of stock or securities acquired by the liquidating corporation after December 31, 1953, or after December 31, 1962, whichever date is applicable;

(3) A statement of the stockholder's ratable share of the earnings and profits of the liquidating corporation accumulated after February 28, 1913, computed without diminution by reason of distributions made during the month of liquidation (other than designated dividends under section 316(b)(2)(B));

(4) A copy of the shareholder's written election to be governed by the provisions of section 333. See Regs. 1.333–3.

**I. Signature.**—If the shareholder making the election is a corporation, the election must be signed either by the president, vice president, treasurer, assistant treasurer, chief accounting officer, or by any other corporate officer (such as tax officer) who is authorized to sign.

A receiver, trustee, or assignee must sign any election which he is required to file on behalf of a corporation.

This election may be executed by the shareholder's attorney or agent, provided such action is specifically authorized by a power of attorney, which, if not previously filed, must accompany the election.

GPO    o70—16—82003-1    464-493         ☆ U. S. GOVERNMENT PRINTING OFFICE: 1976-634-059

**FORM IA 2.20**

(Statutory certificate of election to dissolve corporation voluntarily,
to be filed before Articles of Dissolution are filed)

**CERTIFICATE OF ELECTION TO DISSOLVE[1]**
**JOHN DOE COMPANY, INC.**

The undersigned, duly authorized officers of JOHN DOE COMPANY, INC., a Pennsylvania corporation, hereby certify that the shareholders of the corporation have elected to dissolve the corporation pursuant to Act of May 5, P.L. 364, Article XI, para. 1102, as follows:

1. The name of the corporation is JOHN DOE COMPANY, INC.

2. The address of the registered office of the corporation in the Commonwealth of Pennsylvania is 537 Wood Street, Pittsburgh, Pennsylvania 00000.

3. The names and respective addresses of the corporation's present officers are:

John Doe, President
415 Graham Street
Pittsburgh, Pennsylvania 00000

Richard Roe, Treasurer
100 Main Street
Pittsburgh, Pennsylvania 00000

Mary Doe, Secretary
415 Graham Street
Pittsburgh, Pennsylvania 00000

4. The names and respective addresses of the present board of directors of the corporation are:

John Doe
415 Graham Street
Pittsburgh, Pennsylvania 00000

Mary Doe
415 Graham Street
Pittsburgh, Pennsylvania 00000

Richard Roe
100 Main Street
Pittsburgh, Pennsylvania 00000

5. The election to dissolve was by written agreement of all the shareholders of the corporation, which was signed by all the shareholders of record of the corporation.

Dated this 4th day of June, 1982.

JOHN DOE COMPANY, INC.

By _____
John Doe, President

(imprint of corporate
seal)

By _____
Richard Roe, Treasurer

[1]15 Purdon's Statutes (PA) 2103 and 2105, or appropriate state corporation statute, section on dissolution. Ref. Form IA 2.21.

**FORM IA 2.21**

(Voluntary by stockholders, to be filed after certificate of
dissolution and liquidation)

## ARTICLES OF DISSOLUTION[1]
### of
### JOHN DOE COMPANY, INC.

ARTICLE I

The name of the corporation is JOHN DOE COMPANY, INC.

ARTICLE II

The present address of the registered office of the corporation is 537 Wood Street, Pittsburgh, Pennsylvania 00000.

ARTICLE III

The corporation has heretofore delivered to the Department of State of the Commonwealth of Pennsylvania a Certificate of Election to Dissolve dated June 4, 1982.

ARTICLE IV

All debts, obligations, and liabilities of the corporation have been paid or discharged or adequate provision has been made therefor.

ARTICLE V

All remaining property and assets of the corporation have been distributed among its shareholders, in accordance with their respective rights and interests.

ARTICLE VI

There are no actions pending against the corporation in any court.

ARTICLE VII

Notice of the winding-up proceedings of the corporation was mailed by certified mail to each municipality in which the corporation has a principal or registered office.

ARTICLE VIII

The undersigned have been duly authorized by the corporation to execute these Articles of Dissolution.
Dated this 6th day of December, 1982.

JOHN DOE COMPANY, INC.

BY _____
John Doe, President

(imprint of corporate
seal)

By _____
Richard Roe, Treasurer

[1]*19 Am. Jur. 2d Corporations*, paras. 1596 et seq.; and *33 Am. Jur. 2d Federal Taxation*, paras. 2350–2379 and 2380–2389. Ref. Form IA 2.20 and Form VIIIS 1.08.

## SECTION B        PROFESSIONAL CORPORATIONS

The basic form in Section B may be modified and used for forming a professional corporation for any profession. Dentists, lawyers, architects and other professionals often prefer to operate as a professional corporation. The corporation may be a one-man corporation or its stock may be owned by several or more members of the profession.

If the professional corporation is to have multiple ownership of shares, the forms in Part 1 Section A Subsection 2. Transfer of Stock or Control of a Business Corporation may be modified and used in appropriate circumstances.

Many professionals still prefer to operate together as a partnership. Form IIA 1.03 is a sample professional partnership agreement.

## FORM IB 1.00
### CLIENT QUESTIONNAIRE FOR FORMING A
### PROFESSIONAL CORPORATION[1]

1. Name and address of client(s), the incorporator(s), and the initial board of directors

2. Business and home telephone numbers of client(s)

3. Names and addresses of proposed members of the professional association (form of name used in the professional license)

4. Names and addresses of professional licensing boards or associations with which each proposed member is licensed or registered as required by law to practice the profession

5. Dates of admission or registration of each member. Have client provide certificates from the licensing authority to be attached to the Articles of Incorporation in some states

6. Are any of the members presently operating as a partnership or as members of a professional association? If so, will there be an assignment to the new corporation; who will handle dissolution of the old partnership or corporation and prepare any necessary final tax returns?

7. Corporate name desired

8. Duration of the corporation (perpetual or specified time)

9. Shall all members of the new professional corporation have voting rights? If not, what special voting restrictions shall be required?

10. What is the general purpose of the corporation (practice of medicine, law, architecture, engineering, or other)

11. How broad does client want the investment powers of the corporation to be?

12. Stock to be authorized:[2]
    (a) How many shares?
    (b) Par value of each share
    (c) Restraints on alienation of stock
    (d) Shall the corporation be a Subchapter S corporation?
    (e) Shall the stock be Section 1244 stock?

13. Does client want you to draft the bylaws for the corporation? If so, see checklist appearing in Paragraph 23 of Form IA 1.00

14. Are any fringe benefits to be made available immediately? If so, prepare resolutions for them:
    (a) Employment agreement[3]
    (b) Salary continuation plan
    (c) Purchase of key-man life insurance or purchase of shareholder-owned policy
    (d) Automobile purchase or lease
    (e) Social club or professional association dues of stockholders to be paid by corporation

(f) Death benefits

(g) Deferred compensation, pension, or profit-sharing plans[4]

(h) Other

> [1]*18 Am. Jur. 2d Corporations,* paras. 32, 1052, and 1053. Check state statutes regulating professional corporations and state statutes regulating the particular profession.
> [2]Ref. Form IA 1.00 22.
> [3]Ref. Form IVA 1.00; Form IVA 1.01; Form IVA 1.02.
> [4]Form IVA 1.00; Form IVA 1.03; Form IVA 1.04; Form IVA 1.05.

## FORM IB 1.01

### (Medical professional corporation)

### ARTICLES OF INCORPORATION[1]
### of
### DOE, ROE and POE, P.A.

The subscribers to these Articles of Incorporation are natural persons over the age of 18 years, each duly licensed by the State of Florida to conduct the practice of medicine and surgery, who present these Articles for the formation of a corporation under The Professional Service Corporation Act and other applicable laws of the State of Florida.

I

*Name*

The name of the Corporation is Doe, Roe and Poe, P.A.

II

*Purpose and Powers*

The purpose for which this Corporation is formed is to carry on and conduct the practice of medicine and surgery under the Laws of the State of Florida through individuals authorized by that law to render such services as individuals.

In furtherance of the above purpose, the Corporation shall have the power to do the following:

1. To invest the funds of the Corporation in real estate, mortgages, banks, or any other type of investment, and to own real and personal property to be used for the rendering of medical and surgical services.

2. To do anything necessary and proper for the accomplishment of the purposes or exercise of the powers of the Corporation necessary or incidental to the protection and benefit of the Corporation, and in general, either alone or in association with other corporations, firms, or individuals, to carry on any lawful pursuit necessary or incidental to this accomplishment of the purposes or exercise of the powers of the Corporation.

III

*Capital Stock*

The maximum number of shares of stock that the Corporation is authorized to have outstanding at any one time is 5,000 shares of common stock having a par value of $1 per share. None of the shares of the Corporation may be issued to anyone other than an individual duly licensed to practice medicine and/or surgery in the State of Florida.

IV

*Initial Capital*

The amount of capital with which the Corporation will begin business is $1,500.

V

*Term of Existence*

The term of the Corporation is perpetual.

VI

*Initial Address*

The initial post office address of the principal office of the Corporation in the State of Florida is 100 Main Street, Ocala, Florida.

VII

*Initial Directors*

The names and residence addresses of the members of the first board of directors are:

| | |
|---|---|
| John Doe | 10 West Street<br>Middletown, Florida 32600 |
| Richard Roe | 100 Arbor Circle<br>Middletown, Florida 32600 |
| George Poe | 100 East Drive<br>Middletown, Florida 32600 |

VIII

*Directors*

The business of the Corporation shall be managed by its Board of Directors. The number of directors constituting the entire board shall not be fewer than 3, and subject to such minimum may be increased from time to time by amendment to the bylaws of the Corporation in a manner not prohibited by law.

IX

*Cumulative Voting*

At each election for directors, every holder of the capital stock shall have the right to vote, in person or by proxy, the number of shares registered in his name for as many persons as there are directors to be elected and for whose election he has a right to vote, or to cumulate his votes by giving one candidate as many votes as the number of such directors multiplied by the number of his shares shall equal, or by distributing such votes on the same principle among any number of such candidates.

X

*Restraint on Alienation of Shares*

1. The shareholders of the Corporation shall have the power to include in the bylaws, adopted by a two-thirds majority of the stockholders of the Corporation, any regulatory or restrictive provisions regarding the proposed sale, transfer, or other disposition of any of the outstanding shares of the Corporation by any of its shareholders or in the event of the death of any of its shareholders.

2. The manner and form, as well as the relevant terms, conditions, and details of any regulation or restriction shall be determined by the shareholders of the Corporation; provided, however, that such regulatory or restrictive provisions shall not affect the rights of third parties without actual notice thereof, unless the existence of such provisions shall be plainly written upon the certificate evidencing the ownership of such shares.

3. No shareholder of the Corporation may sell or transfer his shares therein except to another individual who is eligible to be a shareholder of the Corporation, and such sale or transfer may be made only after the same shall have been approved at a stockholder's meeting specially called for such purpose.

4. If any shareholder shall become legally disqualified to practice medicine in the State of Florida, or be elected to a public office, or accept employment that places restrictions or limitations upon his continuous rendering of such professional services, such shareholder's shares of stock shall immediately become subject to purchase by the Corporation in accordance with the bylaws of the Corporation at the time of such act.

XI

*Subscribers*

The names and residence addresses of each person signing the Articles of Incorporation as a subscriber, each of whom is duly licensed to practice medicine in the State of Florida, the number of shares of stock each agrees to take, and the value of the consideration therefor are:

| | | | |
|---|---|---|---|
| John Doe | 10 West Street<br>Middletown, Florida<br>32600 | 500 shares | $500 |
| Richard Roe | 100 Arbor Circle<br>Middletown, Florida<br>32600 | 500 shares | $500 |
| George Poe | 100 East Drive<br>Middletown, Florida<br>32600 | 500 shares | $500 |

IN WITNESS WHEREOF, we have signed and acknowledged these Articles of Incorporation this 10th day of May, 1982.

_____
JOHN DOE

_____
RICHARD ROE

_____
GEORGE POE

STATE OF FLORIDA
COUNTY OF ORANGE

Before me, the undersigned authority, personally appeared John Doe, Richard Roe, and George Poe, who, being duly sworn, acknowledged before me that they signed the foregoing Articles of Incorporation for the uses and purposes therein set forth.

Dated this 10th day of May, 1982.

_____
Notary Public

My commission expires:

[1] *18 Am. Jur. 2d Corporations,* paras. 32, 1052, 1053. Compare Form IIA 1.03 for a professional partnership agreement.

## SECTION C     NOT-FOR-PROFIT CORPORATIONS

This section contains a sample of Articles of Incorporation for a private school, together with a sample membership certificate which is used by a not-for-profit corporation instead of a stock certificate. The forms can be adapted for a church corporation or any other charitable, scientific, educational institution or project which is not to be used for the profit of its members.

Form IC 1.03 provides a sample index for the bylaws of a not-for-profit corporation.

### FORM IC 1.00

### CLIENT QUESTIONNAIRE FOR FORMING NOT-FOR-PROFIT CORPORATION[1]

1. Name and residence address(es) of client(s), the incorporator(s), and intital board of directors
2. Business and home telephone numbers of client(s)
3. What is the purpose of the corporation (charitable, educational, or other-tax exempt purpose?[2]

4. What are the powers of the corporation?
5. Corporate name desired
6. Duration (perpetual or specified time)
7. What are the membership qualifications and limitations (who shall prepare application forms and membership certificates[3])?
8. Names and residence addresses of the persons who will sign the Articles of Incorporation
9. Who will operate the corporation?
   (a) Titles of officers and names and addresses of initial officers
   (b) Number of persons constituting the first board of directors and names and addresses of the initial board of directors
   (c) Who will make, alter, or rescind bylaws for the corporation?
   (d) How shall the Articles of Incorporation be amended and by whom?
   (e) Who shall have voting rights (all members or only certain classes of members)?
10. Does the purpose of the corporation require that any members be licensed by any government entity? If so, have client get certificate from licensing authority for each such member
11. Does client want you to draft the bylaws for the corporation?[4] If so, see checklist appearing in Paragraph 23 of Form IA 1.00
12. Who will be the resident agent for service of process? Get name and address and file the form and acceptance required by your state statute

[1] *18 Am. Jur. 2d Corporations*, para. 10. Check state statutes regarding not-for-profit corporations and private foundations.
[2] 26 U.S.C.A. 4942.
[3] Ref. Form IC 1.02.
[4] Ref. Form IC 1.03.

## FORM IC 1.01

### (Not-for-profit corporation)[1]

### ARTICLES OF INCORPORATION
### of
### SOUTHEAST ASSOCIATION OF PRIVATE SCHOOLS, INC.

### ARTICLE I  NAME

The name of the Corporation is SOUTHEAST ASSOCIATION OF PRIVATE SCHOOLS, INC.

### ARTICLE II  PURPOSE

The purpose for which the Corporation is organized is to promote and advance in all lawful ways the mutual interests of its members engaged in the operation of private educational institutions in the states of Florida, Georgia, North Carolina, and South Carolina and to disseminate all types of information that may improve the quality of education in private schools, including descriptive indexes, reports and abstracts of local and federal government legislation, and regulation of private schools.

### ARTICLE III  QUALIFICATION OF MEMBERS

There shall be two classes of members: regular and associate.
*Regular member:* Any private school licensed to operate in the states of Florida, Georgia, North Carolina, and South Carolina or found to be exempt from licensure in the state where it operates, upon written application and payment of first year's dues.
*Associate member:* (1) any person, representative of education, government, business, or industry; or (2) any firm, corporation, or association directly or indirectly interested in the private-school industry, whose application for associate membership shall have been approved by the Board of Directors.

### ARTICLE IV  DURATION

The term of the Corporation shall be perpetual.

### ARTICLE V  SUBSCRIBERS

The names and addresses of the subscribers are:

> John Doe
> 100 East Street
> Jacksonville, Florida 00000
>
> Richard Roe
> 100 West Street
> Atlanta, Georgia 00000
>
> Peter Poe
> 100 Main Street
> Spartanburg, South Carolina 00000

### ARTICLE VI  OFFICERS

The affairs of the Corporation will be managed by a President, a Vice-President, a Secretary, and a Treasurer who will be elected for a period of two (2) years in the year ending with an even digit.

The names of the initial officers who will serve until the first election of officers held by the Corporation are: John Doe, Richard Roe, and Peter Poe.

### ARTICLE VII  BOARD OF DIRECTORS

The initial Board of Directors to serve until the first election of directors held by the Corporation shall consist of three persons, whose names and addresses are:

> John Doe
> 100 East Street
> Jacksonville, Florida 00000
>
> Richard Roe
> 100 West Street
> Atlanta, Georgia 00000
>
> Peter Poe
> 100 Main Street
> Spartanburg, South Carolina 00000

### ARTICLE VIII   BYLAWS

Bylaws will be adopted by the initial Board of Directors. New bylaws may be adopted or the initial bylaws may be repealed or amended in whole or in part at an annual meeting of the members or at any other meeting of the members called for that purpose, but any such resolution repealing or amending the intial bylaws or adopting new bylaws shall require a vote of not less than two-thirds (2/3) of the members entitled to vote.

### ARTICLE IX   POWERS AND VOTING RIGHTS

The Corporation, its officers, directors, and members shall have all corporate powers provided in Section 617.021 Florida Statutes, except that associate members shall not have the right to vote at corporate meetings.

IN WITNESS WHEREOF, we have signed and acknowledged these Articles of Incorporation this 23rd day of September, 1982.

_____
John Doe

_____
Richard Roe

_____
Peter Poe

STATE OF FLORIDA
COUNTY OF DUVAL

BEFORE ME, a notary public in and for said county and state, personally appeared JOHN DOE, known to me and known by me to be the person who subscribed the foregoing Articles of Incorporation, and he acknowledged before me that he executed those Articles of Incorporation for the purposes set forth therein.

IN WITNESS WHEREOF, I have hereunto set my hand and notarial seal, in the state and county aforesaid, this 23rd day of September, 1982.

_____
Notary Public

My commission expires:


STATE OF GEORGIA
COUNTY OF DEKALB

BEFORE ME, a notary public in and for said county and state, personally appeared RICHARD ROE, known to me and known by me to be the person who subscribed the foregoing Articles of Incorporation, and he acknowledged before me that he executed those Articles of Incorporation for the purposes set forth therein.

IN WITNESS WHEREOF, I have hereunto set my hand and notarial seal, in the state and county aforesaid, this 23rd day of September, 1982.

_____
Notary Public

My commission expires:


STATE OF SOUTH CAROLINA
COUNTY OF SPARTANBURG

BEFORE ME, a notary public in and for said county and state, personally appeared PETER POE, known to me and known by me to be the person who subscribed the foregoing Articles of Incorporation, and he acknowledged before me that he executed those Articles of Incorporation for the purposes set forth therein.

IN WITNESS WHEREOF, I have hereunto set my hand and notarial seal, in the state and county aforesaid, this 23rd day of September, 1982.

_____
Notary Public

My commission expires:

[1] *18 Am. Jur. 2d Corporations*, para. 10. Compare *6 Am. Jur. 2d Associations and Clubs*, paras. 2–4. Compare Form IIA 1.06 for unincorporated association. See Forms IC 1.02 and 1.03 to implement incorporation. Check state non-profit corporation statute for need to file separate designation of resident agent.


## FORM IC 1.02

### (For not-for-profit corporation[1])

## CERTIFICATE OF MEMBERSHIP
## SOUTHEAST ASSOCIATION OF PRIVATE SCHOOLS, INC.

This is to CERTIFY that
CLEARVIEW ACADEMY
is a REGULAR member of the above Corporation, incorporated under the laws of the State of Florida, and is entitled to all the rights and privileges of a regular member, as more fully set forth in the Corporation's bylaws, rules, and regulations.

IN WITNESS WHEREOF, the Corporation has caused this Certificate to be executed by its duly authorized officers, and its corporate seal to be hereto affixed.

Dated this 15th day of August, 1981.

(CORPORATE SEAL)

| | |
|---|---|
| _____ | _____ |
| Secretary of the Corporation | President |

[1]Ref. Form IC 1.01 for articles of incorporation and Form IC 1.03 for sample index to bylaws.

## FORM IC 1.03

### SOUTHEAST ASSOCIATION OF PRIVATE SCHOOLS, INC.
### BYLAWS[1]
### SAMPLE INDEX

ARTICLE I—MEMBERS

Section    1. Classes of Members
           2. Qualifications
           3. Application
           4. Dues and Fees
           5. Rights of Members
           6. Duties of Members
           7. Expulsion
           8. Forfeiture
           9. Termination of Membership
          10. Transfer

ARTICLE II—MEETINGS OF MEMBERS

Section    1. Place of Meetings
           2. Annual Meetings and Notice Thereof
           3. Special Meetings and Notice Thereof
           4. Voting
           5. Quorum

ARTICLE III—BOARD OF DIRECTORS

Section    1. Powers
           2. Number and Qualifications
           3. Term of Office
           4. Voting and Quorum
           5. Meeting of the Board of Directors
           6. Removal and Recall
           7. Resignations
           8. Vacancies
           9. Committees

ARTICLE IV—OFFICERS

Section    1. In General
           2. Subordinate Officers
           3. President
           4. Vice-President
           5. Secretary
           6. Treasurer
           7. Removal and Recall
           8. Resignation
           9. Vacancies

ARTICLES V—ELECTIONS

Section    1. Time and Place
           2. Pre-Election Procedure for Annual Elections

¹Ref. Form IC 1.01 for articles of incorporation and Form IC 1.02 for sample membership certificate.

# PART II
# PARTNERSHIPS AND JOINT VENTURES

# PART II

# Partnerships and Joint Ventures

## INTRODUCTION

The documents in Part II are used to form a business relationship between *two or more* individuals other than a corporation.[1]

The formation of corporations is treated in Part I, Section A. Various contracts that create a particular business status between an individual or corporation and another individual or corporation are presented in Parts III, IV, and V.

Before drafting any document, read the Introduction and the Client Questionnaire for the appropriate Section of this book. A review of the Table of Contents for the Part of the book on the general subject will lead you to the appropriate Section.

Using the applicable Client Questionnaire will provide the *facts* that are to be considered before drafting the instrument.

The footnotes to the Introduction, Client Questionnaire, and the forms will alert you to possible problems and give you an overview of the *law* that affects the particular form.

In the United States since 1950, the corporate form of business entity is the most prevalent.[2] Joint stock companies[3] are rather rare. Business trusts[4] (known as Massachusetts Trusts) are an acceptable form of group business without incorporation in some states. In most states a group of individuals may do business as an unincorporated association[5] as a fairground association, a club, or a trade association.

Joint ventures[6] usually involve one or more particular business projects to be carried on by two or more individuals for a limited time and for a specific purpose.

A general partnership[7] is the most common legal business entity, other than a corporation. A corporation can be a "one-man" business, but either a general or a limited partnership consists of at least two individuals.

Limited partnerships[8] in businesses as varied as owning and using a race horse or breeding horses, owning and operating an apartment building, or owning and renting a railroad car have been utilized as federal income tax shelters[9] in recent

---

[1] *60 Am. Jur. 2d Partnership*, paras. 9–14.
[2] *60 Am. Jur. 2d Partnership*, para. 3.
[3] *46 Am. Jur. 2d Joint Stock Companies*, paras. 1–21.
[4] *13 Am. Jur. 2d Business Trusts*, paras. 1 and 13–21.
[5] *6 Am. Jur. 2d Associations and Clubs*, paras. 1–4.
[6] *46 Am. Jur. 2d Joint Ventures*, paras. 1–6.
[7] *59 Am. Jur. 2d Partnership*, paras. 33–38.
[8] *60 Am. Jur. 2d Partnership*, paras. 372, 374, and 376.
[9] *26 U.S.C.A. 181 et seq. and 465.*

years. The limited partner(s) may contribute money or property but not services. The general partner may contribute services.

All states, as well as the District of Columbia, Guam, and the Virgin Islands, have adopted the *Uniform Partnership Act*[10] with some variations. All states and territories *except* Connecticut, Georgia, Guam, Maryland, Minnesota, Washington, West Virginia, and Wyoming adopted the earlier version of the *Uniform Limited Partnership Act.*[11] Those excepted states have adopted the 1976 version of the Act as of this writing.

The Uniform Acts define a partner or limited partner. Liabilities of the partnership, of the partners to each other and to third parties are spelled out in the Acts. The Acts specifically allow the liabilities of the partners *to each other* to be abrogated or modified by the partnership agreement.

## SECTION A      GENERAL PARTNERSHIP

Before using the forms in this section, the general introduction to PART II and FORM IIA 1.00 CLIENT QUESTIONNAIRE FOR CREATING AN UNINCORPORATED BUSINESS ENTITY should be read. The answers to the FORM IIA 1.00 will determine whether the forms in this section or another section in PART II are appropriate to organize the client's business.

### FORM IIA 1.00

(By two or more persons or corporations)[1]

#### CLIENT QUESTIONNAIRE FOR CREATING AN UNINCORPORATED BUSINESS ENTITY

1. Name and address of client(s)
2. Business and home telephone numbers of clients(s)
3. Names and addresses of all participants in the new business or venture and their proposed relationship to the business or project if it is not to be incorporated:
    (a) General partner[2]
    (b) Limited partner[3]
    (c) Member of a joint stock company[4]
    (d) Member of an unincorporated association[5]
    (e) Joint venturer[6]
    (f) Business trust beneficiary[7] or trustee of the business trust
4. Nature of the business or business project
5. Name of the business entity to be formed
6. Date business or project is to begin

---

[10]See Appendix XIV for all state citations.
[11]See Appendix XIII for all state citations.

7. Amount and nature of capital to be contributed by each person or corporation, and amount and nature of labor or services to be performed by each person or corporation
8. If the entity is to be a partnership or limited partnership, ask client which statutory provisions as to liability of the partners to each other is to be modified or deleted
9. Duration of the agreement—time in which project is to be completed, if any
10. In what proportion will profits be distributed? In case of a proposed partnership agreement, are any payments to be made to any participant in payment for:
    (a) A debt
    (b) Wages of an employee
    (c) Rent to a landlord
    (d) Annuity to a widow or representative of a deceased partner
    (e) Interest on a loan
    (f) Sale of goodwill of a business

If the share in profits is payable solely because of any of the above, the participant may not be a partner. In such case, a security agreement, employment agreement, lease, or deferred compensation or pension agreement or other agreement may be called for instead of a partnership agreement.

[1]Ref. Introduction to this chapter; and *60 Am. Jur. 2d Partnership,* paras. 9–14.
[2]*59 Am. Jur. 2d Partnership,* paras. 33–38.
[3]*60 Am. Jur. 2d Partnership,* paras. 372, 374, and 376; and 26 U.S.C.A. 465.
[4]*46 Am. Jur. 2d Joint Stock Companies,* paras. 1–21; Compare statutory limited partnership *60 Am. Jur. 2d Partnership,* para. 392; *48 Am. Jur. 2d Labor and Labor Relations,* para. 47; *33 Am. Jur. 2d Federal Taxation,* paras. 2005–2013; and C.F.R. 301.7701–2(a). Check state statute for regulation and/or filing requirements.
[5]*6 Am. Jur. 2d Associations and Clubs,* paras. 1–10.
[6]*46 Am. Jur. 2d Joint Ventures,* paras. 1–6.
[7]*13 Am. Jur. 2d Business Trusts,* paras. 1 and 13–21.

## FORM IIA 1.01

### (To operate business for specified time)

### PARTNERSHIP AGREEMENT[1]

AGREEMENT, made in Pittsburgh, Pennsylvania, on January 1, 1983, between John Doe, residing at 5000 Forbes Avenue, Pittsburgh, Pennsylvania 15217 (First Party), and Richard Roe, residing at 400 Graham Street, Pittsburgh, Pennsylvania 15232 (Second Party),

WHEREIN IT IS MUTUALLY AGREED, AS FOLLOWS:

1. PURPOSE

That the parties shall, as partners, engage in and conduct the business of buying, selling, and dealing in goods, at wholesale and retail.

2. NAME

That the name of the partnership shall be John Doe & Co.

3. TERM

That the term of the partnership shall begin January 1, 1983, and shall end on December 31, 1987.

4. LOCATION

That the place of business of the partnership shall be located at 415 Wood Street, Pittsburgh, Pennsylvania 15222.

5. CAPITAL

(a) That the capital of the partnership shall be the sum of Twenty Thousand Dollars ($20,000); and each party shall contribute, contemporaneously with the execution of this Agreement, the sum of Ten Thousand Dollars ($10,000) in cash.

(b) That neither party's contribution to the capital of the partnership shall bear interest in his favor.

(c) That the capital of the partnership, and all other moneys of, as well as all instruments for the payment of moneys to, the partnership, shall be deposited in the name of the partnership, in the Fidelity National Bank, in Allegheny County, Pennsylvania; and all moneys credited to the partnership shall be subject to withdrawal only by check made in the name of the partnership, and signed jointly by the parties.

(d) That neither party shall, without the written consent of the other, advance any moneys to the partnership in excess of the amount of his first contribution to the capital; but any such advance that shall be made by either party, with the written consent of the other, shall bear interest at the rate of Six Percent (6%) per annum.

(e) That if either party shall, with the consent of the other, become indebted to the partnership, such indebtedness shall bear interest at the rate of Nine Percent (9%) per annum.

6. OPERATION

(a) That each party shall devote all of his time and attention to the business of the partnership, and shall not, during the term of this partnership, either directly or indirectly, engage in any other business.

(b) That full and accurate accounts of the transactions of the partnership shall be kept in proper books; and each party shall cause to be entered in the partnership books a full and accurate account of all of his transactions on behalf of the partnership.

(c) That the books of the partnership shall be kept at the place of business of the partnership, and each party shall, at all times, have access to, and may inspect and copy, any of them.

(d) That each party shall be entitled to draw Two Hundred Dollars ($200) a week from the funds of the partnership.

(e) That neither party shall, without the written consent of the other party, make, execute, deliver, endorse, or guaranty any commercial paper, nor agree to answer for, or indemnify against, any act, debt, default, or miscarriage of any person, partnership (other than that of these parties), association, or corporation.

(f) That, at the end of each calendar year, a full and accurate inventory shall be prepared, and the assets, liabilities, and income, both gross and net, shall be ascertained, and the net profits or net loss of the partnership shall be fixed and determined.

(g) That the net profits or net loss shall be divided equally between the parties, and the account of each shall be credited or debited, as the case may be, with his proportionate share.

7. TERMINATION

(a) That, at the termination of this partnership, by the expiration of its term, or by reasons of any other cause, a full and accurate inventory shall be prepared, and the assets, liabilities, and income, both gross and net, shall be ascertained; the debts of the partnership then remaining shall be divided in specie between the parties, share and share alike.

(b) See alternative forms concerning continuing partnership on death of a partner, if that is desired.

8. ARBITRATION

(a) That if any disagreement shall arise between the parties as to the conduct of the partnership business, or as to its dissolution, or as to any other matter, cause, or thing whatever, not otherwise provided for, including the physical or mental disability of a partner to perform his partnership duties, the same shall be decided and determined by arbitrators. Each party shall appoint one (1) such arbitrator, and both of such arbitrators shall appoint a third arbitrator. The decision of two (2) of the three (3) of such arbitrators, when made in writing, shall be conclusive upon the parties.

(b) That the appointment of the arbitrators by the respective parties shall be made, as follows: The party seeking arbitration shall serve a notice in writing upon the other party, setting forth the disagreement or disagreements that he desires to be arbitrated, as well as the name of his arbitrator; and then the other party shall, within five (5) days after the receipt of such notice, serve upon the party seeking arbitration a notice in writing stating the name of his arbitrator.

(c) The failure of a party to appoint an arbitrator shall authorize the other party to make an appointment for the one so in default.

(d) If the two (2) arbitrators appointed shall fail, within five (5) days after the second of the arbitrators shall have been appointed, to select a third arbitrator, then any judgement of the Court of Common Pleas of Allegheny County, upon application made by either party for that purpose, shall be authorized and empowered to appoint such third arbitrator.

(e) The award to be made by the arbitrators shall be made within five (5) days after the third arbitrator shall have been appointed.

(f) Costs of arbitration and reasonable attorney's fees for each partner in the conduct of the arbitration proceedings, if any, shall be paid by the partnership.

IN WITNESS WHEREOF, the parties have signed this Agreement the day and year first above written.

WITNESSES:

 

_____      _____
JOHN DOE

_____      _____
RICHARD ROE

[1]See Appendix XIV for all state citations to Uniform Partnership Act; *59 Am. Jur. 2d Partnership,* paras. 33–38; 26 U.S.C.A. 181.

## FORM IIA 1.02

**(To purchase, develop and operate real estate as partners)**

### PARTNERSHIP AGREEMENT[1]

AND NOW, to wit, this 10th day of March, 1983,
WITNESSETH:

WHEREAS, the parties hereto desire to form a partnership for the sole purpose of acquiring a certain parcel of land located in Central Township, County of Westmoreland and Commonwealth of Pennsylvania; and

WHEREAS, the Partners have stipulated their mutual rights, powers, duties, and liabilities in connection with the business of the partnership;

NOW, THEREFORE, in consideration of the mutual convenants given herein, the Partners agree as follows:

1. *Name.* The name of the partnership shall presently be Doe Industrial Complex, or such other name as the Partners may later agree upon.

2. *Purpose.* The purposes of the partnership shall be to acquire, own, develop, mortgage, lease, sell, or otherwise dispose of land located in Central Township, County of Westmoreland and Commonwealth of Pennsylvania, said land being described in Exhibit A attached hereto, to finance and construct or cause to be constructed improvements thereon, and to do anything necessary or incidental to the foregoing.

3. *Office.* The principal office of the partnership shall be located at 400 Wood Street, Pittsburgh, County of Allegheny and Commonwealth of Pennsylvania, or at such other place as the Partners may agree.

4. *Term.* The provisions of this Agreement shall become binding upon all of the Partners at the time this Agreement is signed by all of the Partners, and said partnership shall continue indefinitely unless terminated by mutual agreement of the Partners, or as may hereinafter be provided.

5. *Management.* No Partner may do any act on behalf of the partnership, without the consent of the other Partners, which act is not within the scope of the purposes of the partnership as set forth in Paragraph 2 above. Any partnership decision having a substantial effect upon the interest of the partnership, or of any Partner, shall require the unanimous agreement of the Partners. Provided however, it is expressly agreed that John Doe may execute any and all documents, including agreement to purchase property described in Exhibit A, notes, mortgages, assignments of lease, etc., to effectuate the foregoing, and the signature of John Doe to any such document shall bind the partnership.

6. *Capital Contributions.*

(a) The Partners shall make initial capital contributions in the following amounts:

| | |
|---|---|
| John Doe | $30,000 |
| Richard Roe | $20,000 |
| Peter Poe | $20,000 |

| John Just | $20,000 |
| Raymond Rich | $10,000 |

(b) The profits and losses of the partnership and distributions of the partnership, including distributions to Partners upon the dissolution of the partnership, shall be allocated to the Partners according to the following percentages:

| John Doe | 30% |
| Richard Roe | 20% |
| Peter Poe | 20% |
| John Just | 20% |
| Raymond Rich | 10% |

7. *Additional Capital.* It is recognized by the Partners that capital, in addition to the intitial contributions set forth above, may be required by the partnership to accomplish the purposes of the partnership. In such event, the Partners shall make additional contributions or loans to the partnership, and such contributions or loans shall be made in proportion to the ownership of the Partners as set forth in Paragraph 6 above.

8. *Other Activities of Partners.* It is acknowledged that each of the Partners has other interest in business, and shall be permitted to continue their other business activities notwithstanding their status as Partners, nor shall any of them be required to devote their full time to the partnership's business, but only such part as may be necessary to reasonably develop and manage the subject property.

9. *Banking.* All funds of the partnership shall be deposited in its name in such checking account or accounts in such bank or banks as agreed upon by the Partners. All withdrawals therefrom are to be made upon checks signed by any Partner or by such person as may be designated by the Partners.

10. *Books.* The books of the partnership shall be maintained at its principal office, in accordance with generally accepted accounting principles, and any Partner or his representative shall have access thereto during all reasonable business hours. The fiscal year of the partnership shall end on December 31st in each year or on such other date as the Partners shall determine, and the books shall be closed and balanced at the end of each year. Statements showing the receipts and disbursements in each calendar month shall be prepared and distributed to the Partners at least quarterly. Periodic balance sheets shall be furnished as often as deemed necessary by the Partners.

11. *Compensation.* No compensation, salaries, fees, or commissions shall be paid by the partnership to any Partner herein for any services rendered to the partnership, except as expressly agreed to, from time to time, by the Partners.

12. *Sale of Partnership Interest.*

(a) Any partner may assign all or portions of his interest in the partnership to another Partner or to his spouse, children, parents, or to a trust created for the benefit of the foregoing. In the event of such assignment, the assignee shall not be admitted as a Partner, but shall have an interest only in the profits of the partnership as set forth in Part 5, Section 27 of the Pennsylvania enactment of the Uniform Partnership Act as in existence on the date hereof.

(b) Except, as set forth in Subparagraph (a) above, no Partner may sell, assign, transfer, or otherwise dispose of his interest in this partnership without the written consent of the other Partners herein, except as follows:

(i) A Partner may sell part or all of his interest in this partnership to any third party provided he shall:

A. First offer such interest to the other Partners herein at the same price and on the same terms as to the third party, whose identity must be stated in the offer; and

B. If such offer is not accepted by the other Partners in the partnership within fifteen (15) days from the date of such offer, the offerer may sell to the designated third party at the price and terms specified within ninety (90) days after the expiration of the said 15-day period.

C. Thereafter, before any contemplated sale, the interest must again be offered to the other Partners.

D. Nothing herein shall imply that the Partners may purchase less than all of the interest being offered.

(ii) Any Partner may sell all or part of his interest to the other Partners.

(iii) Any such sale, transfer, assignment, or other disposition, however, shall not have any operative force or effect unless:

A. The instrument of transfer provides that the assignee shall be bound by all of the terms and conditions of this Agreement as if the assignee were a party who had joined in the execution and delivery hereof; and

B. A duplicate original of the instrument of transfer is delivered to this partnership and to all the Partners herein.

13. *Death of a Partner.*

(a) In the event of the death of a Partner, the partnership shall not be dissolved. The legal representative of the deceased Partner shall, within one hundred twenty (120) days of the death of the Partner, elect either to retain the partnership interest of the deceased Partner, or to sell such interest to the surviving Partners upon the terms and conditions set forth below. Failure of the legal representative of the deceased Partner to make an election pursuant to this paragraph shall be deemed to be an election by said legal representative to retain the partnership interest. In the event the interest of the deceased Partner is retained, the owner of such interest shall not be admitted as a Partner, but shall only have an interest in the profits of the partnership as set forth in Part 5, Section 27 of the Pennsylvania enactment of the Uniform Partnership Act as in existence on the date hereof. In the event the legal representative of the deceased Partner elects to sell the interest to the partnership, the purchase price of such interest shall be the sum of:

(i) Credits to the decedent on the partnership's books for loans made to the partnership;

(ii) Undistributed profits to the date of death;

(iii) The value of the deceased Partner's interest in the partnership and its assets, including his capital account as of the date of death, but exclusive of the amount of preceding items (i) and (ii).

Interest shall accrue on such amount at Nine Percent (9%) per annum from the date of death and shall be paid quarter-annually and without regard to the earnings of the partnership. Items (i) and (ii) shall be determined by the certified public accountants retained by the partnership by reference to the books of account.

(b) If the parties to the sale cannot agree upon the value of item (iii) within fifteen (15) days after the determination of the preceding items (i) and (ii) by the said certified public accountants, then the value thereof shall be determined by appraisal in the following manner:

(i) Within seven (7) days after the expiration of the aforementioned fifteen (15)-day period, one appraiser shall be selected by the surviving Partners and one appraiser shall be selected by the representative of the deceased partner, and written notice thereof shall be given to the other parties, and said two appraisers' determination as to value shall be conclusive and binding.

(ii) In the event either party fails or refuses to select an appraiser and give notice thereof within the seven (7)-day period mentioned in preceding Subparagraph (i), the determination of value made by the appraiser selected by the other party shall be conclusive and binding upon the parties.

(iii) If two appraisers are selected in the foregoing manner but cannot agree on a determination of value within fifteen (15) days after the expiration of the seven (7)-day period mentioned in Subparagraph (i), then said two appraisers shall select a third appraiser, whose determination of value shall be conclusive and binding upon both parties.

(iv) If the said two appraisers cannot agree upon a third appraiser within ten (10) days after the expiration of the fifteen (15)-day period mentioned in preceding Subparagraph (iii), then such third appraiser shall be appointed by the Presiding Judge of Allegheny County, Pennsylvania, upon petition of either party.

(v) The cost of such appraisal shall be shared equally by the parties.

(c) The purchase price determined hereunder shall be payable in no more than ten (10) equal annual installments, the first to be made within thirty (30) days after the determination of the purchase price. The purchase price may be prepaid at any time without penalty.

14. *Bankruptcy.* If any of the Partners shall be adjudicated bankrupt or insolvent pursuant to the provisions of any state or federal insolvency or bankruptcy act, or if a receiver or trustee shall be appointed for all or a portion of such Partner's property, or if any assignment of such Partner's property shall be made for the benefit of creditors, or if any execution or other process

shall issue against any Partner's interest in the partnership, and if not vacated within ninety (90) days (hereinafter under any of the foregoing circumstances called the "Attached Partner") then and in any such event, the other Partners shall have the right and option to acquire all the Attached Partner's interest in the partnership at a price equivalent to the Attached Partner's capital contribution and loans, if any, to the partnership, less any cash distributions previously made by the partnership to the Attached Partner and less any repayments of loans. Such right and option shall be exercisable in writing within thirty (30) days after such adjudication or order appointing receiver or trustee becomes final, or after such assignment for the benefit of creditors has been effected, or after the expiration of such ninety (90)-day period following the issuance of any execution or other process against the Attached Partner's interest in the partnership, and the Attached Partner shall execute and deliver to the other party such deeds, assignments, and other documents as shall be necessary to convey all of his right, title, and interest in the partnership in proper and due form of transfer with all requisite transfer stamps affixed, free and clear of all encumbrances except such encumbrances to which the partnership shall have suffered as against payment of the purchase price. The Partners are hereby granted the irrevocable power of attorney to execute and deliver on behalf of the Attached Partner all such instruments.

15. *Failure of Partner to Make Additional Required Advances.* In the event that one of the Partners shall fail to make an advance to the partnership required of him under this Agreement, and such default shall continue for a period of thirty (30) days after a call for such advance, then the other Partners shall have the following options:

(a) To arrange for a loan to the partnership with interest and to pledge therefore the interest of such defaulting Partner in the partnership, the amount of such loan and the interest thereon to be payable on demand by the defaulting Partner, and any distributions from the partnership otherwise payable to the defaulting Partner being first available for application against the aforesaid indebtedness; or

(b) To purchase, within sixty (60) days after such default, the total interest of the defaulting Partner for the amount of said defaulting Partner's total contribution to the capital of the partnership and loans to the partnership, less any previous cash distributions made by the partnership to the defaulting Partner; or

(c) To make good such deficiency on the part of the defaulting Partner and then to reallocate the interest in the partnership of the defaulting Partner in the capital and profits of the partnership so that such defaulting Partner's participation in the partnership and its profits and losses and his percentage of the cash flow therefrom shall be reduced to reflect his failure to make the aforesaid advances, and the interest in the partnership and in the profits thereof and the percentage of the cash flow therefrom of the Partner making good such deficiency shall be increased to reflect such advances in excess of his original obligation hereunder, and shall thereafter remain fixed as of the date of such default; or

(d) To dissolve and terminate the partnership and have its assets liquidated and distributed, in which event the proceeds of such liquidation shall be distributed to the nondefaulting Partner to the full extent of his capital contributions plus any loans made by him to the partnership, before any distributions shall be made to the defaulting Partner.

16. *Notices.* Any notices and demands hereunder shall be in writing and shall be deemed to have been given and received forty-eight (48) hours after the same shall have been deposited in United States registered or certified mail, postage prepaid, to the following addresses:

John Doe
415 Graham Street
Pittsburgh, PA 00000

John Just
100 West Street
Pittsburgh, PA 00000

Richard Roe
100 Main Street
Butler, PA 00000

Raymond Rich
100 Main Street
McKeesport, PA 00000

Peter Poe
100 Jones Drive
Pittsburgh, PA 00000

Any Partner may change his address as set forth above by giving notice to the other Partners.

17. *Modification and Amendments.* No modifications or amendments to this partnership Agreement shall be valid or binding unless and until each such modification or amendment shall have been reduced to writing and executed by each of the parties hereto.

18. *Successors.* This Agreement shall be binding upon the parties hereto and upon their heirs, successors, and assigns.

IN WITNESS WHEREOF, the parties hereto have affixed their signatures the day and year first above written.

|                          |
|--------------------------|
| JOHN DOE                 |
| RICHARD ROE              |
| PETER POE                |
| JOHN JUST                |
| RAYMOND RICH             |

¹Ref. footnotes to Form IIA 1.01.

## FORM IIA 1.03

### (Professional partnership agreement—dentists)

### PARTNERSHIP AGREEMENT¹

The parties to this agreement, George Painless, of Middletown, Orange County, Florida, and Richard Able, of Middletown, Orange County, Florida, hereby agree to form a partnership on the terms and conditions herein set forth.

#### ARTICLE I

*Name*

The name of the partnership shall be Painless & Able Dentistry.

#### ARTICLE II

*Purpose*

The purpose of the partnership shall be to practice the profession of dentistry and to do all other acts incidental thereto pursuant to the laws of the State of Florida and the rules and regulations of the Florida State Board of Dentistry.

#### ARTICLE III

*Location*

The offices of the partnership shall be at 100 Main Street, Middletown, Florida. Such office location may be changed, and additional offices may be established by the agreement of the parties.

#### ARTICLE IV

*Duration*

The partnership shall commence on January 1, 1983, and shall continue until it is dissolved as provided in Articles XV, XVI, or XVII, or liquidated as provided in Article XVIII of this partnership agreement.

#### ARTICLE V

*Capital*

(a) The initial capital of the partnership shall consist of the sum of Fifty Thousand Dollars ($50,000).

(b) The capital of the partnership shall be contributed equally by the partners.

(c) Subsequent capital contributions, as such are needed by the partnership, shall be made by each partner in proportion to his respective distributive share at the time of such need. In the event any partner fails to make such subsequent capital contribution, the partners who have contributed their shares may consider the same so advanced by them as loans to the partnership.

(d) Interest at the rate of Nine Percent (9%) per annum shall be allowed to a partner for such loan or who loans money to the partnership with the consent of all partners.

## ARTICLE VI

### Management and operation of partnership business

(a) *Full Time.* The partners shall devote their entire time, attention, and influence to the affairs of the partnership.

(b) *Part-time Status.* If, for reasons of health or otherwise, a partner fails to devote substantially all his time to partnership affairs, he shall be entitled to receive such monthly salary (after cessation of his entitlement to sick leave as provided in Article VII(b), if such incapacity results from illness) and such share of future profits as the partners shall determine by a vote of the majority in interest.

(c) *Other Business Activities.* No partner, during the continuance of the partnership, shall pursue, or become directly or indirectly interested in, any business or occupation that is in conflict with either the business of the partnership or with the rights, duties, and responsibilities of such partner to the partnership.

## ARTICLE VII

### Vacation and sick leave

(a) *Vacations.* Each partner shall be entitled to such vacations with salary as may be mutually agreed between the partners.

(b) *Sick Leave.* If a partner is unable to devote full time to partnership affairs due to illness or other incapacity, he shall be entitled to continue to receive his monthly salary as provided in Article XII(c), for a period of 365 days after such illness or other incapacity commences.

## ARTICLE VIII

### Fees and Compensation for Services

(a) *Fees Charged.* Generally fees to be charged shall be determined by majority agreement between the partners, but, in individual cases, fees to be charged shall be determined initially by the partner performing the services, or under whose supervision the work was done, subject to review and modification based on majority vote of the partners.

(b) *Accounting for Fees and Compensation Received.* Unless otherwise agreed by all partners, each partner shall account to the partnership for all compensation received and attributable to his personal services, including, by way of example but without limitations, salaries or fees of any kind for any performed services, appraisal fees, director's fees, and fees for serving as trustee, guardian, executor, or other fiduciary, provided however, that if such personal services do not interfere with or utilize time deemed as normal production time of the partnership, such salary or fee shall not be deemed an accountable activity or reportable under this section. This section shall not be construed to include income from personal monetary or other investments by any one partner.

(c) *Witholdings from Compensation Due Partnership.* If there is withheld from the compensation due to the partnership under Article VIII(b) any amount for taxes or insurance or other contributions inuring to the personal benefit of the partner performing the personal services, the gross amount of the compensation shall be income to the partnership. The deductions shall be charged to the income account of the partner performing the services. If the taxing authority requires the compensation to be returned by the partner performing the personal services, then appropriate equalizing adjustments shall be made in the income accounts of the other partners.

## ARTICLE IX

### Management

(a) *General Policies.* Each partner shall have an interest in the conduct of the affairs of the partnership in proportion to his capital contribution. Except as otherwise provided in this Agreement, all decisions shall be by vote of the majority in interest of the partners.

(b) *Managing Partner.* One partner shall be elected as managing partner to administer the general affairs of the partnership and to carry out and to put into effect the general policies and specific instructions of the majority of the partners in interest, but this provision shall not come into effect until the partnership has been expanded beyond two partners.

## ARTICLE X

### Bank Accounts

All funds of the partnership shall be deposited in its name in the First National Bank of Florida, Middletown, Florida, and all withdrawals therefrom may be made upon checks signed by either partner, until the partnership has been expanded beyond two partners.

## ARTICLE XI

### Records and Accounts

(a) *Time Records.* Each partner shall report daily the time devoted to all matters on which he works.

(b) *Job Sheets.* The partnership shall maintain records showing the total amount of time devoted to all matters handled by each partner.

(c) *Method of Accounting.* All accounts of the partnership shall be kept on a cash basis. All matters of accounting for which there is no provision in this Agreement are to be governed by generally accepted methods of accounting.

(d) *Fiscal Year.* For purposes of partnership accounting and for income tax reporting, a fiscal year ending on the last day of December of each year shall be adopted.

(e) *Place Where Books and Records Are to Be Kept.* The partnership books of account, and all securities, papers, and writings of the partnership shall be kept at the principal place of business at 100 Main Street, Middletown, Florida, or in such other place as the business shall be carried on. All books, records, and accounts of the partnership at all times shall be open to inspection by any or all partners, including withdrawn partners pursuant to the provisions of Articles XV(f), (h), XVI(f).

(f) *Capital Accounts.* A capital account shall be maintained on the partnership books for each partner. Such account shall be credited with that partner's contributions to the capital of the partnership and debited and credited in the manner prescribed in Paragraph (g) of this article.

(g) *Income Accounts.* An income account shall be maintained on the partnership books for each partner. Such account shall be closed to the capital account of the partner at the close of each fiscal year.

Any losses to be debited to a partner's income account that exceed the credit balance of such account shall be debited to that partner's individual capital account. If, as a result of the debiting of a partner's individual capital account with the excess losses, his capital account is depleted, future profits of that partner shall be credited to his capital account until such depletion has been eliminated.

(h) *Drawing Accounts.* A drawing account to which withdrawals shall be debited shall be maintained on the partnership books for each partner. Withdrawals may be made subject to such limitations as the partners may from time to time adopt. The drawing account of each partner shall be closed to his income account at the close of each fiscal year.

(i) *Monthly Statements.* At the end of each month, the books shall be balanced and an operating statement shall be prepared and made available to each partner showing the results of operations of the partnership during the previous month.

(j) *Annual Accounting.* The partnership books shall be closed at the end of each fiscal year, and statements showing the results of operation prepared and supplied to all partners. Such statements shall be prepared or audited by a certified public accountant or an accounting firm agreeable to all partners. When approved in writing by all partners, the annual statements shall be deemed final and binding, except for manifest errors discovered prior to the end of the next fiscal year. Written approval of the annual statements by all partners shall be obtained before final distribution of profits or losses are made at the end of each fiscal year.

(k) *Copies of Statements to Withdrawn Partners.* A copy of each montly operating statement and the annual statements shall be supplied to any withdrawn partner under Articles XV and XVI so long as he is entitled to receive any portion of the net profits.

ARTICLE XII

*Profits, Losses, and Salaries*

(a) *Participation in Profits and Losses.* Subject to the provisions of Article VI(b), the partners shall participate in the profits and losses according to the following percentages until otherwise agreed:

| Name of Partner | Percentage |
| --- | --- |
| George Painless | 50% |
| Richard Able | 50% |

ARTICLE XIII

*Limitations on Rights and Powers of Partners*

No partner shall, without the consent of all other partners:

(a) borrow money in the name of the partnership for partnership purposes or utilize collateral owned by the partnership as security for such loans.

(b) compromise or otherwise settle claims or assign, transfer, pledge, compromise, or release any of the claims or debts due to the partnership except on payment in full, or arbitration or consent to the arbitration of any dispute or controversy of the partnership by all the partners.

(c) transfer partnership assets, or make, execute, or deliver:

(1) any assignment for the benefit of creditors;

(2) any negotiable instrument, bond, confession of judgment, guaranty, indemnity bond, or surety bond; or

(3) any contract to sell, bill of sale, deed, mortgage, or lease relating to any substantial part of the partnership assets or his interest therein.

(d) make any purchases in excess of One Thousand Dollars ($1,000). A majority in interest of the partners may from time to time delegate to the managing partner limited or general authority to make purchases.

ARTICLE XIV

*Admission of New Partners*

The admission of a new partner shall require the unanimous approval of all existing partners. The capital contributions to be made by, and the participation percentage in profits and losses of the new partner shall be determined by vote of a majority in interest of the existing partners.

Each new partner must, before being admitted, agree in writing to be bound by the provisions of this partnership Agreement.

ARTICLE XV

*Withdrawal of Partners*

(a) *Applicability.* The obligation or election of the remaining partners to buy a withdrawing partner's interest under the terms of this Article arises in the following circumstances:

(1) *Retirement After Age 55.* After becoming fifty-five years of age, a partner may elect to retire by giving ninety (90) days' notice, retirement to become effective either on the first day of the next fiscal year, or on the first day of the second half of the fiscal year in which the election to retire is made. The purchase of partnership interest provided herein shall become effective on the retirement date.

(2) *Death.* Upon the death of a partner, the purchase shall become effective on the last day of the next month after the death.

(3) *Incapacity.* On the incapacity of the partner, only if the remaining partners elect to purchase his interest by notice given to him or to his representative, provided such notice is given:

(i) After the partner has been unable to practice his profession for twelve (12) continuous months, and

(ii) While the incapacity continues, and

(iii) If an election to purchase is made, the purchase shall become effective on the last day of the next month after the notice is given.

(4) *Voluntary Retirement Before Certain Age.* If a partner gives ninety (90) days' notice of retirement before reaching fifty-five years of age, to become effective at the end of a month,

and if, within thirty (30) days thereafter, the remaining partners, by notice to such retiring partner, elect to purchase his interest, the purchase shall become effective on the retirement date. If the remaining partners fail to make an election to purchase, the partnership shall be liquidated as provided in Article XVIII, if the liquidation does not violate Articles XVI(a) and XVIII(a) on account of a partner who has previously withdrawn.

(5) *Expulsion.* On expulsion of a partner, the purchase shall become effective as provided in Article XVII.

(b) *Valuation of Withdrawing Partner's Interest.* The value of the interest of any partner withdrawing from the partnership under this Article shall be computed by (1) adding the totals of (i) his capital account, (ii) his income account, and (iii) any other amounts owed to him by the partnership, and (2) subtracting from the sum of the above totals (i) his drawing account and (ii) any amount owed by him to the partnership. (3) For purposes of this Section, it is mutually agreed that all values to be utilized shall be *fair market values,* and that they shall be determined as follows at the time the obligation or election to purchase becomes effective, regardless of how the following assets are carried on the partnership books:

(i) Fair market value of buildings and real property and nondental personal property shall be determined by the use of independent professional appraisers, one to be hired by the partnership and one to be hired by the withdrawing partner or his personal representative at his own expense, and the two appraisers to between themselves agree to hire a third appraiser, this said cost to be shared equally between the partnership and the withdrawing partner, and that each of the three appraisers is to arrive at his evaluation of the aforesaid property independently, the three evaluations to be submitted both to the partnership and to the withdrawing partners, and the partnership and any future withdrawing partner hereby specifically bind themselves to specify that the fair market value of the property in question shall be the sum of the three evaluations divided by three.

(ii) Fair market value of professional dental equipment is hereby agreed by and between the partnership and any future withdrawing partner to be that sum established by a dental equipment distributor who services this area, or who provided the bulk of the dental equipment utilized by the partnership, whichever is available, and that this said portion of the total assets shall be arbitrarily determined by this single appraisal.

(iii) Fair market value of accounts receivable shall be by audit, said audit to be performed by the accountant or accounting firm retained by the partnership at the time the notice of withdrawal is received by the partnership, said total amount of accounts receivable to be reduced by the percent of uncollectable accounts as was experienced by the partnership during the two fiscal years of the partnership prior to the effective withdrawal date from the partnership, the first preceding fiscal year to be arbitrarily determined to be the fiscal year in which said withdrawal becomes effective under the terms of this Article, and the total amount of accounts receivable less uncollectables is to then be divided by the number of active partners at the time of the withdrawal or notice of withdrawal, and this is determined to be the withdrawing partner's share. Should the withdrawing partner object to this determination, he or his authorized representative may, at his own expense, retain an accounting firm of his own choice, and the partnership agrees to make available the partnership books and records or copies of same to that accountant, and the final determination of this valued asset in the event of disagreement between the two auditing firms shall be that sum equal to one-half the difference between the two independent audits, plus the amount of the lesser audit.

(iv) Fair market value of inventory of dental supplies shall be based upon current invoice values, divided by the number of active partners prior to the withdrawal or notice of withdrawal.

(v) It is mutually agreed that the allowance for goodwill shall be determined by the withdrawing partner to be that sum that is equal to the greater of:

(A) One half-year's net income to the active partners divided by the number of active partners prior to the notice of withdrawal, said formula to exclude income from any associate employed by the partnership, and the half-year period shall be limited to either the first or second half of the fiscal year prior to the year in which withdrawal takes place or the notice is received, or

(B) One half-year's net income of the withdrawing partner, to be limited to either the first or second half of any of the preceding two fiscal years before the withdrawal is made, said sum to exclude any of the partnership's associates' fee income during the period elected by the withdrawing partner.

(c) *Payment.* Payments to the withdrawing partner for his interest shall be paid Twenty-five

Percent (25%) in cash, and the balance of the purchase price in ten (10) installments over a period of ten (10) years and shall bear interest on the unpaid balance at the rate of Nine Percent (9%) per annum from the effective date. The payments required in this article shall be the joint and several personal obligations of the purchasing partners.

(d) *Title to Partnership Assets After Payment Under This Article.*

(1) *Transfer on Completion of Payments.* Title to the interest of the withdrawn partner shall vest in purchasing partners as the effective date of the purchase.

(2) *Sale to New Partners.* Nothing herein shall be construed to prevent the purchasing partners from selling a withdrawn partner's interest to a new partner. Such a sale will not relieve the purchasing partners of their joint and several personal obligations under Paragraph (c) of this article.

(e) *Assumption of Partnership Obligations.* The purchasing partners agree to save the withdrawn partner harmless from all obligations of the partnership, past and future, except for any claims against the partnership based on mistakes or defalcations of the withdrawn partner.

(f) *Disposition of Records and Partnership Files.* All partnership records and files, including clients' files, shall be deemed assets of and shall remain with the partnership. The remaining partners may on request deliver certain files to a withdrawn partner or permit him to make copies or to examine the files relating to certain clients so long as such does not offend professional ethics. The withdrawn partner shall be entitled to the files and records relating to his personal matters.

(g) *Partnership Name.* Unless prohibited by statute, regulation, or rules of conduct established within the profession by recognized organizations established to regulate ethical standards, the remaining partners may continue to use the surname of the withdrawn partner as a part of the partnership name.

(h) *Examination of Partnership Books and Files by Withdrawn Partner.* A withdrawn partner, or his authorized representative, shall have the right to examine the books and records of the partnership for a period of three (3) months after the effective date of his withdrawal for the purpose of verifying the amount he is to receive for his interest in the partnership under this article.

## ARTICLE XVI

### Expulsion from Partnership

(a) *Grounds for Expulsion.* The following grounds shall constitute a basis for the remaining partners to expel a partner:

(1) *Disciplinary Action.* If the license of any partner is revoked or suspended, or if such partner is otherwise disciplined by final action of any duly constituted authority, provided none of the remaining partners has participated or acquiesced in the professional misconduct that provided the basis for such action;

(2) *Breach of Professional Ethics.* If any partner persists in professional misconduct in violation of the standards set forth in local or state regulations or statutes, or in rules of conduct established within the profession by recognized organizations established to regulate ethical standards, after being requested by the remaining partners to desist;

(3) *Injury to Partnership Name.* If any partner persists in pursuing a course of action that seriously injures the professional standing of the partnership after being requested by the remaining partners to desist;

(4) *Insolvency or Bankruptcy.* If any partner becomes insolvent, makes an assignment for the benefit of creditors, is declared a bankrupt, or if his assets are administered in any type of creditors' proceeding.

(b) *Notice of Expulsion.* If the remaining partners believe that grounds for expulsion for cause exist, they shall give the partner a thirty (30)-day written notice of expulsion to be effective thirty (30) days after receipt thereof. The notice shall briefly state the ground for expulsion.

(c) *Hearing on Expulsion.* Any partner having received a notice of expulsion shall be entitled, at any time before the effective date of the expulsion, to a hearing by all of the other partners. At such hearing, a unanimous vote of all of the other partners shall be necessary to expel a partner.

(d) *Salary Termination.* An expelled partner shall be entitled to receive his salary or draw only to the effective date of his expulsion.

(e) *Purchase of Interest.* The remaining partners shall be obligated to purchase, and the expelled partner obligated to sell, his interest in the partnership at the price and on the terms provided in Article XV, except that payment in full for his interest shall be made within three hundred and sixty-five (365) days after the effective date of expulsion.

(f) *Accounts Receivable.* An expelled partner shall be entitled to participate in the accounts receivable of the partnership as of the effective date of his expulsion in the same ratio as he shares in the net profits under Article XII(a). His share of the accounts receivable shall be paid to him within sixty (60) days after collected. His share is to be treated as income to him on the day(s) it is paid by the partnership.

(g) *Matters in Process.* An expelled partner shall not be entitled to share in the fees to be charged for matters in process, except that on matters in process for clients customarily served by him and on which he was actually working at the time of his expulsion he shall be entitled to such fees as he ordinarily would have been entitled to receive for the work actually done. If, after expulsion, any client for whom the expelled partner was working at the time of his expulsion elects to have the partnership continue to represent him on such or all matters, the expelled partner shall not be entitled to participate in any subsequent fees on the matters in process.

## ARTICLE XVII

### Liquidation of the Partnership

(a) *Liquidation by Agreement.* The partnership may be liquidated at any time by unanimous agreement of all partners.

(b) *Liquidation After Failure to Purchase.* If the remaining partners fail to elect to purchase the interest of a partner who has given notice of retirement before reaching the age of fifty-five years as they may do under Article XV(a)(4), the affairs of the partnership shall be wound up and liquidated forthwith as provided in Paragraph (c) of this Article.

(c) *Liquidation Procedure.* If, for any reason, the affairs of the partnership are to be wound up and liquidated, the procedure shall be as follows:

(1) *Pending Matters.* All matters in process shall be completed, or their completion assumed by agreement among the partners with the consent of the clients, if such consent is appropriate or necessary.

(2) *Application of Assets.* The assets shall first be used to pay or provide for all debts of the partnership. Thereafter, the available funds shall be applied in the following order:

(i) To repay any loans to the partnership by a partner;

(ii) To pay any earned and unpaid salaries of partners;

(iii) To pay any balances in the income accounts due to partners;

(iv) To pay any balances in the capital accounts due to partners, after crediting or debiting the profits or losses accrued or incurred from the date of the last annual accounting to the completion of the liquidation.

(d) *Disposition of Clients' Documents and Files After Liquidation.* The possession of the documents and files of all clients shall be given to the partner who customarily handled the matters for each client. If the partners are unable to agree, all documents belonging to the particular client shall be returned to the client or transferred in accordance with the client's instructions.

## ARTICLE XVIII

### Notice to Partners

All notices provided in this Agreement shall be in writing and shall be sufficient if sent by registered or certified mail to the last known address of the partner to whom such notice is to be given.

## ARTICLE XIX

### Acts to Make Agreement Effective

The partners agree that they will execute any further instruments, and that they will perform any acts that are or may become necessary to effectuate and to carry on the partnership created by this agreement.

## ARTICLE XX

### Construction: Definitions

Unless the context in which a word or phrase is used is to the contrary, the terms used in this Agreement are defined as follows:

"As the partners may agree" and "otherwise agreed" mean by decision of the majority in interest of the partners according to capital contributions.

"Associate" means a dentist duly licensed to practice said professsion in the State of Florida and employed by the partnership.

"He," "him," or other personal pronouns include the feminine.

"Month" means calendar month.

"Profits" and "losses" mean net profits and net losses as determined in accordance with good accepted accounting practices.

"Withdrawn partner" includes the estate of a deceased partner.

### ARTICLE XXI

*Amendments*

This Agreement may be amended only by written agreement, signed by all of the partners.

IN WITNESS WHEREOF, the parties have executed this agreement at Middletown, Florida, on September 30, 1982.

_____

GEORGE PAINLESS

_____

RICHARD ABLE

[1]May be called Articles of Partnership. *59 Am. Jur. 2d Partnership,* para. 18, as to *junior* and *senior* partners. As to covenants not to compete, see *54 Am. Jur. 2d Monopolies Restraint of Trade and Unfair Trade Practices,* paras. 554 and 555. See also *33 Am Jur. 2d Federal Taxation,* para. 2016. Compare Form IB 1.01.

## SECTION B    LIMITED PARTNERSHIP

Before using the forms in this section, the general introduction to PART II and FORM IIA 1.00 CLIENT QUESTIONNAIRE FOR CREATING AN UNINCORPORATED BUSINESS ENTITY should be read. The answers to the FORM IIA 1.00 will determine whether the forms in this section or another section in PART II are appropriate to organize the client's business.

### FORM IIB 1.00

### PRELIMINARY AGREEMENT TO FORM LIMITED PARTNERSHIP[1]

THIS AGREEMENT made this 5th day of October, 1982, by and among John Doe, residing in Riverton, Fremont County, Wyoming; Richard Roe, residing in Riverton, Fremont County, Wyoming; and Peter Poe, residing in Cheyenne, Laramie County, Wyoming;

WITNESSETH:

WHEREAS, the parties hereto desire to form a limited partnership pursuant to the laws of the State of Wyoming, and in consideration of the sum of One Dollar, each to the other, in hand paid, the receipt whereof is hereby acknowledged, and the mutual convenants and agreements herein contained, do hereby mutually agree as follows:

1. *Formation of limited partnership.* The parties shall form a limited partnership pursuant to the provisions of W.S. 1977 17-14-201 et seq. of the State of Wyoming for the purpose of conducting the business of purchasing or leasing and developing land for recreational purposes and resale or subleasing.

2. *Name.* The said partnership shall be conducted under the firm name and style of Doe and Roe Land Development.

3. *Location.* The principal place of business of such partnership shall be at No. 100 East Street, City of Riverton, State of Wyoming, or such other place or places as may hereafter be agreed upon by the parties.

4. *Designation of partners.* Peter Poe shall be a limited partner, and John Doe and Richard Roe shall be general partners.

5. *Term.* The partnership shall exist for a term of ten (10) years to commence on the 1st day of January, 1983, and to continue until the 31st day of December, 1992.

6. *Contribution by limited partners.* Peter Poe, as a limited partner, shall contribute the sum

of Fifty Thousand Dollars ($50,000) in cash to the partnership on or before the date of filing of the Certificate of Limited Partnership in the State of Wyoming.

7. *Return of limited partner's contribution.* The contribution of the limited partner shall be returned to him in cash upon the dissolution or other termination of this partnership, unless the limited partner agrees to accept other property in lieu of cash.

8. *Contribution of general partners.* The general partners shall contribute the sum of Fifteen Thousand Dollars ($15,000) each to the partnership on or before six (6) months after the date of the issuance of the first certificate of authority to do business under the Certificate of Limited Partnership. In addition, the general partners shall devote their full time and attention to the conduct of the partnership business in which the limited partner shall have no control.

9. *Profits.* The profits from the conduct of the partnership business after deduction of all reasonable expenses and outlays incurred in the conduct of the partnership business shall be divided as follows and paid at the end of each fiscal year during the conduct of the partnership business:

| | |
|---|---|
| John Doe | 25% |
| Richard Roe | 25% |
| Peter Poe | 50% |

10. *Losses.* Any losses suffered or incurred in the conduct of the partnership business shall be borne by all the parties to this Agreement in the same proportion in which they are entitled to share in the profits of the partnership; but the limited partner shall not be liable in any event for any loss in excess of the amount of capital contributed by him, nor shall he be personally liable for any debts, engagements, or losses of the partnership.

11. *Additional limited partners.* Additional limited partners may at any time hereafter be admitted to the partnership hereby created upon the consent in writing of all the general partners. In such event, such additional limited partner(s) when so admitted shall have all the rights of limited partner(s) as herein specified for the limited partner and be subject to all his duties, liabilities, and responsibilities. They shall be entitled to share in the manner herein provided in the profits of the partnership business thereafter earned in proportion to the amounts of the capital contributed to the partnership by them; provided that no right of Peter Poe, the limited partner, shall be subordinated to the rights of any additional limited partner without the written consent of Peter Poe.

12. *Partnership records.*

(a) At all times during the continuation of the partnership, the general partners shall keep full and correct books of account in which shall be entered each and every transaction of the partnership according to accepted standard accounting practice.

(b) On or before March 31st of each year, a profit and loss statement and a balance sheet for the partnership business shall be mailed to the limited partner.

(c) All of the partnership books of account shall, at all reasonable times, be open to the inspection and examination by the limited partner or his representative.

13. *Termination.* In the event of the death, retirement, or physical or mental disability of a general partner during the term provided in Paragraph 5, this partnership shall not be dissolved but shall be continued by the survivors under the following conditions:

(a) *Death.*

(1) In the event of the death of a general partner, the interest of a deceased general partner shall terminate as of the first day of the calendar month next succeeding his death, and the value of the interest of such deceased partner in the partnership as of that date, as determined from the books of the partnership; and the value of that interest, as so determined, shall be paid to the legal representative of the deceased partner's estate within six (6) months, with interest at the rate of Eight Percent (8%) per annum to the date of such payment.

(2) That in the event of the death of a limited partner, during the time fixed for the continuance of the partnership, this partnership shall not be thereby dissolved, but shall be continued by the surviving general partner, and each limited partner covenants, for himself, and for his heirs, executors, and administrators, that the capital contributed by him to the partnership may, at the option of the surviving general partner or partners, either be retained in the partnership, upon the same terms, in respect of participation in profits, as are provided in this Agreement, or be liquidated and paid off at any time after the death of the limited partner, except that it shall be paid at the time of dissolution of the partnership.

(b) *Retirement at age 55.* Upon reaching the age of 55, any general partner may elect to retire and thereby shall withdraw from the partnership, upon giving written notice of his election to retire and intention to withdraw by mailing the notice to the partnership office and a copy of the notice to the last known address of the limited partner(s). The interest of the retiring/withdrawing partner shall be determined as of the date of retirement, and shall be liquidated as provided in Paragraph 13 (a), except that payment shall be made to the retiring/withdrawing partner or to the legal representative of his estate if he should die before the payment is made.

(c) *Physical or mental disability.* Upon affidavit of two physicians that a general partner is permanently disabled mentally or physically, the remaining general partner(s) may elect to terminate the partnership; and in case of such termination, the dissolution of the partnership in accordance with the limited partnership laws of the State of Wyoming shall be begun forthwith.

14. *Modification or amendment of this Agreement.* The terms of this Agreement cannot be modified or amended except by a writing signed by all the parties to this Agreement.

15. *Assignment.* Any interest of any of the parties to this Agreement may not be assigned without the written consent of all other parties to the Agreement.

IN WITNESS WHEREOF, the parties have signed this Agreement on the day and year above written.

_____
JOHN DOE

_____
RICHARD ROE

_____
PETER POE

[1]*60 Am. Jur. 2d Partnership,* para. 379 et seq. See also alternative Form IIB 1.00(a). File Form IIB 1.01 to comply with state statute adopting Uniform Partnership Act. In some states a corporation may be a member of a limited partnership.

## FORM IIB 1.00(a)

### (Limited partnership agreement)

### ALTERNATIVE FORM

### LIMITED PARTNERSHIP AGREEMENT[1]

AGREEMENT made this 15th day of May, 1982, among Richard Roe and Peter Poe, residing at 100 East Street, Middletown, Florida 00000, and 500 Circle Drive, Tampa, Florida 00000, respectively (hereinafter called the "General Partners") and those persons appearing on Schedule A hereto and in Paragraph 3 below (hereinafter collectively called the "Limited Partners").

1. *Name and Business.* The parties do hereby form a limited partnership pursuant to the provisions of Chapter 620 of the Florida Statutes to carry on the business of the acquisition of land, design, development, and construction of a time-sharing resort in Middle County, Florida, under the name of Happy Heath Developers. The principal office of the business shall be at 100 Main Street, Middletown, Florida 00000.

2. *Term.* The partnership shall begin on the date upon which all Limited Partners shall have affixed their signatures hereto, or on June 1, 1982, whichever date shall last occur, and shall continue until May 30, 1987, and thereafter from year to year, until terminated as herein provided.

3. *Capital.* Richard Roe and Peter Poe shall be the General Partners. The persons appearing on Exhibit A hereto shall be the Limited Partners. Richard Roe and Peter Poe are parties to a contract to purchase 50 acres of real estate located in Middle County, Florida, upon which it is proposed to build the time-sharing resort contemplated by this Limited Partnership Agreement, and they do assign all of their rights, title, and interest in said contract to purchase to the Limited Partnership as a part of their contribution to the capital of the Limited Partnership. All of the parties hereto agree that the value of the capital contribution so made by Richard Roe and Peter Poe is $20,000. Each of the Partners shall contribute to the capital of the partnership in cash and in property the amount set opposite their name.

*General Partners*

Richard Roe                              $10,000

Peter Poe                                $10,000

*Limited Partners*

| | |
|---|---|
| Richard Rich | $200,000 |
| George Goe | $100,000 |
| John Doe | $ 40,000 |
| Daniel Doe | $ 40,000 |

The cash and property contributions made by each of the Partners represent his respective interest in the real estate, improvements thereon, and amenities comprising the time-sharing resort to be known as Happy Heath Acres, having an agreed aggregate value of $400,000. The real property is more particularly described in Scheduled B attached hereto. The General Partners will cause said real property to be conveyed by the Seller to James Joe, as Trustee for the Partnership.

4. *Profit and Loss.* The net profits of the partnership shall be divided among the partners and the net losses shall be borne by them in the proportions set opposite their respective name.

| *General Partner* | *Percentage* |
|---|---|
| Richard Roe | 2½% |
| Peter Poe | 2½% |
| *Limited Partner* | *Percentage* |
| Richard Rich | 50% |
| George Goe | 25% |
| John Doe | 10% |
| Daniel Doe | 10% |

However, the liability of any of the Lmited Partners for the losses of the Partnership shall in no event exceed in the aggregate the amount of his contributions to the capital of the Partnership.

5. *Salaries and Drawing Accounts.* Salaries shall be paid to the General Partners and drawing accounts shall be established for all Partners as follows:

(a) *Salaries.* Each of the General Partners shall receive a salary for services to be rendered by him, and these salaries shall be treated as an expense in the determination of the profits and losses of the business. The amount of salary to be paid to each General Partner shall be determined from time to time by a majority in interest of all of the General Partners, and for this purpose the interest of each partner shall be deemed equivalent to the share of profits distributable to him under the terms of this agreement; provided, however, that no General Partner shall receive a salary or a draw from his drawing account during the initial stages of phase 1 of the development, or until such time as the cash flow to the Partnership from the construction and sale of time-sharing units as envisioned herein shall be equal to the total aggregate sum invested by the Limited Partners as their initial capital contribution. Expenses incurred by the General Partners in the course of their activities on behalf of the Partnership business shall be reimbursed upon the unanimous approval of the other General Partners. In no event, however, shall the salary of any General Partner be reduced retroactively.

(b) *Drawing Accounts.* Subject to the limitations on commencement of draws as contained in the penultimate sentence of Subparagraph (a) above, the Partners shall have such drawing accounts as may be fixed by the General Partners, but such drawing accounts shall be in the proportion to which the Partners are entitled to share in the profits of the Partnership.

6. *Interest on Capital.* No interest shall be paid on the initial contributions to the capital of the Partnership or on any subsequent contributions of capital.

7. *Management, Duties, and Restrictions.* During the continuance of this Partnership, the rights and liabilities of the General Partners and Limited Partners, respectively, shall be as follows:

(a) *General Partners.* The General Partners shall have equal rights in the management of the Partnership business, and each General Partner shall devote such of his time as deemed necessary to assure success of the Partnership venture. No General Partner shall, without the consent of the other General Partner, endorse any note, or act as an accommodation party or otherwise become surety for any person other than members of their families. Without the consent of the other General Partner, no General Partner shall on behalf of the Partnership borrow or lend money, or make, deliver, or accept any commercial paper, or execute any mortgage, security agreement, bond or lease, or purchase or contract to purchase, or sell or contract to sell, any property for or of the partnership other than the type of property bought and sold in the regular course of its business. Neither of the General Partners shall assign, mortgage, grant a security interest in, or sell his share in the Partnership or in its capital assets or property, or enter into any agreement as a result of which any person, firm, or corporation shall become interested with him in the Partnership, or do any act detrimental to the best interests of the partnership, or that would make it impossible to carry on the ordinary business of the partnership. Nothing herein shall prohibit the assignment or bequest by a General Partner of all or part of his interest in the Partnership to the other General Partner or to a lineal descendant.

(b) *Limited Partners.* Any Limited Partner shall have the right to withdraw or reduce his contribution to the capital of the partnership on June 30th of any year by giving at least four (4) months' prior written notice of the intention to withdraw or reduce such contribution to all of the General Partners at the principal office of the Partnership. In addition, any limited Partner shall have the right to withdraw his capital contribution upon termination or dissolution of the Partnership. However, no part of the capital contribution of any Limited Partner shall be withdrawn unless all liabilities of the Partnership, except liabilities to General Partners and to Limited Partners on account of their contributions, have been paid or unless the partnership has assets sufficient to pay them. No Limited Partner shall have the right to demand or receive property other than cash in return for his contribution, and no Limited Partner shall have priority over any other Limited Partner either as to contributions to capital or as to compensation by way of income. After any withdrawal of capital by a Limited Partner, his share in the profits and losses shall be in the proportion that his reduced capital bears to the total capital of the Partnership on the date of such withdrawal; and the shares of the other Partners shall be increased in the proportions in which they have theretofore shared the profits and losses of the Partnership. No additional Limited Partners may be admitted into the Partnership, and no Limited Partner shall have the right to substitute an assignee as contributor in his place.

8. *Banking.* All funds of the Partnership shall be deposited in its name in such checking account or accounts, or money market funds, as shall be designed by the General Partners. All withdrawals therefrom shall be made upon checks signed by either of the General Partners.

9. *Books.* The Partnership books shall be maintained at the principal office of the Partnership, and each Partner shall at all times have access thereto. The books shall be kept on a fiscal year basis, beginning October 1 and ending September 30, and shall be closed and balanced at the end of each fiscal year. An audit shall be made as of the closing date.

10. *Retirement.* Either General Partner shall have the right to retire from the Partnership at the end of any fiscal year. Written notice of intention to retire shall be served upon the other General Partner at the office of the Partnership at least three (3) months before the end of such fiscal year. The retirement of either General Partner shall dissolve the Partnership, but shall have no effect upon the continuance of the Partnership business. The remaining General Partner shall have the right either to purchase the retiring Partner's interest in the Partnership, or to terminate and liquidate the Partnership business.

(a) If the remaining General Partner elects to purchase the interest of the retiring Partner, he shall serve notice in writing of such election upon him at the office of the Partnership within two months after receipt of his notice of intention to retire. The purchase price and manner of payment for such interest shall be the same as stated in Paragraph 11(a) with reference to the purchase of a deceased General Partner's interest in the partnership, substituting "retiring Partner" for "decedent" and "representative of the estate of a deceased General Partner" and "retirement" for "death."

The remaining General Partner may conduct the business in accordance with any terms and conditions agreed upon, but no reduction shall be made in the respective percentages of participation of the Limited Partners in the profits and losses of the business, and no obligations shall be imposed upon the Limited Partners other than those set forth in this Agreement.

(b) If the remaining General Partner does not elect to purchase the interest of the retiring Partner, the Partner shall proceed with reasonable promptness to liquidate the business of the Partnership. The procedure as to liquidation and distribution of the assets of the Partnership business shall be the same as stated in Paragraph 11(b) with reference to termination in the event of a Partner's death, substituting "retiring Partner" for "decedent" and "decedent's estate" and "retirement" for "death."

11. *Death of General Partner.* The death of either General Partner shall dissolve the Partnership, but shall have no effect upon the continuance of the Partnership business. The surviving General Partner shall have the right either to purchase the interest of the decedent in the Partnership or to terminate and liquidate the Partnership business. If the surviving General Partner elects to purchase the decedent's interest, he shall serve notice in writing of such election, within

three months after the death of the decedent, upon the personal representative of the decedent, or, if at the time of such election, no personal representative has been appointed, upon any one of the known legal heirs of the decedent at the last known address of such heir.

(a) If the surviving General Partner elects to purchase the interest of the decedent in the Partnership, the purchase price shall be equal to the decedent's capital account as shown on the Partnership books as at the end of the fiscal year immediately prior to his death, increased by his share of Partnership profits or decreased by his share of Partnership losses for the period from the beginning of the fiscal year in which his death occurred until the date of his death, as adjusted for contributions and withdrawals during such period. No allowance shall be made for goodwill, trade name, patents, or other intangible assets, except as those assets have been reflected on the Partnership books immediately prior to the decedent's death. The purchase price shall be paid in foru equal semiannual installments beginning four months after the date of death of decedent. Any balance of the purchase price shall bear interest at the rate of Nine Percent (9%) per annum from the date of death until final payment, and any part or all of the balance may be prepaid at any time. When the personal representative of a deceased General Partner shall have received the payments herein provided, he shall have no further claim upon or interest in the assets or business of the firm. The surviving General Partner may conduct the business in accordance with any terms and conditions agreed upon, but no reduction shall be made in the respective percentages of participation of the Limited Partners in the profits and losses of the business, and no obligations shall be imposed upon the Limited Partners other than those set forth in this Agreement.

(b) If the surviving General Partner does not elect to purchase the interest of the decedent in the Partnership, he shall proceed with reasonable promptness to liquidate the business of the Partnership. The Partnership name shall be sold with the other assets of the business. The profits and losses of the business during the period of liquidation shall be divided among or borne by the surviving General Partner, the decendent's estate, and the Limited Partners in accordance with the provisions of Paragraph 4, except that the decedent's estate shall not be liable for losses in excess of the decedent's interest in the Partnership at the time of his death. The proceeds of liquidation shall be distributed, as realized, in payment of liabilities of the Partnership in the following order: (1) to creditors of the Partnership, (2) to Limited Partners in respect to their share of any undrawn profits, (3) to Limited Partners in respect of their contributions to the capital of the Partnership, (4) to General Partners other than for capital or profits, (5) to General Partners in respect of undrawn profits, and (6) to General Partners in respect of their capital contributions.

12. *Death of a Limited Partner.* The death of a Limited Partner shall not terminate the Partnership business. The estate of any deceased Limited Partner shall have the right to withdraw, subject to the same limitations as are applicable to withdrawals by a Limited Partner, the decedent's contribution to the capital of the Partnership together with any undrawn profits owing to such Partner.

IN WITNESS WHEREOF, the parties hereto have signed this Agreement as of the date and year first above written.

GENERAL PARTNERS

_____

RICHARD ROE

_____

PETER POE

LIMITED PARTNERS          LIMITED PARTNERS

_____     _____

RICHARD RICH               JOHN DOE

_____     _____

GEORGE GOE                DANIEL DOE

(Attach Schedule A, giving the names and addresses of the Limited Partners, and Schedule B, giving the Legal Description of the real estate.)

[1]60 *Am. Jur. 2d Partnership,* para. 379 et seq. See also alternate Form IIA 1.03. File Form IIA 1.04 to comply with state statute adopting Uniform Partnership Act. In some states a corporation may be a member of a limited partnership.

**FORM IIB 1.01**

**(Pursuant to the Uniform Limited Partnership Act)**

**CERTIFICATE OF LIMITED PARTNERSHIP[1]**
**of**
**DOE & ROE LAND DEVELOPMENT**

The undersigned, desiring to form a limited partnership under Section 620.02 Florida Statutes, hereby certify:

1. The name of the Partnership is DOE & ROE LAND DEVELOPMENT.

2. The business to be carried on by the Partnership is the purchase or lease and development of land for recreational purposes and resale or sublease.

3. The principal place of business will be 100 Main Street, Middletown, Orange County, Florida.

4. The names and addresses of the Partners, both general and limited, are:

General Partner:

John Doe
100 Main Street
Middletown, FL 32600

General Partner:

Richard Roe
Star Route 1, Box 40
Middletown, FL 32600

Limited Partner:

Peter Poe
10 East Street
St. Petersburg, FL 00000

5. The Partnership is to exist for a term of ten (10) years, commencing January 1, 1983.

6. The contribution of the Limited Partner is Fifty Thousand Dollars ($50,000) cash.

7. There are no additional contributions required of the Limited Partner.

8. The contribution of the Limited Partner is to be returned upon dissolution or other termination of the Partnership. In the event of death of the Limited Partner before other termination or dissolution, the General Partners may, at their option, retain the contribution and pay the Limited Partner's estate his share in the profits or may elect to return his contribution to his estate.

9. The Limited Partner shall receive Fifty Percent (50%) of the profits of the Partnership by reason of his contribution.

10. The Limited Partner may substitute an assignee as contributor only with the written consent of all the subscribers hereto.

11. The General Partners have the right to admit additional limited parties, but they cannot subordinate the rights of the Limited Partner, Peter Poe, to the rights of any additional Limited Partners.

12. There are no rights given to any Limited Partner to priority over other Limited Partners, as to contributions or as to compensation by way of income.

13. The remaining General Partner has the right to continue the Partnership business on the death, retirement, or insanity of a General Partner.

14. The Limited Partner does not have the right to demand property other than cash in return for his contribution, but he may agree to receive other property in lieu of cash in return for his contribution.

IN WITNESS WHEREOF, the undersigned have signed and sworn to this Certificate of Limited Partnership this 1st day of November, 1982.

_____
JOHN DOE

_____
RICHARD ROE

_____
PETER POE

STATE OF FLORIDA
COUNTY OF ORANGE

BEFORE ME, a notary public in and for said state and county, personally appeared John Doe, Richard Roe, and Peter Poe, who, upon being duly sworn, state that the facts set forth in the foregoing Certificate of Limited Partnership are true and correct to the best of their knowledge and belief.

Dated this 1st day of November, 1982.

_____
Notary Public

My commission expires:

[1]See Appendix XIII for all state citations to Uniform Limited Partnership Act. 60. Am. Jur. 2d Partnership, paras. 372, 374, and 376; 26 U.S.C.A. 465; and 26 C.F.R. 7701. See also Form IIB 1.02

**Form IIB 1.02**

**(Limited partnership to develop and sell time-sharing condominiums)**

**CERTIFICATE OF LIMITED PARTNERSHIP[1]**
**OF**
**HAPPY HEATH DEVELOPERS**

We, the undersigned, desiring to form a limited partnership pursuant to the laws of the State of Florida, being duly sworn, do certify as follows:

1. The name of the Partnership is Happy Heath Developers.

2. The purpose of the Partnership is to carry on the business of the acquisition of land, design, development, and construction of a time-sharing resort in Middle County, Florida, and to engage in any and all general business activities related to or incidental thereto, and to do all other things and exercise all other powers of like partnerships confirmed by the laws of the State of Florida.

3. The principal place of business of the Partnership is 100 Main Street, Middletown, Florida 00000, unless changed by the General Partners by giving written notice to the Limited Partners of such change in location not less than ten (10) days preceding any such change.

4. The name and place of residence of each General Partner interested in the Partnership are as follows:

Richard Roe
100 East Street
Middletown, Fla. 00000

Peter Poe
500 Circle Drive
Tampa, Fla. 00000

The name and place of residence of each Limited Partner interested in the Partnership are as shown on Exhibit A attached hereto.

5. The term for which the Partnership is to exist is from the date upon which all Limited Partners shall have affixed their signatures to the Limited Partnership Agreement, or from June 1, 1982, whichever date shall last occur, and shall continue until May 30, 1987, and thereafter from year to year, until terminated as set forth in the Limited Partnership Agreement.

6. The amount of cash and the description and agreed value of the other property contributed by each Limited Partner are:

| General Partner | Agreed Property Value |
|---|---|
| Richard Roe | $10,000 |
| Peter Poe | $10,000 |
| Limited Partner | Cash Contribution |

Richard Rich
100 Middle Street
Middletown, Fla. 00000                                                    $200,000

George Goe
500 Bay Drive
Miami, Fla. 00000                                                         $100,000

John Doe
500 East Drive
Tampa, Fla. 00000                                                         $40,000

Daniel Doe
300 East Street
Middletown, Fla. 00000                                                    $40,000

7. There shall be no additional contributions required of the Limited Partners for operating expenses or other liabilities of the Partnership.

8. The contribution of each Limited Partner is to be returned to him upon his request per Paragraph 7(b) of the Limited Partnership Agreement.

9. The share of the profits or the other compensation by way of income that a Limited Partner shall receive by reason of his contributions is as set forth hereinbelow:

| *General Partner* | *Percentage* |
|---|---|
| Richard Roe | 2½% |
| Peter Poe | 2½% |

| *Limited Partner* | *Percentage* |
|---|---|
| Richard Rich | 50% |
| George Goe | 25% |
| John Doe | 10% |
| Daniel Doe | 10% |

10. No Limited Partner shall have the right to substitute an assignee as a contributor in his place.

11. No additional LImited Partners may be admitted into the Partnership.

12. There shall be no right of one or more of the Limited Partners to priority over other Limited Partners as to contributions or to compensation by way of income.

13. Upon the death, retirement, or insanity of any General Partner, the remaining General Partner shall have the right to continue the Partnership business by purchasing the deceased, retiring, or insane Partner's interest in the Partnership at a price equal to the deceased, retiring, or insane Partner's capital account as at the end of the fiscal year immediately prior to his death, retirement, or insanity, plus his share of Partnership profits or minus his share of Partnership losses for the period from the beginning of the fiscal year in which his death, retirement, or insanity occurred until the date of his death, retirement, or insanity, as adjusted for contributions and withdrawals during such period.

14. There shall be no right of a Limited Partner to demand and receive property other than cash in return for his contribution.

IN WITNESS WHEREOF, the parties have executed this Certificate of Limited Partnership this 1st day of March, 1982.

WITNESSES:

_____        _____
WITNESS                          Richard Roe, General Partner
                 LIMITED PARTNERS

_____        _____
RICHARD RICH                     JOHN DOE

_____        _____
GEORGE GOE                       DANIEL DOE

STATE OF FLORIDA )
                        )   SS
COUNTY OF PINELLAS )

                  , being first duly sworn, deposes and says that he is one of the Limited Partners named in the foregoing Certificate of Limited Partnership, and that the statements made in the foregoing Certificate are true.

    SWORN to before me this _____ day of _____, 1982. My commission expires:

_____
Notary Public
(Also Jurat for each of the General Partners.)

¹See Form IIB 1.01 for an ordinary Certificate of Limited Partnerships.

## SECTION C    JOINT VENTURE

Before using the forms in this section, the general introduction to PART II and FORM IIA 1.00 CLIENT QUESTIONNAIRE FOR CREATING AN UNINCORPORATED BUSINESS ENTITY should be read. The answers to the Form IIA 1.00 will determine whether the forms in this section or another section in PART II are appropriate to organize the client's business.

### FORM IIC 1.00

### JOINT VENTURE AGREEMENT¹

THIS AGREEMENT made this 8th day of October, 1982, by and between John Doe, residing at 100 Main Street, City of Akron, State of Ohio (herein called "Doe"), and Richard Right residing at East Street, City of Dayton, State of Ohio (herein called"Right"), WITNESSETH,

WHEREAS, Doe has entered into an agreement with one Small Manufacturer, Inc., located in Youngstown, Ohio, wherein and whereby Doe has agreed to purchase and Right has agreed to sell for resale by Doe at retail the following goods: 100,000 feet of 10-inch steel pipe @ $1 per foot; and

WHEREAS, Doe has a selling organization capable of handling and selling the pipe to oil drillers in Ohio and Pennsylvania but lacks the capital necessary for the purchase thereof and the other expenses of selling the pipe; and

WHEREAS, the party of the second part has agreed to furnish capital for the purposes of selling the pipe;

IT IS AGREED AS FOLLOWS:

1. *Consideration.* The consideration for this agreement is payment of the sum of One Dollar ($1) each to the other party, and the mutual covenants and agreements herein.

2. *Funding.* Right shall, as needed on demand of Doe, furnish all funds to an amount not to exceed Sixty Thousand Dollars ($60,000), for the purchase of the pipe and the expenses of selling the pipe, which shall be the cost of transporting the pipe from the factory of Small Manufacturer, Inc., and a customer's location or designated location in Ohio or Pennsylvania only, and sales travel and entertainment expense for Doe and/or others delegated by him, which latter expense shall not exceed Twenty-five Hundred Dollars ($2,500).

3. *Sale.* Doe will use all money paid by Right for the purposes herein stated and will purchase and pay for said goods out of such money and cause the same to be sold and will use all proper and necessary efforts through himself and salesmen to be employed by him to sell such goods for a profit within one (1) year of the execution of this Agreement.

4. *Compensation of parties.* Neither of the parties to this Agreement shall receive any salary or any interest on any money advances, except as follows:

(a) When the pipe has been sold, the sales price thereof collected, and all outstanding debts of this venture paid, this Agreement shall terminate and the proceeds of such sale shall be divided as follows:

(1) There shall first be repaid to Right all moneys advanced by him for the purposes stated herein plus interest at the rate of Six Percent (6%) per annum from the date of the advance of the sum(s) to the date of this repayment.

(2) Of the net profit of this venture then remaining there shall be paid to Doe in full for all services performed by him Fifty Percent (50%) of that net profit.

(3) The remainder of that net profit shall be paid to Right.

(4) For the purpose of determining net profit, only those expenses and outlays authorized in Paragraph 1 may be deducted from the gross sale price of the pipe.

(5) In the event that such transaction does not result in a profit but a loss, such losses shall be paid in full by Doe in that Doe shall pay Right the amount provided in Paragraph 3(a)(1), regardless of profit or loss on this venture.

5. *Operation.* Doe shall have full control of the handling of the business of this venture and shall devote his full time and best efforts to the success.

6. *Arbitration.* If any dispute arises between the parties to this contract, such dispute shall be settled and determined by arbitration as follows:

(a) Each party hereto shall select one arbitrator.

(b) The two so selected shall thereupon appoint a third arbitrator.

(c) Such arbitrators shall thereupon ascertain the facts and shall make a determination.

(d) The determination of a majority of such arbitrators shall be binding and conclusive upon the parties to this agreement.

(e) *Default.* In the event that the arbitrators find default of either party in failing to pay any amount required to be paid under this Agreement, said amount determined by the arbitrators may be recovered in an action at law or in equity, but no consequential damages shall be recovered in such action.

(f) The prevailing party in the arbitration determination shall be entitled to recover from the other party as part of the arbitration award a reasonable attorney's fee for an attorney representing him in the arbitration procedure.

7. *Termination.* If the pipe is not sold within one (1) year of the execution of this Agreement, Doe shall return all moneys advanced by Right as provided in Paragraph 3(a)(1), and this agreement shall terminate.

8. *Relationship of parties.* The parties to this Agreement are not partners nor are they agent of each other. Neither party shall pledge the other's credit for any reason.

IN WITNESS WHEREOF, the parties hereto have set their hands and seals the day and year first above written.

In presence of:

_____        _____ (SEAL)
                                        JOHN DOE

_____        _____ (SEAL)
                                        RICHARD RIGHT

[1]*46 Am. Jur. 2d Joint Ventures,* paras. 7 and 8. In most states a corporation may be a party to a joint venture. See Form IIC 1.00(a) for alternative clause for real estate joint venture.

## FORM IIC 1.00(a)

### (Alternative recital clause for real estate joint venture)

WHEREAS, the parties intend to be Joint Venturers for the purpose of acquiring the fee title interest in the real estate described herein; and

WHEREAS, the parties have agreed to make contributions to a common fund for the purpose of acquiring and holding said real estate for development; and

WHEREAS, the parties have agreed upon limitations upon the right and power to transfer their undivided interests and also to provide for anticipated future contributions to that common fund for the purpose of improving the premises with a suitable building;

NOW, THEREFORE, IT IS AGREED:

1. *Title to property and beneficial interest.*

(a) Legal title to the joint venturer's real property that is described in Exhibit A attached hereto and made part hereof shall be taken in the name of John Doe as trustee for the joint venturers, and he shall hold it for their benefit.

(b) The beneficial interest of each party in the real property, unless changed by other terms of this agreement shall be as follows:

(List percentage of each party's
interest in the real property.)

## SECTION D    UNINCORPORATED ASSOCIATION

Before using the forms in this section, the general introduction to PART II and FORM A1.00 CLIENT QUESTIONNAIRE FOR CREATING AN UNINCORPORATED BUSINESS ENTITY should be read. The answers to the Form IIA 1.00 will determine whether this section or another section in PART II are appropriate to organize the client's business.

### FORM IID 1.00

(Unincorporated association agreement)[1]

### ARTICLES OF ASSOCIATION

1. *Organization.* The persons executing these Articles hereby associate themselves as initial members of an unincorporated association.

2. *Name.* The name of the Association shall be The Blackstone Club.

3. *Principal office.* The principal office of the Association shall be at 437 Wood Street, Pittsburgh, Pennsylvania, and the Association may open such other offices throughout the County of Allegheny as may be designated by its Board of Directors.

4. *Purposes.*

   (a) The purposes of the Association are to maintain club quarters, including a dining room, in Pittsburgh, Pennsylvania, to encourage intraprofessional social activity and healthful relaxation among lawyers in the western Pennsylvania area and among out-of-state lawyers who visit this area.

   (b) No part of the income or assets of this club shall be paid or distributed to any private individual or member of the club. The directors shall hire a bonded club manager.

   (c) The club shall have no capital stock, its object and purpose being solely of a benevolent character, and not for individual pecuniary gain or profit to its members.

5. *Capital.* The initial capital of the Association shall consist of One Hundred Thousand Dollars ($100,000), which has been contributed by the subscribers and deposited in the State National Bank of Pittsburgh in a checking account titled The Blackstone Club.

6. *Dues.* The Board of Directors shall determine from time to time what facilities and services should be offered and shall determine and assess the amount of annual dues necessary to operate the Association in accordance with its purposes. Said dues shall not exceed One Hundred Dollars ($100) annually for any member without a two-thirds (2/3) vote of the majority of the members entitled to vote at a duly called meeting. Initial annual dues shall be:

| | |
|---|---|
| Regular members: | $100 per year |
| Associate members: | $ 50 per year |
| Temporary members: | no charge |

7. *Membership.*

   (a) *Regular members.* Any member of the Pennsylvania Bar who maintains a law office in any one of the following counties may, upon application and payment in advance of the prevailing annual dues for regular members, become a member: Allegheny, Butler, Erie, Fayette, Greene, Lawrence, Washington, and Westmoreland.

(b) *Associate members.* Any member of the Pennsylvania Bar may become an associate member, whether or not he maintains an office in the Commonwealth of Pennsylvania, upon application and payment in advance of the prevailing annual dues for associate members.

(c) *Temporary members.* Any member of the bar of any state in the United States may become a temporary member for a period not to exceed ten (10) days in any one (1) calendar year upon application signed by a regular or associate member in good standing at the time of such application.

(d) Persons who become members of the Association after the execution of these Articles of Association shall be bound by these Articles, unless bylaws or a constitution are adopted by a two-thirds (2/3) vote of the majority of members entitled to vote at a duly called meeting.

8. *Certificate of membership.* An annual certificate of regular or associate membership bearing the signatures of the President and Secretary shall be issued to each regular or associate member upon his acceptance into the Association.

9. *Death of member.* The death of a member shall not cause the dissolution of the Association, which shall continue as before, but such death shall terminate the membership of the deceased.

10. *Meetings.* An annual meeting for the purpose of electing directors, receiving reports, and transacting other business shall be held on the first Friday in March of each year commencing in 1982. Special meetings may be called by the President or Secretary at the request of a majority of the regular members. Notice of all meetings, except as may be otherwise provided by statute, shall be mailed to all members at their last recorded addresses not less than ten nor more than thirty days before the date scheduled for the meeting. At all meetings of the members of the Association, each regular member shall be entitled to one (1) vote. Associate and temporary members shall not have the right to vote. Each regular member shall be entitled to appoint a person to vote for and act for such member by proxy either at the annual or special meetings of the Association. The President shall preside at every meeting of the members, and in his absence the Vice-President shall preside.

11. *Directors.* The Association shall have nine (9) directors, who shall have sole management of its affairs. The Board of Directors shall be elected by the regular members of the Association by ballot at the annual meeting of the Association. Each director shall serve until the next annual meeting or until his or her successor is duly chosen. The Board of Directors to serve from the date of execution of these Articles until the first annual meeting of members shall be John Doe, Richard Roe, Peter Poe, John Just, Arthur Able, George Great, Thomas Trial, David Depo, and Honor Rogatory. Should any vacancy occur in the Board of Directors, it shall be filled by vote of the remaining directors until the next annual meeting or until his or her successor is duly chosen.

12. *Officers.* The officers of the Association shall be a President, Vice-President, Treasurer, and Secretary. Upon the signing of these Articles of Association, the following officers will serve until the next annual meeting of directors or until their successors are duly chosen. Should any vacancies occur in any of said offices, such vacancies shall be filled by vote of the Board of Directors.

13. *Nonassessment of members, and indemnification.*

(a) There shall be no assessment of associate members.

(b) There shall be no assessment of regular members except by a two-thirds (2/3) vote of the majority of members entitled to vote at a duly called meeting.

(c) The Association indemnifies and agrees to reimburse any member against and from any and all loss, liability, expense, or damage arising out of the operation of the Association, except to the extent that such loss, liability, expense, or damage shall result from such member's own gross negligence or willful misconduct. Such indemnity or reimbursement shall be limited to the Association property.

14. *Distribution upon termination.* Upon the termination or dissolution of the Association, the directors then in office shall proceed at once to settle the affairs of the Association. They shall sell and dispose of all property and assets of the Association and convert them into cash. From the amount received they shall pay all outstanding obligations of the Association and the costs and expenses connected with the termination or dissolution. Should the assets be insufficient to pay such obligations, costs, and expenses in full, the regular members shall, pro rata person, pay and discharge any deficiency. Any surplus remaining after the payment in full of such obligations, costs, and expenses in full shall be distributed to a nonprofit charitable organization(s) as may be selected by the directors then in office.

IN WITNESS WHEREOF, all of the initial members of the Association have set their hands and seals this 7th day of September, 1982.

_____ (L.S.)
JOHN DOE

_____ (L.S.)
RICHARD ROE

_____ (L.S.)
PETER POE

_____ (L.S.)
JOHN JUST

_____ (L.S.)
ARTHUR ABLE

_____ (L.S.)
GEORGE GREAT

_____ (L.S.)
THOMAS TRIAL

_____ (L.S.)
DAVID DEPO

_____ (L.S.)
HONOR ROGATORY

[1] *6 Am. Jur. 2d Associations and Clubs,* paras. 1–10. Compare joint stock company, *46 Am. Jur. 2d Joint Stock Companies,* paras. 1–21.

## SECTION E      BUSINESS TRUST

Before using the form in this section, the general introduction to PART II and FORM A 1.00 CLIENT QUESTIONNAIRE FOR CREATING AN UNINCORPORATED BUSINESS ENTITY should be read. The answers to the Form IIA 1.00 will determine whether the forms in this section or another section in PART II are appropriate to organize the client's business.

### FORM IIE 1.00

### DECLARATION OF BUSINESS TRUST[1]

DECLARATION OF TRUST made April 6, 1983, between John Doe of 100 Main Street, Albany, New York, Richard Rich of 100 East Street, Buffalo, New York, and Peter Poor of 100 West Street, Syracuse, New York (herein called "Grantors"); and George Able of 1000 Fifth Avenue, Borough of Manhattan, New York, New York, and John Just of 1000 Madison Avenue, Borough of Manhattan, New York, New York (herein called "Trustees").

1. *Organization and name.* This Declaration of Trust is intended to create a trust of the type known as a business trust, hereinafter called the "Trust," and not a partnership or a joint-stock association. The trust may be designated as the "Opportunity Trust."

2. *Initial Trust property.* The Grantors hereby transfer to the Trustees all of their right, title, and interest in the property described in Exhibit A attached hereto and made a part hereof.

3. *Business of the Trust.*

(a) The principal office of the Trust is located at 100 Wall Street, Borough of Manhattan, New York, New York.

(b) The Trustees shall hold the property described in Exhibit A and all property hereafter acquired, and all income and profits therefrom (hereinafter collectively called the "Trust Property") in trust, and shall manage, administer, collect, and dispose of the Trust Property for the benefit of such persons as acquire shares of beneficial interest in the Trust (hereinafter called the "Beneficiaries").

(c) The Trustees, in the name of the Trust, may engage in general business activity, and perform all acts they consider necessary in furtherance of such activity. The powers and duties of the Trustees are more specifically set forth in Paragraph 9.

4. *Duration.*

(a) The Trust shall begin on the date of the execution of this Declaration of Trust and shall continue for ten (10) years from that date, except that it may be terminated at any earlier time by the Trustees, provided that consent to termination is given by two-thirds (2/3) in value of the outstanding shares of beneficial interest.

(b) Upon the death, insolvency, or adjudged incompetency of a Beneficiary, his legal representative shall succeed as a Beneficiary and shall be bound by the provisions of this Declaration of Trust.

5. *Trust Shares.*

(a) Beneficial interest in the Trust shall consist of Five Thousand (5,000) shares, each with a par value of Five Dollars ($5).

(b) The Trustees may sell, exchange, or acquire such shares for such sums as they consider proper.

(c) The Trustees shall issue certificates (herein called "share certificates") to the purchasers of such shares, in the following form:

Certificate No. 1                                                      No. of shares_____

TRUST CERTIFICATE
for shares in
OPPORTUNITY TRUST

(d) The purchases of the share certificates or their transferees pursuant to Paragraph 6 shall be the Beneficiary of the Trust, and shall be bound by the provisions of this Declaration of Trust, and they shall be entitled to participate in all dividends and other distributions of income or principal, as the Trustees in their discretion, from time to time, shall deem advisable.

(e) Each Beneficiary shall share in dividends or other distributions in the proportion that the number of shares owned by him bears to the total number of shares issued and outstanding.

(f) No Beneficiary shall have the right to ask for partition of the Trust Property during the continuance of this Trust.

(g) No Beneficiary shall have any interest in any portion of the Trust Property as such, and shall have an interest in dividends and other distributions only as herein provided.

(h) In the event of the loss or destruction of a share certificate, the Trustees may issue a new share certificate upon such conditions as they deem expedient.

6. *Transfer of trust shares.* A Beneficiary may transfer a share certificate in person or by. a duly authorized attorney. The transferee shall surrender such share certificate, duly endorsed for transfer, to the Trustees, who shall execute a new certificate representing the share or shares so transferred.

7. *Meetings of Beneficiaries.*

(a) An annual meeting of Beneficiaries shall be held at the principal office of the Trust, unless otherwise designated by the Trustees in writing not less than ten (10) nor more than thirty (30) days before the meeting. The meeting shall be held at 11:00 A.M. on the first Monday in March in each year, or on the following day if such Monday is a legal holiday.

(b) In addition to the annual meeting, the Trustees may call special meetings of the Beneficiaries at such times as the Trustees consider advisable.

(c) Written notice of every meeting, specifying the time, place, and the purpose thereof, shall be sent by registered mail to the Beneficiaries not less than ten (10) nor more than thirty (30) days prior to the holding of such meeting. A notice addressed to a Beneficiary at the address listed in the register of the Trustees shall be sufficient notice under this Paragraph.

(d) The owners of one-half of the issued and outstanding shares of beneficial interest, or their proxies, shall constitute a quorum for the purposes of any meeting, and a majority of the shares represented and voting at the meeting shall control on any issue considered at such meeting, except as otherwise specifically provided herein.

8. *Personal liability of beneficiaries.* The Beneficiaries shall not be personally liable for any act or omission of the Trustees. All persons dealing with the Trustees, or with any agent of the

Trustees, shall look only to the Trust Property for the payment of any sum due as a result of such dealing. In every instrument executed by the Trustees and creating an obligation of any kind, the Trustees shall stipulate that neither they nor the Beneficiaries shall be held to any personal liability under such instrument.

9. *Powers of Trustees.* The Trustees shall have absolute and exclusive power and authority to manage the Trust Property and to conduct the Trust business, exercisable without the consent of the Beneficiaries, to the same extent as if such Trustees were the owners of such property and business, and limited only as specifically set forth in this Declaration of Trust. The concurrence of both Trustees shall be necessary to the validity of any action taken by them. The Trustees' powers shall include, but shall not be limited to or by, the following:

(a) To undertake or engage in any type of commercial, industrial, or other business or venture;

(b) to purchase or otherwise acquire real or personal property, and to sell, exchange, mortgage, grant a security interest in, pledge, or in any manner deal with the Trust Property or any part thereof or any interest therein, upon such terms and for such consideration as they deem proper;

(c) To incur indebtedness, borrow or lend money with or without security, execute, accept, discount, negotiate, and deal in commercial paper and evidence of indebtedness, and execute any written instruments;

(d) to prosecute and defend all actions affecting the Trust, and to compromise or settle any suits, claims, or demands, or waive or release any rights relating to the Trust;

(e) to employ officers, agents, attorneys, and employees; and

(f) to adopt and enforce such bylaws, not inconsistent with this Declaration of Trust, as they may from time to time deem proper.

10. *Liability of Trustees.* The Trustees shall not be personally liable for any loss resulting from an act or omission to act in the execution of any of the powers conferred by this Declaration of Trust, so long as they act in good faith. Neither Trustee shall be personally liable for an act or omission of the other, or for an act or omission of any person appointed by either of them to assist in the execution of the Trust unless such appointment in itself is grossly negligent. All persons dealing with the Trustees shall look only to the Trust Property for the payment of their claims, and every instrument to which the Trustees shall be parties or on account of which any liability may be chargeable against the Trust Property shall so provide.

11. *Indemnification of Trustees.* Each Trustee shall be indemnified by and receive reimbursement from the Trust Property against and from any and all loss, liability, expense, or damage arising out of any action or omission to act as a Trustee hereunder, except to the extent that such loss, liability, expense, or damage shall result from his own gross negligence or willful misconduct. Such indemnity or reimbursement shall be limited to the Trust Property, and no shareholder shall be personally liable therefor to any extent.

12. *Appointment and meetings of Trustees.*

(a) There shall be two Trustees, each of whom shall serve for the entire term of the Trust, unless his tenure is terminated by death, resignation, or incapacity to serve. Each Trustee shall receive an annual salary of Twenty-four Thousand Dollars ($24,000) payable in equal monthly installments. The death, resignation, or incapacity of either or both of the Trustees shall not terminate the Trust or in any way affect its continuity.

(b) Upon the death, resignation, or inability to serve of either of the Trustees, the resulting vacancy shall be filled by the remaining Trustee. The successor Trustee shall execute a written consent to act as Trustee under the terms of this Declaration of Trust. Notice of the appointment of a successor Trustee under this Paragraph shall be mailed to each Beneficiary as provided for mailing of notice of meetings in Paragraph 7.

(c) The Trustees shall meet at such times and at such places as they deem advisable.

13. *Amendment.* This Declaration of Trust may be amended in any particular, except that no change may be made in the provisions governing the liability of the Trustees, or their agents, or of the Beneficiaries. An amendment may be considered at any meeting of the Beneficiaries provided the notice of the meeting states that such amendment is to be considered at the meeting. The consent of the holders of two-thirds in value of the outstanding shares of beneficial interest shall be necessary to adopt any amendment. The amendment shall become effective when certified by the chairman of the meeting that voted it, countersigned by the Trustees, and attached to this Declaration of Trust.

14. *Governing law.* This Declaration of Trust shall be interpreted and governed by the law of the State of New York.

IN WITNESS WHEREOF, the parties have signed and sealed this instrument on the day and year first above written.

Grantors:

_____ (L.S.)
JOHN DOE

_____ (L.S.)
RICHARD RICH

_____ (L.S.)
PETER POOR

Trustees:

_____ (L.S.)
GEORGE ABLE

_____ (L.S.)
JOHN JUST

[1]Also called a Massachusetts or common law trust. *13 Am. Jur. 2d Business Trusts,* paras. 1, 11, and 13–21. Check state business trust law for filing requirements. See also *88 A.L.R. 3rd 704.*

# PART III
# SOLE PROPRIETORSHIP

# PART III

# Sole Proprietorship

## INTRODUCTION

An individual may choose to operate a business without partners or associates. He may wish to conduct a sole proprietorship business under his own name or a fictitious name.[1]

If he chooses a fictitious name, he must register it under the state fictitious name statute in the state where he will operate.

If a corporation or a group of individuals is going to do business in a fictitious name, it or they must also register under the statute, giving the names of all the corporations or individuals who will be operating the business.

A sole proprietor may operate a business in his own name or in a fictitious name as an independent contractor, as an agent for another, as a broker, or as an independent agent or he may be a franchisee operating a business. For forms creating these various relationships, see Part V, Independent Service Contracts and Agency Agreements.

For an individual who is an employee of another individual or legal entity, see contracts in Part IV, Employer-Employee Relationship.

## SECTION A    FICTITIOUS NAME REGISTRATION

The forms in this section are representative of those required by the various state fictitious name registration statutes.

The newspaper which prints the notice which appears as Form IIIA 1.01 will give the attorney a Proof of Publication which is in the form of an affidavit that the notice was published on the required statutory dates.

In the event of legal action by or against a person or persons doing business under a fictitious name, the failure of plaintiff to be registered is grounds for dismissal of his lawsuit and the failure of defendant to be registered is grounds for striking his responsive pleadings. Although most state courts allow a reasonable time for the party to register after the question is raised in a legal action, the need to register before proceeding with the case may cause unnecessary delay and inconvenience.

---

[1] *57 Am. Jur. 2d Name*, paras. 24–36.

## FORM IIIA 1.00

(To be filed, accompanied by proof of publication of Form IIIA 1.01)

### FICTITIOUS NAME AFFIDAVIT[1]

STATE OF FLORIDA
COUNTY OF CITRUS

It is hereby stated under oath pursuant to Section 865.09 of the Florida Statutes that:

1. The undersigned intend to engage in business at 100 East Street, Middletown, Citrus County, Florida, under the fictitious name of: SUPER SERVICE COMPANY.

2. The full and true name of every person interested in SUPER SERVICE COMPANY, and the interest of each person eminent is as follows:

|  |  |
|---|---|
| John Doe | ½ interest |
| Richard Roe | ½ interest |

3. A proof of publication of a notice of intention to register a fictitious name is recorded with this affidavit.

_____
JOHN DOE

_____
RICHARD ROE

Sworn to and subscribed to before me this _____
day of _____ , 1982.

_____
Notary Public

My commission expires:

[1]*59 Am. Jur. 2d Partnership,* para. 27; and *57 Am. Jur. 2d Name,* paras. 24–36. Check state fictitious or assumed name statute for content and publication/filing requirements. See Form IIIA 1.01 for Notice to be published.

## FORM IIIA 1.01

(To be published before filing Form IIIA 1.00)

### NOTICE OF INTENTION TO REGISTER[1]
### FICTITIOUS NAME

NOTICE IS HEREBY GIVEN that the undersigned, John Doe and Richard Roe, desire to engage in business under the fictitious name of Super Service Company at 100 East Street, Middletown, Citrus County, Florida. Notice is further given that the undersigned intend to register such fictitious name with the Clerk of the Circuit Court of such county.

Dated this _____ day of _____ , 1982.

_____
JOHN DOE

_____
RICHARD ROE

[1]Ref. Form IIIA 1.00 and footnotes. Proof of Publication of required notice is usually filed in the clerk of court's office.

# PART IV
# EMPLOYER-EMPLOYEE RELATIONSHIP

**113**

# PART IV

# Employer-Employee Relationship

## INTRODUCTION

The documents in this Part are for use in the creation of and in the operation of the employer-employee relationship.

The contractual relationship between employer and employee, whether the employer is a sole proprietor, partnership, or corporation, has become increasingly important to both parties as fringe benefits, labor relations, and the general economics and government control of business become more urgent and more complicated. The traditional legal term "master-servant relationship" is rather anomalous to describe the modern "employer-employee relationship."[1]

This Part is divided into three Sections: A, B, and C. See introduction to each section for use of the forms in the section.

### SECTION A    EMPLOYMENT CONTRACTS AND RETIREMENT BENEFITS

The forms in Section A are for use in drafting employment contracts and retirement benefits for employees. The latter is a specialized field.

The sample forms given in this part are for the purpose of alerting the general practitioner to some of the problems. The client questionnaire will help get the facts so that one can decide whether the services of a specialist in the field are needed. When the facts are obtained, a lawyer specializing in the field, or a knowledgeable insurance broker or investment counselor may be consulted before drafting a plan. The samples of various U.S. Treasury forms included in this section underscore the need for factual information and will help the lawyer for employee benefit plans determine which forms should be requested from the IRS.

A sample IRA plan that may be used by an individual employee or a sole proprietor is included. The bank, stockbroker, or other trustee for the plan usually provides its own form. The purpose of including this form is to provide a checklist for comparison with another printed IRA plan that an individual is considering.

A checklist for creating a Keogh plan is also included in this section, to be used if the employer is either a sole proprietor or a partnership, but not a corporation.

Section B contains an agreement to engage in collective bargaining and a Checklist for Collective Bargaining. Negotiating and drafting labor contracts is also

---

[1]53 Am. Jur. 2d Master and Servant, paras. 14–59.

**115**

a specialized field. The forms are supplied to pinpoint some of the problems in the field.

Section C contains a sample Organization Certificate for creating an employee credit union under the Federal Credit Union Act. For creating a credit union under a state Act, see the state statute in the state where the union will operate. The general format of the organization certificate Form IVC 1.01 can be followed, using the information required in the state Act.

## FORM IVA 1.00

### CLIENT QUESTIONNAIRE FOR EMPLOYMENT CONTRACTS AND RETIREMENT BENEFITS

1. Name, address, and telephone number of client
2. Social Security and/or Employer's Identification Number of client
3. Client's business
   (a) Nature of
   (b) Union or nonunion operation
   (c) Number and job classification of employees, and job description (if relevant)
   (d) Names and Social Security numbers of employees (if relevant)
4. Type of contract to be drafted or reviewed
   (a) Individual employment contract
       (1) Present compensation[1]
       (2) Deferred compensation[2]
   (b) Employee benefit plan
       (1) Stock option plan:
           Nonqualified[3]
           Incentive stock option (ISO)
           Employee stock purchase plan
       (2) Pension plan
       (3) Profit-sharing plan[4]
   (c) IRA plan (for employer himself or for an employee(s))[5]
   (d) Keogh plan (HR-10) for employer only[6]
   (e) Collective bargaining agreement[7]
   (f) Formation of employee credit union[8]
5. Individual employment contract[9]
   (a) Name and address of employer and employee
   (b) Nature of employee's work and his title, if any; general and specific duties or formal job description
   (c) Salary, commission, or other compensation of employee
   (d) Is there to be any deferred compensation?
   (e) Fringe benefits, if any
   (f) Duration
   (g) Termination for what causes
   (h) Is there to be a noncompetition clause? If so, is it for duration of contract only, or also after termination? For what period of time and in what territory or area? Must be reasonable to avoid unlawful restraint of trade.[10]
   (i) Trade secrets clause
   (j) Is there a pension, stock option, profit-sharing or other employee compensation plan in existence? If so, what is it? Is such a plan part of the consideration for the employment agreement? If so, what part? Will the employment agreement give employee an option to purchase stock? If so, on what conditions?
   (k) Other terms or conditions of employment
6. Stock option plan[11]
   (a) Type of stock (class, par or no-par, voting rights)
   (b) Number of shares authorized
   (c) Number of shares outstanding

(d) Eligibility requirements and number of employees

(e) Basis for apportionment of right to purchase

(f) Is there to be any repurchase obligation on the part of the corporation?[12] If so, what is it?

(g) Is there to be any restriction on resale of the stock by the employee?[13] If so, what are the terms of the restriction?

7. Pension plan[14]

(a) Number and classification of employees

(b) Type of plan, and is it to be integrated with Social Security?

*Defined Benefit Plan* (amount of money contributed varies, but retirement amount is determined in advance)

*Defined Contribution Plan* (amount of money contributed is fixed, but the retirement benefit is not known—also known as an *individual account plan*)

(c) Who will contribute to the plan?

*Employer only*

*Both employer and employee*

*Union dues and assessments*

(d) *How and when will the plan vest? ERISA minimum vesting provisions are as follows:*

*Cliff vesting*[15] (full vesting after 10 years of service, with no vesting before then)

*Graded vesting*[16] (25 percent after 5 years of service, 5 percent for each additional year up to 10 years, plus an additional 10 percent for each year thereafter (benefits will be 100 percent vested after 15 years' service)

*Rule-of-45 vesting*[17] (50 percent vesting for an employee with at least 5 years of service when his or her age and years of service add up to 45, plus 10 percent for each additional year up to 5 years

(e) Types of benefits

*Normal* (what is the retirement age desired?)

*Early retirement* (minimum years of service required)

*Disability* (definition of disability and exceptions as mental, alcohol, drug, or other plus age and service requirements before being eligible for disability)

*Deduction of Social Security Benefits* (will employee's Social Security benefits be deducted from the pension plan benefit? If so, to what extent?)

(f) How will benefits be paid (monthly for life, lump sum or other)? Will the amount of payment be adjusted to the cost of living? If so, what formula or index is to be used?

(g) Survivors' benefits (no survivor benefits, joint and survivor benefits, or other death benefit to survivor)

(h) Termination—Is the plan to be insured on termination by the Pension Benefit Guaranty Corporation (PBGC)? Only vested benefits in certain "defined benefit" plans are insured, and there is a limit on the amount of benefits covered. Get "PBGC Fact Sheet" from PBGC[18] for the insurance information

(i) For obtaining and using the proper identification numbers under ERISA, get Publication 1004 from your LMSA[19] area office

(j) Does client want you to prepare the Summary Sheet on the Plan for distribution to the employees?

8. Profit-sharing plan[20]

(a) Number and classification of employees

(b) Contribution to the plan

(1) Formula for employer's contribution

(2) Will employee voluntary contributions be allowed? If so, on what terms?

(c) How and when will the plan vest?

(d) How and when will benefits be paid?

(e) By whom will the plan be administered—name and address of Trustee for the plan, and name, title, and address of the liaison person between Trustee, employer and employees

(f) Does client want you to prepare the Summary Sheet for the Plan to be distributed to employees?

9. IRA Plan[21]

(a) Name, address, and Social Security number of the person who desires to start an Individual Retirement Account (IRA)

(b) Type of account desired:

Insured savings account (investment value will not fall but will not increase)

Mutual funds (may fall or increase)

Self-directed or other plan with stock brokerage firm (may fall or increase)

Insurance company annuity plan (depends on plan)

(c) Amount of initial annual contribution (present limit $2,000 or 100 percent of earned income, whichever is less)

(d) Will client's contribution be affordable to him to avoid penalty for early withdrawal? What is client's income tax bracket?

(e) Name, address, and financial stability or reputation of the proposed account trustee (bank, savings and loan, brokerage firm, insurance company, etc.)

10. Keogh plan (for employer only)

(a) See Checklist for Review in Form IVA 1.09 and footnotes

[1]Ref. Form IVA 1.01.

[2]Ref. Form IVA 1.02.

[3]Ref. Form IVA 1.06.

[4]Ref. Form IVA 1.07.

[5]Ref. Form IVA 1.08(a), (b), (c).

[6]Ref. Form IVA 1.09.

[7]Ref. Form IVB 1.01.

[8]Ref. Form IVC 1.00.

[9]Ref. Forms IVA 1.01 and 1.02.

[10]Ref. Paragraph 7 of Form IVA 1.01 and Paragraph 2(C) of Form IVA 1.02. Some states have enacted statutes on this subject to supplement restraint of trade provisions of the *Clayton Act.*

[11]Ref. Form IVA 1.06; and see *Employee Stock Purchase Plan* 26 U.S.C.A. 423 and regulations; *Incentive Stock Option Plan (ISO)* 26 U.S.C.A. 320 and 422A (Section 251 ERTA); and 26 U.S.C.A. 162 and 212 for employer deductions; former "qualified" stock options 26 U.S.C.A. 421–425; and *33 Am. Jur. 2d Taxation,* paras. 3320–3373 and 3760–3774; *Money Purchase Pension Retirement Plan* 29 U.S.C.A. 1001–1461; 26 U.S.C.A. 401–403 and 26 C.F.R. 1.401-1(b)(i); and ERISA Appendix to this book. See also *60 Am. Jur. 2d Pensions and Retirement Funds,* paras. 73–75.

[12]Compare Form IA 2.10 and Form IA 2.11.

[13]Compare Form IA 2.12 and Form IA 2.13.

[14]See ERISA in Appendix.

[15]29 U.S.C.A. 1053 (a) (2) (A).

[16]29 U.S.C.A. 1053 (a) (2) (B).

[17]29 U.S.C.A. 1053 (a) (2) (C).

[18]See ERISA in Appendix.

[19]See ERISA in Appendix.

[20]Ref. Form 1VA 1.07.

[21]Ref. Form IVA 1.08(a), (b), (c).

## FORM IVA 1.01

### (Employment agreement with one executive employee)

### EMPLOYMENT CONTRACT[1]

AGREEMENT made this 10th day of May, 1982, between MODERN COMPUTER CENTER, INC., a Pennsylvania corporation, having its principal place of business at 100 Industrial Plaza, Suburbia, Pennsylvania 00000 (herein called "Employer"), and JOHN DOE, of 100 Main Street, Wilkinsburg, Pennsylvania 00000 (herein called "Employee").

1. *TERM OF EMPLOYMENT*

The Employer hereby employs the Employee and Employee hereby accepts employment with the Employer for a period of five (5) years beginning the first day of June, 1982. This Agreement may be terminated earlier or renewed as hereinafter provided.

2. DUTIES OF EMPLOYEE

(a) *General Duties.* The Employee is hereby employed as a Vice-President and Chief Operating Officer of Employer's corporation. The Employee shall carefully and accurately perform all the duties and tasks of the Chief Operating Officer and perform all duties commonly discharged by Vice-Presidents and Chief Operating Officers and such other duties of a similar nature as may be required from time to time by the Employer.

(b) *Specific duties.* The Employee is specifically hired and employed by the Employer to operate, invent, discover, develop, and improve methods, formulas, machines, softwares, and devices relating in any manner whatsoever for data processing. The Employee shall devote his entire productive time, ability, and attention to the business of the Employer during the term of this contract. The services of the Employee shall be performed at any laboratory, research facility, bank, office or other installation in the western Pennsylvania area as determined solely by the Employer. On inventing, discovering, developing, or improving any of the aforesaid methods, formulas, machines, and devices, the Employee shall immediately make a full disclosure thereof to the Employer and shall thereafter keep the Employer fully informed at all times of all progress in connection therewith. Property rights in inventions or patents are governed by Paragraph 6 of this Agreement.

(c) *Other Duties of the Employee.* In addition to the foregoing duties, the Employee shall perform such other work as may be assigned to him subject to the instructions, directions, and control of the Employer, provided only that such additional duties shall be during the hours and at the place of employment specified in this Contract and shall be reasonably related to the purpose of Modern Computer Center, Inc.

(d) *Changes of Duties—Mutual Consent.* The duties of the Employment may be changed from time to time by the mutual consent of the Employer and the Employee. Notwithstanding any such change, the employment of the Employee shall be construed as continuing under this Agreement as modified.

(e) *Change of Duties if Employee Disabled.* If the Employee at any time during the term of this Agreement should be unable because of personal injury, illness, or any other cause to perform his duties under this Contract, the Employer may assign the Employee to other duties, and the compensation to be paid thereafter to the Employee shall be determined by the Employer in its sole discretion. If the Employee is unwilling to accept the modification in duties and compensation made by the Employer, or if the Employee's inability to perform is of such extent as to make a modification of duties hereunder not feasible, this contract shall terminate within 30 days thereafter.

(f) *Place of Performance.* At the commencement of his employment, the Employee shall perform his duties at the office of the Employer located at 100 Industrial Plaza, Suburbia, Pennsylvania. However, at any time deemed necessary or advisable by the Employer for business purposes, the Employee shall work at such other place or places as may be determined by the Employer; provided, however, that if the place designated by Employer is outside the western Pennsylvania area for a period in excess of three (3) months, Employer shall pay employee a Fifty-Dollar ($50) per diem fee in addition to the expenses and other compensation provided herein.

(g) *Hours of Employment.* The Employee shall work those hours necessary to get the functions of the Corporation accomplished. The Employee is of management capacity and as such shall not be held to a minimum or maximum hourly time frame.

3. *COMPENSATION*

(a) *Basic Compensation.* As compensation for services rendered under this Agreement, the Employee shall be entitled to receive from the Employer a salary of Forty Thousand Dollars ($40,000) per year for the first year, payable in semimonthly installments on the 1st and 15th day of each month during the period of employment, prorated for any partial employment period. Employee's salary shall be increased by Five Percent (5%) per annum each year of the Contract. Salary increases pursuant to renewals of the Contract for the two (2) one (1)-year terms described in Paragraph 10 shall be limited to Ten Percent (10%) per annum increases unless otherwise agreed in writing by the parties.

(b) *Additional Compensation.* In recognition of the Employee's peculiar value to the Employer and as a special and specific inducement to the Employee, and in order to retain Employee's peculiar knowledge and expertise, the Employer specifically agrees to pay to the Employee the sum of Sixty Thousand Dollars ($60,000), payable over a three (3)-year period, in equal increments of Twenty Thousand Dollars ($20,000) per year, payable on the 1st day of April of each year, until the total of Sixty Thousand Dollars ($60,000) is paid to the Employee. This employment inducement money shall be paid Employee whether or not he stays with Modern Computer Center, Inc., for a full three-year term or whether he is terminated for cause or otherwise during the first three years of this contract. If termination occurs for any reason, including death, prior to the completion of the three years, the balance then owed Employee under this Paragraph shall be paid in full on termination date. This shall be treated and is in fact additional salary being paid the Employee, but for purposes of the 5% salary increase annually for each year of the contract in chief, shall not be subject thereto. This employment inducement salary shall be for three years only and shall not be included in any renewal of this Contract as provided in Paragraph 9. This Paragraph shall not be construed to preclude the Employee from being eligible to participate in any bonus, dividend, or other monetarily beneficial program for employees established by the Employer.

(c) *Overtime Work Requirements.* Whenever requested by the Employer or required by the nature of the Employee's work, the Employee shall work as many hours in a given workday, in addition to the regular workday term, as is reasonably necessary to complete the work assigned by the Employer. This overtime, if reasonably necessary, shall be performed in the normal course of Employee's duties and responsibilities and within his normal pay.

4. *EMPLOYEE BENEFITS AND BONUSES*

(a) *General.* The Employee shall be entitled to participate in any qualified pension plan, qualified profit-sharing plan, medical and/or dental reimbursement plan, group term life insurance plan, and any other employee benefit plan that may be established by the Employer, such participation to be in accordance with the terms of any such plan, and such participation shall be available only upon the Employer's having or establishing such plan.

(b) *Vacation Privileges.* The Employee shall be entitled, after he has been in the employ of the Employer for a period of one (1) year, to an annual vacation leave of two (2) weeks, at full pay, as increased annually. The Employer reserves the right to determine the vacation time of the Employee in order to assure the efficient and orderly operation of the Employer's business.

5. *REIMBURSEMENT OF EMPLOYEE EXPENSES*

The Employer, in accordance with the rules and regulations that it may issue from time to time, shall reimburse the Employee for business expenses incurred in the performance of his duties.

6. *PROPERTY RIGHTS*

(a) *Inventions and Patents.* The Employee agrees that he will promptly, from time to time, fully inform and disclose to the Employer all inventions, designs, improvements, and discoveries that he now has or may hereinafter have during the term of this Agreement that pertain or relate to the business of the Employer or to any experimental work carried on by the Employer, whether conceived by the Employee alone or with others and whether or not conceived during regular working hours. All such inventions, designs, improvements, and discoveries shall be the exclusive property of the Employer. The Employee shall assist the Employer to obtain patents on all such inventions, designs, improvements, and discoveries deemed patentable by the Employer and shall execute all documents and do all things necessary to obtain letters patent, vest the Employer with full and exclusive title thereto, and protect the same against infringement by others.

(b) *Trade Secrets.* The Employee during the term of employment under this Agreement has had and will have access to and become familiar with various trade secrets, consisting of software formulas, programs, patterns, devices, secret inventions, processes, and compilations of information, records, and specification, of Employer and other records of corporations owned by or associated with the Employer. The Employee shall not disclose any of the aforesaid trade secrets, directly or indirectly, nor use them in any way, either during the term of this Agreement or at any time thereafter, except as required in the course of his employment. All programs, formulas, files, records, documents, drawings, specifications, equipment, and similar items relating to the business of the Employer or others, whether prepared by the Employee or otherwise coming into his possession, shall remain the exclusive property of the Employer and shall not be removed from the premises of the Employer or the premises of any subsidiary or sister corporation under any circumstances whatsoever without the prior written consent of the Employer.

7. *NONCOMPETITION RESTRICTIVE COVENANT BY EMPLOYEE*

In consideration of the Employer's employing the Employee in a position wherein he has and will gain specialized knowledge and experience and will establish personal relationships with the Employer's accounts, confidential files, and other employees, the Employee covenants and agrees as follows:

(a) *During Term of Employment.* During the term of this Contract, the Employee shall not, directly or indirectly, either as an employee, employer, consultant, agent, principal, partner, stockholder, corporate officer, director, or in any other individual or representative capacity, engage or participate in any business that is in competition in any manner whatsoever with the business of the Employer.

(b) *After Termination.* On termination of his employment, whether by termination of this Agreement, by wrongful discharge, or otherwise, the Employee shall not directly or indirectly, within the existing service area of the Employer in the area of western Pennsylvania or any future service area of the Employer begun during employment under the terms of this Agreement, enter into or engage generally in direct competition with the Employer in the business of operating, programming, developing, engineering, designing, manufacturing, and selling like software account processes either as an individual on his own or as a partner or joint venturer, or as an employee or agent for any person, or as an officer, director, or shareholder or otherwise, for a period of two (2) years after the date of termination of his employment hereunder.

(c) These covenants on the part of the Employee shall be construed as an agreement independent of any other provision of this Agreement; and the existence of any claim or cause of action of the Employee against the Employer, whether predicated on this Agreement or otherwise, shall not constitute a defense to the enforcement by the Employer of this covenant. In the event of a breach or threatened breach by the Employee of his obligation under this Restrictive Covenant, the Employee acknowledges that the Employer will not have an adequate remedy at law and shall be entitled to such equitable and injunctive relief as may be available to restrain the Employee from the violation of the provisions hereof. Nothing herein shall be construed as prohibiting the Employer from pursuing any other remedies available for such breach or threatened breach, including the recovery of damages from the Employee.

8. *EMPLOYEE PERFORMANCE AND BOND*

(a) *Qualification for Surety Bond.* The Employee agrees that he will furnish all information and take any other steps necessary to enable the Employer to obtain a fidelity bond conditioned on the rendering of a true account by the Employee of all moneys, goods, or other property that may come into the custody, charge, or possession of the Employee during the term of his employment. The surety company issuing the bond and the amount of the bond must be acceptable to the Employer in the sole discretion of the Employer. All premiums on the bond are to paid by the Employer. Failure by the Employee to qualify for such bond within thirty (30) days from the date of this Agreement will result in immediate termination of this employment Contract, if such bond is required by the Employer.

(b) *Satisfactory Performance of Duties.* This Contract is intended to be three (3) years in length. It also contains a clause allowing for two (2) one (1)-year renewals thereof. However, the employment of the Employee shall continue only as long as the services rendered by the Employee are satisfactory to the Employer, regardless of any other provision contained in this Agreement. The Employer shall be the sole judge as to whether the services of the Employee are satisfactory.

9. *MILITARY SERVICE*

(a) *Military Training Leave.* If the Employee is or becomes a member of a Military Reserve or National Guard unit, he shall be entitled to apply for and be granted a leave of absence for a period of fourteen (14) days plus travel time each year to attend training camp. During such leave, the Employee shall receive full compensation less the amount of military base pay received, and such leave shall be in addition to any vacation to which he may be entitled hereunder.

(b) *Effect of Military Service.* In the event that the Employee is drafted, or is otherwise inducted into the Armed Forces of the United States, he shall not be entitled to receive any compensation under this Agreement during the period of such military service. At the expiration of such military service, the Employee shall be reinstated in his employment under this Agreement and shall be entitled to continue to render services hereunder for the balance of the term of employment provided for herein remaining at the time of his induction into the Armed Forces; for such period the Employee shall receive the compensation provided for under this Agreement or the compensation then paid by the Employer to other employees occupying positions of like status or seniority, whichever is higher. If the Employee is not qualified to resume his former position by reason of a disability sustained during military service, the Employer shall employ him in such other position, the duties of which he is qualified to perform, as will provide him like seniority, status, and pay, or the nearest approximation consistent with the then existing circumstances, unless it is impossible or unreasonable at that time for the Employer to do so.

10. *RENEWAL*

This Agreement may be renewed at the option of the parties for two (2) one (1)-year terms of renewal by the written consent of both parties signed at least ninety (90) days before the expiration of this term of this Agreement or any renewal term.

11. *TERMINATION*

(a) *By Employer for Cause.* If the Employee willfully breaches or habitually neglects the duties that he is required to perform under the terms of this Agreement, the Employer may at his option terminate this Agreement by giving written notice of termination to the Employee without prejudice to any other remedy to which the Employer may be entitled either at law, in equity, or under this Agreement.

(b) *By Employee.* This Agreement may be terminated by the employee by giving thirty (30) days' written notice of termination to the Employer.

(c) *Remedies.* Termination by either party shall not prejudice any remedy that the terminating party may have either at law, in equity, or under this Agreement.

(d) *Option to Terminate in Event of Bankruptcy or Similar Proceedings.* This Agreement may be terminated immediately by the Employer at its option and without prejudice to any other remedy to which it may be entitled either at law, in equity, or under this Agreement by giving written notice of termination to the Employee if the Employee:

(1) Files a petition in bankruptcy court or is adjudicated a bankrupt;

(2) Institutes or suffers to be instituted any procedure in bankruptcy court for reorganization or rearrangement of his financial affairs;

(3) Has a receiver of his assets or property appointed because of insolvency; or

(4) Makes a general assignment for the benefits of creditors.

(e) *Option to Terminate if Employee Permanently Disabled.* If the Employee becomes permanently disabled because of sickness, physical or mental disability, or any other reason, so that it reasonably appears that he will be unable to complete his duties under this Agreement, the Employer shall have the option immediately to terminate this Agreement by giving written notice of termination to the Employee. Such termination shall be without prejudice to any right or remedy to which the Employer or the Employee may be entitled either at law, in equity, or under this Agreement.

(f) *Effect of Termination on Compensation.* In the event of the termination of this Agreement prior to the completion of the term of employment specified herein, the Employee shall be entitled to the compensation earned by him prior to the date of termination as provided for in this Agreement computed pro rata up to and including that date, and said compensation shall be paid by Employer within thirty (30) days of the termination date. The Employee shall be entitled to no further compensation as of the date of termination except that provided in Article 3(b).

12. *GENERAL PROVISIONS*

(a) *Notices.* Any notices to either party required hereunder may be given by personal delivery in writing or by mail, registered or certified, postage prepaid with return receipt requested. Mailed notices shall be addressed to the parties at the addresses appearing in the Introductory Paragraph of this Agreement, but each party may change his address by written notice in accordance with this Paragraph. Notices delivered personally shall be deemed communicated as of time of actual delivery; mailed notices shall be deemed communicated as of 15 day(s) after mailing.

(b) *Entire Agreement.* This Agreement supersedes any and all other agreements, either oral or in writing, between the parties hereto with respect to the employment of the Employee by the Employer and contains all of the representations, covenants, and agreements between the parties with respect to such employment in any manner whatsoever.

(c) *Governing Law.* This Agreement shall be governed by and construed in accordance with the laws of the Commonwealth of Pennsylvania, and the only venue for legal action hereundershall be the Court of Common Pleas of Allegheny County, Pennsylvania.

(d) *Attorney's Fees and Costs.* If any action at law or in equity is brought to enforce or interpret the terms of this Agreement, the prevailing party shall be entitled to reasonable attorney's fees, costs, and necessary disbursements in addition to any other relief to which he may be entitled.

(e) *Written Consent of Employer to Employee Expenditures.* It is expressly agreed that the Employee shall have no right or authority at any time to make any contract or binding promise of any nature, whether oral or written, for an amount or value exceeding One Thousand Dollars ($1,000) without the express written consent of the Chief Executive Officer of the Employer, notwithstanding anything in this Agreement to the contrary.

(f) *Payment of Moneys Due Deceased Employee.* If the Employee dies prior to the expiration of the term of employment, any moneys that may be due him from the Employer under this Agreement as of the date of his death shall be paid to the executor or administrator of his estate.

Signed at Pittsburgh, Pennsylvania, on the day and year first above written.

(SEAL)                                                          MODERN COMPUTER CENTER, INC.

_____          By: _____
Secretary of the Corporation                         President

Witness:

_____          _____
                                                                   JOHN DOE

[13] *3 Am. Jur. 2d Agency*, para. 86. As to covenant not to compete, see *54 Am. Jur. 2d Monopolies, Restraints of Trade and Unfair Trade Practices*, paras. 542–553 and 556. For alternative clauses, see Forms IVA 1.01(a) and (b).

## FORM IVA 1.01(a)

### (Discharge by employer)

### ALTERNATIVE CLAUSE

*Discharge.* Nothing in this Agreement shall prevent Employer from discharging the Employee at any time whenever, in the opinion of the Employer's Executive Officer, the Employee's services are for any reason unsatisfactory to the Employer.

## FORM IVA 1.01(b)

### (Fringe Benefits)

### ALTERNATIVE CLAUSE

*Compensation.* The monthly salary of Employee shall be Two Thousand Dollars ($2,000), payable semimonthly. In addition to the monthly salary, Employer shall provide the following benefits:

A. Employer shall pay up to Two Hundred Dollars ($200) a month toward the leasing of an automobile for Employee's use.

B. Employer shall pay all costs of maintenance of that automobile. Employer shall pay for all gas and oil used in the performance of Employer's business, but excluding Employee's personal use of the automobile.

C. Employer shall pay for insurance coverage on that automobile at standard rates, and the coverage shall include comprehensive and One-Hundred-Dollar ($100) deductible collision. Further, Employer shall pay the deductible amount on collision in the event automobile is damaged while Employee is on Employer's business.

D. Employer shall purchase and pay for an accident and health policy with a 90-day waiting period, which policy will pay the Employee the sum of Five Hundred Dollars ($500) a month for a five (5)-year period. In addition, Employer shall, in the event of disability of the Employee, continue paying Employee's salary for a period not to exceed ninety (90) days.

E. Employer shall pay the premiums for Employee on a major-medical insurance policy providing coverage is furnished to other employees.

F. Employer shall purchase and pay for a term life insurance policy in the amount of Fifty Thousand Dollars ($50,000) subject to Employee's capability of qualifying for said insurance at standard rates.

**FORM IVA 1.02**

(Unfunded direct deferred compensation agreement for one
executive employee—specific amount for each current year of
service—payable to employee or his estate—noncompetition
clause)

## DEFERRED COMPENSATION AGREEMENT[1]

AGREEMENT made this 23rd day of September, 1981, between ABLE MANUFACTURING CO., INC. (herein called "Corporation"), and RICHARD R. ROE (herein called "Roe"), WITNESSETH:

WHEREAS, Roe has worked diligently for the Corporation for many years and is a responsible and effective officer of the Company; his services continue to be of great value to the Corporation, and the loss of his services to a competitor would be damaging to the business and welfare of the Corporation; and

WHEREAS, Roe is willing to have part of the compensation to be earned by him after the signing of this Agreement deferred in accordance with the terms of this Agreement; it is

AGREED AS FOLLOWS:

1. *Service to Corporation.*[2] Roe shall serve the Corporation as Vice-President in charge of production, subject to the control of the Board of Directors.

2. *Compensation and conditions.* The Corporation shall pay Roe as compensation for his services:

(a) A salary of Forty Thousand Dollars ($40,000) per year, payable in equal semimonthly installments.

(b) Additional compensation of Twenty-five Thousand Dollars ($25,000) per year for the year ending September 30, 1982, shall be paid to Roe on January 15 of the first calendar year following the year in which Roe retires, and additional compensation of Twenty-five Thousand Dollars ($25,000) a year for each succeeding year of Roe's employment under this Agreement shall be paid to him on each following year on January 15.

(c) The payments of additional compensation to Roe shall be made only if he is not, when said payments become due, an officer, director, shareholder, or employee of a corporation nor an owner or partner in or otherwise associated in a business that is in competition with the business of the Corporation.

(d) If Roe dies before he retires, the payments of additional compensation earned by him pursuant to this Agreement shall be paid, according to the terms hereof, to his estate (or to his surviving widow or other designated person).

(e) If Roe dies after he retires, the payments of additional income earned by him pursuant to this Agreement shall be paid, according to the terms hereof, to his estate (or to his surviving widow or other designated person).

3. *Term of employment.*

(a) The employment of Roe pursuant to this Agreement shall begin on October 1, 1981, and shall continue through September 30, 1986.

(b) Roe may retire from his service to the Corporation at any time during the time of this Agreement upon giving the Corporation sixty (60) days' written notice. In case such retirement is effective before the thirtieth day of September in that year, he shall receive a pro rata portion of the additional compensation due for that retirement year under the terms of this Agreement. All further payments under this Agreement shall be in full for each year served before the retirement year.

4. *Business expenses.* During the term of this Agreement, the Corporation shall pay reasonable business travel and other business expenses incurred by Roe and shall furnish him with an office, accommodations, and personnel suitable to his position and adequate for the performance of his duties under this Agreement.

5. *Assignment.* The rights or interest of Roe in this Agreement are not assignable by voluntary act of Roe or operation of law, except by written consent of the Corporation.

6. *Waiver.* Any failure by either party to insist upon strict performance of this Agreement or any terms hereof shall not be deemed to be a waiver of any of the terms and provisions hereof.

IN WITNESS WHEREOF, the parties hereto have signed this Agreement, pursuant to a resolution adopted by the corporate party's Board of Directors, a copy of which resolution is attached hereto.

ATTEST:

(SEAL)

ABLE MANUFACTURING COMPANY, INC.

By _____
          President

_____
Secretary of the Corporation

_____
RICHARD R. ROE

(Attach a copy of the resolution authorizing the deferred compensation, certified by the Secretary of the Corporation.)

¹26 U.S.C.A. 1051, 1081, 1101. Compare general deferred compensation plans. See *33 Am. Jur. 2d Federal Taxation*, paras. 3170–3180; and 26 U.S.C.A. 404. See also 26 C.F.R. 1.404(a)-14 and 26 C.F.R. 1.404(b)-1. Ref. Forms IVA 1.03–1.05.
²See also alternative clause, Form IVA 1.02(a).

## FORM IVA 1.02(a)

### (Consultation services)

### ALTERNATIVE CLAUSE

*Consultation services.* During the period of five (5) years following his retirement, Roe will render to the Corporation services of an advisory or consultative nature as reasonably requested by the Corporation. Those services may be rendered by telephone, letter, or in person as reasonably requested by the Corporation; provided, however, Roe's failure to render such services or to give such advice and counsel by reason of illness or other reasonable incapacity shall not affect Roe's right to receive his additional compensation during that period.

| Form **5500** | **Annual Return/Report of Employee Benefit Plan** | OMB No. 1210-0016 |
|---|---|---|

**Form 5500**

Department of the Treasury
Internal Revenue Service

Department of Labor
Pension and Welfare Benefit Programs

Pension Benefit Guaranty Corporation

**Annual Return/Report of Employee Benefit Plan**
**(With 100 or more participants)**

This form is required to be filed under sections 104 and 4065 of the Employee Retirement Income Security Act of 1974 and sections 6057(b) and 6058(a) of the Internal Revenue Code, referred to as the Code. Caution: There is a penalty for late filing of this return/report.

OMB No. 1210-0016

**19**

**This Form is Open to Public Inspection**

For the calendar plan year 19 ___ or fiscal plan year beginning _____ , 19 ___ , and ending _____ , 19 ___

Type or print in ink all entries on the form, schedules, and attachments. If an item does not apply, enter "N/A". File the originals.

This return/report is: (i) ☐ the return/report filed for the plan's first year; (ii) ☐ an amended return/report; or

(iii) ☐ the final return/report filed for the plan.

▶ Church plans (not electing coverage under Code section 410(d)) and governmental plans, **do not file this form.** File Form 5500–G instead.

▶ Welfare benefit plans with 100 or more participants, complete only items 1 through 16 and item 22.

▶ Pension benefit plans, unless otherwise excepted, complete all items. Annuity and custodial account arrangements of certain exempt organizations, and individual retirement account trusts of employers, complete only items 1 through 6, 9 and 10.

▶ If you have been granted an extension of time to file this form, you must attach a copy of the approved extension to this form.

Use IRS label. Otherwise, please print or type.

**1 (a)** Name of plan sponsor (employer if for a single employer plan)

Address (number and street)

City or town, State and ZIP code

**1 (b)** Employer identification number

**1 (c)** Telephone number of sponsor
( )

**1 (d)** If plan year changed since last return/report, check here . ▶ ☐

**2 (a)** Name of plan administrator (if same as plan sponsor enter "Same")

Address (number and street)

City or town, State and ZIP code

**1 (e)** Business code number

**2 (b)** Administrator's employer identification no.

**2 (c)** Telephone number of administrator
( )

**3** Name, address and identification number of plan sponsor and/or plan administrator as they appeared on the last return/report filed for this plan, if not the same as in 1 or 2 above: **(a)** Sponsor ▶ ------------------------------------------------------------

**(b)** Administrator ▶ ------------------------------------------------------------

**4** Check appropriate box to indicate the type of plan entity (check only one box):

**(a)** ☐ Single-employer plan

**(b)** ☐ Plan of controlled group of corporations or common control employers

**(c)** ☐ Multiemployer plan

**(d)** ☐ Multiple-employer-collectively-bargained plan

**(e)** ☐ Multiple-employer plan (other)

**(f)** ☐ Group insurance arrangement (of welfare plans)

**5 (a)** (i) Name of plan ▶ ------------------------------------------------------------

(ii) ☐ Check if name of plan changed since last return/report

**5 (b)** Effective date of plan

**5 (c)** Enter three digit plan number ▶

**6** Check at least one item in (a) or (b) and applicable items in (c):

**(a)** Welfare benefit plan: (i) ☐ Health insurance (ii) ☐ Life insurance (iii) ☐ Supplemental unemployment

(iv) ☐ Other (specify) ▶ ------------------------------------------------------------

**(b)** Pension benefit plan:

(i) Defined benefit plan—(Indicate type of defined benefit plan below):

(A) ☐ Fixed benefit (B) ☐ Unit benefit (C) ☐ Flat benefit (D) ☐ Other (specify) ▶ --------------

(ii) Defined contribution plan—(indicate type of defined contribution plan below):

(A) ☐ Profit-sharing (B) ☐ Stock bonus (C) ☐ Target benefit (D) ☐ Other money purchase

(E) ☐ Other (specify) ▶ --------------

(iii) ☐ Defined benefit plan with benefits based partly on balance of separate account of participant (Code section 414(k))

(iv) ☐ Annuity arrangement of a certain exempt organization (Code section 403(b)(1))

(v) ☐ Custodial account for regulated investment company stock (Code section 403(b)(7))

(vi) ☐ Trust treated as an individual retirement account (Code section 408(c))

(vii) ☐ Other (specify) ▶

Under penalties of perjury and other penalties set forth in the instructions, I declare that I have examined this report, including accompanying schedules and statements, and to the best of my knowledge and belief, it is true, correct, and complete.

Date ▶ ------------------- Signature of employer/plan sponsor ▶ ------------------------------------------------------------

Date ▶ ------------------- Signature of plan administrator ▶ ------------------------------------------------------------

For Paperwork Reduction Act Notice, see page 1 of the instructions.

**6 (c)** Other plan features: *(i)* ☐ Thrift-savings *(ii)* ☐ Keogh (H.R. 10) plan

      *(iii)* ☐ Pension plan maintained outside the United States *(iv)* ☐ Participant-directed account plan

      *(v)* ☐ Master trust (see instructions) _____

**(d)** Single employer plans enter the tax year end of the employer in which this plan year ends . . ▶ Month ____ Day ____ Year ____

**(e)** Is this a plan of an affiliated service group? . . . . . . . . . . . . . . . . . . . . . . . . . ☐ Yes ☐ No

**7** Number of participants as of the end of the plan year (welfare plans complete only (a)(iv), (b), (c) and (d)):

  **(a)** Active participants *(i)* Number fully vested . . . . . . . . . . . . .

                   *(ii)* Number partially vested . . . . . . . . . . .

                   *(iii)* Number nonvested . . . . . . . . . . . .

                   *(iv)* Total . . . . . . . . . . . . . .

  **(b)** Retired or separated participants receiving benefits . . . . . . . . . . . . . .

  **(c)** Retired or separated participants entitled to future benefits . . . . . . . . . . .

  **(d)** Subtotal (add (a), (b) and (c)) . . . . . . . . . . . . . . . . . . .

  **(e)** Deceased participants whose beneficiaries are receiving or are entitled to receive benefits . . . . .

  **(f)** Total (add (d) and (e)) . . . . . . . . . . . . . . . . . . . . .

|  | Yes | No |
|---|---|---|
| **(g)** *(i)* During this plan or prior plan year, was any participant(s) separated from service with a deferred vested benefit for which a Schedule SSA (Form 5500) is required to be attached to this form? . . . . . . . | | |
| *(ii)* If "Yes," enter the number of separated participants required to be reported ▶ | | |
| **8** Plan amendment information (welfare plans do not complete (b)(ii)): | | |
| **(a)** Was any amendment to this plan adopted in this plan year? . . . . . . . . . . . . . | | |
| **(b)** If "Yes," *(i)* And if any amendments have resulted in a change in the information contained in a summary plan description or previously furnished summary description of modifications— | | |
| (A) Have summary descriptions of change(s) been sent to participants? . . . . . . . | | |
| (B) Have summary descriptions of the change(s) been filed with DOL? . . . . . . . | | |
| *(ii)* Does any amendment result in the reduction of the accrued benefit of any participant under the plan? . . . . | | |
| **(c)** Enter the date the most recent amendment was adopted . . ▶ Month ............... Day ............... Year ............... | | |
| **(d)** *(i)* If (a) or (c) is "Yes," have you received a favorable determination letter from IRS for the termination? . . . . . . | | |
| *(ii)* If (i) is "Yes," what was the employer identification number and the plan number used to identify it? | | |
| Employer identification number ▶            Plan number ▶ | | |
| **9** Plan termination information (welfare plans complete only (a), (b), (c) and (f)): | | |
| **(a)** Was this plan terminated during ☐ this plan year or ☐ any prior plan year? . . . . . . . . . | | |
| **(b)** If "Yes," were all trust assets distributed to participants or beneficiaries or transferred to another plan? . . | | |
| **(c)** Was a resolution to terminate this plan adopted during this plan year or any prior plan year? . . . . . . | | |
| **(d)** If (a) or (c) is "Yes," have you received a favorable determination letter from IRS for the termination? . . . . . | | |
| **(e)** If (d) is "No," has a determination letter been requested from IRS? . . . . . . . . . | | |
| **(f)** If (a) or (c) is "Yes," have participants and beneficiaries been notified of the termination or the proposed termination? . . . . | | |
| **(g)** If either item (a) or (c) is "Yes," and this plan is covered under PBGC termination insurance program, has a notice of intent to terminate been filed? . . . . . . . . . . . . . . . . . | | |
| **10 (a)** In this plan year, was this plan merged or consolidated into another plan, or were assets or liabilities transferred to another plan? . . | | |

If "Yes," identify other plan(s):

| **(c)** Employer identification number(s) | **(d)** Plan number(s) |
|---|---|
| | |

**(b)** Name of plan(s) ▶ _____

**(e)** Has Form 5310 been filed? . . . . . . . . . . . . . . . . . . . . . . . ☐ Yes ☐ No

**11** Indicate funding arrangement:

  **(a)** ☐ Trust (benefits provided in whole from trust funds)

  **(b)** ☐ Trust or arrangement providing benefits partially through insurance and/or annuity contracts

  **(c)** ☐ Trust or arrangement providing benefits exclusively through insurance and/or annuity contracts

  **(d)** ☐ Custodial account described in Code section 401(f) and not included in (c) above

  **(e)** ☐ Other (specify) ▶ _____ ▶

  **(f)** If (b) or (c) is checked, enter the number of Schedules A (Form 5500) which are attached . . . . . . ▶

**12** Did any person who rendered services to the plan receive, directly or indirectly, compensation from the plan in the plan year? . . ☐ Yes ☐ No

If "Yes," furnish the following information:

| a.<br>Name | b.<br>Employer identification number (see instructions) | c.<br>Official plan position | d.<br>Relationship to employer, employee organization, or person known to be a party-in-interest | e.<br>Gross salary or allowances paid by plan | f.<br>Fees and commissions paid by plan | g.<br>Nature of service code (see instructions) |
|---|---|---|---|---|---|---|
| | | | | | | |
| | | | | | | |
| | | | | | | |

**13** Plan assets and liabilities at the beginning and the end of the plan year (list all assets and liabilities at current value). A fully insured welfare plan or a pension plan with no trust and which is funded entirely by allocated insurance contracts which fully guarantee the amount of benefit payments should check the box and not complete this item . . . . . . . . . . □

> **Note:** *Include all plan assets and liabilities of a trust or separately maintained fund. (If more than one trust/fund, report on a combined basis.) Include all insurance values except for the value of that portion of an allocated insurance contract which fully guarantees the amount of benefit payments. Round off amounts to the nearest dollar. Trusts with no assets at the beginning and the end of the plan year enter zero on line 13(h).*

| Assets | a. Beginning of year | b. End of year |
|---|---|---|
| **(a)** Cash: *(i)* On hand | | |
| *(ii)* In bank: (A) Certificates of deposit | | |
| (B) Other interest bearing | | |
| (C) Noninterest bearing | | |
| *(iii)* Total cash (add (i) and (ii)) | | |
| **(b)** Receivables: *(i)* Employer contributions | | |
| *(ii)* Employee contributions | | |
| *(iii)* Other | | |
| *(iv)* Reserve for doubtful accounts | | |
| *(v)* Net receivables (subtract (iv) from the total of (i), (ii) and (iii)) | ////// | ////// |
| **(c)** General investments other than party-in-interest investments: | | |
| *(i)* U.S. Government securities: (A) Long term | | |
| (B) Short term | | |
| *(ii)* State and municipal securities | | |
| *(iii)* Corporate debt instruments: (A) Long term | | |
| (B) Short term | | |
| *(iv)* Corporate stocks: (A) Preferred | | |
| (B) Common | | |
| *(v)* Shares of a registered investment company | | |
| *(vi)* Real estate | | |
| *(vii)* Mortgages | | |
| *(viii)* Loans other than mortgages | | |
| *(ix)* Value of interest in pooled fund(s) | | |
| *(x)* Value of interest in master trust | | |
| *(xi)* Other investments | | |
| *(xii)* Total general investments (add (i) through (xi)) | ////// | ////// |
| **(d)** Party-in-interest investments: | | |
| *(i)* Corporate debt instruments | | |
| *(ii)* Corporate stocks: (A) Preferred | | |
| (B) Common | | |
| *(iii)* Real estate | | |
| *(iv)* Mortgages | | |
| *(v)* Loans other than mortgages | | |
| *(vi)* Other investments | | |
| *(vii)* Total party-in-interest investments (add (i) through (vi)) | | |
| **(e)** Buildings and other depreciable property used in plan operation | ////// | ////// |
| **(f)** Value of unallocated insurance contracts (other than pooled separate accounts): | | |
| *(i)* Separate accounts | | |
| *(ii)* Other | | |
| *(iii)* Total (add (i) and (ii)) | | |
| **(g)** Other assets | | |
| **(h)** Total assets (add (a)(iii), (b)(v), (c)(xii), (d)(vii), (e), (f)(iii) and (g)) | | |
| **Liabilities** | ////// | ////// |
| **(i)** Payables: *(i)* Plan claims | | |
| *(ii)* Other payables | | |
| *(iii)* Total payables (add (i) and (ii)) | | |
| **(j)** Acquisition indebtedness | | |
| **(k)** Other liabilities | | |
| **(l)** Total liabilities (add (i)(iii), (j), and (k)) | | |
| **(m)** Net assets (subtract (l) from (h)) | | |
| **(n)** During the plan year what were the: | ////// | |
| *(i)* Total costs of acquisitions for common stock? | | |
| *(ii)* Total proceeds from dispositions of common stock? | | |

**14** Plan income, expenses and changes in net assets for the plan year:

**Note:** *Include all income and expenses of a trust(s) or separately maintained fund(s) including any payments made for allocated insurance contracts. Round off amounts to nearest dollar.*

| Income | a. Amount | b. Total |
|---|---|---|
| **(a)** Contributions received or receivable in cash from— | | |
|    *(i)* Employer(s) (including contributions on behalf of self-employed individuals) . | | |
|    *(ii)* Employees . . . . . . . . . . . . . . . . . . . . . | | |
|    *(iii)* Others . . . . . . . . . . . . . . . . . . . . . . | | |
| **(b)** Noncash contributions (specify nature and by whom made) ▶ | | |
| **(c)** Total contributions (add (a) and (b)) . . . . . . . . . | | |
| **(d)** Earnings from investments— | | |
|    *(i)* Interest . . . . . . . . . . . . . . . . . . . . . | | |
|    *(ii)* Dividends . . . . . . . . . . . . . . . . . . . . | | |
|    *(iii)* Rents . . . . . . . . . . . . . . . . . . . . . . | | |
|    *(iv)* Royalties . . . . . . . . . . . . . . . . . . . . | | |
| **(e)** Net realized gain (loss) on sale or exchange of assets— | | |
|    *(i)* Aggregate proceeds . . . . . . . . . . . . . . . | | |
|    *(ii)* Aggregate costs . . . . . . . . . . . . . . . . | | |
| **(f)** Other income (specify) ▶ | | |
| **(g)** Total income (add (c) through (f)) . . . . . . . . . . . . . . . | | |

| Expenses | a. Amount | b. Total |
|---|---|---|
| **(h)** Distribution of benefits and payments to provide benefits— | | |
|    *(i)* Directly to participants or their beneficiaries . . . . . . . . . . . | | |
|    *(ii)* To insurance carrier or similar organization for provision of benefits . . . | | |
|    *(iii)* To other organizations or individuals providing welfare benefits . . . . . | | |
| **(i)** Interest expense . . . . . . . . . . . . . . . . | | |
| **(j)** Administrative expenses— | | |
|    *(i)* Salaries and allowances . . . . . . . . . . . . . . | | |
|    *(ii)* Fees and commissions . . . . . . . . . . . . . . . | | |
|    *(iii)* Insurance premiums for Pension Benefit Guaranty Corporation . . . . | | |
|    *(iv)* Insurance premiums for fiduciary insurance other than bonding . . . . . | | |
|    *(v)* Other administrative expenses . . . . . . . . . . . . . | | |
| **(k)** Other expenses (specify) ▶ | | |
| **(l)** Total expenses (add (h) through (k)) . . . . . . . . . . . . . . | | |
| **(m)** Net income (expenses) (subtract (l) from (g)) . . . . . . . . . . . . . . | | |

| | a. Amount | b. Total |
|---|---|---|
| **(n)** Change in net assets— | | |
|    *(i)* Unrealized appreciation (depreciation) of assets . . . . . . . . . | | |
|    *(ii)* Net investment gain (or loss) from all master trust investment accounts . . | | |
|    *(iii)* Other changes (specify) ▶ | | |
| **(o)** Net increase (decrease) in net assets for the year (add (m) and (n)) . . . . . . . | | |
| **(p)** Net assets at beginning of year (line 13(m), column a) . . . . . . . . . . | | |
| **(q)** Net assets at end of year (add (o) and (p)) (equals line 13(m), column b) . . . . . . . . | | |

| | Yes | No |
|---|---|---|
| **15** All plans complete (a). Plans funded with insurance policies or annuity contracts also complete (b) and (c): | | |
|   **(a)** Since the end of the plan year covered by the last return/report has there been a termination in the appointment of any trustee, accountant, insurance carrier, enrolled actuary, administrator, investment manager or custodian? . . . . If "Yes," explain and include the name, position, address and telephone number of the person whose appointment has been terminated ▶ | | |
|   **(b)** Have any insurance policies or annuities been replaced during this plan year? . . . . . . . . . If "Yes," explain the reason for the replacement ▶ | | |
|   **(c)** At any time during the plan year was the plan funded with: | | |

     *(i)* ☐ Individual policies or annuities,   *(ii)* ☐ Group policies or annuities, or   *(iii)* ☐ Both.

| | | Yes | No |
|---|---|---|---|
| **16** | Bonding: | | |
| | **(a)** Was the plan insured by a fidelity bond against losses through fraud or dishonesty? . . . . . . . . . . | | |
| | If "Yes," complete (b) through (f); if "No," only complete (g). | | |
| | **(b)** Indicate number of plans covered by this bond ▶ _____ | | |
| | **(c)** Enter the maximum amount of loss recoverable ▶ _____ | | |
| | **(d)** Enter the name of the surety company ▶ _____ | | |
| | _____ | | |
| | **(e)** Does the plan, or a known party-in-interest with respect to the plan, have any control or significant financial interest, direct or indirect, in the surety company or its agents or brokers? . . . . . . . . . . . . | | |
| | **(f)** In the current plan year was any loss to the plan caused by the fraud or dishonesty of any plan official or employee of the plan or of other person handling funds of the plan? . . . . . . . . . . . . . . . | | |
| | If "Yes," see Specific Instructions. | | |
| | **(g)** If the plan is not insured by a fidelity bond, explain why not ▶ _____ | | |
| | _____ | | |

**17** Information about employees of employer at end of the plan year. (Plans not purporting to satisfy the percentage tests of Code section 410(b)(1)(A) complete only (a) below and see Specific Instructions):

**(a)** Total number of employees . . . . . . . . . . . . . . . . . . . . . . .

**(b)** Number of employees excluded under the plan because of:

　*(i)* Minimum age or years of service . . . . . . . . . . . . . . . . .

　*(ii)* Employees on whose behalf retirement benefits were the subject of collective bargaining . . .

　*(iii)* Nonresident aliens who receive no earned income from United States sources . . . . . . .

　*(iv)* Total excluded (add (i), (ii) and (iii)) . . . . . . . . . . . . . . . .

**(c)** Total number of employees not excluded (subtract (b)(iv) from (a)) . . . . . . . . . . .

**(d)** Employees ineligible (specify reason) ▶ _____

_____

**(e)** Employees eligible to participate (subtract (d) from (c)) . . . . . . . . . . . . . . .

**(f)** Employees eligible but not participating . . . . . . . . . . . . . . . . . . .

**(g)** Employees participating (subtract (f) from (e)) . . . . . . . . . . . . . . . . .

| | | Yes | No |
|---|---|---|---|
| **18** | Is this plan an adoption of a: | | |
| | **(a)** ☐ Master/prototype, **(b)** ☐ Field prototype, **(c)** ☐ Pattern, **(d)** ☐ Model plan or **(e)** ☐ Bond purchase plan? . | | |
| | If "Yes," enter the four or eight digit IRS serial number (see instructions) ▶ | | |
| **19** | **(a)** Is it intended that this plan qualify under Code section 401(a) or 405? . . . . . . . . . . | | |
| | **(b)** Have you requested or received a determination letter from the IRS for this plan? . . . . . . . . | | |
| | **(c)** Is this a plan with Employee Stock Ownership Plan features? . . . . . . . . . . . . . . | | |
| | 　*(i)* If "Yes," was a current appraisal of the value of the stock made immediately prior to any contribution of stock or the purchase of the stock by the trust for the plan year covered by this return/report? . . . | | |
| | 　*(ii)* If (i) is "Yes," was the appraisal made by an unrelated third party? . . . . . . . . . . | | |
| | 　*(iii)* If (ii) is "No," was the appraisal made in accordance with the provisions of Revenue Ruling 59–60? . . | | |
| **20** | If plan is integrated, check appropriate box: | | |
| | **(a)** ☐ Social security　　**(b)** ☐ Railroad retirement　　　**(c)** ☐ Other | | |
| **21** | **(a)** If this is a defined benefit plan is it subject to the minimum funding standards for this plan year? . . . . . | | |
| | If "Yes," attach Schedule B (Form 5500). | | |
| | **(b)** If this is a defined contribution plan, i.e., money purchase or target benefit, is it subject to the minimum funding standards? (If a waiver was granted, see instructions.) . . . . . . . . . . . . . . . | | |
| | If "Yes," complete (i), (ii) and (iii) below: | | |
| | 　*(i)* Amount of employer contribution required for the plan year under Code section 412 . . . . | | |
| | 　*(ii)* Amount of contribution paid by the employer for the plan year . . . . . . . . . | | |
| | 　　Enter date of last payment by employer . . . ▶ Month _____ Day _____ Year _____ | | |
| | 　*(iii)* If (i) is greater than (ii), subtract (ii) from (i) and enter the funding deficiency here; otherwise enter zero. (If you have a funding deficiency, file Form 5330.) . . . . . . . . . . . . . . | | |
| **22** | The following questions relate to the plan year. If (a)(i), (ii), (iii), (iv) or (v) is checked "Yes," schedules of those items in the format set forth in the instructions are required to be attached to this form. | Yes | No |
| | **(a)** *(i)* Did the plan have assets held for investment? . . . . . . . . . . . . . . . | | |
| | 　*(ii)* Did any non-exempt transaction involving plan assets involve a party known to be a party-in-interest? . . | | |
| | 　*(iii)* Were any loans by the plan or fixed income obligations due the plan in default as of the close of the plan year or classified during the year as uncollectable? . . . . . . . . . . . . . . . | | |
| | 　*(iv)* Were any leases to which the plan was a party in default or classified during the year as uncollectable? . . | | |
| | 　*(v)* Were any plan transactions or series of transactions in excess of 3% of the current value of plan assets? . | | |

**22** *(Continued)*

**(b)** The accountant's opinion is *(i)* ☐ Required, or *(ii)* ☐ Not required

**(c)** If the accountant's opinion is required attach it to this form and check the appropriate box. This opinion is:

    *(i)*   ☐  Unqualified

    *(ii)*  ☐  Qualified

    *(iii)* ☐  Adverse

    *(iv)* ☐  Other (explain)

**23** Is the plan covered under the Pension Benefit Guaranty Corporation termination insurance

program? . . . . . . . . . . . . . . . . . . . . . . . . . . . . ☐ Yes    ☐ No    ☐ Not determined

If "Yes," list employer identification number(s) and/or plan number(s) used in any filing with PBGC if the number was different from the numbers listed in item 1(b) or 5(c) ▶ --------------------------------------------------------------------------------------

---

**If additional space is required for any item, attach additional sheets the same size as this form.**

---

☆ U.S. GOVERNMENT PRINTING OFFICE : 1981—O—343-194     E.I. #52-1074467

Refer to footnotes for Form IVA 1.02 and Forms IVA 1.06 and 1.07.

| Form **5500-C** | **Return/Report of Employee Benefit Plan** | OMB No. 1210-0016 |
|---|---|---|

Department of the Treasury
Internal Revenue Service

Department of Labor
Pension and Welfare Benefit Programs

Pension Benefit Guaranty Corporation

**(With fewer than 100 participants)**
This form is required to be filed under sections 104 and 4065 of the Employee Retirement Income Security Act of 1974 and sections 6057(b) and 6058(a) of the Internal Revenue Code, referred to as the Code. **Caution: There is a penalty for late filing of this return/report.**

**19**

**This Form is Open to Public Inspection**

For the calendar plan year 19 ___ or fiscal plan year beginning _____ , 19 ___ , and ending _____ , 19 ___ .

**Type or print in ink all entries on the form, schedules, and attachments. If an item does not apply, enter "N/A". File the originals.**

This return/report is: (i) ☐ the return/report filed for the plan's first plan year; (ii) ☐ an amended return/report; or (iii) ☐ the final return/report filed for the plan.

▶ File this form for 1981 if the last digit of the plan sponsor's employer identification number is 4, 5, or 6. This form should also be filed for the initial plan year and for the final plan year (sponsors with other EIN's, see instructions).

▶ Do not file this form for Keogh (H.R. 10) plans with fewer than 100 participants and with at least one owner-employee participant. File Form 5500-K instead.

▶ Pension benefit plans, unless otherwise excepted, complete all items. Annuity and custodial account arrangements of certain exempt organizations, and individual retirement account trusts of employers, complete only items 1 through 6, 9, and 10.

▶ Certain welfare benefit plans are not required to file this form—see instructions. Welfare benefit plans required to file this form do not complete items 7(b), 12, 14 and 24 through 28.

▶ If you have been granted an extension of time to file this form, you must attach a copy of the approved extension to this form.

**Use IRS label. Otherwise, please print or type.**

**1 (a)** Name of plan sponsor (employer, if for a single employer plan)

Address (number and street)

City or town, State and ZIP code

**1 (b)** Employer identification number

**1 (c)** Telephone number of sponsor ( )

**1 (d)** If plan year changed since last return/report, check here ▶ ☐

**2 (a)** Name of plan administrator (if same as plan sponsor enter "Same")

Address (number and street)

City or town, State and ZIP code

**1 (e)** Business code number

**2 (b)** Administrator's employer identification no.

**2 (c)** Telephone number of administrator ( )

**3** Name, address and identification number of plan sponsor and/or plan administrator as they appeared on the last return/report filed for this plan, if not the same as in 1 or 2 above: **(a)** Sponsor ▶ ..........................................
**(b)** Administrator ▶

**4** Check box to indicate the type of plan entity (check only one box):
**(a)** ☐ Single-employer plan
**(b)** ☐ Plan of controlled group of corporations or common control employers
**(c)** ☐ Multiemployer plan
**(d)** ☐ Multiple-employer-collectively-bargained plan
**(e)** ☐ Multiple-employer plan (other)

**5 (a)** (i) Name of plan ▶ ..........................................

(ii) ☐ Check if name of plan changed since the last return/report.

**5 (b)** Effective date of plan

**5 (c)** Enter three digit plan number ▶

**6** Check at least one item in (a) or (b) and applicable items in (c): **(a)** Welfare benefit plan:
(i) ☐ Health insurance
(ii) ☐ Life insurance
(iii) ☐ Supplemental unemployment
(iv) ☐ Other (specify) ▶ ...............

**(b)** Pension benefit plan: (i) Defined benefit plan—(Indicate type of defined benefit plan below):
(A) ☐ Fixed benefit
(B) ☐ Unit benefit
(C) ☐ Flat benefit
(D) ☐ Other (specify) ▶ ...............

(ii) Defined contribution plan—(Indicate type of defined contribution plan below):
(A) ☐ Profit-sharing
(B) ☐ Stock bonus
(C) ☐ Target benefit
(D) ☐ Other money purchase
(E) ☐ Other (specify) ▶

(iii) ☐ Defined benefit plan with benefits based partly on balance of separate account of participant (Code section 414(k))
(iv) ☐ Annuity arrangement of a certain exempt organization (Code section 403(b)(1))
(v) ☐ Custodial account for regulated investment company stock (Code section 403(b)(7))
(vi) ☐ Trust treated as an individual retirement account (Code section 408(c))
(vii) ☐ Other (specify) ▶

Under penalties of perjury and other penalties set forth in the instructions, I declare that I have examined this report, including accompanying schedules and statements, and to the best of my knowledge and belief it is true, correct, and complete.

Date ▶ ..................... Signature of employer/plan sponsor ▶ ..........................................

Date ▶ ..................... Signature of plan administrator ▶ ..........................................

**For Paperwork Reduction Act Notice, see page 1 of the Instructions.**

**6 (c)** Other plan features:     *(i)* ☐ Thrift-savings     *(ii)* ☐ Keogh (H.R. 10) plan

    *(iii)* ☐ Pension plans maintained outside the United States (see instructions)     *(iv)* ☐ Participant-directed account plan

    *(v)* ☐ Master trust (see instructions) ▶ ..........................................................................................................................

**(d)** Single employer plans enter the tax year end of the employer in which this plan year ends ▶ Month ........ Day ........ Year ........

**(e)** Is this a plan of an affiliated service group? . . . . . . . . . . . . . . . . . . . . . ☐ Yes ☐ No

|  |  | Yes | No |
|---|---|---|---|
| **7 (a)** Total participants *(i)* Beginning of plan year ▶...................... *(ii)* End of plan year ▶...................... | | | |
| **(b)** *(i)* During this plan year or the prior plan year, was any pension benefit plan participant(s) separated from service with a deferred vested benefit for which a Schedule SSA (Form 5500) is required to be attached? . . | | | |
| *(ii)* If "Yes," enter the number of separated participants required to be reported . . . . ▶ | | | |
| **8** Plan amendment information (welfare plans do NOT complete (b)(ii)): | | | |
| **(a)** Were any plan amendments to this plan adopted since the end of the plan year covered by the last return/report Form 5500, 5500–C or 5500–K which was filed for this plan? . . . . . . . . . . | | | |
| **(b)** If "Yes," *(i)* And if any amendments have resulted in a change in the information contained in a summary plan description or previously furnished summary description of modifications: | | | |
|     (A) Have summary descriptions of the changes been sent to participants? . . . . . . . . | | | |
|     (B) Have summary descriptions of the changes been filed with DOL? . . . . . . . . . | | | |
| *(ii)* Does any such amendment result in the reduction of the accrued benefit of any participant under the plan? . | | | |
| **(c)** Enter the date the most recent amendment was adopted . . ▶ Month............ Day............ Year............ | | | |
| **(d)** *(i)* Has a summary plan description been filed with DOL for this plan? . . . . . . . . . | | | |
| *(ii)* If (i) is "Yes," what was the employer identification number and the plan number used to identify it? Employer identification number ▶      Plan number ▶ | | | |
| **9** Plan termination information: | | | |
| **(a)** Was this plan terminated during this plan year or any prior plan year? . . . . . . . . . | | | |
| **(b)** If "Yes," were all trust assets distributed to participants or beneficiaries or transferred to another plan? . . . | | | |
| **(c)** If item 12 is to be checked "Yes," and 9(a) is "Yes," has a notice of intent to terminate been filed with PBGC? . | | | |
| **10 (a)** Was this plan merged or consolidated into another plan, or were assets or liabilities transferred to another plan since the end of the plan year covered by the last return/report Form 5500, 5500–C or 5500–K which was filed for this plan? . . . . . . . . . . . . . . . . . . . . . . . . . . | | | |

If "Yes," identify other plan(s):

| **(c)** Employer identification number(s) | **(d)** Plan number(s) |
|---|---|
| **(b)** Name of plan(s) ▶ | | |

**(e)** Has Form 5310 been filed? . . . . . . . . . . . . . . . . . . . . . . ☐ Yes ☐ No

**11** Indicate funding arrangement:

    **(a)** ☐ Trust   **(b)** ☐ Fully insured   **(c)** ☐ Combination   **(d)** ☐ Other (specify) ▶ ..................................................

    **(e)** If (b) or (c) is checked, enter the number of Schedules A (Form 5500) which are attached . . . . ▶

**12** Is the plan covered under the Pension Benefit Guaranty Corporation termination insurance program? . . . ☐ Yes ☐ No ☐ Not determined

If "Yes," or "Not determined," list the employer identification number and/or plan number used in any filing with PBGC if the number was different from the numbers listed in item 1(b) or 5(c) ▶ ..............................................................

|  | Yes | No |
|---|---|---|
| **13** Complete both (a) and (b): | | |
| **(a)** Is the plan insured by a fidelity bond? . . . . . . . . . . . . . . . . . . | | |
| *(i)* If "Yes," enter name of surety company ▶ | | |
| *(ii)* Amount of bond coverage ▶ | | |
| **(b)** Was any loss discovered since the last return/report Form 5500, 5500–C or 5500–K was filed for this plan? . . | | |
| **14 (a)** If this is a defined benefit plan, is it subject to the minimum funding standards for this plan year? . . . . . If "Yes," attach Schedule B (Form 5500). | | |
| **(b)** If this is a defined contribution plan, i.e., money purchase or target benefit, is it subject to the minimum funding standards (if a waiver was granted, see instructions)? . . . . . . . . . . . | | |
| If "Yes," complete (i), (ii) and (iii) below: | | |
| *(i)* Amount of employer contribution required for the plan year . . . . . . . $ | | |
| *(ii)* Amount of contribution paid by the employer for the plan year . . . . . . $ | | |
| Enter date of last payment by employer ▶ Month............ Day............ Year............ | | |
| *(iii)* If (i) is greater than (ii) subtract (ii) from (i) and enter the funding deficiency here. Otherwise enter zero. (If you have a funding deficiency, file Form 5330.) . $ | | |

Refer to footnotes for Form IVA 1.02 and Forms IVA 1.06 and 1.07.

| Form **5500-R**<br>Department of the Treasury<br>Internal Revenue Service<br><br>Department of Labor<br>Pension and Welfare Benefit Programs<br><br>Pension Benefit Guaranty Corporation | **Registration Statement of Employee Benefit Plan**<br>**(With fewer than 100 participants)**<br>This form is required to be filed under sections 104 and 4065 of the Employee Retirement Income Security Act of 1974 and section 6058 of the Internal Revenue Code. Caution: There is a penalty for late filing of this return/report. | OMB No. 1210-0016<br>**1981** Amended ☐<br>**This Form is Open to Public Inspection** |
|---|---|---|

For the calendar plan year 1981 or fiscal plan year beginning                    , 1981, and ending                    , 19    .

▶ File this form for the plan years that Form 5500-C or Form 5500-K is not required to be filed. (See instruction B.) Do NOT file this form for the plan's first year or for the plan's final return/report. Instead file applicable Form 5500-C or Form 5500-K.

▶ If you have been granted an extension of time to file this form, you must attach a copy of the approved extension to this form.
▶ Type or complete in ink and file the original. If any item does not apply, enter "N/A."

| Use IRS label. Otherwise, please print or type. | **1 (a)** Name of plan sponsor (employer, if for a single employer plan) | **1 (b)** Employer identification number |
|---|---|---|
| | Address (number and street) | **1 (c)** Sponsor's telephone number ( ) |
| | City or town, State and ZIP code | **1 (d)** This form is filed instead of ☐ 5500-C ☐ 5500-K |
| | **2 (a)** Name of plan administrator (if same as plan sponsor, enter "Same") | **1 (e)** If plan year changed since last return/report, check here ☐ |
| | Address (number and street) | **2 (b)** Administrator's employer identification no. |
| | City or town, State and ZIP code | **2 (c)** Administrator's telephone number ( ) |

**3** Name, address, and employer identification number of plan sponsor and/or plan administrator as shown on the latest return/report filed for this plan, if different from 1 or 2 above: **(a)** Sponsor ▶ ----------------------------------------------------------------------------------
**(b)** Administrator ▶ ----------------------------------------------------------------------------------

| **4 (a)** (i) Name of plan ▶ ---------------------------------------- | **4 (b)** Effective date of plan ▶ |
|---|---|
| (ii) ☐ Check if name of plan changed since last return/report. | **4 (c)** Enter three digit plan number ▶ |

**5** Type of plan:
(a) ☐ Defined benefit
(b) ☐ Defined contribution (money purchase or profit-sharing)
(c) ☐ Welfare benefit
(d) ☐ Other (specify) ▶

**6** Plan information:

| | Yes | No |
|---|---|---|
| (a) Was this plan terminated during this plan year or any prior plan year? . . . . . . . . . . . . . | | |
| (b) If (a) is "Yes," were all trust assets distributed to participants or beneficiaries, or transferred to another plan? . | | |
| (c) Was this plan amended during this plan year to reduce any participant's accrued benefits? . . . . . . . | | |
| (d) If this is a defined benefit plan or a defined contribution plan subject to the minimum funding standards, has the plan experienced a funding deficiency for this plan year (defined benefit plans, attach Schedule B (Form 5500))? . . . . . . . . . . . . . . . . . . . . . . . . . . . . . | | |
| (e) If (d) is "Yes," have you filed Form 5330 to pay the excise tax? . . . . . . . . . . . . . . . | | |
| (f) Is this plan covered under the Pension Benefit Guaranty Corporation termination insurance program? . . . . . . . . . . . . ☐ Yes ☐ No ☐ Not determined | ░░░ | ░░░ |
| (g) If 6(a) is "Yes" and this plan is covered under PBGC termination insurance program, has a notice of intent to terminate been filed? . . . . . . . . . . . . . . . . . . . . . . . . . . | | |
| (h) Total participants:<br>(i) Beginning of plan year . . . . . . . . . . . . . . . . . ▶ ----------------<br>(ii) End of plan year . . . . . . . . . . . . . . . . . . . ▶ ----------------<br>See back of form for additional questions. | ░░░ | |

Under penalties of perjury and other penalties set forth in the instructions, I declare that I have examined this report, including accompanying schedules and statements, and to the best of my knowledge and belief it is true, correct and complete.

Date ▶ ----------------------  Signature of employer/plan sponsor ▶ ----------------------------------------------------------------------------------

Date ▶ ----------------------  Signature of plan administrator ▶ ----------------------------------------------------------------------------------

For Paperwork Reduction Act Notice, see page 1 of Form 5500-C or Form 5500-K instructions.

| | Yes | No |
|---|---|---|
| **6 (con't)** | | |
| **(i)** If plan benefits were provided by an insurance company, insurance service or similar organization, enter the number of Schedules A (Form 5500) attached . . . . . . . . . . . ▶ | | |
| **(j)** *(i)* During this plan year or the prior plan year, was any participant(s) separated from service with a deferred vested benefit for which a Schedule SSA (Form 5500) is required to be attached? . . . . . . . . . | | |
| *(ii)* If "Yes," enter the number of separated participants required to be reported ▶ | | |
| **7** Fiduciary information during this plan year: | | |
| **(a)** Did any plan fiduciary who is an officer or employee of the plan sponsor receive compensation from the plan for his or her services to the plan? . . . . . . . . . . . . . . . . . . . . . . . | | |
| **(b)** Did the plan acquire any qualifying employer security or qualifying employer real property, when immediately after such acquisition the aggregate fair market value of employer securities and employer real property held by the plan exceeded 10% of the fair market value of the plan assets? . . . . . . . . . . . . . | | |
| **(c)** Did the plan receive any non-cash contributions? . . . . . . . . . . . . . | | |
| **(d)** Has any plan fiduciary had either a financial interest worth more than $1,000 in any party providing services to the plan or received anything of value from any party providing services to the plan? . . . . . . . . | | |
| **(e)** Has any employer owed the plan contributions which were more than three months past due under the terms of the plan? . . . . . . . . . . . . . . . . . . . . . . . . . . . | | |
| **(f)** Were any loans the plan made or fixed income obligations due the plan in default as of the end of the plan year, or classified as uncollectable? . . . . . . . . . . . . . . . . . . . . . . | | |
| **(g)** Were any leases to which the plan was a party in default or classified as uncollectable? . . . . . . . . | | |
| **(h)** Party-in-interest information: | | |
| *(i)* Did the plan lend assets to, borrow from, or guarantee any indebtedness of a party-in-interest? . . . . | | |
| *(ii)* Has the plan purchased any assets from or sold any assets to a party-in-interest? . . . . . . . . . | | |
| *(iii)* Has the plan leased property to or from a party-in-interest? . . . . . . . . . . . . . . . | | |

Refer to footnotes for Form IVA 1.02 and Forms IVA 1.06 and 1.07.

## FORM IVA 1.06

### (Nonqualified [nonstatutory] stock option plan with stock appreciation rights [SAR] for key employees in a close corporation)

### DOE & ROE ADVERTISING, INC.
### KEY EMPLOYEE STOCK OPTION PLAN[1]

This Key Employee Stock Option Plan (herein called the "Plan") of Doe & Roe Advertising, Inc. (herein called the "Agency"), has been adopted by the shareholders of the Agency for the purpose of attracting and retaining competent account executives and officers of the Agency and to provide such key executive personnel with an opportunity to participate in the increased value of the Agency that their effort, initiative, and skill have helped and will continue to help produce.

1. *Administration of the Plan.*

(a) The Plan shall be administered by a Committee that shall consist of three (3) directors appointed by the Board of Directors of the Agency. Any vacancy in the Committee shall be filled by another appointment by the Board.

(b) Members of the Committee shall not be eligible to participate in the Plan while serving on the Committee.

(c) The Committee shall have full and sole power to construe and interpret the Plan as herein established or as amended from time to time by the Board of Directors of the Agency.

(d) No member of the Committee shall be liable for any action or determination in respect to the Plan, if made in good faith. The Company shall indemnify and save harmless each member of the Committee from any legal action arising out of the member's service on the Committee, except for the member's gross negligence or willful neglect.

(e) Options to purchase the stock designated by the Board of Directors under Paragraph 3 shall be granted for the option price provided in Paragraph 4 to such Key Employees and upon such terms and conditions, including stock appreciation rights (SAR) as described in Paragraph 7, as the Committee, in its sole discretion, may prescribe during the year following the designation of stock. A Key Employee is a full-time employee of the Agency who holds the title of Account Executive and Vice-President.

(f) After granting an option to a Key Employee under (e) above, the Committee shall cause the employee to be notified in writing of the grant of the option.

(g) At least thirty (30) days before the regular annual meeting of the Board of Directors, the Committee shall submit a written report to the Board of Directors giving the following information:

(1) Names of Key Employees to whom options were granted during the preceding year.

(2) The number of shares covered by each option.

(3) The applicable option price and terms for each employee, including the number of stock appreciation rights given in each case.

2. *Employee eligibility.* Key personnel, as defined in Paragraph 1(e), shall be eligible to participate in the Plan.

3. *Stock subject to the Plan.*

(a) The Board of Directors of the Agency shall annually determine and designate the number of shares of the Company's One-Dollar ($1) par value common stock that shall be subject to the options provided by the Plan and shall determine its book value on the date of such designation.

(b) Shares for which no option is granted by the Committee or shares that were subject to any option, with or without stock appreciation rights, that ceases to be exercisable under the Plan or otherwise, shall not be available for granting further options, unless that stock is included in the next annual designation of stock by the Board of Directors pursuant to (a) of this Paragraph.

4. *Option price.* The price at which the Committee may grant options under the Plan is the book value of the stock as determined by the Board of Directors on the date of the designation of the stock by the Board of Directors under Paragraph 3, plus Ten Percent (10%) of that book value.

5. *Exercise of option by employee.* The right to purchase the shares covered by the option granted to the employee, of which he is notified pursuant to Paragraph 1(f), shall be exercisable in whole or in part in installments, cumulative or otherwise, only for any period or periods of time specified by the Committee at the time of the grant or subsequent thereto. Said time shall not be less than six (6) months nor more than ten (10) years from the date of the grant of the option.

6. *Termination of option.*

(a) In the event that an optionee's employment with the Company shall be terminated by the Company for cause, each option he has and all rights and obligations thereunder shall immediately terminate, except that any installment payments made by the optionee toward the uncompleted exercise of an option shall be refunded by the Company within thirty (30) days of such termination for cause.

(b) In the event that an optionee's employment with the Company shall terminate as a result of normal retirement, total disability, or early retirement under the terms of a retirement or pension plan maintained by the Company and in which that optionee is a participant, the existing option may be exercised by full payment of the option price within three (3) months of the date the employment terminates but not thereafter, regardless of the time and manner specified in the original grant.

(c) In the event that an optionee's employment ceases by reason of his death, the existing option may be exercised by full payment of the option price by the personal representative of his estate within six (6) months of the date of the optionee's death.

7. *Stock appreciation rights.*

(a) *Definition of stock appreciation right.* The term "stock appreciation right" (herein called SAR), as used in this Plan, means the right of an optionee under this Plan to receive as part of a Related Option the excess of book value plus Ten Percent (10%) of a share of the Company's common stock on the date on which an SAR is exercised over the option price provided for in the original grant of the Related Option. An SAR under this Plan is issued in consideration of services performed for the Company or for its benefit by the optionee.

(b) *Grant of SAR.* A stock appreciation right under this Plan may be granted for the Company under this Plan only in connection with an option right granted under this Plan (herein called "Related Option"). The terms and conditions of an SAR granted with a Related Option under this Plan shall be determined by the Committee in its sole discretion.

(c) *Exercise of SAR.* A stock appreciation right under this Plan shall be exercisable by the optionee at any time the Related Option could be exercised and in the manner prescribed by the Committee.

(d) *Payment of SAR.* The Committee may cause the SAR to be paid in cash or in additional stock of the Company or any combination of cash and shares, in the Committee's sole discretion.

(e) *Termination of SAR.* A stock appreciation right under this Plan shall terminate at the time of the termination of the Related Option.

(f) *Transferability of SAR.* A stock appreciation right under this Plan cannot be transferred by the optionee having the Related Option except by will or the state laws of descent and distribution as provided herein.

8. *Amendment, suspension, or termination of the Plan.*

(a) The Board of Directors of the Company may at any time suspend or terminate the Plan and may amend it from time to time in such respects as the Board may, in its sole discretion, deem advisable in order that the SAR and Related Options granted or to be granted under this Plan shall conform to any change in the law or be necessary for the best interests of the Company.

(b) No amendment, suspension, or termination of the Plan shall, without the optionee's written consent, alter or impair any of the rights or obligations under any option or stock appreciation rights granted to him before such amendment, suspension, or termination.

9. *Effective date of the Plan.* The Plan shall become effective on February 1, 1983.

10. *Duration of the Plan.* Unless this Plan shall have been earlier terminated by the Board of Directors pursuant to Paragraph 8, this Plan shall terminate on January 31, 1993, except as to stock options and stock appreciation rights granted and outstanding under this Plan before that date. Dated November 10, 1982.

(SEAL)                                    DOE & ROE ADVERTISING, INC.

                                          By _____
_____
Secretary of the Corporation                    President

[1]26 U.S.C.A. 83 and 15 U.S.C.A. 78(p). *33 Am. Jur. 2d Federal Taxation,* paras. 3380–3390 and 3820. May be used in addition to an Incentive Stock Option Plan (ISO) where the ISO might otherwise exceed the value limit of $100,000 prescribed by the IRC. For incentive stock option plans for key employees under ERTA of 1981, see 26 U.S.C.A. 320 and 422A (Section 251 ERTA). See also 26 U.S.C.A. 162 and 212 for employer deductions. See also 26 U.S.C.A. 421–425 for *former* "qualified" stock option plans. See 26 U.S.C.A. 422A and temporary regulations for election to treat a former qualified plan as an ISO and creating a new ISO.

**FORM IVA 1.07**

(Cash or deferred payment of profits at employee's election—
employer contributions only—immediate voting—loan provision—
no insurance annuity provision)

**PROFIT-SHARING PLAN AND TRUST[1]
OF
ACME ADVERTISING, INC.**

THIS AGREEMENT made September 30, 1982, between ACME ADVERTISING, INC., an Ohio corporation (herein called the "Company"), and Richard Just and Peter Poe (herein collectively called "Trustee"), WITNESSETH,

WHEREAS, the Company desires to promote in its employees a substantial and loyal interest in the successful operation of the business of the Company and to give its employees certain rights and privileges whereby they will share in the prosperity of the Company's business; and

WHEREAS, the Company, by Action in Lieu of Meeting signed by all the directors of the corporation dated September 1, 1982, approved and adopted the following plan, which is intended to comply with the requirements for a qualified employee benefit plan as set forth in Sections 401 et seq. of the Internal Revenue Code; and

WHEREAS, the Company has paid to the Trustee in trust hereunder the sum of Five Hundred Dollars ($500) as the Company's initial contribution to the Profit-Sharing Trust hereby created;

IT IS AGREED between the Company and the Trustee as follows:

1. *Consideration.* The consideration for this Agreement is the mutual promises and covenants provided herein.

2. *Duration.* The Trust shall become effective on December 1, 1982, and shall continue until terminated as provided herein.

3. *Name.* The Trust shall be known as the Acme Advertising, Inc., Profit-Sharing Trust (herein called "Trust").

4. *Purpose.* The Trust is created for the sole purpose of enabling eligible employees of the Company to share in the profits of the Company's business as provided herein, and the principal and income of the Trust shall not be used for any purpose other than for the exclusive benefit of the eligible employees and their beneficiaries as provided herein.

5. *No reversion to Company.* The Company has no beneficial interest in the Trust, and no part of the Trust fund shall ever revert or be repaid to the Company, directly or indirectly, except that if the Internal Revenue Service determines that the Plan or a yearly contribution to the Plan does not meet the requirements of I.R.C. Section 401, as amended, any assets contributed by the Company to the Trust that fail to qualify under the Code requirement shall be returned to the Company.

6. *Employee eligibility to participate.* Each employee of the Company shall become eligible to participate in the Plan on the Entry Date next following the completion of One Thousand (1,000) Hours of Service after employment or recommencement of employment after a One-Year Break in Service, and shall participate during each Plan Year ending on or subsequent to that Entry Date, provided that in any such Plan Year that employee completes not less than One Thousand (1,000) Hours of Service.

7. *Contributions by Company only.*

(a) Not later than the time prescribed by law for filing its federal income tax return for its current taxable year and for each succeeding taxable year, the Company shall contribute to the Trustee, as its contribution to the Trust pursuant to the Plan for the Plan Year that is coterminous with that taxable year of the Company, an amount or amounts equal to Five Percent (5%) of its net profit for that year.

(b) For the purpose of determining net profit of the Company, the net profit of the Company shall consist of operating profits, exclusive of extraordinary losses arising from the sale, exchange, or other disposition of assets not acquired for resale, and of carryforwards or carrybacks of losses, prior to (a) deduction for contribution to this Plan or other qualified retirement plan(s) maintained by the Company, and (b) the accrual or payment of federal, state, and local income taxes.

(c) The Company shall determine by resolution of its Board of Directors and communicate to the Trustee before the close of each Plan Year the amount in dollars that represents the Five Percent (5%) of net profits to be contributed to the Trust.

(d) The Company alone shall determine the amount of the contribution, and in making such determination, it shall be entitled to rely on statements or estimates prepared by it or by an independent public accountant on the basis of the Company's records at the time of the determination.

(e) The Trustee shall have no duty to inquire into the correctness of the amounts contributed and paid over to the Trustee; nor shall the Trustee or any other person have any duty to enforce the payment of the contributions provided herein.

(f) The Company may make such contributions in cash or in kind at the fair market value at the time of the contribution.

(g) Nothing in this Agreement shall entitle any Trustee, Participating Employee, or beneficiary to inquire into or demand the right to inspect the books or records of the Company.

8. *Election of employee to receive cash distribution.*

(a) Subject to the further provisions of this Paragraph, each Participant shall be given the opportunity to elect to receive, in cash, an amount equivalent to the portion of the Company's contribution for any year that would otherwise have been allocated to such person as provided herein. The Company shall notify each Participant, not later than May 15 of the relevant fiscal year of the Company, of the amount allocable for such year to such Participant. Thereafter, but prior to May 31 of that year, each Participant who elects to receive a cash distribution shall notify the Trustee, in writing, of that election. Said distribution of cash shall be made by the Company contemporaneously with its delivery to the Trustee of its contribution to the Plan for such year.

(b) *Nondiscrimination rule.* Notwithstanding the foregoing, the Trustee shall retain the right, as and to the extent that they in their discretion deem necessary or appropriate, to limit cash distributions to any "highly compensated employee" of the Company. (For this purpose, "highly compensated employee" shall mean any employee who is more highly compensated than two-thirds of all eligible employees, taking into account the total compensation of each employee). The said retained right of the Trustee shall be exercised, if at all, in a manner that is not discriminatory, and to that end Participants in like circumstances shall be treated alike as far as may be practicable under the circumstances. Moreover, said right shall be exercised only for the purpose of and to the extent necessary to assure the compliance by the Plan, for each Plan Year, with at least one of the following tests:

(1) The actual deferral percentage for the highly compensated employees, as a group, is not more than the actual deferral percentage of all other eligible employees multiplied by 1.5.

(2) The excess of the actual deferral percentage for the group of highly compensated employees over that of all other eligible employees is not more than three percentage points, and the actual deferral percentage for the group of highly compensated employees is not more than the actual deferral percentage of all other eligible employees multiplied by 2.5.

For purposes of applying the foregoing provisions, "actual deferral percentage" shall have the meaning set forth at Section 401(k)(3)(B) of the 1954 Internal Revenue Code. Moreover, the Plan shall in all respects be interpreted and operated in a manner as to comply with the provisions of Section 401(k) of the 1954 Internal Revenue Code, and with Treasury Regulations issued from time to time thereunder, and with the comparable provision of any subsequently enacted Internal Revenue Code.

9. *Allocation of benefits.*

*(a) Separate accounts for each participating employee.* The Trustee shall maintain a separate account in the name of each Participating Employee and each Beneficiary having a share in the Trust.

(b) *Allocation of income and expenses to participating employee accounts.* As of the last day of each Plan Year, all income of the Trust and all losses and expenses of the Trust shall be allocated and credited or charged to each Participant's separate account in the proportion that the value of the account bears to all other present accounts.

(c) *Allocation of Company's current contribution.*

(1) *Pro rata share.* As of the date the Company's current contribution is made to the Trustee, the Trustee shall credit to the account of each employee eligible to participate under this Agreement, and who did not elect a cash distribution pursuant to Paragraph 8, a sum for each that shall bear the same ratio to the total thereof as the employee's Considered Compensation for that year shall bear to the aggregate of the Considered Compensation of all the employees listed by the Company in accordance with Paragraph 9(e).

(2) *Termination of employment after close of Plan Year.* In the case of a Participating Employee who is entitled to have credited to his account a portion of the Company contribu-

tion for such year but whose employment is terminated after the close of such year and before such contribution has been made to the Trust, such amount shall be paid to the Trustee, who shall credit the payment to the Participating Employee's account as though employment had not terminated.

(3) *Limitation on annual additions.* Notwithstanding any other provision of the Plan, the aggregate annual addition to the account of any Participating Employee, including accounts established under this Plan and under any other defined contribution plan or plans maintained by the Company, shall not exceed the lesser of Twenty-five Thousand Dollars ($25,000) (or such higher amount prescribed by regulations pursuant to Section 415[d] of the Internal Revenue Code to reflect increases in the cost of living) or Twenty-five Percent (25%) of such Participating Employee's Considered Compensation for the year.

(4) *Allocation of forfeitures.* There shall be no forfeitures under this plan.

(d) *Revaluation of Participating Employee accounts.* As of the last day of each Plan Year, the Trustee shall revalue each of the Participating Employee accounts to reflect any proportionate increase or decrease in fair market value of the assets of the Trust on that date.

(e) *List of Participating Employees.* On or before the last day of each Plan Year, the Company shall deliver to the Trustee a list of all employees eligible on such date to participate in the Plan, together with a statement of the amount of Considered Compensation paid to each employee during the preceding Plan Year.

10. *Payment of benefits.* The Trustee shall pay benefits to which a Participant is entitled under the Plan to the employee, his designee in writing, or to his estate within sixty (60) days after the latest to occur of any one of the following events; upon certificate of the fact and written direction of the Company:

(a) Employee Participant reaches the age of sixty-five (65) years, upon production of birth certificate or its equivalent.

(b) Employee Participant has been a participant in the Plan for ten (10) years.

(c) The termination of the Employee Participant's employment.

11. *Form of payment.*

(a) The amount payable to a Participating Employee or his designated beneficiary may be paid in monthly installments or in a lump sum, as requested by the Participating Employee or his beneficiary in writing to the Trustee within sixty (60) days of the date on which he becomes eligible for payment.

(b) If no preference is expressed by the employee pursuant to (a), the Trustee may determine the method of payment in its sole discretion.

(c) In any event, the Trustee, in its sole discretion, may make payment in cash or in kind at the present market value.

(d) *No guarantee of interests.* Neither the Company nor the Trustee guarantees the Trust fund from loss or depreciation, nor do they guarantee payment to any person. The liability of the Trustee and the Company to make payments hereunder is limited to the available assets of the Trust fund.

12. *Loans to Participating Employees.* The Trustee shall have the power to make loans from the Trust to any Participating Employee in cases of employee need as found by the Trustee in its sole discretion exercised in a consistent and fair manner. No loan shall exceed Eighty-five Percent (85%) of the value of the Participating Employee's account at the time as if his employment were being terminated at the time and less any other indebtedness of the employee to the Trust. The interest on the loan shall be at the rate prevailing in the Dayton, Ohio, area for commercial bank consumer loans.

13. *Trustee's powers and duties.*

(a) The Trustee shall administer the Plan for the benefit of all Participating Employees and their beneficiaries as herein provided, without discrimination in favor of one or some Participating Employees or their beneficiaries.

(b) The Trustee shall have the right to rely upon information or instructions received from the Company in writing and shall be under no duty or responsibility to inquire into any acts or omissions of the Company. The Trustee shall interpret and act under this Plan as written herein in its sole discretion. Mistakes of fact shall be corrected when they appear to have been made, and reasonable adjustment shall be made in the account of Participating Employee. In any event, the Trustee shall be indemnified and held harmless by the Company for any liability hereunder except for fraud or gross negligence.

(c) The Trustee shall have the right to retain, manage, improve, repair, operate, and control any assets of the Trust fund, without any court order.

(d) To purchase, to sell, to convey, transfer, exchange, partition, grant options with respect to, lease for any term, including a lease for a term that extends beyond the duration of the Trust, mortgage, pledge or otherwise deal with or dispose of any asset of the Trust fund in such manner, for such consideration, and upon such terms and conditions as the Trustee, in its sole discretion, shall determine subject to the provisions of Sections 404 and 406 of ERISA.

(e) To settle, compromise, or abandon all claims in favor of or against the Trust fund.

(f) To borrow money for the Trust fund from anyone other than a "party in interest" as defined in Section 3(14) of ERISA, with or without giving security from the Trust fund.

(g) The net income and profits of the Trust fund shall be accumulated, added to the principal of the Trust fund, and invested and reinvested therewith as a single fund.

(h) The Trustee may, in its sole discretion, hold in cash such portion of the Trust fund as shall be reasonable under the circumstances pending investment or payment of expenses or distribution of benefits.

(i) The Trustee may consult with legal counsel who may also be legal counsel for the Company in respect to any of its rights, duties, or obligations hereunder; and may employ such agents and financial or other counsel as may be reasonably necessary to collect, manage, administer, invest, distribute, and protect the Trust fund and to pay them reasonable compensation from the Trust fund.

(j) The Trustee shall maintain accurate and detailed records and accounts of all transactions of the Plan in accordance with sound accounting principles, which shall be available for audit or inspection at all reasonable times by the Company or any Participating Employee or his beneficiary.

(k) The Trustee shall be reasonably compensated for his services hereunder from time to time as agreed upon between the Trustee and the Company. One-half (½) of the agreed reasonable compensation shall be paid by the Company and one-half (½) from the Trust fund.

(l) The Trustee shall deliver a written report to the Company, as soon as practicable after each fiscal year of the Plan, which report shall show all transactions with respect to the Trust fund during the preceding fiscal year and shall list the assets of the Trust fund with the market value thereof at the time of preparing the report, and such other information as may be necessary to the Company to conform with the requirements of Section 103 of ERISA.

(m) Any Trustee hereunder may be removed by resolution of the Board of Directors of the Company upon delivery to such Trustee of a certified copy of the resolution of removal.

(n) Any Trustee hereunder may resign as Trustee, upon written notice of resignation signed by the resigning Trustee delivered to the Company and the remaining Trustee(s).

(o) In the case of death, disability, or removal of a Trustee, a successor Trustee shall be appointed by the Board of Directors of the Company.

(p) In the event of the death or disability of a Trustee after the Company shall have gone out of business or ceased to exist or been dissolved, voluntarily or involuntarily, or had a receiver or trustee in bankruptcy appointed, a successor Trustee may be appointed by election by a majority in interest of Participating Employees or their beneficiaries then having an interest in the Trust.

(q) No bond shall be required of the Trustee named herein or of any of the Trustee's successors.

14. *Spendthrift clause.* The rights of a Participating Employee or his beneficiary to receive payments or benefits hereunder shall not be subject to alienation or assignment, and shall not be subject to anticipation, encumbrance, or claims of creditors. A distribution by the estate of a deceased Participating Employee or his beneficiary to an heir or legatee of a right to receive payments hereunder shall not be deemed an alienation, assignment, or anticipation for the purposes of this Paragraph 14.

15. *Governing law.* The law of Ohio shall be the controlling state law in all matters relating to the Plan and shall apply to the extent that it is not preempted by the laws of the United States of America.

16. *Modification.* This Plan shall not be modified except by a writing signed by both the Company and the Trustee.

ATTEST:

(SEAL)

ACME ADVERTISING, INC.

By _____

_____
Secretary of the Corporation

---
(Witness)                                    RICHARD JUST, Trustee

---
(Witness)                                    PETER POE, Trustee

[1]26 U.S.C.A. 401–405; 26 C.F.R. 1.401(a)(2)(ii); *33 Am. Jur. 2d Federal Taxation* 3400 et seq. Ref. Form IVA 1.07(a) for alternative provision.

## FORM IVA 1.07(a)

### (Allocation of forfeiture)

### ALTERNATIVE CLAUSE

*Allocation of forfeitures.* Any forfeiture occurring by reason of this agreement shall be allocated by the Trustee to each Participating Employee's account, subject to the Limitation on Annual Additions as provided in Paragraph 9(e)(3), in the proportion that the Participant's Considered Compensation during the latest plan Year ending on or before the date of allocation bears to the total compensation of all participants for that year.

## FORM IVA 1.08

## OREGON SAVINGS LEAGUE
## INDIVIDUAL RETIREMENT ACCOUNT PLAN
## AND TRUST AGREEMENT[1]

THIS AGREEMENT, originally made and entered into this 10th day of February, 1975, and as now amended, between OREGON SAVINGS LEAGUE, an unincorporated association organized under Oregon law, hereinafter referred to as the "League," and the Trustee.

### WITNESSETH:

WHEREAS, certain of the financial institutions who are members of the League wish to make their savings accounts available for the investment of funds contributed by individuals under qualified individual retirement plans established pursuant to Section 408 of the Internal Revenue Code; and

WHEREAS, the League and the Trustee have promulgated this plan for individuals which provides for investment of contributed funds in such savings accounts; and

WHEREAS, the League and its members desire to obtain the Trustee's services as a Trustee of such savings accounts and to maintain certain records incidental thereto; and

WHEREAS, the Trustee is willing and able to perform such services upon the terms and conditions listed herein;

NOW THEREFORE, the Trustee agrees with the League and with all individuals who shall adopt this plan and trust agreement that it shall hold and administer in trust all monies and assets delivered to it as Trustee pursuant to the terms of this master plan and trust agreement and any amendments hereto, as follows:

### ARTICLE I

(1) The Trustee may accept contributions in cash from the Grantor deposited with the participating institutions during a taxable year of the Grantor except as limited by Paragraph 2.

(2) Except in the case of a contribution under Article XII hereof, or a rollover contribution as that term is described in Section 402(a)(5), 402(a)(7), 403(a)(4), 403(b)(8), 403(d)(3) or 409(b)(3)(C) of the Code, or an employer contribution to a simplified employee pension as defined in Section 408 (k), the Trustee will only accept cash and will not accept contributions on behalf of the Grantor in excess of $2,000 for any taxable year of the Grantor.

(3) If this is a simplified employee pension as defined in Section 408(k) the Trustee will only accept cash and will not accept contributions on behalf of the Grantor in excess of 15% of compensation or $15,000, whichever is less, for any taxable year of the Grantor.

### ARTICLE II

The interest of the Grantor in the balance in the trust account shall at all times be nonforfeitable.

### ARTICLE III

No part of the trust funds shall be invested in life insurance contracts; nor may the assets of the trust be commingled with other property except in a common trust fund or a common investment fund (within the meaning of section 408(a)(5) of the Code).

### ARTICLE IV

(1) The entire interest of the Grantor in the trust account must be, or commence to be, distributed before the close of the taxable year in which the Grantor attains age 70½. Not later than the close of such taxable year the Grantor may elect, in a form and at such time as may be acceptable to the Trustee, to have the balance in the trust account distributed in:

(a) a single sum payment,

(b) an annuity contract providing equal or substantially equal monthly, quarterly or annual payments commencing not later than the close of such taxable year over the life of the Grantor,

(c) an annuity contract providing equal or substantially equal monthly, quarterly or annual payments commencing not later than the close of such taxable year over the joint and last survivor lives of the Grantor and his/her spouse.

(d) equal or substantially equal monthly, quarterly or annual payments commencing not later than the close of such taxable year over a period certain not extending beyond the life expectancy of the Grantor, or

(e) equal or substantially equal monthly, quarterly or annual payments commencing not later than the close of such taxable year over a period certain not extending beyond the joint life and last survivor expectancy of the Grantor and his/her spouse.

Notwithstanding that distributions may have commenced pursuant to option (d) or (e), the Grantor may receive a distribution of the balance in the trust account at any time upon written notice to the Trustee. If the Grantor fails to elect any of the methods of distribution described above on or before the close of his/her taxable year in which he/she attains the age of 70½, distribution to the Grantor will be made prior to the close of such taxable year by a single sum payment. If the Grantor elects a mode of distribution under (b) or (c) above, such annuity contract must satisfy the requirements of sections 408(b)(1), (3), (4) and (5) of the Code. If the Grantor elects a mode of distribution under (d) or (e) above, figure the payments made in tax years beginning in the tax year the Grantor reaches age 70½ as follows:

(i) For the minimum annual payment, divide the Grantor's entire interest in the trust at the beginning of each year by the life expectancy of the Grantor (or the joint life and last survivor expectancy of the Grantor and his/her spouse, or the period specified under (d) or (e) (whichever applies)). Determine the life expectancy in either case as of the date the Grantor reaches 70½ minus the number of whole years passed since the Grantor became age 70½.

(ii) For the minimum monthly payment, divide the result in (i) above by 12.

(iii) For the minimum quarterly payment, divide the result in (i) above by 4.

(2) If the Grantor dies before his/her entire interest in the trust is distributed to him/her, or if distribution has been commenced, as provided in (e) above, to his/her surviving spouse and such surviving spouse dies before the entire interest is distributed to such spouse, the entire interest of the remaining undistributed interest shall, within five years after the Grantor's death or the death of the surviving spouse, be distributed in a single sum or be applied to

purchase an immediate annuity for the beneficiary or beneficiaries of the Grantor or his/her surviving spouse. The terms of such annuity shall provide for payments over the life of the beneficiary or beneficiaries or for a term certain not exceeding the life expectancy of such beneficiary or beneficiaries. Any annuity contract so purchased shall be immediately distributed to such beneficiary or beneficiaries. However, no such annuity contract shall be required to be purchased if distributions over a term certain commenced before the death of the Grantor and the term certain is for a period permitted under (d) or (e) above.

(3) If the beneficiary elects to not commence distribution within five years or if the beneficiary commences to make contributions, then the beneficiary may treat the balance of account as an account subject to Code Section 408(a)(6) and regulation 1.4022(b)(6).

### ARTICLE V

Except in the case of the Grantor's death or disability (as defined in Section 72 (m) of the Code) or attainment of age 59½, before distributing an amount from the account, the trustee shall receive from the Grantor a declaration of the Grantor's intention as to the disposition of the amount distributed.

### ARTICLE VI

(1) The Grantor agrees to provide information to the Trustee at such time and in such manner and containing such information as may be necessary for the Trustee to prepare any reports required pursuant to Section 408(i) of the Code and the regulations thereunder.

(2) The Trustee agrees to submit reports to the Internal Revenue Service and the Grantor at such time and in such manner and containing such information as is prescribed by the Internal Revenue Service.

(3) The Trustee shall have no obligation to Grantor to select the term or type of savings account.

### ARTICLE VII

Notwithstanding any other articles which may be added or incorporated, the provisions of Articles I through III and this sentence shall be controlling. Furthermore, any such additional article shall be wholly invalid, if it is inconsistent, in whole or in part, with Section 408(a) of the Code and the regulations thereunder.

### ARTICLE VIII

All contributions shall be in cash and shall be invested in savings accounts at the Participating Institution designated by the Grantor in his/her Adoption Agreement.

### ARTICLE IX

The Trustee shall be paid an annual fee for each participant for its services as Trustee hereunder determined from time to time by the League. This fee shall be due and payable each January 1. If the participant account is opened after January 1, the full fee shall be due and payable for the balance of the first year. In the event the Grantor does not pay such fees directly, the same shall be deducted from the savings account.

### ARTICLE X

The following words and phrases, shall when used herein, have the meanings set forth below:

(a) Adoption Agreement means the form to be executed by the Grantor agreeing to becoming a party to the Plan and to be bound by all terms and conditions as if he/she had executed each of them.

(b) Beneficiary means any person or persons designated by the Grantor to receive any benefits under the Plan.

(c) Grantor means a person who is eligible and who does join the Plan.

(d) Participating Institution means a member of the Oregon Savings League and whose savings accounts have been designated by the Grantor as the medium for investment of the Grantor's contributions under the Plan.

(e) Plan means the Oregon Savings League Individual Retirement Account Plan and Trust Agreement, and related Disclosure Statement.

(f) Savings Account means any deposit, withdrawable or repurchasable share, investment certificate, withdrawable account, any other type of savings account or the obligations or securities issued or offered by the Participating Institution designated by the Grantor in his Adoption Agreement and established for each Grantor under the Plan.

(g) Trustee means Service Trust Company or its successor Trustee under this agreement.

### ARTICLE XI

Grantor shall designate in his/her Adoption Agreement the Beneficiary to receive any benefit payable from his/her savings account which may become payable in the event of the death of the Grantor prior to the complete distribution of such benefit.

### ARTICLE XII

Subject to the provisions of Section 220 of the Code, if the Grantor's spouse has no compensation for the taxable year, and the individual and his spouse file a joint tax return, the aggregate limit upon contributions to the individual retirement accounts of both spouses shall be the lesser of $2,250 or an amount equal to the compensation includible in the individual's gross income for the taxable year provided that no more than $2,000 shall be contributed to either spouse's account for the taxable year.

### ARTICLE XIII

This Agreement shall be amended by the Oregon Savings League from time to time, in order to comply with the provisions of the Internal Revenue Code and regulations thereunder.

IN WITNESS WHEREOF, the Oregon Savings League and the Trustee have caused this Agreement to be executed by their duly authorized officer.

OREGON SAVINGS LEAGUE                                      SERVICE TRUST COMPANY

By _____/s/ David S. Barrows_____                    _____/s/ Kenneth L. Schmit_____
                    President                                                                  President

[1] 26 U.S.C.A. 408, 409, 2039(e) and 4973. *34A Am. Jur. 2d Federal Taxation* paras. 44,015-44,078 and 47,958.

## FORM IVA 1.08(a)

## DISCLOSURE STATEMENT [1]

### Oregon Savings League

### Individual Retirement Trust

This disclosure statement describes the statutory and regulatory provisions applicable to the operation and tax treatment of your individual retirement account as of January 1, 1982. Regulations of the Internal Revenue Service require that this disclosure statement be given to a Participant.

**REVOCATION.** This disclosure statement, along with the Adoption Agreement and Trust Agreement, is to be given to each participant when the account is established. Thereafter, the participant is entitled to revoke the IRA within seven days. Such revocation must be in writing mailed or delivered to:

Notice is deemed mailed on the date of the postmark if it is deposited in the mail in the United States, in an envelope, first class postage prepaid, properly addressed. Upon revocation within the seven day period, the participant is entitled to a return of the entire amount paid without adjustment for administrative or other expenses.

**IRA ACCOUNT.** An individual retirement account (IRA) is a trust account which allows certain eligible individuals called either ''participants'' or ''grantors'' to accumulate funds for retirement under favorable tax conditions. On the plan's master trust agreement and on the signature card the term grantor is used because the funds are granted to the trustee to be held for grantor. Contributions to the Oregon Savings League Individual Retirement Account are deductible from the participant's gross income and the earnings on the funds held in the IRA are not subject to Federal income tax until distribution or unless participant has engaged in a prohibited transaction. The plan has been approved as to form by the Internal Revenue Service, but no determination has been made as to the propriety of any individual's participation thereunder.

**ELIGIBILITY.** Any individual who has compensation which is includible in gross income may establish an IRA under this plan *except* one who will attain the age of 70-1/2 years before the end of his current taxable year.

**CONTRIBUTIONS.** Contributions must be made in cash or by check. Contributions must be made prior to filing the tax return for the year for which the deduction is claimed. Except in cases of a non-working spouse, only individuals who have received ''compensation'' during the year, defined to include salaries, wages, professional fees, self-employment income and other income for personal services included in gross income, can make a tax deductible contribution under the Plan. Income from property, such as dividends, interest, and rent, does not qualify as compensation under the Plan. After you attain the age of 70-1/2, no contributions may be made nor will a deduction be allowed during or after that tax year.

## LIMITATIONS ON CONTRIBUTIONS.

Single Account: If contributions are made to an IRA, none of which are for the benefit of a non-working spouse, the deduction is limited to 100% of the participant's compensation, or $2,000, whichever is less.

Account Including Non-Working Spouse: If contributions are made to an individual retirement plan covering a non-working spouse, the deduction for the taxable year is limited to the lesser of the following:

(a)    100% of the compensation includible in the working spouse's gross income for the taxable year, or

(b)    $2,250, provided that no more than $2,000 shall be contributed to either spouse's account for the taxable year.

Although separate savings accounts are maintained for each spouse, the accounts will be considered as one plan. No deduction for contributions to an individual retirement plan is allowed under this rule where a non-working spouse is involved if that spouse received any compensation during the taxable year. In addition, the participant and spouse must file a joint tax return.

Each spouse becomes the owner or ''grantor'' of his or her own IRA account and must execute the documents relating thereto. Once an IRA is established for a non-working spouse, that spouse, as the owner and ''grantor'' of that IRA, becomes subject to all of the privileges, rules and restrictions applicable to IRAs generally, including conditions of eligibility for distribution; penalties for premature distribution, excessive accumulation (failure to take timely distribution at age 70-1/2) and prohibited transactions; designation of beneficiaries and distribution in event of IRA participant's death; income and estate tax treatment of withdrawals and distributions. A contribution by the working spouse to the non-working spouse's IRA may have gift tax implications.

If a husband and wife each receive compensation during the year and are otherwise eligible, each may establish his or her own IRA under this Plan. The percentage limitations are applicable to the separate compensation of each spouse without regard to any state community property laws.

A divorced spouse whose former spouse has made spousal contributions to the divorced spouse's IRA prior to the divorce may contribute and deduct IRA contributions if the divorced spouse's IRA has been in existence for five years preceding the year the divorce occurred, the former spouse has made contributions to that IRA for three out of the five years, and the contribution does not exceed the lesser of $1,125 or the amount of compensation and alimony which is includible in the divorced spouse's gross income.

**TRUSTEE.** The Trustee is Service Trust Company or its successor Trustee under the Trust Agreement. Trustee shall have no obligation to participant to select the term or type of IRA savings account.

**INVESTMENT OF TRUST FUNDS IN LIFE INSURANCE.** No part of the Trust funds will be invested in life insurance contracts. The Trust funds, however, may be commingled with other funds in the ordinary course of business.

**INVESTMENT AND HOLDING OF CONTRIBUTIONS.** Contributions under the Plan are held in a trust account for the exclusive benefit of the participant and his beneficiaries which may include his spouse, his estate, his dependents or any other persons he may designate in writing. The participant's interest in the account is fully vested and non-forfeitable. The funds in this Plan will be invested in savings accounts of the institution. Investment in fixed-term certificates is subject to the usual penalty of reduced interest in event of premature withdrawal.

**DISTRIBUTION OF FUNDS.** Distributions *may* begin as soon as the participant attains age 59-1/2, but they must begin before the close of the taxable year in which the participant attains age 70-1/2. The plan sets forth a number of optional methods for distributing the funds in the Plan, but it is required that the funds be distributed over a period not to exceed the joint life expectancy of the grantor and his spouse. A participant may elect any of these methods of distribution. If he fails to elect any of the methods before the end of the taxable year in which he attains age 70-1/2, the trustee will distribute the full balance in the Plan to the participant in a lump sum prior to the close of that taxable year. Lump sum distributions are includible in gross income and are not subject to the favorable tax treatment granted distributions from other types of qualified retirement plans.

**DISTRIBUTION OF FUNDS IN THE EVENT OF THE PARTICIPANT'S DEATH.** If you (or your surviving spouse) die before receiving the entire interest in the IRA program, the remaining amount must be distributed to the designated beneficiary in one lump sum within five years after death, be applied to purchase an annuity for the beneficiary payable over life, or paid in installments to the beneficiary from the IRA savings account over a period equal to the life expectancy of the beneficiary, determined as of the date such payments commence.

Any annuity contract so purchased must be distributed immediately to the beneficiary. However, no annuity contract is required if you were receiving distributions before your death for a term not exceeding your life expectancy or the joint life expectancy of you and your spouse.

If the beneficiary elects not to commence distribution within five years or if the beneficiary commences to make contributions, the beneficiary may treat the balance of the account as his own and will be subject to all the IRS rules and regulations for IRA accounts.

**TAX DEDUCTION OF CONTRIBUTIONS.** Contributions (subject to the limitations previously set forth and except for rollover transfer contributions described below) are deductible by a participant from his Federal gross income for the taxable year in which the contributions are made. Contributions may be made for less than the maximum amount. Also, no deduction is allowable for contributions made during the taxable year in which the participant attains age 70-1/2. The contribution to your IRA reduces your gross income. Therefore, even if you do not itemize your deductions, and you use the standard deduction, you may still claim a deduction for contributions to your IRA.

To the extent that a union or employer pays any amount to an IRA account on behalf of an individual, such payment constitutes compensation income to the individual. This amount, however, is deductible from gross income as an amount paid to the IRA account on behalf of the individual.

**INCOME TAX TREATMENT OF WITHDRAWALS AND DISTRIBUTIONS.** Funds generally cannot be withdrawn from the IRA without adverse tax consequences prior to the date on which the participant attains age 59-1/2 (with the exception of the rollover transfers later described, returns of excess contributions and payments on account of the participant's death or certified disability). Any other distributions prior to that time are considered to be premature distributions. In addition to being fully taxable to the participant as ordinary income at the time of distribution, such premature distributions are subject to a penalty of 10%.

Distributions after age 59-1/2 or upon a participant's death or disability are to be included in the participant's or beneficiary's income as ordinary income. If the account is distributed in a single payment, although it is not eligible for the 10 year averaging provision as a lump sum distribution, you may be eligible to utilize the income averaging provisions under section 1301 of the Internal Revenue Code. No penalty taxes, however, are applied in these instances.

**FEDERAL ESTATE TAX CONSEQUENCES.** A distribution upon the participant's death is not includible in his estate for federal estate tax purposes if distribution to the beneficiary is in the form of an annuity contract or arrangement providing for regular periodic payments to the beneficiary (other than a person in his capacity as the participant's executor) for life or over a period extending for at least 36 months after the date of the participant's death. If a lump sum distribution of the entire remaining account balance is distributed to a beneficiary, the entire amount is includible in the participant's gross estate and is taxable to the beneficiary as ordinary income (although the beneficiary may be entitled to some relief since such distribution would be deemed income with respect to a decedent). Exercise of an option whereby an annuity or other payment becomes payable to any beneficiary is not considered a transfer for federal gift tax purposes.

**ROLLOVER TRANSFER CONTRIBUTIONS (tax-free transfer of funds.)** Rollover contributions permit you to transfer your retirement savings from one IRA to another without the imposition of any tax. Basically, rollover contributions allow you to change your investment media by withdrawing all or part of your account from an IRA program and reinvesting it in another IRA. You will neither be taxed on nor allowed to take a tax deduction for the amount transferred.

Limitations. Rollover contributions are subject to the following limitations:

(1) Rollover contributions between IRA programs may occur only once a year; and

(2) All money or property distributed from an IRA program must be reinvested within 60 days of the date received. To participate in this program, assets must be converted to cash and all of the proceeds rolled over into the IRA. Failure to rollover the entire IRA account will result in tax consequences.

Transfers from an IRA to a qualified endowment contract will be treated as a rollover contribution. However, the amount of the assets that are used to purchase life insurance protection are considered to be amounts distributed to you, and you must include this amount in your gross income for that tax year. This amount will not be subject to the 10% tax on premature distributions.

**ROLLOVER TRANSFERS FROM QUALIFIED PLANS.** You can transfer from qualified employer's plans (including Keogh) to an IRA savings program. If you as a member of an employer's qualified plan receive a lump sum distribution, you will be able to transfer tax free all or a portion of the total amount of distribution from the plan less any contributions made to the plan by you.

A lump sum distribution is a:

(1) Distribution of the entire balance (except employee's non tax-deductible voluntary contribution) made within one taxable year; and

(2) Distribution made payable because of (a) death, (b) attaining age 59-1/2, (c) termination of employment, (d) certified disability, (e) termination of plan.

This rollover is permissible even though you would not otherwise be eligible to establish an IRA. All or a part of money or property distributed from a qualified plan must be reinvested within 60 days of the date received. To participate in this program, assets must be converted to cash. Any portion not rolled over will be subject to tax consequences.

A separate account should be maintained for rollover contributions. No regular contributions should be made or combined with that account. If you later become a participant in a qualified plan, these funds may be rolled over into that plan if acceptable to that plan. Combining rollover contributions with regular IRA contributions will disqualify such combined account from future rollover to a qualified plan.

A rollover of part or all of a lump sum distribution may be made by the surviving spouse of a qualified plan participant. The surviving spouse may roll over only into an IRA and may not roll over into a qualified plan in which he or she is a participant. Whether an individual can receive a qualified lump sum or plan termination distribution depends upon the provisions of the employee benefit plan in which his or her deceased spouse was a participant.

All Tax Sheltered Annuities owned by you must be rolled over at the same time to qualify. Otherwise, the distribution will be taxable.

**KEOGH PLAN AND ROLLOVER TRANSFERS.** An IRA program that contains assets which were rollovers from a self-employed individual's participation in an HR-10 (Keogh) plan may not subsequently be rolled over into a qualified pension plan.

**PROHIBITED TRANSACTIONS.** If you engage in a prohibited transaction, as defined under Section 4975 of the Internal Revenue Code, the account will lose its exemption from taxation. This will be effective as of the first day of the tax year in which the prohibited transaction occurs. Once your account loses its exempt status, you are required to include the value of the account in your income for that tax year. Total assets on hand are determined as of the first day of the tax year in which the prohibited transaction occurred. In addition, you may be liable for the 10% tax on premature distributions.

**USE OF IRA ACCOUNT AS SECURITY FOR A LOAN IS A PROHIBITED TRANSACTION.** If the participant borrows money and pledges the IRA as security, the portion of the IRA so used will be deemed to be distributed to the participant. In this event, if the participant has not attained age 59-1/2 or is not certified disabled, the distribution will not only be fully taxable as ordinary income but will also incur the 10% penalty tax discussed above for premature distributions. The Plan specifically prohibits pledging the Plan accounts as security for a loan.

**PENALTY FOR EXCESS CONTRIBUTIONS.** An "excess contribution" is a contribution to an IRA in a taxable year in excess of the maximum amount allowed for that taxable year. A penalty tax equal to 6% of the amount of the excess contribution is imposed on a participant who has not withdrawn his excess contribution in his IRA by the date of filing of his tax returns. The participant must not claim a tax deduction with respect to the withdrawn excess contribution and, in addition, any earnings from the IRA attributable to the excess contributions must also be withdrawn and earnings must be included in the participant's gross income in the year they are received. Such earnings will also incur the 10% premature distribution penalty unless the participant has attained age 59-1/2.

The excess contributions may, however, be applied against the deductible limit in the following year. The penalty tax continues to apply to each year in which there is an excess contribution to the IRA.

**ACCUMULATION AFTER AGE 70-1/2.** If the required distribution is not made after a participant attains age 70-1/2, a penalty tax of 50% of the difference between the amount required to be distributed and the amount actually distributed may be imposed. At age 70-1/2, it is required that in that year and each year thereafter, a distribution will be made, determined by dividing the entire balance at the beginning of each year by the life expectancy of participant (or joint life and last survivor expectancy of participant and spouse, if applicable) determined as of the date the participant attains age 70-1/2, reduced by the number of years elapsed since participant attained age 70-1/2. If participant fails to elect any of the methods before the end of the taxable year in which he attains age 70-1/2, the trustee will distribute the full balance in the Plan to the participant in a lump sum prior to the close of that taxable year. The Secretary of the Treasury may waive the penalty if the inadequate distribution is due to reasonable error and reasonable steps are being taken to correct the situation.

**TRUSTEE'S FEES.** The annual fee of the Trustee for its services as Trustee hereunder shall be as determined from time to time by the League. This fee shall be due and payable each January 1. If the participant account is opened after January 1st, the full fee shall be due and payable for the balance of the first year. In the event the participant does not pay such fees directly, the same shall be deducted from the savings account.

**DEDUCTIBILITY FOR STATE INCOME TAXES.** The above description pertains to federal income tax. You should seek independent counsel as to the treatment under the income tax and inheritance tax laws of your state.

**REPORTING REQUIREMENTS.** The participant must file Form 5329 (Return for Individual Retirement Savings Arrangement) with the Internal Revenue Service only for each taxable year during which a penalty tax is imposed for an excess contribution, premature distribution, or an insufficient distribution after age 70-1/2.

**EFFECTIVE DATE.** This Disclosure Statement is effective January 1, 1982, and incorporates all changes in the tax laws as of that date.

**FURTHER INFORMATION.** If any further information is desired, you may contact any district office of the Internal Revenue Service. Due to the income tax consequences of establishing this account, you may want to seek independent counsel.

[1] IRA ($2,000 and $2,500 for non-working spousal IRA) may be created in addition to employer-employee retirement plan. See Internal Revenue Service Publication 590, *Tax Information on Individual Retirement Savings Programs* for a simple IRA tax explanation. For help in choosing the appropriate IRA plan, the FTC has published a *Buyer's Guide* on IRAs which is free from: Legal and Public Records, Federal Trade Commission, Washington, D.C. 20580.

| | | |
|---|---|---|
| Form **5305** (Rev. Dec. 1981) Department of the Treasury Internal Revenue Service | **Individual Retirement Trust Account** (Under Section 408(a) of the Internal Revenue Code) ▶For Paperwork Reduction Act Notice, see back of this form. | OMB No. 1545-0365 Expires 10-31-84 **Do NOT File with Internal Revenue Service** |

State of ▶ .................................................................................................................. ⎫ SS ☐ Amendment

County of ▶ .............................................................................................................. ⎭

Grantor's name .................................................. Grantor's date of birth ................................. Grantor's social

security number ................................................ Grantor's address ...............................................................

Trustee's name .................................................................. Trustee's address or principal place of business ...................................

The Grantor whose name appears above is establishing an individual retirement account (under section 408(a) of the Internal Revenue Code) to provide for his or her retirement and for the support of his or her beneficiaries after death.

The Trustee named above has given the Grantor the disclosure statement required under the Income Tax Regulations under section 408(i) of the Code.

The Grantor has assigned the trust ................................... dollars ($........................) in cash.

The Grantor and the trustee make the following agreement:

### Article I

1. The Trustee may accept additional cash contributions on behalf of the Grantor for a tax year of the Grantor. The additional cash contributions are limited to $2,000 for the tax year unless the contribution is a rollover contribution described in section 402(a)(5), 402(a)(7), 403(a)(4), 403(b)(8), 405(d)(3), 408(d)(3), or 409(b)(3)(C) of the Code or an employer contribution to a simplified employee pension plan as described in section 408(k).

### Article II

The Grantor's interest in the balance in the trust account is nonforfeitable.

### Article III

No part of the trust funds may be invested in life insurance contracts, nor may the assets of the trust account be commingled with other property except in a common trust fund or common investment fund (within the meaning of section 408(a)(5) of the Code).

### Article IV

1. The Grantor's entire interest in the trust account must be, or begin to be, distributed before the end of the tax year in which the Grantor reaches age $70\frac{1}{2}$. By the end of that tax year, the Grantor may elect, in a manner acceptable to the trustee, to have the balance in the trust account distributed in:

(a) A single sum payment.

(b) An annuity contract that provides equal or substantially equal monthly, quarterly, or annual payments over the life of the Grantor. The payments must begin by the end of that tax year.

(c) An annuity contract that provides equal or substantially equal monthly, quarterly, or annual payments over the joint and last survivor lives of the Grantor and his or her spouse. The payments must begin by the end of the tax year.

(d) Equal or substantially equal monthly, quarterly, or annual payments over a specified period that may not be longer than the Grantor's life expectancy.

(e) Equal, or substantially equal monthly, quarterly, or annual payments over a specified period that may not be longer than the joint life and last survivor expectancy of the Grantor and his or her spouse.

Even if distributions have begun to be made under option (d) or (e), the Grantor may receive a distribution of the balance in the trust account at any time by giving written notice to the trustee. If the grantor does not choose any of the methods of distribution described above by the end of the tax year in which he or she reaches age $70\frac{1}{2}$, distribution to the Grantor will be made before the end of that tax year by a single sum payment. If the Grantor elects as a means of distribution (b) or (c) above, the annuity contract must satisfy the requirements of section 408(b)(1), (3), (4), and (5) of the Code. If the Grantor elects as a means of distribution (d) or (e) above, figure the payments made in tax years beginning in the tax year the Grantor reaches age $70\frac{1}{2}$ as follows:

(i) For the minimum annual payment, divide the Grantor's entire interest in the trust account at the beginning of each year by the life expectancy of the Grantor (or the joint life and last survivor expectancy of the Grantor and his or her spouse, or the period specified under (d) or (e), whichever applies). Determine the life expectancy in either case on the date the Grantor reaches $70\frac{1}{2}$ minus the number of whole years passed since the Grantor became $70\frac{1}{2}$.

(ii) For the minimum monthly payment, divide the result in (i) above by 12.

(iii) For the minimum quarterly payment, divide the result in (i) above by 4.

2. If the Grantor dies before his or her entire interest in the account is distributed to him or her, or if distribution is being made as provided in (e) above to his or her surviving spouse, and the surviving spouse dies before the entire interest is distributed, the entire remaining undistributed interest will, within 5 years after the Grantor's death or the death of the surviving spouse, be distributed in a single sum or be applied to purchase an immediate annuity for the beneficiary or beneficiaries of the Grantor or the Grantor's surviving spouse. Under the terms of the annuity, payments will be made either over the life of the beneficiary or beneficiaries, or, over a specified term not longer than the life expectancy of the beneficiary or beneficiaries. Any annuity contract purchased will be immediately distributed to the beneficiary or beneficiaries.

3. Exceptions.—

(a) No annuity contract needs to be purchased if distributions over a specified term began before the death of the Grantor and the term is for a period permitted under (d) or (e) above.

(b) No distribution need be made if the beneficiary elects to treat the entire interest in the trust under the distribution rules in paragraph 1 of this article.

## Article V

Unless the Grantor dies, is disabled (as defined in section 72(m) of the Code), or reaches age 59½ before any amount is distributed from the trust account, the Trustee must receive from the Grantor a statement explaining how he or she intends to dispose of the amount distributed.

## Article VI

1. The Grantor agrees to provide the Trustee with information necessary for the Trustee to prepare any reports required under section 408(i) of the Code and the related regulations.

2. The Trustee agrees to submit reports to the Internal Revenue Service and the Grantor as prescribed by the Internal Revenue Service.

## Article VII

Notwithstanding any other articles which may be added or incorporated, the provisions of Articles I through III and this sentence will be controlling. Any additional articles that are not consistent with section 408(a) of the Code and related regulations will be invalid.

## Article VIII

This agreement will be amended from time to time to comply with the provisions of the Code and related regulations. Other amendments may be made with the consent of the persons whose signatures appear below.

**Note:** *The following space (Article IX) may be used for any other provisions you wish to add. If you do not wish to add any other provisions, draw a line through this space. If you add provisions, they must comply with applicable requirements of State law and the Internal Revenue Code.*

## Article IX

Grantor's signature ...............................................................................

Trustee's signature ...............................................................................

Date ...................................................

Witness ..............................................................................................
(Use only if signature of the Grantor or
the Trustee is required to be witnessed.)

## Instructions

*(Section references are to the Internal Revenue Code.)*

**Paperwork Reduction Act Notice.**—The Paperwork Reduction Act of 1980 says that we must tell you why we are collecting this information, how it is to be used, and whether you have to give it to us. The information is used to determine if you are entitled to a deduction for contributions to this trust. Your completing this information is only required if you want a qualified individual retirement account.

## Purpose

This model trust may be used by an individual who wishes to adopt an individual retirement account under section 408(a). When fully executed by the Grantor and the Trustee not later than the time prescribed by law for filing the Federal income tax return for the Grantor's tax year (including any extensions thereof), an individual will have an individual retirement account (IRA) trust which meets the requirements of section 408(a). This trust must be created in the United States for the exclusive benefit of the Grantor or his/her beneficiaries.

## Definitions

**Trustee.**—The trustee must be a bank or savings and loan association, as defined in section 581, a Federally insured credit union, or other person who has the approval of the Internal Revenue Service to act as trustee.

**Grantor.**—The grantor is the person who establishes the trust account.

## IRA for Non-Working Spouse

Contributions to an IRA trust account for a non-working spouse must be made to a separate IRA trust account established by the non-working spouse.

This form may be used to establish the IRA trust for the non-working spouse.

An employee's social security number will serve as the identification number of his or her individual retirement account. An employer identification number is not required for each individual retirement account, nor for a common fund created for individual retirement accounts.

For more information, get a copy of the required disclosure statement from your trustee or get **Publication 590,** Tax Information on Individual Retirement Arrangements, from your local Internal Revenue Service office.

## Specific Instructions

**Article IV.**—Distributions made under this Article may be made in a single sum, periodic payment, or a combination of both. The distribution option should be reviewed in the year the Grantor reaches age 70½ to make sure the requirements of section 408(a)(6) have been met. For example, if a Grantor elects distributions over a period permitted in (d) or (e) of Article IV, the period may not extend beyond the life expectancy of the Grantor at age 70½ (under option (d)) or the joint life and last survivor expectancy of the Grantor (at age 70½) and the Grantor's spouse (under option (e)). For this purpose, life expectancies must be determined by using the expected return multiples in section 1.72-9 of the Income Tax Regulations (26 CFR Part 1). The balance in the account as of the beginning of each tax year beginning on or after the Grantor reaches age 70½ will be used in computing the payments described in (d) and (e) of Article IV. Article IV does not preclude a mode of distribution different from those described in (a) through (e) of Article IV prior to the close of the tax year of the Grantor in which he/she reaches age 70½.

**Article IX.**—This Article and any that follow it may incorporate additional provisions that are agreed upon by the grantor and trustee to complete the agreement. These may include, for example: definitions, investment powers, voting rights, exculpatory provisions, amendment and termination, removal of trustee, trustee's fees, State law requirements, beginning date of distributions, accepting only cash, treatment of excess contributions, prohibited transactions with the grantor, etc. Use additional pages if necessary and attach them to this form.

**Note:** This form may be reproduced and reduced in size for adoption to passbook or card purposes.

FORM IVA 1.08(c)

| | | |
|---|---|---|
| **Form 5305-A**<br>(Rev. (Dec. 1981)<br>Department of the Treasury<br>Internal Revenue Service | **Individual Retirement Custodial Account**<br>**(Under Section 408(a) of the Internal Revenue Code)**<br>▶ For Paperwork Reduction Act Notice, see back of this form. | OMB No. 1545–0365<br>Expires 10–31–84<br>**Do NOT File**<br>**with Internal**<br>**Revenue Service** |

State of ▶ ...........................................................................................................   } SS   ☐ Amendment

County of ▶ ...............................................

Depositor's name ...................................................... Depositor's date of birth ...............................

Depositor's social security number ..............................................

Depositor's address ................................................................................................................

Custodian's name ...................................... ...................................... Custodian's address or principal place of business

.........................................................................................................................................

The Depositor whose name appears above is establishing an individual retirement account (under section 408(a) of the Internal Revenue Code) to provide for his or her retirement and for the support of his or her beneficiaries after death.

The Custodian named above has given the Depositor the disclosure statement required under the Income Tax Regulations under section 408(i) of the Code.

The Depositor has deposited with the Custodian ............................... ($ ....................) in cash.

The Depositor and the Custodian make the following agreement:

### Article I

The Custodian may accept additional cash contributions on behalf of the Depositor for a tax year of the Depositor. The additional cash contributions are limited to $2,000 for the tax year unless the contribution is a rollover contribution described in section 402(a)(5), 402(a)(7), 403(a)(4), 403(b)(8), 405(d)(3), 408(d)(3), or 409(b)(3)(C) of the Code or an employer contribution to a simplified employee pension plan as described in section 408(k).

### Article II

The Depositor's interest in the balance in the custodial account is nonforfeitable.

### Article III

No part of the custodial funds may be invested in life insurance contracts, nor may the assets of the custodial account be commingled with other property except in a common trust fund or common investment fund (within the meaning of section 408(a)(5) of the Code).

### Article IV

1. The Depositor's entire interest in the custodial account must be, or begin to be, distributed before the end of the tax year in which the Depositor reaches age 70½. By the end of that tax year, the Depositor may elect, in a manner acceptable to the Custodian, to have the balance in the custodial account distributed in:

    (a) A single-sum payment.

    (b) An annuity contract that provides equal or substantially equal monthly, quarterly, or annual payments over the life of the Depositor. The payments must begin by the end of that tax year.

    (c) An annuity contract that provides equal or substantially equal monthly, quarterly, or annual payments over the joint and last survivor lives of the Depositor and his or her spouse. The payments must begin by the end of the tax year.

    (d) Equal or substantially equal monthly, quarterly, or annual payments over a specified period that may not be longer than the Depositor's life expectancy.

    (e) Equal, or substantially equal monthly, quarterly, or annual payments over a specified period that may not be longer than the joint life and last survivor expectancy of the Depositor and his or her spouse.

Even if distributions have begun to be made under option (d) or (e), the Depositor may receive a distribution of the balance in the custodial account at any time by giving written notice to the Custodian. If the Depositor does not choose any of the methods of distribution described above by the end of the tax year in which he or she reaches age 70½, distribution to the Depositor will be made before the end of that tax year by a single-sum payment. If the Depositor elects as a means of distribution (b) or (c) above, the annuity contract must satisfy the requirements of section 408(b)(1), (3), (4), and (5) of the Code. If the Depositor elects as a means of distribution (d) or (e) above, figure the payments made in tax years beginning in the tax year the Depositor reaches age 70½ as follows:

    (i) For the minimum annual payment, divide the Depositor's entire interest in the custodial account at the beginning of each year by the life expectancy of the Depositor (or the joint life and last survivor expectancy of the Depositor and his or her spouse, or the period specified under (d) or (e), whichever applies). Determine the life expectancy in either case on the date the Depositor reaches 70½ minus the number of whole years passed since the Depositor became 70½.

    (ii) For the minimum monthly payment, divide the result in (i) above by 12.

    (iii) For the minimum quarterly payment, divide the result in (i) above by 4.

2. If the Depositor dies before his or her entire interest in the account is distributed to him or her, or if distribution is being made as provided in (e) above to his or her surviving spouse, and the surviving spouse dies before the entire interest is distributed, the entire remaining undistributed interest will, within 5 years after the Depositor's death or the death of the surviving spouse, be distributed in a single sum or be applied to purchase an immediate annuity for the beneficiary or beneficiaries of the Depositor or the Depositor's surviving spouse. Under the terms of the annuity, payments will be made either over the life of the beneficiary or beneficiaries, or over a specified term not longer than the life expectancy of the beneficiary or beneficiaries. Any annuity contract purchased will be immediately distributed to the beneficiary or beneficiaries.

3. Exceptions.

    (a) No annuity contract needs to be purchased if distributions over a specified term began before the death of the Depositor and the term is for a period permitted under (d) or (e) above.

    (b) No distribution need be made if the beneficiary elects to treat the entire interest in the account under the distribution rules in paragraph 1 of this article.

### Article V

Unless the Depositor dies, is disabled (as defined in section 72(m) of the Code), or reaches age 59½ before any amount is distributed from the account, the Custodian must receive from the Depositor a statement explaining how he or she intends to dispose of the amount distributed.

### Article VI

1. The Depositor agrees to provide the Custodian with information necessary for the Custodian to prepare any reports required under section 408(i) of the Code and the related regulations.

2. The Custodian agrees to submit reports to the Internal Revenue Service and the Depositor as prescribed by the Internal Revenue Service.

## Article VII

Notwithstanding any other articles which may be added or incorporated, the provisions of Articles I through III and this sentence will be controlling. Any additional articles that are not consistent with section 408(a) of the Code and related regulations will be invalid.

## Article VIII

This agreement will be amended from time to time to comply with the provisions of the Code and related regulations. Other amendments may be made with the consent of the persons whose signatures appear below.

**Note.** The following space (Article IX) may be used for any other provisions you wish to add. If you do not wish to add any other provisions, draw a line through this space. If you add provisions, they must comply with applicable requirements of State law and the Internal Revenue Code.

## Article IX

Depositor's Signature .......................................................................................................................................................................

Custodian's Signature .......................................................................................................................................................................

Date ......................................................................................................

Witness .......................................................................................................................................................................

(Use only if signature of Depositor or Custodian is required to be witnessed.)

## Instructions

*(Section references are to the Internal Revenue Code.)*

**Paperwork Reduction Act Notice.**—The Paperwork Reduction Act of 1980 says that we must tell you why we are collecting this information, how it is to be used, and whether you have to provide it. The information is used to determine if you are entitled to a deduction for contributions to this custodial account. Your completing this information is only required if you want to adopt this model custodial account.

### Purpose

This model custodial account may be used by an individual who wishes to adopt an individual retirement account under section 408(a). When fully executed by the Depositor and the Custodian not later than the time prescribed by law for filing the Federal income tax return for the Depositor's tax year (including any extensions thereof), a Depositor will have an individual retirement account (IRA) custodial account which meets the requirements of section 408(a). This custodial account must be created in the United States for the exclusive benefit of the Depositor or his/her beneficiaries.

### Definitions

**Custodian.**—The Custodian must be a bank or savings and loan association, as defined in section 581, a Federally insured credit union, or other person who has the approval of the Internal Revenue Service to act as custodian.

**Depositor.**—The Depositor is the person who establishes the account.

### IRA for Non-Working Spouse

Contributions to an IRA custodial account for a non-working spouse must be made to a separate IRA custodial account established by the non-working spouse.

This form may be used to establish the IRA custodial account for the non-working spouse.

An employee's social security number will serve as the identification number of his or her individual retirement account. An employer identification number is not required for each individual retirement account, nor for a common fund created for individual retirement accounts.

For more information, get a copy of the required disclosure statement from your Custodian or get **Publication 590,** Tax Information on Individual Retirement Arrangements, from your local Internal Revenue Service office.

### Specific Instructions

**Article IV.**—Distributions made under this Article may be made in a single sum, periodic payment, or a combination of both. The distribution option should be reviewed in the year the Depositor reaches age 70½ to make sure the requirements of section 408(a)(6) have been met. For example, if a Depositor elects distributions over a period permitted in (d) or (e) of Article IV, the

period may not extend beyond the life expectancy of the Depositor at age 70½ (under option (d)) or the joint life and last survivor expectancy of the Depositor (at age 70½) and the Depositor's spouse (under option (e)). For this purpose, life expectancies must be determined by using the expected return multiples in section 1.72–9 of the Income Tax Regulations (26 CFR Part 1). The balance in the account as of the beginning of each tax year beginning on or after the Depositor reaches age 70½ will be used in computing the payments described in (d) and (e) of Article IV. Article IV does not preclude a mode of distribution different from those described in (a) through (e) of Article IV prior to the close of the tax year of the Depositor in which he/she reaches age 70½.

**Article IX.**—This article and any that follow it may incorporate additional provisions that are agreed upon by the Depositor and Custodian to complete the agreement. These may include, for example: definitions, investment powers, voting rights, exculpatory provisions, amendment and termination, removal of custodian, custodian's fees, State law requirements, beginning date of distributions, accepting only cash, treatment of excess contributions, prohibited transactions with the depositor, etc. Use additional pages if necessary and attach them to this form.

**Note:** This form may be reproduced and reduced in size for adoption to passbook or card purposes.

## FORM IVA 1.09

### (Keogh [HR-10 Plan] plan checklist)

## CHECKLIST FOR REVIEW OF COMMERCIAL BANK KEOGH PLAN AND TRUST[1]

1. Eligibility to participate in a Keogh Plan.
   (a) Only an individual or a partnership (not a corporation) that operates a business may adopt the Plan. Compare Form IIIB 1.08 (IRA for any individual) and Form IIIB 1.06 and 1.07 (for corporations).
   (b) If individual or partners control more than 50 percent of two or more businesses, equal retirement plans must be set up for both or all such businesses.
   (c) Eligibility period to participate may not be longer then three years (a Year of Service is a twelve-month period during which an employee has 1,000 hours of service, unless a shorter year, which cannot be varied from year to year, is elected). The eligibility period applies to both owner/employee and his participating employees.
   (d) *Minimum* age for participation *may* be age 25, but *no maximum* age limit is allowed.
   (e) Employees who may be excluded from participation:
      (1) Employees covered by a collective bargaining agreement that has a retirement plan.
      (2) Nonresident aliens.
   (f) *Maximum* deductible contributions by the owner are the *lesser* of 15 percent of earned income or $30,000. To determine earned income:
      (1) For owner/employee—net income from bottom line on IRS Form Schedule C (up to maximum of $100,000).
      (2) Employee—employee's gross pay as shown on his W-2 form.
   (g) Voluntary employee contributions to the Plan by *participating* employees *to supplement the employer's deductible contribution* may be made up to the maximum limit of 10 percent of compensation up to $2,500 by the owner and up to 10 percent of compensation with no specific dollar limit for the participating employee.
2. Time for establishing participation in a Keogh Plan.
   (a) Before end of calendar year.
   (b) Before end of fiscal year if it is not the calendar year.
3. Ask your commercial bank for a copy of its *trust or custodial plan that has been approved by the IRS.*
4. After reading the bank's plan and its adoption or joinder agreement, decide on the elections you desire *as allowed in the Plan* (waiting period, employer contribution formula [including percentage of contribution], collective bargaining agreement with retirement benefits exception, profit-sharing or pension-type plan, and other).
5. Fill in all blanks and make all elections provided in the adoption or joinder agreement supplied by the bank.
6. If you are the owner/employee (you have no employees), complete and sign the "consent to participate" form and a "designation of beneficiary" form (at the bank).
7. If you have one or more employees, each employee must also complete and sign a "consent to participate" form and a "designation of beneficiary" form (get from bank).
8. An owner/employee contribution to the plan for his own account is deducted each year on his federal income tax Form 1040 (line 26).
9. Contributions made by an owner on an employee's behalf are deducted each year on Schedule C of the owner's federal income tax Form 1040 (Schedule C, line 22).
10. Contributions made by the owner on an employee's behalf *are based on, but not included in,* the employee's W-2 form as gross income, so employee cannot deduct the amount of the owner's contribution.
11. Voluntary owner/employee or participating employee contributions may be made and may be withdrawn at any time without IRS penalty (the income tax was already paid) for the amount of the principal contributed. Tax on the interest must be paid in the year of withdrawal. Interest earned on the voluntary contribution is not reportable as income until it is withdrawn.

[1]26 U.S.C.A. 401(c), 401, 404, 408, 1379, and 4972, as amended by ERTA Section 312 (1981); and 26 U.S.C.A. 415, as amended 1974. For self-employed Keogh Plan ($15,000 with 15% limit), see also *33 Am. Jur. 2d Federal Taxation*, paras. 3830–3879.1.

## SECTION B    LABOR RELATIONS (COLLECTIVE BARGAINING)

The length and intricacy of labor contracts prevents inclusion of a form for a major labor contract in this section. However, Forms IVB 1.00 QUESTIONNAIRE FOR COLLECTIVE BARGAINING and IVB 1.02 EMPLOYER'S CHECKLIST FOR COLLECTIVE BARGAINING are invaluable aids to the general practitioner who may be entering the labor field or assisting in labor negotiation for a business client.

FORM IVB 1.01 is the initial agreement to bargain collectively in order to settle a threatened strike against a non-union employer.

### FORM IVB 1.00

### CLIENT QUESTIONNAIRE FOR COLLECTIVE BARGAINING

1. Name and address of employer and its labor relations, personnel, or other management representative in this particular agreement
2. Name and address of the union and its representative or negotiator in this particular agreement
3. Nature of employer's business and its legal status (as: sole proprietorship, partnership, corporation/state of incorporation, and subsidiaries, if any)
4. Nature of union organization
   (1) Independent or local chapter of a national union
   (2) Nonprofit corporation/state of incorporation or unincorporated association
   (3) Copy of Articles of Association or Incorporation of union
   (4) Copy of Union Bylaws
   (5) Eligibility requirements for union members
   (6) Voting rights of union members
   (7) Fringe benefits for members provided by union (as: credit union, strike fund, etc.)
   (8) Dues and assessments
5. Number of employees to be covered by this agreement and nature of their work
6. Wages, hours, fringe benefits demanded by union, if known. See Checklist Form IVB 1.02 for preparation of employer's proposal on these subjects

### FORM IVB 1.01

### (Agreement recognizing union as collective bargaining agent for employees, and agreement of union to end strike)

### COLLECTIVE BARGAINING AGREEMENT[1]

THIS AGREEMENT, made in Maintown, Ohio, on June 1, 1982, between Electronics Corporation, an Ohio corporation, having an office at 100 Main Street, Maintown, Ohio (herein called the "Corporation"), and Eastern Electrical Workers of America, having an office at 100 East Street, Maintown, Ohio (herein called the "Union"), WITNESSETH:

WHEREAS, both parties and the employees of the Corporation are desirous of entering into a collective bargaining agreement on behalf of the employees of the Corporation, IT IS AGREED AS FOLLOWS:

1. *Recognition of Union.* The Corporation recognizes the Union[2] as the collective bargaining agency for such employees of the Corporation as are, or may become, members of the Union.

2. *Corporation duty.* The Corporation recognizes, and will not interfere with, the right of any of its employees to be, or become, a member of the Union; and the Corporation covenants that it will not discriminate, interfere with, restrain, or coerce any of its employees because of membership in the Union.

3. *Union duty.* During the pendency of the negotiations of the collective bargaining agreement, no attempts shall be made by the Union to discriminate, interfere with, restrain, or coerce any employee of the Corporation for any reason.

4. The parties to this Agreement shall commence collective bargaining negotiations on June 5, 1982, for the prupose of entering into a collective bargaining agreement or agreements looking to a final and complete settlement of all matters in dispute between them.

5. The Union shall forthwith terminate the existing strike against the Corporation, and shall evacuate, or cause to be evacuated, all plants now occupied by strikers; and, during the pendency of the negotiations, there shall be no strikes called, or any other interruption to, or interference with, production of the Corporation by the Union or its members.

6. All plants of the Corporation on strike or otherwise idle shall resume operations as speedily as possible; and all employees now on strike or otherwise idle shall return to their usual work when called, and no discrimination shall be made, or prejudice exercised by the Corporation, against any employee because of his former affiliation with, or activities in, the Union or the present strike. Dated June 1, 1982

ATTEST:

(SEAL)

ELECTRONICS CORPORATION

By _____
                 President

_____
Secretary of the Corporation

EASTERN ELECTRICAL WORKERS OF AMERICA
By _____
                 President

_____
(Witness)

_____
(Witness)

(See Form IVB 1.02 for Employer's Checklist for Collective Bargaining.)

[1] *48 Am. Jur. 2d Labor and Labor Relations*, paras. 620–627, 1839, and 1843, and paras. 44 and 45 for outlawing "yellow dog contracts"; 29 U.S.C.A. 185. Check state statute governing collective bargaining.
[2] *48 Am. Jur. 2d Labor and Labor Relations*, paras. 46–53, 54–67, 73–79, and 80–86. See also state right-to-work laws in *48 Am. Jur. 2d Labor and Labor Relations*, paras. 12–20.

## FORM IVB 1.02

### EMPLOYER'S CHECKLIST FOR COLLECTIVE BARGAINING[1]

1. (a) If company has more than one operating department, conduct staff meetings with major operating department heads to discover the nature and extent of present labor problems and demands.
    (b) If company is small and the Board of Directors and managing officers are familiar with the nature and extent of present labor problems and demands, conduct a meeting of those persons.
2. Appoint a negotiating team or committee—desirable qualities: respected but not necessarily liked by the employees and the union; patient; self-controlled; affable but firm; has or will gain extensive knowledge of labor law, particularly the law of collective bargaining (may include a lawyer who is familiar with labor law as a member of the team or as chief negotiator).
3. Get copies of collective bargaining agreements, including copies of original proposals and copies of final agreements:
    (a) From employers in the local area with the same union, if any.
    (b) From employers in the local area with other union(s).
    (c) From employers in other areas who are in a business similar to yours with any union.
4. Study the copies obtained per Paragraph 3 to compare your present practices with the bargained practices—in order to respond to criticism in an area where it is likely to come.
5. Have negotiating team analyze and compare the copies obtained per Paragraph 3 and make a chart, list, or other format dramatizing the information gleaned by comparing your present practices with bargained practices.
6. Employee survey:
    (a) Poll supervisory employees about specific grievances or complaints expressed by employees.

(b) How have past grievances been settled?

(c) What contract language, if any, led to unjust results if you had a former contract?

7. Learn as much as possible about the nature and personality of the union's chief negotiator and his committee (other local management negotiators may help with this):

(a) What is his general attitude to negotiation?

(b) Does he control his committee or is he controlled by them?

(c) Will he usually try for a quick settlement or refuse to move until there is absolutely no hope?

(d) Is he in firm standing with his union so he can deliver on his promises?

(e) Does he make deals or follow an open formal format of bargaining?

(f) Is he emotional or hot-tempered?

8. Get your economic data together and in order, making it available to the negotiating team or committee:

(a) Your company's budget information (how much more in annual cost are you willing or able to pay, bearing in mind that if this is a *first* collective bargaining contract, union demands will get greater, not less, as the contract is renegotiated in future years).

(b) Cost of living figures from the U.S. Bureau of Labor Statistics (quarterly figure for your nearest metropolitan area).

(c) Average wages in your types of business throughout the country.

(d) Local wage settlements, including fringe benefits that were obtained and job descriptions. Do they show a trend?

9. Get your employment history data together and in order, making it available to the negotiating team or committee:

(a) Recruitment and retention figures.

(b) If recruitment of employees or retention of employees has been difficult, find out why—it may be something other than wages.

(c) Check age distribution of employees. Why?

(d) Check longevity of service distribution of employees. Why?

10. First Meeting with Union (procedure for negotiation):

(a) Place where future meetings will be held.

(b) Sharing of cost for future meeting rooms.

(c) Number of hours per meeting and dates for future meetings (allow time between for both sides to consult with their committees and principals and for cooling tempers).

(d) "No-publicity" agreement?

(e) Shall minutes of the meetings be kept? If so, by whom, and time when transcripts will be available.

(f) Authority of the union negotiator—are his decisions subject to a vote by the entire union membership, etc.?

(g) Order of business—economic vs. noneconomic demands.

(h) Evidence of agreement required:

(1) Any agreed clause must be initialed and dated.

(2) Agreement to one clause not binding unless *complete* agreement on *all* proposals is reached.

(i) Get union's written proposal.

11. Subsequent meetings with Union (procedure before and after subsequent sessions):

(a) Analyze the union proposal by separating the demand into a list (indicating the paragraph number of the proposal).

(1) Categories may be: wages; union security (as union shop, agency shop, modified union shop, maintenance of membership, checkoff, open shop); vacations and holidays; seniority (as job elimination, plantwide length of service, departmental seniority, etc.); contract length; job training with pay; hospitalization, health, life insurance; retirement benefits (pension, profit sharing, or employee stock purchase plans); grievance procedures; and/or other.

(b) Compare each item on the list from (a) with similar items in other proposals and contracts you have obtained per Paragraph 3.

(c) Compare each item with the employee information you have gathered per Paragraph 6.

(d) Analyze the effect of each item on the control and efficiency of your business, and consider whether nonunion employers have similar provisions.

(e) Take all the union's economic proposals and have the accountant convert them to annual costs to your company.

(f) Compute how much a one-cent-an-hour increase would cost your company in annual figures.

(g) Be familiar with industrial and labor relations terms.[2]

(h) Review all the above with the negotiating team. Where there is any question, bring in the supervisory or management person or staff affected and review the item with him for suggestions.

(i) Prepare a draft of your company's proposal or of your substitute clauses for the union's proposal clauses.

12. Arbitration—will disputes arising from or related to the agreement be settled by arbitration? If so:

(a) Who will be the arbitrator?

(b) How will the arbitrator be chosen?

(c) Will the Rules of the American Arbitration Association[3] for Voluntary Labor Arbitration be used?

[1]Ref. footnotes to Form IVB 1.01.

[2]Inexpensive pamphlet is available from: Publications Division, New York State School of Industrial and Labor Relations, Cornell University, Ithaca, N.Y. 14850, titled *Industrial and Labor Relations Terms, ILR Bulletin 44.*

[3]American Arbitration Association, 140 West 51st Street, New York, N.Y. 10020.

## SECTION C    EMPLOYEE CREDIT UNION (FORMATION)

The sample form in this section is drafted in accordance with the federal statute governing federal credit unions.[1]

The form may be adapted for use under any state statute governing incorporating and operating a state credit union. Include all information in the articles of incorporation for the state credit union that are set forth in the state statute.

### FORM IVC 1.00

### CLIENT QUESTIONNAIRE FOR FORMING EMPLOYEE CREDIT UNION[1]

(a) Names and addresses and telephone numbers of the organizers of the credit union

(b) Social Security numbers of the organizers

(c) Name of the credit union

(d) Address of the office of the credit union

(e) What type of shares will be issued (par, no-par, voting rights)?

(f) Field of membership (what business, what area, what type of employment, and other)

(g) Duration (usually perpetual)

(h) Purpose (if created pursuant to the Federal Credit Union Act or other statute, note citation to the Act or statute)

(i) Are you to prepare the bylaws for the credit union? If so, get the following information:
Number of directors
Titles and duties of officers
Time and place of meetings (quorum and voting requirements)
Membership requirements
Requirements and duties for management of the fund
Name of initial bank where funds will be deposited

[1]Ref. Form IVC 1.01 and footnotes.

[1]*Federal Credit Union Act* 12 U.S.C.A. 1751–1795i.

**FORM IVC 1.01**

## ORGANIZATION CERTIFICATE
## ABLE MANUFACTURING, INC., FEDERAL CREDIT UNION[1]
### Charter No. _____

We, the undersigned, hereby associate ourselves as a Federal Credit Union for the purposes indicated in and in accordance with the provisions of the Federal Credit Union Act, Public Law 86-354, "An Act to amend the Federal Credit Union Act," Public Law 467, 73rd Congress, as amended, titled "An Act to establish a Federal Credit Union System, to establish a further market for securities of the United States and to make more available to people of small means credit for provident purposes through a national system of corporative credit, thereby helping to stabilize the credit structure of the United States"; we hereby request approval of this Organization Certificate; we agree to comply with the requirements of the Act, with the terms of this Organization Certificate, and with all laws, rules, and regulations now or hereafter applicable to Federal Credit Unions; and we hereby certify that:

### SECTION ONE

### NAME

The name of this credit union shall be Able Manufacturing, Inc., Federal Credit Union.

### SECTION TWO

### OFFICE

This credit union will maintain its office at 100 East Street, City of Pittsburgh, County of Allegheny, State of Pennsylvania, and will operate in the territory described in the field of membership.

### SECTION THREE

### SUBSCRIBERS

The names and addresses of the subscribers to this Certificate and the number of shares, subscribed by each are as follows:

| NAME | ADDRESS | SHARES |
|---|---|---|
| John Doe | 100 East St., Pittsburgh, PA 00000 | 500 |
| Richard Roe | 100 Main St., Butler, PA 00000 | 400 |
| Mary Poe | 400 Graham St., Pittsburgh, PA 00000 | 400 |
| Ruth Rich | 100 Arbor Circle, Allison Park, PA 00000 | 250 |
| James Joe | 100 West St., Butler, PA 00000 | 250 |
| Terry Tool | 1000 Forbes Ave., Pittsburgh, PA 00000 | 100 |
| John Rule | 1000 Fifth Ave., Pittsburgh, PA 00000 | 100 |

### SECTION FOUR

### PAR VALUE OF SHARES

The par value of the shares of this credit union shall be Five Dollars ($5).

### SECTION FIVE

### FIELD OF MEMBERSHIP

The field of membership shall be limited to those having the following common bond: employees of the plant and offices of Able Manufacturing, Inc., located on Highway 100, Butler, Pennsylvania, and 100 East Street, Pittsburgh, Pennsylvania, respectively.

### SECTION SIX

### TERM OF EXISTENCE

The term of this credit union's existence shall be perpetual. However, if a finding is made that this credit union is bankrupt or insolvent or has violated any provision of this Organization Certificate, of the bylaws, of the Federal Credit Union Act including any amendments thereto, or of any regulations issued thereunder, this Organization Certificate may be suspended or revoked under the provisions of Section 21(b) of the Federal Credit Union Act.

## SECTION SEVEN

## PURPOSE OF CERTIFICATE

This Certificate is made to enable the undersigned to avail themselves of the advantages of the Act.

## SECTION EIGHT

## MANAGEMENT

The management of this credit union, the conduct of its affairs, and the powers, duties, and privileges of its directors, officers, committees, and membership shall be set forth in the approved bylaws and any approved amendments thereto.

IN WITNESS WHEREOF, we have hereunto subscribed our names this 10th day of November, 1982.

_____
JOHN DOE

_____
RICHARD ROE

_____
MARY POE

_____
RUTH RICH

_____
JAMES JOE

_____
TERRY TOOL

_____
JOHN RULE

STATE OF PENNSYLVANIA
COUNTY OF ALLEGHENY

Before me, the undersigned authority, personally appeared JOHN DOE, RICHARD ROE, MARY POE, RUTH RICH, JAMES JOE, TERRY TOOL, and JOHN RULE, who, being duly sworn, acknowledged to me that they subscribed the foregoing Organization Certificate of the ABLE MANUFACTURING, INC., FEDERAL CREDIT UNION for the purposes stated therein.

Dated this 10th day of November, 1982.

_____
Notary Public
My commission expires:

[1] *13 Am. Jur. 2d Building and Loan Associations*, para. 5; and 12 U.S.C.A. 1751 et seq. See also *13 Am. Jur. 2d Building and Loan Associations*, para. 4, for state credit unions. Check your state's specific credit union statute for incorporating and regulating operation of a state credit union.

# PART V
# INDEPENDENT SERVICE CONTRACTS
# AND AGENCY AGREEMENTS

# PART V

# Independent Service Contracts and Agency Agreements

## INTRODUCTION

Part V presents sample contracts for use in creating the relationship of independent contractor or agent for another as distinguished from an employer-employee relationship. These relationships may be created between individuals, corporations, partnerships, or groups of any one or all of them.

This Part is divided into two sections. Section A provides forms for professional services contracts; and B, commercial service contracts.

Section A contains an advertising agency agreement, an attorney-client contingent fee agreement, an auction agreement, a business brokerage agreement, and alternative clauses to be used in connection with standard printed real estate listing agreement forms.

Section B contains a race track concession agreement, a distributor's agreement for the sale of goods, a factoring agreement, a restaurant franchise agreement, and an independent sales agency agreement for the sale of goods.

Other service contracts will be found in Part VIII. The contracts in that part are samples of consumer "sale of services" contracts as opposed to "sale of goods" contracts, which appear in Part VI, Business Personal Property Contracts.

The language used in the following contracts can be adapted for use in many other contracts for the sale of services. In using the forms, the attorney must be sure of the nature of the relationship his client wants to create. Does the client want to be an agent or a completely independent contractor? The client questionnaire and the footnotes included with forms in Part V will be helpful in determining what relationship should be and is being created.

## SECTION A  PROFESSIONAL SERVICE CONTRACTS

Before using the forms in this section, the general introduction to PART V and FORM VA 1.00 CLIENT QUESTIONNAIRE FOR PROFESSIONAL SERVICE CONTRACTS should be read.

See Section B of this part for commercial service contracts.

## FORM VA 1.00

### CLIENT QUESTIONNAIRE FOR PROFESSIONAL SERVICE CONTRACTS

1. Names, addresses, and telephone numbers of all parties
2. Social Security and Employer's Identification Number for parties, if applicable
3. Correct names of all corporations and fictitious names registrations
4. What is the purpose and nature of the contract desired by client?
5. What is the business of the contractor or agent? Is he or it properly licensed and/or registered as required by applicable law?
6. Specific information needed for various types of professional service agreements:
    a. *Advertising agency contract*
        (1) Services to be performed by agency
        (2) Control of services—will written or other approval be required?
        (3) Compensation of agency for production work vs. media payments
        (4) Billing procedure and payment
        (5) Will there be idemnification by agency for all claims for libel, false advertising, etc.? If so, determine insurance requirements
        (6) Term of agreement (usually at least one year)
        (7) Disposition of artwork, manuscripts, and other production items when unneeded or on termination
    b. *Attorney-client agreement*
        (1) Contingent, fixed, hourly, or other fee. Percentage or amount
        (2) Special powers, duties, and privileges
        (3) Right to retain associate counsel
    c. *Auction agreement*
        (1) Is it to be auction of "bulk transfer" property?[1] If so, get list of creditors from owner. If you are to represent the auctioneer, prepare required notice to creditors
        (2) Place and time of auction
        (3) Auctioneer's compensation
        (4) How will sale be promoted? Who will handle and pay for the promotion, and when?
        (5) Any condition(s) of sale?—If so, list the condition(s) in the contract or in a rider or exhibit attached to the contract
    d. *Business Brokerage Agreement*
        (1) Name and address of business broker
        (2) Name and address of buyer or seller who will be retaining the business broker
        (3) Exclusive or nonexclusive?
        (4) Effective date of agreement and length of term
        (5) Duties of broker
        (6) Duties of buyer or seller who will be retaining the business broker
        (7) Compensation of broker; retainer, expenses, total fee (formula for determining)
        (8) Rules as to confidentiality
        (9) Representations and warranties to be made by the seller as to the business and by the buyer as to his ability to pay and operate the business
    e. *Real estate listing agreement*
        (1) Is a printed form prepared for real estate board members to be used? If so, does the exclusive listing form, a general listing form, or multiple listing form reflect the basic terms?
        (2) When one of the prepared printed forms is chosen or is to be reviewed: fill in all blanks and delete all inapplicable provisions; make all indicated choices of alternative provisions that appear on the form
        (3) Exclusive, nonexclusive, or multiple listing
        (4) Term of listing
        (5) Price and all terms of sale that are acceptable to seller
        (6) Broker's commission: amount (percent of selling price, fixed sum, graduated percent, percent over net to owner, payment in installments), when commission is earned, when payable (as closing, or entering agreement to purchase, on procuring ready, willing, and able party; or default by owner; in case purchaser defaults and owner recovers damages or other relief)

(7) If there may be an exchange of properties, is permission given broker to represent and receive commission from both parties?

(8) Deposits from purchaser—are they to be nonrefundable? If refundable, on what conditions? If not refundable, does broker share deposit with owner?

(9) Any time limit or other condition for broker to receive commission after end of listing period?

¹U.C.C. 6–102 et seq.


## FORM VA 1.01

### (Agreement between advertiser and general advertising agency)

### ADVERTISING AGENCY AGREEMENT¹

BY this Agreement for advertising services made between Delicious Food Products, Inc., of 100 North Street, St. Louis, Missouri 00000 (herein called "Client"), and John Doe Company, Inc., of 1000 High Building, Chicago, Illinois 00000 (herein called "Agency"), IT IS AGREED AS FOLLOWS:

1. *Appointment of Agency.* Client hereby retains and appoints Agency to serve as its exclusive advertising agency for Client's Honey Bee food products developed and processed by its Honey Bee Division in Des Moines, Iowa.

2. *Term.* This Agreement shall become effective on January 1, 1983, and shall continue in force for a period of twelve months unless sooner terminated as provided herein.

3. *Mutually exclusive.* During the term of this Agreement, Agency shall not serve as advertising agency for the advertising of any product(s) directly competitive with the product(s) being advertised for Client, nor shall Client engage any other advertising agency to advertise Honey Bee products, without first obtaining the written consent of the other party.

4. *Third-party contracts.* Agency is authorized to enter into contracts with third parties to carry out the purposes of this Agreement, and Agency shall be primarily liable to those parties for payment due thereunder. Agency shall exert its best efforts to prevent any loss to Client resulting from failure of proper performance by those third parties, but the Agency shall not be liable to Client by reason of any default of those third parties or other parties who are not the agents or employees of the Agency.

5. *Advertising services.*

(a) Consult with Client and study and analyze Client's business and products and survey the market therefor.

(b) Consult with Client on its overall merchandising program for the products, or plan such a program.

(c) Analyze advertising media and select those that are most suitable for use by the Client.

(d) Prepare and submit an advertising campaign plan and/or merchandising plan for Client's approval with estimates of the cost thereof.

(e) Plan, create, write, and prepare layouts and copy to be used in advertisements of all types to be submitted to Client's attorney for approval, if requested by Client within ten (10) days after submission of the material for Client's approval.

(f) Negotiate, arrange, and contract for any special talent required to implement Client's approved advertising/merchandising campaign, and for photography, models, special effects, layouts, artwork, printing, engravings, electrotypes, typography, and/or any other technical material or personnel required for use in Client's approved advertising/merchandising campaign.

(g) Make contracts with advertising media for space or time and with others to implement the advertising/merchandising plan approved by the Client.

(h) Check and follow up on all media and other contracts for proper and timely performance.

6. *Advertising fees.* The Agency shall not incur any third-party obligations or provide any services for Client except after obtaining written approval from the Client's designated representative for that purpose. The Agency shall not be responsible for missed deadlines, closing dates, or other omissions caused by the delay of the Client in approving the advertising to be used in connection therewith. The following compensation shall be paid to the Agency in accordance with the billing and payment provisions of Paragraph 7:

(a) Agency market, merchandising, and media research done for the purpose of assisting Agency in planning an advertising program for Client shall be at Agency's expense and nonbillable to Client; provided that such investigation and research is not made to secure information at Client request for Client's own use. Research and/or investigation provided at the request of and for the use of Client shall be paid for by Client at the rate of the cost to Agency plus a Twenty Percent (20%) service charge.

(b) Agency shall receive a commission of Fifteen Percent (15%) of the published rates of owners of media on all space in media purchased by agency for Client, except that Agency's commission on outdoor advertising space shall be Sixteen Percent (16%) of such purchase price. Agency shall deduct this commission from the published rate for any such space, and shall pay the net sum after such deduction to the owner of the medium in which such space was purchased.

(c) Noncommissionable items purchased by Agency on Client authorization, such as finished art, comprehensive layouts, type composition, photostats, engravings, typesetting, preparation of mechanicals, printing, radio and television programs, talent, literary, dramatic, and musical works, records, and exhibits, shall be billed to Client at Agency's cost plus a Twenty Percent (20%) service charge.

(d) Client shall pay Agency for direct costs of mailing, packaging, shipping, taxes, and duties on production items used in the performance of this Agreement.

(e) Client shall pay Agency for any necessary travel done on behalf of Client other than travel to and from the main office of Agency to the main office of Client.

(f) Should Client desire Agency to perform special services involving no commissions to Agency from owners of media, such as direct-mail advertising, speechwriting, and publicity and public relations work, Agency and Client shall, before such services are performed, mutually agree in writing upon Agency compensation therefor on a straight-time or fixed-fee basis.

(g) In the event Client, after having approved any planned advertising, cancels all or part of it, Client shall pay all costs incurred therefor to the date of cancellation, and unavoidable costs incurred thereafter, including the cost of any noncancelable commitments for media time or space. Agency shall receive its standard commission on all such costs incurred.

(h) Client guarantees Agency a minimum fee for services performed and materials furnished pursuant to this Agreement of Ten Thousand Dollars ($10,000), which minimum fee shall be paid to Agency upon termination, despite any other provision of this Agreement, unless amounts paid to Agency by Client pursuant to this Agreement have been equal to or exceed that amount.

(i) All advertising ideas and compaigns, television and radio scripts, copy, illustrations, and all other materials prepared by Agency for Client approval that are rejected or disapproved by Client shall remain the property of the Agency and may be used by Agency as it sees fit.

7. *Billing and payment.* Agency shall bill Client on the Agency's standard forms, which conform with the standards recommended by the American Association of Advertising Agencies, a copy of which forms are attached hereto as Rider A. The bills shall be sent as follows:

(a) Media bills shall be mailed to Client on the first day of the month in which any such services are performed, and shall be due and payable on the 10th day of the following month. If Client shall pay any bill for space in media on or before the due date thereof, so as to enable Agency to obtain any cash discount offered by owners of such media, Agency shall credit client with the full amount of such discount.

(b) Other bills shall be mailed to Client on the 10th of each month, unless the parties hereto otherwise agree, and shall be due and payable on the 10th day of the following month.

(c) Agency shall make all payments to third parties entitled thereto by this Agreement. However, Agency reserves the right to discontinue making such payments if Client is in default in any payment to Agency required by this Agreement.

(d) If Client defaults in any payment required by this Agreement, or if, in Agency's reasonable opinion, Client's credit has become impaired so as to endanger future payments hereunder, Agency may change its method of billing and times of payment, and may require payment in advance from Client.

8. *Termination and rights of parties on termination.* Either party may terminate this agreement by giving the other party written notice at least sixty (60) days prior to the effective date of termination. Upon receipt of notice of termination:

(a) Agency shall not commence work on any new advertisements, but it shall complete and place all advertisements previously approved by Client if notice of termination is given by Client, and Client shall be responsible to the Agency for the advertising heretofore approved and for third-party obligations of Agency incurred as a part of the completion after notice.

(b) Client shall be liable for all noncancelable contracts made by Agency in accordance with the terms of this Agreement.

(c) Agency shall render a final bill to Client for all services rendered by Agency under this Agreement within thirty (30) days of the completion of the last service performed.

(d) All plans, preliminary outlines, sketches, copy, and all other property and materials that are produced under this Agreement shall be the property of Client as soon as payment has been made therefor. Upon termination of this Agreement, all such property and materials shall be the property of Agency unless Client has paid or pays therefor in accordance with the terms of this Agreement, even though Client or another party has physical possession thereof.

(e) If the property described in Paragraph 8(d) belongs to Client but is in possession of Agency at the time of receipt of final payment under this Agreement, Agency shall notify Client in writing and shall clearly describe the particular item or items. Client shall then be obligated to notify Agency in writing of the disposition Client desires with respect to such items. All shipping and transportation costs shall be borne by Client, and Agency shall not be obligated to store such material at its own expense except for a period of thirty (30) days after such notice has been given. This provision shall apply whether the item(s) in question are in the possession of Agency or of third parties. In the event that Client shall fail to respond to Agency notice within the thirty-day period, Agency shall have the option of storing such items in public storage facilities in the name of Client and at Client expense and risk, or Agency shall have the right to otherwise dispose of the item(s) as it sees fit. If Agency elects to store the item(s), Agency shall notify Client in writing of such storage and give Client the necessary storage receipts.

9. *Arbitration.* Any controversy or claim arising out of or relating to this Agreement, or the breach thereof, shall be settled by arbitration in the City of Chicago in accordance with the rules then obtaining of the American Arbitration Association, and judgment upon the award rendered by the arbitrator or arbitrators may be entered in any court of competent jurisdiction.

10. *Entire agreement.* This writing contains the entire agreement of the parties. No representations were made or relied upon by either party, other than those that are expressly set forth. No agent, employee, or other representative of either party is enpowered to alter any of the terms hereof, unless done in writing and signed by an executive officer of the respective parties.

11. *Governing law.* The validity, interpretation, and performance of this Agreement shall be controlled by and construed under the laws of the State of Illinois.

12. *Waiver.* The failure of either party to this Agreement to object to or to take affirmative action with respect to any conduct of the other that is in violation of the terms of this Agreement shall not be construed as a waiver thereof, or of any future breach or subsequent wrongful conduct.

Agreed and signed this 10th day of September, 1982.

ATTEST:                                DELICIOUS FOOD PRODUCTS, INC.

                                          By _____

_____
Secretary of the Corporation                           President

ATTEST:                                JOHN DOE COMPANY, INC.

                                          By _____

_____
Secretary of the Corporation                           President

[1] *3 Am. Jur. 2d Agency*, para. 22; and Alternative Clause Form IIIA 1.01(a).

## FORM VA 1.01(a)

### (Indemnification of advertiser by advertising agency and insurance)[1]

### ALTERNATIVE CLAUSE

1. Agency shall indemnify and hold Client harmless from and against (a) any and all claims arising from contracts between Agency and third parties made to effectuate the purposes of this Agreement, and (b) any and all claims, liabilities, or damages arising from the preparation or presentation of any advertising covered by this Agreement, including but not limited to libel, deceptive advertising, or violation of any government regulation of advertising. Costs of litigation and counsel fees for Client are included in damages.

2. Agency shall, at its own cost and expense, during the term of this Agreement, continuously maintain in force a Client's liability policy for the benefit of the Client in a minimum amount of Two Million Dollars ($2,000,000). In the event insurance is not available in the amount herein provided, Agency shall not commence performance of this Agreement until the time that such insurance coverage or a mutually satisfactory insurance arrangement is in full force and effect.

[1]Ref. Form IIIA 1.01 and footnote.

## FORM VA 1.02

### (Attorney-client contingent-fee agreement with provision for associate counsel)

### FEE AGREEMENT[1]

*READ CAREFULLY:* This is your contract. It protects both you and your attorney and will prevent misunderstanding. If you do not understand it, or if it does not contain all the agreements we discussed, please call it to my attention. *Do not sign this contract until you have thoroughly read it, have completely understood it and are in agreement with its terms.*

1. *Definitions:* Wherever used herein, the term "Attorney" shall mean Richard Able, P.A., 100 Main Street, Middletown, Florida 32600, or associate counsel as designated in Paragraph 8 hereof; and the term "Client" shall include the plural.

2. *Consideration:* In consideration of the legal services to be rendered by Attorney for any claims that Client may have against the party or parties responsible for injuries and/or damages sustained by *JOHN DOE and MARY DOE*, on or about *November 22, 1982*, in *Middle* County, Florida, Client employs Attorney to commence and prosecute such claims for a fee and lien of:

   a. 33-1/3 percent of any sum or sums recovered for Client before suit is filed.

   b. 40 percent of any sum or sums recovered for Client after suit is filed, but before trial of the case.

   c. 50 percent of any sum or sums recovered for Client after trial of the case.

3. In the event that an appeal is filed at the request of Client, the amount of the legal fees for the appeal shall then be subject to renegotiation.

4. All necessary costs and expenses incurred in the litigation of this claim will be borne and paid by Client.

5. All medical expenses and related charges of any nature, including doctors' fees for Client accrued as a result of the Client(s) claim(s), are not litigation costs and will be paid by Client. In the event of a recovery, Client agrees that Attorney may pay any of those unpaid bills from Client's share of the recovery. Should Client recover nothing, it is understood that Attorney is not bound to pay any of those bills.

6. If no recovery is obtained, no fee shall be payable to Attorney except as set forth in Paragraph 9.

7. Attorney, in his absolute discretion, may withdraw at any time from the case if investigation discloses no insurance coverage or Defendant(s) liability.

8. Associate counsel may be employed at no additional expense to Client. If associate counsel is employed, it may be *Rich, Trial & Just, P.A.*, whose address is *100 Large Building, Tampa, Florida 00000*. If associate counsel is employed, he shall sign this Agreement, be bound by it, and be entitled to its benefits. Client hereby consents to the employment of such associate counsel and understands that a division of fees between the attorneys will be made in proportion to the services performed and the responsibility assumed by each. Associate counsel shall be available to Client for consultation.

9. In the event that any party makes a claim for damages against Client, or any person in whose behalf Client has executed his Agreement, then, in that event, Client agrees to pay Attorney a reasonable attorney's fee for defending or negotiating a settlement of every such claim. It is expressly understood that any attorney's fee payable to Attorney pursuant to the provisions of this Paragraph shall be in addition to, and not in lieu of, all other fees payable to him in accordance with the other provisions of this Agreement.

10. Client agrees not to compromise the suit without Attorney's consent, and Attorney is not authorized to compromise the suit without Client's consent.

11. Client agrees to keep Attorney advised of his whereabouts at all times and to cooperate in the preparation and trial of this case, to appear on reasonable notice for depositions and Court appearances, and to comply with all reasonable requests made of him in connection with the preparation and presentation of his case.

12. Client hereby authorizes Attorney to turn over all information, including doctors' reports, hospital records, and any and all pictures, to the insurance company of the Defendant(s).

13. No representation has been made as to what amount, if any, Client may be entitled to recover in this case.

DATED at Middletown, Florida, this 6th day of December, 1982.

_____
(John Doe)
CLIENT

_____
(Mary Doe)
CLIENT

RICHARD ABLE, P.A.

Accepted by:

_____
Richard Able

ASSOCIATE COUNSEL
(Rich, Trial & Just, P.A.)

_____

100 Large Building

_____

Tampa, FL 00000

Accepted by:

_____
Thomas Trial

[1] *7 Am. Jur. 2d Attorney at Law*, paras. 118–120. Note: There are more than 90 federal statutes providing for or regulating awards of attorney's fees. State statutes provide for reasonable attorney's fees to the prevailing party in certain types of legal action. The fees must be pleaded and demanded or prayed for in the complaint filed under such a statute in most cases.

### FORM VA 1.03

#### (Auction contract between seller and auctioneer)

#### AUCTION AGREEMENT[1]

AGREEMENT made May 1, 1983, between Able Manufacturing Co., Inc., 100 Main Street, Buffalo, New York 00000, Owner, and Glenn Articulate, Auctioneer, 500 East Street, Buffalo, New York 00000.

1. *Appointment and acceptance.* The Owner employs the Auctioneer and the Auctioneer accepts and agrees to sell at public auction the goods set forth in the Schedule of Property attached hereto and made part hereof, the sale to be held at the sales rooms of the Auctioneer at 500 East Street, in the City of Buffalo, on June 1, 1983.

2. *Auctioneer's compensation.* The Owner shall pay to the Auctioneer for his services under this Agreement a commission of Ten Percent (10%) of the selling price of all the goods actually sold at such auction, which commission is payable out of the gross amount realized at the sale. In the event that any of the property described in this Agreement shall be withdrawn from the sale by the Owner or shall be bid on by or for the Owner at the sale or shall be sold at private sale before the holding of such auction, the Owner shall pay to the Auctioneer an amount equal to Seven Percent (7%) of the value of all such items shown on the Schedule of Property attached to this Agreement.

3. *Promotion of sale.* The Auctioneer shall cause such auction to be advertised in such newspapers published in the City of Buffalo as the Auctioneer deems necessary, and send out circulars

and other matter in the manner in which he ordinarily advertises such sales, and the Owner shall pay for such advertising the actual cost thereof, up to but not exceeding the sum of Five Hundred Dollars ($500). The Auctioneer shall prepare the goods to be sold and shall cause them to be displayed at the place of sale, shall furnish at the time of sale such assistants and other help as may be required to handle the sale and delivery of the goods, and shall use his best efforts to sell the goods for as high a price as may be obtained for them.

4. *Memorandums of sale.* The Auctioneer shall have full authority to sign any memorandum or bill of sale either in the name and on behalf of the Owner or in his own name, and to receive from the purchasers of such goods the purchase price thereof as agent for the Owner to be held subject to the provisions of Paragraph 5.

5. *Proceeds of sale.* At the completion of the sale, the Auctioneer shall furnish the Owner a complete list of all goods sold at the sale, together with the sales price obtained for each of the items on the list, and after deducting therefrom the amounts due him pursuant to this Agreement, shall pay to the Owner that net amount.

6. *Bulk transfer compliance.*

(a) The Owner shall prepare and deliver to the Auctioneer, on or before May 10, 1983, a List of Creditors in accordance with the following instructions: (1) the List of Creditors will be completed upon forms supplied by the Auctioneer; (2) the List of Creditors will contain the names and addresses of all creditors of the Owner, both personal and business, and whether general or secured, with the amounts owing when known, and, in addition, the names of all persons who are known to the Owner to assert claims against him even if such claims are disputed. The Owner agrees to swear or affirm that the List of Creditors furnished in accordance with this Paragraph is true and accurate to the best of his knowledge, information, and belief.

(b) The Owner shall also furnish the Auctioneer, on or before May 10, 1983, a true and accurate list of all names and business addresses used by the Owner within three (3) years of the date of this Agreement.

7. *Conditions of sale.* The Auctioneer shall conduct the sale in accordance with the attached Conditions of Sale, and shall conspicuously post such conditions at the time and place of sale. The auction sale shall be "with reserve." The Owner reserves the right to bid at the auction on any of the property described in this Agreement.

8. *Governing law.* The terms used in this Agreement shall be construed and interpreted pursuant to the provisions of the Uniform Commercial Code as adopted in the State of New York.

Dated: May 1, 1983

Able Manufacturing Co., Inc.

Glenn Articulate, Auctioneer
500 East Street
Buffalo, New York

by _____
           John Doe, President
           100 Main Street
           Buffalo, New York

(Attach Schedule of Property and copy of Conditions of Sale of Goods. Ref. Form IIIA 1.03 [a].)

[1] *7 Am. Jur. 2d Auctions and Auctioneers,* paras. 55–59. Ref. Forms IIIA 1.03(a) and (b) for use with this form.

## FORM VA 1.03(a)

**(To be attached to Auction Agreement and be posted at the place of the auction sale)**

### CONDITIONS ON SALE OF GOODS OF ABLE MANUFACTURING CO., INC., AT AUCTION ON JUNE 1, 1983[1]

1. HIGHEST BIDDER TO BE PURCHASER. The highest bidder for each lot shall be the buyer, and if any dispute arises as to any bidding, the lot so disputed shall be immediately put up again and resold.

2. AUCTIONEER MAY REFUSE BID. The Auctioneer may, without giving any reason therefor, refuse any bid.

3. BIDDINGS. No lot will be offered at a less sum than Twenty Dollars ($20). No bidder shall advance less than Ten Dollars ($10) more than the preceding bid; or, if above One Thousand Dollars ($1,000), less than One Hundred Dollars ($100) more than the preceding bid, and so on in proportion.

4. SELLER MAY BID. The Seller may bid for any lot or lots, either personally or through the Auctioneer, or through any other person.

5. NAMES AND DEPOSIT. The buyers shall give in their names and addresses, if required, and shall pay down Thirty Percent (30%) of the purchase money as earnest and in part payment; and in default of compliance with these conditions, the lot so purchased may, if the auctioneer sees fit, be put up again and resold. If upon such resale a lower price is obtained for any such lot than was obtained at the first sale, the difference in price shall be a debt due from the buyer in default upon the first sale.

6. BUYER'S RISK. PAYMENT AND REMOVAL. Each lot shall be at the buyer's risk from the fall of the hammer and shall be paid for and taken away by the buyer within ten (10) days from the end of the sale.

7. FAULTS OR MISDESCRIPTION. No warranty is given with any lot; and no sale shall be invalidated by reason of any fault in any lot or by reason of any lot being incorrectly described in the catalog or otherwise, and no sum shall be paid for any such fault or error of description.

8. FAILURE TO COMPLY WITH CONDITIONS. If default be made by any buyer in any of the above conditions, the money deposited by him in part payment shall be forfeited, and all lots not paid for and taken away within the time aforesaid shall be resold either by public auction or private sale, and the deficiency, if any, arising upon such resale, together with the expenses thereof, shall be made good by the buyer in default of this sale.

GLENN ARTICULATE, Auctioneer
500 East Street
Buffalo, New York

[1]An auction is "with reserve" unless the condition "without reserve" is specified. See U.C.C. 328(3). Ref. Forms IIIA 1.03 and A1.03(b) for use with this form.

## FORM VA 1.03(b)

### (To be signed by purchaser and auctioneer after successful bid by purchaser)

### MEMORANDUM OF SALE AT AUCTION[1]

I, Richard Roe, as Agent for Super Manufacturing, Inc., of 100 Main Street, Erie, Pennsylvania, hereby acknowledge that I, on behalf of Super Manufacturing, Inc., a Pennsylvania corporation, have this day purchased one (1) International rolling machine, the property described in Item 3 of Schedule of Property, subject to the posted Conditions on Sale of Goods by Auction, and have paid to Glenn Articulate, Auctioneer, the sum of Thirty-three Hundred Dollars ($3,300) by way of deposit and part payment of the purchase money, and I hereby agree to complete the purchase in accordance with said Conditions of Sale.

Dated this 1st day of June, 1983.

Richard Roe, as Agent for
Super Manufacturing, Inc.

| | |
|---|---|
| Purchase price | $10,000.00 |
| Deposit paid | − 3,300.00 |
| Balance Due | $ 6,700.00 |

As Agent for the Seller, I ratify the sale, and as Auctioneer acknowledge recepit of the deposit.

Glenn Articulate, Auctioneer

[1]Ref. Forms IIIA 1.03 and IIIA 1.03(a).

## FORM VA 1.04

### (Business brokerage agreement)

### AGREEMENT[1]

This Agreement made and entered into this 30th day of September, 1982, by and between Able Manufacturing Corporation, a Delaware corporation having its principal office at 100 East Street, Atlanta, Georgia 00000 (herein called "Seller"),

A
N
D

George Superior, trading and doing business as George Superior and Associates, merger brokers and acquisition consultants, having their principal office at 100 Mt. Royal Boulevard, Allison Park, Pennsylvania 15101 (herein called "GS"),

WITNESSETH:

WHEREAS, GS is engaged in the business of merger brokerage and acquisition consulting and, as a result thereof, is possessed of certain skills that Seller desires to utilize; and

WHEREAS, Seller desires to sell all or part of the assets of the Seller (herein called "Assets"); and

WHEREAS, Seller desires to retain GS as an independent contractor in order to avail itself of the services of GS in connection with the sale of the Assets;

NOW THEREFORE, intending to be legally bound hereby, the parties agree as follows:

1. *Engagement of GS.* Seller hereby retains GS and GS hereby accepts engagement by Seller upon the terms and conditions hereinafter set forth.

2. *Term.* Subject to the provisions contained herein, the term of this Agreement shall commence on the date hereof and shall terminate on the 31st day of March, 1983, unless the Seller extends the term of the contract in writing prior to March 31, 1983. Notwithstanding the termination of the Term of this Agreement, the commission payable to GS in accordance with Paragraph 4 hereof shall be paid by Seller to GS in the event that the Seller, within thirty (30) months of the date hereof as a result of negotiations initiated through the services of GS, agrees in writing to sell or otherwise dispose of the Assets. GS must provide the Seller with a list in writing, within seven (7) calendar days of the date of termination, of all contacts to which this thirty-month provision will apply. Under no condition, unless agreed to at the sole discretion of the Seller, will a commission be paid to GS under this thirty-month provision if the buyer's name is not on the list supplied by GS.

3. *Duties of GS.* GS agrees to endeavor to procure a purchaser for the Assets. In performing such services, GS shall be the exclusive agent of Seller for such purpose. GS shall compile from Seller's books and records, as well as from other information furnished by Seller, a written profile of the Seller for use by GS in performing the services herein provided for. The Seller agrees to indemnify, defend, and save harmless GS from and against any and all claims, demands, costs, and liabilities arising from or connected with the use of such information by GS that has been approved by Seller prior to use by GS.

4. *Compensation.*

(a) *Retainer.* Seller shall pay GS a nonrefundable retainer upon execution of this Agreement in the amount of Five Thousand Dollars ($5,000).

(b) *Reimbursement of Expenses.* Seller shall reimburse GS for all travel and travel-related expenses incurred or paid by him that relate directly or indirectly or are necessary to the performance of the services contemplated by or are required by GS under this Agreement, whether or not a transaction is or is not consummated. Such expenses shall be verbally approved by the Seller before they are incurred. Any advertising of Seller's Assets will be done after its approval in writing and at Seller's expense.

(c) *Commission Compensation.* As compensation for the services of GS rendered hereunder and contingent upon final settlement of the sale of the Assets, Seller shall pay to GS a commission (herein called the "Commission") in an amount to be computed as follows based on the total consideration received by the Seller:

| *Consideration* | *Commission Percentage Applicable* |
|---|---|
| $     0  –$   500,000 | 7% |
| $ 500,001–$1,000,000 | 6% |

| | |
|---|---|
| $1,000,001–$2,000,000 | 4½% |
| $2,000,001–$3,000,000 | 3% |
| $3,000,001–$4,000,000 | 2% |
| $4,000,001–$5,000,000 | 1% |
| Over $5,000,000 | ½% |

whether the sale price is paid in the form of money or other valuable consideration. Furthermore, consideration shall be treated as having been paid as part of the sale of the Seller's assets if it is paid to the Seller, or to the shareholders, directors, or employees of the Seller or any affiliated entity.

(c) *Commission Compensation.* As compensation for the services of GS rendered hereunder and contingent upon final settlement of the sale of the Assets, Seller shall pay to GS a commission (herein called the "Commission") in an amount to be computed as follows based on the total consideration received by the Seller:

| *Consideration* | *Commission Percentage Applicable* |
|---|---|
| $    0  –$  500,000 | 7% |
| $  500,001–$1,000,000 | 6% |
| $1,000,001–$2,000,000 | 4½% |
| $2,000,001–$3,000,000 | 3% |
| $3,000,001–$4,000,000 | 2% |
| $4,000,001–$5,000,000 | 1% |
| Over $5,000,000 | ½% |

whether the sale price is paid in the form of money or other valuable consideration. Furthermore, consideration shall be treated as having been paid as part of the sale of the Seller's assets if it is paid to the Seller, or to the shareholders, directors, or employees of the Seller or any affiliated entity.

For purposes of this Subparagraph (c), the term "consideration" shall be defined to include, but not be limited to, all cash, the face amounts of all bonds, notes, or other evidence of indebtedness; the fair market value of all stock and options to purchase stock; all consideration paid for convenants not to compete; and all consideration paid under or for consulting contracts, deferred compensation plans, and employment contracts to the extent that the amounts paid under such agreements exceed the fair market value of the services rendered pursuant thereto. In the event the parties hereto cannot agree as to the fair market value of such services, then GS and the Seller shall jointly appoint an independent third party to make such determination, which shall be conclusive.

(d) *Payment of Compensation.* GS shall credit the retainer against the Commission. GS shall invoice Seller at the end of each month for all expenses incurred through each month. Seller shall pay such invoices within twenty (20) days of their date. Commission amounts shall be paid to GS upon closing of an acquisition transaction. Upon termination of this Agreement, Seller shall immediately pay to GS all amounts due and payable to GS.

5. *Confidentiality.* The Seller agrees to regard and preserve as confidential all information developed by GS or obtained by him in the course of his engagement by Seller. The Seller, without the written authority from GS to do so, shall not use for their benefit or purposes, nor disclose to others, either during the term of GS's engagement hereunder or thereafter, any such information. This provision shall not apply after the information has been voluntarily disclosed to the public, independently developed and disclosed by others, or otherwise enters the public domain through lawful means.

6. *Disclosure of Relationship.* Any of the parties to this Agreement may disclose the existence of the relationship hereby created, and GS may use Seller as a business reference; provided, however, that neither of them shall disclose the terms and conditions set forth in Paragraphs 2–5 hereof.

7. *Incorporation into Acquisition Agreement.* Seller agrees that it shall cause the existence of this Agreement and the obligation of the Seller to pay the Commission to GS to be referenced in the acquisition agreement between the Seller and the purchaser from Seller. Such reference shall include the statement that GS is to be paid his commission at the time of closing of the acquisition.

8. *Representations and Warranties.* Seller hereby represents and warrants as follows:

(a) The officer signing in the name and on behalf of the Seller is the duly authorized officer of the Seller and has the right and authority to bind the Seller to the performance of its obligations and duties hereunder.

(b) That it owns the Assets and that it is legally able to sell or exchange the Assets.

(c) That neither Seller on its own behalf, nor others, including employees or servants of Seller, are presently involved in or actively negotiating the sale contemplated hereunder with any person, firm, or corporation, and that there exist no agreements of sale or other documents relating to this sale, and that there are no active buyers with whom any negotiations are taking place.

9. *Miscellaneous.*

(a) *Independent Contractor.* In making and performing this Agreement, GS acts and shall act at all times as an independent contractor, and nothing contained in this Agreement shall be so construed or applied as to create or imply the relationship of partners, of agency, joint adventurers, or of employer and employee between the parties hereto.

(b) *Notices.* Any notice required or permitted to be given under this Agreement shall be sufficient if in writing, and if sent by registered or certified mail to the principal office of the party to whom such notice is directed, listed on Page 1 hereof, or such other address as such party may hereafter designate in writing.

(c) *Invalidity.* If any term or provision of this Agreement shall, to any extent, be invalid or unforceable, the remainder of this Agreement shall not be affected thereby, and each provision of this Agreement shall be valid and enforceable to the fullest extent permitted by law.

(d) *Entire Agreement.* It is understood and agreed that this Agreement expresses the complete and final understanding of the parties hereto, that any and all negotiations and representations not included herein or referred to herein are hereby abrogated, and that this Agreement cannot be changed, modified, or varied except by a written instrument signed by all parties hereto.

(e) *Successors; Assigns.* This Agreement shall be binding upon and inure to the benefit of the successors of Seller and GS, but shall not be assignable by GS except with the written permission of the Seller.

(f) *Governing Law.* This Agreement shall be construed, interpreted, and governed by the laws of the State of Georgia.

IN WITNESS WHEREOF, the parties have set their hands and seals on the day and year first above written.

ATTEST:

SELLER:

Able Manufacturing Corporation

_____

Secretary of the Corporation

By _____

President

WITNESS:

George Superior and Associates

_____

By _____

George Superior, trading and doing business as George Superior and Associates

[1]*12 Am. Jur. 2d Brokers,* paras. 15, 30–53; and *41 Am. Jur. 2d Independent Contractors,* para. 2. Ref. Form VID 1.00(a) for Business Valuation Checklist.

## FORM VA 1.05

### (To be used, *if applicable,* with local printed forms of real estate listing agreements)[1]

### ALTERNATIVE CLAUSES

*Nonexclusive.* I hereby give you the nonexclusive right and authority to sell the following property for the price and terms described herein for a period of four (4) months from this date; provided the property is not sold to John Doe and Company, 100 Jones Road, Middletown, Florida, with whom Owner is presently negotiating.

*Multiple listing.* The advantages of multiple listing have been explained to me, and I desire that the property be listed (not be listed) with the Multiple Listing Service of the Midstate Board of Realtors.

*Amount of commission.* Owner agrees to pay broker (a sum amounting to Five Percent [5%] of the selling price) (the fixed sum of Five Thousand Dollars [$5,000]) (a sum equal to Five Percent [5%] of the first Fifty Thousand Dollars [$50,000] of the selling price, together with Two Percent [2%] of the selling price in excess of Fifty Thousand Dollars ($50,000) up to and including One Million Dollars [$1,000,000] and One Percent [1%] of all above One Million Dollars [$1,000,000]) (a sum amounting to Five Percent [5%] of the selling price less [specified] expenses or encumbrances) (a sum amounting to Five Percent [5%] of the purchase price when title passes under the sale contract, which sum is to be paid by Owner to Broker in installments in direct proportion to the percentage of purchase price received by Owner from Purchaser under the terms of the sale contract, for which installment obligation Owner shall, at closing, give Broker a promissory note bearing interest at the rate of Six Percent [6%] per annum).

*Commission earned.* The commission shall be earned and payable as follows:

(a) The Broker's commission shall be earned, due, and payable when (the sale is closed through the efforts of the Broker, and the proceeds of the sale shall be the sole source of commission) (Owner, through the efforts of Broker, executes an agreement to sell with the purchaser) (Broker procures a prospective buyer who is ready, willing, and able to buy the property) (Other).

(b) If completion of the sale is prevented by default of Owner, the Broker's commission shall remain due and payable by Owner.

(c) If completion of the sale is prevented by default of Purchaser, the Broker shall be entitled to his commission only if the Owner collects damages from Purchaser by suit or otherwise, and then only in an amount not to exceed one-fourth (1/4) of the damages collected after first deducting title and closing expenses and the expenses of collection including a reasonable attorney's fee, but in no event shall the Broker be entitled to receive an amount in excess of the Broker's compensation provided in this listing.

*Exchange of property.*[2] The parties agree as follows:

(a) Broker is hereby authorized to solicit offers to exchange for other real property acceptable to Owner the property of the Owner described herein.

(b) Owner reserves the right to accept or reject any offer of property in exchange if it is not satisfactory to Owner.

(c) If Broker presents Owner with a written offer to exchange for property of Owner a property acceptable to Owner and the exchange is completed, Owner agrees to pay Broker a fee of Ten Thousand Dollars ($10,000). Owner is liable to Broker for that amount if Owner accepts the offer but the exchange is not completed as a result of default by Owner.

(d) Owner is liable to Broker for that fee during the term of this agreement or any extension hereof, whether a sale, lease, or exchange of the Owner's property described herein is effected by Owner with or without the assistance of the Broker.

(e) Owner is liable to Broker for that fee if Owner's property described herein is sold, exchanged, or leased within six (6) months after termination of this Agreement to parties who have negotiated in regard to that property before the termination; provided the Broker has notified Owner in writing before the termination of the name and address of that party.

(f) Owner gives Broker permission to represent and receive commissions from both parties to the exchange contemplated by this Agreement, provided similar permission is obtained from the other party.

[1] *3 Am. Jur. 2d Agency*, paras. 117–129; and *12 Am. Jur. 2d Brokers*, paras. 66–68. See also 26 U.S.C.A. 1031 and 26 U.S.C.A. 453.

[2] See Footnote 1 to this form. An exchange of property may be a two-party/two-property exchange, a three-party/two-property exchange with the developer as middleman, a three-party/two-property exchange with the seller as middleman, or a three-party/three-property exchange.

## SECTION B     COMMERCIAL SERVICE CONTRACTS

Before using the forms in this section, the general introduction to PART V and FORM VB 1.00 CLIENT QUESTIONNAIRE FOR COMMERCIAL SERVICE CONTRACTS should be read.

See Section A of this Part for professional service contracts.

**FORM VB 1.00**

**CLIENT QUESTIONNAIRE FOR COMMERCIAL SERVICE CONTRACTS**

1. Names, addresses, and telephone numbers of all parties
2. Correct registered corporate name or registered fictitious name of parties, if applicable
3. Information needed for specific types of commercial service contracts:
    a. *Concession agreement*
        (1) Description of the premises where concession will be located and operated
        (2) Purpose of the concession
        (3) Description of the part of the premises to be used by the concessionaire, *plus* his rights and duties in regard to use of adjacent and adjoining area(s) or facilities
        (4) Duties of owner and concessionaire as to maintenance and/or repair
        (5) Term and termination conditions
        (6) Rent to be paid: fixed, base rent plus percentage of gross, net, or other
        (7) Who is to provide insurance? On what terms and conditions?
        (8) Is the concession agreement assignable by either party?
    b. *Distributorship agreement (sale of goods)*
        (1) Nature and description of goods to be sold—is there a minimum amount to be bought, or other amount as "full output" etc.?
        (2) Territory
        (3) Term
        (4) Where and how are goods to be delivered?
        (5) When and how are goods to be paid for?
        (6) Price of goods. Is there any resale price condition?
        (7) Who shall be responsible for sales promotion and advertising?
        (8) Is distributor allowed to sell competitive products?
    c. *Factoring agreement*[1]
        (1) Is the arrangement to be the traditional sale of goods to the factor or is it to be in the nature of a loan from the factor to the seller of goods with the accounts receivable as security?
        (2) If sale of goods:
            (a) Nature and description of goods to be sold
            (b) Minimum, "full output," or other supply requirement
            (c) Possession and title to goods—delivery of goods, where, when, and how
            (d) Price of goods and payment
            (e) Factor's lien
        (3) If accounts receivable as security:
            (a) Prepare a form of assignment to be endorsed on all seller's invoices
            (b) Get following information:
                Time accounts are to be rendered by factor,
                How will returns or nonacceptance of goods or disputed accounts be handled?
                How will advances by factor be handled?
                Amount of factor's fee or commission
                Does seller guarantee a certain amount of accounts each year or month, etc.?
                Shall factor have a lien, acceleration, waiver, or other conditions?
    d. *Franchise agreement*[2]
        (1) If the client is to be the franchisee, recommend that he read pages 42–55 of the publication of the U.S. Small Business Administration titled *The Starting and Managing Series,* Volume I, 3rd Edition, for sale by the Superintendent of Documents, U.S. Government Printing Office, Washington, D.C. 20402.
        (2) What is the product or service? What is franchisee's territory, and should it be protected by a noncompetition clause?
        (3) What is the franchiser's reputation and success?
        (4) What is the franchise fee (is it reasonable)?
        (5) What are the continuing royalty or percent of gross sale payments (are they reasonable)?
        (6) Is the franchise fee to be paid in full in advance, or will franchiser finance a balance of the fee (what are the finance terms)?

(7) What does the franchise fee cover (does it include fixtures and equipment)?

(8) Who will do promotion and advertising? Will franchisee have to contribute? If so, what percentage or amount?

(9) Product or service liability insurance or patent rights—how should franchisee be protected?

(10) Is there a minimum certain purchase amount, and what are the return-of-merchandise provisions?

(11) Is there a minimum annual sales quota as a condition of the franchise?

(12) Can the franchise be terminated? On what grounds ? By which party?

(13) Can franchisee engage in other business, or is spending full time a condition?

(14) Terms of assignment, if any allowed

(15) Training terms—initial and/or continuing by the franchiser

e. *Independent sales agent agreement*

(1) Nature of manufacturer's business and name and address of the manufacturer

(2) What goods are to be sold by agent?

(3) How are goods ordered and shipped (to agent or to customer direct)?

(4) Will manufacturer supply samples and/or advertising?

(5) Description and location of premises to be maintained by the sales agent, if any; expense of maintaining the premises

(6) Term

(7) Territory—exclusive or nonexclusive

(8) Right to sell competitive products and time to be devoted. Can sales duties be delegated by agent to others? If so, under what conditions?

(9) Is there to be any product liability indemnity of agent by manufacturer? Insurance?

[1]Ref. footnotes to Form VB 1.03.
[2]Ref. footnotes to Form VB 1.04.

## FORM VB 1.01

### (Concession agreement—raceway at fairgrounds)

### RACETRACK CONCESSION AGREEMENT[1]

This Concession Agreement made this 1st day of November, 1982, between the MIDDLE COUNTY FAIR ASSOCIATION, INC., an Alabama nonprofit corporation, the "Lessor," and JOHN DOE and RICHARD ROE, whose address is Route 1, Box 00, Montgomery, Alabama 00000, the "Concessionaire."

WHEREAS, the Lessor owns and operates the Middle County Fairgrounds located on U.S. Highway 00 North, Middletown, Middle County, Alabama; and

WHEREAS, on the land owned by Lessor is located an automobile racetrack, commonly known as the Middle County Speedway, (herein called "Speedway"); and

WHEREAS, Concessionaire is ready, willing, able, and qualified to operate an automobile racetrack; and

WHEREAS, Lessor is interested in leasing its automobile ractrack to Concessionaire for operation by Concessionaire; and

WHEREAS, Concessionaire is desirous of operating the automobile racetrack owned by Lessor;
NOW, THEREFORE, IT IS AGREED:

### ARTICLE I

### PREMISES AND PURPOSE

For and in consideration of the terms, conditions, and convenants of this Agreement to be performed by Concessionaire, Lessor leases to Concessionaire and Concessionaire hires and takes from Lessor that certain automobile racetrack, commonly known as the Middle County Speedway, which is located on the Middle County Fairgrounds, together with the lighting system, bleacher seats, rest rooms, and concession stands thereto pertaining, and expressly including the parking areas adjacent to said Speedway, for the purpose of holding automobile races at the times specified as limited herein.

ARTICLE II

MAINTENANCE, REPAIRS, AND ALTERATIONS

A. The Racecourse
   (1) Concessionaire agrees to maintain and repair the racecourse in such a manner as to keep it reasonably clean and safe for its employees and the public, and to pay for any and all repairs necessary to accomplish this purpose.
   (2) Concessionaire shall provide and pay for:
      (a) Cleaning services, normal service maintenance during operating hours, and such other services as needed for the reasonable safety and comfort of its employees and the public.
      (b) All equipment, furniture, furnishings, and fixtures necessary in the proper conduct of Concessionaire's business of operating an automobile racetrack.
      (c) Concessionaire shall obtain prior written approval from Lessor before installing, at Concessionaire's expense, any equipment that requires new electrical or plumbing connections or changes in those installed on the Middle County Fairgrounds as of the date of occupancy.
      (d) Approval of Plans and Construction. If Concessionaire desires to make alterations, additions, replacements, or major repairs to the demised premises, it shall submit to Lessor final plans and specifications, layout, and architectural renderings for the improvements, which may be made only upon written approval by Lessor. Such approved installations or changes shall become a part of this Agreement. Lessor hereby agrees that Concessionaire may place leased bleachers on the premises and move the existing bleachers into pit area and other unused parts of the premises; the Concessionaire shall, at the Lessor's option, return any moved bleachers to the present position before the last day of this contract or any extension thereof.
      (e) The following improvements shall be made by the Concessionaire before track opening and maintenance of same shall be continued by the Concessionaire:
         (1) Proper lighting, to racing specifications, in the pit area, on the track, and in the area of the concession stands and rest rooms. This shall be accomplished by properly cleaning and replacing, if necessary, to comply with the building code of Middle County, Alabama.
         (2) Repaint all retaining walls.
         (3) Repair surface of track.
         (4) Build tire-retention fence.
         (5) Repack and reinforce dirt packings to correct drainage problem.
         (6) Construct rest rooms in the pit area where septic tanks exist.
         (7) Any other improvements to the track necessary to bring the track and associated facilities up to proper safety standards as set forth in the building codes of Middle County, Alabama.
      (f) The following improvements shall be made by the Concessionaire within two (2) years of signing this contract:
         (1) Resurfacing of track.
         (2) Concessionaire agrees to allow Lessor, at any reasonable times, free access to the racecourse for the purpose of examining or exhibiting the same and of making any needful repair or alteration thereof that the Lessor, in its sole discretion, may want to make. Lessor may, in connection with such alterations, additions, or repairs, erect scaffolding, fences, and similar structures, post relevant notices, and place movable equipment without any obligation to reduce Concessionnaire's obligation for rent of the premises during such period, and without incurring liability to Concessionaire for disturbance of quiet enjoyment of the premises, or loss of occupation thereof.
B. Parking Spaces and Overflow Parking Spaces
   (1) Lessor shall make available one hundred (100) parking spaces in the public parking area for vehicles of patrons of the racecourse.

(2) Concessionaire will maintain and repair the parking area; and Concessionaire shall pay for any damage to the existing parking area caused by its intentional or negligent acts.

(3) Not later than the Tuesday following each Saturday night race event, Concessionaire shall remove from the parking area all debris resulting from its operation of the raceway.

## ARTICLE III

### OPERATION OF AUTOMOBILE RACETRACK

A. Hours of Operation

(1) Lessor agrees that the racetrack can be used by the Concessionaire any Saturday except the Saturday before and during the Annual Middle County Fair. Races may also be scheduled by the Concessionaire for any day, other than Saturday, provided the Concessionaire gives the Lessor written notice thirty (30) days in advance of such use.

(2) Lessor agrees not to have any conflicting program in the barn building south of the Fairgrounds and adjacent to the track from 6:00 P.M. Saturday through Sunday 6:00 A.M., when a race program will be in progress.

(3) Concessionaire agrees that no race will start at the racetrack after 11:00 P.M.

(4) Concessionaire agrees that no race may start earlier than 1:00 P.M. on Sundays.

B. Type of Operation

(1) Concessionaire shall allow participation in the races on a fair, reasonable, and nondiscriminatory basis.

(2) Concessionaire agrees to formulate a set of racecourse rules to be known as Middle County Speedway Course Rules, and the same shall be presented to Lessor prior to Concessionaire's operation, and the same must be acceptable to Lessor and shall be made available to each race driver and care owner that participates in the Concessionaire's race program or uses the racecourse prior to the driver's and/or owner's entry onto the course or pit area.

(3) Concessionaire shall maintain and operate the racetrack concession in a first-class manner and shall keep the premises in a safe, clean, orderly, and inviting condition at all times, satisfactory to Lessor.

(4) Laws, Ordinances, etc. Concessionaire shall observe and obey all laws, ordinances, regulations, and rules of federal, state, and municipal governments that may be applicable to its operation at the Fairgrounds. Concessionaire shall maintain continuously the necessary licenses, state and local, as applicable.

(5) Concessionaire shall at all times retain an active, qualified, competent, and experienced manager to supervise the automobile racetrack operation, and he shall be authorized to represent and act for Concessionaire at all times.

(6) Concessionaire shall maintain a close check over attendants and employees to ensure the maintenance of a high standard of service to the public, the performance of such obligation to be determined at the sole discretion of Lessor.

(7) Concessionaire shall make a formal written request to the Middle County Sheriff's Department, furnishing a copy thereof to Lessor, for adequate police protection necessary during any race meeting, at Concessionaire's expense if any is incurred.

(8) Concessionaire agrees not to permit the sale or consumption of any alcoholic beverages on the demised premises.

(9) Concessionaire agrees to have an ambulance and/or emergency vehicle, together with a paramedic and a driver therefor; a minimum of two (2) wreckers; and adequate fire-fighting equipment present for each and every race held at said racetrack, at Concessionaire's expense if any is incurred.

(10) Concessionaire, its agents, servants, and employees shall so conduct the automobile racetrack business on the Fairgrounds as to maintain a friendly and cooperative relationship with other concessionaires and users of the Fairgrounds; Concessionaire shall not engage in open public disputes, disagreements, or conflicts that would tend to deteriorate the quality of the service of Concessionaire and would be incompatible with the best interests of the public at the Fairgrounds. Lessor shall have the right to resolve any dispute, disagreement, or conflict of this nature; and Lessor's determination of the manner in which Concessionaire shall subsequently operate shall be binding upon Concessionaire.

Concessionaire shall be permitted to advertise its business on the Fairgrounds in a manner that does not interfere with the use of the Fairgrounds by other authorized concessionaires and users of the Fairgrounds.

ARTICLE IV

TERM OF AGREEMENT

The term of this Agreement shall be for a period of three (3) years commencing with January 1, 1983. However, Concessionaire, at its sole and exclusive options, may renew this Agreement on the same terms and conditions for an additional two (2) periods of two years each, except that annual rental rates for renewal shall be renegotiated by the parties ninety (90) days in advance of each renewal period. Lessor and Concessionaire each agree that Concessionaire or Lessor have the right to cancel this contract for cause upon thirty (30) days' written notice to the other.

ARTICLE V

PAYMENT OF RENT

A. Concessionaire shall pay to Lessor as rental for the premises described herein the sum of Thirty-five Hundred Dollars ($3,500) for each year of this contract, payable at least thirty (30) days in advance each year.

B. Concessionaire shall pay, in addition to the rent specified above, all water rents, electric bills, and any and all other bills for public utilities or otherwise that are levied or charged to the demised premises during the term of this agreement as the result of the operation of the automobile racetrack.

C. Lessor shall, at all times, have the right to distrain for rent due or any other sum due under this Agreement and shall have a first lien upon all personal property placed upon the premises by the Concessionaire as security for the payment of rent or any other obligations assessed against the leased premises.

ARTICLE VI

DEFAULT

Should Concessionaire default in any of the terms and conditions of this Agreement, default of this Agreement may be declared by Lessor. Notice of default shall be required to be written and sent by certified mail to Concessionaire's address as shown on Page 1 hereof. Default once declared may be waived or forgiven at Lessor's option. Waiver of a default shall not be construed as estoppel to declare another default. Default when declared shall void Concessionaire's rights under this Agreement and shall preclude his reentry on Lessor's premises as other than a guest. Damages, if any exist, shall be assessable for Concessionaire's obligations due Lessor at time of default declaration, and the balance of the annual rent still becomes immediately payable.

ARTICLE VII

TERMINATION

A. Upon the end of the term of this Agreement as provided herein, or any extension hereof, or sooner termination of this Agreement, Concessionaire shall surrender to Lessor all the demised premises, together with all improvements as herein above provided in the same condition as when received or constructed by Concessionaire, reasonable wear and tear excepted. Following such surrender, Lessor shall promptly inspect the premises, and, in the event the same are not in the condition required by the previous sentence, in addition to any other remedy reserved to Lessor herein or provided in law or equity, Lessor shall have the right, at Lessor's option, to cause to be done for Concessionaire's account all repairs or other work as may be required to restore the demised premises to the required condition. This provision shall survive the termination of the Agreement and surrender of the premises.

B. At the time of termination, Concessionaire agrees to remove from the Fairgrounds any and all personal property owned by Concessionaire, its agents, or employees. Upon failure to remove such personal property, Concessionaire agrees that Lessor shall have the right to ownership of said personal property, and it shall become the personal property of the Lessor to use of dispose of as the Lessor, in its sole discretion, desires.

ARTICLE VIII

INSURANCE

Concessionaire agrees to carry public liability insurance providing coverage for premises, and operations liability and products liability insurance on the premises and all operations conducted thereon during the term of this Lease in the amount of not less than One Million Dollars ($1,000,000) combined single limits bodily injury liability and property damage liability per occurrence and aggregate. Lessor shall be named as additional insured on such policy and shall be provided a certificate of said insurance. Concessionaire agrees to hold Lessor harmless from any claim or injury of any person arising out of the leased premises and all operations conducted thereon.

Due to the unique type of function performed at this racetrack, and due to the unique type of insurance applicable to racetrack operations, Concessionaire agrees to pay applicable premiums in advance of any race date, and shall be required to pay all such premiums by cashier's check thirty (30) days to Lessor in advance of said race date, and is further required to provide a copy of the cashier's check in advance of a race date. Failure to provide such proof of payment in advance of a race date shall be grounds for the Lessor to enter upon the premises and cause the cessation of race activities thereon or prevent the commencement of race activities thereon until proof of payment is produced by Concessionaire. Any race activity performed without proof of race insurance being conveyed to Lessor in advance shall constitute immediate breach of this Agreement and shall be construed as a default and be dealt with accordingly, except that notice of this default may be oral, at option of the Lessor only. Due to the extreme risks and serious nature of race activities, Concessionaire agrees to comply fully with this provision and further agrees that failure of Concessionaire to properly perform hereunder shall constitute serious breach of contract and shall void this Agreement upon the sale of one or more admission tickets to any noninsured race meet, and Concessionaire further agrees that should this sale occur, he shall be immediately dispossessed of control until resolved to the satisfaction of Lessor.

ARTICLE IX

GENERAL PROVISIONS

A. Manner of Giving Notice. Notices given pursuant to the provisions of this Agreement, or necessary to carry out its provisions, shall be in writing, and delivered personally to the person to whom the notice is to be given, or mailed postage prepaid, addressed to such person. Lessor's address for this purpose shall be 100 County Office Building, Middletown, Alabama 00000, or such other address as it may designate to Lessee in writing. Notices to Concessionaire may be addressed to Concessionaire at the address of Concessionaire as shown on Page 1 of this Agreement.

B. Concessionaire to Pay Lessor's Attorney's Fees. If Lessor files an action to enforce any covenant of this lease, or for breach of any convenant herein, Concessionaire agrees to pay Lessor reasonable attorney's fees for the services of Lessor's attorney in the action, such fees to be fixed by the court.

C. Time of Essence. Time is of the essence of this lease.

D. No Waste, Nuisance, or Unlawful Use. Concessionaire shall not commit, or allow to be committed, any waste on the premises, create or allow any nuisance to exist on the premises, or use or allow the premises to be used for any unlawful purpose.

E. Assignability of Agreement. This Agreement is not assignable by Concessionaire. Any assignment thereof or attempt to assign shall immediately render this Agreement null and void.

F. Entire Agreement. This Agreement contains the entire agreement of the parties hereto with respect to the matters covered hereby, and no other agreement, statement, or promise made by any party hereto, or to any employee, officer, or agent of any party hereto, that is not contained herein shall be binding or valid. No modification of this Agreement shall be binding on the parties unless it is in writing and executed by both Concessionaire and Lessor.

IN WITNESS WHEREOF, the parties have executed this Agreement at Middletown, Alabama, on this 1st day of November, 1982.

ATTEST:                                                      MIDDLE COUNTY FAIR ASSOCIATION

_____                    _____
Secretary of the Corporation                              Richard Able, President
              (Seal)
        (as to Concessionaire)

                                                            _____
                                                            JOHN DOE
        (as to Concessionaire)

_____
                                                            _____
                                                            RICHARD ROE

[1]*4 Am. Jur. 2d Amusements and Exhibitions,* paras. 63, 64, 76, and 78. See also *49 Am. Jur. 2d Landlord and Tenant,* paras. 163 and 204.

## FORM VB 1.02

### (No resale price maintenance, minimum quantity to be purchased, and no competitive product)

### DISTRIBUTOR'S AGREEMENT[1]

AGREEMENT made June 18, 1982, between Able Manufacturing Company, Inc., an Iowa corporation with its principal place of business at 100 East Avenue, Des Moines, Iowa 00000 (herein called "Manufacturer"), and Fast Sales, Inc., a Pennsylvania corporation located at 537 Wood Street, Pittsburgh, Pennsylvania 00000 (herein called "Distributor").

WHEREAS, Manufacturer is in the business of manufacturing a polishing compound sold under the trademark of Quik-Dri (herein called "Quick-Dri"); and

WHEREAS, it is the desire of Manufacturer to establish Distributor as the sole distributor for such product in the territory herein described, upon the terms herein set forth;

IT IS THEREFORE AGREED:

1. *Territory.* Manufacturer hereby grants to Distributor the exclusive right to sell Quik-Dri in all of the United States east of the Mississippi River.

2. *Duration and termination.* The term of this Agreement shall be for a period of five (5) years from the date thereof, unless terminated as follows:

(a) For a period of six (6) months from the date thereof, Distributor may purchase such quantities of Quik-Dri as Distributor may from time to time require. After that six (6)-month period, Distributor shall purchase and pay for a minimum quantity of one hundred thousand (100,000) pounds of Quik-Dri for each six-month period commencing with December 1, 1982. If Distributor fails to purchase that minimum, Manufacturer may terminate this Agreement upon thirty (30) days' written notice to Distributor. If the Distributor does not make up the deficiency within that thirty-day period, this Agreement shall terminate upon the date set in this notice, except for Manufacturer's right to collect sums due and owing to Manufacturer under this Agreement to the date of termination.

(b) If Distributor becomes bankrupt or insolvent, or if Manufacturer reasonably fears that Distributor's credit is substantially impaired, Manufacturer may, upon thirty (30) days' written notice to Distributor, terminate this agreement, except for Manufacturer's right to collect sums due and owing to Manufacturer under this Agreement to the date of termination.

3. *Price.* Distributor shall pay to Manufacturer Thirty Cents (30¢) per pound, f.o.b. Des Moines, Iowa, for each pound of Quik-Dri sold hereunder. Payment of such purchase price shall be net cash thirty (30) days, or Two Percent (2%) each discount for payment in ten (10) days from date of each invoice.

4. *Delivery.* Distributor shall give Manufacturer two weeks' written notice before each shipment is required. Manufacturer shall not be liable for any failure to deliver hereunder, where such failure has been occasioned by fire, embargo, strike, failure to secure materials from usual source of supply, or any circumstance beyond Manufacturer's control that shall prevent Manufac-

turer from making deliveries in the normal course of its business. Manufacturer shall not, however, be relieved from making delivery, nor Distributor from accepting delivery, at the agreed price, when the causes interfering with deliveries shall have been removed.

5. *Sales promotion.* Manufacturer has arranged for and will pay for a one (1)-year national advertising campaign for the product Quik-Dri to be advertised in national trade magazines beginning September 1, 1982. Advertising and sales promotion by Manufacturer after August 31, 1983, shall be done in the sole discretion of Manufacturer.

6. *Restrictive covenant.* Distributor, during the term of this Agreement, shall not engage in the manufacture, compounding, or sale, directly or indirectly, of any other metal-polishing products.

7. *Assignability.* This Agreement may not be assigned by Distributor without the written consent of Manufacturer, which consent shall not be unreasonably withheld.

8. *Governing law.* This Agreement shall be construed and interpreted under the laws of the State of Iowa.

IN WITNESS WHEREOF, the parties have signed and affixed their corporate seals to this Agreement the day and year first above written.

ATTEST:                                                            ABLE MANUFACTURING COMPANY, INC.

_____   By: _____
Secretary of the Corporation

                                                   FAST SALES, INC.

_____   By: _____
Secretary of the Corporation

[1] *62 Am. Jur. 2d Private Franchise Contracts,* para. 1; U.C.C. 2-306(2); and 15 U.S.C.A. 13 and 13(a), (b), and (c). Compare Form IVA 1.01 and see Chapter VIC of this book.

## FORM VB 1.03

### (Factoring agreement—loaning money on accounts receivable. Compare Form IVC 1.05 for consignment of goods)[1]

THIS AGREEMENT, made in New York, New York, on June 1, 1982, between Best Discount, Inc., a New York corporation having its principal place of business at 100 Broadway, Borough of Brooklyn, New York, New York 00000 (herein called "Owner"), and Ready Cash, Inc., a New York corporation having its principal place of business at 100 Wall Street, Borough of Manhattan, New York, New York 00000 (herein called "Factor").

Now, THEREFORE, IT IS AGREED, AS FOLLOWS:

1. *Assignment of accounts receivable.* The Owner agrees to assign to the Factor each and every account receivable created by the Owner in the course of its business by sales of merchandise; and the Owner further agrees not to apply for or secure any advances upon any of its accounts receivable to any person(s) other than the Factor, during the term of this agreement.

2. *Percentage of advance and minimum.*

(a) The Factor agrees to advance to the Owner up to Eighty Percent (80%) of the net amount of all accounts receivable created by the Owner in the course of its business, which are acceptable to, approved by, and assigned to, the Factor, but approval shall not be unreasonably withheld by the Factor.

(b) The Owner guarantees that the net amount of accounts assigned in each year of this Agreement, including extensions, if any, shall be not less than One Million Dollars ($1,000,000).

3. *Form of assignment.*

(a) The assignments of accounts receivable in the following form shall be accompanied by shipping receipts and such other documents as the Factor may require and in the form prescribed by the Factor.

"For value received, we sell, assign, transfer, and set over unto Ready Cash, Inc., its successors and assigns, the within account receivable and all of our right, title, and interest in and to any described merchandise that may be returned to us; and we guaranty to Ready Cash, Inc., that such account is just and true, that no payments have been made on account, that there are no advances, counterclaims or offset, that the terms of credit are as specified, and that no part of any of this account has been assigned, transferred, or in any other manner encumbered, except as stated herein.

THIS ASSIGNMENT IS MADE PURSUANT TO THE AGREEMENT BETWEEN US AND READY CASH, INC., DATED JUNE 1, 1982."

(b) The assignment shall be endorsed on all copies of invoices made for the Factor and retained by the Owner, and shall be properly entered in Owner's books and records of account.

4. *Notice of claim or payment.*

(a) *Claims.* No claims or deductions on any account assigned to the Factor shall be allowed by the Owner without the prior written consent of the Factor, except that the Owner may allow such claim if it shall immediately notify the Factor and repay to the Factor the amount of any such allowance.

(b) *Payment.* Immediately upon the receipt by the Owner of payment from its customers of accounts receivable assigned to the Factor, the Owner shall immediately notify the Factor, and the Owner further agrees to immediately turn over to the Factor the identical check, note, draft, money, or other form of payment constituting such payment, and, until the same shall be turned over, the Owner shall hold it in trust for the sole use and benefit of the Factor.

5. *Power of attorney.* The Owner irrevocably constitutes and appoints Richard Rich, President of Ready Cash, Inc., as Owner's true and lawful attorney for it, and in its name, including the power of substitution, to endorse the name of the Owner to any check, note, draft, or other form of payment that shall, under the terms of this Agreement, come into the possession of the Owner or the Factor, and to deposit such checks, notes, or other form of payment in any depository to the credit of the Factor and for its sole use and benefit.

6. *Certain advances secured by merchandise.* The Factor may, in Factor's sole discretion, upon request of the Owner, advance to the Owner up to a percentage of the net cash or marked value of merchandise of the Owner, as determined by the Factor, and in amounts as determined by the Factor, provided in any and/or all cases that such merchandise shall be delivered and pledged to the Factor as security for such advances and/or at the option of the Factor that such merchandise shall be placed in a storage warehouse at the expense of the Owner, in which case the Owner shall obtain either a negotiable or nonnegotiable receipt in the name of the Factor, stating that such merchandise is the property of the Factor, but the amount of the advances in any event shall be in the sole discretion of the Factor.

7. *Books and records of Owner.* The Factor shall have the right to examine any and all of the books and records of the Owner at any and all reasonable times, for the purpose, among other things, of verifying the validity of all accounts assigned hereunder or to be assigned.

8. *Accounting by Factor and compensation.*

(a) The Factor agrees to render an account of each month's transactions within fifteen (15) days after the end of each calendar month, and if it shall appear from such account that any moneys are due from the Factor to the Owner over and above the amount advanced upon accounts, together with interest, commissions, and other charges of the Factor, and a reserve of Twenty Percent (20%) of the gross amount of all outstanding accounts assigned to the Factor, which the Factor shall at all times during the continuance of this Agreement be entitled to retain as a reserve, such amount shall be paid by the Factor to the Owner.

(b) In the event of the return or nonacceptance for any reason, in whole or in part, of any of the merchandise, the sale of which resulted in, or is represented to have resulted in, the assigned accounts, or any of them, the Owner agrees to give the Factor immediate written notice of such return or nonacceptance, and any amount advanced by the Factor to the Assignor upon the security of the account shall be repaid by the Owner to the Factor; and until the advance shall have been so repaid, the Owner agrees to turn over the returned or nonaccepted merchandise to the Factor.

(c) In the event that the advance shall not be repaid as provided in 8(b) within ten (10) days after the return of the merchandise as provided to the Owner, the Factor shall have the right to sell such merchandise in the manner provided for the sale of merchandise by the Factor upon the termination of this Agreement and without notice to the Owner, and the net proceeds of such sale shall be applied toward the liquidation of the amount advanced by the Factor upon such account.

(d) The Factor shall charge and receive interest at the rate of Eight Percent (8%) per annum upon all moneys advanced to or paid out for the account of or that may be due from time to time from the Owner. Interest shall be paid from the date of an advance to the date of actual payment. That interest shall be charged and credited to current accounts receivable. In addition to interest, the Factor shall charge and receive a commission of Three and One-Half Percent (3½%) of the net amount of each account assigned by the Owner to the Factor.

(e) The Factor shall not be responsible for the failure of any carrier to deliver merchandise sold by the Owner, nor for any delay of the carrier in delivering such merchandise, nor for any damage to merchandise while in the possession of the carrier, nor for any negligence or default of any carrier, nor shall the Factor be required to deduct any such loss in his accounting.

(f) The Owner shall pay to the Factor, upon its request, the amount of any assigned account that shall be more than thirty (30) days past due the maturity date, or the Factor may, at its option, charge the amount of such account to the Owner's account.

(g) Interest, commissions, and other charges due the Factor shall be due and payable by the Owner monthly on the first day of each and every month following receipt of the Factor's accounting.

9. *Default by Owner.*

(a) Upon any default by Owner under this agreement, all amounts due the Factor hereunder shall immediately become due and payable without demand or notice to Owner.

(b) If the Owner shall fail or refuse to make repayment of any part of the amount of any account as required herein, the Factor may immediately give such notice as it may deem proper to any customer of the Owner that such account or accounts have been assigned to the Factor, and any claim against such customer may be asserted, approved, and sued upon in the name and for the benefit of the Factor.

(c) The Factor shall also have the right to settle or compromise any account, after giving the Owner an opportunity to pay the amount or to take such steps as it may deem necessary for the protection of its rights in the accounts or under this Agreement.

(d) As security for its advances now or later to be made, the Factor shall, at all times, in addition to all other available legal remedies, have a general lien upon any and all moneys and other property of any kind or character, tangible or intangible, of the Owner at any time in the possession or control of the Factor.

(e) All legal or other expenses paid or incurred by the Factor in collecting the accounts or in collecting a sum payable by any debtor or in the assertion or protection of the Factor's rights shall be paid by the Owner to the Factor.

(f) Upon default by Owner, the Factor, in addition to all other rights and remedies given to Factor by this Agreement or by law, shall have the right, privilege, and authority to sell any and all assigned accounts, merchandise, or other collateral in its control or possession, at its sole option, at public or private sale, with or without notice, for cash or credit, and upon such terms as it may deem proper; and, at such sale or sales, it may become the purchases of all or any part. The net proceeds, after deducting all costs of such sales, commissions, and charges, and any and all expenses, including legal costs and attorney's fees that may be incurred, shall be applied to the indebtedness of the Owner to the Factor under this Agreement. Any surplus remaining, after the deduction of all such charges, shall be turned over to the Owner, and, in the event that there shall be a deficit, the Owner shall remain liable.

10. *Waiver.* The failure of the Factor to exercise any rights given under this Agreement upon any breach or any default by the Owner shall not constitute a waiver of any rights arising by reason of other or similar breaches or defaults.

11. *Notice.* All notices or other communications to be given hereunder shall be deemed sufficient if sent by United States certified or registered mail by either party to the other directed to the address shown herein, unless other express written instructions for notice have been given by the party to be notified.

12. *Duration.* This Agreement shall commence on June 1, 1982, and shall continue in full force and effect until May 31, 1983, and from year to year thereafter, unless either party shall give three (3) months' notice in writing to the other of an intention to terminate the same on June 1, in any year commencing with 1983.

13. *Assignability.* This Agreement is not assignable without the written consent of the other party.

14. *Governing law.* This Agreement shall be interpreted according to the laws of the State of New York.

15. *Entire agreement.* This Agreement expresses the entire understanding between the parties and cannot be modified except by a writing signed by both parties.

IN WITNESS WHEREOF, the subscribers, upon due grant of authority by the corporate parties hereto, have hereunto set their hands and caused the corporation seals of the corporations to be imprinted the day and year first above written.

ATTEST:                                         BEST DISCOUNT, INC.

(SEAL)

_____     By _____
Secretary of the Corporation                          President

(SEAL)                                          READY CASH, INC.

_____     By _____
Secretary of the Corporation                          President

[1]32 *Am. Jur. 2d Factors and Commission,* paras. 1–43; and 67 *Am. Jur. 2d Sales,* para. 17. See U.C.C. 2–306, 2–326, 2–401 through 2–403, and 9–201, 9–202, 9–205, 9–302(1), 9–306, and 9–501 through 507.

## FORM VB 1.04

### (Restaurant franchise—dealer owns premises)

### FRANCHISE AGREEMENT[1]

THIS AGREEMENT made and entered into this 3rd day of July, 1981, by and between John Cook and Ruth Cook, of 100 East Street, Middletown, Middle County, Virginia 00000, d/b/a Super Snackery (herein called "Company"), and John Doe and Mary Doe of 500 Main Street, Middleville, Central County, State of Maryland 00000 (herein called "Dealer").

WITNESSETH:

WHEREAS, Company has expended time, effort, and money to acquire experience and knowledge with respect to franchising, and to the business of the buying, selling, and merchandising of food, food products, sandwiches, and beverages, together with related restaurateur activities; and

WHEREAS, Company has developed a format for the operation of mercantile establishments featuring food, food products, sandwiches, and beverages, together with related restaurateur activities under the trade name of "Super Snackery" and does train and assist its dealers in the operation of that business, and does provide services and assistance throughout Dealer's tenure; and

WHEREAS, Company has established a reputation with the public for a specialized type of business establishment with unique merchandising procedures and has, as an entity, established certain purchasing and merchandising techniques to the benefit of Company; and

WHEREAS, Dealer wishes to engage in the described business as a "Super Snackery" dealer, to be trained and assisted in the operation of that business; and

WHEREAS, Dealer recognizes and acknowledges the importance to Company of maintaining the relationship created in the Agreement, each with the other, and the equal importance of maintaining the distinctive features of the business to the public in order that the reputation of "Super Snackery" restaurants to the public be maintained; and

WHEREAS, Dealer recognizes and acknowledges there is a unique relationship under the trade name of "Super Snackery," and further recognizes and acknowledges the mutual benefits to be derived through the maintenance of the standards and policies set by Company, and the reliance of each upon the other for the faithful performance of the terms and conditions of this Agreement;

NOW, THEREFORE, in consideration of the promises and the mutual covenants contained in this Agreement, it is agreed as follows:

1. *Franchise Grant.*

(a) In consideration of the sum of Five Thousand Dollars ($5,000), receipt whereof is hereby acknowledged, Company grants to the Dealer and the Dealer accepts a franchise as a "Super Snackery" dealer upon the terms and conditions contained in this Agreement, for use on property owned by Dealer at 1000 Highway 22 South, Middletown, Virginia, together with the use of the trademarks, trade names, insignia, and other connected indicia of operation of the franchise.

(b) The relationship between the parties is only that of independent contractors. No partnership, joint venture, or relationship of principal and agent is intended.

2. *Term.* The term of this franchise shall commence September 1, 1981, and shall continue for a period of five (5) years.

3. *Area restrictions on Company.* Company, while this Agreement is in force, shall not operate or grant a franchise for any other restaurant operating as "Super Snackery" within the following described area:

Within a radius of two (2) miles of the Super Snackery to be operated hereunder.

4. *Design and construction of premises.* Dealer shall install and use on his premises such fixtures, equipment, machinery, and accessories as shall conform to the specifications designed and approved by Company, as described in Exhibit A attached hereto and made part hereof.

5. *Operation control.*

(a) In order to continue the uniformity of operation and of product, Company shall make available to Dealer the specifications and requirements of ingredients, commodities, supplies, and merchandise recommended for use in the restaurant of Dealer, and Dealer shall purchase only those approved ingredients, commodities, supplies, and merchandise; provided, however, that Dealer may make purchases from any source selected by Dealer as long as the items purchased meet the specifications set by Company. Company reserves the right to test any items purchased by Dealer to assure Company of compliance. Company, upon request by Dealer, will test any product submitted by Dealer to determine its compliance with the standards set by Company, at a charge to Dealer not to exceed the actual costs of the testing.

(b) In order to protect the goodwill associated with the Company name and to prevent any deception to the public, Dealer shall operate his business in accordance with the standards and requirements of quality, production, appearance, cleanliness, and services as are from time to time prescribed by Company, and as are followed by other restaurants having the same franchise. Dealer shall maintain the premises in a neat, attractive condition and shall make such repairs and renovations as may be required by the Company to meet the standards set by Company. Dealer also, at all times, shall maintain adequate inventories and trained personnel to serve the public in a manner commensurate with the reputation of other restaurants bearing the trade name of Company.

(c) In order that there shall be common identity of products and service to the public, Dealer shall use products bearing the name, insignia, or service mark of Company on all applicable merchandise or items used or connected with the sale, dispensing, or display of merchandise on or about Dealer's premises, and shall submit those articles to Company for its approval prior to use. For purposes of identifying applicable merchandise or items, Company will issue to Dealer a list of merchandise or items of Company and to give further common identity between dealers.

(d) Dealer also shall erect, use, and display advertising signs of such color, number, location, illumination, and size as Company shall specify.

(e) Company agrees to supply and Dealer agrees to purchase all menus and other printed paper goods from Company and to pay for same upon delivery, or to use Company-approved designs or to obtain Company approval prior to purchasing new designs of printed materials. The menus supplied Dealer will provide for the food, food products, sandwiches, and beverages to be provided by Dealer to guests and will be provided by Dealer to guests in accordance with the menus. Dealer will not amend, alter, or change the menus provided by Company in any manner except upon consent of Company, except that Dealer can alter prices on the menus.

(f) In order to assure uniformity of operation and to make maximum effectiveness of the available information concerning restaurant operation, marketing, and financial data, Dealer shall submit to Company such financial and operating information as Company shall request and in such frequency as Company, in its sole discretion, shall request. Dealer, by these presents, gives consent to the use of such information by Company as it, in its sole discretion, shall determine. Company shall not identify that information, when and if released, with the name of Dealer without the prior consent of Dealer.

(g) Dealer agrees to pay all suppliers, including Company, promptly, and if any supplier of meats, groceries, and beverages is not paid by Dealer within thirty (30) days following any said purchase, any purchases thereafter will be made cash on delivery, and Company may at its option give notice to Dealer on his failure to so pay any supplier of meats, groceries, and beverages, and

Dealer shall have ten (10) days in which to correct the default and to pay such supplier, and if not paid within said ten (10) days, this Agreement shall be terminated.

(h) In the event Dealer shall fail to operate his restaurant within the framework of the standards and requirements prescribed in this Agreement or set out elsewhere as operating procedure of Company, Company, at its option and at the expense of Dealer, may place a representative of Company in the store of Dealer for periods of fifteen (15) days each, which representative shall be authorized by Dealer to do those things necessary for compliance with the standards of Company.

(i) Dealer shall obtain prior written consent of Company before offering through public advertisement or making any sale, transfer, assignment, mortgage, lease, or sublease of Dealer's premises or any personal property used on said premises in connection with said business except as otherwise expressly provided in this Agreement.

(j) Dealer shall pay all federal, state, county, and local taxes attributable to the existence or operation of the business contemplated by this Agreement, and shall obtain and pay all license fees required by any federal, state, county, and local government because of the existence or operation of the business contemplated by this Agreement.

6. *Trade secrets.* Dealer agrees that information provided by Company concerning the operations, economics, trade secrets, financing, and other important factors regarding the operation of the franchise are considered as confidential and proprietary, and are valuable business and property rights, and agrees that any information disclosed, whether written, oral, physical, or otherwise, will not be used or disclosed by Dealer except as may be necessary to fulfill the purpose for which it has been disclosed. At Company's request, Dealer shall have each officer, employee, or agent of Dealer agree to and be bound to a reasonable employment agreement provided by Company.

7. *Noncompetition clause.* During the term of this Agreement and for a period of two (2) years thereafter, Dealer shall not in any capacity, except with the written consent of Company, engage in the same or any similar business to "Super Snackery" method, either directly or indirectly, or in any capacity or in conjunction with others within any of Company's territorial sales areas. Dealer shall not during the term of this Agreement or for two (2) years thereafter do any act prejudicial or injurious to the business or goodwill of Company. Upon violation of this Paragraph 7, Dealer agrees to submit to an injunction restraining it from further competition, in addition to actual damages.

8. *Insurance.* Dealer, at his own expense, shall maintain insurance against all types of public liability, including products liability, with companies satisfactory to Company and in such amounts as Company shall reasonably determine. All insurance of Dealer shall cover Company and Dealer as their interest may appear.

9. *Assignability.*

(a) The rights of Dealer under this Agreement are not transferable or assignable in whole or in part, except as provided in Paragraph 10, without the written consent of Company, which consent shall not be unreasonably withheld.

(b) The rights of Company may be assigned, and its successors and assigns shall be bound by the terms of this Agreement.

10. *Right of first refusal.* If Dealer desires to transfer or sell Dealer's rights under this Agreement to a bona fide purchaser, he may do so and be relieved of further obligation under this Agreement (other than those contained in Paragraph 7), provided Dealer shall first offer to sell to this Company upon the same terms and conditions as those of the bona fide purchaser, and Company shall have seven (7) days in which to accept, subject to obtaining reasonable financing, and Company shall have thirty (30) days thereafter to obtain a commitment on such financing. If Company has not accepted the offer, Dealer may conclude the sale to the prospective purchaser, subject to the following terms and conditions:

(a) The prospective purchaser has a credit rating reasonably satisfactory to Company.

(b) The prospective purchaser is willing to and satisfactorily completes all training routinely required by the Company at the time of the purchase.

(c) The prospective purchaser enters into any and all agreements that Company is then requiring of newly franchised dealers.

(d) All of the obligations of Dealer to Company, suppliers, and others are fully satisfied.

(e) Dealer is not in default under this Agreement.

(f) Dealer executes a general release under seal to Company.

11. *Termination.*

(a) If Dealer shall make any general assignment or trust mortgage for the benefit of his creditors, or if Dealer shall commit or suffer a default under any contract of conditional sale, mortgage, or other security instrument, or if a petition shall be filed by or against Dealer initiating a proceeding under any provision of the Bankruptcy Act, or if a receiver, guardian, conservator, or similar officer shall be appointed by a court of competent jurisdiction to take charge of all or any part of Dealer's property, or if Dealer shall fail to perform or observe any of the provisions required to be performed or observed by Dealer under this Agreement or under any lease or sublease of Dealer's premises or under any equipment agreement promissory note, conditional sale contract, or other instrument executed by Dealer in connection with obtaining equipment for use on Dealer's premises and shall not remedy that failure within five (5) days after notice to that effect by Company, or if Dealer shall commit repeated and persistent violations of any of those provisions, or fail to make payment of amounts owed to Company under this Agreement or otherwise, Company forthwith may terminate this Agreement and all rights of Dealer under it shall cease.

(b) Upon the expiration or termination of this Agreement for any cause, Dealer shall immediately discontinue the use of all trade names, service marks, signs, structures, and forms of advertising indicative of Company, its symbols or service marks or its business or products; and as far as Dealer lawfully may do so, Dealer shall make or cause to be made such removals or changes in signs, buildings, and structures as Company shall reasonably direct so as to eliminate the name of Company from Dealer's premises, and to distinguish the premises effectively from their former appearance and from any other Company restaurant.

12. *Waiver.* No failure of Company to exercise any power given to it under this Agreement, or to insist upon strict compliance by Dealer with any obligation or condition under it, and no custom or practice of the parties at variance with its terms shall constitute a waiver of Company's rights to demand exact compliance with those terms upon any subsequent default.

13. *Entire agreement.* This Agreement contains the entire agreement between the parties concerning its subject matter, and no representations, inducements, promises, or agreements, oral or otherwise, between the parties with reference to it and not embodied in this Agreement shall be of any force or effect.

14. *Notices.* All notices pursuant to this Agreement shall be sent by registered or certified U.S. mail to Company at the address of Company shown above and to Dealer at the premises on which Dealer is conducting his business under this Agreement, unless Company or Dealer, as the case may be, from time to time may send to the other written notice of change of address.

15. *Construction.* If Dealer consists of two or more individuals, those individuals shall be jointly and severally liable, and reference to Dealer in this Agreement shall include all those individuals. Reference to Dealer as male also shall include a female dealer or a corporation or any other entity, except that if Dealer is a corporation, the persons signing on behalf of said corporation warrant that said corporation complies with and will comply with the conditions set forth in this Agreement, and the persons signing on behalf of said corporation shall also be signing on their own behalf.

16. *Separability.* If any provision of this Agreement, or its application to any person or circumstance, is invalid or unenforceable, then the remainder of this Agreement or the application of that provision to other persons or circumstances shall not be affected.

17. *Governing law.* This Agreement shall be interpreted according to laws of the Commonwealth of Virginia.

IN WITNESS WHEREOF, the parties have executed and sealed this Agreement the day and year first above written.

_____          _____
JOHN DOE                                  JOHN COOK

_____          _____
MARY DOE                                  RUTH COOK

[1] *62 Am. Jr. 2d Private Franchise Contracts,* paras. 1–17; and *54 Am. Jur. 2d Monopolies, Restraints of Trade and Unfair Trade Practices,* para. 518. See 16 C.F.R. et seq. for disclosure requirements if offered to public.

## FORM VB 1.05

### (Manufacturer with independent sales agent)

### SALES AGREEMENT[1]

AGREEMENT made September 1, 1982, between ABLE MANUFACTURING CO., INC., an Ohio corporation with its principal place of business at 100 East Street, Dayton, Ohio 00000 (herein called "Corporation"), and John Doe, residing at 80 Circle Drive, Clearwater, Florida 00000 (herein called "ISA").

1. *Appointment of exclusive sales agent.* The Corporation hereby appoints ISA as its exclusive sales agent in Florida, Georgia, and Alabama to sell the electronic products manufactured by the Corporation.

2. *Sales office.* ISA maintains an office and showroom for the display and sale of similar products and shall maintain such office, or one similar thereto, during the term of this Agreement for the purpose of selling the Corporation's products.

3. *Compensation of agent.* The Corporation shall pay to ISA as his entire compensation for his services a commission of Ten Percent (10%) of the net invoice value of all shipments of its electronics products to any part of ISA territory for which payment shall have been received by the Corporation. The commissions are to be paid on the 15th day of each month for all shipments paid for during the preceding calendar month.

4. *Term.* The term of the agency shall be five (5) years from the date hereof. If ISA violates any provision of this Agreement, or becomes insolvent or bankrupt, the Corporation may on five (5) days' written notice to ISA terminate this Agreement, but the Corporation shall be obligated to pay ISA the commissions earned by him up to the date of termination.

5. *Restrictive covenant.* ISA shall devote ISA's entire time and attention to the sale of the Corporation's electronics products while this Agreement is in effect.

6. *Sales.* ISA shall not solicit any sales outside Florida, Georgia, and Alabama. In obtaining sales of the Corporation's electronics products, ISA shall quote only the prices and terms set forth in the annexed schedule, or such prices and terms as may be fixed hereafter by the Corporation. ISA shall forward all orders promptly to the Corporation, and each order shall be subject to the Corporation's acceptance. The Corporation shall forward to ISA a copy of invoice covering shipments of its electronic products to any part of his territory.

7. *Expenses.* ISA shall pay all the costs of conducting the agency hereunder, including commission or other compensation to salesmen employed by ISA.

8. *Samples.* The Corporation shall furnish ISA, at the Corporation's expense, a reasonable supply of samples and advertising matter to be used by ISA in connection with his agency hereunder. Such samples are the exclusive property of the Corporation, and ISA shall return them to the Corporation, at the Corporation's expense, upon the termination of this Agreement.

9. *Indemnification.* The Corporation agrees to indemnify and hold ISA harmless from any claim or damages for injuries resulting from product defects, including costs and reasonable attorney's fees in the event that ISA is included as a party in any product liability suit or government proceeding.

10. *Assignment.* This agency appointment is personal in nature, and ISA shall not assign his rights nor delegate the performance of his duties under this Agreement except as provided herein, without the prior written consent of the Corporation.[2]

IN WITNESS WHEREOF, the parties have signed and sealed this Agreement.

ATTEST:                      ABLE MANUFACTURING CO., INC.

(SEAL)

By ———————————————
                                President

———————————————
Secretary of the Corporation

———————————————
JOHN DOE

[1] *3 Am. Jur. 2d Agency*, paras. 99–116; and *53 Am. Jur. 2d Master and Servant*, para. 4.
[2] Ref. Form VB 1.05(a) for alternative clause.

## FORM VB 1.05(a)

### (Independent sales contract is assignable)[1]

## ALTERNATIVE CLAUSE

*Assignment.* As the ISA operates a going business, this Agreement is assignable to a bona fide purchaser or transferee of the business of ISA, provided the transferee executes an assumption agreement with the Corporation.

[1]Internal Revenue Service may or may not treat an assignment as a capital gain rather than income, depending on the circumstances.

# PART VI
# BUSINESS PERSONAL PROPERTY CONTRACTS

# PART VI

# Business Personal Property Contracts

## INTRODUCTION

This Part is divided into six Sections lettered A through F. The Sections provide forms for bailments (leases of personal property); barter agreement; agreements for the sale or purchase of "goods," as distinguished from the sale of other personal property; sale of a business; documents required for bulk transfer compliance; and documents to create and perfect a security interest in personal property.

There is a Client Questionnaire for each Section. Before drafting any document under this Part, read the Client Questionnaire for the Section.

Using the appropriate Client Questionnaire will provide the *facts* that are to be considered before drafting the instrument, and will indicate what supplemental documents may need to be drafted. For example, it is necessary to file a Financing Statement, which appears as Form VIF 1.03, to perfect the security interest created in the Security Agreement, which appears as Form VIF 1.02.

The footnotes to this Introduction and to the Client Questionnaires and forms in this Part will alert you to possible problems and to the need for supplemental documents and give you an overview of the *law* that affects the particular form.

Section C of this Part provides forms for the sale and purchase of "goods" as defined in the Uniform Commercial Code.

Since 1954, when Pennsylvania was the first state to adopt the Uniform Commercial Code,[1] the Code has been adopted in all states except Louisiana, which has adopted its own Commercial Laws that include certain U.C.C. provisions with variations.

Appendix VI to this book provides citations to the commercial code of every state. Citations in this Part are to the U.C.C. Since most of the states follow the format and section numbering of the Code, it will be simple to convert the U.C.C. citations to your state commercial code citations.

Commercial personal property contracts include leases of personal property, (bailments),[2] barter agreements,[3] sales of goods,[4] bulk transfers,[5] and security agree-

---

[1]*15A Am. Jur. 2d Commercial Code*, paras. 2–4.

[2]*8 Am. Jur. 2d Bailments*, paras. 54–61. And see also *48 ALR 3rd 668* for divergent views on application of U.C.C. warranty provisions to commercial bailments.

[3]*30 Am. Jur. 2d Exchange of Property*, paras. 5–28; and Vol. 68, April 1982 *American Bar Association Journal*, Page 409.

[4]Article II, Uniform Commercial Code.

[5]Article VI, Uniform Commercial Code.

ments.[6] In drafting any of these contracts, one should be familiar with the provisions of the Code. One should also have knowledge of "usages of the trade" involved and of any "course of dealing" between the parties involved.[7] Code definitions of terms will be used to interpret a commercial contract that is subject to the Code, unless the contract specifically provides its own applicable definitions. For Uniform Commercial Code Definitions, see Appendix VII.

The "unconscionable" provision[8] of the U.C.C., and the "implied warranty" provisions,[9] are both philosophically and practically different from the common law doctrine of "caveat emptor."

Federal legislation and regulation of consumer sales, real estate development, and the sale of securities, as well as federal labor, safety, and civil rights legislation, must also be considered in drafting commercial contracts, whether the contract is formal or informal as by letter, estimate, purchase order, and invoice or in any other form prescribed by custom or usage.

Disclosure requirements in consumer contracts[10] may appear as language contained in the body of a consumer contract being capitalized or otherwise emphasized as required by law, or they may appear in separate documents incorporated in the contract by reference or implication. The applicable statute and regulations under the statute must be consulted to ensure compliance.

If a commercial consumer contract is being drafted for repeated use, it is usually printed. The fine print on the back should be readable, and its presence as part of the contract should be clearly indicated on the front of the contract to comply with *basic* disclosure regulations.

When the attorney drafts the consumer contract, it will be typed. The client will then send it to the printer. To avoid future regulatory problems, the attorney should check the printer's proof before the final printing of the contract.

### SECTION A      BAILMENT (LEASE OF PERSONAL PROPERTY)

Before using the forms in this section, the general introduction to PART VI should be read. Use Form VIA 1.00 CLIENT QUESTIONNAIRE FOR LEASE OF PERSONAL PROPERTY (BAILMENT).

There are divergent views on the application of the Uniform Commercial Code to commercial bailments. Consult your state law on the subject. If in doubt, use the philosophy of the Code in drafting a commercial bailment.

#### FORM VIA 1.00

#### CLIENT QUESTIONNAIRE FOR LEASE
#### OF PERSONAL PROPERTY (BAILMENT)

1. Client's name, address, and telephone number
2. Will client be the lessor (bailor) of the property, or will he be handling, renting, or using the personal property?

---

[6]Article IX, Uniform Commercial Code.

[7]U.C.C. 1–201(3)(11) and 1–205.

[8]U.C.C. 2–302; and *67 Am. Jur. 2d Sales*, para. 116.

[9]U.C.C. 2–314 and 315.

[10]For example, see the Truth in Lending Act, 15 U.S.C.A. 1601–1665; Regulation Z, 12 C.F.R. 226; and the new Regulation M, 12 C.F.R. 213. See also state trade regulation statutes. See also Appendixes I, IX, X, and XI of this book.

3. Description of the personal property: Manufacturer's name and identification and serial numbers of machines or other equipment
4. *Condition of property and duty to repair*
   (a) Is the property new or used?
   (b) Is the property leased "as is"?
   (c) Does lessor (bailor) or lessee have duty to keep it in repair?
   (d) Will substitute equipment be provided during repair time? If so, what are the substitution terms?
5. What is the duration of the lease?
6. Are there any limitations on place and manner of use of the personal property? If so, what are they?
7. Is there an option to purchase? If so, what are the terms and conditions, including price, notice, and warranties?
8. Who is to be responsible for damage to the equipment? Who will carry insurance, if any, and on what terms?

## FORM VIA 1.01

### (Lease of manufacturing equipment)

#### EQUIPMENT LEASE[1]

AGREEMENT, made this 10th day of September, 1982, between Manufacturer's Equipment Corporation, a Pennsylvania corporation having its principal place of business at Suite 1248 Great Building, Philadelphia, Pennsylvania 00000 (herein called "Owner"), and Able Manufacturing, Inc., a Pennsylvania corporation having its principal place of business at 100 East Street, Pittsburgh, Pennsylvania 00000 (herein called "Bailee"), WITNESSETH,

WHEREAS, Owner is engaged in the business of leasing certain manufacturing equipment owned by it to manufacturers in the Commonwealth of Pennsylvania; and

WHEREAS, Bailee desires to lease the manufacturing equipment described herein; and

WHEREAS, Owner has inspected Bailee's plant and operation, and believes that the equipment is suitable for use in Bailee's manufacture of steel pellets.

IT IS AGREED:

1. *Description of leased property.* Owner shall furnish and install in the plant owned by Bailee on Highway 40, Butler, Pennsylvania, the steel pellet manufacturing equipment (herein called "Equipment") described in Exhibit A signed and annexed hereto and made part hereof.

2. *Warranty.* Owner warrants that the Equipment to be installed by Owner in Bailee's plant will produce 10 mg. uniform round steel pellets at the rate of 1,000 a second.

3. *Payment by Bailee.* Bailee shall pay to Owner, for the cost of installing and parts and service for the equipment, for the license to use the same under the Owner's letters patent, and for the right to use the Equipment in the Bailee's plant during the term of this Agreement, the sum of One Thousand Dollars ($1,000) in advance for the first three-month period after the installation provided in Paragraph 5, and at the beginning of each three-month period thereafter, during the balance of the term of this Agreement or any extension hereof.

4. *Repair of leased property.*[2] Owner shall, at its own cost and expense, upon written request of the Bailee, supply the Bailee with all parts and service necessary to keep the Equipment in proper repair and good working order, except when such parts shall be required because of the negligence of the Bailee or if the Bailee shall be in default in payments required by this Agreement.

5. *Location and use of leased property.* Bailee shall not remove the Equipment from the location in its plant where it is installed by Owner, nor part possession with any part of the Equipment, nor allow it to be used by anyone except the Bailee and its employees and agents, without the prior written consent of the Owner.

6. *Duration.* This Agreement shall become effective and continue for a period of five (5) years from the date of the installation of the equipment, which shall be completely installed within sixty (60) days of the signing of this Agreement, and shall continue from year to year unless either party shall notify the other in writing sixty (60) days before the expiration of the original five-year term, or any extension thereof, of its desire to terminate this Agreement.

7. *Time(s)*. Time is of the essence of this Agreement.

8. *Insurance*. Bailee shall, at its own cost and expense, but also for the Owner as its interest may appear, immediately insure the Equipment and keep it insured for Fifty Thousand Dollars ($50,000) against loss or damage by fire, and shall deliver to Owner photocopies of receipts for premiums paid showing this coverage. The proceeds of insurance received by Owner may be used by Owner to repair the damaged Equipment and substitute other Equipment of the same design and quality, which substituted Equipment shall be subject to all the terms and provisions of this Agreement; provided the substitution can be accomplished within sixty (60) days after Bailee's plant is ready for its use.

9. *Default*. In the event of default by Bailee in making any quarterly payment under this Agreement, or in the event of a breach by Bailee of any of the covenants and promises contained in this Agreement, or in the event of any of the following contingencies, then the balance of payments due to the end of this Agreement or extension thereof shall immediately become due and payable without notice or demand from Owner, and Owner shall have the right to enter the Bailee's premises, take possession of and remove the Equipment, and terminate all the rights and interests of the Bailee in the Equipment:

    (a) Bailee discontinues its business at the plant for more than sixty (60) days.

    (b) Bankruptcy or insolvency proceedings are commenced by or against Bailee.

    (c) Lessee makes an assignment for the benefit of creditors.

    (d) A receiver is appointed to take possession of the business of the Bailee.

10. *Successors and assigns of the parties*. This Agreement shall legally bind each party hereto and its respective successors and assigns.

IN WITNESS WHEREOF, the duly authorized officers of the parties have hereunto set their hands and caused their corporate seals to be affixed on the day and year written.

(CORPORATE SEAL)        MANUFACTURER'S EQUIPMENT CORPORATION

By _____

Secretary of the Corporation        President

(CORPORATE SEAL)        ABLE MANUFACTURING, INC.

By _____

Secretary of the Corporation        President

[1] *8 Am. Jur. 2d Bailments,* paras. 39, 163, 170; and *67 Am. Jur. 2d Sales,* para. 31. See also *48 A.L.R. 3rd 668* for divergent views on application of U.C.C. to commercial bailments.
[2] Ref. Form VIA 1.01(a) for alternative clause providing bailee duty to repair.

## FORM VIA 1.01(a)

### (Bailee's duty to repair)

### ALTERNATIVE CLAUSE

*Repair of leased property*. Bailee shall, at its own cost and expense, keep the Equipment in good and efficient working condition and repair and shall at all times exercise reasonable care in using the Equipment. Bailee shall, at its own cost and expense, at the end or other expiration of this Agreement, replace any damaged part and shall surrender the Equipment to the Owner in as good order and condition as it is now, reasonable wear and tear excepted. The care required of Bailee under this Paragraph shall include, but not be limited to:

    (a) Furnishing all electric and water power connections necessary for the installation and use of the Equipment as prescribed in writing by Owner.

    (b) Properly use the Equipment in accordance with Owner's written manual of instructions, which is annexed hereto and made part hereof.

    (c) Properly maintain the Equipment by regular cleaning, oiling, and inspection in accordance with Owner's manual of instructions, which is annexed hereto and made part hereof.

    (d) Pay all taxes and assessments that may be imposed by any taxing authority upon the Equipment or its use.

## FORM VIA 1.02

### (Computer lease with provision for granting of a security interest in the leased property by the Lessee to Lessor)

#### EQUIPMENT LEASE[1]

BY THIS AGREEMENT made October 1, 1982, between MODERN ELECTRONICS CORPORATION, a Florida corporation with plant and offices at No. 1 Industry Park, Tampa, Florida 00000 (herein called "Lessor"), and LOCAL AIRLINES, INC., a Florida corporation with offices at 100 Main Street, Miami, Florida 00000 (herein called "Lessee"), IT IS AGREED AS FOLLOWS:

1. *Description of leased property.* Lessor shall deliver for rental computer equipment described by trade name and serial number in Schedule A (herein called the "Equipment") to Lessee at its office at 100 Main Street, Miami, Florida, and its office at the Albert Ace Airport, Neartown, Florida, as indicated on the Schedule.

2. *Duration of lease.* Lessor leases the Equipment to Lessee for a term of three (3) years beginning on the date of delivery.

3. *Rent.* Leasee shall pay to Lessor as rent for the use of the Equipment the sum of Seven Hundred Dollars ($700) per month, the first payment to be made on completed delivery of the Equipment and the balance of the rent to be paid monthly, in advance for the term of this Agreement.

4. *Ownership and security interest of Lessor.*[2] Equipment is solely owned by Lessor, subject to the Lessee's rights hereunder. The Lessee's rights hereunder are to use the Equipment in the normal course of its business at the two locations to which the Equipment shall be delivered in accordance with the terms of this Agreement.

   (a) Notice of Lessor's ownership shall be displayed on each article of the Equipment by means of a suitable label or plaque affixed thereto, which shall not be removed or damaged by the Lessee. If such identification becomes illegible or damaged, Lessee shall notify Lessor and shall permit Lessor to repair or replace the illegible or damaged identification.

   (b) Equipment shall remain personal property of Lessor even if installed in or attached to real property.

   (c) Lessee shall not pledge or create any security interest in the Equipment other than the security interest of the Lessor created hereunder, and shall not sublet or remove the Equipment or any part of it, without the Lessor's written permission, from the locations to which it is delivered hereunder.

   (d) Lessee shall keep the Equipment free and clear of all claims, levies, liens, and encumbrances at all times and shall immediately give Lessor notice (to be confirmed in writing) of any such claim or judicial process affecting the Equipment or any part of it leased hereunder.

   (e) Lessee hereby grants Lessor a security interest in the Equipment in the amount of the market value of the Equipment as shown on Schedule B, subject to the terms of this Lease.

5. *Use, repairs, and replacement.*

   (a) Lessee shall cause the Equipment to be operated by competent and qualified personnel in accordance with the manufacturer's manual of instructions to be provided by Lessor.

   (b) Lessee shall keep the Equipment in good condition and, at its own cost and expense, make all repairs and part replacements necessary for its use and preservation, and all replacement parts shall forthwith become the property of the Lessor, except that Lessee may purchase a Service Contract for the Equipment from Lessor, which shall modify this Paragraph in accordance with the terms of the Service Contract.

   (c) Lessee shall be responsible for any damages to the Equipment while in Lessee's possession and shall pay to Lessor the value of the Equipment or any part thereof that is damaged or destroyed. Upon receipt of such payment, Lessor shall, to the extent of the amount paid, assign to the Lessee any rights Lessor may have with respect to the damaged or destroyed item of Equipment under any insurance together with all of Lessor's right, title, and interest in the item of Equipment.

   (d) At the end of the term of this Lease, Lessee shall return the Equipment to Lessor in as good condition as when received, reasonable wear and tear excepted, by allowing Lessor to pick up the equipment at Lessee's places of business.

6. *Insurance.* Lessee, at its cost and expense, shall insure the Equipment against burglary, theft, fire, windstorm, and vandalism in the amount of Twenty Thousand Dollars ($20,000), and maintain public liability insurance with minimum limits of One Hundred Thousand Dollars/Three Hundred Thousand Dollars ($100,000/$300,000) for bodily injury and Twenty-five Thousand Dollars ($25,000) for property damage in such form as shall be satisfactory to Lessor, naming Lessee and Lessor as insureds as their interest appear, with the right to payment of all losses direct to each insured. A copy of the policy and premium receipt shall be supplied by Lessee to Lessor forthwith upon completed delivery of the Equipment.

7. *Default and termination.*

(a) Upon default in the payment of any installment of rent, or upon a breach of any other conditions of this Lease Agreement, or if, during the term of this Lease, bankruptcy, insolvency, or receivership proceedings are instituted by or against Lessee, of if Lessee discontinues business at both office locations for a period of thirty (30) days, the Lessee shall be in default under this Lease Agreement and the Lessor shall have the right, without notice or demand, to terminate this Lease, but such termination shall not release Lessee from payment of damages sustained by Lessor.

(b) If, on default or termination of this Lease as provided in (a) above, Lessee fails or refuses to deliver the Equipment forthwith to Lessor, the Lessor shall have the right to enter Lessee's premises or any other premises where the Equipment may be found and to take possession of and remove the Equipment without legal process.

(c) The remedy allowed Lessor under (b) above does not limit Lessor in enforcing its rights under this contract but is cumulative with all other remedies at law available to Lessor to which it might be otherwise entitled.

8. *Assignability.* This Lease Agreement is not assignable without the written consent of Lessor. IN WITNESS WHEREOF, the parties have executed this Lease Agreement by their respective duly authorized officers.

(CORPORATE SEAL)                                  MODERN ELECTRONICS CORPORATION

                                                                     By _____
——————————————————————————
Secretary of the Corporation                                   President

(CORPORATE SEAL)                                  LOCAL AIRLINES, INC.

                                                                     By _____
——————————————————————————
Secretary of the Corporation                                   President

(Note: to perfect the security interest granted in Paragraph 4, a Financing Statement must be filed referring to this Lease Agreement. If the Equipment described in the Schedule B would ordinarily become fixtures, file the county financing form in the county where the plant is located. If it is movable equipment, file with the state the financing form similar to Form VIF 1.03.)

[1] *8 Am. Jr. 2d Bailments*, paras. 39–44; and *67 Am. Jur. 2d Sales*, paras. 30 and 31. If the lease is a consumer lease, see Consumer Leasing Act, 15 U.S.C.A. 1667–1667E (part of the Truth in Lending Act) and Appendix for Basic Federal Consumer Protection Law citations. Since computer leases and sales are proliferating in business and in the professions, it is interesting to note that Hamline University School of Law in St. Paul, Minnesota, requires a "computer literacy course." Ref. footnotes to Form VIA 1.03 for business purpose (not consumer) lease.

[2] Ref. Chapter VIF for other security agreements.

### FORM VIA 1.03

#### (Truck fleet lease with option to purchase)

### LEASE AGREEMENT[1]

AGREEMENT made this 8th day of May, 1982, between ALPHA MOTOR SALES & LEASING SERVICE, INC., a New York corporation with offices at 100 East Street, Borough of Queens, New York, New York 00000 (herein called "Owner"), and ABC FOODS, INC., a New York corporation with offices at 100 West Street, Borough of Queens, New York, New York 00000 (herein called "Lessee"), WITNESSETH:

WHEREAS, Owner is the owner of certain motor vehicles and is engaged in the business of leasing those vehicles and servicing them; and

WHEREAS, Lessee desires to lease certain of those vehicles for use in its food distribution business;

NOW THEREFORE, in consideration of the following mutual promises and convenants, it is AGREED AS FOLLOWS:

1. *DESCRIPTION OF LEASED PROPERTY*

Owner leases to Lessee and Lessee hires the trucks *described and valued in Schedule A* attached hereto and made part hereof, for the purpose of transporting packaged food products in the State of New York for the period beginning June 1, 1982, and ending May 31, 1985, subject to the terms and conditions of this Agreement.

2. *RENT*

(a) Lessee shall pay Owner for the use of each truck operated and used hereunder a sum that shall consist of a mileage charge of One Dollar ($1) a mile for the total number of miles each truck is operated each week, plus an operating service charge of One Hundred Dollars ($100) per week for each truck, computed on the number of continuous weeks that each truck is used. The rent shall be payable on or before each succeeding Wednesday.

(b) On Saturdays of each week, Owner shall furnish to Lessee a Check Sheet that will show the time Lessee's drivers leave and return to Owner's garage and odometer readings for each truck on leaving and returning to the garage, with the number of miles run each day. Both Owner's employee in charge of its garage and Lessee's drivers shall sign the Check Sheet. If Lessee does not dispute the information appearing on the Check Sheet within a reasonable time, not to exceed thirty (30) days, the Check Sheet shall be conclusive evidence of the amount due Owner from Lessee for the mileage charge provided herein for the week represented by the Check Sheet.

3. *ADDITIONAL TRUCKS*

In the event that Lessee temporarily requires more trucks in the operation of its business than the number of trucks listed on Schedule A, it may lease additional trucks from Owner on the same terms and conditions as provided in this Lease Agreement, except that the rent payable by Lessee for the temporary additional vehicles shall be at rates to be mutually agreed upon at the time; provided it gives Owner one (1) month's notice in writing, and further provided that Owner has such additional trucks available for leasing.

4. *TERMINATION WITHOUT CAUSE*

(a) Lessee may terminate this Agreement at any time by giving at least sixty (60) days' written notice of intention to terminate mailed to Owner at its place of business as shown herein, subject to the provisions of Paragraph 5 hereof.

(b) Owner may terminate this Agreement on May 31 of any year by giving Lessee ninety (90) days' written notice of intention to terminate mailed to Lessee at its place of business as shown herein, subject to the provisions of Paragraph 5 hereof.

5. *TERMINATION FOR CAUSE*

Time is of the essence of this Agreement, except that Owner shall not be liable to Lessee for failure to supply a truck, repair a truck, or substitute a truck for a disabled vehicle if such failure is due to war, strike, or accident, or other cause beyond Owner's control. Prompt payment of rent by Lessee under this Agreement is of the essence of the Agreement. If Lessee shall fail to make payment when due, Owner may give Lessee written notice of nonpayment by registered or certified mail, and if Lessee does not pay within five (5) days after the receipt of that notice, Owner may terminate this Agreement and take, retain, or regain possession of the trucks on or off the premises of Lessee without liability to Lessee in any suit or action by Lessee, except that Owner shall retain the right to recover all payments due and/or damages suffered by Lessee's default or breach of this Agreement.

6. *OPTION TO PURCHASE*

(a) In the event that Owner or Lessee shall elect to terminate this Agreement pursuant to Paragraph 4, Lessee shall have the option to purchase the Owner's trucks then in use in Lessee's business, not to exceed the number of trucks listed in Schedule A less the amount arrived at by applying the depreciation formula set forth in Schedule A.

(b) If this Agreement is not terminated by either party during the term thereof, Lessee shall not be obligated to purchase but Lessee shall have the right and option to purchase the trucks then in use in Lessee's business, not to exceed the number of trucks listed in Schedule A, for the price set forth in Schedule A less the amount arrived at by applying the depreciation formula set forth in Schedule A.

7. *SERVICE OF TRUCKS*

(a) Owner agrees, as its own expense, to maintain each truck leased hereunder in good repair and appearance in all respects, properly supplied with oil and lubricated, painted, and lettered to the reasonable satisfaction of Lessee; and to furnish all tires and tire replacements for each truck as needed for safety and efficiency of operation of the truck.

(b) Owner shall pay for oil lubricants and like articles purchased by drivers and shall pay all necessary towing charges, upon submission of authentic vouchers from the service supplier. Lessee shall, at its own expense, furnish the gasoline or diesel fuel necessary to operate the trucks in Lessee's business.

(c) Lessee shall not permit its drivers or other employees to make any repair or adjustment on the trucks, except to substitute spare tires in cases of trucks equipped with pneumatic tires when tire trouble occurs away from the garage.

(d) Lessee shall hire and use only safe and careful licensed chauffeurs as drivers, who shall be selected by and under the orders, directions, employment, and pay of Lessee. Upon written demand of Owner specifying any reckless or abusive handling of a truck, or other incompetence, Lessee shall forthwith remove that driver and substitute another, subject to the rights of Lessee's driver to a hearing on such removal and/or substitution.

(e) In the event any of the trucks to be used under this Agreement shall be disabled for any cause, Owner shall repair or cause the truck to be repaired forthwith if brought to its service department at 100 East Street, Borough of Queens, or within a reasonable time after receipt by Owner of notice from Lessee or its agents given in writing (if notice is originally given orally) as to the location of the truck and the nature of the disability if known.

(f) In the event that Owner determines that it is impracticable to repair any disabled truck pursuant to the notice given under (c) above, Owner shall substitute another truck of substantially equivalent carrying capacity, in good operating condition, for the transshipment of products at any point at which the truck shall have been disabled. In the event that the substituted truck is not reasonably satisfactory to Lessee, or in the event that the repair time is unreasonably long in the opinion of the Lessee, it may rent a truck on the open market to take the place of the truck substituted by owner for the disabled truck, and the operating charge for the week in which the truck was disabled shall not be made, nor shall the operating charge for the disabled truck be resumed, until the repaired truck or a substitute reasonably satisfactory to Lessee is provided.

(g) Owner shall furnish garage storage at its service department. There shall be no mileage charge to Lessee for trips from Lessee's warehouse to Owner's garage or for towing of a disabled truck to Owner's garage and storage space.

(h) Lessee shall cause each truck to be returned to Owner's service department for a minimum of four (4) hours in each and every twenty-four (24) hours, except with Owner's consent in writing.

(i) Owner shall cause each truck to be duly registered, licensed, and put and kept in an operating condition to comply with all laws and regulations, and shall furnish all licenses and permits applying to the trucks required by any governmental subdivision within the State of New York.

8. *LIABILITY AND INSURANCE*

(a) Lessee's drivers shall be solely responsible for individual fines and penalties for speeding, parking, or other violation of any statute, ordinance, or regulation of any governmental subdivision regulating the operation of the truck.

(b) Lessee shall not use nor allow any truck leased hereunder to be used for any illegal purpose, and shall be liable to Owner for any damages resulting from or damage to or forfeiture of any truck leased hereunder by reason of any illegal use.

(c) Owner shall assume the liability of Lessee to third parties (excluding Lessee's drivers) for death or injury to persons or properties resulting from the operation of the trucks used or operated hereunder in Lessee's usual course of business, and shall insure that liability of Lessee, at Owner's sole expense, by obtaining public liability insurance against liability arising out of the operation of each truck, from an insurance company or companies approved by the Insurance Department of the State of New York and reasonably satisfactory to Lessee, in the amount of Five Hundred Thousand Dollars ($500,000) per accident, and Two Hundred Thousand Dollars ($200,000) per individual for death or personal injury, and Fifteen Thousand Dollars ($15,000) for property per accident. Owner shall provide Lessee with a certificate of that insurance at or before the time of delivering the first truck to Lessee under this Agreement.

(d) Lessee shall give Owner written notice within twenty-four (24) hours of any accidents or collisions involving any truck, stating the time, place, and persons involved in the collision, plus complete details and the names and addresses of any witnesses known to Lessee or its agents.

(e) Lessee shall cooperate sincerely and fully with Owner and its insurance company in the preparation, prosecution, and/or defense of any settlement attempt or legal action arising from any accident or collision described in this Paragraph. Compliance with this Paragraph (e) is a condition precedent to Owner's liability under Paragraph (c).

9. *ASSIGNABILITY*

This Agreement is not assignable by the Lessee without the written consent of the Owner.

IN WITNESS WHEREOF, the parties have caused this Agreement to be signed and sealed by their respective duly authorized corporate officers on the day above written.

(CORPORATE SEAL)                                    ALPHA MOTOR SALES & LEASING SERVICE, INC.

                                                    By _____
_____
Secretary of the Corporation                            President

(CORPORATE SEAL)                                    ABC FOODS, INC.

                                                    By _____
_____
Secretary of the Corporation                            President

[1]U.C.C. 9-105(1)(b), 9-308. *68 Am. Jur. 2d Secured Transactions,* paras. 117–121. Business purpose lease is specifically excluded from the Consumer Leasing Act, 15 U.S.C.A. 1667–1667E (part of the Truth in Lending Act), but ordinary rent-a-car leases to the public are regulated by the Act. See *8 Am. Jr. 2d Bailments,* paras. 5–13 and 241. See also I.R.C. 168(f)(8) of ERTA (1981) for "safe harbor" leasing and I.R.C. 465. See also 12 C.F.R. 226 for required disclosure in *consumer* leases with option to purchase; and new Regulation M, 12 C.F.R. 213, effective April 1, 1981.

## FORM VIA 1.04

### (Aircraft lease of company aircraft to an individual)

### AIRCRAFT LEASE[1]

AGREEMENT between ACE SALES AND SERVICE CORPORATION, a Pennsylvania corporation having offices at 100 Clark Building, Pittsburgh, Pennsylvania 00000 (herein called "Lessor", and John Doe of 100 Oak Drive, Allison Park, Pennsylvania 00000 (herein called "Lessee", WITNESSETH:

WHEREAS, Lessor is the owner of the airplane described herein that has been used in the operation of its company business; and

WHEREAS, Lessee is desirous of renting said aircraft for his personal business use;

IT IS AGREED:

1. *Description of leased aircraft.* The following aircraft, presently parked in Hangar No. 4 at the North Borough Airport, Route 4, Pittsburgh, Pennsylvania, is hereby leased to Lessee for a period of one (1) year:

Cessna Model 111
FAA Registration No. T46 12345
Aircraft Serial No. 1234567
Engine Make and Model Super Model 88X
Engine Serial No. 891011
Propeller Make Epic
Propeller Serial No. 45678910

2. *Warranty.* Lessor warrants that the aircraft is owned by Lessor and is duly registered with the FAA and is in airworthy condition.

3. *Rent.* Lessee shall pay Lessor as rental for the use of the aircraft by Lessee and his agents the sum of One Thousand Dollars ($1,000) per month, payable on the 5th day of each month, beginning June 1, 1982, for the term of one (1) year, being a total rent of Twelve Thousand Dollars ($12,000).

4. *Use.*

(a) Lessee shall use the aircraft in conformance with all requirements of state and federal statutes and regulations, and the aircraft shall be based at Pittsburgh, Pennsylvania.

(b) Lessee shall allow the aircraft to be operated only by competent and qualified personnel, who shall at all times be considered agents of Lessee in the operation and use of the aircraft.

(c) Lessee shall not pledge, loan, mortgage, sublet, or part with possession of the aircraft or permit any liens to be incurred upon the aircraft. In the event that any claim of lien or judicial process is directed to the aircraft, Lessee shall forthwith notify Lessor of that claim or action and shall confirm that notice in writing.

5. *Repairs and replacements.* Lessee shall keep the airplane in good condition and shall make all repairs necessary for its airworthy operation at Lessee's expense. At the termination of this Lease, the aircraft shall be surrendered to Lessor at a Pittsburgh, Pennsylvania, airport in the same condition it was leased, reasonable wear and tear excepted.

6. *Insurance.* Lessor shall insure the aircraft against loss in such manners and amounts as Lessor deems necessary. Lessee shall procure reasonable public liability insurance for any claim for personal injury or property damage resulting from the operation or storage of the aircraft during the term of this Lease. In any event, Lessee indemnifies and hereby agrees to hold Lessor harmless from any claim by reason of the operation or storage of the aircraft by Lessee or his agents.

7. *Default.* Upon default of payment of rental or breach of any of the conditions of this Lease Agreement, Lessor shall have the right, without notice or demand, to terminate this Lease and shall forthwith have the right to take possession of the aircraft and to remove it, without legal process, wherever found. Such termination shall not release Lessee from the payment of any damages sustained by Lessor as provided herein. The remedy of repossession shall be cumulative with any other remedies the Lessor may have against the Lessee as a matter of law.

Dated and signed this 20th day of May, 1982.

(CORPORATE SEAL)                              ACE SALES AND SERVICE CORPORATION, Lessor

                                             By _____
_____
Secretary of the Corporation                             President

                                             _____
                                             JOHN DOE, Lessee

[1]*8 Am. Jur. 2d Aviation,* para. 25. See also 49 U.S.C.A. 1401 and 1403.

## SECTION B     BARTER

Before using the form in this section, the general introduction to PART VI should be read as well as FORM VIB 1.00 CLIENT QUESTIONNAIRE FOR BARTER AGREEMENTS.

### FORM VIB 1.00

### CLIENT QUESTIONNAIRE FOR BARTER AGREEMENTS[1]

1. Names and addresses of both parties
2. Telephone number(s) of client
3. Exact names in which the personal properties to be exchanged are registered if registration is required as: motor vehicle, aircraft, mobile home (corporate name or joint names)
4. Description of *both* properties, including trade name, model number, serial number, or other appropriate identification of the particular item
5. Are services to be exchanged for property? If so, nature and value of services
6. Are either or both parties "merchants" under the U.C.C.?[2]
7. Capacity and authority to contract. Are both parties of age and sui juris? If the property is owned by a corporation or owned jointly, who will sign the agreement and by what authority?

8. Time for performance or delivery of services. Is performance by one a condition precedent to performance by the other?

9. Who pays the cost of transferring title, if such transfer is necessary?

[1]*30 Am. Jur. 2d Exchange of Property*, paras. 5–28; and Vol. 68, April 1982, *American Bar Association Journal*, Page 409. See also U.C.C. 1–201(9), wherein "buying" includes exchange of goods.
[2]U.C.C. 2–104.

## FORM VIB 1.01

### (Agreement to barter corporate services for purchase of motor vehicle)

#### BARTER AGREEMENT[1]

BY AGREEMENT made in Miami, Florida, on November 1, 1982, between ACE AUTO SALES, INC., a Florida corporation having its principal office at 100 East Boulevard, Miami, Florida 00000 (herein called "Seller"), and ARTHUR DOE, P.A., a Florida professional accounting corporation having its principal office at 100 Flagler Street, Miami, Florida 00000 (herein called "Accountant"), Accountant shall perform the accounting services described herein, in consideration of One Dollar ($1) paid, the receipt of which is hereby acknowledged, and in further consideration of the transfer of title to the motor vehicle described herein by Seller to Accountant as provided herein, as follows:

1. *Accounting Services.*

(a) During the two (2)-year period beginning January 1, 1983, Accountant shall prepare monthly profit and loss statements for Seller's corporate business, an annual balance sheet for Seller's corporate business, and Seller's Florida Annual Report and federal corporate income tax returns. Said statements, reports, and tax returns shall be prepared in accordance with good and accepted accounting practice.

(b) The monthly statements shall be completed by the 15th of each month, beginning February 15, 1983, unless the completion is prevented by actions or conduct of the Seller.

(c) The information for the monthly statements shall be obtained from Seller's bookkeeping records at Seller's office, which records shall be kept by Seller in accordance with the advice and instruction of Accountant to be given to Seller on or before January 1, 1983. The bookkeeping records shall be available to Accountant's representative(s) during Seller's business hours from the 5th to the 15th of each month during the term of this Agreement.

(d) The information for all other statements, reports, and tax returns of Seller to be prepared by Accountant hereunder shall be made available to Accountant by Seller at all reasonable times, upon demand by Accountant.

(e) The value of the accounting services is Thirty-five Hundred Dollars ($3,500) per year.

2. *Delivery of Motor Vehicle and transfer of Title.*

(a) On January 1, 1983, Seller shall deliver the following described motor vehicle to Accountant at Seller's place of business: New '83 American Motors Concord 4D ID. No. A0A055C 300248

(b) Title in the motor vehicle shall remain in Seller until Accountant has completed its performance under this Agreement. Seller shall maintain collision, fire, and theft insurance during that period.

(c) Beginning on the date of delivery, Accountant shall obtain and maintain public liability One Hundred Thousand Dollars/Three Hundred Thousand Dollars ($100,000/300,000) personal injury and Ten Thousand Dollars ($10,000) property for the operation of the motor vehicle. Proof of payment of that insurance shall be provided to Seller on delivery of the motor vehicle by Seller to Accountant.

(d) Accountant shall have the right to use the motor vehicle as its own during the term of this Agreement, provided Miami, Florida, is its base of operation.

(e) While the motor vehicle is being used by Accountant, Accountant shall be responsible for all repairs and parts required that are not covered in Seller's standard new-car warranty agreement for the motor vehicle described above. When title to the motor vehicle is transferred to Accountant pursuant to this Agreement, the new-car warranty date shall be considered to be January 1, 1983, or the date of delivery of the motor vehicle to Accountant hereunder, whichever is later.

(f) Upon completion of Accountant's services under this Agreement, Seller shall cause the title to the motor vehicle to be transferred free and clear to Accountant, at the cost and expense of Seller, within ten (10) days of the completion of performance.

3. *Default and termination.*

(a) In the event that Accountant fails to provide statements, balance sheets, annual reports, or tax returns within the time required by this Agreement, he shall be in default, and Seller shall have the right, without notice or demand, to terminate this Agreement and to recover possession of the motor vehicle, wherever located, without judicial process. This right to terminate and repossess shall not limit Seller's right to any damages suffered by it as a result of Accountant's breach of any provision of this Agreement.

(b) Upon any termination of this Agreement, whether for cause or not, Accountant shall surrender to Seller, or to anyone designated by Seller, all contracts, deeds, papers, bookkeeping records, and other instruments and documents in Accountant's possession or under his control relating to the business of the Seller.

IN WITNESS WHEREOF, the parties hereto have caused this Agreement to be signed and their corporate seals to be attached by their duly authorized corporate officers on the day and year above written.

(CORPORATE SEAL)                              ACE AUTO SALES, INC.

_____   By _____
Secretary of the Corporation                    President

(CORPORATE SEAL)                              ARTHUR DOE, P.A.

_____   By _____
Secretary of the Corporation                    President

¹72 *Am. Jur. 2d Statute of Frauds,* paras. 132 and 133; *67 Am. Jur. 2d Sales,* paras. 29 and 61. See also *30 Am. Jur. 2d Exchange of Property,* paras. 1–5, 8, 13, 15–19, 28, 30, 34, 35, and 50.

## SECTION C     SALE OR PURCHASE OF GOODS

Before using the forms in this section, the general introduction to PART VI should be read as well as FORM VIC 1.00.

The forms in this section include formal and informal sale contracts and contracts for both cash and credit sales.

If a form in this section is used for a "consumer" sale, special attention must be given to the size and placement of certain consumer sale disclosure requirements of federal and state statutes as illustrated in FORM VIC 1.04 and FORM VIC 1.04(a).

For forms of additional documents required where a sale of personal property is a bulk transfer as defined in the Uniform Commercial Code, see Section E of PART VI.

Section F of this section provides FORM VIF 1.01 for use when a security interest in consumer goods is to be created.

If a formal sale of goods contract is being drafted, check Appendix VII of this book for citations to the Uniform Commercial Code definitions of commercial words and phrases. Appendix VI gives the state citations to state statutes which have enacted the Code.

## FORM VIC 1.00
### CLIENT QUESTIONNAIRE FOR SALE OR PURCHASE OF GOODS[1]

1. Name, address, and telephone number of buyer and seller
2. Is either buyer or seller a "merchant" under U.C.C. 2-104?
3. Is buyer a "consumer" under the Consumer Protection Laws?[2]
4. Description of goods to be bought or sold. Are they included as "goods" under U.C.C. 2-105? Get manufacturer's serial number or other ID numbers as well as brand name, color, size, year of manufacture, and other information necessary to describe the goods, as: specifications (U.C.C. 2-301 and 2-313[1][b]) or sample (U.C.C. 2-301 and 2-313[1][c])
5. Is the transaction a "sale" under U.C.C. 2-106?
6. Is the transaction a "bulk transfer" under U.C.C. Article 6?[3]
7. When and where are the goods to be delivered? U.C.C. 1-204, 2-301, 2-307, 2-308, 2-309(3), 2-311, 2-503, and 2-504
8. Price. U.C.C. 2-305 and terms. U.C.C. 2-319, 2-320, 2-322, 2-504
9. Any deposit? If so, terms of forfeiture of deposit. U.C.C. 2-718
10. Is there a trade-in? U.C.C. 2-304
11. Is payment to be made at time of delivery or in the future after delivery? Will there be a cash discount? If so, time and amount. U.C.C. 2-301 and 2-304. Inspection of goods? U.C.C. 2-310, 2-321, and 2-513
12. If payment is to be made in the future after delivery, is it to be made in installments? If so, see U.C.C. 2-612 and get the following information:
    (a) Amount and time of installment payments
    (b) Interest rate, if any
    (c) Discount or penalty for early payment
    (d) Will there be acceleration for nonpayment and/or provision for late charges on note given in payment? U.C.C. 1-208, 2-301, and 2-305
    (e) Is time of the essence of the contract? U.C.C. 2-612(3)
    (f) Any presupposed conditions? U.C.C. 2-615
13. Are you to prepare the security agreement, if any?[4] U.C.C. 1-208
14. Are the goods to be sold "as is"? U.C.C. 2-316(2)
15. Are there to be any express warranties? If so, what are they? Is there to be a time limit? U.C.C. 2-313
16. The U.C.C. provides for the following warranties, unless they are excluded or modified by the sale agreement. Are any of them to be limited in time or otherwise excluded or otherwise modified?
    (a) Of title and against infringement. U.C.C. 2-312
    (b) Express warranty of description used in the contract or in representations inducing the sale. U.C.C. 2-313 and 2-202
    (c) Implied warranty based on usage or trade. U.C.C. 2-314
    (d) Implied warranty of fitness for particular purpose. U.C.C. 2-315
    (e) Implied warranty of merchantability. U.C.C. 2-315
    (f) Express warranty that goods will conform to a sample. U.C.C. 2-317
    (g) Warranties apply to third parties as to consumer goods. U.C.C. 2-318
    Note that the buyer must agree to any warranty exclusion or modification. U.C.C. 2-316
17. Terms of acceptance. U.C.C. 2-316, 2-508, 2-509, 2-510, 2-513(3), 2-602, and 2-606
18. Will client want or get all output of the manufacturer, or does buyer want or get all his requirements from the seller? U.C.C. 1-201, 2-203(1)(b), and 2-306
19. Is there to be an exclusive dealings clause? U.C.C. 2-306
20. Risk of loss. U.C.C. 2-319, 2-311, 2-327, 2-501, 2-509, 2-510, 2-722(b). Do the parties wish to allocate the risk of loss? U.C.C. 2-303. Identification of goods? U.C.C. 2-501. Transfer of title? U.C.C. 2-401
21. Are there to be any "return" provisions? U.C.C. 2-326 and 2-327
22. How will the sale contract be terminated or canceled? U.C.C. 1-204, 2-106, 2-301, and 2-309(3)
23. Will there be a provision for limited or liquidated damages or for arbitration? U.C.C. 2-316(4) in conjunction with 2-718 and 2-719 For remedies generally, see U.C.C. 2-701 through 2-724
24. Will there be any limitation on the time in which suit can be brought on the contract? The time may be reduced, but it cannot be extended. U.C.C. 2-725

25. Is there any course of dealing or usage of trade that may affect the contract if not specifically dealt with in the contract?[5] U.C.C. 1-205 and 1-102(2), (3), and (4)
26. Is delegation or assignment of the contract to be prohibited? U.C.C. 2-210
27. How may the contract be modified? U.C.C. 2-207 and 2-209. See also U.C.C. 2-202
28. Have any representations been made to induce the contract that are not included in the contract? U.C.C. 2-202 and 2-313(1)(a) and 2-313(2)
29. Is a "resale price maintenance"[6] clause to be included? U.C.C. 2-306, and see U.C.C. 1-103
30. What state law shall govern the contract? U.C.C. 1-105

[1]Article 2 Uniform Commercial Code; and 67 *Am. Jur. 2d Sales,* paras. 14 and 15.
[2]See Appendix for consumer protection laws.
[3]Ref. Forms VIE 1.00-1.02(a).
[4]Article 9 Uniform Commercial Code. Ref. Forms IV 1.00–1.04.
[5]67 *Am. Jur. 2d Sales,* paras. 22–26.
[6]32 *Am. Jur. 2d Fair Trade Laws,* paras. 1–3; and 54 *Am. Jur. 2d Monopolies, Restraints of Trade and Unfair Trade Laws,* para. 53. See also 15 U.S.C.A. 1, as amended December 12, 1975, Pub. L. 94–145, para. 2, 89 Stat. 801. Ref. Form VIC 1.05.

## FORM VIC 1.01

(Formal sale of goods contract—*according to specification,* delivery
of specified total number of items as ordered monthly by buyer)

### AGREEMENT[1]

THIS AGREEMENT made this 12th day of June, 1982, between MUSIC MANUFACTURING CORPORATION of Fort Worth, Texas (herein called "Seller"), and RECREATION SALES, INC., of Tampa, Florida (herein called "Buyer"), WITNESSETH:

1. *Description of goods.* That the Seller agrees to deliver to Buyer the following described goods upon the terms and conditions hereinafter set forth:

| QUANTITY | DESCRIPTION & SPECIFICATIONS | UNIT PRICE |
|---|---|---|
| 100 | Star Sound speaker systems, according to the following specifications:<br>Frequency response—20–20,000 Hz<br>Impedance—8 ohms<br>Speaker Complement—10″ high-compliance woofer;<br>  2 extended-range, high-compliance 3″ tweeters<br>Enclosure—sealed oiled walnut veneer with removable grille<br>Control—tweeter level switch<br>Dimensions—23″ H × 12″ W × 11½″ D<br>Shipping weight—34 lbs. | $50<br>f.o.b. Fort Worth |

2. *Total purchase price.* The total purchase price is Five Thousand Dollars ($5,000) f.o.b. Fort Worth, Texas, to be paid in installments as the goods are delivered pursuant to the terms of this Agreement. This term is a price term only, and buyer shall also bear and pay all shipping and delivery costs.[2]
3. *Delivery of goods.* Ten (10) speaker systems shall be shipped from Fort Worth, Texas, to the Buyer on August 15, 1982. The balance of the speakers shall be shipped by Seller in lots as required by the Buyer on fifteen (15) days' written notice by Buyer during the term of this Agreement. If no notice to ship shall be given by the Buyer in any one (1) month, the Seller shall have a right to ship a lot of one-third (1/3) of the remaining speaker systems to the Buyer each month; and Buyer hereby agrees to accept and pay for the lot of speaker systems shipped upon the Seller tendering to the Buyer the railroad bill of lading.
4. *Payment of purchase price.* The purchase price shall be paid in installments as the speakers are shipped pursuant to this Agreement, as follows: Two Percent (2%) ten (10) days, thirty (30) days net cash against railroad bill of lading and documents, at the time the goods leave the Seller's factory at Fort Worth, Texas.
5. *Time of essence.* Time is of the essence of this contract, in that Buyer is purchasing the

goods for Christmas 1982 promotion and sale. Each month's shipment shall be treated as a separate and independent contract; but if Buyer shall fail to fulfill the terms of payment provided herein, the Seller, at its option, may cancel the contracts, or defer further shipments until payment due shall have been made.

6. *Excuse for nonperformance.* The Seller shall not be responsible for contingencies beyond its control that may or shall prevent shipment at the time or times provided in this Agreement.

7. *Taxes.* Any tax or taxes that may be imposed upon the finished goods that are the subject of this sale, or upon the sale or delivery, shall be added to and become a part of the contract price and shall be paid by the Buyer.

Dated this 12th day of June, 1982.

(SEAL)                                                 MUSIC MANUFACTURING CORPORATION

                                                       By _____

Secretary of the Corporation                                          President

(SEAL)                                                 RECREATION SALES, INC.

                                                       By _____

Secretary of the Corporation                                          President

[1]U.C.C. 2-302 and 2-313(1)(b); *67 Am. Jur. 2d Sales,* paras. 8, 10, 57–117, and 448–451.
[2]To avoid U.C.C. 2-319(1).

## FORM VIC 1.01(a)[1]

### (Consumer express warranty and disclosure required after July 4, 1975)

### ALTERNATIVE CLAUSE

### FULL ONE-YEAR WARRANTY

Able Manufacturing, Inc., warrants this product to be free of manufacturing defects for a *one-year* period after the original date of consumer purchase or receipt as a gift. This warranty does not include damage to the product resulting from accident or misuse.

If the product should become defective within the warranty period, *we will elect to repair or replace it free of charge,* including free return transportation, provided it is delivered prepaid to the Able Manufacturing, Inc., Service Division, 1000 Industrial Park, Birmingham, Alabama 00000-0000.

THIS WARRANTY GIVES YOU SPECIFIC LEGAL RIGHTS, AND YOU MAY ALSO HAVE OTHER RIGHTS THAT VARY FROM STATE TO STATE.

[1]See Appendix I, X and XI for consumer protection laws and disclosure requirements.

## FORM VIC 1.01(b)[1]

### (Manufacturer's express warranty to merchant)

### ALTERNATIVE CLAUSE

*Warranty of conformity to label.* Seller warrants that the goods supplied by it will conform to the promises, descriptions, and statements of fact made on the containers and labels of the goods.
(or)
*Warranty.* Seller warrants that the inert matter in the polishing compound does not exceed Two Percent (2%) by volume.

[1]*67 Am. Jur. 2d Sales,* paras. 434–441; and U.C.C. 2-313.

## FORM VIC 1.01(c)[1]

### (Exclusion of oral warranties)

### ALTERNATIVE CLAUSE

*Exclusion of oral warranties.* There are no understandings, agreements, or representations, express or implied, written or oral, not specified in this order and the terms hereof, and this instrument contains the entire agreement of the parties and is binding on both parties.

[1]U.C.C. 2-202, 2-313; *67 Am. Jur. 2d Sales,* paras. 492 and 493.

## FORM VIC 1.01(d)[1]

### (Disclaimer of implied warranties)

### ALTERNATIVE CLAUSE

*DISCLAIMER OF IMPLIED WARRANTIES.* The Seller shall in no way be deemed or held to be obligated, liable, or accountable upon or under any guaranties or warranties, EXPRESS OR IMPLIED, STATUTORY, BY OPERATION OF LAW, OR OTHERWISE, in any manner or form beyond its express warranty and agreement relating to the capacity of the steel pellet machine sold hereunder as provided herein.

(or)

All goods delivered to the buyer under this contract "AS IS."

[1]U.C.C. 2-316; *67 Am. Jur. 2d Sales,* paras. 460–478 and 495–501.

## FORM VIC 1.01(e)[1]

### (Sale of goods to conform to sample or model)

### ALTERNATIVE CLAUSE

*Warranty of conformity.* Seller agrees to supply to buyer goods according to the sample supplied by the Seller. The sample has been marked for identification purposes by the manufacturer's indelible stamp containing the words "Sample 6041—January 1982."

[1]U.C.C. 2-313(1) (c); *67 Am. Jr. 2d Sales,* paras. 452–459.

## FORM VIC 1.01(f)

### (Sale or return—seller to repurchase unsold goods)[1]

### ALTERNATIVE CLAUSE

Seller agrees that it will repurchase any of the YOU-CONSTRUCT-CHAIRS from Buyer upon thirty (30) days' written notice from Buyer at any time during the term of this Contract; provided said chairs are unused and in the original shipping containers, at a price equal to Eighty Percent (80%) of the original invoice price, less return freight and shipping charges to Seller's warehouse at 100 Industrial Park, Middletown, Pennsylvania.

The Buyer may, without the notice or consent of Seller, assign this right to require repurchase of all or any of these goods to any bank or other financier to whom any security interest in the goods, or any of them, may be granted, and, in such event, Seller will not assert as against any such bank or other secured party any right of setoff, recoupment, or counterclaim that may now exist or hereafter arise under or by virtue of any transaction between Buyer and Seller.

Seller shall not be obligated to repurchase any goods under this Contract unless and until it shall have been furnished reasonable assurance that the goods will be redelivered to Seller free and clear of any and all liens, encumbrances, security interests, and other claims of third parties to the goods.

[1]U.C.C. 2-326. Distinguish between "sale on approval" and "sale or return" per this section of the U.C.C.

## FORM VIC 1.02

### (Letter sale contract to be signed by both buyer and seller)[1]

June 1, 1982

Distribution and Sales, Inc.
100 Market Street
Pittsburgh, Pa. 15200

Attention: John Doe

Dear John:

This will confirm and thank you for your order by telephone to our Richard Roe for five hundred (500) cases of Bay's condensed Clam Chowder (10½ oz.—297 g) at our market price in Boston on the date of shipment, which order is accepted on the following terms and conditions:

*Terms of payment:* One Percent (1%) ten (10) days; thirty (30) days net.

*Shipment:* Buyer shall furnish shipping instructions within ten (10) days from date; and Seller shall have ten (10) days from receipt of instructions to make shipment. Shipment shall be f.o.b. car at point of shipment, freight prepaid.

*Failure to furnish shipping instructions.* Failure of Buyer to furnish shipping instructions within twenty (20) days from date will entitle Seller, without further notice, to cancel order or to ship at its convenience within the succeeding thirty (30) days at the agreed price.

*Delay in shipping.* Seller shall not be held responsible for any damages arising from delay in shipment caused by strike, accident, or interruption of manufacture beyond its control. Delay in shipping beyond twenty (20) days, due to Seller's default, shall entitle Buyer to any lower market price of Seller in effect on date of shipment, or Buyer may cancel delayed order to Seller's Boston office, provided same is received by Seller before shipment of the order.

*Acceptance and Modification.* No sale shall be binding upon Seller until accepted in writing by Buyer. Salesmen and local brokers are not empowered to execute or modify this contract on behalf of Seller.

Please return the enclosed copy with your acceptance at your early convenience. We look forward to a mutually profitable and pleasant relationship.

Cordially,

BAY'S SEA PRODUCTS, INC.                    Agreed to and accepted _____
                                                                      (date)

                                            DISTRIBUTION AND SALES, INC.

Peter Poe                                   By _____
President                                        (title)

[1]U.C.C. 2-201 through 2-206, particularly 2-201(2); *67 Am. Jur. 2d Sales*, para. 101. Compare Form VIC 1.02(a).

## FORM VIC 1.02(a)

### (Confirmation letter sale contract signed by seller only)[1]

### ALTERNATIVE FORM

September 1, 1982

Mr. John Doe, President
Distribution and Sales, Inc.
100 Market Street
Pittsburgh, PA 15200

Dear Sir:

We confirm having sold to Distribution and Sales, Inc., the following goods for shipment within twenty (20) days:

Quantity:   five hundred (500) cases Bay's Condensed Clam Chowder (10½ oz.—297 g)

Price:   $4.80 per case

Terms:   Net cash against truck bill of lading and documents, at the time the goods leave our factory in Boston, Mass.

Dated September 1, 1982

Very truly yours,

BAY'S SEA PRODUCTS, INC.
Richard Roe, Sales Manager

[1]U.C.C. 2-201 through 2-206; and compare Form VIC 1.02; *67 Am. Jr. 2d Sales,* para. 102.

## FORM VIC 1.03

### (Purchase money security interest using traditional conditional sale contract form)

### CONDITIONAL SALE AGREEMENT[1]

AGREEMENT made in Pittsburgh, Pennsylvania, November 10, 1982, by Restaurant Distribution and Sales, Inc., of Pittsburgh, Pennsylvania (herein called "Seller"), and John R. Doe d/b/a Jack's Restaurant, 100 Liberty Avenue, Pittsburgh, Pennsylvania (herein called "Buyer"), is as follows:

1. *Description of goods.* Seller hereby agrees to deliver, and Buyer hereby agrees to accept from Seller, at 100 Liberty Avenue, Pittsburgh, Pennsylvania, one (1) Ace refrigeration unit, bearing the Serial No. C89543 (herein called "the goods"), upon and subject to the terms and conditions herein provided.

2. *Purchase price.* Seller agrees to sell, and Buyer agrees to buy, the goods for the cash price of Three Thousand Dollars ($3,000), to be paid: Two Hundred Fifty Dollars ($250) upon the signing of this Agreement, and the unpaid balance of said cash price is to be paid to the Seller, except as otherwise provided herein, by the Buyer in ten (10) equal monthly installments of Two Hundred Fifty Dollars ($250) each month in advance, beginning on December 10, 1982, until the remaining sum of Twenty-five Hundred Dollars ($2,500) is paid.

3. *Conditional title.*[2] Title to the goods shall vest in the Buyer only upon payment in full of the purchase price and only upon complete performance by the Buyer of all of the other terms and conditions of this Agreement required to be performed by the Buyer. The Buyer shall have the right to retain possession of the goods so long as he shall not be in default under this Agreement.

The goods shall be, and continue to be, personal property, irrespective of the extent or manner in which it may be affixed or attached to any building or other structure, or any part of them, or the manner in which it may be placed in that building or other structure.[3]

4. *Use of goods.* The Buyer shall keep the goods in good condition in his own custody at the delivery address, except with the written consent of Seller, and shall keep the goods free and clear of all taxes, liens, and encumbrances.

5. *Acceleration of payments.* If the Buyer shall be in default in payment of any payment due hereunder for a period of five (5) days, or if any debtor relief or proceeding in bankruptcy, receivership, or insolvency shall be instituted or filed by or against the Buyer, or if the Buyer shall enter into any arrangement or composition with his creditors, the full amount of the purchase price then remaining unpaid shall, at the option of the Seller, be immediately due and payable; but the exercise of that option by the Seller shall not transfer the title in the goods to the Buyer.

6. *Right to repossession by Seller.* If the Buyer shall be in default under any of the terms or conditions of this Agreement, the Seller shall have the right to take immediate possession of the goods, and, for such purpose, the Seller may enter upon any premises where the goods may be, and may remove the same from the premises with or without notice of his intention to retake and remove.

7. *Obligations of Seller after repossession.*

(a) If the Seller shall not give notice of intention to retake possession, the Seller shall retain the goods for ten (10) days after retaking the same, and during that period the Buyer, upon payment or tender of the amount due under this Contract at the time of the retaking and upon payment of the expenses of retaking, keeping, and storing, may redeem the goods, and become entitled to take possession of them, and to continue performance of the Contract as if no default had occurred.

(b) If the Buyer shall have paid at least Sixty Percent (60%) of the purchase price at the time of the repossession by the Seller, and if the Buyer shall not redeem the goods within the ten (10)-day period, the Seller shall sell the same at public auction in the state where the goods were at the time of the repossession, the sale to be held not more than ninety (90) days after the repossession; but if the Buyer shall not have paid at least Sixty Percent (60%) of the purchase price at the time of the retaking, the Seller shall not be under a duty to resell the goods as prescribed in this Paragraph, unless the Buyer shall serve upon the Seller, within ten (10) days after the retaking, a written notice demanding a resale, delivered personally or by registered or certified mail; and if there shall be no resale required, the Seller may retain the goods as his own property without obligation to account to the Buyer, and the Buyer shall be discharged of all further obligation.

(c) In the event of resale, the proceeds of the resale shall be applied to (1) the payment of the expenses of the resale, (2) payment of the expenses of retaking, keeping, and storing the goods, (3) satisfaction of the balance due under this Contract. Any excess from the proceeds of the resale shall be paid to the Buyer; and the Seller may recover any deficiency from the Buyer, who hereby agrees to pay that deficiency, if any.

(d) Seller shall have the right to rescind this Agreement for any default by the Buyer described in Paragraph 5, and Seller may, at Seller's sole option, repossess the goods and retain them as he sees fit without right of redemption or without resale as provided herein, provided Seller credits Buyer's account under this Contract and/or other indebtedness of Buyer to Seller with the full purchase price of the goods sold under this Agreement, and repays to the Buyer, on written demand by the Buyer, any surplus not required to satisfy such indebtedness of the Buyer to the Seller.

8. *Warranties and representations.* No promise, representation, or warranty, express or implied by statute or by operation of law, not set forth in this Agreement shall bind either party hereto.

9. *Separability.* This Agreement is drawn with the intent of complying with the Pennsylvania Commercial Code, Purdon's Pennsylvania Statutes, Title 12A, and any provision of this Agreement that shall violate that Code shall be severable and shall not affect any other provision or provisions of this Agreement that do comply.

10. *Governing Law.* This agreement shall be interpreted and enforced according to the laws of the Commonwealth of Pennsylvania.

Signed in Pittsburgh, Pennsylvania, this 10th day of November, 1982.

(SEAL)                                         RESTAURANT DISTRIBUTION AND SALES, INC.

                                              By _____
_____
Secretary of the Corporation                        President

                                              _____
                                              JOHN R. DOE d/b/a JACK'S RESTAURANT

[1]"Rent to own contract." U.C.C. 9-102, 9-202, 9-310, and 9-505; 67 *Am. Jur. 2d Sales,* para. 32; and 68 *Am. Jur. 2d Secured Transactions,* paras. 99, 103, and 108–112.
[2]See Forms VIF 1.03 and 1.04 for filing financing statement.
[3]U.C.C. 9-313 and 9-401.

## FORM VIC 1.04

(Retail purchase by consumer of used mobile home from dealer disclaiming implied warranties and providing for assignment by seller)

### ACE MOBILE HOMES, INC.

### RETAIL INSTALLMENT SALE CONTRACT AND SECURITY AGREEMENT[1]
### (SEE TERMS ON FACE AND BACK HEREOF)

BUYER(S)  Name   *John Doe and Mary Doe*
          Address   *480 Maple Lane*
          City   *Pittsburgh* County   *Allegheny* State *Pa.*
          Telephone No.   *(412) 345-6789* Zip Code   *15200*
Buyer(s) means all persons who sign this Contract as Buyer or Co-Buyer, jointly and severally.
*THE TERMS OF THIS CONTRACT ARE STATED ON THE FACE OF THIS CONTRACT AND ON THE*

*BACK HEREOF. DO NOT SIGN THIS CONTRACT BEFORE YOU READ IT OR IF IT CONTAINS ANY BLANK SPACES.*[2]

*GOODS SOLD.* Buyer(s) agree to purchase, receive, and accept the following used mobile home, including its furnishings, equipment, appliances, and accessories (herein called "Vehicle") AS IS in its present condition from Seller:

    Description of vehicle: NEW_____USED _X_____

    MAKE: *Comfy Home*   YEAR: *1980*

    LENGTH:   *52'*     WIDTH:     *24'*

    SERIAL NUMBER  *2345 – 1234*

    ACCESSORIES:   *aluminum skirt and tie-downs*

to be delivered and set up by Seller on Lot No. 3 in Home Park, Ridge Avenue, Tarentum, Pennsylvania, within ten (10) days of the signing of this Contract and security agreement.

*ASSIGNMENT BY SELLER. It is anticipated that this Contract, when signed and delivery hereunder is completed, will be submitted to Atlas Credit Corporation, 100 Park Avenue, New York, New York 10000 (herein called "ACC"), or its local branch office for purchase of this Contract by ACC, and, if approved, this Contract will be assigned to ACC.*

*SECURITY INTEREST.* Seller has retained a security interest in the Vehicle, and Buyer hereby grants to Seller a security interest therein (including any furnishings, equipment, appliances, and accessories that may hereafter be attached thereto) as security for the payment and performance of Buyer's obligation under this Contract to Seller (or an assignee of this Contract from Seller) and all proceeds, if any. The said security interest in the Vehicle shall also secure all amendments, rentals, extensions, or refinancing of any part or all of the obligations hereunder.

*PROPERTY INSURANCE.* Buyer shall have and maintain, at Buyer's expense, insurance against physical damage to the Vehicle for the term of the Contract, with a less payable clause protecting lienholder (as interest may appear) with provision for ten (10)-day notice of cancellation to lienholder (minimum coverage—fire, theft, and combined additions coverage and Vendor's Single Interest protection). The cost of this required insurance by Buyer, *if procured through Seller*, is Three Hundred Dollars ($300), and Buyer's election to obtain such insurance through Seller is shown by the inclusion of this cost in the coverages checked in Item 4 A below. *BUYER HAS THE RIGHT TO OBTAIN SUCH INSURANCE THROUGH AN AGENT OR OTHER PERSON OF BUYER'S CHOICE AS WELL AS THROUGH SELLER.*

*CREDIT LIFE INSURANCE OPTION.* The Buyer(s) elects to purchase decreasing term credit life insurance on the life of the person designated below as the proposed Insured (initial coverage in the amount of the Total of Payments hereunder, or, if less, in the amount of *Ten Thousand Dollars ($10,000)*, decreasing in either instance in proportion with the indebtedness hereunder. Buyer understands and acknowledges that such insurance was not required as a condition of the extension of credit by the Seller, and Buyer's decision to purchase such insurance was voluntarily made after the disclosure of its cost of *Seven Hundred Dollars ($700)* for the term shown below.

PERSON DESIGNATED AS PROPOSED INSURED. *John Doe*  AGE *30*

                                     (Person designated must be contract signer or spouse.)

LIABILITY INSURANCE FOR BODILY INJURY AND PROPERTY DAMAGE TO OTHERS IS NOT INCLUDED UNLESS SUCH COVERAGE IS PART OF A MOBILE HOMEOWNERS POLICY PURCHASED HEREUNDER.

Date   *October 10, 1982*      Signature of Insured *(John Doe)*

TERMS OF PAYMENT

1. Cash Price _____                                                     $10,000.00
    Cash Down Payment_____  $1,500.00
    Trade in: Year & Make   *N/A*
    Model  *N/A*  Serial No.  *N/A*           Seller to
    Gross Allowance  *N/A*  Owing  $*N/A* pay off  Net  $*N/A*
2. Total Down Payment _____                                              $1,500.85
3. Unpaid Balance of Cash Price (1 minus 2)_____  $8,500.00
4. Other Charges
    A. Insurance Charges (note: coverage expires on date shown under "Expiration Date." No coverage unless box is checked and cost is included in Total Other Charges).

| | | Expiration Date (mo., day, year) |
|---|---|---|
| (1) Property Insurance |  |  |
| —Fire, Theft, and combined additional coverage | $ —0— |  |
| *X* or Comprehensive | $300.00 | 10/10/85 |
| —Mobile Homeowners coverage | $ —0— |  |
| *X* Vendor's Single Interest Protection | $20.00 | 10/10/85 |
| (2) __ $ _____ Deductible Collision Coverage | $ —0— |  |
| (3) Total Property Insurance (1) plus (2) | $320.00 |  |
| (4) *X* Credit Life Insurance | $700.00 | 10/10/85 |
| B. Official Fees | $ —0— |  |
| C. Additional Charges |  |  |
| Sales Taxes | $400.00 |  |
| License fees | $ 27.35 |  |
| Tags | $ 81.50 |  |
| Total Additional Charges | $508.85 |  |

Total Other Charges (sum of (3), (4), B, and C) ____     $1,528.85

5. Amount Financed (3 plus 4) ____ $10,028.85

6. FINANCE CHARGE (includes, if amount is stated here, Vendor's Single Interest insurance premium of $20.00)     $10,028.85

7. Deferred Payment Price (sum of 1, 4, 6) ____ $10,028.85

8. ANNUAL PERCENTAGE RATE     12.05%     $11,000.00

9. Total of Payments (7 plus 8) ____ $21,028.85

The Total of Payments is payable in *144* consecutive monthly installments beginning November 10, 1982. Regular Installment *$146.03* Final Installment *$146.56*. Payments made shall first be applied to interest, then to principal.

10. *LATE PAYMENT AND DEFAULT CHARGES*. In addition to the regular installment, Buyer agrees to pay as a delinquency and collection charge on each installment in default for 10 days or more 5% of such installment or $5, whichever is less. Buyer also agrees to pay court costs plus reasonable attorney's fees incurred by holder if this Contract is referred to an attorney who is not a salaried employee of holder.

11. *PREPAYMENT REBATE*. Under the law you have a right to pay off in advance the full amount due. Should balance be prepaid in full prior to maturity date, a refund of the unearned portion of the *FINANCE CHARGE and INTEREST* will be calculated by Rule of 78 and deducted after deduction of a *$25* acquisition charge.

YOU ARE ENTITLED TO AN EXACT COPY OF THE CONTRACT YOU SIGN. KEEP THIS CONTRACT TO PROTECT YOUR LEGAL RIGHTS. THIS CONTRACT WAS PREPARED BY SELLER. SEE REVERSE SIDE FOR CONTINUATION. ACCEPTED: The foregoing Contract is hereby accepted. See reverse side for assignment.

BUYER ACKNOWLEDGES RECEIPT OF A TRUE COPY OF THIS RETAIL INSTALLMENT CONTRACT AND SECURITY AGREEMENT.

ACE MOBILE HOMES, INC. _____

Seller

By Richard Roe, Sales Mgr. _____

(title)

Seller's
Address 100 Rich Blvd, Pgh, Pa. 00000 _____

John Doe     (L.S.)

(Signature of Buyer)

Mary Doe     (L.S.)

(Signature of Co-Buyer)

480 Maple Lane, Pgh., Pa. 15200 _____

(Address of Co-Buyer)

Date October 10, 1985

12. *LOCATION OF COLLATERAL.* The Vehicle will be kept at Buyer's address shown on the front hereof unless another address is stated here *Lot 3 Home Park Ridge Avenue, Tarenton, Pa. 00000.* All equipment, tires, heaters, radios, television sets, accessories, and parts shall become part of the Vehicle by accession. Buyer agrees not to remove the Vehicle from the address designated herein unless he first notifies holder and receives its express written consent, and not to sell, encumber, or abandon the Vehicle or use it for hire or illegally, and to keep it free of liens. Wherever placed, the Vehicle shall remain personal property and shall not become part of the freehold.

13. *DEFAULT.* Time is of the essence of this Agreement. If Buyer fails to pay the Total Payments or any part thereof when due, or fails to observe or perform any of the terms and conditions of this Retail Installment Sale Contract and Security Agreement, or any warranty, representation, or statement of fact made to Seller at any time by Buyer is false or misleading in any material respect when made, or if there shall occur any substantial damage to or destruction of the Vehicle, or the making of any levy upon seizure or attachment of the Vehicle, or if Buyer shall become insolvent or commit an act of bankruptcy or make an assignment for the benefit of creditors, or if there shall be filed by or against Buyer any petition for any relief under the bankruptcy laws of the United States now or hereafter in effect, or under any insolvency, readjustment of debt, dissolution or liquidation law or statute of any jurisdiction now or hereafter in effect (whether at law or in equity), Seller may, without notice to (except as herein set forth) or demand upon Buyer, declare any part or all of the obligations and indebtedness immediately due and payable, and Seller shall have the following rights and remedies in addition to all of the rights and remedies of a secured party under any statute. Seller rights and remedies are cumulative and enforceable alternatively, successively, or concurrently: Seller may, at any time or times, with or without judicial process and the assistance of others, enter upon any premises upon which the Vehicle may be located and, without interference by Buyer, take possession of the Vehicle; and/or dispose of any part of the Vehicle or the Vehicle on any premises of the Buyer; and/or require Buyer, at Buyer's expense, to assemble and make available to Seller the Vehicle at any place and time designated by Seller and reasonably convenient to both parties; and/or remove the Vehicle from any premises on which the same may be located, for the purpose of effecting sale or other disposition thereof; and/or to sell, resell, lease, assign, and deliver, grant options or otherwise dispose of any part of the Vehicle or the Vehicle in its then condition or following any commercially reasonable preparation or processing, at public or private sale or proceedings, with or without having the Vehicle at the place of sale or other disposition, for cash and/or credit, upon any terms, and to such persons, firms, or corporations as Seller deems best, all without demand for performance or any notice or advertisement whatsoever, except where an applicable statute requires reasonable notice of sale or other disposition. Buyer agrees that the sending of ten (10) days' notice by ordinary mail, postage prepaid, to any address of Buyer set forth in this Contract, of the place and time of any public sale or of this time after which any private sale or other intended disposition is to be made, shall be deemed reasonable notice thereof. If the Vehicle is sold by Buyer upon credit or for future delivery, Seller shall not be liable for the failure of the purchase to pay for same, and in such event Seller may resell or otherwise dispose of the Vehicle. Seller may apply the cash proceeds actually received from any sale or other disposition to the costs and expenses in connection therewith, including the expense of retaking, holding, preparing for sale, selling, or otherwise disposing of the Vehicle, to reasonable attorney's fees, to legal and travel expenses, premiums on bonds, sheriff's, marshal's, and auctioneer's fees (including advertising and labor), and all other expenses that may be incurred by Seller in attempting to collect the indebtedness hereunder, proceed against the Vehicle or otherwise enforce this Installment Sales Contract and Security Agreement, or in the prosecution or defense of any action or proceeding related to the indebtedness hereunder of this Vehicle Security Agreement, or in the balance of such cash proceeds actually received shall be applied to the indebtedness hereunder, and Buyer shall remain liable and will pay Seller on demand, any deficiency remaining, together with any charges specified herein or in any instruments evidencing any of the obligations and indebtedness of the Buyer to the Seller, and the balance of any expenses unpaid, with any surplus to be paid to Buyer subject to any duty of Seller as a secured party imposed by law in favor of the holder of any subordinate security interest in the Vehicle known to Seller. Any personal property in the Vehicle when so retaken, other than that sold under this Contract or that which has become part of the Vehicle by accession, may be temporarily held by Seller for Buyer without liability.

14. CONTINUING INSURANCE. As indicated on the front hereof, Buyer will obtain and maintain for the duration of this Contract, at Buyer's expense, insurance against physical damage to the Vehicle with a minimum coverage of fire, theft, and combined additional coverage and Vendor's Single Interest protection. If the subject matter of this Contract is a recreational vehicle, then collision coverage is also required. Should Buyer fail to procure or maintain such insurance, which shall constitute a default hereunder, holder may do so on Buyer's behalf, and, in such event, Buyer will immediately reimburse holder for the cost thereof or such cost, plus interest at the highest lawful contract rate, will be added to Buyer's indebtedness hereunder.

   Buyer hereby designates holder as loss payee and assignee of any moneys not in excess of the unpaid balance hereunder that may become payable under such and other insurance, including return of unearned premiums, and directs any insurance company to make payment direct to holder to be applied to said unpaid balance and appoints holder as attorneys-in-fact to endorse any draft. In the event of any repossession for any default, holder is authorized to cancel insurance and credit any premiums refund received against said unpaid balance.

15. TAXES AND ASSESSMENTS. Buyer agrees to pay promptly all taxes and assessments upon the Vehicle and for its use.

16. BUYER'S CREDIT. Buyer hereby authorizes Seller to mail to Buyer any credit card, coupon book, or similar device for purposes of establishing the Buyer's identity and credit; and Buyer authorizes any holder of this Contract to release to credit bureaus, credit interchanges, and other grantors of credit such information relating to this transaction and Buyer's creditworthiness as may be determined pertinent by such holder.

17. WAIVERS. If Seller assigns this Agreement, he shall not be assignee's agent for any purpose. Buyer will not assert against assignee any claim or defense arising from this sale or that Buyer may otherwise have against Seller. Buyer waives all debtor's exemptions (and homestead laws) and assigns to holder all rights thereunder.

18. FORBEARANCE. Waiver of any default shall not constitute a waiver of any other waiver.

19. MODIFICATION. No provision of this Agreement shall be modified, changed, or altered unless in writing and executed by an officer of Seller. This Contract constitutes the entire agreement between the parties, and Buyer agrees that no representations, oral or implied, have been made to Buyer to induce Buyer to enter into this Contract other than those expressly set fortherein.

20. SEVERABILITY. Wherever possible, each provision of this Agreement shall be interpreted in such manner as to be effective and valid under applicable law, but if any provision of this Agreement shall be prohibited by or invalid under applicable law, such provision shall be ineffective to the extent of such prohibition or invalidity, without invalidating the remainder of such provision or the remaining provisions of this Agreement.

## ASSIGNMENT BY DEALER

TO ATLAS CREDIT CORPORATION:

   To induce you to purchase the within instrument, signed by one or more buyers (herein called "Buyer") the assignor warrants that (1) Buyer's credit statement submitted herewith is substantially true unless otherwise specified; (2) Buyer was not less than 21 years of age and otherwise legally competent to contract at the time of the execution of said instrument; (3) said instrument arose from the bona fide sale of the merchandise described in said instrument; (4) the down payment was received in cash and not its equivalent unless otherwise specified, and no part thereof was loaned directly or indirectly by the assignor to Buyer; (5) there is now owing on said instrument the amount as set forth therein; (6) said instrument and each guaranty submitted in connection therewith is in all respects legally enforceable against each purported signatory thereof; (7) the assignor has the right to assign said instrument and thereby convey good title to it and to said merchandise; and (8) in accordance with the Fair Credit Reporting Act, the assignor has notified the Buyer that this Agreement is to be submitted for purchase to Atlas Credit Corporation, or its local branch office, and the Buyer has been notified of the appropriate address of same.

   For value received, the assignor hereby assigns to you all its interest in said instrument and property and authorizes you to do everything necessary to collect and discharge the same.

   All the terms of any existing written agreement between the assignor and you are made a part hereof by reference, and assignor understands that you rely upon the above warranties and upon said agreements in purchasing said instrument.

Neither the repossession of the said merchandise from the Buyer for any cause, nor failure to file or record this instrument when required by law (it being the duty of the assignor to file or record the instrument), shall release the assignor from assignor's obligation hereunder, and in said agreements, with you.

ACE MOBILE HOMES, INC.

By _____

President

[1]U.C.C. 9-203(2), 9-206(1), 9-318(4); 69 *Am. Jur. 2d Secured Transactions,* paras. 34, 331, and 361. See also Chapter VIF for other security agreements. See Appendix I for citations to basic Federal Consumer Credit Protection Laws. See also 67 *Am. Jur. 2d Sales,* para. 408. For Home Solicitation Sales Cancellation Notice, see 15 U.S.C.A. 1245 and 16 C.F.R. 429, and state statute notice requirement, which should be included if it is not inconsistent with the federal.

[2]Include this warning on the *face* of the contract if it is a one-page printed form to be printed on both sides.

FORM VIC 1.04(a)

# FLORIDA RETAIL INSTALLMENT CONTRACT [1]

WHITE — ORIGINAL
PINK — FILING
BLUE — BUYER

_____, hereinafter called "Buyer," residing at _____
(Typewrite or Print Name of Buyer)     (Street—Rural Route—Box Number)

_____, _____, for the Deferred Payment Price
(City)    (State)

and upon the terms and conditions set forth below, hereby purchases from _____
(Dealer)

hereinafter called the "Seller," whose principal place of business is _____ Street, **in the**

City of _____, Florida, the following described vehicle, together with all parts, equipment and accessories now upon or
in the vehicle, or hereafter substituted by the Buyer.

| | New or Used | Make of Motor Vehicle | No. Cyl. | Year | Model No. | Type of Body | Serial Number | Motor Number | License Number |
|---|---|---|---|---|---|---|---|---|---|
| One | | | | | | | | | |

| Radio | Heater | Automatic Transmission | Power Seats | Power Steering | Power Brakes | Power Windows | Air Conditioning | Other |
|---|---|---|---|---|---|---|---|---|
| ☐ | ☐ | ☐ | ☐ | ☐ | ☐ | ☐ | ☐ | ☐ |

## OPTIONAL INSURANCE
(No Insurance Included Unless Checked)

Buyer authorizes Seller to obtain the following insurance coverages:

(a) PHYSICAL DAMAGE INSURANCE:
Coverages checked below for a term of _____ months (or for such shorter term as the insurer to whom Seller shall apply therefor will provide for the amount included herein) from the date hereof, payable to Buyer or Seller as interests may appear:

☐ Comprehensive
☐ Road Service
☐ $ _____

☐ Fire-Theft & Combined Additional Coverage
} $ _____
_____ Deductible Collision

(b) CREDIT INSURANCE:
☐ Credit Life Insurance .............. $ _____
☐ Credit Accident and Health Insurance .............. $ _____

TOTAL COST OF OPTIONAL INSURANCE .............. $ _____

## DISCLOSURES REQUIRED BY FEDERAL LAW

1. CASH PRICE .............. $ _____
2. DOWN PAYMENT
  Cash Down Payment. $ _____
  Trade-In .............. $ _____
    (Describe)
  TOTAL DOWN PAYMENT .............. $ _____
3. UNPAID BALANCE OF CASH PRICE (Item 1 minus Item 2) .............. $ _____
4. OTHER CHARGES
  Optional Insurance .............. $ _____
  Official Fees .............. $ _____
  License, Title, and Registration Fees .............. $ _____
  Documentary Stamps $ _____
  Other .............. $ _____
    (Describe)

TOTAL OTHER CHARGES ............... $ _____

5. AMOUNT FINANCED (Item 3 plus Item 4) .. $ _____

6. **FINANCE CHARGE** ................ $ _____

7. TOTAL OF PAYMENTS (Item 5 plus Item 6).. $ _____

8. DEFERRED PAYMENT PRICE (Items 1, 4 & 6). $ _____

9. DATE **FINANCE CHARGE** BEGINS TO ACCRUE (if different from the Contract date): _____ , 19 ___ .

**ANNUAL PERCENTAGE RATE** _____ %

Physical Damage Insurance may be obtained by the Buyer through the person of his choice. Credit Life and/or Credit Accident and Health Insurance is not required by the Seller.

Buyer acknowledges the foregoing optional insurance coverages and charges indicated and hereby requests and authorizes Seller to obtain each insurance coverage checked above

BUYER _____ Date _____
(Cost of Insurance to be included only if signed and dated by Buyer)

**BODILY INJURY AND PROPERTY DAMAGE LIABILITY INSURANCE NOT INCLUDED**

Buyer hereby promises to pay at the office of _____ monthly installments of $ _____ and a final installment of _____ payable on the Total of Payments (Item 7 above) in _____ , 19 ___ , except for a Balloon Payment of $ _____ , due the like day of each succeeding month commencing _____ , 19 ___ , together with interest after maturity at the highest lawful contract rate. If any of said installments be not paid when due, then all unpaid installments shall immediately become due at the option of the owner hereof without notice or demand. Buyer also promises to pay to the Seller or other holder of this Contract a delinquency and collection charge on each installment of this Contract in default more than 10 days in an amount equal to 5% of each such installment or $5.00, whichever is less.

The Buyer may prepay the balance due hereunder, in whole or in part, at any time. Upon prepayment in full, the Buyer will receive a rebate of the unearned portion of the **finance charge**, after first deducting an acquisition charge of $25.00, computed by the sum-of-the-digits method, commonly known as the "Rule of 78's." No rebate of less than $1.00 will be paid.

Title to the vehicle and a security interest therein shall remain in the Seller or his assignee under the Uniform Commercial Code until this Contract is fully performed. Buyer hereby acknowledges delivery and possession of the vehicle. Buyer shall not sell, encumber or lease the vehicle or transfer or assign any of his interest therein or in this Contract, or use said vehicle in violation of any State or Federal laws. Buyer will not remove it from the county or filing district in which he now resides without written permission from the holder of this Contract.

Buyer covenants and agrees with Seller as follows:

(1) The vehicle shall remain personal property and shall not become real property no matter how affixed thereto.

(2) The vehicle is now and shall at all times be kept in good condition and repair, and may be inspected by the Seller from time to time as it may demand.

(3) No delays or omission to exercise any right, power of remedy accruing to Seller upon any breach by Buyer under this Agreement shall impair any such right, power or remedy by Seller, nor be construed as a waiver of any such breach or default, or of any similar breach or default thereafter occurring; nor shall any waiver of a single breach or default be deemed a waiver of any subsequent breach or default. All waivers under this Agreement must be in writing. All remedies either under this Agreement or by law afforded to Seller shall be cumulative and not alternative.

The Buyer and Seller agree to the "Statement of Additional Covenants" set forth on the reverse side hereof, which the undersigned each agree shall constitute a part of this Contract.

**NOTICE TO THE BUYER:** 1. Do not sign this Contract before you read it or if it contains any blank spaces.
2. You are entitled to an exact copy of the Contract you sign.
3. The REVERSE SIDE is part of this contract.

**Executed by the Buyer and Seller this _____ day of _____ , 19 ___ .**

**BUYER** hereby acknowledges receipt of a true copy of this Contract and warrants to each purchaser of the Seller's interest herein that this instrument contains all of the agreements of the parties regarding the property herein described.

SELLER _____

(Dealer)

BY _____

(Name)

(Title)

BUYER _____

BUYER _____
(Credit Life, Accident and Health Insurance, as included herein, covers only the person signing above.)

## STATEMENT OF ADDITIONAL COVENANTS

Buyer further covenants and agrees with Seller as follows:

(4) Time is of the essence hereof and if Buyer shall fail to pay when due any installment hereof, or if Buyer shall fail to observe any provisions of this Agreement, or if Buyer ceases doing business as a going concern, or if a petition is filed by or against Buyer under the Bankruptcy Act or any amendment thereto, or if Buyer shall make an assignment for the benefit of creditors or take advantage of any law for the relief of debtors, or if a receiver or any officer of a court be appointed to have control of the property or assets of the Buyer, or if Seller shall deem the vehicle in jeopardy or feel insecure, the unpaid balance hereof shall become due and payable forthwith and Seller may, at its option, and in addition to and without prejudice to any other remedy, without notice or demand and without legal process, take possession of the vehicle wherever it may be located (with all additions and substitutions). Seller may at its option sell the vehicle at public or private sale with or without notice at which sale Seller may become the purchaser. Any personal effects in or upon the vehicle at the time of retaking may be taken and such property may be held without liability until demanded by me. Each party hereunder shall have the rights and privileges with respect to repossession, resale and disposition of proceeds thereof as are accorded by the Uniform Commercial Code of the State of Florida. In the event of such a sale there shall be due from the Buyer and Buyer will immediately pay to Seller the difference between the purchase price at such sale and the remaining unpaid total of payments, plus all costs and expenses of Seller in repossessing, transporting, repairing, selling or otherwise handling the vehicle, including reasonable attorney fees.

**Buyer hereby authorizes the holder hereof to cancel** any policy of insurance upon said vehicle or other insurance purchased under this Contract and transfer, set over, and assign to the holder any and all refunds and returned premiums from such insurance to be receipted by the holder in Buyer's name or holders for application to any existing indebtedness hereunder with excess, if any, to be returned to Buyer.

(5) The Seller may assign this Contract and in the event of assignment to _____ the Buyer agrees that after such assignment, **the Buyer will settle all** the Buyer shall perform all promises herein contained to such assignee as the **owner** hereof and the Buyer agrees that after such assignment, **the Buyer will settle all** claims against the Seller directly with it and agrees not to set up any claim which the Buyer may have against the Seller as a defense, set-off, cross complaint or otherwise to any action for the purchase price or possession of the vehicle brought by the owner hereof. Buyer further agrees to pay reasonable attorneys' fees and court costs in the event this Agreement is assigned to an attorney not a salaried employee of the holder for collection or repossession of the vehicle.

(6) All risk of loss to the vehicle shall be that of Buyer. During the term of this Contract, Buyer shall procure and maintain, at his expense, to protect the interests of Buyer and Seller in the vehicle insurance against all physical damage risks in such form and for the actual cash value of the vehicle with such deductible and written by such insurance carrier as Seller may accept. If Buyer fails to so insure, Seller may purchase such insurance, or any part thereof, including insurance protecting only the interests of Seller, but shall not be obligated to do so. To the extent that the cost of the premiums for such insurance is not included in this Contract, Buyer promises to pay to Seller, upon demand, as an additional obligation secured hereunder, the cost of any such insurance so purchased by Seller together with interest thereon until paid at the highest lawful contract rate.

**Buyer hereby assigns to Seller** all refunds of unearned insurance premiums on policies paid for by Seller hereunder and hereby authorizes and empowers Seller **to collect and receipt for the same** in its **name or Buyer's.** Seller may use such refunds to purchase replacement insurance for the then remaining term of this Contract, but shall not be obligated to do so. To the extent not so used, such refunds shall be credited to the final installment of Buyer's obligation secured hereunder.

(7) All of the terms and conditions of this Contract shall apply to and be binding upon the Buyer, his heirs, personal representatives, successors, and shall inure to the benefit of the Seller, its successors and assigns.

## ASSIGNMENT WITHOUT RECOURSE

For Value Received, the undersigned hereby assigns this Contract to _____ hereinafter called "Assignee," its successors and assigns and hereby transfers title to the motor vehicle described therein to said Assignee, and warrants that the facts set forth in the Contract are true; that said motor vehicle is free of all liens and encumbrances of whatever nature or kind; that said Contract is genuine and in all things what it purports to be; that the undersigned has good title to said motor vehicle and has the right to transfer title thereto; that the said motor vehicle was sold to the Buyer in a bona fide time sales transaction; that a certificate of title with Assignee's interest noted thereon has or will be issued for the said motor vehicle; that all parties thereto have capacity to contract; that none of the parties thereto is a minor; and that the undersigned has no knowledge of any facts which impair the validity of said Contract or render it less valuable or valueless. If any of the warranties herein contained be untrue, the undersigned hereby promises to purchase on demand this Contract from the Assignee for the balance remaining unpaid on said Contract.

Dated this _____ day of _____, 19____

_____ By _____
(Dealer — Firm Name)      (Official Title)

## ASSIGNMENT WITH RECOURSE

For Value Received, the undersigned hereby assigns this Contract to _____ hereinafter called "Assignee," its successors and assigns, with full recourse, and hereby transfers title to the motor vehicle described therein to said Assignee, and warrants that the facts set forth in the Contract are true; that said motor vehicle is free of all liens and encumbrances of whatever nature or kind; that said Contract is genuine and in all things what it purports to be; that the undersigned has good title to said motor vehicle and has the right to transfer title thereto; that the said motor vehicle was sold to the Buyer in a bona fide time sales transaction; that a certificate of title with Assignee's interest noted thereon has or will be issued for the said motor vehicle; that all parties thereto have capacity to contract; that none of the parties thereto is a minor; and that the undersigned has no knowledge of any facts which impair the validity of said Contract or render it less valuable or valueless. If any of the warranties herein contained be untrue, the undersigned hereby promises to purchase on demand this Contract from the Assignee for the balance remaining unpaid on said Contract.

The undersigned guarantees payment of the unpaid balance on said Contract as and when the same shall become due and payable under the terms of said Contract, hereby waiving notice of acceptance and notice of defaults and consents that the Assignee may, without affecting the undersigned's liability, compromise or release, by operation of law or otherwise, any rights against and grant extensions of time of payment to Buyer and other obligors.

Dated this _____ day of _____, 19____

_____ By _____
(Dealer — Firm Name)      (Official Title)

## ASSIGNMENT

For Value Received, the undersigned hereby assigns this Contract to _____ hereinafter called "Assignee," its successors and assigns and hereby transfers title to the motor vehicle described therein to said Assignee, and warrants that the facts set forth in the Contract are true; that said motor vehicle is free of all liens and encumbrances of whatever nature or kind; that said Contract is genuine and in all things what it purports to be; that the undersigned has good title to said motor vehicle and has the right to transfer title thereto; that the said motor vehicle was sold to the Buyer in a bona fide time sales transaction; that a certificate of title with Assignee's interest noted thereon has or will be issued for the said motor vehicle; that all parties thereto have capacity to contract; that none of the parties thereto is a minor; and that the undersigned has no knowledge of any facts which impair the validity of said Contract or render it less valuable or valueless. If any of the warranties herein contained be untrue, the undersigned hereby promises to purchase on demand this Contract from the Assignee for the balance remaining unpaid on said Contract.

As a part of the foregoing instrument, the undersigned's obligation in addition to those stated in the preceding paragraph are governed by the paragraph set forth opposite the undersigned's signature below.

### 1. FULL REPURCHASE AGREEMENT

The undersigned further agrees that if the Assignee repossesses the said motor vehicle described in said Contract, the undersigned will purchase from Assignee the said motor vehicle in accordance with the provisions of Dealer's Protection Agreement No. 1, and will so purchase said motor vehicle although Assignee has without undersigned's consent, waived defaults made by the Buyer in performing said Contract and/or granted extensions of time to said Buyer in which to perform.

### 2. LIMITED REPURCHASE AGREEMENT

The undersigned further agrees that if the Buyer fails to pay the first _____ installments of his obligation as set forth in the Contract hereby assigned and if Assignee repossesses the said motor vehicle described in said Contract, the undersigned will purchase from Assignee the said motor vehicle in accordance with the provisions of Dealer's Protection Agreement No. 1, and will so purchase said motor vehicle although Assignee has without undersigned's consent, waived defaults made by the Buyer in performing said Contract and/or granted extensions of time to said Buyer in which to perform.

### 3. PARTIAL REPURCHASE AGREEMENT

The undersigned further agrees that if the Assignee repossesses the said motor vehicle described in said Contract, the undersigned upon demand will pay to Assignee $ _____ or purchase the motor vehicle from Assignee for the then unpaid balance in its then condition and location, and will so pay or purchase although Assignee has without undersigned's consent, waived defaults made by the Buyer in performing said Contract and/or granted extensions of time to said Buyer in which to perform.

Dated this _____ day of _____, 19____

By _____
(Dealer)

_____
(Official Title)

_____
(Address of Dealer)

Dated this _____ day of _____, 19____

By _____
(Dealer)

_____
(Official Title)

_____
(Address of Dealer)

Dated this _____ day of _____, 19____

By _____
(Dealer)

_____
(Official Title)

_____
(Address of Dealer)

**NOTE: If a corporation, signature must be in name of corporation by officer having authority from board of directors to sign. If a partnership, by one of the partners.**

[1] See footnotes to Form VIC 1.04.

## FORM VIC 1.05

### (Consignment of goods for sale by consignee)

### CONSIGNMENT AGREEMENT[1]

AGREEMENT made on June 1, 1982, between COUNTRY KITCHENS, INC., a Connecticut corporation (herein called "Owner"), and John Doe d/b/a COOK'S CORNER, at 100 Main Street, Middletown, Pennsylvania (herein called "Consignee"), in consideration of the mutual obligations and undertakings herein set forth, WITNESSETH:

1. *Description of goods consigned.* Owner agrees to deliver, from time to time, such culinary gadgets and accessories manufactured and distributed by Owner (herein called the "Goods") as it shall deem suitable for the location of the Consignee and the volume of business of Consignee beginning September 1, 1982, upon the terms and conditions of this Agreement.

2. *Acceptance and sale by Consignee.* Consignee agrees to accept possession of the Goods delivered to the Consignee, at Owner's sole expense, and to hold and care for the same as the property of the Owner, it being agreed that the title to the Goods, or their proceeds, is always vested in the Owner until their sale in the ordinary course of business of the Consignee. The Goods shall be subject to and under the direction and control of the Owner at all times unless sold in the manner and upon the terms herein contained.

3. *Resale price.*[2] All sales will be made by Consignee at the prices printed on the packages by Owner, and no discounts or rebates will be allowed by Consignee. All sales shall be for cash, except that Consignee may sell the Goods on credit, provided Consignee remits for such sales to Owner from Consignee's own funds as though the sales had been made for cash.

4. *Consignment notice and display.* Consignee agrees to keep the Goods in a partitioned display area designed by Owner and to display the Goods in the area in a neat and pleasing manner. Consignee also agrees to erect and maintain a suitable and conspicuous sign in the area, which sign shall be provided by Owner, evidencing the relationship of Consignor-Consignee.

5. *Payment and accounting to Owner.* On or before the tenth day of each month, Consignee shall remit to Owner the amount of all moneys received by Consignee during the previous month from the sale of Owner's Goods, less the difference between the Consignee's sales price and the invoice price from the Owner. The invoice price is subject to the usual trade discount of One Percent (1%) ten (10) days, thirty (30) days net. All returns must be accounted for at the time of that remittance. All Goods not accounted for as sold and not returned to Owner shall be conclusively presumed to have been sold by Consignee.

6. *Duration and termination.* This Agreement may be terminated by either party upon ninety (90) days' written notice to the other party. All notices to Owner shall be sent to 100 Main Street, Middletown, Connecticut 00000, and all notices to Consignee may be sent to the above address of the Consignee. Any breach on the part of the Consignee of any of the provisions contained herein shall, at the option of the Owner, terminate this Agreement. On any termination or cancellation of this Agreement for any reason, Owner shall be entitled to remove any unsold Goods from the premises of Consignee and shall be afforded a reasonable time to take possession thereof.

7. *Insurance.* The Consignee agrees to keep the Goods fully insured for the benefit of the Owner. All Goods damaged or otherwise rendered unmerchantable by fire, vandalism, flood, or other casualty shall be accounted for as having been sold by Consignee.

8. *Security documents.*[3] Consignee agrees to execute any and all other documents, including such financing statements and other assurances as Owner shall deem advisable to protect its ownership of the Goods, in order to carry out the purpose of this Agreement.

IN WITNESS WHEREOF, the parties hereto have executed this Agreement on the day and year first abovewritten.

COUNTRY KITCHENS, INC.

By _____     _____
    President                      John Doe d/b/a COOK'S CORNER

[1] U.C.C. 2-326(3)(c), 9-402, and 9-102(2); *32 Am. Jur. 2d Factors and Commissions*, paras. 1–43, 53–57; *67 Am. Jur. 2d Sales*, paras. 35–38, 274, 278, 279, and 282; *68 Am. Jur. 2d Secured Transactions*, paras. 113–116.

[2] *54 Am. Jur. 2d Monopolies, Restraints of Trade, and Unfair Trade Laws*, para. 53; and *32 Am. Jur. 2d Fair Trade Laws*, paras. 1–3. See also 15 U.S.C.A. 1, as amended December 12, 1975, Pub. L. 94–145, para. 2, 89 Stat. 801.

[3] Ref. Chapter VIF for security agreements and filing forms.

## FORM VIC 1.06

### (Bill of sale for goods sold)

### BILL OF SALE[1]

KNOW ALL MEN BY THESE PRESENTS, that ECONOMY FARM SALES, INC., of Middletown, Nebraska (herein called "Seller"), for and in consideration of the sum of Two Thousand Dollars ($2,000) paid to it by JOHN DOE, of Middletown, Nebraska (herein called "Buyer"), the receipt whereof is hereby acknowledged, has granted, bargained, sold, transferred, and delivered, and by these presents does grant, bargain, sell, transfer, and deliver unto Buyer, his executors, administrators, and assigns, the following goods and chattels:

1 Deere Tractor 1962 No. TR1234567.

TO HAVE AND HOLD the same unto the Buyer, his executors, administrators, and assigns forever.

AND does for Seller's successors and assigns covenant to and with the Buyer and his heirs, executors, administrators, and assigns that ECONOMY FARM SALES, INC., is the lawful owner of the tractor described herein, that it is free from all encumbrances, that it has the right to sell the same as aforesaid, and that it will warrant and defend the sale of said tractor unto the Buyer, his executors, administrators, and assigns against the lawful claims and demands of all persons whomsoever.

IN WITNESS WHEREOF, we have hereunto set our hands and seals this 10th day of February, 1982.

Signed, sealed, and delivered in the presence of:     ECONOMY FARM SALES, INC.

                                                 By _____
_____
Witness                                                         President

_____        _____
Witness                                                         JOHN DOE

[1]U.C.C. 2-201, 2-206, 8-31º, and 9-203. Note that in ordinary cash sale transactions the invoice marked "paid" operates as a bill of sale. Ref. Form IIIA 1.03(b) for a memorandum of sale at auction. Compare Form VIC 1.07 for bill of sale of growing crops. See also 67 *Am. Jur. 2d Sales*, paras. 60, 243–245.

## FORM VIC 1.07

### (Sale of growing crop to be harvested by Buyer)[1]

### BILL OF SALE

I, Fred Farmer, residing at Star Route #1, Box 16, Middletown, Kansas 00000 (herein called "Seller"), in consideration of One Dollar ($1) paid to me by Grain Products Inc., a Kansas corporation (herein called "Buyer"), sell to Buyer all crop of wheat now standing and/or growing upon the certain parcel of land near Middletown, Kansas, known as the "Farmer Farm," and more particularly bounded and described as follows:

(Insert legal description of the farm by metes and bounds or by government survey description, as: section, township, and range description, rectangular survey or monument description, as applicable.)

And I, the Seller, hereby authorize and license the Buyer to enter upon the parcel of land for the purpose of harvesting and removing the crop in any reasonable manner and time as it sees fit.

To induce the Buyer to pay the agreed consideration for this bill of sale, and to induce the Buyer to accept this bill of sale, I the Seller, represent and covenant:

1. That I am lawfully seized of the crop;
2. That I have the right to sell, transfer, and convey the crop;
3. That the same is free and clear of any and all encumbrances whatever; and
4. That I will forever warrant and defend the same against any person or persons.

Dated May 15, 1982, and signed by the Seller on that date in the presence of:

WITNESS

_____

FRED FARMER

WITNESS

¹U.C.C. 2-105(1) and 2-107; *21 Am. Jur. 2d Crops,* paras. 47 et seq. Compare Form VIF 1.02(a) for crop security agreement. See also Form VIC 1.08.

## FORM VIC 1.08

### (Sale of crop to be harvested by Seller)

### CONTRACT FOR SALE OF CROP¹

AGREEMENT made March 1, 1982, between FRESH FARM PRODUTS, INC., a Pennsylvania corporation having its principal place of business at 100 Main Street, Middletown, Pennsylvania 00000 (herein called "Buyer"), and FRED FARMER of R.F.D. 4, Grove Mill, Pennsylvania 00000 (herein called "Seller"), is as follows:

1. *Description of crop.* Buyer agrees to and shall purchase and Seller agrees to and shall sell to Buyer all the potato crop now grown or being grown on Seller's farm located on State Route 11 two (2) miles north of Grove Mill, Middle County, Pennsylvania, more particularly described as follows:

(Insert description by metes and bounds or other appropriate legal description.)
for the price of One Dollar ($1) per bushel.

2. *Harvest and delivery.* Seller will harvest the crop at his own expense and deliver to Buyer or Buyer's representative at the farm where produced. That delivery by Seller to Buyer shall be made between August 31 and September 30 upon ten (10) days' written notice from Buyer.

3. *Seller's warranties.* Seller agrees that all the potatoes delivered hereunder shall be in good marketable and merchantable condition and the whole thereof fit for human consumption.

4. *Liquidated damages.* Inasmuch as it is impracticable to determine the actual damage resulting to Buyer should Seller fail to deliver to Buyer the potato crop as herein agreed, Seller agrees to pay to Buyer Ten Cents (10¢) per bushel for all potatoes agreed to be delivered that are undelivered, as liquidated damages for the breach of this Contract by failure to deliver, subject to the exceptions by way of excuse set forth in Paragraph 5.

5. *Excuse for nonperformance.*

(a) In case of fire, strike, or other labor disturbances, lack of transportation facilities, shortage of labor or supplies, floods, earthquakes, action of the elements, invasion, war, riots, insurrection or rebellion, interference by civil or military authorities or passage of laws, or any unavoidable casualty or cause beyond the control of Buyer, affecting in any way the conduct of Buyer's business, Buyer will be excused from performance hereunder during such period of inability to perform.

(b) The happening of any of the foregoing events shall excuse Seller from all or any part of the potato crop that is destroyed by frost, flood, or other natural casualties.

6. *Modification.* Should there be any changes, additions, modifications of the terms, stipulations, and conditions of this Contract, or any of them, such changes, modifications, additions, or revisions shall be signed by the respective parties hereto or their authorized agents.

IN WITNESS WHEREOF, the parties have executed this Contract for sale on the day and year first above written.

FRESH FARM PRODUCTS, INC.

FRED FARMER

By _____
AGENT

¹U.C.C. 2-105(1) and 2-107; *21 Am. Jur. 2d Crops,* paras. 47 et seq. Compare Form VIF 1.02(a) for crop security agreement. See also Form VIC 1.07.

## FORM VIC 1.09

### (Billing mistakes notice under Truth in Lending Act)[1]

### NOTICE

In Case of Errors or Inquiries About Your Bill

The Federal Fair Credit Billing Act requires prompt correction of billing mistakes.

1. If you want to preserve your rights under the Act, here's what to do IF YOU THINK YOUR BILL IS WRONG OR IF YOU NEED MORE INFORMATION ABOUT AN ITEM ON YOUR BILL:

    a. Do not write on the bill. On a separate sheet of paper write within 60 days after date bill was mailed (you may telephone your inquiry, but doing so will not preserve your rights under this law) the following:

        i. Your name and account number.

        ii. A description of the error and an explanation (to the extent you can explain) why you believe it is an error. If you need only more information, explain the item you are not sure about and, if you wish, ask for evidence of the charge, such as a copy of the charge slip. Do not send in your copy of a sales slip or other document unless you have a duplicate copy for your records.

        iii. The dollar amount of the suspected error.

        iv. Any other information (such as your address) that you think will help us to identify you or the reason for your complaint or inquiry.

    b. Send your billing error notice to: Doe's Department Store Inc., P.O. Box 12430, Sumter Branch, Bigtown, Pennsylvania 00000.

Mail it as soon as you can, but in any case, early enough to reach us within 60 days after the bill was mailed to you.

2. We must acknowledge all letters pointing out possible errors within 30 days of receipt, unless we are able to correct your bill during that 30 days. Within 90 days after receiving your letter, we must either correct the error or explain why we believe the bill was correct. Once we have explained the bill, we have no further obligation to you even though you still believe that there is an error, except as provided in Paragraph 5.

3. After we have been notified, neither we nor an attorney nor a collection agency may send you collection letters or take other collection action with respect to the amount in dispute; but periodic statements may be sent to you, and the disputed amount can be applied against your credit limit. You cannot be threatened with damage to your credit rating or sued for the amount in question, nor can the disputed amount be reported to a credit bureau or to other creditors as delinquent until we have answered your inquiry. However, you remain obligated to pay the parts of your bill not in dispute.

4. If it is determined that we have made a mistake on your bill, you will not have to pay any finance charges on any disputed amount. If it turns out that we have not made an error, you may have to pay finance charges on the amount in dispute, and you will have to make up any missed minimum or required payments on the disputed amount. Unless you have agreed that your bill was correct, we must send you a written notification of what you owe; and if it is determined that we did make a mistake in billing the disputed amount, you must be given the time to pay that you normally are given to pay undisputed amounts before any more finance charges or late payment charges on the disputed amount can be charged to you.

5. If our explanation does not satisfy you, and you notify us in writing within 10 days after you receive this explanation that you still refuse to pay the disputed amount, we may report you to credit bureaus and other creditors and may pursue regular collection procedures. But we must also report that you think you do not owe the money, and we must let you know to whom such reports were made. Once the matter has been settled between you and us, we must notify those to whom we reported you as delinquent of the subsequent resolution.

6. If we do not follow these rules, we are not allowed to collect the first $50 of the disputed amount and finance charges, even if the bill turns out to be correct.

7. If you have a problem with property or services purchased with a credit card, you may have the right not to pay the remaining amount due on them, if you first try in good faith to return them to Doe's Department Store, Inc.

[1]See Appendix I for citations to basic Federal Consumer Credit Protection Laws and 12 C.F.R. 226.14.

## SECTION D    SALE OF BUSINESS

Before using the forms in this section, the general introduction to PART VI should be read as well as FORM VID 1.00.

If the attorney is assisting in the negotiation of a contract for the sale of a business, the business evaluation checklist which appears as FORM VID 1.00(a) will be invaluable both for negotiation and drafting the contract.

If the sale of the business includes inventory, the state commercial code must be consulted. Forms for bulk transfer compliance appear in Section E of PART VI.

If a security interest is to be retained in the assets of the business which is being sold, see Section F of PART VI for forms necessary to create and perfect the security interest.

### FORM VID 1.00

CLIENT QUESTIONNAIRE FOR SALE OF BUSINESS ASSETS OR OF AN UNINCORPORATED BUSINESS[1]

1. Name, address, and telephone number(s) of client
2. Is client the buyer or seller?
3. Is the business a sole proprietorship, partnership, corporation, or other?
4. Does the business have an Employer's Identification Number? If so, what is it?
5. Does the business operate under an assumed or fictitious name? If so, is the name registered and in which county? Get the official record number at which it is recorded and the *exact* name
6. If the business is a corporation that is selling its business assets but not its stock, have the proper corporate steps been taken to authorize the sale? Get certified (by corporate secretary) copies of the corporate resolutions or written consents in lieu of meeting(s), or prepare them if client is the seller
7. Does the sale of assets involve a Bulk Transfer?[2]
8. List of assets (including inventory and other personal property) being sold. Get brand names, model numbers, and manufacturer's identification numbers where applicable. If real estate is included, get the legal description that will be used in the deed
9. Is it a cash sale, an exchange, or an installment sale? If it is an installment sale, what are the terms, and is a security interest to be held by the seller?[3]
10. Are the assets free from encumbrances? If not, list all liens and encumbrances in detail
11. *Price*
    (a) Has the *price* been agreed upon? If not, who will appraise or evaluate the business or its assets?[4]
    (b) Is there a business broker involved? If so, who is it and what are the terms of the business brokerage agreement?[5]
    (c) Is buyer to assume any liens or encumbrances as part of the purchase price? If so, list in detail
12. See Form IVD 1.00(a) for Business Valuation Checklist

[1] 26 U.S.C.A. 111-114 for capital gain or loss on sale of individual or partnership business or assets. See 26 U.S.C.A. 331 et seq. for liquidation of corporate assets. See 26 U.S.C.A. 368(a); and Form IA 2.00 for sale of corporate stock or corporate reorganization.
[2] U.C.C. Article 6; and Forms VIE 1.00–1.02(a).
[3] U.C.C. Article 9; and Forms VIF 1.00–1.07.
[4] Ref. Form VID 1.00(a).
[5] Ref. Form VA 1.04.

**FORM VID 1.00(a)**

**BUSINESS VALUATION CHECKLIST**[1]

PRELIMINARY INFORMATION

1/ Name of Business entity
2/ Address
_____
_____
_____

3/ Name of contact & position
_____

4/ Phone number
5/Names of 4 top senior
   management personnel
_____
_____
_____
_____
_____

GENERAL

1/Type of entity
2/Date & place of
   incorporation
_____

_____

3/Principal stockholders
      a/ # of Shares and
      b/ % owned
_____
4/History of company
      a/Date established or purchased.
      b/Size when purchased if applicable
      c/Changes in ownership
         Dates & impact
      d/Significant years for sales & profit-
         ability—good, bad & turnaround
      e/Significant changes in company or indus-
         try—(e.g., marketing, production, expan-
         sion, new capital)
_____
5/Obtain minimum of past three years' statements including interims
_____
6/Obtain fixed asset listing
7/Obtain product literature
_____
8/Industry outlook
   Recent changes and expected changes, estimated impact
_____

SALES & MARKETING

1/Sales channels—#
   (e.g., salesmen, reps, etc.)
2/Distribution channels—#
_____
   and location
3/Georgraphical coverage
_____
   and product
4/Markets currently
   corvioo  % of business
_____
5/How many customers?
_____
6/Who are your 3 largest customers?
      a/% of their business to total
      b/Their recent trend—past three years
_____
7/Average price increases—prior three years
      a/How does this compare to competitors'?
_____
8/What has produced recent sales trends?—
   past 3 yrs.
_____

9/Who are your major competitors? Compare them as to:
    a/Distribution & sales channels
    b/Type of machinery & process used & cost implication

10/Who is the industry leader?—share of market

11/Any seasonal fluctuations in sales?

12/Annual expense for advertising & sales promotion. How does it compare to industry?

13/What are potential markets with current products?
    a/Why are we not currently servicing?
    b/What is potential volume if entered?

14/Where is next major sales expansion?
    a/What is required to accomplish this?
    b/Who is major competitor?

15/Sales by product line—$ and units, if possible

16/What are your competitive advantages?

17/What are the competition's competitive advantages?

18/Have any exclusives been granted that would limit sales penetration or expansion?
a/licenses, franchises, etc.
b/expiration dates for exclusives

19/What is current sales backlog?

20/Any product warranties?—terms and impact

21/Any patents, etc.? impact

22/Any unusual jobs that resulted in significantly different profitability?—either greater or lesser

## MANUFACTURING & PRODUCTION

1/Description of major pieces of equipment
    a/Size (12″ boring mill)
    b/Manufacturer
    c/Year of manufacture
    d/Estimated value to going concern

2/Your machinery technology and process—compare to competitors' for capability of producing low-cost or quality product

3/Any significant needs for new machinery?
    a/To reduce current bottlenecks
    b/To compete with current technology

4/Any recent changes in technology?
    a/Impact on you
    b/Cost to get current

5/Any major recent purchases or disposals of fixed assets?

6/Production volume capabilities
    a/With current machinery
    b/With minor machinery additions
    Cost—describe

7/Capabilities to produce other products that you might market

8/Product production capabilities that would make you an attractive suitor for a particu-

lar industry. These would not encompass
products you would market (in [7] above)

9/Any significant limitations on energy
availability?

10/Any OSHA problems?

Any EPA problems?

11/Availability of raw materials

12/Sources of raw materials

13/Transportation factors

    a/Availability of rail siding

    b/Ownership of road vehicles

    c/Access to Interstate

14/Product liability insurance

    a/Cost

    b/Recent increases

    c/Future expectations

15/Appraised value of fixed assets and basis of
valuation

## FACILITIES

1/Estimation of current market value for land
and buildings

2/Acres of Land

3/Buildings—date built

    a/Amount of sq. ft. under roof

    b/Amount of production sq. ft. under roof

    c/Amount of warehousing sq. ft. under roof

    d/Height (clearance) of production building

    e/Heaviest crane capacity—currently

    f/Heaviest crane capacity—feasible

4/Type of building construction

5/If facilities not owned, lease terms

    a/Length of lease

    b/Any options?

    c/Monthly payment

    d/Any escalator or tax clauses?

    e/Will owner extend current lease for pro-
spective purchaser?

6/Availability of land for future expansion

## FINANCIAL INFORMATION

1/Depreciation method and lives

2/Any long-term binding agreements (over 1
yr.) that must be assumed by purchasor if
"stock" deal?

    a/Long-term sales contracts

    b/Long-term purchase agreements (in-
ventory or capital equipment)

    c/Distributors agreement

    d/Mfr. rep. agreement

3/Any large purchase orders outstanding—
either raw materials or capital equipment—
to be completed in current year?

4/Any accounting treatments used to provide
owner's benefits that would tend to misstate
true company profit?

Could be expensive capital items, excessive

salaries or fringes, etc. Last item to be determined by GMS from notes in personnel section

5/Are accruals adequate—federal & state taxes among others?

6/Condition & collectability of accounts receivable

7/Inventory—nonprime material (e.g., obsolete mdse., discontinued product line, severe overstock)

8/Significant nonrecurring profit or loss items—past three years

9/Rough segregation of fixed vs. variable costs

10/Intangible assets—value and describe

11/Any contingent liabilities (e.g., claims in litigation)?
   —status

12/Specifics of long-term loans
   a/Collateral pledged
   b/Negative covenants—especially pertaining to management rights
   c/Interest rates
   d/Termination clauses

13/State taxes and rates

14/Is tooling expensed as purchased?
   —estimate of value of tooling on hand

## PERSONNEL & EMPLOYEE BENEFIT PLANS

1/Employee status
   a/Number of hourly, salary, key management (include owners) employees
   b/Average wage rate—hourly employees
   c/Hourly employees—unionized or not?
   d/If not, any attempts?
   e/Hourly, if unionized
   (1) Current contract expires
   (2) Date of union election
   (3) Strikes and description
   (4) Condition of union relations
   (5) Specified amount of changes under current contract

2/Availability of skilled labor—at your rate of pay?

3/Employee benefits package: hourly, salary

4/Impact of ERISA on pension costs. Any future projection?

5/Owner & key officer profile
   a/Age
   b/Responsibilities with company
   c/Time with company
   d/Advancement with company (for officers)
   e/Pay
   f/ Fringes
   g/Brief background
   h/Physical condition
   i/ Specialized knowledge

SALES AGREEMENTS CONSIDERATIONS

1/Terms & conditions of sales agreement
  a/Any absolute musts?
  b/Any that are totally unacceptable? _____
2/Specific conditions
  a/Sale of assets or stock
  b/Installment Sale
  c/Personal guarantees acceptable for installment payments
  d/Employment agreement—length & amount
  e/Complete or partial sale of company
  f/ Relinquishment of patent and trademark
   rights _____
3/Asking price _____
4/Desired price _____
5/Reasons for selling _____
6/Are any personal loans to company to be
  satisfied _____
7/Are there any companies to whom we should
  not talk (if appraiser is the business broker)? _____

POINTS PERTINENT TO MARKETING OF COMPANY

1/Company's SEC # _____
2/Trade associations
  a/Of which you are a member
  b/Other pertinent or related to your industry _____
3/How long have you tried to sell? _____
4/Were any offers made?
  a/When
  b/Amount and terms
  c/Reasons for rejection _____
5/Whom else have you contacted re
  purchasing? _____
6/Authorization to advertise company _____
7/Do you know of any leads? _____
8/Industries using similar distribution or product retailing network _____
9/Industries utilizing seller's products as component of theirs _____
10/Industries whose product is a component of
  seller's _____
11/Complementary products—(e.g., customer
  would use both buyer's and seller's product
  for a job or product) _____

[1]Contributed by George Spilka and Associates, Merger Brokers & Acquisition Consultants, 4084 Mt. Royal Boulevard, Allison Park, Pennsylvania 15101.

## FORM VID 1.01

(Sale of manufacturing business, including patents, trademarks, and
real estate—with covenant not to compete)

### AGREEMENT[1]

AGREEMENT made in East Town, Pennsylvania, on July 1, 1982, between John Doe d/b/a ART TOYS at 100 Main Street, East Town, Pennsylvania 00000 (herein called "Seller"), and SUPER

GAMES, INC., a New York Corporation having its principal place of business at One Park Avenue, New York, New York 00000 (herein called "Buyer"), WITNESSETH:

WHEREAS, Seller is the owner of a factory and of certain patents and patent rights to manufacture toys and does and has been manufacturing the line known as Art Toys at his factory building located in East Town, Eastern County, Pennsylvania, and has been selling them by direct-mail advertising throughout the eastern United States, and has established, in connection with this business, a valuable goodwill; and

WHEREAS, Buyer is a manufacturer and distributor of toys throughout worldwide market, and Buyer desires to buy and Seller desires to sell the business of Seller, including the factory, the goodwill, the inventions, improvements, letters patent, and other property, interest, and rights relating to Seller's business of manufacturing and dealing in the line known as Art Toys upon the conditions and terms set forth in this Agreement;

IT IS AGREED:

1. *Description of property to be sold.* The Seller hereby agrees to sell, assign, transfer, set over, and deliver to Buyer the following property, free and clear of all liens and encumbrances:

   (a) The real estate and factory building erected thereon (herein called "Factory") located in East Town, Eastern County, Pennsylvania, described in Schedule A attached hereto and make part hereof.

   (Schedule A contains legal description of the real estate and factory by metes and bounds, or other appropriate legal description that will be used in the deed from Seller to Buyer.)

   (b) All the articles, machinery, tools, models, patterns, implements, and appliances of all kinds used or designed to be used in the manufacture of toys that are now in or on the Factory, as more particularly described in Schedule B attached hereto and made part hereof.

   (Schedule B contains the list of machinery tools, etc., giving trade names, model numbers, and manufacturer's identification numbers as applicable, and the list of models, patterns, and other personal property and furnishings located in or on the premises that are to be included in the sale.)

   (c) The goodwill of the Seller's toy business and the exclusive use of the name ART TOY(S).

   (d) The exclusive right to all Seller's trademarks and labels are used and owned by him in connection with the Art Toy business.

   (e) All inventions, improvements, letters patent, and patent licenses, as more fully and particularly described in Schedule C attached hereto and made part thereof.

   (Schedule C contains the patent numbers and copies of patent license agreement(s), and accurate descriptions of any inventions or improvements that are being sold.)

   (f) Seller's entire stock of finished and unfinished toys at a price to be agreed upon by the parties at the closing of this Agreement.[2]

2. *Warranties.* Seller is the sole and absolute owner of all of the property and interests included in this Agreement and in the schedules attached hereto and made part hereof. Seller has the right, title, and authority to sell and transfer all of the property, business, and goodwill and all interests of every kind included within the terms of this Agreement, and Seller will warrant and defend the same against the claims and demands of any and all persons whatever.

3. *Implementation of this Agreement.* Seller will, at any and all times, upon request of Buyer, its successors or assigns, execute any and all further instruments and documents, and will perform any and all further acts necessary or desired by the Buyer, its successors and assigns, to assure and vest in the Buyer, its successors and assigns, the full right, title, and interest of the Buyer in, to, and under all the property, business, and goodwill sold and transferred under this Agreement.

4. *Arbitration.* If there is any dispute as to the delivery of items listed in any Schedule attached hereto, except as to the real estate described in Schedule A, or as to the reasonable value of the stock of toys described in Paragraph 1(f), either party may give written notice to the other of his or its desire to submit the matter to arbitration and may designate an arbitrator. Within five (5) days after the receipt of that written notice, the other party shall serve upon the party requesting arbitration, a written notice designating an arbitrator in his or its behalf. The two (2) arbitrators so chosen shall, within five (5) days, designate a third arbitrator. The three (3) arbitrators shall promptly proceed to hear and determine the controversy by fixing a time and place when and where the matter shall be submitted to them by both parties. The arbitrators shall render their decision on the matter within ten (10) days after final submission by the parties. A decision by the majority of the arbitrators shall be final and binding on the parties. The cost of the arbitration shall be borne equally by the parties.

5. *Price.* In consideration of the foregoing sale, assignment, transfer covenants, and agreements of the Seller, the Buyer agrees to pay the Seller, on or before September 1, 1982, the sum of Two Hundred Thousand Dollars ($200,000) by paying the Seller One Hundred Twenty Thousand Dollars ($120,000) in cash and issuing and delivering to Seller Eight Hundred (800) shares of Buyer's capital stock of the par value of One Hundred Dollars ($100) each, upon the execution and delivery of a general warranty deed of conveyance of the land and factory to Buyer and Seller and upon the sale and delivery by Seller to Buyer of all the articles, machinery, tools, appliances, and personal property described herein, with the goodwill, use of name, patents, trademarks, and all other rights and interests of the Seller described herein.

6. *Covenant not to compete.* Seller covenants that, upon delivery to him of the cash and shares of stock provided herein, he, the Seller, shall not and will not, at any later time, directly or indirectly, engage in the manufacture or sale of Art Toys within the limits of the United States and its territories, nor aid or assist anyone else to do so within these limits, nor have any interest, directly or indirectly, in any business of manufacturing and/or selling Art Toys within these limits, except as an employee of the Buyer, and shall not and will not, within two (2) years, directly or indirectly, engage in the manufacture or sale of any toys within the Commonwealth of Pennsylvania, except as an employee of the Buyer.

7. *Complete agreement of the parties.*[3] It is understood and agreed that this Contract contains all the covenants, stipulations, and provisions agreed upon by the parties. It is understood and agreed that the real, fixed, and personal property described herein has been inspected by the Buyer or the Buyer's duly authorized agent; that the same is and has been purchased as a result of the inspection and not upon representations made by the Seller; and that the Buyer hereby expressly waives any and all claims for damages or for cancellation of this Contract because of any representation made by the Seller or any selling agent or person whatsoever other than as contained in this Agreement; and the Seller will not be responsible for or liable on account of any inducements, promises, representations, or agreements not set forth in this Agreement.

8. *Limitation of Seller's liability.*[4] In the event of a breach of any covenant hereunder, Seller shall not be liable for prospective profits or indirect or consequential damages of the Buyer, nor shall any recovery of any kind against Seller be greater in amount that the proportionate purchase price of the item or interest affected by the breach.

9. *Separability.* Should any portion of this Contract be judicially determined to be illegal or unenforceable, the remainder of the Agreement shall not be affected by such determination.

10. *Governing law.* This Agreement shall be interpreted and enforced according to the laws of the Commonwealth of Pennsylvania.

IN WITNESS WHEREOF, the parties hereto have duly executed this Agreement on the day and year first above written.

JOHN DOE d/b/a ART TOYS

(CORPORATE SEAL)      SUPER GAMES, INC.

By _____

Secretary of the Corporation      President

[1] 26 U.S.C.A. 111–114. See Chapter V for sale or lease of business real estate. Ref. Form IVD 1.00(a) for Business Valuation Checklist.
[2] U.C.C. Article 6; and Forms VIE 1.00–1.02(a).
[3] U.C.C. 2–202.
[4] U.C.C. 2–710 and 2–715.

## FORM VID 1.02

### (Sale of retail store business including goodwill—covenant not to compete)[1]

### AGREEMENT

THIS AGREEMENT made in Middletown, Minnesota, this 12th day of February, 1982, between John Doe d/b/a HAPPY HUNTER SUPPLIES (herein called "Seller"), and Richard Roe (herein called "Buyer"), WITNESSETH:

WHEREAS, Seller represents and warrants that he is the owner of the real estate and building known as 100 Main Street, Middletown, Minnesota, and has been and is presently operating a retail store for the sale of sporting goods at that location under the name HAPPY HUNTER SUPPLIES; and

WHEREAS, Seller desires to retire from the business not later than May 1, 1983; and

WHEREAS, Buyer operates a retail store for the sale of sporting goods at 500 East Street, Middletown, Minnesota, and desires to buy the stock, franchises, fixtures, and goodwill of Seller's business;

NOW, THEREFORE, IT IS AGREED:

1. *Description of property purchased.*[2] The Seller sells and the Buyer buys all of the Seller's right, title, and interest in the goodwill and name of the sporting goods business known as Happy Hunter Supplies, together with all manufacturer's franchises, more particularly described in Schedule A attached hereto and made part hereof, and all display cases, office furniture, and fixtures used in the business, more particularly described in Schedule B attached hereto and made part hereof, and the Seller's sporting goods inventory stock that has not been sold by Seller at the time of delivery of the business pursuant to this Agreement.

2. *Delivery.* Seller shall deliver all tangible personal property, including sporting goods inventory stockand duly executed assignments of manufacturer's franchise agreements, to Buyer no later than May 1, 1983, at the Seller's premises. The Buyer shall remove the purchased property from the Seller's premises at the Buyer's sole cost and expense, within ten (10) days after receiving written notice of the Seller's readiness to deliver the same; but, pending such removal by the Buyer, the Seller may continue his business without accounting to the Buyer.

3. *Warranties.* The tangible personal property and inventory stock of the Seller is sold AS IS. The Seller covenants that all the property and goods sold are free and clear of all liens and encumbrances; that Seller is the owner of and has the right to sell same; that Seller has the right to assign the franchises listed in Schedule A; and that Seller is not indebted to any person, firm, association, or corporation for any debt arising out of the operation of the business known as Happy Hunter Supplies. The Seller agrees to hold Buyer harmless from any and all claims by anyone against the Buyer for or by reason of the execution and delivery of this Agreement.

4. *Insurance.* Seller shall, pending delivery, insure the tangible personal property and inventory stock of the Seller, at Seller's expense, for the benefit of the Buyer, against loss or damage by fire in the amount of Ten Thousand Dollars ($10,000).

5. *Covenant not to compete.* Seller covenants that he will not, directly or indirectly, sell or otherwise deal in sporting goods in Middle and Northern counties, Minnesota, in any capacity, for a period of five (5) years following the delivery of the business assets pursuant to this Agreement.

6. *Liquidated damages for breach of covenant not to compete.* As it would be difficult and impracticable to prove the damages resulting from the breach of the covenant of the Seller not to compete, any breach of that covenant shall require the payment of liquidated damages by Seller to Buyer in the amount of One Hundred Dollars ($100) for each week in which the Seller violated that covenant in any manner and to any extent.

7. *Price.*

(a) In consideration for the sale of the business as provided herein, except for the sporting goods stock described in Paragraph 1 and the covenants of the Seller contained herein, the Buyer shall pay to Seller upon the execution of this instrument the sum of Three Thousand Dollars ($3,000) and shall simultaneously deliver to Seller the Buyer's three (3) promissory notes drawn to the order of the Seller for Ten Thousand Dollars ($10,000) each, bearing annual interest of Eight Percent (8%), payable as follows: May 1, 1984, May 1, 1985, and May 1, 1986. In the event that Buyer fails to pay any note when due, the then remaining unpaid balance of the purchase price as evidenced by the notes shall become immediately due and payable without notice or protest by the holder.

(b) The sporting goods stock described in Paragraph 1 shall be purchased by Buyer at the time of delivery hereunder at the Seller's invoice price, not to exceed Five Thousand Dollars ($5,000).

8. *Complete agreement of the parties.* The making, execution, and delivery of this Agreement has been induced by no representations, statements, or warranties other than those set forth herein. The Buyer has inspected the goods and assignments sold hereby and has relied on his inspection of the goods and documents in executing this Agreement.

IN WITNESS WHEREOF, the parties have hereunto signed this Agreement in Middletown, Middle County, Minnesota, on the day and year first above written.

ATTEST

_____

WITNESS

_____

WITNESS

_____

JOHN DOE d/b/a HAPPY HUNTER SUPPLIES

_____

RICHARD ROE

(Attach schedules.)

¹26 U.S.C.A. 111–114. See Chapter VII for sale or lease of business real estate. Ref. Form VID 1.00(a) for Business Valuation Checklist.
²U.C.C. Article 6; and Forms VIE 1.00–1.02(a).

## FORM VID 1.03

(Sale of service business [insurance]—goodwill, commissions, and accounts receivable)

### AGREEMENT TO SELL¹

AGREEMENT made this 10th day of July, 1982, between John Doe, residing at 100 East Boulevard, Little Rock, Arkansas 00000 (herein called "Seller"), and Peter Poe, residing at West Boulevard, Little Rock, Arkansas 00000 (herein called "Buyer"), WITNESSETH:

WHEREAS, Seller has operated as a soliciting independent insurance agent in the name John Doe Insurance Agency, with offices located at 100 Main Street, Little Rock, Arkansas 00000; and

WHEREAS, Buyer is a duly licensed insurance broker under the laws of the State of Arkansas; and

WHEREAS, Seller has agreed to sell to Buyer all his right, title, and interest in the insurance agency business;

IT IS THEREFORE MUTUALLY AGREED AS FOLLOWS:

1. *Description of property and interests sold.* Seller sells and Buyer buys, the following:
   (a) The business known as John Doe Insurance Agency, together with its name and goodwill.
   (b) Any and all commissions due, or that may become due, on any policies or renewals of policies sold by the agency business as shown on the books of account of the agency.
   (c) Any and all accounts receivable shown on the books of account of the agency.

2. *Price.* Buyer shall pay Seller the sum of Ten Thousand Dollars ($10,000) upon the execution of this agreement.

3. *Delivery.* Upon the execution of this Agreement and payment of the purchase price by Buyer, Seller shall deliver to Buyer at the present agency office located at 100 Main Street, Little Rock, Arkansas, the books of account of the John Doe Insurance Agency, together will all files and client lists pertaining to the past or future sale of insurance by the agency, which property and documents delivered hereunder shall be removed by Buyer within ten (10) days of that delivery.

4. *Collection of accounts receivable.* Upon delivery and payment as provided in Paragraph 3, the Seller hereby authorizes the Buyer, in the Seller's name (John Doe Insurance Agency), but at the Buyer's own cost and expense, to collect all outstanding accounts of the agency business, to give receipts, and to receive, endorse, and collect any and all checks made to the order of the Seller or the John Doe Insurance Agency, and delivered or sent in payment of any of these accounts. If any such payments are made directly to Seller, he shall forthwith deliver them to the Buyer for the Buyer's exclusive use.

5. *Covenant not to compete.* Seller shall not, within five (5) years of the date of the execution of this Agreement.
   (a) Canvass, solicit, or accept any business from any customer or customers named in the books or records of the agency, now or in the past.
   (b) Permit, allow, or give any other person, firm, association, or corporation the right or permission to canvass, solicit, or accept insurance business from any of those customers.
   (c) Directly or indirectly, in any way, request or advise any customers now on the books or

records of the agency, or who have been, to withdraw or cancel his, or any of their, insurance business with the Buyer.

(d) Disclose to any person, firm, association, or corporation, directly or indirectly, the name or address of any customer or customers of insurance from the agency.

6. *Liquidated damages.* As it would be difficult and impracticable to prove the damages resulting from the Seller's breach of his covenant not to compete, any breach of that covenant shall require the payment of the Seller to the Buyer of the sum of Five Thousand Dollars ($5,000) and, in addition, Buyer may seek relief from a court of equity to enjoin further breach of that covenant, as the damage from further breach would be irreparable. This provision for liquidated damages shall not limit the right of the Buyer to seek any other remedy and to recover any other damages for breach of any other terms or provisions of this Agreement.

7. *General warranty.* The Seller shall warrant and defend this sale against any and every corporation, association, person, or persons whatsoever and whomsoever.

IN WITNESS WHEREOF, the parties hereto have executed this Agreement on the day and year first above written.

---

John Doe d/b/a JOHN DOE INSURANCE      PETER POE
AGENCY

¹26 U.S.C.A. 111–114. Compare other forms in this section for sale of business involving inventory, and see Chapter VII for sale or lease of business real estate.

## FORM VID 1.04

### (Sale of all assets of sole proprietorship, including stock in trade— bulk transfer compliance)

### SALE OF BUSINESS ASSETS¹

This Agreement made the 10th day of August, 1982, between JOHN DOE of Middletown, Middle County, Florida, (herein called "Seller"), and RICHARD ROE of 200 Main Street, Middletown, Middle County, Florida (herein called "Buyer").

1. *BUSINESS AND PROPERTY SOLD AND DELIVERY.* Seller agrees to sell and transfer and Buyer agrees to buy the business known as DOE'S APPLIANCES, located at 100 Main Street, Middletown, Middle County, Florida, including the stock in trade; and also fixtures, equipment, licenses, or any other rental or use of equipment at the said premises, more particularly described in Schedule A, attached hereto and made part hereof. The property listed in Schedule A is free and clear of any debts, mortgages, security interest, or other liens or encumbrances, except as herein stated. Transfer of title shall take place on August 31, 1982, at 10:00 A.M. in the office of John Just, Esq., 100 East Avenue, Middletown, Florida. Keys to the premises shall be delivered to the Buyer at the closing. The present lease of the premises has been assigned by Seller to Buyer with the written consent of the landlord, which assignment shall be delivered at the closing.

2. *PURCHASE PRICE AND TERMS OF PAYMENT.* The purchase price is Twenty Thousand Dollars ($20,000), to be paid by the Buyer as follows:

By executing and delivering one promissory note dated August 31, 1982, payable to Seller, to be secured by a purchase money security interest² hereby granted by the Buyer to the Seller upon the existing and after acquired fixtures, equipment, stock in trade, and all other goods and chattels used in connection with said business; together with the property or accessories thereafter acquired as replacement or substitution or additon or accession to or with the said collateral. Terms of Note: Dated Middletown, Florida, August 31, 1982, in the amount of Twenty Thousand Dollars ($20,000) principal amount; maker promising to pay Six Hundred Dollars ($600) on or before the 1st day of each and every month thereafter, commencing October 1, 1982, including interest on the unpaid principal balance at the rate of Eight Percent (8%) per annum, interest payable monthly; said payments to be made to the Seller at P.O. Box 111, Middletown, Florida, or at such place as Seller may designate. Said monthly payments of Six Hundred Dollars ($600) to continue until the aggregate amount paid on principal shall be equal to the sum of Twenty Thousand Dollars ($20,000). Said Note shall have standard provisions as to acceleration in case of default for a period of thirty (30) days and shall provide for the payment of all expenses of collecting, including a reasonable attorney's fee.

3. *COMPLIANCE WITH BULK TRANSFER LAW.*[3] Following the execution of this Agreement, the Seller shall furnish a list of his existing creditors to the Buyer, signed and sworn to and affirmed by the Seller, and such list shall contain the names and business addresses of all creditors of the Seller, both personal and business, whether general or secured, with the amounts owing when known, also the names of all persons who are known to the Seller to assert claims against him, even though such claims are contested or disputed. The Seller and Buyer shall prepare a schedule of the property transferred under this Agreement sufficient to identify it, and have done so, and the same is attached to this Contract as Schedule A. The Buyer shall preserve said list of Creditors and Schedule of Property for six (6) months next following the transfer, during which time he shall permit inspection of either or both and copying therefrom at all reasonable hours by any creditor of the Seller, or shall file said list and schedule in the office of the Clerk of the Circuit Court of Middle County, Florida. Seller has been in business under the name Doe's Appliances at 100 Main Street, Middletown, Florida, for the past ten (10) years.

4. *APPLICATION OF PROCEEDS OF SALE.* Seller is retiring from the appliance business and asserts that he has only one creditor or supplier other than monthly expenses for utilities, and Seller shall pay said creditors promptly when billed therefor. It is understood between the parties that accounts receivable of Doe's Appliances are not included in this Sale.

5. *ASSIGNABILITY.* All the terms, covenants, and conditions herein contained shall be for and shall inure to the benefit of and shall bind the respective parties hereto, and their legal representatives, successors, and assigns respectively.

6. *COMPLETE AGREEMENT OF THE PARTIES. THIS WRITING CONTAINS THE ENTIRE AGREEMENT BETWEEN THE BUYER AND SELLER.* There are no warranties, express or implied, of merchantability, fitness, or otherwise, that extend beyond the description herein; all tangible personal property being sold hereunder is being sold "AS IS."

IN WITNESS WHEREOF, the parties hereto have hereunto set their hands and seals the day and year first above written.

---
JOHN DOE

---
RICHARD ROE

(Prepare creditors list for Seller as shown in Form IVE 1.01. Buyer shall notify the creditor(s) as shown in Form IVE 1.02.)

[1]U.C.C. 6-102(1) and 9-109(4); 26 U.S.C.A. 111–114. See Forms VIE 1.00–1.02(a) for bulk transfer compliance. Also check whether your state has adopted U.C.C. 6-106.
[2]U.C.C. Article 9.
[3]U.C.C. Article 6 and Forms VIE 1.00–1.02(a) for bulk transfer compliance

## VID 1.05

### (Sale of all tangible assets of a corporation, including stock in trade, through an escrow agent—bulk transfer compliance)

### AGREEMENT OF SALE[1]

BY THIS AGREEMENT made in Pittsburgh, Pennsylvania, on June 1, 1982, by DOE RESTAURANT EQUIPMENT, INC., a Pennsylvania corporation having its principal place of business at 100 Penn Avenue, Pittsburgh, Pennsylvania 00000 (herein called "Seller"); ACME RESTAURANT SUPPLY, INC., an Ohio corporation having its principal place of business at 100 Main Street, Cleveland Ohio 00000 (herein called "Buyer"), and RICHARD ABLE, having a law office at Suite 554, Main Building, Pittsburgh, Pennsylvania 00000 (herein called "Escrow Agent"); the parties, in consideration of the mutal promises and covenants contained herein, agree as follows:

1. *Description of property sold.* Seller agrees to sell and Buyer agrees to buy all of the Seller's stock in trade consisting of restaurant fixtures, appliances, equipment, and supplies, and all articles of merchandise now in and on the premises of the Seller at 100 Penn Avenue, Pittsburgh, Pennsylvania, together with all fixtures and furnishings on the premises used in the business of Seller operating its restaurant supply business.

2. *Warranties.*

(a) The property sold is sold AS IS; the Seller having inspected the property before entering into this Agreement.

(b) Seller warrants that it is operating and has operated the restaurant supply business from which the property is being purchased exclusively at 100 Penn Avenue, Pittsburgh, Pennsylvania, for the period of the past fifteen (15) years.

3. *Price.* The price to be paid by Buyer to Seller shall be:

(a) the cost price to Seller of each article sold plus Ten Percent (10%) of that cost price. The cost shall be determined *as provided* in Paragraph 3.

(b) The price shall be paid by the Buyer to the Escrow Agent as follows: Five Thousand Dollars ($5,000) upon the execution of this Agreement, to be applied on the purchase price when this sale is consummated as provided herein; an additional Five Thousand Dollars ($5,000) immediately upon the completion of the inventory list and evaluation and the list of Seller's creditors, which sum shall also be applied on the purchase price when this sale is consummated as provided herein; and the balance of the purchase price shall be paid not less than ten (10) days prior to the closing of this sale as provided in Paragraph 7, and not less than one (1) day prior to the date on which the Buyer shall notify creditors of Seller of this proposed sale and of the price terms and conditions of this sale, in the manner provided for in Article 6 Title 12 A Purdon's Statutes.

4. *Determination of cost base for price.* For the purpose of determining the cost of the stock in trade, furnishings, and fixtures sold.

(a) The Seller shall close and lock its business premises and deliver the keys to the premises to the Escrow Agent upon the execution of this Agreement.

(b) From the date of delivery of the keys, provided Buyer performs as required by this Agreement, the Escrow Agent shall permit only persons designated in a writing signed by both Seller and Buyer authorizing their designated representatives to enter the premises for the purpose of preparing a written inventory and cost determination of the property sold hereunder. Any such designated person shall be entitled to admission to the premises and the right to remain thereon only in the presence of the other designee.

(c) The Buyer and Seller shall equally share the cost of the inventory and cost determination.

(d) The persons designated shall have full and complete access to the Seller's premises as provided herein, and to the books, accounts, data, and all business records of Seller in order to ascertain and value the property to be sold, and, if desired by Buyer to verify the list of creditors to be supplied by Seller as provided in paragraph 5.

(e) In the event that the value of the property cannot reasonably be determined as above provided, the parties shall each choose one (1) appraiser, and the two (2) appraisers chosen shall choose a third (3rd) appraiser to determine the value of the property as provided herein. The decision of any two (2) of the three (3) appraisers shall be binding on the parties. The Buyer and Seller shall equally share the cost of the appraisal.

5. *Bulk transfer compliance.*[2] The Seller and Buyer shall respectively comply with the bulk transfer provisions of Article 6 of the Pennsylvania Uniform Commercial Code, Title XII A Purdon's Statutes.

6. *Default.* In addition to any other legal rights and remedies either Buyer or Seller may have for breach of this Agreement:

(a) Upon default in any payment by the Buyer to the Escrow Agent as required hereunder, and proof of the default satisfactory to the Escrow Agent, the Seller may, at its option, demand and receive payment by Seller of all moneys in the hands of the Escrow Agent as liquidated damages. Furthermore, the Escrow Agent shall, under that circumstance, return the keys to Seller's premises to the Seller, and the Escrow Agent shall then be forever discharged from any liability or duties under this Agreement.

(b) Upon failure of Seller to furnish and cooperate in the preparation of the inventory and valuation provided herein and/or upon the failure of Seller to furnish the written list of creditors as required herein, and upon proof satisfactory to the Escrow Agent of such failure, the Buyer may, at its option, demand and receive payment by Buyer of all moneys in the hands of the Escrow Agent as liquidated damages, and the Escrow Agent shall return the keys to Seller's premises to the Seller, and the Escrow Agent shall then be forever discharged from any liability or duty under this Agreement.

7. *Closing.* The sale and transfer of the property sold hereby shall take place at the law offices of Richard Able, Esq., Suite 554 Main Building, Pittsburgh, Pennsylvania, at 10:00 A.M. on June

25, 1982, at which time and place all keys to the premises, bills of sale, and other instruments of transfer of the property shall be delivered and the moneys in escrow shall be paid over. At the closing, all transfers and payments to the parties, creditors, or others shall be duly supported by appropriate identification of parties and evidence of appropriate corporate action and authority.

8. *Escrow.* Richard Able is hereby appointed and accepts the appointment as Escrow Agent to perform in accordance with the provisions of this Agreement. The Escrow Agent shall not be personally liable for any act he may do or fail to do hereunder while acting in good faith and in the exercise of his own best judgment. The Escrow Agent may disregard, in his sole discretion, any and all notices of the parties provided hereunder or by any other person or legal entity, except that the Escrow Agent shall comply with any order, judgment, or decree of any court made, filed, entered, or issued, whether with or without jurisdiction.

9. *Governing law.* This Agreement shall be interpreted and construed pursuant to the laws of the Commonwealth of Pennsylvania.

IN WITNESS WHEREOF, the parties hereto have duly signed and caused their respective corporate seals to be affixed on the day and year above written.

DOE RESTAURANT EQUIPMENT, INC.

By _____
Secretary of the Corporation          President

ACME RESTAURANT SUPPLY, INC.

By _____
Secretary of the Corporation          President

_____
Richard Able, ESCROW AGENT

(Prepare creditors list for Seller as shown in Form VIE 1.01. Buyer shall notify *all* creditors as shown in Form VIE 1.02.)

[1]26 U.S.C.A. 331 et seq.
[2]U.C.C. Article 6 and Forms VIE 1.00–1.02(a) for bulk transfer compliance.

## SECTION E      BULK TRANSFER COMPLIANCE

Before using the forms in this section, the general introduction to PART VI should be read as well as FORM VID 1.00.

The forms in this section are to be used where there is a bulk transfer of personal property as defined in the Uniform Commercial Code Article 6 as enacted in the state where the transfer takes place.

### FORM VIE 1.00

### CLIENT QUESTIONNAIRE FOR BULK TRANSFER COMPLIANCE

1. Read your state's version of Article 6 of the Uniform Commercial Code and follow it exactly
2. Is the seller a "merchant" within the definition of U.C.C. 2-104?
3. Is the seller's business one that sells from Inventory? U.C.C. 6-102?
4. Is the seller's business exempt from Article 6 under U.C.C. 6-103?
   The following transfers are exempt under that section, but see public notice requirements in the section
   a. Security for performance
   b. General assignment for benefit of creditors
   c. Settlement of lien
   d. Sales by executors, administrators, receivers, trustees in bankruptcy, or other judicial sales
   e. Sales in course of judicial or administrative proceedings where notice is given in the proceeding
   f. Where transferee (buyer) assumes the debts and has known place of business in state

    g. New business enterprise

    h. Property that is exempt from execution.

5. Is the seller selling a "major part" of his business?

6. Will the sale bring enough to pay all seller's creditors? To be safe, all creditors should be paid. Even so, all creditors must be notified before the actual transfer of assets on the closing date pursuant to U.C.C. 6-104, 6-105, and 6-106, and 6-107(1)(c) and (2)

7. Present business names and addresses of the seller and buyer. U.C.C. 6-107(1)(b)

8. Business names and business addresses seller has used in the past three years. U.C.C. 6-107(1)(b)

9. Does the buyer, or a new business enterprise organized by seller to take over his business, maintain a known place of business in the state where the sale is made, and does the Buyer or new business enterprise undertake, by the contract, to pay the debts of the seller in full? U.C.C. 6-103(6)? If so, Public Notice of Assumption of Debts may be advertised per U.C.C. 6-103(6) and 6-103(7) instead of using the creditors list and notice procedure. Check your state statute to see if U.C.C. 6-106 was adopted

10. Names and addresses of all creditors of seller (include matured and unmatured debts, liquidated and unliquidated amounts of debts, tort and contract debts, secured and unsecured debts, contingent or fixed debts, and business and nonbusiness debts of the seller). U.C.C. 6-104

    Seller must furnish this list. See Form IVE 1.01

11. Schedule of property to be transferred. U.C.C. 6-104(1)(b)

12. Notice to Creditors. See Forms IVE 1.02 and 1.02(a). Be specific about closing date: give date, time of day, and place, including suite or room number, if possible. U.C.C. 6-107

13. Will there be a substantial down payment by buyer? If so, it should be put in escrow until the closing if there are numerous creditors or if the amounts owing are substantial. U.C.C. 6-106

## FORM VIE 1.01

### (Creditors list for bulk transfer—where major part of business assets, including inventory, is being sold)

### CREDITORS LIST AFFIDAVIT[1]

    Pursuant to the bulk transfer provisions of the Pennsylvania Uniform Commercial Code, John Doe, President of DOE RESTAURANT EQUIPMENT, INC., a Pennsylvania corporation, Transferor, states as follows:

1. Transferor conducts a restaurant appliance and supply business at 100 Penn Avenue, Pittsburgh, Pennsylvania 00000.

2. Transferor has contracted to sell the assets of its business, including all inventory, fixtures, and equipment, to ACME RESTAURANT SUPPLY, INC., an Ohio corporation having its principal place of business at 100 Main Street, Cleveland, Ohio 00000.

3. Pursuant to Article 6-104, Title 12 A Purdon's Statutes, Transferor has prepared the following list of names and business addresses of all creditors of Transferor. These claims are admitted, and the amounts of the claims are set forth when known:

| Creditor and address | Amount |
|---|---|
| A-1 Stove Company<br>100 Main Street<br>Butler, Pa. 00000 | $ 647 |
| Roe China, Inc.<br>100 Main Street<br>Erie, Pa. 0000 | $1,200 |
| Poe Steele Products, Inc.<br>100 Main Street<br>Syracuse, N.Y. 00000 | $ 900 |
| Richard Roe<br>8 River Drive<br>Pittsburgh, Pa. 00000 | $1,000 |

In further compliance with Article 6-104, Title 12 A Purdon's Statutes, Transferor has also prepared the following list of all creditors who assert claims against Transferor, even though the claims are disputed or admitted only in part:

*Claimant and address*                                                   *Amount*

Poe Manufacturing, Inc.
100 Main Street
Buffalo, N.Y. 00000                                                      $1,200

STATE OF PENNSYLVANIA)
                     )  SS
COUNTY OF ALLEGHENY  )

John Doe, as President acting on behalf of Doe Restaurant Equipment, Inc., of 100 Penn Avenue, Pittsburgh, Pennsylvania, who, being first duly sworn by me, deposes and says on his oath that the above lists of names of all creditors and claimants, including their business addresses and the amounts claimed when known, against the business of Doe Restaurant Equipment, Inc., is a complete list of all known creditors and claimants against said business, and that the above list is being delivered to Acme Restaurant Supply, Inc., at 100 Main Street, Cleveland, Ohio, by certified mail, return receipt requested and postage prepaid, in answer to demand of Acme restaurant Supply, Inc., on June 1, 1982.

                                             DOE RESTAURANT EQUIPMENT, INC.

                                             By _____
                                                JOHN DOE, President

Subscribed and sworn to before me this 10th day
of June, 1982.

_____

Notary Public

My commission expires:

    [1]U.C.C. 6-104; *68 Am. Jur. 2d Secured Transactions,* para. 12. Ref. Form VIE 1.02 for actual notice to creditors on the list. See Form VIE 1.03 for constructive notice under U.C.C. 6-103.

## FORM VIE 1.02

### (Actual notice to creditors of bulk transferor)

### NOTICE TO CREDITORS[1]
### of
### DOE RESTAURANT EQUIPMENT, INC.

To:  A-1 Stove Company[2]
     100 Main Street
     Butler, Pa. 00000

Pursuant to the provisions of Article 6-107 (2), Title 12 A Purdon's Statutes, notice is hereby given to the creditors of Doe Restaurant Equipment, Inc., whose present business address is 100 Penn Avenue, Pittsburgh, Pennsylvania 00000, that a bulk transfer is about to be made to Acme Restaurant Supply, Inc., an Ohio corporation whose present mailing address is 100 Main Street, Cleveland, Ohio 00000.

The property transferred is located at 100 Penn Avenue, Pittsburgh, Pennsylvania, at the Seller's place of business and is described in general as follows: all stock in trade, fixtures, furnishings, and equipment of that restaurant appliance and supply business known as Doe Restaurant Equipment, Inc., and located at that address.

The bulk transfer will be consummated on June 25, 1982, at 10:00 A.M. at the law offices of Richard Able, Esq., in Suite 554 Main Building, Pittsburgh, Pennsylvania.

So far as is known to the Transferee, all other business names and addresses used by the Transferor within three (3) years last past are:

DOE RESTAURANT EQUIPMENT, INC.
100 Penn Avenue
Pittsburgh, Pennsylvania

Dated June 12, 1982 ACME RESTAURANT SUPPLY, INC.

(Buyer must send the above notice to each and every creditor and claimant that appears on the Seller's Creditors List as shown in Form VIE 1.01.)

[1]U.C.C. 6-107. Compare Form VIE 1.03 for constructive notice to creditors under U.C.C. 6-103.

[2]This notice must be sent to every creditor listed on Form VIE 1.01.

## FORM VIE 1.03

**(Constructive notice to creditors of bulk transfer by advertising, where Buyer assumes the debts of Seller and Buyer maintains a known place of business in the state or the transfer is to a new business enterprise organized to take over and continue the business)**

### NOTICE OF ASSUMPTION OF DEBTS[1]

Notice is hereby given pursuant to Uniform Commercial Code, as enacted in Section 676-103 Florida Statutes, that John Doe, located at 100 Main Street, Middletown, Florida, transferred the entire business known as Doe's Furniture Mart to the undersigned on May 1, 1982, and that we have assumed all of the debts of the Seller

DOE'S SUPER DISCOUNT FURNITURE, INC.
100 Main Street
Tampa, Fla. 00000

(Caution:　If transferor is an individual partnership or close corporation that may have debts unrelated to the business, it may be safer to follow U.C.C. 104 and 107[2] instead of this section, if the purchaser is a stranger.)

[1]U.C.C. 6-103. Compare From VIE 1.02 for actual notice to creditors on the creditors list provided pursuant to U.C.C. 6-104.

## SECTION F　　SECURITY INTEREST IN PERSONAL PROPERTY

Before using the forms in this section, the general introduction to PART VI should be read as well as FORM VIF 1.00.

A set of representative state filing forms for perfecting a security interest in personal property is included in this section. See FORM VIF 1.03 through FORM VIF 1.05.

For forms to be used as a supplement or addition to security agreements, see PART VII of this book.

### FORM VIF 1.00

### CLIENT QUESTIONNAIRE FOR CREATING SECURITY INTEREST IN PERSONAL PROPERTY[1]

1. Name, address, and telephone number of client
2. Is client the debtor or the secured party?
3. What is the amount of money to be secured?
4. Will the security agreement include future advances?[2]
5. What is the collateral (consumer goods being purchased,[3] tangible personal property, stocks, bonds, other)? Get detailed description of the collateral, including ID and serial numbers where applicable

6. Location of collateral. Be specific. If in the hands of a third party, get third party's name and address.[4]
7. Are there any limitations on the debtor's use of the collateral until the debt is paid? If so, what are they? Note: If secured party holds the security, it is a pledge, and a written agreement is *not* required, but it is advisable.[5]
8. Does the collateral include after-acquired property of the same kind?[6]
9. What interest is to be paid?
10. Date(s) payment is due
11. Will there be acceleration in case of default?
12. In case of dispute, will the prevailing party be entitled to attorney's fees?
13. Does client want you to prepare and file Financing Statement?[7] If so, advise client of the date it is filed for his future reference if there is need to file a continuation statement[8]

[1]*69 Am. Jur. 2d Secured Transactions*, paras. 269-351.
[2]*68 Am. Jur. 2d Secured Transactions*, para. 315.
[3]15 U.S.C. A 1602(f) and 1671–1677.
[4]U.C.C. 9-304 (3), 9-305, and 9-112(b).
[5]U.C.C. 9-305.
[6]*68 Am. Jur. 2d Secured Transactions*, paras. 178–184; and 69 Am. Jur. 2d Secured Transactions, paras. 297–302.
[7]U.C.C. 9-401, 9-402, 9-403(2), and 9-110; and Form VIF 1.03.
[8]Ref. Form VIF 1.05.

## FORM VIF 1.01

### (Security agreement and note for purchase price of consumer goods for business use)

### SECURITY AGREEMENT[1]

(consumer goods)
FIRST NATIONAL BANK OF MIDDLETOWN
*JOHN DOE and MARY DOE d/b/a DOE'S RESTAURANT*
(Name[s] of Borrower[s])
(and if more than one, each of them jointly and severally), hereinafter called
"Borrower," of *Star Rt. 1 Box 27 G-1          Middletown*
                    (No. and Street)            (City)
*Middle          Virginia*, for value received and intending to be
 (County)   (State)
legally bound, hereby grant to FIRST NATIONAL BANK OF MIDDLETOWN, hereinafter called "Secured Party," a security interest in the following property, title to which is or will become vested in the Borrower:

| New or Used | Description of Collateral (Year, model, trade name,) | Model or Serial Number | Manufacturer's Serial No. |
|---|---|---|---|
| New | ACME SUPER UPRIGHT COMMERCIAL FREEZER (18 Cu. ft.) 1982 | MODEL 220 | Serial No. XT 1903 |

together with all increases, parts, fittings, accessories, equipment, and special tools now or hereafter affixed to any or any part thereof or used in connection with any or any part thereof, and all replacements of all or any part thereof (all of which is hereafter called "Collateral"), to secure the payment of a promissory note or notes executed by Borrower in the amount of *Two Thousand Seven Hundred Fifty* Dollars (*$2,750*), of even date herewith, and any and all extensions or renewals thereof, and any and all other liabilities or obligations (primary, secondary, direct, contingent, sole, joint, or several) due or to become due that may be hereafter contracted or acquired, of each Borrower (including each Borrower and any other person) to Secured Party (all the foregoing being hereafter called the "liabilities"), and also to secure the performance by Borrower of the Agreements hereinafter set forth.

Borrower hereby warrants and agrees that:

1. (a) Borrower is the owner of the Collateral clear of all liens and security interests except the security interest granted hereby; (b) Borrower has the right to make this Agreement; and (c) the Collateral is used or acquired for us primarily for the purpose checked: personal, family, or household purposes; farm purposes; or business purposes; and (d) if checked here, the Collateral is being acquired with the proceeds of the loan provided for in or secured by this Agreement, and said proceeds will be used for no other purpose, and Borrower hereby authorizes Secured Party to disburse such proceeds or any part thereof directly to the seller of the Collateral or to the insurance agent or broker, or both, as shown on Secured Party records.

2. (a) The Collateral will be kept at *DOE'S RESTAURANT, 100 Main St.,*
                                                              (No. and Street)
*Middletown, Middle, Virginia,* or, if left blank, at the address shown at the beginning of
  (City)   (County) (State)
this Agreement; Borrower will promptly notify Secured Party of any change in the location of the Collateral within said state; and Borrower will not remove the Collateral from said state without the written consent of Secured Party. (b) If the Collateral is used or acquired for use primarily for personal, family, or household purposes, or for farm purposes, Borrower's residence in Virginia is that shown at the beginning of this Agreement, and Borrower will immediately notify Secured Party of any change in the location of said residence.

3. (a) If the Collateral is acquired or used primarily for business use and is of a type normally used in more than one state whether or not so used, and Borrower has a place of business in more than one state, the chief place of business of Borrower is:
*100 Main Street,*        *Middletown,*        *Middle,*        *Virginia,* or, if left blank, is that shown at
  (No. and Street)          (City)          (County)          (State)
the beginning of this Agreement, and Borrower will immediately notify Secured Party in writing of any change in Borrower's chief place of business. (b) If certificates of title are issued or outstanding with respect to any of the Collateral, Borrower will cause the interest of Secured Party to be properly noted thereon and deliver such certificates of title to Secured Party.

4. Borrower will defend the Collateral against the claims and demands of all persons at any time claiming the same or any interest therein.

5. No Financing Statement covering any Collateral or any proceeds thereof is on file in any public office; Borrower authorizes Secured Party to file, in jurisdictions where this authorization will be given effect, a Financing Statement signed only by the Secured Party describing the Collateral in the same manner as it is described herein; and from time to time, at the request of Secured Party, execute one or more Financing Statements and such other documents (and pay the cost of filing or recording the same in all public offices deemed necessary or desirable by the Secured Party), and do such other acts and things, all as the Secured Party may request to establish and maintain a valid security interest in the Collateral (free of all other liens and claims whatsoever) to secure the payment of the liabilities, including, without limitation, deposit with Secured Party of any certificates of title issuable with respect to any of the Collateral, and notation thereon of the security interest hereunder.

6. Borrower will not (a) permit any liens or security interests (other than Secured Party's security interest) to attach to any of the Collateral; (b) permit any of the Collateral to be levied upon under any legal process; (c) sell, transfer, lease, or otherwise dispose of any of the Collateral or any interest therein, or offer so to do, without the prior written consent of Secured Party; (d) permit anything to be done that may impair the value of any of the Collateral or the security intended to be afforded by this Agreement; or (e) permit the Collateral to be or become a fixture (and it is expressly covenanted, warranted, and agreed that the Collateral, and every part thereof, whether affixed to any realty or not, shall be and remain personal property), or to become an accession to other goods or property.

7. Borrower will (a) at all times keep the Collateral insured against loss, damage, theft, and such other risks as Secured Party may require in such amounts and companies and under such policies and in such form, and for such periods, as shall be satisfactory to Secured Party, and each such policy shall provide that loss thereunder and proceeds payable thereunder shall be payable to Secured Party as its interest may appear (and Secured Party may apply any proceeds of such insurance that may be received by Secured Party toward payment of the liabilities, whether due or not due in such order of application as Secured Party may determine), and each such policy shall provide for a ten (10)-day written minimum cancellation notice to Secured Party; and each such policy shall, if Secured Party so requests, be deposited with Secured Party; and Secured Party may act as attorney for Borrower in obtaining, adjusting, settling, and canceling such insurance

and endorsing any drafts; (b) at all times keep the Collateral free from any adverse lien, security interest, or encumbrances and in good order and repair, and will not waste or destroy the Collateral or any part thereof, unless Borrower, in Borrower's sole discretion, chooses the optional insurance plan that can be provided by Secured Party and included in the note for which this security Agreement is given.

8. At its option, Secured Party may discharge taxes, liens, or security interests or other encumbrances at any time levied or placed on the Collateral, may pay for insurance on the Collateral, and may pay for the maintenance and preservation of the Collateral. Borrower agrees to reimburse Secured Party on demand for any payment made, or any expense incurred, by Secured Party, pursuant to the foregoing authorization. Until default, Borrower may have possession of Collateral and use it in any lawful manner not inconsistent with this Agreement and not inconsistent with any policy of insurance thereon.

9. (a) Borrower will not use the Collateral or permit the same to be used in violation of any statute or ordinance; and Secured Party may examine and inspect the Collateral at any time, wherever located; (b) Borrower will pay promptly when due all taxes and assessments upon the Collateral, or for its use or operation, or upon this Agreement, or upon any note or notes, or other writing evidencing the liabilities, or any of them.

10. Borrower shall be in default under this Agreement upon the happening of any of the following events or conditions: (a) failure or omission to pay when due any liability (or any installment thereof or interest thereon), or default in the payment or performance of any obligation, covenant, agreement, or liability contained or referred to herein; (b) any warranty, representation, or statement made or furnished to Secured Party by or on behalf of any Borrower proves to have been false in any material respect when made or furnished; (c) loss, theft, substantial damage, destruction, sale, or encumbrance to or of any of the Collateral, or the making of any levy, seizure, or attachment thereof or thereon; (d) any Obligor (which term, as used herein, shall mean each Borrower and each other Party primarily or secondarily or contingently liable on any of the liabilities) becomes insolvent or unable to pay debts as they mature, or makes an assignment for the benefit of creditors, or any proceeding is instituted by or against any Obligor alleging that such Obligor is insolvent or unable to pay debts as they mature; (e) entry of any judgment against any Obligor; (f) death of any Obligor who is a natural person, or of any partner of any Obligor that is a partnership; (g) dissolution, merger, or consolidation, or transfer of a substantial part of the property of any Obligor that is a corporation or a partnership; (h) appointment of a receiver for the Collateral or any thereof or for any property in which any Borrower has any interest.

11. Upon the occurrence of any such default or at any time thereafter, or whenever the Secured Party feels insecure for any reason whatsoever, Secured Party may, at its option, declare all liabilities secured hereby, or any of them (notwithstanding any provisions thereof) immediately due and payable without demand or notice of any kind, and the same thereupon shall immediately become and be due and payable without demand or notice (but with such adjustments, if any, with respect to interest or other charges as may be provided for in the promissory note or other writing evidencing such liability), and Secured Party shall have and may exercise from time to time any and all rights and remedies of a Secured Party under the Uniform Commercial Code and any and all rights and remedies available to it under other applicable law; and upon request or demand of Secured Party, Borrower shall, at its expense, assemble the Collateral and make it available to the Secured Party at a convenient place acceptable to Secured Party; and Borrower shall promptly pay all costs of Secured Party of collection of any and all the liabilities, and enforcement of rights hereunder, including reasonable attorney's fees and legal expenses, and expenses of any repairs to any of the Collateral, and expenses of any repairs to any realty or other property to which any of the Collateral may be affixed. Any notice of sale, disposition, or other intended action by Secured Party, sent to Borrower at the address of Borrower specified above or at any other address shown on the records of Secured Party, at least five (5) days prior to such action, shall constitute reasonable notice to Borrower. Expenses of retaking, holding, preparing for sale, selling, or the like shall include Secured Party's reasonable attorney's fees and legal expenses. Any excess or surplus of proceeds of any disposition of any of the Collateral may be applied by Secured Party toward payment of such of the liabilities, and in such order of application, as Secured Party may from time to time elect.

12. No waiver by Secured Party of any default shall operate as a waiver of any other default or of the same default on a future occasion. No delay or omission on the part of Secured Party in exercising any right or remedy shall operate as a waiver thereof, and no single or partial exercise by Secured Party of any right or remedy shall preclude any other or further exercise thereof or

the exercise of any other right or remedy. Time is of the essence of this Agreement. The provisions of this Agreement are cumulative and in addition to the provisions of any note secured by this Agreement, and Secured Party shall have all the benefits, rights, and remedies of and under any note secured hereby. If more than one party shall execute this Agreement, the term "Borrower" shall mean all parties signing this Agreement and each of them, and all such parties shall be jointly and severally obligated and liable hereunder. The singular pronoun, when used herein, shall include the plural, and the neuter shall include masculine and feminine. If this Agreement is not dated when executed by the Borrower, the Secured Party is authorized, without notice to the Borrower, to date this Agreement. This Agreement shall become effective as of the date of this Agreement. All rights of Secured Party hereunder shall inure to the benefit of its successors and assigns; and all liabilities of Borrower shall bind the heirs, executors, administrators, successors, and assigns of each Borrower.

13. This Agreement has been delivered in the Commonwealth of Virginia and shall be construed in accordance with the laws of Virginia. Wherever possible, each provision of this Agreement shall be interpreted in such manner as to be effective and valid under applicable law, but if any provision of this Agreement shall be prohibited by or invalid under applicable law, such provision shall be ineffective to the extent of such prohibition or invalidity, without invalidating the remainder of such provision or the remaining provisions of this Agreement.

IN WITNESS WHEREOF, this Agreement has been duly executed as of the 1st day of March, 1982.

NOTICE TO THE BUYER:

1. Do not sign this Contract before you read it or if it contains any blank spaces.

2. You are entitled to an exact copy of the Contract you sign.

Signed, sealed, and delivered
in the presence of:

_____     _____ (SEAL)
WITNESS                           JOHN DOE Borrower

_____     _____ (SEAL)
WITNESS                           MARY DOE Borrower

(Note:  Secured Party need sign this agreement *only if* the agreement itself is to be used as a Financing Statement per U.C.C. 9-402, 9-403[2], and 9-110.)

[1]15 U.S.C.A. 1601 et seq.; and Regulation Z, 12 C.F.R. 226; and Regulation B, 12 C.F.R. 202; 67 *Am. Jur. 2d Sales*, para. 408; and 69 *Am. Jur. 2d Secured Transactions*, paras. 269–331, 332, 333, 345, and 457. For filing, see Forms VIF 1.03 and 1.04.

## FORM VIF 1.01(a)

(Installment loan note for use with Form VIF 1.01)

### FIRST NATIONAL BANK OF MIDDLETOWN

Loan No. *82-454*                         Total amount of loan *$3,022.50*
INSTALLMENT LOAN NOTE FOR PURCHASE OF CONSUMER GOODS[1]
*March 1*, 1982

FOR VALUE RECEIVED, the undersigned, jointly and severally, promise to pay to the order of *FIRST NATIONAL BANK OF MIDDLETOWN*, the sum of *three thousand twenty-two and 50/100* DOLLARS, payable in *48* successive monthly installments of *$100.00*, and a final installment of *$142.45*, commencing on *May 5*, 1982. The amount of this note includes the purchase price of *$2,750.00*, PROPERTY INSURANCE (include only if premium financed hereunder) as more particularly described in Paragraph 6 below, of *$120.00*, CREDIT LIFE INSURANCE PREMIUM of *$130.00*, and other charges *for credit investigation and filing* of *$22.50* (resulting in an AMOUNT (Describe and state cost of each)
FINANCED of *$3,022.50*, plus a FINANCE CHARGE of *$1,363.40* (which amount includes interest of *$1,348.40* and credit investigation cost of *$15.00*), resulting in an ANNUAL PERCENTAGE RATE of *12.25%*.

CREDIT LIFE INSURANCE IS VOLUNTARY AND NOT REQUIRED FOR CREDIT. Such Insurance coverage is available at a cost of $*130.00* for the term of the credit.

Credit Life Insurance is desired on the life of *John Doe*

*March 1, 1982*                                                    X *(to be signed by the insured maker).*
(Date)                                                                           (Insured)

This note is executed with a Security Agreement dated *March 1, 1982* made by the Maker with the Payee of this note, and the holder hereof is entitled to all of the benefits of the security described as follows:

*New Acme Super Upright Commercial Freezer (18 cu. ft.) 1982 Model 220 Serial No. XT1903*
THE SECURITY AGREEMENT SECURING THIS NOTE WILL SECURE FUTURE OR OTHER INDEBTEDNESS AND WILL COVER AFTER ACQUIRED PROPERTY.

The Maker and any endorser hereof also agree that:

(1) The undersigned has the right to prepay this loan in full and obtain a refund of the unearned portion of the finance charge computed under the Sum of the Digits method.

(2) The undersigned promises to pay late charges not to exceed 5%, or $5, whichever is less, of the amount of any principal payment or payments in default. All payments made hereunder shall be credited first to interest and lawful charges then accrued and the remainder to principal.

(3) In the event any installment of principal is not paid when it becomes due, the entire amount of this note, less the amount of any rebates required by law, shall become due and payable at the election of the holder, together with costs of collection, including attorney's fees equal to 10% of the principal sum, or such larger amounts as may be reasonable and just if collected by legal proceedings or through an attorney-at-law.

(4) The holder is hereby authorized to apply, on or after maturity, to the payment of this debt, any funds or property in possession of holder belonging to the Maker, surety, endorser, guarantor, or any one of them, and all endorsers and sureties agree that this note may, in whole or in part, be extended or renewed from time to time without notice to them and without release of their liability hereon.

(5) Presentment, notice of dishonor, and notice of nonpayment are hereby waived by each maker, endorser, and other party to this note, and each of them do hereby waive the right to be sued after default in the county of their residence.

(6) PROPERTY INSURANCE, if written in connection with this loan, may be obtained by the undersigned through any person of his choice. If the undersigned desires *comprehensive fire and theft* insurance to be obtained through the creditor, the cost will be $*120.00* for a term of *48* months. BODILY INJURY AND PROPERTY DAMAGE LIABILITY INSURANCE IS NOT INCLUDED IN THE PROPERTY INSURANCE PROVIDED HEREIN.

(7) THE UNDERSIGNED ACKNOWLEDGES RECEIPT OF A COMPLETED COPY OF THIS NOTE ON THE ABOVE DATE.

ADDRESS: (Give complete address and              SIGNATURES: (Write in full)
Business Phone No.)

Star Rt. 1 Box 27 G-1 _____ (1)  Maker: __JOHN DOE_____ (SEAL)

Middletown, Virginia 00000 _____ (2)  Co-Maker __MARY DOE_____ (SEAL)

_____ (3)  Co-Maker _____ (SEAL)

In addition to the liability as endorsers, which the undersigned hereby assume, and intending to be legally bound, the undersigned (and if more than one, each of them jointly and severally) (a) hereby become surety[2] to FIRST NATIONAL BANK OF MIDDLETOWN, its successors, endorsees, and assigns, for the payment of this note; and (b) consent (i) that the Collateral may be exchanged, surrendered, or sold from time to time, (ii) that the payment of the note, or any of the liabilities of the Maker hereof, or of any Collateral, may be extended in whole or in part, and (iii) that any of the provisions of the note may be modified, all without notice to and without affecting the liability of the undersigned as endorsers and sureties.

_____ (SEAL)

_____ (SEAL)

_____ (SEAL)

[1] For other notes, see Part VIII P.
[2] For other guaranty agreements, see Part VIII K.

## FORM VIF 1.02

(Security agreement for operating capital loan by a business—
secured by business personal property, not inventory, as collateral)[1]

### SECURITY AGREEMENT

JOHN DOE, d/b/a DOE'S SUPER GARAGE at 100 Main Street, Middletown, Middle County, Florida (herein called "Borrower"), for value received and intending to be legally bound, hereby grants to RICHARD ROE, residing at 100 East Drive, Middletown, Middle County, Florida (herein called "Secured Party"), a security interest in the property located on the premises of Doe's Super Garage, 100 Main Street, Middletown, Middle County, Florida, as described in Schedule A attached hereto and made part hereof, and any other miscellaneous new and/or used personal property, excluding stock in trade, of any and all description located on the premises of the Borrower, on the hereinbelow date of this security Agreement, together with all increases, parts, fittings, accessories, equipment, and special tools now and which are hereafter affixed to any or all part thereof or used in connection with any thereof, and all replacements of all and any part thereof (all of which is hereafter called "Collateral"), to secure the payment of a promissary note executed by the Borrower in the amount of Five Thousand Dollars ($5,000) of even date herewith, and any and all extensions or renewals thereof, and any and all other liabilities (primary, secondary, direct, contingent, sole, joint, or several) due or to become due that may be hereafter contracted or acquired, of the Borrower to Secured Party (all the foregoing being here called "Liabilities"), and also to secure the performance by Borrower of the agreements hereinafter set forth.

### 1. WARRANTIES

Borrower hereby warrants and agrees that:

1.1 Borrower is the owner of the Collateral free and clear of all liens and security interests except the security interest granted hereby.

1.2 Borrower has the right to make this Agreement.

1.3 The Collateral is used or was acquired for use primarily for the specific business purpose of operating a garage business.

1.4 No Financing Statement presently covering any Collateral or any part thereof is on file in any public office. Borrower authorizes Secured Party to file, in jurisdictions where this authorization will be given effect, a Financing Statement signed only by the Secured Party describing the Collateral in the same manner as it is described herein; and from time to time at the request of Secured Party, Borrower shall execute one or more Financing Statements and such other documents (and pay the cost of filing or recording the same in all public offices) as may be deemed necessary or desirable by the Secured Party, and Borrower shall do such other acts and things, all as the Secured Party may request to establish and maintain a valid security interest in the Collateral free of all other liens and claims whatsoever.

1.5 Borrower will defend the Collateral against the claims and demands of all persons at any time claiming the same or any interest therein.

### 2. USE OF COLLATERAL AND PROCEEDS

2.1 Additional Collateral may be acquired with the proceeds of the loan provided for in or secured by this Agreement, and said proceeds will be used for no other purpose than to purchase additional Collateral or to in any other necessary manner operate the garage business.

2.2 Until default, Borrower may have possession of Collateral and use it in any lawful manner not inconsistent with this Agreement and not inconsistent with any policy of insurance thereon.

2.3 The Collateral will be kept at DOE'S SUPER GARAGE at 100 Main Street, Middletown, Florida.

2.4 Borrower will not remove the Collateral from the Main Street premises without the written consent of the Secured Party.

2.5 The chief and only place of business of the Borrower is: 100 Main Street, Middletown, Middle County, Florida.

2.6 Borrower will immediately notify Secured Party in writing of any change in Borrower's chief place of business or of any additional place of business.

2.7 If certificates of title are issued or outstanding with respect to any of the Collateral, Borrower will cause the interest of the Secured Party to be noted thereon and deliver such certificates of title to the Secured Party.

2.8 Borrower will not (a) permit any liens or security interests (other than Secured Party's security interest) to attach to any of the Collateral; (b) permit any of the Collateral to be levied upon under any legal process; (c) sell, transfer, lease, or otherwise dispose of any of the Collateral or any interest therein, or offer to do so, without the prior written consent of Secured Party; (d) permit anything to be done that may impair the value of any of the Collateral or the security intended to be afforded by this Agreement; or (e) permit the Collateral to be or become a fixture (and it is expressly covenanted, warranted, and agreed that the Collateral, and every part thereof, whether affixed to any realty or not, shall be and remain personal property).

2.9 Borrower will at all times keep the Collateral insured against loss, damage, theft, and such other risks as Secured Party may require in such amounts and companies and under such policies and in such form, and for such period, as shall be satisfactory to Secured Party, and each such policy shall provide that loss thereunder and proceeds payable thereunder shall be payable to Secured Party as its interest may appear (and Secured Party may apply any proceeds of such insurance that may be received by Secured Party toward payment of the Liabilities, whether due or not due, in such order of application as Secured Party may determine), and each such policy shall provide for ten (10) days' written minimum cancellation notice to Secured Party; and each such policy shall, if Secured Party so requests, be deposited with Secured Party; and Secured Party may act as attorney for Borrower in obtaining, adjusting, settling, and canceling such insurance and endorsing any drafts.

2.10 Borrower will not use the Collateral or permit the same to be used in violation of any statute or ordinance; and Secured Party may examine and inspect the Collateral at any time, wherever located.

2.11 Borrower will pay promptly when due all taxes and assessments upon the Collateral, or for its use or operation, or upon this Agreement, or upon any note or notes or other writing evidencing the Liabilities, or any of them.

2.12 At its option, Secured Party may discharge taxes, liens, or security interests or other encumbrances at any time levied or placed on the Collateral; may pay for insurance on the Collateral and may pay for the maintenance and preservation of the Collateral. Borrower agrees to reimburse Secured Party on demand for any payment made or any expense incurred by Secured Party pursuant to the foregoing authorization.

## 3. DEFAULT

3.1 Borrower shall be in default under this Agreement upon the happening of any of the following events or conditions: (a) failure or omission to pay when due any Liability, or default in the payment or performance of any obligation, covenant, agreement, or liability contained or referred to herein; (b) any warranty, representation, or statement made or furnished to the Secured Party by or on behalf of any Borrower proves to have been false in any material respect when made or furnished; (c) loss, theft, substantial damage, destruction, sale, or encumbrance to or of any part of the Collateral, or the making of any levy, seizure, or attachment thereof or thereon; (d) any Obligor (which term, as used herein, shall mean the Borrower and each other party primarily or secondarily or contingently liable on any of the Liabilities) becomes insolvent or unable to pay debts as they mature, or makes an assignment for the benefit of creditors, or any proceeding is instituted by or against any Obligor; (e) death of any Obligor who is a natural person, or of any partner of any Obligor that is a partnership; (f) dissolution, merger, or consolidation, or transfer of a substantial part of the property of any Obligor that is a corporation or a partnership; (g) appointment of a receiver for the Collateral or any part thereof or for any property in which any Borrower has any interest.

3.2 Upon the occurrence of any such default or at any time thereafter, or whenever the Secured Party feels insecure for any reason whatsoever, Secured Party may, at his option, declare all Liabilities secured hereby, or any of them (notwithstanding any provisions thereof), immediately due and payable without demand or notice of any kind, and the same thereupon shall immediately become and be due and payable without demand or notice (but with such adjustments, if any, with respect to interest or other charges as may be provided for in the promissory note or other writing evidencing such Liability), and Secured Party shall have, and may exercise from time to time, any and all rights and remedies of a Secured Party under the Uniform Commercial Code, and any and all rights and remedies available to it under any other applicable law, and upon request or demand of Secured Party, Borrower shall at its expense assemble the Collateral and make it available to the Secured Party at a convenient place acceptable to the Secured Party; and Borrower shall promptly pay all costs of Secured Party of collection of any and all the Liabilities, and enforcements of rights hereunder, including reasonable attorney's fees and legal expenses, and expenses of any repairs to any of the Collateral, and expenses of any repairs to any realty or other property to which any of the Collateral may be affixed. Any notice of sale, disposition, or other intended action by Secured Party sent to Borrower at the address of Borrower specified above or at any other address shown on the records of Secured Party at least five (5) days prior to such action, shall constitute reasonable notice to Borrower. Expenses of retaking, holding, preparing for sale, selling, or the like shall include Secured Party's reasonable attorney's fees and legal expenses. Any excess or surplus of proceeds of any disposition of any of the Collateral may be applied by Secured Party toward payment of such Liabilities, and in such order of application, as Secured Party may from time to time elect. Time is of the essence of this Agreement.

### 4. MISCELLANEOUS

4.1 *Forbearance.* No waiver by Secured Party of any default shall operate as a waiver of any other default or of the same default on a future occasion. No delay or omission on the part of Secured Party in exercising any right or remedy shall operate as a waiver thereof, and no single or partial exercise by Secured Party of any right or remedy shall preclude any other or future exercise thereof or the exercise of any other right or remedy.

4.2 *Remedies cumulative.* The provisions of this Agreement are cumulative and in addition to the provisions of any note secured by this Agreement, and Secured Party shall have all the benefits, rights, and remedies of and under this Agreement and any note secured hereby in addition to all other remedies provided by the law of the State of Florida.

4.3 *Construction of Agreement.* The singular pronoun, when used herein, shall include the plural, and the neuter shall include masculine and feminine. If this Agreement is not dated when executed by the Borrower, the Secured Party is authorized, without notice to the Borrower, to date this Agreement. This Agreement shall become effective as of the date of this Agreement.

4.4 *Governing law.* This Agreement has been delivered in the State of Florida and shall be construed in accordance with the laws of Florida.

4.5 *Assignability and persons bound.* All rights of Secured Party hereunder shall inure to the benefit of its successors and assigns; and all liabilities of Borrower shall bind the heirs, executors, administrators, successors, and assigns of each Borrower.

4.6 *Separability.* Wherever possible, any provision of this Agreement shall be interpreted in such manner as to be effective and valid under applicable law, but if any provision of this Agreement shall be prohibited by or invalid under applicable law, such provision shall be ineffective to the extent of such prohibition or invalidity, without invalidating the remainder of such provision or the remaining provisions of this Agreement.

IN WITNESS WHEREOF, this Agreement has been duly executed on the 1st day of May, 1982. Signed, sealed, and delivered

_____   _____ (SEAL)
WITNESS as to Doe                  JOHN DOE

_____
WITNESS as to Doe

_____   _____ (SEAL)
WITNESS as to Roe                  RICHARD ROE

_____
WITNESS as to Roe

STATE OF FLORIDA )
                )
COUNTY OF MIDDLE )

I HEREBY CERTIFY that on this day, before me, an officer duly authorized to take acknowledgments, personally appeared JOHN DOE and RICHARD ROE, to me known to be the persons described in and who executed the foregoing instrument, and they acknowledged before me that they executed the same.

WITNESS my hand and official seal in the county and state last aforesaid this 1st day of May, 1982.

_____
Notary Public

My commission expires:

[1] U.C.C. 9-105, 9-304, 9-305, and 1-201(15); 69 *Am. Jur. 2d Secured Transactions,* paras. 269–331, 332, and 333, 345. For filing, see Forms VIF 1.03 - F1.05. To determine place of filing, see U.C.C. 9-401.

**FORM VIF 1.02(a)**

(Description of crops in security agreement)[1]

**ALTERNATIVE CLAUSE**

*Description of collateral.* All the right, title, and interest of the Borrower in and to any and all crops of every nature and description, including grass, which have been or may be sown, grown, planted, cultivated, or harvested during the year 1982 on the Borrower's farm, known as "Farmer's Farm," which is more particularly bounded and described as follows:

(Insert legal description of the farm by metes and bounds or by government survey description as section, township, and range description, rectangular survey or monument description, as applicable.)

[1]U.C.C. 2-105, 9-105(h), 9-109(3), 9-110. For filing in county, get County Financing Statement. Compare state financing statement Form VIF 1.03. To determine place of filing, see U.C.C. 9-401.

FORM M-701

PRINTED AND FOR SALE BY
FRANKLIN PRINTING CO.
TAMPA, FLORIDA

FORM VIF 1.03'

STATE OF FLORIDA
UNIFORM COMMERCIAL CODE — FINANCING STATEMENT — FORM UCC — 1

Any forms used for filing with the Office of Secretary of State pursuant to the Uniform Commercial Code must be approved by Secretary of State, State of Florida.

INSTRUCTIONS:
1. PLEASE TYPE this form. Fold only along perforation for mailing.
2. Remove Secured Party and Debtor copies and send other 3 copies with interleaved carbon paper to the filing officer. Enclose filing fee of $5.00.
3. If the space provided for any item(s) on the form is inadequate the item(s) should be continued on additional sheets, preferably 5'' x 8'' or 8'' x 10''. Only one copy of such additional sheets need be presented to the filing officer with the first three copies of the financing statement. Long schedules of collateral, indentures, etc., may be on any size paper that is convenient for the secured party. Indicate the number of additional sheets attached. Enclose filing fee of $2.00 for each additional sheet.
4. If collateral is crops or goods which are or are to become fixtures, give the legal description of the real estate and name of record owner or record lessee.
5. When a copy of the security agreement is used as a financing statement, it is requested that it be accompanied by a completed but unsigned set of these forms. An additional fee of $3.00 is required.
6. Please sign this form with a ball point pen. Signature must be legible on alphabetical and numerical copies.
7. If filing with Clerk of Circuit Court consult Chapter 28, F. S., or local clerk for proper fees.

THIS FINANCING STATEMENT is presented to a filing officer for filing pursuant to the Uniform Commercial Code:

1. Debtor(s) (Last Name First) and address(es)

2. Secured Party(ies) and address(es)

3. Maturity date (if any):

For Filing Officer (Date, Time, Number, and Filing Office)

4. This financing statement covers the following types (or items) of property:

5. Assignee(s) of Secured Party and Address(es)

6. The secured party(s), whose signature(s) appears below, states that the stamps required by Chapter 201, Florida Statutes, if any, have been placed on the promissory instruments secured hereby, and will be placed on any additional and similar instrument that may be so secured.

This statement is filed without the debtor's signature to perfect a security interest in collateral.   (Check ☒ if so)
☐ Already subject to a security interest in another jurisdiction when it was brought into this state.
☐ which is proceeds of the original collateral described above in which a security interest was perfected:

Check ☒ if covered:  ☐ Proceeds of Collateral are also covered.  ☐ Products of Collateral are also covered. No. of additional Sheets presented:

Filed with:

By: _____
Signature(s) of Debtor(s)

By: _____
Signature(s) of Secured Party(ies)

STANDARD FORM — FORM UCC-1
Approved by the Secretary of State, State of Florida

(1) Filing Officer Copy - Alphabetical

' U.C.C. 9–401, 9–402 and 9–403.

FORM VIF 1.04[1]

State of Florida Uniform Commercial Code — REQUEST FOR INFORMATION OR COPIES — Form UCC-11

FORM M-702

IMPORTANT — Read instructions on back before filling out form.

PRINTED AND FOR SALE BY FRANKLIN PRINTING CO., TAMPA, FLA.

REQUEST FOR COPIES OR INFORMATION. Present in DUPLICATE to Filing Officer.

1. Debtor (Last Name First) and Address

Party requesting information or copies: (Name and Address)

For Filing Officer (Date, Time, Number, and Filing Office)

☐ INFORMATION REQUEST:    ☐ PHOTO COPY    ☐ CERTIFICATE UNDER SEAL    ☐ CERTIFIED COPY

Filing Officer, please furnish as requested above showing whether there is on file as of _____, 19___ at _____ M., any presently effective financing statement naming the above named debtor(s), and any statement of assignment thereof, and if there is, giving the date and hour of filing of each such statement, and the name(s) and address(es) of each secured party(ies), therein. Enclosed is uniform fee of $3.50 for Certified Copy plus $.50 for each additional page thereof, $5.00 for Certificate Under Seal or $2.00 for Search of Information on each debtor.

Filing Officer, please furnish photo copies of each page of financing statements and statements of assignment listed below, at the rate of $.50 each, which are on file with your office. Enclosed is $_____ fee for copies requested. In case any said statements contain more than one page the undersigned agrees to pay the sum of $.50 for each additional page payable in advance..

Date _____

(Signature of Requesting Party)

| File No. | Date and Hour of Filing | Name(s) and Address(es) of Secured Party(ies) and Assignee(s), if any |
|---|---|---|
| | | |
| | | |
| | | |
| | | |
| | | |
| | | |

STANDARD FORM — FORM UCC—11    Approved by Richard (Dick) Stone, Secretary of State, State of Florida

[1] U.C.C. 9-407.

FORM VIF 1.05[1]

FORM M-703

**STATE OF FLORIDA UNIFORM COMMERCIAL CODE**

**STATEMENTS OF CONTINUATION, PARTIAL RELEASE, ASSIGNMENT, ETC. — FORM UCC-3**

Any forms used for filing with the Office of Secretary of State pursuant to the Uniform Commercial Code must be approved by Secretary of State, State of Florida.

INSTRUCTIONS:

1. PLEASE TYPE this form. Fold only along perforation for mailing.
2. Remove Security Party and Debtor copies and send other 3 copies with interleaved carbon paper to the filing officer. Enclose Filing Fee of $5.00.
3. Fill in original Financing Statement number and date filed.
4. If the space provided for any item(s) on the form is inadequate the item(s) should be continued on additional sheets, preferably 5'' x 8'' or 8'' x 10''. Only one copy of such additional sheets need be presented to the filing officer with a set of three copies of Form UCC-3. Long schedules of collateral etc., may be on any size paper that is convenient for the secured party. Indicate the number of additional sheets attached. Enclose Filing Fee of $2.00 for each additional sheet.
5. If collateral is crops or goods which are or are to become fixtures, give the legal description of the real estate and name of record owner or record lessee.
6. Please sign this form with a ball point pen. Signatures must be legible on alphabetical and numerical copies.
7. If filing with Clerk of Circuit Court consult Chapter 28, F. S., or local clerk for proper fees.

THIS STATEMENT is presented to a filing officer for filing pursuant to the Uniform Commercial Code:

| 1. Debtor(s) (Last Name First) and address(es) | 2. Secured Party(ies) and address(es) | 3. Maturity date (if any): |
|---|---|---|
| | | For Filing Officer (Date, Time, Number, and Filing Office) |

4. This statement refers to original Financing Statement bearing File No. _____

Filed with _____ Date Filed _____ 19____

5. ☐ Continuation. The original financing statement between the foregoing Debtor and Secured Party, bearing file number shown above, is still effective.

6. ☐ Termination. Secured party no longer claims a security interest under the financing statement bearing file number shown above.

7. ☐ Assignment. The secured party's right under the financing statement bearing file number shown above to the property described in Item 11 has been assigned to the assignee whose name and address appear in Item 11.

8. ☐ Amendment. Financing Statement bearing file number shown above is amended as set forth in Item 11.

9. ☐ Release. Secured Party releases the collateral described in Item 11 from the financing statement bearing file number shown above.

10. ☐ Check if true. All documentary stamp taxes due and payable or to become due and payable pursuant to Chapter 201, F. S. have been paid.

11.

No. of additional sheets presented: _____

By: _____

Signature(s) of Debtor(s) (necessary only if Item 8 is applicable).

By: _____

Signature(s) of Secured Party(ies)

**STANDARD FORM — FORM UCC-3**

Approved by the Secretary of State, State of Florida

(1) **Filing Officer Copy - Alphabetical**

[1] U.C.C. 9-403, 9-404, 9-405, 9-406.

# PART VII
# BUSINESS REAL PROPERTY CONTRACTS

# PART VII

# BUSINESS REAL PROPERTY CONTRACTS

## INTRODUCTION

This Part is divided into six Sections, A through F, that cover leases, licenses and easements, sales and purchases, mortgages, building construction contracts, and documents for creating condominiums and cooperatives.

Each Section has its own introduction with citations to *American Jurisprudence 2d* as to the general law covering the forms, and to statutes that are applicable in some cases.

Section A contains forms for memorandum of lease for recording, a mortgage of a leasehold interest, notice to tenant by landlord in event of sale of property, assignment of lease, and a sublease, in addition to the forms for both long- and short-term leases.

Section B has forms for creating rights of way over adjoining landowner's property, easement for air and light use, agreement for construction of a party wall, outdoor advertising license, and a grazing lease. These forms can be easily adapted for creating other easements and licenses.

Section C concerns itself with agreements to sell or purchase real property for business use. It contains an agreement to purchase vacant land and an agreement to purchase an office building. The introduction to the Section and the Client Questionnaire for the section should be read before using the forms.

Section D includes forms for mortgage deed, installment note to be secured by mortgage, bond to be secured by mortgage, agreement for deed, and deed in trust. The various forms of mortgages are used in various states as indicated in the forms for each. For example, Florida uses both mortgages and agreements for deed; Pennsylvania often uses mortgage and bond as opposed to mortgage and note. The deed in trust is a form of mortgage used in California, Illinois, Missouri, Virginia, and the District of Columbia.

Releases of mortgages, assignments of mortgages, and satisfactions of mortgages are represented in the forms contained in Section D as well as the original mortgages. A review of the Table of Contents for Part VII, which contains a list of each form affecting business real property contracts, is a quick way for finding the exact form you need.

Section E presents a detailed introduction and client questionnaire to aid in drafting or reviewing a construction contract or the construction loan contract used to finance the construction. A sample construction loan agreement is given.

The last section of Part VII contains samples and checklists for drafting condominium agreements for the development and sale of condominiums. The sample is for a time-sharing condominium. The attorney must always be familiar with the state statutes regulating condominium development before advising a client or drafting the necessary documents.

Form VIIF 1.06 provides a form for Articles of Incorporation for a cooperative office building corporation. It is followed by a Proprietary Lease for the office space.

Because of the length of Part VII, there is an *Introduction to each Section* in addition to this general Introduction.

## SECTION A LEASE OF PREMISES FOR BUSINESS USE

The forms in Section A of Part VII include real property leases and supplemental forms for assignment, sublease, mortgage of a leasehold interest, notice to lessee of sale by landlord, and a memorandum of lease for recording.

For licenses and easements, which have some characteristics of a lease, see Part VII, Section B.

Both leases of real property and licenses and easements are distinguished from leases of personal property, which are presented in Part VI, Section A.

Business or commercial leases[1] are usually not subject to state residential landlord and tenant acts.[2] Such acts usually do not cover *temporary* rentals in hotels, motels, or rooming houses; residence in institutions such as a nursing home or school dormitory; occupancy under a contract of purchase;[3] or leases in a cooperative apartment[4] or ownership of a condominium unit even if it involves timesharing.[5]

Long-term leases of business real estate may be preferred to a sale in certain circumstances.

Sale and leaseback to the seller of business real estate has tax consequences that should be considered before such a lease is executed.[6]

### FORM VIIA 1.00

### CLIENT QUESTIONNAIRE FOR COMMERCIAL LEASE[1]

1. Name and address of client (usually the landlord). If landlord is a corporation, get exact registered corporate name and check that the deed to the real estate is in that name
2. Telephone number of client landlord. If client is the proposed tenant, get landlord's exact name, address, and telephone number
3. Exact corporate, association, *or* business name of tenant. Get correct name and initials of tenant(s) if tenant is an individual or partnership
4. Description of the premises
    (a) Legal description, if appropriate
    (b) Address and/or unit number to be leased
    (c) Access and parking
    (d) Nature of tenant's business and use of the premises. Shall landlord be restricted from

---

[1]*49 Am. Jur. 2d Landlord and Tenant,* paras. 162 et seq.

[2]Check your state landlord and tenant statute. Some states now also regulate commercial leases by statute.

[3]Ref. Part VII, Section C.

[4]Ref. Form VIIF 1.07.

[5]Ref. Form VIIF 1.04.

[6]*34 Am. Jur. 2d Federal Taxation,* paras. 6410–6415.

leasing to similar business within the complex or within a certain area? Are there building rules and regulations? If so, are they written? If not, does client want you to prepare them?

    (e) Is the building or the particular premises constructed, under construction, or to be constructed?

    (f) Landlord's right to alter, expand, or subdivide, or use adjacent or balance of property, if appropriate

    (g) Services to be supplied by landlord

    (h) Landlord's right to inspect and duty to maintain the property

5. Duration of term of lease
    (a) Date rent begins
    (b) Date or other condition for possession (if not date rent begins)
    (c) Does landlord have any duty to prepare the premises? If so, what is he to do and what is the time limit?

6. Rent
    (a) Certain amount annually, payable monthly or otherwise
    (b) Fixed minimum (base rent) plus percentage of gross sales or income. *Definition* of gross sales or income
    (c) Rent adjustments, if any, after a certain number of years: certain amount *or* adjusted in accordance with Consumer Price Index for All Items (United States City Average Index), *or other formula.* If a formula is to be used, what year is to be used as the base year?
    (d) Is rent to increase if real estate taxes increase or there are extraordinary real estate assessments, etc.
    (e) Will there be any security deposit? If so, how much?

7. Maintenance and repairs
    (a) Landlord's duties (if shopping center, condominium, or cooperative—duty as to premises in general and as to maintenance of common areas)
    (b) Tenant's duties (if shopping center, condominum, or cooperative—duty as to the unit and as to pro rata payment)
    (c) Landlord's right to inspect premises or show premises to prospective tenants or buyers of the property
    (d) Rights of parties as to signs, awnings, and advertising displays in or on the premises

8. Insurance
    (a) Public liability and property damage
    (b) Damage to or destruction of building or premises
    (c) Landlord *or* tenant *or* shared responsibility for insurance
    (d) Should landlord have option to rebuild? or
    (e) Should lease be canceled in case of destruction of premises?

9. Condemnation or eminent domain proceedings
    (a) What should tenant's rights be?
    (b) What should landlord's rights be?

10. Renewal rights
    (a) Tenants option in writing at or before specified time
    (b) Renewal for what length of time
    (c) On renewal, what increase in rent, if any amount or formula

11. Will tenant have option to purchase? If so, what are the terms of the option?

12. If property is sold during term, will tenant have right of first refusal to purchase or other options?

13. Shall assignment of lease or sublease or mortgage of leasehold interest by the tenant be restricted?[2]
    (a) Not assignable *or* not assignable without written consent of landlord—cannot be unreasonably withheld
    (b) Should subleasing or mortgage of leasehold interest also require written consent of landlord, and should such written consent be required for subsequent subletting or mortgaging?
    (c) Should tenant remain liable for rent after consensual assignment or subletting? If so, on what conditions?
    (d) Should landlord have right to assign rent payments without sale of premises?

14. Landlord's rights and remedies[3]
    (a) In addition to or cumulatively with remedies given by law or equity
    (b) Acceptance of rent after default or termination not a waiver of landlord's rights or remedies
    (c) Right to reenter and terminate lease
    (d) Right to relet—writ of possession
    (e) Right to damages
    (f) Writ of distress—landlord's lien
15. Tenant's rights and remedies[4]
    (a) In case of mortgage foreclosure of the premises
    (b) Cure landlord's default and deduct from rent
    (c) Damages and specific performance
    (d) Terminate lease for landlord default
16. Are there to be any guarantors of the rent?
    (a) Personal
    (b) Corporation (check its registration with secretary of state)
    (c) Pledge of assets or corporate stock (if to be held in escrow, get name of escrow holder)

[1] *49 Am. Jur. 2nd Landlord and Tenant,* para 18.

[2] *49 Am. Jur. 2d,* para.

[3] Check your state statute for landlord-tenant rights under a *commercial* lease. Rights vary from those under a *residential* lease in most states. In case of bankruptcy of either landlord or tenant, the *U.S. Bankruptcy Code,* 11 U.S.C.A. 365, controls over state law. In case of bankruptcy of tenant, an Adversary Proceeding by the landlord in the Bankruptcy court may be necessary to modify the bankruptcy stay order and to regain possession or modify the terms of the lease.

[4] See Footnote 3, supra.

## FORM VIIA 1.01

### (Lease with option to purchase)

### LEASE WITH OPTION TO PURCHASE

BY THIS LEASE entered into between CHARLES COE and MARY COE of 100 Main Street, Middletown, Florida 00000 (herein called "Lessor", and RICHARD ROE and JANE ROE of 100 East Street, Middletown, Florida 00000 (herein called "Lessee"), each in consideration of the agreements to be performed by the other, on this 7th day of March, 1977, agree as follows:

1. *Description of property.* The Lessors hereby lease unto the Lessees the following described real property, building located thereon, and equipment as shown in *Rider A attached hereto and made part hereof* for the term beginning March 7, 1982, and ending March 6, 1987, to be used for the operation of a gas station, garage, and/or retail business.

2. *Rent.* The Lessee will pay to the Lessor, as rent for the property leased during the term, the sum of Five Hundred Dollars ($500) per month, plus utilities and Five Percent (5%) sales tax, on or before the 21st day of each month.

3. *Maintenance and repair.* Lessee agrees to maintain and repair the buildings and equipment thereon and to keep the immediate surrounding land and parking area in good appearance and substantial repair during the term of this Lease.

4. *Liens.* The Lessor's interest shall not be subject to liens for improvements made by the Lessee upon the herein demised premises, per F.S.A. 713.10:
    (b) The Lessee shall not construct any additional structure of a permanent nature on the demised premises, without the specific written consent of the Lessor.

5. *Insurance.* The Lessee shall, at its expense, keep the land, and any improvements made thereon, adequately insured against public liability, and agrees to include the Lessor in said policy as additional insureds, and agrees to deliver to Lessor current certificates of said liability insurance during the term(s) of the Lease. The limits of that insurance shall be not less than One Hundred Thousand Dollars/Three Hundred Thousand Dollars ($100,000/$300,000).

6. *Assignability.* There shall be no assigning of this Lease, or subleasing of any part of the leased property, without the specific written consent of the Lessor.

7. *Default.*

(a) If any rent or payment required by this Lease shall not be paid within fifteen (15) days of the date due, the Lessor shall have the option to:

    (1) Terminate this Lease, resume possession of the property for its own account, and recover immediately from the Lessee the difference between the rent specified in the Lease and the fair rental value of the property for the remainder of the term, reduced to present worth.

    (2) Resume possession and release or rerent the property for the remainder of the term for the account of the Lessees, and recover from the Lessee, at the end of the term, or at the time each payment of rent comes due under this Lease, as the Lessors may choose, the difference between the rent specified in the Lease and the rent received on the releasing or rerenting.

    (3) In either event, the Lessor shall also recover all expenses incurred by reason of the breach, including reasonable attorney's fees.

(b) If either the Lessor or the Lessee shall fail to perform, or shall breach any agreement of this Lease, other than the agreement of the Lessee to pay rent, for fifteen (15) days after a written notice specifying the performance required shall have been given to the party failing to perform, the party so giving notice may institute action in a court of competent jurisdiction to terminate this Lease or to compel performance of the Agreement, and the prevailing party in that litigation shall be paid by the losing party all expenses of such litigation, including a reasonable attorney's fee.

8. *Option to purchase during term.* It is agreed that Lessee shall have the option to purchase the leased real and personal property during the term of this Lease, on the following terms and conditions:

    (a) The purchase price shall be the current market value of the real property on the date the option to purchase is exercised, plus Five Thousand Dollars ($5,000) for the equipment listed in Rider A. That market value shall be determined in accordance with the formula set forth in Rider B, which is attached hereto and made part hereof.

    (b) The purchase price shall be payable at no more than Twenty-five Percent (25%) down at closing, and the balance of the purchase price remaining to be paid shall be paid to Lessors by a note and mortgage to Lessors from Lessees payable at the rate of Six Hundred Dollars ($600) per month on principal, plus Eleven Percent (11%) annual interest, until the note is paid in full.

    (c) Credit shall be given to Lessee toward the down payment required at the closing of the purchase pursuant to this Agreement, for all basic rent payments may by Lessee under this Lease up to the time of closing of the purchase.

    (d) This purchase option must be exercised no later than ninety (90) days before the expiration or termination of this Lease to be effective, and shall not be effective at any time if the Lessee is in default under the terms of his Lease at the time of its attempt to exercise this option.

*WITNESSES:*
                                                *LESSOR*

_____

_____                 CHARLES COE

_____                 MARY COE

*WITNESSES:*                                              *LESSEE*

_____

_____                 RICHARD ROE

_____                 JANE ROE

STATE OF FLORIDA)
COUNTY OF MIDDLE)

    I HEREBY CERTIFY that on this day, before me, a notary public duly authorized to take acknowledgements in the state and county named above, personally appeared CHARLES COE and

MARY COE, Lessors, to me well known to be the persons described in and who executed the foregoing instrument, and they acknowledged to and before me that they executed the said instrument for the purposes therein expressed.

WITNESS my hand and official seal, this 7th day of March, 1982.

_____

Notary Public

My commission expires:

STATE OF FLORIDA)
COUNTY OF MIDDLE)

I HEREBY CERTIFY that on this day, before me, a notary public duly authorized to take acknowledgments in the state and county named above, personally appeared RICHARD ROE and JANE ROE, Lessees, to me well known to be the persons described in and who executed the foregoing instrument, and they acknowledged to and before me that they executed the said instrument for the purposes therein expressed.

WITNESS may hand and official seal, this 7th day of March, 1982.

_____

Notary Public

My commission expires:

## RIDER A

*Real property and building:*

All that Part of Lot 10, Doe Acres Subdivision, lying North of New State Road No. 20, and all that portion of a certain 35 Street, lying North of Lot 10, all in Doe Acres Subdivision, according to Plat thereof, as recorded in Plat Book 1, at page 00, Public Records of Middle County, Florida, and also including a portion of the SE¼ of SW¼ lying South of State Road No. 14 and more particularly described as follows:

Commence at the SW Corner of SE¼ of SW¼ of section 12, Township 19 South, Range 19E, and run North on the West line of the above described SE¼ of SW¼, 71.2' to the North right-of-way line of State Road No. 20, thence S. 55 deg. 06' 40" E. along said right-of-way line 76.17 feet to the point of beginning, thence N. 34 deg. 20 deg. E. 130.05' to the South right-of-way line of State Road No. 14, thence along a curve to the left on said South right-of-way a chord bearing and distance of S. 57 deg. 58' E., 264.6' to a point on the East line of Lot 12, Doe Acres Subdivision, extended North, thence S. 1 deg. 21' W. across a closed street and along said East line of Lot 10, 169.8 feet to the North right-of-way line of State Road 20, thence N. 55 deg. 06' 40" W. along North right-of-way line 359 feet to the Point of Beginning, including one-story block building located thereon.

*Equipment:*

Battery charger (12-volt, 50-amp; 6-volt, 100-amp), adding machine (Remington), bubble balancer, grease, oil-change equipment (drain, pump, greaser), two vending machines (cold-drink machine, coin coffee machine), one air jack, one hydraulic car lift.

## RIDER B

Current market value shall be determined as follows:

1. By mutual agreement between Lessee/Purchaser and Lessor/Seller as to current market value at the time of the exercise of the option to purchase. This agreement as to value shall be in writing and executed by both parties. If there is no mutual written agreement as to the current market value within thirty (30) days of the option date, then

2. The Lessee/Purchaser and the Lessor/Seller shall each hire, at its own expense, a certified real estate appraiser. Within thirty (30) days, each of the two appraisers shall independently prepare his certified appraisal, and the average of the two appraisals shall be deemed current market value, except that if the two appraisals vary by more than Three Thousand Dollars ($3,000) in total value, then

3. The two appraisers shall select a third appraiser, costs of this to be borne equally by the Purchaser and Seller. The third appraiser's evaluation shall be added to the two other appraisals, and the total of the three (3) evaluations shall be divided by three (3) to determine the current market value for the purpose of the option, and shall be final and unchallengeable by either party.

## FORM VIIA 1.02

### (Lease of part of premises for use as beauty shop or other retail business)[1]

### LEASE

THIS LEASE entered into by and between John Doe and Mary Doe, his wife, of 100 East Street, Middletown, Florida 00000 (herein called "Lessor"), and Mary Jane Roe of 100 West Street, Middletown, Florida (herein called "Lessee"), and Mary Jane Roe of 100 West Street, Middletown, Florida (herein called "Lessee"), each in consideration of the agreements to be performed by the other, hereby on this 1st day of March, 1982, agree as follows:

1. *Description of property, term and renewal.* The Lessor hereby leases unto the Lessee #100 of Doe Plaza (20′ × 30′ room) located on the following described property:

Lots 12 and 13, in Block 10 of NEW HEIGHTS SUBDIVISION, according to the map or plat thereof recorded in Plat Book 0, Page 10, Public Records of Middle County, Florida.

for a term beginning April 1, 1982, and ending March 31, 1984, with an option to renew on the same terms for three (3) years.

2. *Use.* The leased property shall be used for and only for the specific purpose of operation of a beauty shop in compliance with all laws regulating such business.[2]

3. *Rent, "first and last."* The Lessee will pay unto the Lessor as rent for the property leased during the term the sum of Two Hundred and Twenty-Five Dollars ($225) per month, beginning April 1, 1982, and a like sum on the 1st day of each month thereafter, plus Four Percent (4%) sales tax. Receipt of the first and last monthly payments to be made by Lessee hereunder is hereby acknowledged by the Lessor.

4. *Maintenance by Lessee.*
   (a) The Lessee accepts the premises "as is" except as provided in (b), and hereby assumes the complete maintenance of the interior of the premises #100, and the cleaning and order of the sidewalk and rear parking area, and convenants that the premises will be kept in good and substantial repair.
   (b) Lessor shall construct as an addition in the rear of the premises a 5′ × 8′ metal storage room to include four (4) shelves and two (2) electrical outlets. Lessee shall pay One Hundred Dollars ($100) toward that construction, receipt of which is acknowledged by Lessor.
   (c) Beauty shop equipment (such as booths, chairs, hydraulic chairs, supplies, hot-water heater, sinks, dryers, furniture, and supplies) installed by Lessee shall be removed by Lessee at her sole expense within ten (10) days of the termination of this Lease, provided Lessee is not in default in the payment of rent under this Lease. If said equipment is not removed and the time is not extended by Lessor in writing, the equipment and all personal property of the Lessee shall be considered fixtures and part of the real estate, and title shall vest in the Lessor.
   (d) Lessee shall, at the termination of this Lease, upon removal of beauty equipment, restore the leased premises to their present condition, with consideration being given for ordinary wear and tear. No part of plumbing or electrical fixtures inside the walls or ceilings shall be removed by Lessee.

5. *Insurance.*
   (a) The Lessee, at her expense, shall keep the leased premises adequately insured against public liability, and shall include the Lessor in said policy as additional insured, and shall deliver and continue to deliver to Lessor a current copy of said liability insurance, during the term of the lease, the limit to be not less than One Hundred Thousand Dollars/Three Hundred Thousand Dollars ($100,000/$300,000).
   (b) All personal property placed in or on the premises shall be there at the risk of the Lessee or the owner thereof, and Lessor shall not be liable for any damage to that personal property by any cause not insured by the Lessor.

6. *Assignability.* There shall be no assigning of this Lease or subleasing of any part of the leased property without specific written consent of the Lessor.

7. *Business time.* Lessee convenants to be open for business from 9:00 A.M. to 5:00 P.M. not less than five (5) out of seven (7) days of the calendar week and for not less than eleven (11) out of twelve (12) months of each lease year.

8. *Default.*
   (a) Any failure of Lessee to pay the rent or comply with any term or condition of this Lease

shall, at the option of Lessor, work a forefeiture of this Lease and all of the rights of the Lessee hereunder, and thereupon the Lessor, his agents, or attorneys, shall have the right to enter the premises and remove all persons and property therefrom forcibly or otherwise, and the Lessee hereby expressly waives any and all notice required by law to terminate the tenancy hereunder, and also waives the right to any and all legal proceedings to recover possession of the premises.

(b) The foregoing right of the Lessor shall be cumulative, and failure by the Lessor to exercise promptly the foregoing right or any other right of the Lessor under this Lease shall not operate as a waiver of that or any other right of the Lessor hereunder.

(c) If the Lessee shall abandon or vacate the premises before the end of the term of this Lease, the Lessor may, at his option, forthwith cancel this lease or he may enter the premises as the agent of the Lessee, by force or otherwise, and relet the premises with or without any furnishings or fixtures that may be therein, as the agent of the Lessee, at such price and upon such terms and for such duration of time as the Lessor may determine, and receive the rent therefor, applying the same to the payment of the rent due Lessor from Lessee under this Lease. If the full rental provided herein shall not be realized by Lessor over and above the reasonable expenses to Lessor in such reletting, Lessee shall pay the difference between the rent realized by the Lessor and the rent due under this Lease. If more than the rent due under this Lease is realized by the Lessor, he shall pay that excess over to Lessee on written demand by the Lessee.

9. *Attorney's fees.* If either the Lessor or the Lessee shall fail to perform or shall be in breach of any term or condition of this Lease for fifteen (15) days after a written notice specifying the performance required shall have been given to the party failing to perform, the party so giving notice may institute action in a court of competent jurisdiction to terminate this Lease or to compel performance of the Agreement, and the prevailing party in that litigation shall be paid by the losing party all costs of such litigation, including a reasonable attorney's fee.

Witnesses:                                            Lessor:

_____      _____

                                           JOHN DOE

_____      _____

(As to Lessor)                             MARY DOE

Witnesses:                                            Lessee:

_____      _____

(As to Lessee)                             MARY JANE ROE

STATE OF FLORIDA:
COUNTY OF MIDDLE:

I HEREBY CERTIFY that on this day, before me, a notary public duly authorized in the state and county named above to take acknowledgments, personally appeared JOHN DOE and MARY DOE, his wife, as Lessor, and MARY JANE ROE, as Lessee, to me well known and known to me to be the persons described in and who executed the foregoing instrument, and acknowledged to and before me that they executed the said instrument for the purposes therein expressed.

WITNESS my hand and official seal, this 1st day of March, 1982.

_____

                                  Notary Public

                                  My commission expires:

[1] *49 Am. Jur. 2d Landlord and Tenant*, paras. 162–165 and 179.

[2] *10 Am. Jur. 2d Barbers and Cosmetologists*, paras. 2, 3, and 17. See also *50 Am. Jur. 2d Laundries, Dryers and Drycleaners*, paras. 5, 11, 16–32; and *38 Am. Jur. 2d Garages and Filling and Parking Stations*, paras. 12–21, for statutory regulation of other businesses.

## FORM VIIA 1.03

### (Lease of building for use as a retail furniture store)[1]

### LEASE AGREEMENT

THIS LEASE AGREEMENT entered into on the 10th day of April, 1983, by and between John Doe and Mary Doe, his wife, of Middletown, Florida 00000 (herein called "Lessor"), and ROE BROS. STORES, INC., a corporation organized under the laws of Delaware with its principal office and place of business at 100 Southeast Street, Maintown, North Carolina, 00000 (herein called "Lessee"):

WITNESSETH:

1. *Leased Premises.* The Lessor leases to the Lessee the following described premises:
(Insert legal description.)

Included as a part of the leased premises is the store building currently in use as a furniture store.

2. *Term.* The term of this Lease shall be ten (10) years, commencing on May 1, 1982, and ending April 30, 1992. Lessee shall have an option to extend said lease term for an additional period of five (5) years, beginning at the end of the initial term, on the same terms and conditions in effect for the initial lease period. Notice of exercise of this option by Lessee shall be given in writing by mail addressed to Lessor at the address stated above at least ninety (90) days before expiration of the initial lease period.

3. *Rent, base and percentage.*
(a) The annual base rental to be paid by the Lessee to Lessor at the address shown above shall be Twenty Thousand Dollars ($20,000), payable in equal monthly installments in advance.
(b) In addition to said base rental, Lessee shall pay to Lessor Five Percent (5%) of all net sales made in and on the leased premises in excess of Three Hundred Fifty Thousand Dollars ($350,000) during each lease year.
(c) The term "net sale" is defined as the gross sales made in and on the premises, less discounts, trade-ins, exchanges, repossessions, allowances, returns, and sales tax upon sales paid by customers or otherwise, and shall not include "sales" made to any other stores of Lessee, or to employees working upon the premises.
(d) Lessee shall, within ninety (90) days after the expiration of each lease year, furnish Lessor a statement in writing executed by an official of the Company, which statement shall show the net sales, as above defined, made by it in and on the premises for the preceding lease year, or any part thereof, upon which a percentage of sales shall be owing to Lessor, and the amount owing shall be transmitted with the statement before referred to. If for any reason the Lease shall terminate or be suspended prior to the expiration of any lease year, then the percentage rent, if any, shall be determined by proration. Lessee agrees to keep accurate record of sales made by it on the demised premises, and Lessor or his agent shall have the privilege, at Lessor's expense and at reasonable times, to examine the books and records of Lessee with respect thereto.
(e) Lessee shall pay any increase in real estate taxes and fire and extended coverage insurance on the leased premises paid by Lessor pursuant to Paragraph 4(e) over the amount of such taxes and insurance for the first full tax year following the effective date of this Lease Agreement. The Lessee shall not pay for real estate tax or fire insurance increase due to the use of the parts of the Lessor's building excluded from the Lease.

4. *Covenants of Lessor.* Lessor agrees to the following:
(a) Lessor convenants to keep Lessee in quiet possession of the premises.
(b) Lessor convenants that all entrances and driveways now enjoyed by the leased premises shall be and remain intact and uninterrupted such during the term of this Lease, and shall not by any act of Lessor diminish the light and air now enjoyed by the leased premises. If now-existing egress and ingress to the public streets and sidewalks shall be materially obstructed, Lessee shall have the option to terminate this Lease.
(c) Lessor shall keep in good condition and repair all structural portions of the building, the foundation, roof, exterior walls, windows, and exterior parts of the building, except plate-glass and exterior doors, including awnings, painting, and guttering, and shall repair damage caused by natural decay or termites, and shall maintain water, sewer, and power connections to the premises. Lessor shall pay for all repairs to the heating and air-con-

ditioning system in access of Five Hundred Dollars ($500) for each separate occurrence or failure in said system requiring repairs or service, and Fifty Percent (50%) of the cost of repairs to water pump & septic system. If Lessor fails to begin such repairs within thirty (30) days after written notice by Lessee, the Lessee is authorized to make the repairs and deduct the cost from rental payments. Lessor or its representatives shall have the right to enter the premises at reasonable hours of any business day during the term of this Lease to ascertain if the premises are in proper repair and condition.

(d) Lessee may from time to time, at its own expense, alter, renovate, or improve the interior of the demised premises without the consent of the Lessor except when structural parts are affected, in which case the Lessor's written consent will be necessary but shall not be unreasonably withheld.

(e) Lessee shall have the right to attach such legally permissible signs to the building as it believes necessary, and Lessee shall remove tham at the expiration of this Lease.

(f) Lessor shall purchase and carry fire and extended coverage insurance on the building in an amount equal to the full insurable value thereof or the required coinsurance amounts with appropriate replacement cost endorsement, and shall pay all real estate taxes levied on the premises during the term of this Lease.

(g) That Lessee may sublease the leased premises or any part thereof, provided that Lessee shall continue to be liable for rents and other covenants of this Lease.

5. *Convenants of Lessee.* Lessee agrees as follows:

(a) Lessee shall not commit a nuisance on the premises or violate any state laws or city ordinances, and it will not, by any act on its part, render the Lessor liable in respect thereof. However, commission of a nuisance by Lessee shall not give Lessor power to terminate this lease.

(b) Lessee shall maintain and repair the interior of the building except for structural portions, including repairs to the heating and air-conditioning system costing less than Five Hundred Dollars ($500), and Fifty Percent (50%) of the cost of repairs to water pump & septic system for each separate occurrence of such repairs, and shall return the premises to Lessor at the expiration of this Lease in as good order as received, with the exception of ordinary wear and tear, natural decay, damage or destruction by termites, lighting, fire, or act of God, and damage that it is Lessor's duty to repair.

6. *Fire clause.*

(a) Should the premises be destroyed by fire, lightning, tornado, or the like, or be so damaged as to render them unfit for Lessee's use and occupancy, then this lease shall terminate on the date of such destruction or damage, and all unearned rental shall be returned to Lessee. If in the opinion of a bona fide building contractor selected by mutual agreement of Lessor and Lessee, the premises can be restored within one hundred twenty (120) days to its condition immediately before such destruction or damage, then Lessee shall permit Lessor to enter and restore the premises, and Lessor shall enter and restore the premises promptly and within a reasonable period of time at Lessor's expense. If Lessor and Lessee cannot agree on a contractor from whom an opinion is to be solicited regarding the time required to restore the premises, then each shall select a building contractor, and the two contractors shall select a third contractor, whose opinion as to the time required to restore the premises shall be binding on all parties. If the premises are to be restored, this Lease shall remain in full force and effect, except that the rent shall abate for the period from the date of the damage to the premises until completion of the restoration. Should the premises be partially destroyed or damaged to the extent that a portion of the premises is unfit for Lessee's use, the rent shall abate proportionately on a square footage basis of the area of the destroyed portion to the area of the entire building, and Lessor shall repair the damage, at Lessor's expense.

7. *Waiver of claims.* Lessor and Lessee waive all right of recovery for claims of one against the other arising out of loss covered by fire and extended coverage insurance and public liability insurance obtained by either of the parties. Each releases the other from all liability for any loss or damage to the extent permissible under contract regardless of the origin of the fire, occurrence, or casualty and including fires, occurrences, or casualties caused by the negligence or intentional acts of the party's employees, agents, sublessees, and assigns, and releases all rights to which an insurance company may become subrogated. Any insurance procured by either party shall carry a waiver of subrogation endorsement. In the event of fire or other casualty, Lessor shall not be required to repair or replace Lessee's stock in trade, fixtures and furnishings, or floor coverings and equipment.

8. *Default.* No demand for rent need at any time be made on the premises or elsewhere, but it shall be the duty of the Lessee to pay all sums due hereunder without demand, If Lessee remains in default of payment of rent or any sum due hereunder for thirty (30) days, Lessor may at its option declare this Lease forfeited and resume possession of the premises after ten (10) days' written notice of such default is given by registered or certified mail by Lessor to Lessee at Lessee's principal office in Middletown, North Carolina, provided, however, that Lessee may always prevent a forfeiture by paying the defaulted amount before the end of the ten-day period.

9. *Binding upon successors.* This Lease shall be binding upon the heirs, successors, and assigns of the parties.

IN WITNESS WHEREOF, the parties have duly set their hands and seals the day and year first above written.

| | |
|---|---|
| WITNESS | JOHN DOE, Lessor |
| WITNESS | MARY DOE, Lessor |
| (CORPORATE SEAL) | ROE BROS. STORES, INC. |
| (John Roe) | (Richard Roe) |
| Secretary of the Corporation | President |
| | LESSEE |

STATE OF FLORIDA)
          SS.[2]
COUNTY OF MIDDLE)

The foregoing instrument was acknowledged before me this 10th day of April, 1982, by John Doe and Mary Doe, his wife.

(NOTARIAL SEAL)

Notary Public

My commission expires:

STATE OF NORTH CAROLINA)
          SS.[3]
COUNTY OF MAIN     )

I, Charles Coe, a notary public in and for the aforesaid state and county, CERTIFY that JOHN ROE personally came before me this day and acknowledged that he is the Secretary of Roe Bros. Stores, Inc., a Delaware corporation, and that by authority duly given and as the act of the corporation, the foregoing instrument was signed in its name by its President, sealed with its corporate seal, and attested by himself as its Secretary.

My commission expires October 4, 1984.

WITNESS my hand and official seal this 10th day of April, 1982.

(NOTARIAL SEAL)

Notary Public

[1]*49 Am. Jur. 2d Landlord and Tenant,* paras. 195 and 198.
[2]Florida statutory short form of acknowledgement.
[3]North Carolina statutory short form of acknowledgment.

## FORM VIIA 1.04

### (Lease of farm for annual minimum cash rental plus crop share)[1]

### FARM LEASE

THIS IS A LEASE made January 25, 1983, between John Doe of 100 West Street, Pittsburgh, Pennsylvania 00000 (herein called "Landlord"), and Charles Coe of Box 100, Pine Mills, Pennsylvania 00000 (herein called "Tenant").

LANDLORD and TENANT AGREE AS FOLLOWS:

1. *Description of farm.* In consideration of the rent specified herein, Landlord leases to Tenant his farm of four hundred (400) acres, more or less, known as the Doe Farm, located on State Route 100 in Middle County, Pennsylvania, two miles west of Pine Mills, together with all the buildings and improvements thereon, and the furnishings in the buildings and farm equipment on the premises as shown in Rider A, attached hereto. The legal description of the farm is as follows:

(Insert legal description of the land by metes and bounds or other appropriate legal description.)

2. *Term.* This is a one (1)-year lease beginning February 1, 1983, and ending on January 31, 1984, and continuing thereafter from year to year unless either party shall give written notice of termination to the other on or before the 1st day of November of the lease year. The written notice may be delivered or mailed by registered or certified U.S. mail addressed to the Landlord at 100 West Street, Pittsburgh, Pennsylvania 00000, or such other address as he shall designate in writing to the Tenant; and to the Tenant at the leased farm or by registered or certified U.S. mail addressed to the Tenant at R.F.D. 1, Box 20, Pine Mill, Pennsylvania 00000.

3. *Rent.*

(a) The Tenant shall pay to the Landlord as a minimum rent for the entire farm an annual cash rent of Six Hundred Dollars ($600), payable monthly in advance beginning February 1, 1983; receipt of the first month's rent by Landlord is hereby acknowledged.

(b) All utilities shall be paid by Tenant as they become due. Landlord shall post any refundable deposit required by utility companies for utility service for the farm to effect billing to Tenant and shall guaranty the payment of utilities by the Tenant, if required by the utility companies. The obligation of the Tenant to pay all utilities shall be deemed to be additional rent hereunder.

(c) In addition to the minimum cash rent and the payment of utilities by the Tenant, the Tenant shall pay as additional rental to the Landlord a share of the crop as provided herein.

4. *Crop sharing.*[2] The Tenant agrees to pay the Landlord as the additional rental provided in Paragraph 3(c) as follows: provided the Landlord contributes as provided herein the following shares of crop expense:

(a) The crop shall be a minimum of eighty (80) acres of potatoes (variety).

(b) The Landlord's share of the crop shall be Sixty Percent (60%)

(c) The Landlord's share of the crop expense shall be Fifty Percent (50%) of the cost of seed potatoes, fertilizer, and spraying materials. The Landlord's share of the crop expense shall be paid within ten (10) days of the receipt by him of copies of invoices approved in writing by the Tenant.

(d) The Landlord reserves storage facilities on the farm proportionate to his share of the crop as provided in (b) above, and the Tenant agrees to dig and store as much of the Landlord's share of the crop as possible in the reserved storage space.

(e) When the Landlord sells or desires to remove his share or any part of his share of the crop, the Tenant agrees to deliver it to a point designated by the Landlord not to exceed one hundred fifty (150) miles from the farm, in a conveyance supplied by Landlord, at a cost to the Landlord of 00¢ a mile for the round trip to the designated delivery point. Tenant shall pay for the fuel needed to operate the conveyance out of the mileage rate paid by Landlord.

5. *System of farming.* The potato crop shall be rotated each year with a soil-conserving crop during the term of this Lease (or other agreeable system).

6. *Farm operation (rights and duties of Landlord).*[3] The Landlord shall:

(a) Pay his share of crop expenses as provided herein.

(b) Furnish materials which are reasonably necessary for repair and maintenance of the fixed improvements on the farm property, including the house, barn, fences, and other permanent structures.

(c) To pay for both labor and materials to construct any permanent improvements.

(d) To repair or replace as soon as practicable buildings or other improvements essential to the operation of the farm that may be destroyed by fire, accident, or other casualty unless the parties otherwise agree in writing. To assure the performance of this convenant, Lessor agrees to carry sufficient casualty insurance to cover the replacement costs of such buildings and improvements.

(e) To warrant and defend the Tenant's possession against any and all persons during the terms of this Lease.

(f) To enter and inspect the farm land and its buildings and structures at any reasonable time and manner.

7. *Farm operation (rights and duties of Tenant)*. The Tenant shall:

(a) Manage and operate the farm in an efficient and husbandmanlike manner, following the cropping system and land practices provided herein, and otherwise in accordance with tillage and husbandry practices recognized in the community.

(b) Provide such labor, machinery, and equipment, in addition to that listed in Rider A, as shall reasonably be required to produce and harvest the crop to be shared by Landlord.

(c) Keep the entire farm in as good condition as it is at present, reasonable wear and tear and acts of God excepted, and to allow Landlord or his agent(s) to enter the land to work and make improvements as the Landlord deems expedient, provided such entry and work does not interfere with the tenant in carrying out his farm operation or in his use of the manse.

(d) Perform unskilled labor necessary in making minor repairs, maintenance, and minor improvements on the farm buildings and structures and farm machinery and tools.

(e) Not plow or otherwise destroy permanent pasture, drainageways, dams, streams, or remove timber or stone without the written consent of the Landlord, or undertake any operation that will injure or damage the land.

(f) Reasonably control noxious weeds along fence rows and roadsides by mowing only, refraining from the use of chemical sprays for that purpose.

(g) Shall not burn hay, straw, or crop residues without the written consent of the Landlord.

(h) Apply fertilizer, cultivate and spray potato crop in accordance with potato husbandry practice recognized in the community.

(i) Account for the Landlord's rental share of any potatoes left in the field after harvest in excess of *000* bushels per acre either in potatoes or cash at the option of the Landlord.

(j) Participate in and fully comply with any program offered by the United States Department of Agriculture or any other government agency, if such participation is elected by the Landlord.

(k) Not sublease or license the use of any part of the farm, including, but not limited to, land, buildings, pasture, or use of water, or water rights, without the written consent of the Landlord.

(l) Allow the Landlord to enter and inspect the farm land and its buildings and structures at any reasonable time requested by the Landlord.

(m) Peaceably surrender possession and occupancy of the leased premises at the termination of the Lease for any cause, and leave the leased premises, including all improvements and farm equipment, in as good condition as they were on the date of first occupancy, reasonable wear and tear and acts of God excepted.

8. *Termination (rights of Landlord)*.

(a) Landlord shall have the right to reenter forthwith upon the land upon termination for any cause under this Lease or provided by law.

(b) Upon termination, for any cause, Landlord shall have the right to recover from Tenant any damage to the leased premises or the equipment described in Rider A for which Tenant is responsible, including a reasonable attorney's fee for the recovery thereof by arbitration as provided herein or by other legal proceedings chosen by the Landlord.

(c) Landlord shall have the right to retain all permanent improvement made by the Tenant, with or without the consent of the Landlord, during the term without further compensation to the Tenant, except that Landlord shall pay the Tenant for the unexhausted value of the improvements for which the Landlord gave his written consent. The unexhausted value shall be determined in accordance with the formula in Rider C titled Compensation for Making Improvements, attached hereto and made part thereof.

9. *Default*.

(a) *Grace period*. If either party shall fail to carry out any of the provisions of this Lease, he shall be in default if the other party serves a written notice demanding compliance within a specified time, and the default is not corrected or in the process of correction within ten (10) days of receipt of that written notice; this Lease may be terminated, at the option of the complaining party, and no further notice need be given before taking legal action. This grace period shall not extend to the provision requiring the payment of cash monthly rent, utilities, or in the event that Tenant commits any criminal act, or act of gross negligence or waste.

(b) *Forbearance not waiver*. No forbearance as to any provision of this Lease by either party shall constitute a waiver by that party of any right to enforce a subsequent violation against the other party.

10. *Arbitration.*

(a) Any dispute between the Landlord and the Tenant arising hereunder before the termination of this Lease for any cause shall be first submitted to arbitration by one disinterested person agreeable to both parties, whose fee shall be shared equally by the parties. The decision of the arbitrator shall be binding upon the parties.

(b) In the event that the parties cannot agree on an arbitrator, either party may sue in a court of competent jurisdiction, and the prevailing party shall, in such case, recover all costs of the proceeding including reasonable attorney's fees.

11. *Recording.* This Lease shall be recorded by Landlord in Middle County, Pennsylvania.

12. *Assignability.* The Landlord may sell the farm at any time, subject to the terms of this Lease, and assign his rights hereunder to the purchaser. Other than by bona fide sale by Landlord, neither party may assign, sublease, or sublet any part of the leased premises or his rights hereunder without the written consent of the other.

Dated and signed this 25th day of January, 1983.

WITNESS _____

WITNESS _____

WITNESS _____          _____
                                              JOHN DOE, Lessor

WITNESS _____

WITNESS _____          _____
                                              CHARLES COE, Lessee

[1]*49 Am. Jur. 2d Landlord and Tenant,* paras. 68, 151, 196, 197, 199, and 588; and *77 Am. Jur. 2d Vendor and Purchaser, para. 87.*

[2]For crop share or stock share farm lease forms, check with your state or state university agricultural extension services; *21A Am. Jur. 2d Crops,* paras. 35–46 and compare 47–54.

[3]*49 Am. Jur. 2d Landlord and Tenant, para.* 400.

## FORM VIIA 1.05

**(Long-term lease of vacant land requiring erection of building, containing right of lessee to mortgage leasehold, and option to purchase)[1]**

### LEASE

THIS LEASE made in Pittsburgh, Pennsylvania, on April 1, 1982, between John Doe and Mary Doe, his wife, of 100 West Street, Pittsburgh, Pennsylvania 00000 (herein called "Lessors"), and National Manufacturing, Inc., a Delaware corporation having its principal place of business at 100 Main Street, Buffalo, New York 00000 (Herein called "Lessee"), WITNESSETH:

WHEREAS, the Lessors are the owners in fee simple of 200 acres, more or less, of vacant land located in Middle County, Pennsylvania, which land is more particularly described herein; and

WHEREAS, the Lessee desires to lease that land for the purpose of erecting buildings and structures for the operation of a computer hardware manufacturing business;

IT IS AGREED AS FOLLOWS:

1. *Description and term.*

(a) In consideration of the rents provided and mutual covenants contained herein, Lessors hereby lease, let, rent, and demise the following real property to the Lessee, its successors, and assigns:

(Insert description of the land by metes and bounds or other appropriate legal description.)

TO HAVE AND TO HOLD the premises, together with all and singular the tenements, hereditaments, and appurtenances thereunto belonging, or incident or appertaining thereto, for a period of ninety-nine (99) years commencing on May 1, 1982.

(b) Lessors covenant that they have lawful fee simple title to the premises, free and clear of all liens, mortgages, and encumbrances, and that they have the right to make this Lease on the terms set forth herein, subject to any state of facts that an accurate survey may show.

(c) Lessee will, at its own expense, procure a survey of the land before erecting any of the proposed structures or buildings thereon as shown in Schedule A attached hereto and made part hereof; and will supply Lessors with a copy of that survey, which will indicate the proposed location of those structures. Updated surveys showing the location and size of all buildings or permanent structures actually erected on the land by Lessee at any time shall be procured by the Lessee and provided to the Lessors, without charge, within ten (10) days of receipt of such surveys by the Lessee.

(d) The parties intend, understand, and agree that the relationship between them is that of landlord and Tenant under a commercial lease, and Lessee specifically acknowledges that all statutory proceedings provided by the law of the Commonwealth of Pennsylvania applicable to the relationship of commercial landlord and tenant, and the remedies accruing to the landlord upon default of the tenant as to collection of rent or repossession of the leased premises, accrue to the Lessors hereunder, regardless of the length of the term of this Lessee.

2. *Net rent.*

(a) The Lessee shall pay to Lessors, at any place in the United States or its possessions designated by Lessors in writing, an annual rental of Twenty Thousand Dollars ($20,000), payable in advance on the 1st day of May of each and every year beginning May 1, 1983. The first year's rent, in the sum of Ten Thousand Dollars ($10,000), shall be paid in advance upon the executions of this Lease, receipt of which is hereby acknowledged.

(b) The Lessee shall pay all taxes, charges, assessments, government service fees of any description, or like payments as shall, during the term of this Lease, be imposed upon or grow out of, or become a lien upon the premises or any part of them or the improvements thereon within thirty (30) days after they shall be payable, except that such payments due for the year 2081 shall be apportioned between the Lessors and the Lessee. Furthermore, during the term of this Lease, Lessee shall pay all charges or taxes of any kind that may be imposed by virtue of any present or future law of the United States or of the Commonwealth of Pennsylvania or of any other governmental body having authority to levy or impose them, upon the reversionary or any other right or estate of the Lessors in or to the leased premises or any portion thereof, or upon the rents reserved by this Lease; except for any tax imposed upon the transfer by Lessors of any interest in the leased premises or any inheritance or estate tax or income tax payable by the Lessors measured by the general income of the Lessors and not by their income from the leased premises; it being the intention of the parties that the rents reserved under this Lease shall be received by Lessors as a net sum.

3. *Building and insurance covenants by Lessee.*

(a) Lessee shall, at its sole cost and expense, erect and fully complete the buildings and permanent structures (herein called "Buildings") as shown on Schedule A according to the general plans and specifications prepared by Peter Poe and Associates, Architects, which have been submitted and approved in writing by Lessors, which general plans and specifications are incorporated herein by reference.

(b) Lessee shall cause the Buildings shown in Schedule A to be constructed in a workmanlike manner in conformity with those general plans and specifications, and under the direction of Peter Poe and Associates, Architects (herein called "Directing Architects"), on or before May 1, 1983, and the decision of the Directing Architects as to the construction and meaning and execution of the plans and specifications for the Building shall be final and binding on the Lessors and the Lessee.

(c) Any and all charges of any architect for the general plans and specifications incorporated herein and for any future additional plans, drawings, specifications, or explanations of these plans or plans for the Buildings or for future buildings, shall be paid by Lessee and all charges of the Directing Architects or their successors shall be paid by the Lessee.

(d) Lessee will not permit any mechanic's or other liens for work, services, or materials, to attach to the leased premises or to any portion thereof; and if any such liens shall be filed or shall attach, Lessee will pay and satisfy the same or get some canceled by giving security for some or in such other manner as may be prescribed by law at the time of such filing or attachment.

(e) Until the Buildings are completed, the Lessors or their representatives shall have the right to enter the premises at reasonable times.

(f) After the Buildings are completed, they shall not be taken down, removed, or substantially altered by the Lessee without the prior written consent of the Lessors, and the Lessors or their representatives shall have the right to enter the premises for inspection purposes only with the consent of the Lessee, which consent shall not be unreasonably withheld.

(g) If the completion of the Buildings should be delayed by the act, neglect, or default of Lessors, or by any damage caused by fire or other casualty beyond the control of Lessee, then the time fixed for the completion of the Buildings shall be extended for a period equivalent to the time lost by reason of the cause(s), which extended period shall be determined and fixed by the Directing Architects. Notice of the delay and its cause shall be given by Lessee to Lessors and the Directing Architects within seventy-two (72) hours of the occurrence of the event causing such delay.

(h) In the event that the Buildings are not completed within the time provided, and if the Lessors shall give written notice to Lessee to complete the Buildings by a date specified in the notice at least ninety (90) days from the date of the notice, and if Lessee shall fail to complete the Buildings within the time so specified, then the term of this Lease shall cease on the date specified for completion as though that were the expiration date of the original term of this Lease.

(i) As work on the Buildings progresses, and upon completion of the Buildings, it shall be the sole responsibility of Lessee to insure the Buildings for comprehensive casualty damage, naming Lessors as additional insureds as their interest may appear. Proof of that insurance at all times during the term of this Lease shall be provided to Lessors by Lessee. If Lessee fails to provide that insurance or proof thereof to Lessors, Lessors may, after five (5) days' written notice to Lessee, at Lessors' option and without waiver of the default by Lessee, procure or renew the insurance. The premiums paid by Lessors plus interest on the amount paid at the rate of Twelve Percent (12%) per annum, shall constitute rent hereunder, and Lessee's failure to make reimbursement within thirty (30) days of demand therefor shall constitute a default under this Lease.

(j) In any event, including total destruction of the Buildings, Lessee shall be liable for the rent provided herein for the duration of the term of this Lease.

(k) Lessee shall at all times, during construction and after completion of the Buildings, keep the leased premises, and all property that is subject to the Landlord's lien hereunder during the term of this Lease, in good condition, order, and repair, and shall hold Lessors harmless from any and all personal or property damage claims and liability arising by use of the leased premises by anyone directly or indirectly; and Lessee shall provide policies of insurance against all such claims or demands as public liability, landlord/tenant, boiler policies, elevator policies, and others necessary to implement this indemnification to the extent of not less than One Hundred Thousand Dollars ($100,000) for claim or damage from any single cause by any one person, and to the extent of not less than Three Hundred Thousand Dollars ($300,000) to cover the aggregate of any claims from any one accident or occurrence. Said policies shall be taken only with insurance companies that are duly authorized to do business in the Commonwealth of Pennsylvania.

4. *Option to purchase.*

(a) Lessors hereby grant to Lessee an option to purchase the leased premises, said option to become effective May 1, 1987, and not prior to that time. This option to purchase shall terminate on May 1, 1992. The purchase price shall be Two Hundred Fifty Thousand Dollars ($250,000) in cash, payable in U.S. legal tender at the time of closing.

(b) The closing shall take place within sixty (60) days of receipt of notice from Lessee to Lessors of Lessee's intention to exercise the option.

(c) In the event the option is not exercised or not closed within the specified time, the option shall cease, and all other conditions of this Lease shall remain in full force and effect for the remainder of the term as though no such option had ever existed.

5. *Mortgage of leasehold interest.* Lessee shall have the right to mortgage its leasehold interest hereunder for the purpose of obtaining a construction loan for the Buildings, and, if Lessee decides to obtain such a construction loan within one (1) year from the date hereof, Lessors will, at the written request of the Lessee, join in the execution of that mortgage but not the note, only upon the following terms and conditions:

(a) That the mortgage and note shall specifically state that Lessors shall not be personally responsible for payment of the debt secured by the mortgage.

(b) That the total cost of securing that mortgage and all expenses thereof shall be paid by Lessee.

(c) That the proceeds of the construction loan shall be disbursed by an institutional lender qualified to do business in the Commonwealth of Pennsylvania in a manner to assure completion of the Buildings and the payment of all bills and liens in connection therewith.

(d) That a commitment from that institutional lender has been executed and an executed copy thereof has been delivered to Lessees.

(e) That Lessors shall be required to join in only one (1) construction loan mortgage, which may be for the construction of all the Buildings or part of the Buildings, as determined by Lessee.

(f) If the commitment for the construction loan is not obtained within one (1) year from the date hereof, Lessors shall not be required to join in the execution of any mortgage or mortgages encumbering the leasehold created herein.

(g) Lessee shall keep the mortgage in good standing at all times and will not permit it to become in default for any reason, and shall deliver to Lessors a receipt evidencing payment of principal and interest due as such payments mature. If Lessee should default in its undertakings under the mortgage, Lessors may, at their sole takings under the mortgage, Lessors may, at their sole option, make such payments as are necessary to cure the default, and all payments are made by Lessors shall bear interest at the rate of Fifteen Percent (15%) per annum from the date on which the payments were made until Lessors are reimbursed by Lessee, and shall be considered due or additional rent hereunder. The election by Lessors to make the payments shall not cure the default committed by Lessee hereunder by its failure to keep the mortgage in good standing. Lessors may elect to treat that failure as a default under this Lease enforceable according to the terms hereof.

6. *Default.*

(a) *Reentry by Lessors.* In the event Lessee fails to keep or perform any covenants, conditions, or provisions of this Lease, the Lessors, at their sole option, may declare the lease term ended and the Lease void, and reenter upon the leased premises and the Buildings and improvements thereon, or any part thereof, and retake possession of them and any furniture or equipment contained therein or thereon, with or without process of law. The liability of Lessee to pay rent and all other sums it is required to pay under this Lease shall not cease upon reentry and repossession by Lessors. But Lessors shall have a duty to make a reasonable effort to rent the leased premises and improvements, including the Buildings and person property, and shall credit Lessee's obligation hereunder with the rents, if any, received by Lessors as that obligation accrues.

(b) *Cumulative remedies in addition to Lessors' rights under Paragraph (a).* Lessors shall have such other remedies as the law and this Lease afford, now or as the law may later confer upon the Lessor. Lessors' rights and remedies on default by Lessee are cumulative and not exclusive of those other remedies.

(c) *Grace period.* Before Lessors may declare Lessee in default under Paragraph (a), the violation of the term(s) of this Lease constituting a default must have continued for a period of fifteen (15) days beyond the time the payment was due or the action was required.

(d) *Receivership on default.* Lessee hereby pledges with Lessors all of the rents, issues, and profits that otherwise would be Lessee's hereunder to Lessors, and Lessee agrees that if Lessors, upon default of Lessee, elect to file an action to enforce this Lease and protect Lessors' rights hereunder, the Lessors may as ancillary to that suit apply to any competent court having jurisdiction for the appointment of a Receiver of the leased premises and improvements thereon, including the Buildings and all personal property located therein. Lessee agrees that the Receiver may be appointed without reference to the adequacy or inadequacy of the value of the property that is subject to the landlord's lien, or to the solvency or insolvency of the Lessee; and without reference to the commission of waste.

(e) *Liquidated damages on default.* In the event of the termination of this Lease by reason of the default of Lessee, all of the rights, estate, and interest of the Lessee in the leased premises, and all improvements, buildings and Lessee's interest in furniture, furnishings, fixtures, and equipment in or on the leased premises, together with all rents, issues, and profits of the leased premises and the improvements thereon, whether then accrued or to accrue, and all insurance policies, and all insurance moneys paid or payable thereunder, shall, without any compensation made therefor to Lessee, at once pass and vest in Lessors, not as a penalty or forfeiture, but as liquidated damages are hereby fixed by the Lessor and Lessees and agreed to by them because they recognize the impossibility of precisely ascertaining the amount of damages that will be sustained by Lessors in consequence of a default, and they have taken into account the cost and effect of a default in consequence of that forfeiture in fixing and agreeing upon the amount of rent to be paid by the Lessee to the Lessors hereunder for the period of time provided herein.

7. *Notices to Lessee.* If any notice or demand on Lessee is required by this Lease or desired by Lessors to be given or made, it shall be sufficient service of that demand or notice, including declaration of default hereunder, to be made by delivering a copy thereof to the Lessee or by mailing a copy thereof by registered or certified U.S. mail addressed to the Lessee at the leased premises. If, at any time during the term of this Lease, the Lessor consists of more than one lessor or the Lessee consists of more than one lessee, then the default of one shall be the default of all and notice to one shall be notice to all.

8. *Return of premises to Lessors on termination.* Upon termination of this Lease by lapse of time or otherwise, Lessee shall at once, peaceably and quietly, deliver up to Lessors all of the leased premises, including the improvements and Buildings thereon and all the fixtures therein, including manufacturing equipment and personal property necessary to operation of the manufacturing business even though not physically attached to the land or Buildings, and no compensation shall be allowed or paid to the Lessee therefor.

9. *Assignability.*

  (a) This Lease shall be assignable by the Lessee only upon the following terms and conditions:

     (1) An assignment cannot be made by Lessee before the completion of the Buildings shown in Schedule A.

     (2) Any and all defaults under the Lease must be cured on or before the date of the assignment.

     (3) Written notice of the proposed assignment must have been given to the lessors at least thirty (30) days before the date of execution of any assignment of the Lease.

     (4) Lessee shall be jointly and severely liable with the assignee for the moneys due under this Lease for a period of two (2) years from the date of the executed assignment.

     (5) Lessors shall, upon the written request of Lessee, furnish a written statement to any proposed assignee, within five (5) days of the request, that this lease is or is not in default.

     (6) This right to receive rents under this Lease shall be freely assignable by Lessors. Any sale or mortgage of Lessors' interest in the leased premises shall be subject to this Lease, and the existence of this Lease and the Middle County Public Record number when it is recorded shall be duly stated on any document of conveyance or assignment by the Lessor.

10. *Covenants running with the land.* The terms, promises, and conditions of this Lease are covenants running with the land leased herein and shall inure to the benefit of and shall bind and be obligatory upon the heirs, executors, administrators, successors, and assigns of the Lessors and the Lessee.

11. *Forbearance not waiver.* No forbearance to enforce the breach of any of the promises or covenants of this Lease shall be construed as a waiver of any succeeding breach of the same or any other convenant hereof.

12. *Modification.* No modification, release, discharge, or waiver of any provisions hereof shall be of any force or effect unless signed by the party against whom it is claimed or that party's duly authorized agent.

13. *Time of the essence.* Time is of the essence of every term, condition, promise, or covenant of this Lease.

14. *Security interest in personal property.* In addition to the rights of Lessors as a landlord hereunder, as provided by the landlord and tenant law of the Commonwealth of Pennsylvania, the Lessee hereby grants to Lessors a security interest in the personal property from time to time used as manufacturing equipment in or on the leased premises, whether or not it is affixed to the real property. Lessee shall, at the request of Lessor, execute any and all documents necessary to perfect this security interest in accordance with 13 P.S.C. 9101 et seq.[2]

15. *Entire agreement.* This instrument contains the entire agreement of the parties as of this date, and the execution hereof has not been induced by either party by any representations, promises, or understandings not expressed herein. There are no collateral agreements, stipulations, promises, or undertakings that are not extremely contained herein or incorporated herein by specific reference.

IN WITNESS WHEREOF, the Lessors have hereunto affixed their hands and seals, and the Lessee has caused this Lease to be signed and executed in its corporate name by its President and its corporate seal to be affixed and attested to by its Secretary, at Pittsburgh, Allegheny County, Pennsylvania, on this 1st day of April, 1982.

Signed, sealed, and delivered in the presence of

_____ (SEAL)
JOHN DOE

_____

WITNESS as to Lessor's

_____ _____ (SEAL)

WITNESS as to Lessor's                                      MARY DOE

(CORPORATE SEAL)                                           NATIONAL MANUFACTURING, INC.

(Charles Coe)                                              By   (Peter Poe) _____

Secretary of the Corporation                              President

COMMONWEALTH OF PENNSYLVANIA
COUNTY OF ALLEGHENY

On this 4th day of April, 1982, before me, Mary Brown, the undersigned officer, personally appeared John Doe and Mary Doe, his wife, known to me or satisfactorily proven to be the persons whose names are subscribed to the within instrument, and acknowledged that they executed the same for the purposes therein contained.

IN WITNESS WHEREOF, I hereunto set my hand and official seal.

(NOTARIAL SEAL)                       _____Notary Public

My commission expires:

STATE OF NEW YORK
COUNTY OF MIDDLE

On the 1st day of April, 1982, before me personally came Peter Poe, to me known, who being by me duly sworn, did depose and say that he resides at 100 East Drive, Buffalo, New York; that he is President of National Manufacturing, Inc., the corporation described in and which executed the above instrument; that he knows the seal of said corporation; that the seal affixed to said instrument is such corporate seal; that it was so affixed by order of the Board of Directors of said Corporation; and that he signed his name thereto by like order.

_____

Notary Public

My commission expires:

(Attach Schedule A.)

[1] *49 Am. Jur. 2d Landlord and Tenant,* paras. 68, 184, and 191–213.
[2] U.C.C. 9–104(b) and U.C.C. 9–313(3).

## FORM VIIA 1.06

### (Lease of office space in building)
### LEASE[1]

THIS LEASE made this 20th day of April, 1982, by and between The Doe Building of the City of Pittsburgh, Allegheny County, Pennsylvania, by their agent, Charles J. Greve Co. ("Lessors"), and Roe Johnson, Inc., a Pennsylvania corporation ("Lessee").

1. LEASED PREMISES

Lessors hereby lease to the Lessee and Lessee hereby rents from Lessors the following described premises, hereinafter referred to as the "leased premises," situated in that certain office building known as The Clark Building, and known and numbered as 717 Liberty Avenue, Pittsburgh, Allegheny County, Pennsylvania.

A. All those certain offices, the total area of which is approximately *000* square feet, including common space, that are on the fifth (5th) Floor of the Real Estate.

2. TERM

The term of this Lease shall be five (5) years, commencing on May 1, 1982, and ending on April 30, 1987.

3. ALTERATIONS

(List description of alterations and specifications. Attach list by reference if it is lengthy.)

4. MINIMUM RENT

Lessee shall pay to Lessors, at the office of their agent, Charles J. Greve & Co., Clark Building, Pittsburgh, Pennsylvania 15222, or as otherwise designated, minimum rent for said leased premises and minimum rent for the use of the common areas of The Clark Building, the total area of both of which is *0000* square feet, apportioned as follows:

A. The total sum of Fifty Thousand Dollars ($50,000), payable in sixty (60) monthly installments, the first of which shall be due on the first day of the term and the remainder of which shall be due on the corresponding date in each succeeding month during said term. Said installments shall be in the following amounts:

Each Month Per Term Year

Year 1: *000*   Year 3: *000*   Year 5: *000*   Year 7: *000*   Year 9: *000*
Year 2: *000*   Year 4: *000*   Year 6: *000*   Year 8: *000*   Year 10: *000*

B. In addition to any other right or remedy given hereunder to Lessors for nonpayment by Lessee of any sum due as rent under this Lease, in the event that Lessee shall fail to pay an installment of minimum rent by a date that is ten (10) days after it is due, Lessee shall pay to Lessors a late charge in a sum equal to Four Percent (4%) of the total of such installment.

5. ADDITIONAL RENT

A. If the expenses for maintaining and operating the Real Estate during the calendar year beginning January 1, 1985, or during any calendar quarter thereafter, exceed the expenses for maintaining and operating the Real Estate during the respective calendar quarters beginning January 1, 1982, Lessee shall pay to Lessor, as Additional Rent, a sum equal to 0% of such excess.

(1) The term "expenses for maintaining and operating the Real Estate" shall be deemed to mean those expenses incurred during such operating year in respect of the operation of the Building in accordance with accepted principles of sound management and accounting practices as applied to the operation of first-class buildings, including, but not limited to, real estate taxes (which shall mean all taxes and assessments and governmental charges, whether federal, state, county, or municipal, that are levied on or charged against real estate or rents, or on the right or privilege of leasing real estate or collecting rents thereon, and any other taxes and assessments attributable to the Real Estate, or its operation, excluding, however, federal and state income taxes), employees' wages (which shall include payroll taxes and other related costs such as payments to welfare and pension funds in compliance with provisions of union contracts in force at that time), casualty and liability insurance, utilities (which shall include heating, electricity, water, and sewerage), and maintenance costs relating to the normal operation of the Real Estate covering elevator service contracts, janitor service contracts, and normal service supplies that are necessary to the efficient operation of the Real Estate.

(2) The term "expenses for maintaining and operating the Real Estate" shall not include expenses for any capital improvements made to the Real Estate, expenses for painting, redecorating, or other work that Lessors perform as a special service for other tenants in the Real Estate, and expenses incurred in renovating space for new lessees.

B. All such Additional Rent shall be due and payable not later than twenty (20) days after Lessee has received a bill for same.

C. In addition to any other right or remedy given hereunder to Lessors for nonpayment by Lessee of any sum due as rent under this Lease, in the event that Lessee shall fail to pay a bill for Additional Rent by a date that is ten (10) days after it is due, Lessee shall pay to Lessors a late charge in a sum of Four Percent (4%) of the total such bill.

6. UTILITIES

A. Lessors will keep in operation in the Real Estate heating facilities for the use of Lessee between October 1 and May 1 of each year of the term of this Lease. Lessors shall not be liable in any way for failure to supply the same, unless such failure has been caused by the gross negligence of Lessors, nor shall such failure be construed to be a breach of this Lease on the part of the Lessors.

B. Lessors shall furnish a reasonable amount of electricity for the use of Lessee during the term of this Lease. Lessors shall not be liable in any way for the failure to supply same, unless such failure has been caused by the gross negligence of Lessors, nor shall such failure be construed to be a breach of this Lease on the part of the Lessors. Said obligation of Lessee to pay for electricity shall be considered as rent and shall be due and payable not later than twenty (20) days after Lessee has received a bill for same.

C. Lessors shall not be required to provide heating or air-conditioning service or equipment that is or may be specially necessary to control temperatures of computer equipment. In the event that Lessee deems such service or equipment to be necessary, Lessee may purchase such equipment, provided, however, that (1) such equipment shall not be installed without the advance written consent of Lessors; (2) such equipment shall not be installed if it will adversely affect other heating and air-conditioning equipment, lines, and facilities owned by Lessors; and (3) Lessors shall perform any such installation at the sole expense of Lessees. The limitations on damage claims and offsets contained in Subparagraph B above apply with equal force to any services now or later provided pursuant to this subparagraph.

7. POWERS AS TO UTILITIES

Lessors, without notice to Lessee, may cut off and discontinue gas and electricity and any or all other utilities whenever and during any period when Minimum Rent or Additional Rent are not paid by Lessee when due or whenever discontinuance is necessary in order to make repairs or alterations. No such action by Lessors shall be construed as an eviction or disturbance of possession or as an election by Lessors to terminate this lease, nor shall Lessors be in any way responsible or liable for such action.

8. OTHER SERVICES

A. Lessors shall, at times set by them, provide such ordinary janitor service for the leased premises as Lessors shall deem necessary.

B. Lessors shall provide such elevator service as shall be necessary to the use of the leased premises by Lessee. Lessors shall not be liable in any way for failure to supply the same, unless such failure has been caused by the gross negligence of Lessors, nor shall such failure be construed to be a breach of this Lease on the part of the Lessors.

9. USE OF LEASED PREMISES.

A. Lessee shall utilize the leased premises for the purpose of conducting an executive and administrative office for the business of the Lessee corporation.

B. Lessee shall not commit, or suffer to be committed, any waste on the leased premises, nor shall Lessee maintain, commit, or permit the maintenance or commission of any nuisance on the leased premises or use the leased premises for any unlawful purpose.

C. Lessee shall comply with any and all laws, ordinances, orders, and regulations of any governmental authority that are applicable to its use of the leased premises.

D. Lessee shall comply with any and all Rules and Regulations of the Real Estate, as contained in Exhibit A, which is attached hereto and made a part hereof.

E. Lessee shall neither abandon nor vacate the leased premises during the term of this Lease.

10. REPAIRS

A. If any damage to the leased premises is caused by any act or omission of Lessee, its employees, agents, or invitees, such damage shall be promptly repaired by Lessee, at his sole cost and expense.

(1) If Lessee refuses or neglects to commence or complete repairs promptly and adequately, Lessors may, but shall not be required to do so, make complete repairs, and Lessee shall pay the cost thereof, as Additional Rent, to Lessors immediately upon demand.

11. DAMAGE TO OR DESTRUCTION OF PREMISES

A. If, during the term of this Lease, the leased premises are damaged by any casualty or event that is covered by an applicable insurance policy, to the extent that the same are rendered wholly unfit for occupancy, and if the leased premises cannot, in the judgment of a reputable contractor satisfactory to Lessors, be repaired within ninety (90) days from the time of such damage, then this Lease, at the option of Lessors, may be terminated as of the date of such damage. In the event

Lessors elect to terminate this Lease, Lessee shall pay the rent apportioned to the time of damage and shall immediately surrender the leased premises to Lessors, who may enter upon and repossess the same, and Lessee shall be relieved from any further liability hereunder. If Lessors do not elect to terminate this Lease, or if any damage by way of the above casualties, rendering the leased premises wholly unfit, can, in the judgment of such contractor, be repaired within ninety (90) days thereafter, Lessors agree to repair such damage promptly, and this Lease shall not be affected in any mannor, except that rent shall be suspended and shall not accrue from the date of such damage until such repairs have been completed. If the leased premises shall be so slightly damaged by any of the above casualties as not to be rendered wholly unfit for occupancy, Lessors shall repair the premises promptly, and during the period from the date of such damage until the repairs are completed, the rent shall be apportioned so Lessee pays as rent an amount that bears the same ratio to the entire monthly rent as the portion of the leased premises that Lessee is able to occupy without substantial disturbance during such periods bears to the entire leased premises. If the damage by any of the above casualties is so slight that Lessee is not substantially disturbed in its possession and enjoyment of the leased premises, then Lessors shall repair the same promptly, and in that case the rent accrued or accruing shall not abate.

B. If, during the term of this Lease, the leased premises are damaged by any casualty not covered by an applicable insurance policy, either rendering the leased premises partially untenantable or totally untenantable, then in that event, Lessors shall, within thirty (30) days from the date when said damage has occurred, notify Lessee in writing as to whether or not Lessors elect to rebuild or repair the leased premises, at their own sole cost and expense. Not later than fifteen (15) days after it has received such election not to rebuild, Lessee shall give written notice to Lessors, in which Lessee elects either to cause the leased premises to be rebuilt or repaired, at its sole cost and expense, and in accordance with the provisions contained in Paragraph 15 of this Lease, OR in which Lessee elects to terminate this Lease. If the leased premises have been rendered wholly untenantable by any such casualty, rent shall be suspended and shall not accrue from the date of such damage until such repairs, if elected, shall be completed. If the leased premises have been rendered partially untenantable, the rent shall be apportioned so Lessee pays as rent, until such repairs shall have been completed or until such termination has been elected, an amount that bears the same ratio to the entire monthly rent as the portion of the leased premises that Lessee is able to occupy without disturbance during such period bears to the entire leased premises. In the event Lessee fails to give timely written notice of such election to Lessors, this Lease shall terminate without further liability to either party, except as to rent that is or may be due.

12. ACTION OF PUBLIC AUTHORITIES

In the event that any exercise of the power of eminent domain by any governmental authority, federal, state, county, or municipal, or by any other party vested by law with such power, shall at any time prevent the full use and enjoyment of the leased premises by Lessee for the purpose set forth in Paragraph 9, Lessee shall have the right thereupon to terminate this Lease. In the event of any such action, both Lessors and Lessee shall have the right to claim, recover, and retain from the governmental authority or other party taking such action the damages suffered by them respectively as a result of such action.

13. LIABILITY, INDEMNITY

A. Lessee shall be liable for any injury or death of persons and for any loss and/or damage to property caused by the negligent act or omissions of its agents, employees, or invitees, or caused by the failure of Lessee to perform the maintenance and repairs required to be performed by him under the provisions of Paragraph 10 of this Lease. Lessee shall indemnify and save harmless Lessors against any and all liability, claims, demands, actions, costs, and expenses that may be sustained by Lessors by reason of any of the causes for which Lessee is liable pursuant to this Paragraph.

B. Lessee shall hold Lessors harmless or any loss or damage that Lessee, its agent, employees, or invitees may sustain from:

(1) theft or burglary in or about the Real Estate, including the leased premises, by whomsoever committed;
(2) interruptions in any service from any cause whatsoever;
(3) fire, water, rain, snow, steam, sewage, gas, or odors, from any source whatsoever;
(4) damage or injury not caused by the gross negligence of Lessors.

14. FIXTURES

All fixtures, including carpeting and permanent shelving installed by Lessee during the term of this Lease, whether on permanent foundation or in whatever manner affixed or attached to the leased premises, shall be deemed to have attached to the Real Estate and to have become the property of Lessors. Provided, however, that at the expiration of the term of this Lease, Lessee shall remove any or all of such property if Lessors demand that Lessee effect such removal. In the event that such removal is demanded, Lessee shall repair all damage to the leased premises to the condition in which they were prior to the installation of the articles so removed.

15. ALTERATION, ADDITIONS, AND IMPROVEMENTS

A. Lessee shall not make any alterations, additions, or improvements to the leased premises without the prior written consent of Lessors or their said agent.

(1) Any alterations, additions, or improvements approved in writing by Lessors or their said agent shall be performed by laborers and materialmen and with materials furnished by Lessors.

(2) Lessee shall pay to Lessors, within ten (10) days of billing, the cost to Lessors of labor and materials in making such alterations, additions, or improvements, plus Ten Percent (10%) of said cost and overhead on account of profit.

B. All alterations, additions, and improvements to the leased premises shall at once, when made, be deemed to have attached to the Real Estate and to have become the property of Lessors. At the expiration of the term of this Lease, nevertheless, Lessee shall remove any or all such alterations, additions, and improvements upon demand by Lessors that it do so.

16. DEFAULT

A. If Lessee shall fail to pay any rent to Lessors when the same is due and payable under the terms of this Lease, and such default shall continue for a period of fifteen (15) days, or if Lessee shall fail to perform any other duty or obligation imposed upon him by this Lease, and such default shall continue for a period of twenty (20) days, or if Lessee shall be adjudged bankrupt or shall make a general assignment for the benefit of its creditors, or if a receiver of any property of Lessee in or upon the leased premises be appointed in any action, suit, or proceeding by or against Lessee and such appointment shall not be vacated or annulled within sixty (60) days, or if the interest of Lessee in the leased premises shall be sold under execution or other legal process, then and in any such event, Lessors have the right to enter upon the leased premises and again have, repossess, and enjoy the same as if this Lease had not been made, and thereupon this Lease shall terminate without prejudice, however, to the right of Lessors to recover from Lessee all rent and other sums unpaid up to the time of such reentry. In the event of any such default and reentry, Lessors shall have the right to relet the leased premises for the remainder of the then existing term for the highest rent then obtainable, and to recover from Lessee the difference between the rent reserved by this Lease and the amount obtained through such reletting, less the costs and expenses reasonably incurred by Lessors in such reletting. In the event that the amount obtained exceeds the rent herein reserved, Lessors shall not be required to pay such excess to Lessee.

B. If Lessee shall default in the payment of any installment of rent or of any other sum provided for under this Lease as the same becomes due, or if Lessee breaches any covenant, duty, agreement, or obligation imposed upon Lessee by this Lease, and if such default or breach shall continue for a period of thirty (30) days, Lessee hereby authorizes and empowers any attorney of any court of record within the United States or elsewhere to appear for Lessee and to confess judgment[2] against Lessee in favor of Lessors as often as necessary, as of any term, with or without declaration filed, for the sum due by reason of said default in the payment of rent, including unpaid rent for the balance of the term of this Lease if the same shall have become due and payable under the provisions herein, and/or for the sum due by reason of any breach of covenant, duty, agreement, or obligation by Lessee herein, together with costs of suit and Five Percent (5%) added as attorney's fees, with release of all errors. Lessee waives any right to stay of execution and extension of any levy on property from levy and execution thereon, as well as any levy on property pursuant to any such judgment, and expressly waives the exemption statute now in force or enacted hereafter by any state or nation, to the extent such statutes may be waived.

C. Lessee further, at the option of Lessors, authorizes and empowers any such attorney, either in addition to or without such judgment for the amount due according to the terms of this Lease, to appear for Lessors and confess judgment forthwith against Lessee and in favor of Lessors in an amicable action of ejectment for the leased premises, with all the conditions, fees, releases, waivers of stay of execution, and waiver of exemption to accompany said confession of judgment in ejectment as are set forth herein for confession of judgment therein, and the immediate issuing of a writ of possession with clause of execution for the amount of such judgment and costs, without leave of Court, and Lessors may without notice reenter and expel Lessee from the leased premises, and also any person holding under it, and in each case, this Lease or a true copy thereof shall be a sufficient warrant of any person.

D. All rights and remedies of Lessors under this Lease shall be cumulative, and none shall exclude any other right or remedy at law. Such right and remedies may be exercised and enforced concurrently and whenever and as often as occasion thereof arises.

### 17. SUBORDINATION

This lease shall be subject and subordinate at all times to the lien of existing mortgages and of mortgages that hereafter may be made a lien on the Real Estate, including the leased premises. Lessee shall, if requested so to by Lessors, execute and deliver such documents as may be desired by any such mortgagee to effectuate such subordination.

### 18. SIGNS

Lessee shall not erect any sign in, on, or about the leased premises and/or the Real Estate without prior written consent of Lessors. When such written consent has been obtained from Lessors, Lessee agrees and covenants that all such signs shall be in accordance with any applicable statutes, ordinances, codes, rules, and/or regulations of any governmental authority, and that Lessee shall maintain such signs and keep the same in good state of repair. Upon vacating the leased premises, Lessee agrees, at its expense, to remove all signs and to repair any and all damages caused by said removal. Lessor shall have absolute discretion on all sign matters.

### 19. SURRENDER

A. Lessee covenants and agrees to deliver up and surrender to Lessors possession of the leased premises upon expiration of this Lease, or its earlier termination as may be herein provided, broom clean and in as good condition and relief as the same shall be at the commencement of the term of this Lease or may have been put by Lessors during the continuance, ordinary wear and tear and damage by fire or the elements excepted.

B. Lessors shall also have the right to enter upon the leased premises for a period commencing one hundred twenty (120) days prior to the termination of this Lease for the purpose of exhibiting the same to prospective tenants or purchasers.

C. Lessee shall, at the expense of Lessee, remove all property of Lessee and all fixtures, alterations, additions, and improvements as to which Lessors shall have made the demand as provided in Paragraphs 14 and 15 hereof, repair all damages to the leased premises caused by such removal, and restore the leased premises to the condition in which they were prior to the installation of the articles so removed. Any property not so removed, and as to which Lessors shall have not made such demand, shall be deemed to have been abandoned by Lessee and may be retained or disposed of by Lessors as Lessors shall desire. This obligation of Lessee to observe or perform this covenant shall survive the expiration or termination of the term of this Lease.

### 20. WAIVER OF DEFAULT

Acceptance by Lessors of part payment on any installment of rent by Lessee shall not constitute an accord and satisfaction as to the rental obligation of Lessee. Failure of either party to complain of any act or omission on the part of the other party, no matter how long the same may continue, shall not be deemed to be a waiver by said party of any of their rights hereunder. No waiver by either party at any time, express or implied, of any breach of any provision of this Lease shall be deemed a waiver of a breach of any provision of this Lease or a consent to any subsequent breach of the same or any other provision.

### 21. HOLDING OVER

If Lessee lawfully occupies the leased premises after the end of the term hereof, this Lease and all its terms, conditions, provisions, and covenants herein specially given and agreed to shall be in force for another month, and so on from month to month, unless either party gives notice to the other party in writing at least thirty (30) days prior to the end of any such month, in which event Lessee covenants and agrees that it will vacate the leased premises on or before the end of any such month.

### 22. REIMBURSEMENT

All terms, covenants, and conditions herein contained to be performed by Lessee shall be performed at its sole expense, and if Lessors shall pay any sum of money to do any act that requires the payment of money, by reason of the failure, neglect, or refusal of Lessee to perform such term, covenant, or condition, the sum of money to be paid by Lessors shall be payable by Lessee to Lessors with the next succeeding installment or rent.

### 23. RIGHTS AND REMEDIES CUMULATIVE

The rights and remedies provided by this Lease are cumulative, and the use of any right or remedy by either party shall not preclude or waive the right of either party to use any or all other remedies. Said rights and remedies are given in addition to any other rights the parties may have by law, statute, ordinance, or otherwise.

24. ASSIGNMENT AND SUBLEASE

Lessee shall not assign this lease, nor shall he sublet all or any portion of the leased premises, without the prior written consent of Lessors.

25. NOTICES AND ADDRESSES

All notices provided to be given under this Lease shall be given by certified mail or hand-delivered to Lessors and Lessee by the representative of each of them, hereinafter named at the following address, unless later otherwise designated:

| LESSORS | LESSEE |
|---|---|
| Charles J. Greve & Co., Agent | Roe Johnson, Inc. |
| for the Doe Building | |
| 717 Liberty Avenue, Pittsburgh, | Suite 500 Doe Building |
| Pa. 00000 | 100 Main Street, Pittsburgh, Pa. 00000 |

26. PROVISIONS BINDING

Except as herein otherwise expressly provided, the terms and provisions hereof shall be binding upon and shall insure to the benefit of the heirs, executors, administrators, successors, and permitted assigns, respectively, of Lessors and Lessee. The reference contained to successors and assigns of Lessee is not intended to constitute a consent to assignment by Lessors, but has reference only to those instances in which Lessors may have given written consent to a particular assignment.

27. CAPTIONS OF ARTICLES

The captions of the articles throughout this Lease are for convenience and reference only, and the words contained therein shall in no way be held to explain, modify, amplify, or aid in the interpretation, construction, or meaning of the provisions of this instrument.

28. ENTIRE AGREEMENT

This writing contains the entire agreement between the parties hereto, and no agent, representative, salesman, or officer of Lessors hereto has the authority to make or has made any statement, agreement, or representation, either oral or written, in connection therewith, modifying, adding, or changing the terms and conditions herein set forth. No dealings between the parties or custom shall be permitted to contradict various additions or to modify the terms hereof. No modifications of this Lease shall be binding unless such modifications shall be in writing and signed by the parties hereto. IN WITNESS WHEREOF, and intending to be legally bound hereby, the parties have set their hands and seals to this Lease this 20th day of April, 1982.

WITNESS:                                                    THE DOE BUILDING

_____    By _____
                                                        Charles J. Greve & Co., Agent
        (CORPORATE SEAL OF LESSEE)

_____    By __ROE JOHNSON, INC._____
Secretary of the Corporation               President

DOE BUILDING
RULES AND REGULATIONS
EXHIBIT A

1. The streets, sidewalks, entrances, halls, passages, elevators, and stairways shall not be obstructed by Lessee, or used by it for any purpose other than for ingress and egress.

2. Toilet rooms, water closets, and other water apparatus shall not be used for any purpose other than those for which they were constructed.

3. Lessee shall not do anything in the leased premises or in the Real Estate, or bring or keep anything therein, that will in any way increase or tend to increase the risk of fire or the rate of fire insurance, or that shall conflict with the regulations of the Fire Department or the fire laws, or with any insurance policy on the Real Estate or any part thereof, or that shall in any way conflict with any law, ordinance, rule, or regulation affecting the occupancy and use of said leased

premises, which are or may hereafter be enacted or promulgated by any public authority or by the Board of Fire Underwriters.

4. In order to ensure proper use and care of the premises, Lessee shall not be permitted to:

(a) Keep animals or birds on the leased premises.

(b) Use the leased premises as sleeping apartments.

(c) Allow any sign, advertisement, or notice to be fixed to the Real Estate, inside or outside, without the written consent of Lessors, which may be refused for any reason. Lessor shall have sole and absolute discretion on sign matters.

(d) Commit improper noises or disturbances of any kind. Sing, or play or operate any musical instrument, radio or television without first securing consent of Lessors.

(e) Mark or defile elevators, water closets, toilet rooms, walls, windows, doors, or any part of the Real Estate.

(f) Allow any article to be placed upon window ledges or dropped from windows, skylights, or stairways; or throw dirt or other substances into halls, stairways, elevators, or light-wells of Real Estate.

(g) Cover or obstruct any window, skylight, door, or transom that reflects light.

(h) Fasten any article, drill holes, or drive nails or screws into the walls, floors, or partitions; nor shall the same be painted, papered, or otherwise covered or in any way marked or broken.

(i) Operate any machinery within the leased premises, other than desktop equipment, or manufacture any commodity or prepare or dispense any foods or beverages in the leased premises without the written consent of Lessors.

(j) Interfere with the heating apparatus if it is provided by Lessors.

(k) Allow anyone but the janitor of Lessors to clean the leased premises. Lessors shall not be responsible for damage to furniture or other effects of Lessee caused by janitor or any other person.

(l) Leave leased premises without closing windows, locking doors, and extinguishing all lights.

5. Lessors shall not be responsible to Lessee for any nonobservance of rules and regulations on the part of other tenants.

6. Lessors shall have the right to prohibit any advertising by Lessee that, in their opinion, tends to impair the reputation of the Real Estate or its desirability as a building for offices, and upon written notice from Lessors, said Lessee shall refrain from or discontinue such advertising.

7. Lessee shall not purchase spring water, ice, towels, or other like service from any company or person not approved by Lessors.

8. Lessors reserve the right to designate the time when and method whereby freight, furniture, safes, goods, merchandise, and other articles may be brought into, moved, or taken from the Real Estate and the leased premises.

9. Lessors reserve the right to inspect the leased premises at any reasonable time, and in case of emergency, to enter the leased premises.

10. Lessee shall, upon termination or cancellation of this lease, deliver to Lessors all keys to the leased premises, including keys to Toilet Rooms.

11. Lessors shall have the right to make such other and further reasonable rules and regulations as, in the judgment of Lessors, may from time to time be needed for the safety, care, and cleanliness of the leased premises and for the preservation of good order therein.

[1]49 Am. Jur. 2d Landlord and Tenant, paras. 193 and 198.
[2]Check your state statute as to the validity and enforceability of "confession of judgment" clause.

## FORM VIIA 1.07

### (Lease of restaurant concession in a building)[1]

### CONCESSION AGREEMENT

THIS AGREEMENT made this 6th day of December, 1982, by and between DOE DEPARTMENT STORES, INC., a Pennsylvania corporation having its principal place of business at 100 Penn Avenue, Pittsburgh, Pennsylvania 00000 (herein called "Lessor"), and MODERN FOODS, INC., a Delaware corporation having its principal place of business at 100 Main Street, Wilmington, Delaware 00000 (herein called "Concessionaire"), WITNESSETH:

WHEREAS, Lessor owns and operates a department store and branches of same in Allegheny County, Pennsylvania; and

WHEREAS, Lessee operates a chain of restaurants in office buildings and department stores throughout the Eastern United States and is prepared, equipped, and qualified to operate a full-menu restaurant suitable to the ordinary needs of a city department store at prices comparable to those generally prevailing in the Greater Pittsburgh Area; and

WHEREAS, the operation of a restaurant in the Allegheny County stores owned by Lessor is an essential service to the customers of Lessor's department store, and its branches; and

WHEREAS, it is the intent and desire of Lessor that its customers and employees shall have a suitable restaurant in the Lessor's stores available for their patronage;

IT IS THEREFORE AGREED AS FOLLOWS:

1. *Consideration and grant of concession.* In consideration of the mutual promises and covenants contained herein, Lessor leases to Concessionaire and Concessionaire hires and takes from Lessor that part of the basement premises presently used as a restaurant in the Doe Department Store at 100 Penn Avenue, Pittsburgh, Pennsylvania, and that part of the stores located in the East Mall located on East Drive, Eastown, Allegheny County, and in West Mall, West Drive, Westown, Allegheny County, Pennsylvania, as more particularly described and designated in Rider A, attached hereto and made part hereof, together with the improvements and furniture and equipment therein, and certain attendant privileges and rights as spcifically set forth in Rider A and in this Agreement (herein called the Demised Premises).

2. *Conditions of the grant.* This grant is conditioned on the Concessionaire's obtaining licenses to operate the existing restaurants from the proper government authorities. Alcoholic beverages may be sold in the restaurants if Concessionaire duly obtains a liquor license from the proper government authorities for the retail sale of alcohol in any of the restaurants. It is warranted by Lessor that a duly licensed restaurant without a liquor license is being operated by Lessor on each of the Demised Premises at the time of the execution of this Agreement. Lessor makes no representation as to the availability of or the ability of Concessionaire to obtain a retail liquor license for any or all of the restaurants.

3. *Alterations, additions, or replacements.*

(a) Lessor shall provide and pay for all alterations, additions, or replacements to the Demised Premises (herein called "Improvements"), including, but not limited to, interior partitions, wiring, plumbing, lighting and plumbing fixtures, decorations, and all other fixtures and equipment described in Rider B, attached hereto and made part hereof.

(b) Concessionaire shall provide all additional equipment, furniture, furnishings, and fixtures necessary in the proper conduct of Concessionaire's restaurant business.

(c) Concessionaire shall not dispose of any of the present furniture, fixtures, or equipment listed in Rider A, without the written consent of the Lessor, as title to present furniture, fixtures, or equipment shall remain in Lessor at all times during this Agreement.

(d) If Concessionaire desires to make Improvements other than those shown in Rider B, it shall submit final plans and specifications, layout and architectural renderings for the Improvement(s) for the written approval of Lessor. Concessionaire shall also obtain prior written approval from Lessor for the installation, at Concessionaire's expense, of any equipment that requires new electrical or plumbing connections or changes in those installed on the Demised Premises on the date of occupancy as modified pursuant to Rider B.

(e) All Concessionaire's interest and title to all additional furniture, fixtures, or equipment provided by Concessionaire pursuant to this Paragraph 3 shall immediately vest in Lessor upon its installation or placement on the leased premises, whether or not it is permanently affixed to the building.

4. *Services to be performed by Concessionaire.*

(a) *Type of operation.* Concessionaire shall furnish restaurant service and alcoholic beverage service, if Concessionaire is duly licensed, on a fair, legal, reasonable, and nondiscriminatory basis to the public and employees of Lessor's department store in each of the Demised Premises. Service shall be prompt, courteous, and efficient, and shall be adequate to meet the demands for the service at each of the Demised Premises. Concessionaire shall maintain each restaurant, at its sole expense, in a first-class manner comparable to other department store restaurants in the Greater Pittsburgh Area, and shall keep the each and all of the Demised Premises in a safe, clean, orderly, and inviting condition at all times satisfactory to Lessor. All services provided by Concessionaire shall comply with all federal, state, and municipal laws and regulations. Concessionaire shall obtain and maintain continuously all necessary licenses for the operation of its business hereunder.

(b) *Hours of operation.* Concessionaire shall, in the operation of its restaurant business hereunder, maintain and make available to the public and employees of Lessor's department stores an adequate number of tables, food, legally permissible beverages, and other usual restaurant services from the hours of 11:00 A.M. to 4:00 P.M. each day Monday through Saturday each week of the year, except on the following holidays: New Year's Day, 4th of July, Thanksgiving Day, and Christmas.

(c) *Personnel.*

(1) Concessionaire shall at all times retain an active, qualified, competent, and experienced manager on one of the Demised Premises to supervise the concession operations on all premises, and who is authorized to represent and act for the Concessionaire in all respects except to modify the terms of this Agreement.

(2) Concessionaire shall require all its employees to be properly dressed or uniformed at all times; they shall be neat and courteous at all times and shall not use improper language or act in a loud, boisterous, or other improper or illegal manner.

(3) The performance of these personnel requirements by the Concessionaire shall be determined at the sole discretion of the Lessor. Concessionaire shall replace any employee or manager whose conduct Lessor determines is detrimental to the best interests of the Lessor's department store business.

(d) *Quality, selection of food, and price.* Proposed sample menus and prices of food and beverages have been submitted in writing to Lessor by Concessionaire, and are incorporated herein by reference for the purpose of defining the quality, selection, and price of food to be supplied in Concessionaires restaurants on the Demised Premises. It is recognized that the cost of food, supplies, and service from the sample menus and lists may increase during the term of this Agreement. It is agreed that any increase in cost exceeding Fifteen Percent (15%) shall be approved in writing by Lessor. Any decrease in selection or quality shall be reasonable in comparison to selections and quality available in similar restaurants in the Greater Pittsburgh Area.

(e) *Operation costs.* All costs of the restaurant operations shall be paid by Concessionaire. Those costs shall include maintenance, repairs, utilities, liability and casualty insurance policies in which Lessor shall be named as additional insured, and any and all taxes, cost of permits and licenses, and alterations or improvements to the Demised Premises during the term required by law in the operation of the restaurant business on the Demised Premises.

5. *Term of Agreement and renewal.* The term of this Agreement shall be for a period of three (3) years beginning January 1, 1983; but Concessionaire, at its option, may renew this Agreement on the same terms and conditions for an additional period of three (3) years.

6. *Percentage rent.*

(a) Concessionaire shall pay to Lessor a minimum rental of Thirty-six Thousand Dollars ($36,000) per year, payable monthly in advance beginning January 1, 1983. Concessionaire shall pay an additional rental of Five Percent (5%) of gross sales of the combined restaurants in excess of One Hundred Fifty Thousand Dollars ($150,000) that are made on the Demised Premises during each lease year beginning January 1, 1983.

(b) A report of sales for the preceding lease year shall be given to Lessor by Concessionaire within thirty (30) days after the close of the lease year, and if the report discloses that gross sales were sufficient to require a payment of the additional percentage rent hereunder, a payment for that amount shall accompany that report.

(c) Concessionaire shall keep accurate accounts and records of its sales under this Agreement, and shall not unreasonably withhold permission of Lessor or its representative to examine Concessionaire's records of sales of the restaurants on the Demised Premises at any time during the term of this Agreement or within one (1) year after termination hereof for any reason, including the lapse of the time of this Agreement.

7. *Benefit and obligations.* All the terms, covenants, and promises of this Agreement shall inure to the benefit of and be binding upon the successors and assigns of the parties hereto.

8. *Modification.* No modification, release, discharge, or waiver of any provision hereof shall be of any force or effect unless it is in writing signed by both parties or their duly authorized agent, which agent shall be only an officer or officers of the respective parties and not merely an employee of the parties, except for the General Manager of the Lessor, who is hereby given the authority and power to act and sign for the Lessor in such matters.

9. *Governing law.* This Agreement shall be governed and interpreted by and pursuant to the laws of the Commonwealth of Pennsylvania.

IN WITNESS WHEREOF, the parties hereto have duly authorized and have caused the signing and sealing of this Agreement on their behalf in Pittsburgh, Pennsylvania, on the day and year above written.

| (CORPORATE SEAL) | DOE DEPARTMENT STORES, INC. |
|---|---|
| (Richard Roe) | By (Richard Smith) |
| Secretary of the Corporation | General Manager |
| (CORPORATE SEAL) | MODERN FOODS, INC. |
| (Charles Coe) | By (Peter Coe) |
| Secretary of the Corporation | President |

(Attach Riders A and B.)

[1] *49 Am. Jur. 2d Landlord and Tenant*, paras. 162–165, 179; and *40 Am. Jur. 2d Hotels, Motels and Restaurants*, paras. 28–48.

## FORM VIIA 1.08

### (Shopping center or shopping mall lease for retail store)[1]

### LEASE

THIS LEASE AGREEMENT, made this 1st day of April, 1983, by and between SUNCOAST ENTERPRISES, INC., a Florida corporation with offices at Suite 800 Big Building, St. Petersburg, Florida 00000 (herein called "Landlord"), and DOE'S SHOES, INC., a Florida corporation (herein called "Tenant"), provides as follows:

1. *DESCRIPTION AND GRANT*

(a) Landlord leases to Tenant and Tenant rents from Landlord those certain premises, a part of the Shopping Center known as the Suncoast Mall (herein called the "Shopping Center"), located on East Boulevard and N.W. 90th Avenue, Middletown, Middle County, Florida, which premises are more particularly described as follows:

A storeroom having an area of approximately two thousand (2,000) square feet and storage space having approximately five hundred (500) square feet (herein called the "Leased Premises").

(b) The Shopping Center consists of that portion of the property owned by the Landlord or controlled by the Landlord under a leasehold interest.

(c) The boundaries and location of the Leased Premises are outlined in red on a diagram of the Shopping Center, which is attached hereto as Exhibit A.

(d) Landlord may increase or reduce the number or size of interior retail spaces and may change the number, dimensions, or locations of the walks, buildings, parking areas, and other common facilities in any manner as Landlord shall deem proper, and Landlord reserves the right to make alterations or additions to, and to build additional stories on, the building in which the Leased Premises are contained and to add buildings adjoining the same or elsewhere in the Shopping Center.

(e) Use and occupancy by Tenant of the Leased Premises shall include the use in common with others of the common areas and facilities, as hereinafter more fully described and provided.

(f) Nothing herein contained shall be construed as a grant or rental by Landlord to Tenant of the roof and exterior walls of the building or buildings of which the Leased Premises form a part, or of the walks and other common areas beyond the Leased Premises.

(g) Landlord shall have the right to relocate various facilities and premises within the Shopping Center if Landlord shall determine such relocation to be in the best interest of the development of the Shopping Center; but Landlord shall not have the right to relocate the Leased Premises after the execution of this Lease, without the written consent of the Tenant.

2. *Term*

The term of the Lease shall be for five (5) years commencing upon the earlier of the following dates: June 1, 1983, or the date five (5) days after the existing tenant has vacated the Leased Premises and it is ready for occupancy. In the event Tenant shall take possession of the Leased Premises on a day other than the first day of the month, then the rent shall be immediately paid for the remainder of that month, prorated on the basis of a thirty (30)-day month, and the term of this Lease shall be extended for the number of days from the commencement date to the first day of the month next succeeding.

3. *AFFIDAVIT OF LEASE STATUS*

Tenant shall, upon request by Landlord, execute and deliver to Landlord a written affidavit (1) ratifying this Lease; (2) expressing the commencement and termination dates thereof; (3) certifying that this Lease is in full force and effect and has not been assigned, modified, supplemented, or amended (except by such writings as shall be stated); (4) that all conditions under this Lease to be performed by Landlord have been satisfied; (5) that there are no defenses or offsets against the enforcement of this Lease by the Landlord or stating those claimed by Tenant; (6) the amount of advance rental, if any (or none, if such is the case), paid by Tenant; (7) the date to which rental has been paid; and (8) the amount of security deposited with Landlord. Such declaration shall be executed and delivered by Tenant from time to time as may be requested by Landlord. Landlord's mortgage lenders and/or purchasers shall be entitled to rely upon the affidavit.

4. *USE OF LEASED PREMISES*

Tenant shall use the Leased Premises solely for the purpose of conducting the retail business of selling footwear and accessories. Tenant shall not use or permit or suffer the use of the Leased Premises for any other business or purpose.

5. RENT[2] (Minimum, Percentage, Additional, and Past Due)

## I. MINIMUM RENT

(a) The fixed minimum rent during the term of this Lease shall be payable by Tenant at the annual rate of Thirty-six Hundred Dollars ($3,600), payable in advance in equal monthly installments of Three Hundred Dollars ($300) on the first day of each month.

(b) The phrase "minimum rent" shall mean the fixed minimum rent above specified, without any setoffs or deductions whatsoever and without any prior demand being required therefor. Further, the fixed minimum rent shall be increased by any sales or rent tax that is or may be chargeable against the Leased Premises, the minimum rent, the additional rent, and/or the percentage rent as herein defined.

## II. PERCENTAGE RENT

(a) In addition to the minimum rent and all other sums specified herein, and as part of the total rent to be paid, Tenant shall pay to Landlord quarterly, as percentage rent for each lease year or fractional period thereof, a sum equal to One Percent (1%) of the Tenant's gross sales (as hereinafter defined) for each lease year in excess of Three Hundred Thousand Dollars ($300,000). Each lease year shall be considered as an independent accounting period for the purpose of computing the amount of percentage rent, if any. The amount of gross sales of any preceding lease year shall not be carried over into any other lease year.

(b) The percentage rent shall be determined and paid quarterly within fifteen (15) days after the last day of each three (3)-month period during the term of the Lease (or fractional period prior to the commencement of the first lease year or subsequent to the end of the last lease year) with respect to gross sales during the preceding three (3)-month period.

(c) The amount of the payment of percentage rent shall be equal to One Percent (1%) of the gross sales for said period in excess of three-twelfths of $300,000.

(d) At the end of each lease year, the balance of percentage rental due, if any, shall be adjusted to a yearly basis and shall be paid within thirty (30) days after the end of each lease year. If the total amount of rent paid by Tenant exceeds the total amount of fixed and percentage rent required to be paid by Tenant during each lease year, Tenant shall receive a credit equivalent to such excess, which may be deducted by Tenant from the next accruing payment of percentage rent.

## III. ADDITIONAL RENT

(a) In addition to the foregoing minimum and percentage rent, all other payments to be made by Tenant, either to Landlord or to the Merchant's Association as provided herein, shall be deemed to be and shall become additional rent hereunder, whether or not the same be designated as such; and shall be due and payable on demand or together with the next succeeding installment of rent, whichever shall first occur, together with interest thereon at the then prevailing legal rate; and Landlord shall have the same remedies for failure to pay the same as for any other nonpayment of rent.

(b) Landlord, at its election, shall have the right to pay or do any act that requires the expenditure of any sums of money by reason of the failure or neglect of Tenant to perform any of the provisions of this Lease, and in the event Landlord shall at its election pay such sums or do such acts requiring the expenditure of moneys, Tenant agrees to pay Landlord, upon demand, all such sums, and the sum so paid by Landlord, together with interest thereon, in the amount of Twelve Percent (12%) per annum, shall be deemed additional rent hereunder.

## IV. PAST-DUE RENT

If Tenant shall fail to pay, when the same is due and payable, any minimum rent, any percentage rent, additional rent, or other amounts or charges to be paid to Landlord by Tenant, as provided in this Lease, such unpaid amount shall bear interest from the due date thereof to the date of payment at the rate of Twelve Percent (12%) per annum until paid.

### 6. DEFINITION OF "GROSS SALES"

The term "gross sales," as used herein, is the entire amount charged by Tenant and any subtenant, concessionaire, or licensee, on all sales of merchandise made or services rendered in, at, or from the Leased Premises, and sales wherever made of merchandise stored on the Leased Premises, or any business conducted from the Leased Premises, whether made on a cash basis, or on credit, paid or unpaid, collected or uncollected, including deposits not refunded to customers and the amount of any orders received at or solicited from the Leased Premises although such orders may be filled elsewhere.

The term "gross sales" shall not include, and Tenant shall be entitled to deduct from gross sales to the extent Tenant has included them therein:

(a) Any sales or excise tax imposed by any government authority and added to the price of a sale or service or absorbed therein, and collectable from the customer and in turn payable by Tenant to such governmental authority;

(b) If Tenant operates additional stores, transfers of merchandise from the Leased Premises to warehouses or other stores of Tenant, where the transfer was made for the convenient operation of the Tenant's business and not to consummate or to deprive Landlord of the amount of a sale made in, at, or from the Leased Premises;

(c) The amount of any returns of goods to suppliers to Tenant;

(d) The amount of any credit or refund for any merchandise returned or exchanged or any allowance made for the loss of or damage to merchandise sold;

(e) For the purpose of determining "gross sales" hereunder, Tenant shall prepare and keep, for a period of not less than two (2) years following the end of each lease year, adequate books and records, including, but not limited to, inventories, purchases, and receipts of merchandise, and all sales and other transactions by Tenant. Tenant shall record at the time of sale each receipt from sales or other transactions, whether for cash or on credit, in a sealed cash register or registers having a cumulative total. Tenant shall keep, for at least two (2) years following the end of each lease year, all pertinent original sales records, which records shall include (1) cash register tapes; (2) serially numbered sales slips; (3) mail orders; (4) telephone orders; (5) settlement report sheets of transactions with subtenants, concessionaires, and licenses; (6) records showing that merchandise returned by customers was purchased by such customers; (7) receipts or other records of merchandise taken out on approval; (8) such other records that would normally be examined and required to be kept by an independent accountant pursuant to accepted auditing standards in performing an audit of Tenant's gross sales; and (9) all income, sales, and occupation tax returns.

### 7. TENANT'S REPORTS AND AUDIT ON DEMAND OF LANDLORD

(a) Tenant shall submit to Landlord, on or before the 15th day following the end of each quarter during the term hereof (including the 15th day of the quarter following the end of the term), a written statement signed by Tenant and certified by it to be true and correct, showing the amount of gross sales during the preceding quarter. Tenant shall submit to Landlord, on or before the 30th day following the end of each lease year, a written statement signed by Tenant and certified by it to be true and correct, setting forth the amount of gross sales during the preceding lease year. The statements referred to herein shall be in such form and style and contain such details and breakdowns as Landlord may reasonably require.

The acceptance by Landlord of payments of percentage rent or reports thereon by Tenant shall be without prejudice and shall not constitute a waiver of Landlord's right to examine Tenant's books and records of its gross sales and inventories of merchandise.

(b) Landlord shall have the right to cause, upon five (5) days' written notice to Tenant, a complete audit by a certified public accountant of Tenant's entire business affairs and of all records, including those specified in the preceding two Paragraphs, and Tenant shall make all such records available for said examination at the Leased Premises. If the results of such audit shall show that Tenant's statement of gross sales or other information required hereunder for any period has been understated by Three Percent (3%) or more, then Tenant shall pay Landlord the cost of such audit in addition to any deficiency payment required. A report of the findings of Landlord's certified public accountant shall be binding and conclusive upon Landlord and Tenant. The furnishing by Tenant of any grossly inaccurate statement shall constitute a breach of this Lease. Any information obtained as a result of such audit shall be held in strict confidence by Landlord, except in any proceeding or action to collect the cost of such audit or deficiency or with respect to a prospective sale, mortgage, lease, or leaseback of the Shopping Center.

8. *PLACE OF PAYMENTS AND REPORTS*

All payments required to be paid to Landlord hereunder and all reports required to be made by Tenant to Landlord shall be delivered to the office of Landlord set forth above without any prior demand for the same, and without deduction, withholding, or offset.

9. *CONSTRUCTION AND REPAIRS*

(a) Except as otherwise provided herein, Tenant leases the Leased Premises "AS IS."

(b) Tenant is responsible for the installation of all trade fixtures in accordance with the provisions herein, at Tenant's sole cost.

(c) Tenant shall not do any construction work or alterations, nor shall Tenant install any equipment other than its usual trade fixtures, without first obtaining Landlord's written approval and consent. Such consent shall not be unreasonably withheld, but the consent may be conditioned upon the Tenant's supplying reasonable completion and/or payment bonds and appropriate insurance.

(d) Landlord shall not be required to make any repairs or improvements of any kind upon the Leased Premises except for necessary structural repairs, including plumbing and wiring inside of interior walls that has been installed by Landlord. Tenant shall, at its own cost and expense, maintain and make necessary repairs to the interior of the Leased Premises, and the fixtures and equipment therein and appurtenant hereto, including the exterior and interior windows, window frames, doors, doorframes, and entrances, storefronts, signs, showcases, floor coverings, nonstructural interior walls, columns, and partitions; lighting, electrical equipment, plumbing and sewerage facilities, and equipment protruding from interior walls; and any heating and/or air-conditioning equipment installed by Tenant.

(e) If Tenant refuses or neglects to make repairs required hereunder, or if Landlord is required to make exterior or structural repairs by reason of Tenant's negligent acts or omissions, Landlord shall have the right, but shall not be obligated, to make such repairs on behalf of and for the account of Tenant. In such event, such work shall be paid for in full by Tenant as additional rent promptly upon receipt of a bill therefor.

(f) Should any mechanic's or other lien be filed against the Leased Premises or any part thereof for any reason whatsoever by reason of Tenant's acts or omissions or because of a claim against Tenant, Tenant shall cause the same to be canceled and discharged of record by bond or otherwise within ten (10) days after written notice by Landlord.

(g) If required by the Landlord, the Tenant shall purchase identification signs for the exterior of the Leased Premises, said signs to be of a size and design to be approved in writing by Landlord, and installed at the place designated by Landlord. Other than the foregoing, Tenant shall not place or suffer to be placed or maintain any sign, awning, or canopy in, upon, or outside the Leased Premises or in the Shopping Center or within a half mile of the Shopping Center; nor shall Tenant place in the display window of the Leased Premises any sign, decoration, lettering, or advertising matter of any kind without first obtaining Landlord's approval and consent in each instance. Tenant shall maintain any such signs or other installation as may be approved in good condition and repair.

(h) Landlord shall have the right to place, maintain, and repair all utility equipment of any kind in, upon or under the Leased Premises as may be necessary for the servicing of the Leased Premises and other portions of the Shopping Center. Landlord shall also have the right to enter the Leased Premises at all times to inspect or to exhibit the same to prospective purchasers, mortgagees, and tenants and to make such repairs, additions, alterations, or improvements as Landlord may deem desirable. Landlord shall be allowed to take all material in, to, and upon said premises that may be required therefor without the same constituting an eviction of Tenant in whole or in part, and the rents reserved shall in no wise abate while said work is in progress by reason of loss or interruption of Tenant's business or otherwise, and Tenant shall have no claim for damages. If Tenant shall not be personally present to permit an entry into said premises when for any reason an entry therein shall be permissible. Landlord may enter the same by a master key or by the use of force without incurring liability therefor and without in any manner affecting the obligations of this Lease. The provisions of this Paragraph shall in no wise be construed to impose upon Landlord any obligation whatsoever for the maintenance or repair of the Leased Premises except as otherwise specifically provided herein.

(i) During the six (6) months prior to the expiration of this Lease or renewal thereof, Landlord may place a reasonable "To Let" sign on the Leased Premises.

10. *OPERATION OF BUSINESS BY TENANT*

Tenant shall:

(a) conduct its business in the entire Leased Premises excepting as provided in (h);

(b) remain open for business during such customary business days and hours as the majority of the tenants located within the Shopping Center are open for business or for such further days or additional hours as required by Landlord;

(c) adequately staff its store with sufficient employees to handle the maximum business and carry sufficient stock of merchandise of such size, character, and quality as necessary to accomplish the same;

(d) maintain reasonably attractive displays of merchandise in the display windows of the Leased Premises, if any;

(e) keep the Leased Premises and exterior and interior portions of windows, doors, and all other glass or plate-glass fixtures in a neat, clean, sanitary, and safe condition,

(f) warehouse, store, or stock only such goods, wares, and merchandise as Tenant intends to offer for sale at retail from the Leased Premises;

(g) if the Demised Premises contain a mezzanine, the use thereof for storage purposes or sales purposes shall be subject to Landlord's written approval;

(h) except for mezzanine space, use for office or other nonselling purposes only such space as is reasonably required for Tenant's business, but in no event shall the space used for such purposes exceed Five Percent (5%) of the square foot area of the Leased Premises;

(i) neither solicit business or distribute advertising matter in the parking or other common areas;

(j) not change the advertising name of the business operated in the Leased Premises without the written permission of Landlord; and

(k) use the insignia or other identifying mark of the Shopping Center designated by Landlord in Tenant's advertising, whether printed or visual, and make reference to the name of the Shopping Center in each instance of audio advertising.

(l) Tenant shall, at its own cost and expense: install fire extinguishers in accordance with insurance and governmental requirements; comply with all governmental laws, ordinances, orders, and regulations affecting the Leased Premises now in force or that hereafter may be in force; and shall comply with and execute all rules, requirements, and regulations of the Board of Fire Underwriters, Landlord's insurance companies, and other organizations establishing insurance rates;

(m) not suffer, permit, or commit any waste or nuisance;

(n) not conduct any auction, distress, fire, or bankruptcy sale;

(o) abide by and conform to reasonable rules and regulations promulgated in writing from time to time by Lessor and delivered to Lessee at the Leased Premises, the first Rules and Regulations being attached hereto, made part hereof, and marked Exhibit B.

(p) not open another store for any similar or competing business within a radius of three (3) miles from the outside boundary of the Shopping Center. Landlord, for breach of this covenant and in addition to any other remedy otherwise available, may require that all sales made from any such other store be included in the computation of the percentage rent as though said sales had actually been made from the Leased Premises.

11. *UTILITIES*

(a) From the date the work of the Landlord in the Leased Premises is substantially complete or from the date Tenant begins its work in the Leased Premises, whichever first occurs, Tenant agrees to pay for all public utility services rendered or furnished to the Leased Premises, including heat, water, gas, electricity, sewer rental, sewage treatment facilities, and the like, together with all taxes levied or other charges on such utilities and governmental charges based on utility consumption. Landlord will provide electricity (and water if necessary) to the Leased Premises. Tenant will pay all charges, as additional rent to Landlord, within ten (10) days after mailing by Landlord to Tenant of statements therefor, at the applicable rates based on Tenant's demand determined by Landlord from time to time, which Landlord agrees shall be reasonable and not in excess of the public utility rates for the same service if applicable.

(b) Landlord will provide, install, operate, and maintain a basic heating and air-conditioning system covering the entire Shopping Center, including the Leased Premises and the common facilities. Heating and air conditioning shall be thermostatically controlled in the Leased Premises, and same shall be operated so that the temperature within the Leased Premises will be within a comfortable range established by Landlord. Landlord will also provide, install, and maintain a sprinkler system in the Shopping Center. Tenant agrees to reimburse Landlord for its cost in operating and maintaining said heating and air-conditioning and sprinkler systems by paying, as additional rent, an annual charge equal to its pro rata share of said cost as provided in Paragraph 14 (b) hereof, except that the denominator of any fraction used in computing said pro rata share shall be reduced by the amount of space separately heated, ventilated, and air-conditioned by the Tenant.

(c) Landlord reserves and shall at all times have the right to cut off and discontinue, on five (5) days' written notice to Tenant, water, electricity, heating, and air conditioning, or other utilities and services, when Tenant has failed to pay any amount in rents or otherwise in accordance with the terms of this Lease. Landlord shall not be liable to Tenant for any interruption in service of water, electricity, heating, air conditioning, or other utilities and services caused by unavoidable delay, by the making of any necessary repairs or improvements, or by any cause beyond Landlord's reasonable control.

(d) Tenant agrees that it will not install any equipment that will exceed or overload the capacity of any utility facilities, and that if any equipment installed by Tenant shall require additional utility facilities, the same shall be installed at Tenant's expense in accordance with plans and specifications to be approved in writing by Landlord.

12. *TAX ESCALATION*

(a) Landlord shall pay in the first instance all real property taxes, including extraordinary and/or special assessments (and all costs and fees incurred in contesting the same), hereinafter collectively referred to as "Taxes," that may be levied or assessed by the lawful taxing authorities against the land, buildings, and all other improvements in the Shopping Center.

(b) In the event those Taxes, in any lease year after the first lease year, shall exceed the Taxes assessed on the Shopping Center for the first lease year, Tenant shall pay to Landlord that portion of such excess equal to the product obtained by multiplying said excess by a fraction, the numerator of which shall be the gross leasable area of the Leased Premises, and the denominator of which shall be the gross leasable area of the Shopping Center as a whole.

(c) Tenant's proportionate share of those Taxes shall be paid in full as additional rent within twenty (20) days after demand therefor by Landlord. A tax bill submitted by Landlord to Tenant shall be sufficient evidence of the amount of taxes assessed or levied against the parcel or real property to which such bill relates. Should the taxing authorities include in such Taxes the value of any improvements made by Tenant, or include machinery, equipment, fixtures, inventory or other personal property or assets of Tenant, then Tenant shall also pay the entire personal and real estate taxes for such items.

(d) Should any governmental taxing authority, acting under any present or future law, ordinance, or regulation, levy, assess, or impose a tax, excise, and/or assessment (other than an income or franchise tax) upon or against or in any way related to the land and buildings comprising the Shopping Center, either by way of substitution for or in additional to any existing tax on land and buildings or otherwise, Tenant shall be responsible for and shall pay to Landlord, as additional rent, its proportionate share as set forth above of such tax, excise, and/or assessment.

13. *LICENSE TO USE COMMON AREAS*

In order to establish that the Shopping Center, and any portion thereof, is and will continue to remain private property, the Landlord shall have unrestricted right, in the Landlord's sole discretion, with respect to the entire Shopping Center, and/or any portion thereof owned or controlled by the Landlord, to close the same to the general public for one (1) day in each calendar year, and in connection therewith, to seal off all entrances to the Shopping Center, or any portion thereof. All common areas and facilities that Tenant may be permitted to use and occupy are to be used and occupied under a revocable license, and if any such license be revoked or if the amount of such areas be changed or diminished, Landlord shall not be subject to any liability, nor shall Tenant be entitled to any compensation or diminution or abatement of rent, nor shall revocation or diminution of such areas be deemed constructive or actual eviction.

14. *COMMON AREA MAINTENANCE AND COST*

(a) All common areas and other facilities in or about the Shopping Center provided by Landlord shall be subject to the exclusive control and management of Landlord. Landlord shall have the right to construct, maintain, and operate lighting and other facilities on all said areas and improvements; to police the same; to change the area, level, location, and arrangement of parking areas and other facilities; to build multistory parking facilities; to restrict parking by Tenant, their officers, agents, and employees, to enforce parking charges (by operation of meters or otherwise), and in such event the net proceeds from such charges after deduction of the cost of the same shall be applied toward the reduction of maintaining the parking facilities; to close all or any portion of said areas or facilities to such extent as may be legally sufficient to prevent a dedication thereof or the accrual of any right to any person or the public therein; to close temporarily all or any portion of the parking areas or facilities to discourage noncustomer parking. Landlord shall operate and maintain the common facilities in such manner as Landlord in its reasonable discretion shall determine, and Landlord shall have the full right and authority to employ and discharge all personnel with respect thereto.

(b) The Tenant agrees to pay to the Landlord, as additional rent, that proportion of the annual total cost incurred by the Landlord in operating and maintaining the common areas in the Shopping Center, as the gross leasable area of the premises demised to the Tenant shall bear to the gross leasable area of the Shopping Center as a whole. Said sum shall be payable monthly during each rent year of the term of this Lease immediately after presentation of a bill therefor by the Landlord.

(c) For purposes of the preceding Paragraph, the cost incurred by the Landlord in the operation and maintenance of the common areas shall include, without limitation, the cost of gardening and landscaping; the cost of all Landlord's insurance, including but not limited to, bodily injury, public liability, property damage liability, automobile insurance, sign insurance, and any other insurance carried by Landlord for the common areas in limits determined by Landlord; assessments; repairs; line repainting; rental of signs and equipment; lighting; storm water control; sanitary control; removal of snow, trash, rubbish, garbage, and other refuse; depreciation of machinery and equipment used in such maintenance; repair and/or replacement; the cost of personnel to implement such services to direct parking and to police the common areas and facilities; and Fifteen Percent (15%) of all of the foregoing costs to cover Landlord's administrative and overhead costs. "Common Facilities" and "Common Areas," whether such terms are used individually or collectively, shall mean all areas, space, equipment, signs, and special services provided by Landlord for the common or joint use and benefit of the Tenants and occupants of the Shopping Center, and their employees, agents, servants, customers, and other invitees, including, without limitation, parking areas, access roads, driveways, retaining walls, landscaped areas, truck serviceways or tunnels, loading docks, pedestrian malls (enclosed or open), courts, stairs, ramps, and sidewalks, comfort and first-aid stations, washrooms, community hall or auditorium (if any), and parcel pickup stations.

15. *INSURANCE*

(a) Existing structures, new structures, and structural repairs, whether performed or paid for by Landlord or Tenant, shall be insured by Landlord against fire and such other risks as are from time to time included in standard extended coverage endorsements in an amount equal to at least Eighty Percent (80%) of full insurable value thereof.

(b) For all other decorations and improvements, Tenant shall maintain at its own cost and expense fire and extended coverage, vandalism, malicious mischief and special extended coverage insurance in an amount adequate to cover the cost of replacement of all decorations and improvements in the Leased Premises in the event of a loss, and Fifty Thousand Dollars ($50,000) for water or other damage.

(c) For the Leased Premises generally for any act or omissions of Tenant, its agents, contractors, employees, servants, or licensees within the Shopping Center; the Tenant shall maintain, at its own cost and expense, PUBLIC LIABILITY INSURANCE on all-occurrence basis, with minimum limits of liability in an amount of Five Hundred Thousand Dollars ($500,000) for bodily injury, personal injury, or death with respect to any one person, and One Million Dollars ($1,000,000) for bodily injury, personal injury, or death with respect to any one accident.

(d) Tenant agrees to insure and keep insured in the name of Tenant and for and in the name of Landlord, at Tenant's expense, all outside plate glass in the Demised Premises.

(e) Any and all insurance procured by Tenant as herein required shall be issued in the name of Landlord and Tenant by a company licensed to do business in the State of Florida where the Shopping Center is located, and in the event of payment of any loss covered by such policy, Landlord shall be paid first by the insurance company for its loss; and Tenant waives its right of subrogation against Landlord for any reason whatsoever (any insurance policies herein required to be procured by Tenant shall contain an express waiver of any right of subrogation by the insurance company against the Landlord).

(f) The original policies of all insurance obtained by Tenant within ten (10) days of the effective date of such policy by the insurance company. The minimum limits of any insurance coverage required herein shall not limit Tenant's liability for indemnification of Landlord hereunder.

(g) Tenant shall not stock, use, or sell any article or do anything in or about the Leased Premises that may be prohibited by Landlord's insurance policies or any endorsements or forms attached thereto, or that will increase any insurance rates and premiums on the Leased Premises, the building of which they are a part, and all other buildings in the Shopping Center.

(h) Tenant shall pay on demand any increase in premiums for Landlord's insurance that may be charged on such insurance carried by Landlord resulting from Tenant's use and occupancy of the Demised Premises or the Shopping Center, whether or not Landlord has consented to the same.

(i) In determining whether increased premiums are the result of Tenant's use, occupancy, or vacancy of the Leased Premises, a schedule issued by the organization making the rates for said premises, or any rule books issued by the rating organization or similar bodies, or by rating procedures of rules of Landlord's insurance companies shall be conclusive evidence of the several items and charges that make up the insurance rates and premiums on the Leased Premises and the Shopping Center.

(j) If due to the company of Tenant or of Tenant's failure to occupy the Leased Premises as herein provided, any insurance of Landlord or Tenant shall be canceled or increased, then Tenant shall pay on demand the increased cost of the insurance.

(k) If the Leased Premises shall be partially damaged by any casualty insurable under the Landlord's insurance policy, Landlord shall, upon receipt of the insurance proceeds, repair the same, and the minimum rent shall be abated proportionately as to that portion of the Leased Premises rendered untenantable.

(l) If the Leased Premises are rendered wholly untenantable or if the building of which they are a part, whether the Leased Premises are damaged or not, or all of the buildings that then comprise the Shopping Center should be damaged to the extent of Fifty Percent (50%) or more of the then monetary value thereof, or if any or all of the buildings or common areas of the Shopping Center are damaged, whether or not the Leased Premises are damaged to such an extent that the Shopping Center cannot, in the sole judgment of Landlord, be operated as an integral unit, then or in any of such events, Landlord may either elect to repair the damage or may cancel this Lease by notice of cancellation within one hundred eighty (180) days after such event, and thereupon this Lease shall expire, and Tenant shall vacate and surrender the Leased Premises to Landlord, and Tenant's liability for rent upon the termination of this Lease shall cease as of the day following the event or damage.

(m) In the event Landlord elects to repair the damage insurable under Landlord's policies, any abatement of rent shall end five (5) days after notice by Landlord to Tenant that the Leased Premises have been repaired. Nothing in this Paragraph shall be construed to abate percentage rent, but the computation of such rent shall be based upon the time minimum rent is to be paid as it is abated.

(n) If the damage is caused by the negligence of Tenant or its employees, agents, invitees, or concessionaires, there shall be no abatement of rent.

(o) Unless this Lease is terminated by Landlord, Tenant shall repair and refixture the interior of the Leased Premises in a manner and condition equal to that existing prior to its destruction or casualty, and the proceeds of all insurance carried by Tenant on its property and improvements shall be held in trust by Tenant for the purpose of that repair or replacement.

16. *INDEMNIFICATION AND RELEASE*

(a) Tenant shall indemnify Landlord and save it harmless from suits, actions, damages, liability and expense, loss of life, bodily or personal injury, or property damage arising from, or out of the use or occupancy of, the Leased Premises or any part thereof, or occasioned wholly or in part by any act or omission of Tenant, its agents, contractors, employees, servants, invitees, licensees, or concessionaires, including the sidewalks and common areas and facilities within the Shopping Center development, except in the case of negligence on the part of Landlord or its agents or employees.

(b) Tenant shall store its property in and shall occupy the Leased Premises and all other portions of the Shopping Center at its own risk, and hereby releases Landlord, to the full extent permitted by law, from all claims of every kind resulting in loss of life, personal or bodily injury, or property damage, any loss or damage to either the person or property of Tenant that may be occasioned by or through the acts or omissions of persons occupying adjacent, connecting, or adjoining premises.

(c) Landlord shall not be responsible or liable to Tenant for any defect, latent or otherwise, in any buildings in the Shopping Center or any of the equipment, machinery, utilities, appliances, or apparatus therein, nor shall it be responsible or liable for any injury, loss, or damage to any person or to any property of Tenant or other persons caused by or resulting from bursting, breakage, or by or from leakage, steam or snow or ice, running, backing up, seepage, or the overflow of water or sewerage in any part of said premises, or for any injury or damage caused by or resulting from any defect or act or omission in the occupancy, construction, operation, or use of the same by any person.

17. *CONDEMNATION*

(a) *Total:* If the whole of the Leased Premises shall be acquired or taken by eminent domain for any public or quasi-public use or purpose, then this Lease and the term herein shall cease and terminate as of the date of title vesting in such proceeding.

(b) *Partial:* If any part of the Leased Premises shall be taken and such partial taking shall render that portion not so taken unsuitable for the business of Tenant, then this Lease and the term hereof shall cease and terminate as aforesaid. If such partial taking is not extensive enough to render the premises unsuitable for the business of Tenant, then this Lease shall continue in effect, except that the minimum rent shall be reduced in the same proportion that the floor area of the Leased Premises (including storage space) taken bears to the original floor area leased, and Landlord shall, upon receipt of the award in condemnation, make all necessary repairs or alterations to the building in which the Leased Premises are located, so as to constitute the portion of the building not taken a complete architectural unit, but Landlord shall not be required to spend for such work an amount in excess of the net amount received by Landlord as damages for the part of the Leased Premises so taken. "Net Amount received by Landlord" shall mean that part of the award in condemnation, after deducting all expenses in connection with the condemnation proceedings, which is free and clear to Landlord of any collection by mortgagees for the value of the diminished fee. If more than Twenty Percent (20%) of the floor area of the building in which the Leased Premises are located shall be taken as aforesaid, Landlord may, by written notice to Tenant, terminate this Lease.

(c) *Award:* Tenant shall not be entitled to and expressly waives all claim against Landlord to any condemnation award for any taking, whether whole or partial, and whether for diminution in value of the leasehold or to the fee, but Tenant shall have the right, to the extent that the same shall not reduce Landlord's award, to claim from the condemner, but not from Landlord, such compensation as may be recovered by Tenant in its own right for damage to Tenant's business and fixtures, if such claim can be made separate and apart from any award to Landlord and without prejudice to Landlord's award. Any advance rent or other payment under this Lease made to Landlord shall be refunded to Tenant in the event of termination, in addition to any separate claim recovered by Tenant.

18. *MERCHANTS' ASSOCIATION*

A Merchants' Association has been established for the Shopping Center, and the Tenant will promptly become a member of, and during the term of this Lease, participate fully, and remain in good standing in, said Merchants' Association. Members will abide by the regulations of such Association. The Tenant agrees to pay minimum dues to the Merchants' Association in such amount as the Association shall establish from time to time by a majority vote of the members of the Association. The Tenant agrees to advertise in any and all special Merchants' Association newspaper sections or advertisements, and agrees to cooperate in the Merchants' Association special sales and promotions. Nothing in the bylaws or regulations of the said Association shall affect Tenant's obligations under this Lease. The failure of any other tenant to become a member of or to participate in the Association does not relieve the Tenant from Tenant's obligations hereunder, membership and participation in the Association being a covenant of this lease.

19. *DEFAULT*

The following acts of Tenant shall constitute a default under this Lease:

(a) Failure of Tenant to pay the rent reserved hereunder for a period of ten (10) days after it becomes due and payable.

(b) Failure of Tenant to perform any covenant or agreement contained in this Lease for a period of ten (10) days after written notice of such default is given by the Landlord to the Tenant, unless Tenant has remedied such default or continues to remedy such default to conclusion with reasonable diligence.

(c) Tenant files a voluntary petition in bankruptcy, or takes the benefit of any insolvency act, or is dissolved or adjudicated a bankrupt, or if a receiver is appointed for its business or its assets and the appointment of such receiver is not vacated within sixty (60) days after such appointment, or if Tenant shall make an assignment for the benefit of its creditors, or if the Tenant's interest herein shall be sold under execution.

(d) In the event of any default by Tenant, Landlord may, at Landlord's option and without prejudice to his rights hereunder, terminate this Lease and reenter and take possession of the Leased Premises, or the Landlord, without such reentry, may recover possession of the Leased Premises in the manner prescribed by the statute relating to summary process, and any demand for rent, reentry for condition broken, and any and all notices to quit, or other formalities of any nature, to which the Tenant maybe entitled in such event, are hereby specifically waived,

(e) In the event of any default by Tenant, the acceptance of rent or failure to reenter by the Landlord shall not be a waiver of Landlord's right to terminate this Lease, and the Landlord may reenter and take possession thereof the same as if no rent had been accepted after such default.

(f) In addition to the above rights of Landlord in the event of any default by Tenant, the Landlord may, at its option, declare immediately due and payable all the remaining installments of rent herein provided, and such amount, less the fair rental value of the premises for the remainder of said term, shall be construed as liquidated damages and shall constitute a debt provable in bankruptcy or receivership. For purposes of this Paragraph, "fair rental value" of the premises shall be deemed to be, at any time during the term of this Lease, Seventy-five Percent (75%) of the minimum rent as of the date of the execution of this Lease.

20. *SUBORDINATION*

At the option of Landlord or any mortgagee, this Lease and the Tenant's interest hereunder shall be subject and subordinate to any mortgage, deed of trust, ground or underlying leases, or any method of financing or refinancing now or hereafter placed against the land, and/or the Leased Premises and/or any and all of the buildings now or hereafter built or to be built in the Shopping Center by Landlord; and to all renewals, modifications, replacements, consolidations, and extensions thereof.

If the holder of record of the first mortgage covering the Leased Premises shall have given prior written notice to Tenant that it is the holder of said first mortgage and that such notice includes the address at which notices to such mortgagee are to be sent, then Tenant agrees to give to the holder of record of such first mortgage notice simultaneously with any notice given to Landlord to correct any default of Landlord as hereinabove provided, and agrees that the holder of record of such first mortgage shall have the right, within sixty (60) days after receipt of said notice, to correct or remedy such default before Tenant may take any action under this Lease by reason of such default.

21. *ATTORNMENT*

Tenant shall in the event of the sale or assignment of Landlord's interest in the Shopping Center or in the Leased Premises, or in the event of any proceedings brought for the foreclosure of, or in the event of exercise of the power of sale under, any mortgage made by Landlord covering the Leased Premises, attorn to the purchaser or foreclosing mortgagee and recognize such purchaser or foreclosing mortgagee as Landlord under this Lease.

22. *ATTORNEY-IN-FACT TO EFFECT SUBORDINATION OR ATTORNMENT*

Tenant shall, within ten (10) days after written request from Landlord, execute and deliver to Landlord such instruments to evidence the intent of Paragraphs 19 and 20. Tenant hereby irrevocably appoints Landlord as attorney-in-fact for Tenant with full power and authority to execute and deliver such instruments for and in the name of Tenant. If Tenant shall not have executed and delivered such instruments as aforesaid, and Tenant's actual execution is required by the party requesting the instrument(s), Landlord may cancel this Lease without incurring any liability on account thereof, and the term hereby granted is expressly limited accordingly.

23. *CONDITIONS OF QUIET ENJOYMENT*

Tenant, upon paying the rents and performing all of its covenants and promises hereunder, shall peaceably and quietly enjoy the Leased Premises, subject, nevertheless, to the terms of this Lease and to any mortgage, ground lease, or agreements to which this Lease is subordinated.

24. *VIS MAJOR*

The parties hereto shall be excused for the period of any delay in the performance of any obligations hereunder, when prevented from so doing by cause or causes beyond the nonperforming party's control, which shall include, without limitation, all labor disputes; civil commotion; war; warlike operations; invasion; rebellion; hostilities; military or usurped power; sabotage; governmental regulations or controls; fire or other casualty; inability to obtain any material, services, or financing; or through acts of God.

25. *END OF TERM*

At the expiration of this Lease, Tenant shall surrender the Leased Premises to the Landlord in the same condition as they were upon delivery of possession under this Lease, reasonable wear and tear excepted, and shall deliver all keys and combinations to locks, safes, and vaults to Landlord. Before surrendering said premises, Tenant shall remove all its personal property, including all trade fixtures, and shall repair any damage caused thereby. Tenant's obligations to perform this provision shall survive the end of the term of this Lease. If Tenant fails to remove its property upon the expiration of this Lease, within fifteen (15) days thereof, the said property shall be deemed abandoned and shall become the property of Landlord.

26. *HOLDING OVER*

Any holding over after the expiration of this Lease term or any renewal term shall be construed to be a tenancy at will at the rents herein specified (prorated on a daily basis), and shall otherwise be on the terms herein specified so far as applicable.

27. *FORBEARANCE*

Failure of Landlord to insist upon the strict performance of any provision of this Lease, or to exercise any option or any rules and regulations herein contained, shall not be construed as a waiver for the future of any such provision, rule, or option. The receipt by Landlord of rent with knowledge of the breach of any provision of this Lease shall not be deemed a waiver of such breach. No provision of this Lease shall be deemed to have been waived unless such waiver be in writing signed by Landlord. No payment by Tenant or receipt by Landlord of a lesser amount than the monthly rent shall be deemed to be other than on account of the earliest rent then unpaid, nor shall any endorsement or statement on any check or any letter accompanying any check or payment as rent be deemed an accord and satisfaction, and Landlord may accept such check or payment without prejudice to Landlord's right to recover the balance of such rent or pursue any other remedy in this Lease provided, and no waiver by Landlord in respect to one tenant shall constitute a waiver in favor of any other tenant in the Shopping Center. Any payments made by Tenant to Landlord may be applied by Landlord, in its discretion, to any item then due and owing to Landlord, notwithstanding any specification of the payment by Tenant.

28. *NOTICES*

Any notice, demand, request, or other instrument that may be or are required to be given under this Lease shall be delivered in person or sent by United States Certified or Registered Mail, postage paid, and shall be addressed (a) if to Landlord, at the address above given; and (b) if to Tenant, at the Leased Premises. Either party may designate another address by written notice to the other party at least (5) days before the mailing of any notice hereunder.

29. *RECORDING*[3]

Tenant shall not record this lease but will, at the request of Landlord, execute a memorandum or notice thereof, in recordable form satisfactory to both the Landlord and Tenant, specifying the date of commencement and expiration of the term of this Lease and other information required by statute. Either Landlord or Tenant may then record said memorandum or notice of lease.

30. *SEPARABILITY*

If any provision of this Lease or application thereof to any person or circumstance shall to any extent be invalid, the remainder of this Lease or the application of such provision to persons or circumstances other than those as to which it is held invalid shall not be affected thereby, and each provision of this Lease shall be valid and enforced to the fullest extent permitted by law.

31. *BROKER'S COMMISSION*

Tenant represents and warrants that there are no claims for brokerage commissions or finder's fees incurred by him in connection with the execution of this Lease.

32. *BENEFITS AND OBLIGATIONS*

Except as otherwise expressly provided, all provisions herein shall be binding upon and shall inure to the benefit of the parties, their legal representatives, successors, and assigns. Each provision to be performed by Tenant shall be construed to be both a covenant and a condition, and if there shall be more than one Tenant, they shall all be bound jointly and severally by this Lease. In the event of any sale of the Shopping Center, or of a lease of Landlord's interest in the Shopping Center, or of a sale or lease of Landlord's interest in this Lease, the Landlord that is executing this Lease shall be entirely relieved of all further obligations hereunder. "Landlord" under the terms of this Lease shall be deemed to be the Landlord in possession of the Leased Premises from time to time as fee owner or as ground lessee under a ground lease.

33. *ENTIRE AGREEMENT*

This Lease and the Exhibits, Riders, and/or Addenda, if any, attached, set forth the entire agreement between the parties. Any prior conversations or writings are merged herein and extinguished. If any provision contained in a rider or addenda is inconsistent with any other provision of this Lease, the provision contained in said rider or addenda shall supersede said other provision.

### 34. *MODIFICATION*

No amendment, alteration, or modification of this Lease shall be effective or binding upon either party unless it is reduced to writing and signed by both parties.

### 35. *CAPTIONS*

The captions of paragraphs appearing herein are inserted only as a matter of convenience and are not intended to define, limit, construe, or describe the scope or intent of any paragraph, nor in any way affect this Lease.

### 36. *LIABILITY OF LANDLORD LIMITED*

Anything in this Lease to the contrary notwithstanding, Tenant agrees that it shall look solely to the estate and property of the Landlord in the land and buildings comprising the Shopping Center of which the Leased Premises are a part, and subject to the prior rights of any mortgagee of the premises and subject to Landlord's rights under a leasehold interest of the Shopping Center or part thereof, if any, for the collection of any judgment or other judicial process requiring the payment of money by Landlord in the event of any default or breach by Landlord with respect to any of the terms, covenants, and conditions of this Lease to be observed and/or performed by Landlord; and no other assets of the Landlord shall be subject to levy, execution, or other procedures for the satisfaction of Tenant's remedies.

### 37. *SECURITY DEPOSIT*

It is agreed that the Tenant will deposit with the Landlord at the time of the execution of this Lease the sum of Five Hundred Dollars ($500) in cash, as security for the faithful performance by the Tenant of all of the terms and covenants of this Lease. In the event that the Tenant shall fail to perform or observe any of the terms, covenants, conditions, or agreements to be observed or performed by the Tenant hereunder, and such default shall not be cured within the grace period provided in this Lease, the Landlord shall retain said sum of Five Hundred Dollars ($500) or such remaining portion as the Landlord's absolute property, which sum shall be applied toward any and all damages owed to the Landlord by the Tenant as a result of such default, and shall not be construed as the sole or liquidated damages owed to Landlord. In the event the Tenant is not in default as aforesaid, Landlord agrees to return said sum within thirty (30) days after the expiration of the term of this Lease. Landlord shall not be obligated to place said deposit in an interest-bearing account, and Tenant shall not be entitled to any interest on said deposit.

### 38. *ADVERTISING*

Each year during this Lease, Tenant shall spend not less than One Percent (1%) of its annual gross sales as defined herein in advertising its business in the Leased Premises in newspapers, radio, or television, or other media approved by Landlord. Tenant shall also spend an additional amount of not less than One Percent (1%) of its annual gross sales as defined herein, in advertising its business in the Leased Premises in advertising medium or media designated by the Merchants' Association for the promotion of the Shopping Center. Any amounts spent by Tenant in advertising in the medium or media selected by the Merchants' Association in excess of One Percent (1%) of Tenant's annual gross sales shall be credited against the advertising expenditures required pursuant to the first sentence of this Paragraph. Tenant shall furnish Landlord, together with the annual statement furnished under Paragraph 7 hereof, a statement showing the amount spent by Tenant in advertising hereunder during the preceding lease year.

### 39. *GOVERNING LAW*

This lease shall be construed, and the rights and obligations of Landlord and Tenant shall be determined, according to the laws of the State of Florida.

### 40. *PREJUDGMENT REMEDY, REDEMPTION, COUNTERCLAIM, AND JURY TRIAL*

(a) The Tenant, for itself and for all persons claiming through or under it, hereby acknowledges that this Lease constitutes a commercial transaction and hereby expressly waives any and all rights that are or may be conferred upon the Tenant to any notice or hearing prior to a prejudgment remedy.

(b) Tenant further waives any and all rights it may acquire by any present or future law to redeem the said premises, or to any new trial in any action of ejection under any provision of law, after reentry thereupon, or upon any part thereof, by the Landlord, or after any warrant to dispossess or judgment in ejection. If the Landlord shall acquire possession of the said premises by summary proceedings, or in any other lawful manner without judicial proceedings, it shall be deemed a reentry within the meaning of that word as used in this Lease.

(c) In the event that the Landlord commences any summary proceedings or action for nonpayment of rent or other charges provided for in this Lease, the Tenant shall not interpose any counterclaim of any nature or description in any such proceeding or action.

(d) The Tenant and the Landlord both waive trial by jury of any or all issues arising in any action or proceeding between the parties hereto or their successors, under or connected with this Lease or any of its provisions.

41. *ATTORNEY'S FEES*

The prevailing party in any dispute under this Lease shall recover all costs and expenses, including reasonable attorney's fees incurred or paid by the prevailing party in enforcing the terms of this Lease, whether or not a legal action is filed.

IN WITNESS WHEREOF, the parties have duly signed and caused their corporate seals to be affixed to this Lease on the day and year first above written.

SUNCOAST ENTERPRISES, INC., Lessor

_____　　By: _____
Secretary of the Corporation　　　　　　General Manager

DOE'S SHOES, INC., Lessee

_____　　BY: _____
Secretary of the Corporation　　　　　　President

(Attach Exhibits A and B and prepare appropriate acknowledgment[s] for recording, if desired by the parties.)

[1] *49 Am. Jur. 2d Landlord and Tenant*, paras. 197, 198, 203, 209, and 517.
[2] Ref. also Form VIIA 1.08(a).
[3] Ref. Form VIIA 1.13.

## FORM VIIA 1.08 (a)

### (Minimum rent escalation clause for long-term lease containing minimum and percentage rent provisions)

### ALTERNATIVE CLAUSE

*MINIMUM RENT ESCALATION CLAUSE*

At the end of the third year of this lease term, the minimum rent specified herein shall be increased during the term beginning with the fourth year of the term according to the following formula:

(a) The minimum rent shall be adjusted in accordance with the Consumer Price Index for Urban Wage Earners and Clerical Workers—U.S. City Average: All Items—Series A, issued by the Bureau of Labor Statistics of the U.S. Department of Labor, using the year 1983 as a base of 100. The annual minimum rent specified herein shall be designated the Original Base Rent. The Index for the first month of the third lease year shall be designated the Base Price Index. At the end of the third lease year and of each three-year period thereafter, the annual rental shall be adjusted so that the ratio of the Index for the first month following the end of each such three-year period to the adjusted rental is the same as the ratio of the Base Price Index to the Original Base Rent. In the event that the Index herein referred to ceases to be published during the term of this Lease, or if a substantial change is made in the method of establishing such Index, then the figure upon which adjustment of the Base Rent is to be calculated shall be the Index that would have resulted had no termination or change in the method of establishing the Index been made. In no event shall the Base Rent, as adjusted, be less than the annual minimum rent specified herein.

## FORM VIIA 1.08(b)

### (For shopping mall rules and regulations compliance)

### ALTERNATIVE CLAUSE

*MALL RULES AND REGULATIONS*

(a) Tenant shall observe and abide by such reasonable rules and regulations for the use of the Leased Premises and Common Areas as Landlord may from time to time adopt and distribute to Tenant by written communication. Tenant further agrees to cause its employees, servants, visitors, agents, and customers to comply with said rules and regulations. The failure of Landlord to enforce any such rules and regulations against Tenant or other tenants in the Building shall not be a waiver of its right to do so.

(b) Parking for Tenant, its employees, and customers shall be exclusively in those areas designated in the Building rules and regulations as they are from time to time adopted by Landlord and distributed to Tenant.

(c) The common loading dock shall be used by Tenant only in accordance with the Loading Schedule that is a part of the Mall rules and regulations. Tenant shall not receive merchandise, freight, or similar bulk shipments through any Mall access entrance except the common loading dock, except with Landlord's express consent.

(d) A copy of the current rules and regulations for the use of the Leased Premises and the Common Areas of the Mall is attached hereto, made part hereof, and marked Exhibit B.

### FORM VIIA 1.09

(Assignment of business lease, with consent of lessor, waiving
lessor's rights against original lessee)

### ASSIGNMENT OF LEASE[1]

THIS ASSIGNMENT made March 2, 1983, between Doe Appliances, Inc., a Pennsylvania corporation (herein called "Assignor"), and National Discount Appliances, Inc., a New York corporation having its principal place of business at 100 Broadway, New York, New York 00000 (herein called "Assignee"), is made on the following terms and conditions:

1. This Assignment is made in consideration of One Dollar ($1) and other good and valuable consideration in hand paid to Assignor by Assignee.

2. Assignor hereby grants, conveys, assigns, transfers, and sets over to Assignee, its successors, and assigns, that certain lease agreement dated May 1, 1980, executed by Assignor as Lessee and Peter Coe as Lessor for premises located in Pittsburgh, Pennsylvania, more particularly described in the lease agreement, a copy of which is attached hereto and made part hereof as Exhibit A.

3. The Assignee shall take possession, occupancy, and take over operation of the above described leased property on May 1, 1983, subject to the same terms and conditions appearing in Exhibit A.

4. The lease attached as Exhibit A requires the original Lessor to consent to any subleasing or assignment.

5. This Assignment is conditioned on obtaining the written consent of the original Lessor to this Assignment.

6. Assignee agrees to hold Assignor harmless for any future claim by the original Lessor under the terms of the assigned lease, including costs and reasonable attorney's fees for defending any such claim.

7. The security deposit in the amount of Five Hundred Dollars ($500) now being held by the original Lessor is hereby assigned to the Assignee, and that security deposit shall be returned to the Assignee by the original Lessor at the conclusion of the terms of the lease.

8. The Assignee agrees to take tenancy on May 1, 1983, under the terms of the existing lease for the term of the lease, subject to the conditions and covenants contained therein.

9. All payments required by the lease shall be made by Assignee directly to the original Lessor.

10. This Assignment includes any renewal of the original lease effected between the original Lessor and the Assignee.

11. All equipment and personal property presently contained in the leased premises that is owned by Assignor under the terms of the lease is hereby granted and assigned to Assignee, and it is agreed that the Assignor herein has and shall have no further interest in or right to enter the premises or retake possession of the premises or of any equipment or other personal property now contained in the leased premises.

12. All other provisions of the original lease are incorporated herein and are to be and shall continue in full force.

Dated this 2nd day of March, 1983.

DOE APPLIANCES, INC., Assignor

By _____

_____

Secretary of the Corporation President

NATIONAL DISCOUNT APPLIANCES, INC.
Assignee

By _____

_____

Secretary of the Corporation General Manager

### CONSENT BY LESSOR

I, Peter Coe, Lessor in lease attached as Exhibit A to the foregoing Assignment of Lease, here by consent to the foregoing Assignment and hereby release the Assignor from any and all liability thereunder.

The assigned leased premises have been inspected, and I am satisfied with their general condition.

Dated this 4th day of March, 1983.

_____

PETER COE, Lessor

(Attach copy of original lease. Prepare appropriate acknowledgment for this Assignment of Lease if the original lease or a memorandum of the original lease was recorded or may be recorded.)

[1]6 *Am. Jur. 2d Assignments,* paras. 9, 21, 22, and 86; *49 Am. Jur. 2d Landlord and Tenant,* paras. 391, 392, 398, 399, 402, 410, and 412. Compare Forms VIIA 1.10 and 1.11.

## FORM VIIA 1.09(a)

### (Lessor retains rights against original lessee/assignor of lease)

### ALTERNATIVE CLAUSE

### CONSENT BY LESSOR

I, Peter Coe, Lessor in lease attached as Exhibit A to the foregoing Assignment of Lease, hereby consent to the foregoing Assignment and hereby release the Assignor from any and all liability thereunder.

The assigned leased premises have been inspected, and I am satisfied with their general condition.

Dated this 4th day of March, 1983.

_____

PETER COE, Lessor

## FORM VIIA 1.10

### (Notice to tenant from landlord of sale of leased property by landlord)

### NOTICE TO LESSEE[1]

To: Doe Appliances, Inc., Tenant
100 Main Street
Middletown, Pennsylvania 00000

YOU ARE HEREBY NOTIFIED that the real property containing the premises known as 100 Main Street, Middletown, Middle County, Pennsylvania, leased to you by the undersigned pursuant to written Lease dated March 4, 1980, has been sold to Peter Coe Associates of 500 East Street, Harrisburg, Pennsylvania 00000, subject to all terms and conditions of that Lease.

All of the terms and conditions of that Lease shall be binding and remain in full force and effect, except that all payments thereunder that have heretofore been made by you to the undersigned shall hereafter be made by you directly to the new owner, Peter Coe Associates, at the foregoing address.

Dated this 10th day of April, 1983.

JOHN DOE
100 Circle Drive
Middletown, Pennsylvania
Telephone: (000) 123-4567

(Send copy of this Notice to the new owner of the property.)

[1] *49 Am. Jur. 2d Landlord and Tenant*, paras. 95, 98, 102, and 103–108.

## FORM VIIA 1.11

### (Sublease of portion of leased premises, with consent of lessor, retaining all rights against original lessee)

### SUBLEASE[1]

THIS SUBLEASE entered into between JOHN DOE of 100 Main Street, Middletown, Indiana 00000 (herein called "Sublessor"), and RICHARD ROE of 100 Circle Drive, Middletown, Indiana 00000 (herein called "Sublessee"), each in consideration of the agreements performed by the other, on this 1st day of April, 1983, agree as follows:

1. *Description and grant.* The Sublessor hereby leases unto the Sublessee the following described property:

(give size or square footage of the portions of the area being subleased and the legal description of the whole premises originally leased)

beginning the 1st day of May, 1983, and ending the 30th day of April, 1987.

The subleased premises are part of the premises referred to in a lease between Peter Coe and John Doe as the landlord and tenant, respectively, which lease is dated May 1, 1982, and recorded in Record Book No. 000, Page 000, in the public records of Middle County, Indiana.

Lessee represents that he has received a copy of that lease and has read that lease, which is incorporated herein by reference, subject to any exception provided herein,

Paragraphs 3, 7, and 9 of that lease, concerning security deposit, repairs, and insurance respectively, shall not apply to this Sublease, except as specifically amended herein.

2. *Use.* The subleased premises are to be used and occupied by the Sublessee as a law office.

3. *Rent.* The Sublessee will pay to the Sublessor as rent for the property subleased during the term of the Sublease the sum of Two Hundred Twenty-five Dollars ($225) per month in advance on the first day of each month beginning May 1, 1983, during the term of this Sublease, except for the first installment, receipt of which is hereby acknowledged. No security deposit for the rent provided herein shall be required of the Sublessee.

4. *Rent escalation.* The monthly rent rate established at $225 per month is based on the rent payable under the lease from Peter Coe to John Doe, described in Paragraph 1. In the event that during the remaining four (4)-year period of the existence of that lease and this Sublease, the original landlord does increase the rent pursuant to Paragraph 3 of that lease, the rent due from Sublessee shall be increased and paid by Sublessee in the proportion that the square footage of the subleased premises bears to the total square footage leased by the original Lessor to the Sublessor.

5. *Repairs and maintenance.* Sublessee shall have no duty to repair and maintain the subleased premises, except for damages caused by his own gross negligence or intention to damage. Sublessee shall keep the subleased premises in a clean and orderly condition, including prompt snow removal from the front of the subleased premises.

6. *Insurance.*

(a) The Sublessee agrees to keep the subleased property adequately insured for public liability, at his expense, and further agrees to include the Sublessor in said policy as an additional insured, and agrees to deliver to said Sublessor a current copy of said liability insurance, and to ascertain that the Sublessor is always in possession of a current insurance policy during the terms of the Sublease, limit of liability not less than One Hundred Thousand Dollars/Three Hundred Thousand Dollars ($100,000/$300,000). .

(b) Sublessee shall insure the contents of the subleased premises at his own expense and shall hold Sublessor and the original Lessor harmless from any claim for destruction thereof or damage thereto.

7. *Default in payment of rent.* If any rent required by this Sublease shall not be paid within fifteen (15) days of the date due, the Sublessor shall have the option to:

(a) Terminate this Sublease, resume possession of the property for its own account, and recover immediately from the Sublessee the difference between the rent specified in the Sublease and the fair rental value of the property for the remainder of the term, reduced to present worth.

(b) Resume possession and release or rent the property for the remainder of the term for the account of the Sublessee, and recover from the Sublessee, at the end of the term or at the time each payment of rent comes due under this Sublease, as the Sublessor may choose, the difference between the rent specified in the Sublease and the rent received on the releasing or renting.

In either event, the Sublessor shall also recover all expenses incurred by reason of the breach, including reasonable attorney's fees.

8. *Other default.* If either the Sublessor or the Sublessee shall fail to perform, or shall breach any agreement of this Sublease other than the agreement of the Sublessee to pay rent, fifteen (15) days after a written notice specifying the performance required shall have been given to the party failing to perform, the party so giving notice may institute action in a court of competent jurisdiction to terminate this Sublease or to compel performance of this Agreement, and the prevailing party in that litigation shall be paid by the losing party all expenses of such litigation, including a reasonable attorney's fees.

WITNESSES:                                              SUBLESSOR:

_____

_____        _____
                                                            John Doe

                                                        SUBLESSEE:
_____

_____        _____
                                                          Richard Roe

STATE OF INDIANA
COUNTY OF MIDDLE

BEFORE ME, Mary Coe, a notary public authorized to take acknowledgments in the state and county aforesaid, this 1st day of April, 1983, JOHN DOE and RICHARD ROE acknowledged the execution of the annexed Sublease.

IN WITNESS WHEREOF, I hereunto set my hand and official seal.

                                    _____

                                    Notary Public

                                    My commission expires:

CONSENT OF LESSOR

The undersigned Lessor of the premises described in the annexed Sublease between John Doe and Richard Roe dated April 1, 1983, hereby consents to the terms of the foregoing Sublease between those parties, but in no way releases John Doe or waives any rights against John Doe under the Lease between us dated May 1, 1982.

Dated this 2nd day of April, 1983.

                                    _____

                                    PETER COE

STATE OF INDIANA
COUNTY OF MIDDLE

BEFORE ME, Mary Coe, a notary public authorized to take acknowledgments in the state and county aforesaid, this 2nd day of April, 1983, PETER COE acknowledged the execution of the annexed Consent of Lessor.

IN WITNESS WHEREOF, I have hereunto set my hand and official seal.

_____

Notary Public

My Commission expires:

¹49 Am. Jur. 2d Landlord and Tenant, para. 18.

## FORM VIIA 1.12

### (Mortgage of a business lease in states where mortgage creates a lien but does not pass legal title to mortgaged real estate)

### MORTGAGE OF LEASEHOLD INTEREST¹

THIS MORTGAGE made August 12, 1982, between Able Manufacturing Inc., a Pennsylvania corporation having its principal place of business at 100 South Highway, Middletown, Pennsylvania 00000 (herein called "Mortgagor"), and Commercial Mortgages, Inc., a New York corporation having its principal place of business at 100 Wall Street, New York, New York 00000 (herein called "Mortgagee"), WITNESSETH:

WHEREAS, Mortgagor is the lessee under a certain Lease, dated May 1, 1981, under which there was leased to Mortgagor, as lessee, and to its successors, and assigns, the premises herein described, together with their appurtenances; for the term of twenty-one (21) years, from May 1, 1981, at a yearly rental of Twenty-Four Thousand Dollars ($24,000), which Lease is recorded in the Recorder of Deeds office in Middle County, Pennsylvania, Deed Book 000, Page 000 (herein called the "Lease"); and

WHEREAS, Mortgagor is justly indebted to Mortgagee in the sum of Fifty Thousand Dollars ($50,000), evidenced by a bond dated August 12, 1982, conditioned on the payment of such sum on August 11, 1992, with interest thereon to be computed from August 12, 1982, at the rate of Twelve Percent (12%) per annum, and to be paid monthly in advance beginning August 12, 1982.

PROVIDED HOWEVER,, it is expressly agreed that the whole of such principal sum shall become due at the option of Mortgagee after default in the payment of any installment of interest or principal, or any taxes, assessments, or rents, as hereinafter provided; and

PROVIDED FURTHER, that Mortgagor, as additional security for the payment of such sum of money mentioned in the condition of the bond and interest thereon, but also for and in consideration of the further sum of One Dollar ($1), paid by Mortgagee, the receipt of which is acknowledged, does hereby grant, bargain, sell, alien, enfeoff, release, and confirm to the Mortgagee, its successors, and assigns forever, all of the following described real property, together with the appurtenances and all the estate and right of Mortgagor in and to the premises under the above-mentioned Lease:

(Insert legal description of the property.)

TO HAVE AND TO HOLD the Lease and renewals, and the estate of lessee thereunder, and the above-granted premises, unto Mortgagee, its successors, and assigns for and during the remainder of the unexpired term thereunder and in any renewals thereof; subject, however, to the rents, covenants, conditions, and provisions in the Lease.

PROVIDED FURTHER, that if Mortgagor shall pay to Mortgagee the sum of money mentioned in the condition of the bond and the interest thereon, at the time or times and in the manner mentioned in such condition, then these presents and the estate hereby granted shall cease, determine, and be void, anything herein to the contrary thereof in any wise notwithstanding.

PROVIDED FURTHER, that Mortgagor hereby covenants with Mortgagee as follows:

1. Mortgagor will pay the indebtedness as provided in such bond and perform all covenants hereunder, and if default shall be made in the payment of any part thereof or in the performance of any covenants hereunder, Mortgagee shall have the power to foreclose and sell the leasehold interest hereinabove described according to the law of Pennsylvania or to recover on the bond all sums due, and costs of recovery, including reasonable attorney's fees.

2. Such leasehold interest is now free and clear of all encumbrances whatsoever, and Mortgagor has good right and lawful authority to convey the same in the manner and form hereby conveyed.

3. Mortgagor will keep the buildings on the leased premises insured against loss by fire, for the benefit of Mortgagee, regardless of any duty of Mortgagor to insure under the terms of the Lease.

4. Mortgagor will pay the rents and other charges mentioned and provided for and made payable by the Lease within fifteen (15) days after such rent or charges are payable.

5. Mortgagor will at all times fully perform and comply with all agreements, convenants, terms, and conditions imposed on or assumed by him as lessee under the Lease, and if Mortgagor shall fail to do so, Mortgagee may, but shall not be obligated to, take any action Mortgagee deems necessary or desirable to prevent or to cure any default by Mortgagor in the performance of or compliance with any of Mortgagor's covenants or obligations under the Lease. On receipt by Mortgagee from the lessor under the Lease of any written notice of default by the lessee thereunder, Mortgagee may rely thereon and take any action as aforesaid to cure such default even though the existence of such default or the nature thereof is questioned or denied by Mortgagor or by any party on behalf of Mortgagor. Mortgagee may pay and expend such sums of money as Mortgagee in its sole descretion deems necessary for any such purpose, and Mortgagor hereby agrees to pay to Mortgagee, immediately and without demand, all such sums so paid and expended by Mortgagee, together with interest thereon from the date of each such payment at the rate of Twelve Percent (12%) per annum. All sums so paid and expended by Mortgagee, and the interest thereon, shall be added to and be secured by the lien of this Mortgage.

6. Mortgagor hereby expressly grants to Mortgagee, and agrees that Mortgagee shall have, the absolute and immediate right to enter in and on the leased premises or any part thereof to such extent and as often as Mortgagee, in its sole discretion, deems necessary or desirable in order to prevent or to cure any default by Mortgagor under the Lease or under the terms of this Mortgage.

7. Mortgagor will not surrender his leasehold estate and interest hereinabove described, nor terminate or cancel the Lease, and will not, without the express written consent of Mortgagee, modify, change, supplement, alter, or amend the Lease either orally or in writing, and any such termination, cancellation, modification, change, supplement, alteration, or amendment of the Lease without the prior written consent thereto by Mortgagee shall be void and of no force and effect. As further security to Mortgagee for the performance of the covenant. Mortgagor does hereby deposit with Mortgagee his lessee's original of the Lease and all amendments thereto or certified copy thereof, to be retained by Mortgagee until all indebtness secured by this Mortgage is fully paid.

PROVIDED FURTHER, that no release or forbearance of any of Mortgagor's obligations under the Lease, pursuant to the Lease or otherwise, shall release Mortgagor from any of his obligations hereunder, including his obligations with respect to the payment of rent as provided for in the Lease and the performance of all of the terms, provisions, covenants, conditions, and agreements contained in the Lease, to be kept, performed, and complied with by the lessee therein.

PROVIDED FURTHER, that unless Mortgagee shall otherwise expressly consent in writing, the fee title to the property demised by the Lease and the leasehold estate shall not merge, but shall always remain separate and distinct, notwithstanding the union of such estates either in the lessor or in the lessee, or in a third party by purchase or otherwise.

PROVIDED ALSO, and it is hereby expressly agreed, that the whole of the principal sum and all accrued interest thereon shall become due at the option of Mortgagee after default in the payment of any installment of principal or after default in the payment of any interest, for fifteen (15) days, or after default in the payment of any rent or other charge made payable by the Lease for fifteen (15) days, or after default in the payment of any tax or assessment for fifteen (15) days after notice and demand by the Mortgagee to cure such default.

IN WITNESS WHEREOF, Mortgagor has executed this Mortgage at Pittsburgh, Pennsylvania, the day and year first above written.

(CORPORATE SEAL)

(Richard Roe)
Secretary of the Corporation

(CORPORATE SEAL)

(Charles Coe)
Secretary of the Corporation

ABLE MANUFACTURING, INC., Mortgagor

(John Doe)
By President

COMMERCIAL MORTGAGES, INC., Mortgagee

(Peter Poe)
By President

COMMONWEALTH OF PENNSYLVANIA
COUNTY OF ALLEGHENY

On this the 12th day of August, 1982, before me, Mary Jones, the undersigned officer, personally appeared John Doe and Peter Poe, who acknowledged themselves to be the presidents respectively of Able Manufacturing, Inc., and Commercial Mortgages, Inc., both corporations, and that they, as such Presidents, being authorized to do so, executed the foregoing instrument for the purposes therein contained by signing the names of the respective corporations by themselves as respective Presidents.

IN WITNESS WHEREOF, I hereunto set my hand and official seal.

_____

Notary Public

My commission expires:

> [1] *49 Am. Jur. 2d Landlord and Tenant,* para. 413; and *55 Am. Jur. 2d Mortgages,* paras. 106 and 110.

### FORM VIIA 1.13

#### (Memorandum of lease for recording)

#### LEASE MEMORANDUM

THIS MEMORANDUM OF LEASE is made for the purpose of recording and giving notice of a lease between John Doe of 100 Cricle Drive, Middletown, Florida 00000 (herein called "Lessor"), and Roe Developers Inc., a Florida corporation having its principal place of business at 100 Main Street, Middletown, Florida 00000 (herein called "Lessee"), of the following described premises:

> (Insert legal description of parcel leased or building, suite, or other number to identify premises included in a description of multileased premises.)

The lease was executed between the Lessor and Lessee in Middletown, Florida, on May 1, 1983, for a term of ten (10) years beginning May 1, 1983.

The lease prohibits assignment by Lessee without the written consent of Lessor and, inter alia, contains a rent escalation clause and an option to the Lessee to renew for an additional ten (10) years.

IN WITNESS WHEREOF, the parties to that lease have executed this Memorandum on the 1st day of May, 1983.

ATTEST:

_____        _____

WITNESS                                                         JOHN DOE, Lessor

(CORPORATE SEAL)                                     ROE DEVELOPERS, INC.

(Peter Poe)_____        (Richard Roe)_____

Secretary of the Corporation                        By President

STATE OF FLORIDA
COUNTY OF MIDDLE

The foregoing Memorandum of Lease was acknowledged before me this 1st day of May, 1983, by John Doe, Lessor.

(NOTARIAL SEAL)                                       _____

Notary Public

My commission expires:

STATE OF FLORIDA
COUNTY OF MIDDLE

The foregoing Memorandum of Lease was acknowledged before me this 1st day of May, 1983 by, Richard Roe, President of Roe Developers, Inc., a Florida corporation, on behalf of the corporation.

(NOTARIAL SEAL)

_____

Notary Public

My commission expires:

## SECTION B LICENSES AND EASEMENTS FOR BUSINESS USE

The forms in Section B of Part VII have some of the characteristics of leases of real property, but they have the distinguishing characteristics discussed below and in the citations to the forms in this Section.

The Table of Contents of Chapter VII and the Introductions and Client Questionnaires for this section and for Section A of this Part VII are quick references to determine whether the client wants or needs a lease, license, or an easement and to choose the appropriate form.

An easement is the right to use another's land for a specified purpose not inconsistent with his ownership of the land. An easement, being an interest in land, may be created only by a deed, will, or contract (express or implied), or by prescription (use), and it cannot be created by parol (orally).

A license is distinguished from an easement in that it is a mere privilege to use the land of another rather than an interest in the land. Although a license may be given by parol, a business license to use the land of another should be in writing.

Examples of licenses are given in this Section in the form of an advertising billboard agreement and a grazing lease.

Examples of easements are the forms for adjoining landowners' agreement for use of right of way, party wall agreement, right of way over another's land, and an air and light use agreement.

Since a license to use real property is not an estate in land, it is usually revocable and unassignable.

In drafting a license or an easement from the forms in this Section, *be specific* as to the use, the person(s) using, the time, the ownership and disposition of personal property brought on the land for the use, and the care of the land during the use.

## FORM VIIB 1.00

### CLIENT QUESTIONNAIRE FOR LICENSES AND EASEMENTS FOR BUSINESS USE

1. Name and address of owner of the real estate to be used (servient estate)
2. Name and address of person who will use or who owns real estate that will use the servient estate (dominant estate)
3. Legal description of the real estate involved, preferably from the deed(s)
4. Exact location and description of the *part* of the land to be used
5. For whose benefit is the easement granted?
6. What is the purpose of the easement (ingress and egress or some other use)?

7. Are there any conditions or duties on the owner of the easement (dominant estate)? Ordinarily the owner of the easement has the right to keep it in repair, but he has no duty to do so
8. Are there any restrictions on the use of the easement?
9. Is the easement to be exclusive? If it is not exclusive, the owner of the servient estate may also use it
10. If the document to be prepared is a license and not an easement, get the same information as for the easement
11. If the document to be prepared is a license, do the parties want to record it? If so, prepare appropriate acknowledgments. If not, omit acknowledgments
12. If the document to be prepared is an easement, it should be acknowledged for recording

## VIIB 1.01

### (Easement: adjoining landowners agreement establishing mutual rights of way over adjoining parcels)[1]

### AGREEMENT

AGREEMENT made this 1st day of June, 1982, between John Doe, unmarried, of 100 East Street, Middletown, Pennsylvania 00000 (herein called "Owner A"), and George Hotel, Inc., a Pennsylvania corporation having its principal place of business at 100 Main Street, Middletown, Pennsylvania 00000 (herein called "Owner B"), WITNESSETH:

WHEREAS, Owner A is the owner in fee of the following parcel of land located in Middletown, Middle County, Pennsylvania;

(Give legal description.)

(herein called "Parcel A"); and

WHEREAS, Owner B is the owner in fee of the following abutting parcel of land located in Middletown, Middle County, Pennsylvania:

(Give legal description.)

(herein called "Parcel B"); and

WHEREAS, the Owners hereby mutually agree to establish mutual rights of way over their respective parcels;

IT IS AGREED AS FOLLOWS:

1. *Consideration.* The consideration for this Agreement is One Dollar ($1) each to the other Owner paid and the mutual promises and covenants contained herein.

2. *Grant.* A strip of land twenty (20) feet wide along the east side of Parcel A and the west side of Parcel B, one half of said strip to be on each side of the parcels described above from Main Street in the front to the street known as Blind Alley in the rear, is hereby set aside by both parties and granted each to the other as a right of way of ingress and egress for the joint use of the parties as described herein, TO HAVE AND TO HOLD the said easement to the Owners, their heirs, successors, and assigns forever.

3. *Construction and maintenance.* The Owners and their successors in title shall jointly construct, maintain, and repair an asphalt driveway, or its mutually agreed equivalent, the width of the right of way. The expense of the construction, maintenance, and repair shall be borne equally by the Owners, their respective heirs, and assigns.

4. *Use.* Both Owners may use the right of way for ingress and egress to, and reasonable loading and unloading time for, their respective Parcels.

IN WITNESS WHEREOF, the Owners have duly executed this Agreement on the day and year above written.

ATTEST:

_____

WITNESS

_____          _____

WITNESS                                          JOHN DOE

(CORPORATE SEAL)                                 GEORGE HOTEL, INC.

_____(Carrie Coe)_____          By (Peter Poe)_____

Secretary of the Corporation                     President

COMMONWEALTH OF PENNSYLVANIA
COUNTY OF MIDDLE

On this the 1st day of June, 1982, before me, Jane Roe, the undersigned officer, personally appeared John Doe, known to me or satisfactorily proven to be the person whose name John Doe subscribed to the within instrument, and acknowledged that he executed the same for the purposes therein contained.

IN WITNESS WHEREOF, I hereunto set my hand and official seal.

_____

Notary Public

My commission expires:

COMMONWEALTH OF PENNSYLVANIA
COUNTY OF MIDDLE

On this the 1st day of June, 1982, before me, Jane Roe, the undersigned officer, personally appeared Peter Poe, who acknowledged himself to be the President of George Hotel Inc., a Pennsylvania corporation, and that he, as such, being authorized so to do, executed the foregoing instrument for the purposes therein contained, by signing the name of the corporation by himself as President.

_____

Notary Public

My commission expires:

(Record the above agreement
when it is executed.)

[1]*25 Am. Jur. 2d Easments and Licenses,* paras. 123–126.

## FORM VIIB 1.02

### (Air and light use—express easement in an agreement separate from a deed)[1]

### AGREEMENT

AGREEMENT made this 1st day of January, 1982, between John Doe, unmarried, of 100 Main Street, Middletown, Pennsylvania 00000 (herein called "Owner A"), and Peter Poe and Mary Poe, his wife, of 102 Main Street, Middletown, Pennsylvania 00000 (herein called "Owner B"), WITNESSETH:

WHEREAS, the Owners A and B each own adjoining lots on the north side of Main Street, Middletown, Middle County, Pennsylvania; and

WHEREAS, the Owners A and B each intend to improve their respective lots by constructing a building or buildings thereon in the future; and

WHEREAS, the Owners A and B believe that it will be to their mutual advantage to protect the air and light use of each other's properties;

IT IS AGREED AS FOLLOWS:

1. *Consideration.* The consideration for this Agreement is One Dollar ($1) each to the other Owner paid and the mutual promises and covenants contained herein.

2. *Covenant of air and light use.* A strip of land fifty (50) feet wide running from Main Street to Blind Alley, one half (½) of said strip to be on the north and south sides, respectively, of the following properties shall be reserved by the respective Owners for the use described herein:

Parcel A, known as 100 Main Street
(Give legal description.)

Parcel B, known as 102 Main Street
(Give legal description.)

Said strip of land shall remain unobstructed by any building or enclosure of any nature forever, except by necessary uncovered steps or courtyards and/or ventilated fences and the foundations and railings connected with them, so as not to obstruct air or light of any building that may exist or be constructed by either party on the balance of his property in the future.

3. *Covenants running with the land.*[2] The covenants and agreements contained here in shall be covenants running with the respective parcels of land described herein and with the title to them, and shall be obligatory and binding upon the heirs, successors, and assigns of both Owners.

IN WITNESS WHEREOF, the parties have duly executed this Agreement on the day and year first above written.

ATTEST:

_____

WITNESS

_____      _____

WITNESS                                   JOHN DOE

_____

WITNESS

_____      _____

WITNESS                                   PETER POE

_____

WITNESS

_____      _____

WITNESS                                   MARY POE

COMMONWEALTH OF PENNSYLVANIA[3]
COUNTY OF MIDDLE

On this 1st day of January, 1982, before me, Jane Roe, the undersigned officer, personally appeared John Doe, Peter Poe, and Mary Poe, his wife, known to me or satisfactorily proven to be the persons whose names John Doe, Peter Poe, and Mary Poe subscribed to the within instrument and acknowledged that they executed the same for the purposes therein contained.

IN WITNESS WHEREOF, I hereunto set my hand and official seal.

_____

Notary Public

My commission expires:

(Record the above agreement when it is executed.)

[1] *1 Am. Jur. 2d Adjoining Landowners*, paras. 89–105.
[2] Easement need not be created in the original deed to create a covenant running with the land. *1 Am. Jur. 2d Adjoining Landowners*, para. 90. See also *77 Am. Jur. 2d Vendor and Purchaser*, para. 228. See also *49 Am. Jur. 2d Landlord and Tenant*, paras 205–207.
[3] Acknowledgment is required for recording in the public records in most states.

## FORM VIIB 1.03

**(Express agreement to build a party wall by one building owner—
cost to be shared by both the building owner and the nonbuilding
owner of the adjoining land)[1]**

### AGREEMENT

AGREEMENT made this 1st day of May, 1982, between John Doe, unmarried, of 100 Main Street, Middletown, Pennsylvania 00000 (herein called "Owner A"), and Peter Poe and Mary Poe, his wife, of 102 Main Street, Middletown, Pennsylvania 00000 (herein called "Owner B"), WITNESSETH:

WHEREAS, the parties own certain adjoining lots in the city of Middletown, Middle County, Pennsylvania, which are more particularly described herein; and

WHEREAS, Owner A desires to erect a two-story office complex on Parcel A, as described herein, and Owner B may desire to erect a similar complex on Parcel B, as described herein; and

WHEREAS, the parties believe that it will be to the mutual benefit of both parties to have a party wall erected between the respective east and west sides of the properties; and

WHEREAS, the parties desire that Owner A shall erect or cause to be erected the party wall described herein as part of a building to be erected by him, and that both parties shall pay the cost of construction of the party wall.

IT IS MUTUALLY AGREED AS FOLLOWS:

1. *Description of land.*

(a) Owner A is the owner in fee simple of the following described real property located in Middletown, Middle County, Pennsylvania, known as 100 Main Street:

(Insert legal description.)

(herein called "Parcel A"), which adjoins Parcel B on the west side.

(b) Owner B is the owner in fee simple of the following described real property located in Middletown, Middle County, Pennsylvania, known as 102 Main Street.

(Insert legal description.)

(herein called "Parcel B"), which adjoins Parcel A on the east side.

2. *Construction of party wall.*

(a) Owner A, in erecting a building on Parcel A, shall make the wall on the side adjoining the parcel of land of Owner B, a party wall in accordance with the drawing and specifications and for the party wall price shown in a writing dated this day and titled Schedule A, signed by the parties hereto, which writing is incorporated herein by this reference; and

(b) The wall shall run fifty (50) feet along the length of the boundary line between the east and west sides of Parcels A and B respectively, beginning at the northeast corner of Parcel A; and

(c) the wall shall be placed one-half (½) in width on the land of Owner A and one-half (½) in width on the land of Owner B, and when built, it shall become and remain a party wall; and

(d) during the construction of the party wall and its foundation, Owner A may enter onto Parcel B for reasonable purposes of construction, but Owner A shall protect the property of Owner B from damage and shall make good and repair all damages that may be sustained by Owner B on Parcel B as a result of the operations of Owner A in building the party wall or its foundation. In any event, this right to use Parcel B shall cease on or before three (3) months from the date hereof, unless that time is extended in writing by Owner B, who shall not unreasonably withhold his consent to such extension.

3. *Payment and use of party wall.*

(a) Whenever Owner B, his heirs, successors, or assigns shall use the party wall in whole or in part for any building or other construction on Parcel B, he or they shall pay to Owner A, or those claiming under him, the sum of One Thousand Dollars ($1,000), which is one-half (½) of the original cost of erecting the party wall as set forth in Schedule A, and shall pay in addition thereto one-half (½) of the cost of (any other agreement as to cost of addition, extension, etc.)

(b) The cost of maintenance or loss of the party wall when it is used by both parties shall be borne equally for that portion of the wall being used by both parties. If the party wall or any part of it is being used exclusively by one party, that party shall bear all the expense of maintenance or loss of the party wall.

4. *Conditional covenants running with the land.* The covenants and agreements contained herein shall be covenants running with the respective parcels of land described herein and with the title to them, and shall be obligatory and binding upon the heirs, successors, and assigns of both Owners; except that the obligations of each of the parties and those claiming under them or either of them shall cease with the termination of their, or either of their, ownership of the respective parcels of land, except the duties and obligations growing out or any erection or use made during his or their ownership.

IN WITNESS WHEREOF, the parties have duly executed this Agreement on the day and year first above written.

ATTEST:

_____

WITNESS

_____          _____

WITNESS                                                          JOHN DOE

_____

WITNESS

| | |
|---|---|
| WITNESS | PETER POE |

WITNESS

| | |
|---|---|
| WITNESS | MARY POE |

COMMONWEALTH OF PENNSYLVANIA
COUNTY OF MIDDLE

On this 1st day of January, 1982, before me, Jane Roe, the undersigned officer, personally appeared John Doe, Peter Poe, and Mary Poe, his wife, known to me or satisfactorily proved to be the persons whose names John Doe, Peter Poe, and Mary Poe subscribed to the within instrument and acknowledged that they executed the same for the purposes therein contained.

IN WITNESS WHEREOF, I hereunto set my hand and official seal.

Notary Public

My commission expires:

(Record the above agreement when it is executed.)

¹60 Am. Jur. 2d Party Walls, paras. 1–2 and 6–8.

## FORM VIIB 1.04

### (Grant of right of way to use private driveway on grantor's property, with conditions for joint maintenance and reversion for nonuse.)

### GRANT OF RIGHT OF WAY¹

THIS INDENTURE made in Queens Borough, City of New York, New York, between Doe Warehouses, Inc., a New York corporation having its principal place of business at 100 New Boulevard, Queens, New York, New York 00000 (herein called "Grantor"), and Roe Distributors, Inc., a New York corporation having its principal place of business at 102 New Boulevard, Queens, New York, New York 00000 (herein called "Grantee") WITNESSETH:

That Grantor, in consideration of the sum of One Thousand Dollars ($1,000), in hand paid to Grantor by Grantee, grants to Grantee, its successors and assigns, and their heirs and assigns, forever, as an appurtenance to Grantee's premises, the full and free right, in common with Grantor and its successors and assigns, and their heirs and assigns, forever, to enter upon and use the private driveway that is forty (40) feet in width and extends along the entire westerly side of Grantor's property extending from New Boulevard to Blind Alley in the Borough of Queens, City of New York, State of New York, which property is known as and by the street number, 100 New Boulevard, Queens, New York City, New York. The use hereby granted is for the right of free entry, egress, and regress on foot or otherwise, but shall not include the right to park in said right of way,

TO HAVE AND TO HOLD the right of way to Roe Distributors, Inc., its successors and assigns, and their heirs and assigns forever, in common with the Grantor, its successors and assigns and their heirs and assigns, forever, as provided herein,

SUBJECT, however, to the following conditions subsequent to this Grant:

1. Payment of the equal one-half (½) part of all of the necessary expenses that, from time to time, shall accrue for paving, repairing, cleaning, and maintaining the right of way, for the use described herein; and

2. That if, at any time, the Grantee, its successors and assigns, or their heirs and assigns shall abandon use of the right of way as a means of entry, egress, or regress to its property in the normal course of its business for a period of one (1) year, all right, title, and interest of the Grantee, its successors and assigns, and their heirs and assigns shall revert to the Grantor, its successors and assigns, and their heirs and assigns.

Signed, sealed, and delivered by the Grantor through its duly authorized officers this 1st day of June, 1982.

(CORPORATE SEAL)                                    DOE WAREHOUSES, INC.

(Mary Doe)                                          By (John Doe)

Secretary of the Corporation                        President

STATE OF NEW YORK
COUNTY OF QUEENS

On the 1st day of June, 1982, before me personally came John Doe, to me known, who, being by me duly sworn, did depose and say that he resides at 100 Main Street, Queens, City of New York, NY; that he is the President of Doe Warehouses, Inc., the corporation described in and which executed the above instrument; that he knows the seal of said corporation; that the seal affixed to said instrument is such corporate seal; that it was so affixed by order of the Board of Directors of said corporation; and that he signed his name thereto by like order.

(NOTARIAL SEAL)

Notary Public

My commission expires:

(Record the above agreement when it is executed.)

[1]25 Am. Jur. 2d Easements and Licenses, paras. 73–81. See also 49 Am. Jur. 2d Landlord and Tenant, para. 199.

## FORM VIIB 1.05

### (Use of land for erecting and maintaining advertising billboards)[1]

### LEASE

BY THIS LEASE made January 2, 1982, between John Doe of Star Route 1 Box 100, Middletown, Florida 00000 (herein called "Lessor"), and Outdoor Advertising, Inc., a Florida corporation havings its principal place of business at 500 East Blvd., Tampa, Florida 00000 (herein called "Lessee"), it is agreed as follows:

1. *Description of property and term.*

   In consideration of the rent provided for herein, Lessor leases to Lessee that real property owned by Lessor, located in the County of Middle, State of Florida, and more particularly described as follows (insert legal description and size of the area leased) for a term of three (3) years beginning on March 1, 1982.

2. *Rent.*

   Lessee shall pay Lessor an annual rent of Three Hundred Dollars, ($300), payable annually in advance.

3. *Use of property.*

   Lessee shall use the leased property for the construction and maintenance of three (3) billboards, each measuring no more than twenty (20) feet in length by ten (10) feet in width, and for no other purpose whatsoever.

4. *Compliance with law.*

   In its use of the leased property, Lessee shall comply with all applicable federal, state, county, and municipal statutes, rules, regulations, and ordinances, and shall secure from the proper authorities all required licenses and permits before commencing construction of said billboards.

5. *Repairs and maintenance of improvements and premises.*

   (a) Lessee shall, at all times during the term of this Lease, keep all improvements placed by Lessee on the leased property in good repair, and shall maintain them at all times in a clean and orderly condition.

   (b) Lessee shall remove by the roots or otherwise effectively destroy all unsightly or noxious weeds growing on the leased property; provided, that Lessee shall use no chemical weed killers containing _____ , and Lessee shall keep the leased property mowed.

6. *Insurance.*

Lessee shall obtain, and keep in full force and effect at all times during the term of this Lease, a policy of public liability insurance, with an insurer satisfactory to Lessor, for the protection of Lessor and Lessee against liability arising out of the condition of the leased property and the improvements erected thereon. The liability limits of said policy shall be Fifty Thousand Dollars ($50,000) each occurrence.

7. *Ownership of improvements.*

All improvements erected by Lessee on the leased property shall remain the property of Lessee, and shall be removed by it at the termination of this lease, or any renewal thereof, within a period of ninety (90) days from the date of the termination. If not removed within the specified time, Lessor shall, at his option, have the right to remove and dispose of the improvements as he sees fit, without any accounting to Lessee.

8. *Access easement.*

Lessor grants Lessee the right to pass to and from the leased property over Lessor's private road leading from County Highway 280 at all times during the term of this lease.

9. *Termination.*

(a) *By Lessor.* If Lessor should make a bona fide contract for the sale of the real property of which the leased property is a part, Lessor may, at his option, terminate this Lease by giving Lessee ninety (90) days' notice in writing, and refunding to Lessee the rental paid in advance pro rata for the unexpired term of this lease.

If Lessee defaults in the payment of rent, or breaches any other covenant or condition of this Lease, Lessor may, in addition to any other remedy that he may have, declare a forfeiture of this Lease for such default, reenter the leased property, and remove all improvements therefrom, without any accounting to Lessee.

(b) *By Lessee.* During the term of this Lease, should the use of the leased property for the purpose permitted by this Lease be prohibited, limited, or restricted by the terms of any restriction, covenant, regulation, ordinance, or zoning resolution affecting the property, Lessee, at its option, may terminate this Lease by giving Lessor thirty (30) days' notice in writing of its election to do so.

10. *Effect of condemnation.*

If the leased property, or any part thereof, is taken by eminent domain, the Lease shall terminate on the date when title vests pursuant to such taking.

11. *Option to renew.*

Lessor grants Lessee an option to renew this Lease for a period of three (3) years after expiration of the term of this Lease, at an annual rental of Four Hundred Dollars ($400), the other terms, covenants, and conditions of the renewal lease to be the same as those herein. To exercise such option, Lessee shall give Lessor written notice of its intention to renew at least three (3) months before expiration of this Lease.

IN WITNESS WHEREOF, the parties have executed this Lease at Middletown, Florida, the day and year first above written.

JOHN DOE

OUTDOOR ADVERTISING, INC.

By_ (Richard Roe)
General Manager

STATE OF FLORIDA
COUNTY OF MIDDLE

The foregoing instrument was acknowledged before me this 2nd day of January, 1982, by John Doe.

Notary Public

My commission expires:

STATE OF FLORIDA
COUNTY OF HILLSBOROUGH

The foregoing instrument was acknowledged before me this 2nd day of January, 1982, by Richard Roe, General Manager of Outdoor Advertising, Inc., a Florida corporation, on behalf of the corporation.

_____

Notary Public

My commission expires:

[1] *3 Am. Jur. 2d Advertising,* para. 4; and *25 Am. Jur. 2d Easements and Licenses,* para. 22.
[2] Short form of acknowledgment. See Appendixes III and IV for *uninformed acknowledgment acts.* See also Part VIIIA of this book.

## FORM VIIB 1.06

### (Grazing lease—license to graze cattle on part of land owned by lessor)[1]

### AGREEMENT

THIS IS AN AGREEMENT to allow Charles Coe of Box 100, Pine Mills, Pennsylvania 00000 (herein called "Lessee"), to graze cattle on land located in Middle County, Pennsylvania, owned by John Doe of 100 West Street, Pittsburgh, Pennsylvania 00000 (herein called "Lessor").

In consideration of the payment of the sum of One Hundred Dollars ($100), in hand paid to Lessor by Lessee, receipt whereof is hereby acknowledged, Lessor does hereby grant to Lessee the use of the forty (40)-acre pasture on the northwest corner of the following property for the sole purpose of grazing cattle thereon for the period of six (6) months beginning May 1, 1983, and ending October 31, 1983:

400 acres, more or less, known as the Doe Farm, located on State Route 100 in Middle County, Pennsylvania, two miles west of Pine Mills

on the following terms and conditions:

1. Lessee accepts the pasture, fences, and gates "as is," and agrees to keep them in good repair to prevent Lessee's cattle from straying onto adjacent land of others or of the Lessor.

2. Lessee or Lessee's agents shall have the right to use the private unpaved road on Lessor's property from State Highway No. 100 to the southeast corner of the pasture for the purpose of transporting Lessee's cattle by truck from the highway to the pasture from time to time during the term of this Lease, as desired by Lessee.

3. Lessee shall not sublet the pasture or any part thereof or assign the use of the right of ingress and egress to any person or persons without the written consent of the Lessor.

4. In the event the Lessee should not comply with any of the foregoing conditions, Lessor may cancel this Lease forthwith, in Lessor's discretion, and reenter, hold, occupy, and repossess the pasture, upon giving Lessee five (5) days' notice in writing to remove Lessee's cattle from the pasture. In the event that Lessee does not remove the cattle within five (5) days after written receipt of that notice from Lessor, Lessor shall have a lien on the cattle in the amount of Ten Dollars ($10) per day until the cattle are removed by Lessee or his agents.

Dated and signed this 5th day of March, 1983.

_____

JOHN DOE, Lessor

_____

CHARLES COE, Lessee

[1] *49 Am. Jur. 2d Landlord and Tenant,* paras. 5 and 199; and *25 Am. Jur. 2d Easements and Licenses,* paras. 127 and 128.

## SECTION C SALE OR PURCHASE OF REAL PROPERTY FOR BUSINESS USE

The sample forms in this Section are agreements to purchase business real estate of various kinds, on various conditions, for various purposes. A sample closing statement is also included.

Since forms and formalities for deeds vary from state to state, and local printed deed forms are often suitable, deed forms are not included.

On the other hand, the ordinary printed real estate purchase contracts usually supplied by the real estate broker may not be suitable for a contract to purchase commercial real estate. Before using such printed forms or before reviewing one, the attorney should have answers to the questions contained in Form VIIC 1.00, Client Questionnaire for the Sale or Purchase of Real Property for Business Use.

If the client is wise enough to consult the attorney before he has signed the real estate broker's listing agreement, the attorney should also *review* that *proposed* contract. For reference to alternate phrases the client may want in a listing agreement, see Form VA 1.05.

### FORM VIIC 1.00

### CLIENT QUESTIONNAIRE FOR SALE OR PURCHASE OF REAL PROPERTY FOR BUSINESS USE.

1. Names and addresses of buyer and seller
   (a) If the seller is a corporation, get a corporate status report from the state Department of State, and a certified copy of corporate resolution or written consent in lieu of corporate meeting signed by all stockholders authorizing the sale of the property
2. Legal description of the land. Copy description from the latest deed, adding new conditions and restrictions, if any.
3. Are any buildings, fixtures, or personal property included in the sale? If personal property is included, see Client Questionnaires for purchasing personal property and perfecting a purchase money security interest
4. What are the annual taxes and insurance? Have they been paid for the current year? Are they to be prorated between buyer and seller for year of purchase?
5. Is there a present mortgage on the property? If so, get copy of it
6. Are there any present leases of the land or any part of it? If so, get copies of the lease(s)
7. Are there are easements or restrictions of record? Are they to be purchased or removed, or is the land to be sold subject to them?
8. Is anyone in physical possession of the land at the present time? If so, by what right or authority? Get their name(s)
9. Is there to be title insurance? Who is to order it? From what title company, or is lawyer to certify the title? Who is to pay for the title insurance or the title search?
10. What is the price? How is it to be paid?
11. Is there to be a purchase money mortgage, or is there to be an assumption of an existing mortgage? If so, see Client Questionnaire for Mortgages
12. Is the deal an outright sale or a long-term lease with a quitclaim deed from seller to buyer to be held in escrow until the termination of the lease?[1]
13. Are any express warranties to be made in the purchase agreement?
14. Is the purchase to be conditioned on seller having marketable title, on changed zoning or restrictions, or other conditions? If so, spell out carefully in the purchase agreement
15. Is any hand money or earnest money to be paid by buyer? If so, when is it to be paid? Spell out whether it is refundable, and on what conditions
16. Has there been a recent survey? If so, get copy
17. If land is to be surveyed, who is to pay for it?
18. On what date is the closing? Who will prepare the closing statements?

19. Is the property being bought subject to a mortgage? If so, get or prepare a Mortgagee's Estoppel Certificate, a Mortgage Reduction Certificate, or Affidavit of Balance on Mortgage.[2]

[1]*28 Am. Jur. 2d Estates,* para. 130; and *23 Am. Jur. 2d Deeds,* paras. 14 and 16. Compare Form VIIA 1.05, which provides option to purchase instead of quitclaim deed.
[2]Ref. Forms VIIIB 1.07 and 1.08.

## FORM VIIC 1.01

### (Option to buy vacant land for commercial use, providing for purchase money mortgage and option money to be applied to purchase price)

### OPTION[1]

THIS OPTION is granted to Able Manufacturing, Inc., a Pennsylvania corporation having its principal place of business at 100 Wood Street, Pittsburgh, Pennsylvania 00000 (herein called "Optionee/Buyer"), by John Doe and Mary Doe, his wife, of 100 East Street, Middletown, Pennsylvania 00000 (herein called "Optionor/Seller").

In consideration of Five Thousand Dollars ($5,000) paid to Optionor/Seller, receipt of which is hereby acknowledged, we hereby give Optionee/Buyer, its successors, and assigns, the option of buying, for the price of One Hundred Thousand Dollars ($100,000), the following described vacant land situated in Middle County, Pennsylvania:

(Insert legal description of the land.)

on or before June 21, 1983, at 12:00 noon, time being of the essence of this Option, upon the following terms and conditions:

1. The purchase price shall be paid as follows:
   (a) The Five Thousand Dollars ($5,000) paid for the Option shall be credited to the purchase price.
   (b) An additional Twenty Thousand Dollars ($20,000) in cash or certified check, shall be paid to Optionor/Seller at the time of the closing.
   (c) The balance of the purchase price shall be paid by a bond in the amount of Seventy-five Thousand Dollars ($75,000), plus annual interest of Twelve Percent (12%), executed by Optionee/Buyer and secured by a mortgage on the real property in form satisfactory to Optionor/Seller.

2. Optionor/Seller agrees to deliver fee simple title, free and clear of all liens and encumbrances, by a general warranty deed at the time of closing, upon payment of the purchase price.

3. If Optionee/Buyer does not exercise the Option granted herein on or before June 21, 1983, the consideration of Five Thousand Dollars ($5,000) paid for the Option shall be retained by Optionor/Seller in full satisfaction for making, executing, and delivering this Option.

Dated and signed in Middletown, Pennsylvania, on December 21, 1982.

_____
JOHN DOE

_____
MARY DOE

COMMONWEALTH OF PENNSYLVANIA
COUNTY OF MIDDLE

On this 21st day of December, 1982, before me, Jane Roe, the undersigned officer, personally appeared John Doe and Mary Doe, his wife, known to or satisfactorily proven to be the persons whose names John Doe and Mary Doe subscribed to the within instrument and acknowledged that they executed the same for the purposes therein contained.

_____
Notary Public

My commission expires:

[1]*77 Am. Jur. 2d Vendor and Purchaser,* paras. 27–49.

## FORM VIIC 1.02

(Agreement to purchase residential building "as is" for commercial
use, conditioned on rezoning, obtaining financing, and prospective
commercial tenant agreeing to lease the premises)[1]

### AGREEMENT

THIS AGREEMENT made January 1, 1983, by and between John Doe, unmarried, of 100 East Drive, Tulsa, Oklahoma 00000 (herein called "Seller"), and Rich Enterprises, Inc., an Oklahoma corporation having its principal place of business at 400 South Harvard Street, Tulsa, Oklahoma 00000 (herein called "Purchaser"), is as follows:

1. *Description of property and conditions of sale.* Seller agrees to sell and convey and Purchaser agrees to purchase all that parcel of land, with the residential buildings and improvements thereon, located in the City of Tulsa, Oklahoma, herein called the "Property," and more particularly bounded and described as follows:

(Insert legal description.)

provided and conditioned upon the following:

(a) The Property shall be sold AS IS, except that the present R-1 residential zoning shall be changed to C-3 commercial zoning before the closing of this Purchase Agreement, it being understood and agreed that such zoning change is in the process of being made by the proper zoning authorities; and

(b) The Purchaser can obtain financing from the First Bank of Tulsa in the amount of Eighty Thousand Dollars ($80,000) for the purchase and remodeling of the building on the property as a professional office building. Application for the loan shall be presented to the First Bank of Tulsa within five (5) days of the signing of this agreement; and

(c) The Purchaser is able to obtain a written commitment from Medical Clinics, Inc., to lease the main building upon completion of the remodeling. Reasonable effort shall be made by Purchaser to obtain that commitment.

(d) The Property is not subject to any lease, and no tenant will be in possession on the closing date.

2. *Purchase price.* The Purchaser shall pay for the Property that is to be conveyed the sum of One Hundred Thousand Dollars ($100,000), payable as follows:

(a) Five Thousand Dollars ($5,000) upon the signing of this Contract, receipt whereof is hereby acknowledged. It is agreed that this payment is earnest money and is refundable to the Purchaser by the Seller if the above conditions cannot be met on or before the closing date of this Contract, unless the Purchaser fails to make the loan application and a reasonable attempt to secure the lease commitment as provided above, in which latter case the Five Thousand Dollars ($5,000) shall be retained by Seller as reasonable liquidated damages for either of those breaches of this Contract.

(b) Ninety-five Thousand Dollars ($95,000) in cash or certified check, at the closing, upon the delivery of the deed by Seller.

3. *Insurance.* Risk of loss or damage to the Property by fire or other casualty until the delivery of the deed to Purchaser shall be continued in Seller, and Seller does and shall continue to insure the Property against such loss or damage. Any amount recovered by Seller for such loss or damage prior to delivery of the deed hereunder shall, at Purchaser's option, be paid over to Purchaser or, if adjustment of the loss thereunder shall not have been made, Seller shall assign to Purchaser all of such policies of insurance and all Seller's rights and claims thereunder. Purchaser may elect to cancel this Contract at its option if any such loss or damage in excess of Ten Thousand Dollars ($10,000) occurs prior to the delivery of the deed by Seller.

4. *Deed.*

(a) The Property shall be conveyed by general warranty deed, free and clear of all liens and encumbrances or leases, but subject to covenants and restrictions contained in former deeds or other instruments of record covering the Property if they are still in force; provided they do not limit or restrict the use of the Property beyond the limitations or restrictions imposed by the Tulsa, Oklahoma, building zone regulation known as "Commercial C-3."

(b) The Property shall be vacant at the time of delivery of the deed.

5. *Apportionment of expenses and costs.*

(a) The parties agree that Roe Realty, Inc., brought about this sale, and Seller agrees to pay the real estate broker's commission therefor.

(b) Seller shall pay for documentary transfer stamps.

(c) Purchaser shall pay for title insurance.

(d) Taxes, casualty insurance, water and sewerage rates shall be apportioned and paid pro rata as of the closing date.

6. *Benefit and obligation.* This Contract of Purchase shall inure to the benefit of and bind the respective heirs, executors, administrators, or personal representatives, successors, and assigns of the parties.

7. *Closing date.* This Purchase Contract shall be closed at the offices of Peter Poe, attorney-at-law, in Suite 1000, Tulsa Building at 10:00 A.M. on March 1, 1983.

SIGNED and duly executed by the parties hereto this 1st day of January, 1983

<br>

|  |  |
|---|---|
|  | JOHN DOE, Seller<br>RICH ENTERPRISES, INC. |
| (CORPORATE SEAL) |  |
| (Peter Poe) | By  (John Rich) |
| Secretary of the Corporation | President |

STATE OF OKLAHOMA
COUNTY OF TULSA

Before me, a notary public in and for said state, on this 1st day of January, 1983, personally appeared John Doe, to me known to be the identical person John Doe who executed the within and foregoing instrument and acknowledged to me that he executed the same as his free and voluntary act and deed for the uses and purposes therein set forth.

Notary Public

My commission expires:

STATE OF OKLAHOMA
COUNTY OF TULSA

Before me, a notary public in and for said state, on this 1st day of January, 1983, personally appeared John Rich, to me known to be the identical person who subscribed the name of the maker thereof, to the foregoing instrument as its President and acknowledged to me that he executed the same as his free and voluntary act and deed and as the free and voluntary act and deed of such corporation for the uses and purposes therein set forth.

Notary Public

My commission expires:

[1] *77 Am. Jur. 2d Vendor and Purchaser,* paras. 63–70 and 87. Check state statute for requirement that spouse of vendor join in the deed.

<br>

### FORM VIIC 1.02(a)

### (Improvements to be made by Seller as condition precedent to closing by Purchaser)[1]

### ALTERNATIVE CLAUSE

*Condition precedent—improvements by Seller.* Before the closing date of this Contract, Seller shall, at its sole expense, cause the following improvements to be made to the Property, in a workmanlike manner and in accordance with all Middletown city building code regulations and requirements:

(List improvements to be made, or refer to a list of improvements and specifications attached as Rider A.)

The completion of those improvements by the Seller shall be a condition precedent to the closing of this Agreement by the Purchaser.

[1] *77 Am. Jur. 2d Vendor and Purchaser,* paras. 87 and 337–342.

## FORM VIIC 1.03

### (Agreement to buy office building, subject to existing leases and a mortgage)[1]

### SALE CONTRACT

BY THIS CONTRACT made on May 1, 1983, between John Doe Enterprises, Inc., of 100 Wood Street, Pittsburgh, Pennsylvania 00000 (herein called "Seller"), and Richard Roe Associates, Inc., of 100 Madison Avenue, New York City, New York 00000 (herein called "Purchaser"), the parties agree as follows:

1. *Title warranty.*

(a) Seller warrants and represents that it owns the real property described herein in fee simple, free of all liens and encumbrances, except a mortgage in favor of First Bank of Pittsburgh upon which there is now due the sum of One Hundred Twenty-five Thousand Dollars ($125,000), due on or before June 1, 1988, bearing interest at the rate of Eight Percent (8%) per annum, principal and interest payable quarterly in installments of Eight Thousand Seven Hundred Sixty-six Dollars ($8,766), to be applied first to interest and then to principal. Purchaser has read and understands that mortgage. At the closing of this Contract, Seller shall deliver to Purchaser a certified copy of that mortgage and a Certificate of Reduction[2] of that Mortgage, executed by the Mortgagee showing the amount of principal and interest due on the mortgage at the time of delivery of the deed pursuant to this contract.

(b) Seller further warrants that it has title, free and clear of all liens and encumbrances, to all fixtures, apparatus, machinery, fittings, awnings, shades, screens, and other equipment and furnishings contained in the premises and used in connection with heating, air conditioning, lighting, plumbing, refrigeration, and the general operation of the premises as an office building, including the furniture and fixtures in the building manager's office in Suite 202 of the building, and fixtures and furnishings in the restaurant concession being operated on the 18th floor of the building.

(c) The property described herein is subject to the leases and rights of tenants and others of or in the property or any part thereof as shown by the list of tenants and/or leases, and concession and license agreements appearing in Schedule A, annexed hereto and made part hereof by reference.

2. *Representation as to broker.* The parties represent to each other and agree that the only real estate broker entitled to any claim for commission for this transaction is Coe & Company, Realtors, of Pittsburgh, Pennsylvania, and that Seller shall pay that claim. If any other broker's commission or finder's fee is claimed against Seller by any other person as a result of acts or actions of the Purchaser, then the Purchaser shall indemnify the Seller from any and all damages resulting from such claim, including reasonable attorney's fees and the cost of litigation.

3. *Representations as to building law compliance.* All notes or notices of or known violation of any governmental building law, code, or ordinance or any regulation thereunder against or affecting the Property on the date hereof shall be complied with by Seller, and the Property shall be conveyed free and clear of same; and this provision of this Contract shall survive delivery of the deed.

4. *Description of property and agreement to sell.* Seller hereby agrees to sell and Purchaser agrees to buy the following described real property:

(Give legal description of real estate.)

together with all buildings and improvements thereon and fixtures and furnishings therein, as more particularly described in Schedule B, annexed hereto and made part hereof by reference.

5. *Price.* Purchaser shall pay for the property described herein the sum of Two Hundred Fifty Thousand Dollars ($250,000) as follows:

(a) Five Thousand Dollars ($5,000) upon the signing of this Contract, receipt whereof is hereby acknowledged.

(b) Ninety-five Thousand Dollars ($95,000) in cash or certified check upon delivery of the deed.

(c) One Hundred Twenty-five Thousand Dollars ($125,000) to be paid by the Purchaser's taking the property subject to the mortgage of the First Bank of Pittsburgh, described in Paragraph 1, and assuming payment of that mortgage and performance of all its terms and conditions. Seller shall secure the written consent of the mortgagee to the assumption, and Purchaser agrees to provide all reasonable information required by the mortgagee to give its consent.

6. *Apportionment of income and expenses at closing.* The following items of income and expense are to be apportioned on the date of the closing of this Contract:

(a) Rents, concession, and license fees.

(b) Interest on the present mortgage.

(c) Insurance premiums on existing policies, except liability and worker's compensation insurance.

(d) Taxes, water and sewerage rates. If the closing occurs before the current tax rate is fixed, the apportionment of taxes shall be upon the basis of the tax rate for the last preceding year, applied to the latest assessed valuation.

(e) Wages for building employees.

(f) Electric and gas.

(g) Rental commissions.

(h) The following contracts for services, equipment, furnishings, supplies, and other materials in and about the building premises (which have been shown to the Purchaser and duly initialed by Purchaser's representative and the Seller for purposes of identification) are to be assumed by the Purchaser at the time of the closing, and are to be apportioned to that time:

> (List contracts, as: contracts for advertising, carpet and rug cleaning, purchase contracts for fixtures and appliances, management employment contract, fire alarm system, mail chute system, collection of rents contract, uniforms for employees, vermin extermination, building cleaning, and/or others.)

7. *Risk of loss or damage.* The risk of loss or damage to the building by fire, until the delivery of the deed, is assumed by the Seller.

8. *Deed.* The deed from Seller to be delivered at the closing of this Contract shall be a general warranty deed containing all covenants required under the laws of the Commonwealth of Pennsylvania and shall be in proper statutory form for recording in the County of Allegheny, Commonwealth of Pennsylvania, and shall be duly acknowledged by the Seller for recording.

9. *Refund and lien for deposit and title expense.* All sums paid on account of this Contract, including the Five Thousand Dollar ($5,000) deposit and the reasonable expense of the examination of the title paid by Purchaser, shall be refundable by Seller and shall be a lien on the property to be conveyed if Seller fails to convey in accordance with this Contract; but such liens shall not continue, and these sums shall not be refundable, in the event of default by the Purchaser under this Contract.

10. *Closing.* The deed shall be delivered by Seller, together with the written consent of the mortgagee for Purchaser to assume the mortgage and all necessary documentary revenue stamps for the deed, upon receipt of the cash payment required of the Purchaser at the office of Peter Poe in Suite 554, First Bank Building, Pittsburgh, Pennsylvania, at 10:00 A.M. on July 1, 1983.

11. *Benefit and obligation.* This Contract shall inure to the benefit of and bind the respective heirs, administrators, executors, personal representatives, successors, and assigns of the parties.

Dated this 1st day of May, 1983.

JOHN DOE ENTERPRISES, INC., Seller

By  (John Doe)

(Mary Doe)

Secretary of the Corporation         President

RICHARD ROE ASSOCIATES, INC., Purchaser

By  (Richard Roe)

(Peter Poe)

Secretary of the Corporation         President

COMMONWEALTH OF PENNSYLVANIA
COUNTY OF ALLEGHENY

On this 1st day of May, 1983, before me, Mary Jones, the undersigned officer, personally appeared John Doe and Richard Roe, who acknowledged themselves to be the Presidents, respectively, of John Doe Enterprises, Inc., and Richard Roe Associates, Inc., both corporations, being authorized to do so, executed the foregoing instrument for the purposes therein contained by signing the names of the respective corporations by themselves as respective Presidents.

IN WITNESS HEREOF, I hereunto set my hand and official seal.

---

Notary Public

My commission expires:

(Attach Schedules A and B.)

[1]Ref. Form VIID 1.07 and footnotes. See also "due on sale clause," Form VIID 1.01(c).
[2]Ref Form VIIIB 1.08.

## FORM VIIC 1.04

### (Agreement to exchange business real property)[1]

### CONTRACT FOR EXCHANGE

THIS AGREEMENT made and entered into on the 2nd day of February, 1983, between Doe Associates, Inc., a Florida corporation having its principal place of business at 100 Main Street, Middletown, Florida 00000 (herein called "First Party"), and Roe & Company, Inc., a Florida Corporation having its principal place of business at 500 Industrial Drive, Tampa, Florida 00000 (herein called "Second Party"),

WITNESSETH, that the parties hereto, in consideration of the sum of One Dollar ($1), to each in hand paid by the other, and in further consideration of the conveyance to each other of the premises described herein according to the terms and conditions hereof.

1. *Description of Property A.* The real and personal property owned by First Party, and more particularly described in Exhibit A, attached hereto and made part hereof (herein called "Property A"), is valued for the purpose of this Contract at Five Hundred Thousand Dollars ($500,000).

2. *Description of Property B.* The real and personal property owned by Second Party, and more particularly described in Exhibit B, attached hereto and made part hereof (herein called "Property B"), is valued for the purposes of this Contract at Four Hundred Fifty Thousand Dollars ($450,000).

3. *Grant.* The parties will sell and convey to each other, by good and sufficient warranty deed with all necessary state and federal documentary stamps affixed thereto, their respective properties located in the State of Florida, described in Exhibits A and B; subject to the restrictions upon the use thereof, if any, set forth in the list of restrictions in Exhibits A and B; and also subject to any liens, encumbrances, easements, or conditions, if any, described and set forth in Exhibits A and B, for the purchase price hereinafter stated.

4. *Title insurance binder.* The parties will, within fifteen (15) days of the signing of this Agreement, pay for and deliver to each other title insurance binders from good and reputable title insurance companies authorized to do business in the State of Florida, guaranteeing that upon the recording of the warranty deed from the respective party conveying the land to the other in accordance with the next preceding paragraph hereof, said title insurance company will insure the title of the grantee of said land in the amount of the purchase price for said land as herein stated, subject to the restrictions, liens, encumbrances, easements, and conditions, if any, described and set forth in the attached Exhibits A and B, and subject to any state of facts an accurate survey would disclose, as well as any other exceptions usually and customarily placed in title insurance policies by said title insurance company on lands similarly situated.

5. *Curing title defects.* In the event the title insurance binder for either property so delivered lists any other exception, restriction, lien, encumbrance, easement, or condition, the other party may either accept the same and close this transaction at the time and place and in the manner hereafter provided, accepting title from the Seller in its then existing condition, or within ten days after delivery of said title insurance binder, notify the Seller in writing of the exception, restriction, lien, encumbrance, easement, or condition in said binder that prevents the title from being insurable as herein provided and to which the Buyer objects, in which event the Seller shall, with due diligence and within a reasonable period of time, not exceeding sixty (60) days, remove the designated exception, restriction, lien, encumbrance, easement, or condition and furnish satisfactory evidence thereof to the Buyer, provided, however, that any lien, encumbrance, or other defect in the Seller's title that may be removed by money payment may be paid and removed upon closing.

6. *Refund and lien.* In the event this Contract is not closed because of a failure of either party's title, the party whose title is defective shall refund to the Buyer all sums paid by the Buyer to the Seller pursuant to this Contract, and the Buyer is hereby given a lien upon said land to secure payment thereof. In such case the Buyer shall not be required to refund to the party whose title is defective any sum paid by that party hereunder, but shall retain same as compensation for expenses incurred in negotiating and entering into this Contract.

7. *Difference in exchange price.* The difference between the values of the properties being exchanged is Fifty Thousand Dollars ($50,000).

8. *Payment by First Party.* The First Party will pay for and purchase the property of the Second Party upon the terms and conditions set forth in this Contract, paying to the Second Party a total purchase price of Four Hundred Fifty Thousand Dollars ($450,000) as follows:

A. First Party shall deliver to Second Party a recordable general warranty deed to Property A, subject to the restrictions, liens, encumbrances, easements, and conditions, if any, described and set forth in Exhibit A, upon closing.

B. First Party will assume the first mortgage on Property B in the approximate amount of Seventy-five Thousand Dollars ($75,000), as shall be evidenced by a Mortgagee's Estoppel Certificate[2] not to exceed that amount to be delivered by Second Party, upon closing.

9. *Payment by Second Party* The Second Party will pay for and purchase the property of the First Party upon the terms and conditions set forth in this Contract, paying to the First Party a total purchase price therefor of Five Hundred Thousand Dollars ($500,000) as follows:

A. Five Hundred Dollars ($500), in cash upon the execution hereof, the receipt of which is hereby acknowledged.

B. Five Thousand Dollars ($5,000), in cash upon closing.

C. Second Party will deliver to First Party a recordable general warranty deed to Property B, subject to the restrictions, liens, encumbrances, easements, and conditions, if any, described and set forth in Exhibit B, upon closing.

D. Second Party will assume the first mortgage in Property A in the approximate amount of Forty-four Thousand Five Hundred Dollars ($44,500), as shall be evidenced by a Mortgagee's Estoppel certificate[2] not to exceed that amount, to be delivered by First Party, upon closing.

10. *Possession.* Possession of the respective properties shall be delivered upon closing, and if delivered prior to closing, the respective Buyer shall keep said property in as good a state of repair as the same is at the present time, shall pay all taxes and assessments thereon within sixty (60) days after due, and shall further keep the property so insured as to protect the Seller against all loss to the extent of the unpaid purchase price, with a loss payable clause payable to the Seller, the policy to be approved by and held by the Seller until closing. All taxes, insurance, rent, and other items ordinarily prorated in the closing of a real estate transaction shall be prorated upon closing as of the date of delivery of possession of the property to the Buyer.

11. *Closing.* Within ten (10) days after the parties furnish the title insurance binders provided for in Paragraph 4 hereof, or remove defects in title as provided for in Paragraph 5 hereof, this Contract shall be closed at Middle County Title Company, 500 Main Street, Middletown, Florida, and at the closing, all parties shall pay all sums and execute all instruments necessary for the purpose of this contract.

12. *Liquidated damages.* Parties agree that time is of the essence of this Agreement, and should either party fail to make any payment or keep and perform any other covenant herein contained to be kept and performed by him within the time herein limited, then this Contract shall automatically become null and void without notice, and no part of the purchase price or other sums paid by him to the other party shall be refunded by the other party, but shall be retained by the other party as liquidated damages incurred by reason of the failure to keep and perform this Contract, the parties hereby recognizing and agreeing that the amount of such damages would be difficult, if not impossible, to ascertain and that the amount so paid would be a reasonable amount for the respective party to pay as said damages. If the defaulting party is in possession of the other's property, it shall, upon the demand of the other party, immediately surrender possession thereof to the owner, and should it fail to do so, the defaulting party shall pay all cost of any proceeding instituted to regain possession thereof, including reasonable attorney's fees for the owner's attorney.

13. *Notice.* Notice to the respective parties, given by registered or certified United States mail and addressed to the party at the address herein given, shall be deemed notice to said party wherever notice is required or permitted under this Contract, whether received or not. The place of receiving notice may be changed by either party by written notice to the other at least five (5) days before the notice is given.

14. *Warranties.* It is warranted by each of the parties to the other that it has no knowledge or notice that its property is in violation of any law, ordinance, or government regulation of any government or department of government having jurisdiction, against or affecting the premises hereby exchanged, and if any such notice or knowledge is received by a party before the closing hereof, the notice or knowledge shall be complied with by the respective Seller, and the premises shall be conveyed free of such violation, unless waived in writing by the respective Buyer.

15. *Entire agreement.* This Contract constitutes the entire agreement between the parties hereto, and any statement, promise, or agreement not included or specifically mentioned herein shall not be binding upon either party.

IN WITNESS WHEREOF, the parties hereto have executed this Contract in duplicate on the day and year first above written.

(CORPORATE SEAL)                                    DOE ASSOCIATES, INC.

___(Peter Poe)___                          By___(John Doe)___
Secretary of the Corporation                        President

(CORPORATE SEAL)                                    ROE & COMPANY, INC.

___(Charles Coe)___                        By___(Richard Roe)___
Secretary of the Corporation                        President

(Attach Exhibits A and B, each containing the legal description of the respective property, and the respective restrictions on use and all liens, encumbrances, easements, and conditions to which the sale of the respective properties are subject, plus a description of personal property or fixtures included in the sale, if any.)

STATE OF FLORIDA
COUNTY OF MIDDLE

I HEREBY CERTIFY that the foregoing instrument was acknowledged this 2nd day of February, 1983, by John Doe and Richard Roe, Presidents, respectively, of Doe Associates, Inc., and Roe & Company, Inc., both Florida corporations, on behalf of their respective corporations.

_____
Notary Public

My commission expires:

[1] *30 Am. Jur. 2d Exchange of Property*, para. 20 et seq.
[2] Ref. Form VIIIB 1.07.

## SECTION D MORTGAGE OF REAL PROPERTY

This Section contains various types of documents by which a mortgage can be created as discussed below. In addition, there are forms for assignment, assumption, release, subordination, and satisfaction of a mortgage.

In choosing from the mortgage forms in this Part and Section, choose the form that is appropriate for the state in which the land is located. The forms have been drafted for use in particular states, but they may also be used in any other state that utilizes that *type* of mortgage document. Citations to the forms will aid in making the choice.

The Client Questionnaire Form VIID 1.00 will aid in getting the *facts* required for drafting any of the *types* of mortgage documents.

In some cases a sale or loan that is to be secured by a mortgage may involve both real and personal property. If that is the case, one *may* prepare separate documents for the personal property. The documents required for securing an interest in the personal property appear in Part V D and F. Read the Introduction to Part V and the Client Questionnaires for Sections D and F.

If you choose to include both the real and personal property in the mortgage, the mortgage serves the purpose of creating a security interest in the personal as well as the real property, *if the mortgage complies with the Uniform Commercial Code filing requirements*. To perfect the security interest in the land secured by the mortgage, the mortgage must be recorded in the county where the land is located. To perfect the security interest in the personal property[1] described in the mortgage, a financing statement making reference to the mortgage must also be recorded, using Form VIF 1.03.

In most states, a mortgage of real estate creates a lien on the property by the mortgagee for the amount of his interest under the mortgage.

States vary as to the use of a bond or a note to evidence the debt that is secured by the mortgage. Samples of both bonds and notes are given in this Section. See the Table of Contents for this Part VII.

A "deed in trust"[2] is used in California, Illinois, Missouri, Virginia, and Washington, D.C., and may be used in some other jurisdictions to create a mortgage interest. In Florida an "agreement for deed"[3] has the practical effect of a mortgage.

Because of the recent increase in interest rates, the conditions under which a mortgage may be assumed is very relevant for consideration in drafting a mortgage.

A recent United States Supreme Court case upheld a "Due on Sale Clause"[4] contained in a federal savings and loan mortgage. The language originated in federal home loan mortgages, as the government wanted recourse against both the original mortgagor and his purchaser. If there is no provision in the original mortgage that it is due on sale, the purchaser from a mortgagor can ordinarily assume the mortgage on sale. Some states allow assumption "unless security is jeopardized" if there is no due on sale clause in the mortgage.

Form VIID 1.07 is an Assumption of Mortgagee Agreement between a mortgagor/vendor and his purchaser, consented to by the mortgagee wherein the mortgagee releases the mortgagor/vendor from liability.

If the mortgagee does not specifically consent to the assumption and release the mortgagor, the assumption is still binding between the parties to the assumption, but it will not relieve the mortgagor/vendor from liability in case his purchaser defaults in paying the mortgage.

For the above reasons, it is necessary to understand the desires of the parties and obtain the consent of the mortgagee, as shown in Form VIID 1.07, if you represent the mortgagor/vendor who wants to be released from further obligation on the mortgage.

## FORM VIID 1.00

### CLIENT QUESTIONNAIRE FOR MORTGAGE OF REAL PROPERTY

1. Names and addresses of both mortgagor and mortgagee
2. Description of the real property. Get copy of the deed to the mortgagor
3. Is the mortgage for purchase money?
4. What is the total amount of the purchase price? What amount is to be financed?

---

[1]Ref. Part VI, Section F and see Form VIID 1.01(b).
[2]Ref. Form VIID 1.04 and 1.04(a).
[3]Ref. Form VIID 1.03.
[4]Ref. Form VIID 1.01(c).

5. Is a bond or note for the amount to be paid appropriate as the evidence of the debt to be created? Or does client want an agreement for deed instead (in jurisdictions that recognize such agreement as a mortgage instead of as a contract to purchase)?
6. How is the debt to be paid?
    (a) Is the debt to be paid in installments, including interest?
    (b) Is interest to be paid on a yearly or other basis and the debt to be paid in full by a certain date?
    (c) Is there a "balloon" payment at the end?[1]
    (d) If the debt will be paid in installments, have an amortization schedule prepared including agreed interest
7. Percentage of interest (fixed or variable). If variable, how and when will any increase start and be paid?
8. Where and to whom are the payments on the note, bond, or agreement for deed to be paid?
9. Are there any guarantors[2] of the note? If so, get their name(s) and address(es). Get any conditions of the guaranty as to time and amount. Will guarantors sign the note or a separate guaranty agreement?
10. Are any of the parties corporations? If so, get:
    (a) a corporate status report from the state Department of State
    (b) a certified copy of corporate resolution[3] or written consent in lieu of corporate meeting,[4] signed by all stockholders authorizing the note or bond and mortgage or the agreement for deed, and the signing of those documents
    (c) same evidence as to the names of the officers entitled to act and sign for the corporation
11. Are there any other mortgages on the property? If so, is a Subordination of Mortgage[5] to be prepared?
12. If the document you are to prepare is:
    (a) a partial release of mortgage[6]
    (b) satisfaction of mortgage[7]
    (c) assignment of mortgage[8] or
    (d) assumption of mortgage[9]
get a copy of the original mortgage before drafting the document affecting the mortgage. What is the amount or nature of the consideration for the release, cancellation, or satisfaction?

[1]Ref. Form VIIF 1.05.
[2]Ref. Chapter VIIIK.
[3]Ref. Form IA 1.09.
[4]Ref. Form IA 1.07.
[5]Ref. Form VIID 1.10.
[6]Ref. Form VIID 1.08.
[7]Ref. Form VIID 1.09.
[8]Ref. Form VIID 1.06.
[9]Ref. Form VIID 1.07.

## FORM VIID 1.01

(Purchase money mortgage deed securing installment note)

### MORTGAGE DEED[1]

THIS MORTGAGE, made the 1st day of May, A.D. 1983, by DOE APPLIANCES, INC., a Florida corporation having its principal place of business at 100 Main Street, Middletown, Florida, party of the first part (herein called the "Mortgagor") to First Bank of Middletown, Florida, a Florida banking corporation, of the County of Middle State of Florida, party of the second part (herein called the "Mortgagee");

WITNESSETH, that for good and valuable consideration and also in consideration of the aggregate sum named in the promissory note of even date herewith, the Mortgagor does grant, bargain, sell, convey, and confirm unto the Mortgagee, its successors, and assigns all that certain tract of land, of which the Mortgagor is now seized and possessed, and in actual possession, situation in Middle County, State of Florida, described as follows:

(Insert legal description.)

TO HAVE AND TO HOLD the same, together with the tenements, hereditaments and appurtenances, unto the Mortgagee, and its successors and assigns, in fee simple,

AND Mortgagor, for itself and its successors and assigns, covenants with Mortgagee, its successors and assigns, that Mortgagor is indefeasibly seized of said land in fee simple; that the Mortgagor has full power and lawful right to convey said land in fee simple as aforesaid; that it shall be lawful for Mortgagee, its successors, and assigns, at all times peaceably and quietly, to enter upon, hold, occupy, and enjoy said land; that said land is free from all incumbrances; that Mortgagor, its successors, and assigns will make such further assurances to perfect the fee simple title to said land in Mortgagee, its successors, and assigns, as may reasonably be required; and that Mortgagor does hereby fully warrant the title to said land and will defend the same against the lawful claims of all persons whomsoever.

PROVIDED ALWAYS, that if Mortgagor, its successors, or assigns, shall pay unto the Mortgagee, its successors, or assigns, the certain promissory note, of which the following in words and figures is a true copy, to wit:

> (Attach photocopy of the purchase money note or type in every word and figure of the note, indicating the affixing of the signatures. See Form VIID 1.01 [a] for sample purchase money mortgage installment note.)

and shall perform, comply with, and abide by each and every stipulation, agreement, condition, and covenant of said promissory note and of this deed, then this deed and the estate hereby created shall cease and be null and void.

AND the Mortgagor, for itself and its successors and assigns, hereby covenants and agrees:

1. To pay all and singular the principal and interest and other sums of money payable by virtue of said promissory note and this deed, or either, promptly on the days respectively the same severally come due.

2. To pay all and singular the taxes, assessments, levies, liabilities, obligations, and incumbrances of every nature on said described property each and every, and if the same be not promptly paid, the Mortgagee, its successors, or assigns, may at any time pay the same without waiving or affecting the option to foreclose or any right hereunder, and every payment so made shall bear interest from the date thereof at the rate of Twelve Percent (12%) per annum.

3. To pay all and singular the costs, charges, and expenses, including attorney's fees, reasonably incurred or paid at any time by Mortgagee, its successors, or assigns, because of the failure on the part of the Mortgagor, its successors, or assigns, to perform, comply with, and abide by each and every one of the stipulations, agreements, conditions, and covenants of said promissory note and this deed, or either, and every such payment shall bear interest from the date thereof at the rate of Twelve Percent (12%) per annum.

4. To keep the buildings now or hereafter on said land insured in a sum not less than One Hundred Sixty Thousand Dollars ($160,000), in a company or companies to be approved by Mortgagee, and the policy or policies held by and payable to Mortgagee, its successors, or assigns, and in the event any sum of money becomes payable under such policy or policies, the Mortgagee, its successors, or assigns shall have the option to receive and apply the same on account of the indebtedness hereby secured, or to permit the Mortgagor to receive and use it, or any part thereof, for other purposes, without thereby waiving or impairing any equity lien or right under or by virtue of this Mortgage, and may place and pay for such insurance, or any part thereof, without waiving or affecting the option to foreclose or any right hereunder, and each and every such payment shall bear interest from the date thereof at the rate of Twelve Percent (12%) per annum.

5. To refrain from committing or allowing waste, impairment, or deterioration of said property or any part thereof.

6. To perform, comply with, and abide by each and every stipulation, agreement, condition, and covenant in said promissory note and in this deed set forth.

7. If any sum of money herein referred is not promptly and fully paid within ten (10) days next after the same severally become due and payable, or if each and every stipulation, agreement, condition, and covenant of said promissory note and this deed, or either, are not duly performed, complied with, and abided by, the aggregate sum mentioned in said promissory note shall become due and payable forthwith or thereafter, at the option of the Mortgagee, its successors, or assigns, as fully and completely as if the said aggregate sum of One Hundred Twenty Thousand Dollars ($120,000) were originally stipulated to be paid on such day, anything in said promissory note or herein to the contrary notwithstanding.

8. THIS IS A PURCHASE MONEY MORTGAGE securing a PURCHASE MONEY NOTE evidencing the balance due on the purchase on this date of the property described herein by the Mortgagor from the Mortgagee.

IN WITNESS WHEREOF, the party of the first part has caused these presents to be signed in its name by its President, and its corporate seal to be affixed, attested by its Secretary the day and year above written.

(CORPORATE SEAL)                 DOE APPLIANCES, INC.

(Peter Poe)                                By_ (John Doe)

Secretary of the Corporation              President

STATE OF FLORIDA
COUNTY OF MIDDLE

I, an officer authorized to take acknowledgments of deeds according to the laws of the State of Florida, duly qualified and acting, HEREBY CERTIFY that John Doe and Peter Poe, respectively, as President and Secretary of DOE APPLIANCES, INC., a Florida corporation, to me personally known, this day acknowledged before me that they executed the foregoing mortgage for the corporation as such officers of said corporation, and that they affixed thereto the official seal of said corporation; all with the full authority of the Board of Directors of the corporation.

IN WITNESS WHEREOF, I hereunto set my hand and official seal at Middletown, Florida, this 1st day of May, 1983.

                                      Notary Public

                                      My commission expires:

(Record the Mortgage Deed simultaneously with the Purchase Deed to Mortgagor, presenting the Purchase Deed first.)

[1] *55 Am. Jur. 2d Mortgages,* paras 13 (balloon mortgage) and 348–351.

## FORM VIID 1.01(a)

### (Purchase money mortgage installment note made by corporation)

### MORTGAGE INSTALLMENT NOTE[1]

                                      Middletown, Florida

$120,000                                      May 1, 1983

FOR VALUE RECEIVED, the undersigned corporation, a Florida corporation having its principal place of business at 100 Main Street, Middletown, Florida 00000, promises to pay to FIRST BANK OF MIDDLETOWN on order, in the manner herein specified, the principal sum of One Hundred Twenty Thousand Dollars ($120,000), with interest from date at the rate of Twelve Percent (12%) per annum on the balance from time to time remaining unpaid. The said principal and interest shall be payable in lawful money of the United States of America at the main office of the bank at 100 Main Street, Middletown, Florida 00000, or at such place as may hereafter be designated by written notice from the holder to the maker hereof, on the date and in the manner following:

(List dates and amounts of payments for each period [usually monthly], with dates payments begin and end.)

THIS IS A PURCHASE MONEY NOTE evidencing the balance due on the purchase price of lands sold by the Payee to the Maker.

THIS NOTE with interest is secured by a purchase money mortgage on real estate of even date herewith, made by the Maker hereof in favor of the said Payee, and shall be construed and enforced according to the laws of the State of Florida. The terms of said mortgage are by this reference made a part hereof.

IF DEFAULT be made in the payment of any of the sums or interest mentioned herein or in said mortgage, or in the performance of any of the agreements contained herein or in said mortgage, then the entire principal sum and accrued interest shall, at the option of the holder hereof, become at once due and collectible without notice, time being of the essence; and said principal sum and accrued interest shall both bear interest from such time until paid at the highest rate allowable under the laws of the State of Florida. Failure to exercise this option shall not constitute a waiver of the right to exercise the same in the event of any subsequent default.

EACH PERSON liable hereon, whether maker or endorser, hereby waives presentment, protest, notice, notice of protest, and notice of dishonor and agrees to pay all costs, including a reasonable attorney's fee, whether suit be brought or not, if, after maturity of this note or default hereunder, or under said mortgage, counsel shall be employed to collect this note or to protect the security of said mortgage.

WHENEVER used herein, the terms "holder," "maker," and "payee" shall be construed in the singular or plural as the context may require or admit.

(CORPORATE SEAL)                              DOE APPLIANCES, INC.

_____     By _____
Secretary of the Corporation               President

[1]Ref. Chapter VIIIP, and compare Form VIID 1.02(a) which is a mortgage bond.

## FORM VIID 1.01(b)

### (Where personal property is included in real property mortgage)

### ALTERNATIVE CLAUSE

### SECURITY AGREEMENT AS TO PERSONAL
### PROPERTY LOCATED ON MORTGAGED PREMISES[1]

This mortgage shall constitute a security agreement with respect to any and all personal property included within the description of the mortgage property as shown on Exhibit A, attached hereto. Mortgagor shall join with the Mortgagee in executing one or more financing statements under the Commercial Code of Pennsylvania, 12A P.S. 9-101 seb seq., to be filed by the Mortgagee pursuant to said Code at Mortgagor's expense.

[1]Ref. Chapter VIF.

## FORM VIID 1.01(c)

### (Mortgage "due on sale")[1]

### ALTERNATIVE CLAUSE

*Due on sale.*

(a) No conveyance may be made of the mortgaged premises without approval of Mortgagee, upon such forms as it shall require, and upon payment of its standard assumption fee prevailing at the time of such transfer. Failure to comply with this provision of this mortgage shall entitle Mortgagee, at its option, immediately or thereafter, to declare the entire principal balance, interest, and other charges immediately due and payable, and upon failure to make such payment, the mortgage shall be deemed in default, and all rights shall then accrue to Mortgagee for foreclosure and other remedies afforded herein.

(b) That if conveyance should be made by the Mortgagor of the Premises herein described or any part thereof, without the written consent of the Mortgagee and without assumption in regular form of law by the grantee of the obligation of the Mortgagee created hereunder, then and in that event, and at the option of the Mortgagee, and without notice to the Mortgagor, all sums of money secured hereby shall immediately and concurrently with such conveyance become due and payable and in default, whether the same are so due and payable and in default by the specific terms hereof or not.

[1]Recent cases re enforceability of due-on-sale clauses: *Price v. Florida Federal Sav. & Loan Ass'n,* 524 F. Supp 175 (M.D. Fla. 1981); *First Fed. Sav. & Loan Ass'n. of Gadsden City v. Peterson,* 516 F. Supp. 732 (N.D. Fla. 1981); *Krause v. Columbia Sav. & Loan Ass'n.* 631 P. 2d 1158 (Colo. CA 1981); *Garber v. Fullerton Sav. & Loan Ass'n,* 172 Cal. Rptr. 423 (4th Dist., Div. Two 1981); *Dunham v. Ware Sav. Bank,* 423 N.E. 2d 998 (Mass. 1981); *Wellenkamp v. Bank of America,* 148 Cal. Rptr. 379 (1978); *De La Cuesta v. Fidelity Federal Sav. & Loan Ass'n,* 175 Cal. Rptr. 467 (Cal. 1981).

## FORM VIID 1.02

### (Mortgage securing bond for operating loan to corporation for manufacturing plant)[1]

### MORTGAGE

THIS INDENTURE, made this 1st day of March, 1983, between ABLE MANUFACTURING, INC., a Pennsylvania corporation (herein called "Mortgagor") of the one part, and the FIRST BANK OF PITTSBURGH (herein called "Mortgagee") of the other part.

WHEREAS, the Mortgagor, in and by its bond and warrant obligatory under its hand and seal duly executed, bearing even date herewith, stands bound unto the said Mortgagee in the sum of Fifty Thousand Dollars ($50,000) lawful money of the United States of America, conditioned for the payment of the just sum of that lawful money as aforesaid together with interest thereon, payable at the rate of Twelve Percent (12%) per annum, without any fraud or further delay; and for the production to the Mortgagee, its successors, or assigns, on or before the 1st day of April of each and every year, of receipts for all taxes and water rents of the current year assessed upon the mortgaged premises, and also, from time to time, and at all times, until payment of said principal sum, for the keeping of the buildings herein mentioned insured against loss or damage by fire for the benefit of the Mortgagee in the sum of Fifty Thousand Dollars ($50,000).

PROVIDED, HOWEVER, and it is thereby expressly agreed, that if at any time default shall be made in the payment of interest as aforesaid for the space of ten (10) days after any payment thereof shall fall due or in such production to the Mortgagee, its successors, or assigns, on or before the first day of April of each and every year, of such receipts for taxes and water rates of the current year upon the mortgaged premises, or in the maintenance of such insurance, then, and in such case, the whole principal debt aforesaid shall, at the option of the said Mortgagee, its successors, or assigns, become due and payable immediately; and payment of said principal debt, and all interest thereon, may be enforced and recovered at once, anything therein contained to the contrary notwithstanding.

AND PROVIDED FURTHER, HOWEVER, and it is thereby expressly agreed, that if at any time hereafter, by reason of any default in payment, either of said principal sum at maturity, or of said interest, or in production of said receipts for taxes and water rents within the time specified, or the maintenance of such insurance, a writ or execution is properly issued upon the judgment obtained upon said obligation, or by virtue of said warrant of attorney, or an action of mortgage foreclosure is brought upon this indenture of mortgage, an attorney's commission for collection, viz.: Five Percent (5%) shall be payable, and shall be recovered in addition to all principal and interest then due, besides costs of suit, and all expenses of effecting such insurance, and thereby waiving the right of inquisition on any real estate that may be levied upon under a judgment obtained by virtue hereof and voluntarily condemning the same, and authorize the entry of such condemnation upon said writ of execution and agreeing that the said real estate may be sold under the same; and also, waiving and relinquishing all benefit of each and every law now or hereafter in force to exempt from levy and sale on execution the said mortgaged premises or any other property whatsoever, or any part of the proceeds arising from any sale thereof; as in and by the said recited obligation and the condition thereof, relation being thereunto had, may more fully and at large appear.

NOW THIS INDENTURE WITNESSETH, that the said Mortgagor, as well for and in consideration of the aforesaid debt or principal sum of Fifty Thousand Dollars ($50,000), and for the better securing the payment of the same, with interest unto the said Mortgagee, its successors, and assigns, in discharge of the said recited obligation, as for and in consideration of the further sum of One Dollar ($1), unto it in hand well and truly paid by the said Mortgagee at and before the sealing and delivery hereof, the receipt whereof is hereby acknowledged, has granted, bargained, sold, aliened, enfeoffed, released, and confirmed, and by these presents does grant, bargain, sell, alien, enfeoff, release, and confirm unto the said Mortgagee its successors, and assigns, all that property described as follows:

(Insert legal description of the real property and fixtures and personal property included, or insert a reference to a "Rider A, attached hereto and made part hereof," in which you give those descriptions.)[2]

TOGETHER WITH ALL AND SINGULAR, the ways, waters, watercourses rights, liberties, privileges, improvements, hereditaments, and appurtenances whatsoever, thereunto belonging, or in any wise appertaining, and the reversions and remainders, rents, issues, and profits thereof.

TO HAVE AND TO HOLD, the said hereditaments and premises hereby granted, or mentioned and intended so to be, with the appurtenances, unto the said Mortgagee, its successors, and assigns, to and for the only proper use and behoof of the said Mortgagee, its successors and assigns forever. And the said Mortgagor, for its successors and assigns, does hereby covenant, promise, and agree, to and with the said Mortgagee, its successors, and assigns, that if the said Mortgagor, its successors, and assigns, shall neglect or refuse to keep up the aforesaid insurance, it shall be lawful for the said Mortgagee, its successors, or assigns, to insure the said building in a sum sufficient to fire, and all costs and expenses of effecting such insurance shall be treated as part of the principal debt in a suit upon this mortgage.

PROVIDED ALWAYS, NEVERTHELESS, that if the said Mortgagor, its successors, or assigns, do and shall well and truly pay, or cause to be paid, unto the said Mortgagee, its successors, or assigns, the aforesaid debt or principal sum of Fifty Thousand Dollars ($50,000) on the days and times hereinbefore mentioned and appointed for payment of the same, together with interest as aforesaid, and shall produce to the said Mortgagee, its successors, or assigns, on or before the first day of April of each and every year, receipts for all taxes and water rents of the current year assessed upon the mortgaged premises, without any fraud or further delay, and without any deduction, defalcation, or abatement to be made of anything herein mentioned to be paid or done, and shall keep the buildings herein mentioned insured as aforesaid, then, and from thenceforth, as will this present indenture, and the estate hereby granted, as the said recited obligation shall cease, determine, and become void, anything hereinbefore contained to the contrary thereof in any wise notwithstanding.

AND PROVIDED, ALSO, that is, shall, and may be lawful for the said Mortgagee, its successors, or assigns, when and as soon as the principal debt or sum hereby secured shall become due and payable as aforesaid, or in case default shall be made for the space of ten (10) days in the payment of interest on the said principal sum after any payment thereof shall fall due, or in case there shall be default in the production to the said Mortgagee, its successors, or assigns, on or before the first day of April of each and every year, of such receipts for taxes and water rents the current year assessed upon the mortgaged premises, or in the maintenance of the insurance as aforesaid, to bring an action of mortgage foreclosure upon this indenture of mortgage, and to proceed thereon to judgment and execution for the recovery of the whole of said principal debt, and all interest due thereon, together with an attorney's commission for colllection, viz.: Five Percent (5%) besides cost of suit, and all expenses of effecting such insurance without further stay, any law usage, or custom to the contrary notwithstanding.

IN WITNESS WHEREOF, the said Mortgagor to these presents has hereunto duly caused its corporate seal to be affixed and its corporate name to be signed on its behalf by its duly authorized Vice-President on the day and year first above written.

(CORPORATE SEAL)    ABLE MANUFACTURING, INC.

(John Doe) _____    By_(Richard Able)_____
Secretary of the Corporation    Vice-President

It is hereby certified that the address of the mortgagee within named is 100 Wood Street, Pittsburgh, PA 00000.

_____
(signature of a representative of Mortgagee)

COMMONWEALTH OF PENNSYLVANIA
COUNTY OF ALLEGHENY

On this the 1st day of March, 1983, before me, the undersigned officer, personally appeared Richard Able, who acknowledged himself to be a Vice-President of Able Manufacturing, Inc., a Pennsylvania corporation, and that he, as such Vice-President, being authorized so to do, executed the foregoing Mortgage for the purposes therein contained, by signing the name of the corporation by himself as Vice-President.

IN WITNESS WHEREOF, I hereunto set my hand and official seal.

_____
Notary Public

My commission expires:

[1] *55 Am. Jur. 2d Mortgages*, paras. 106–109.
[2] Ref. Form VIID 1.01(b) and Part VI F.

**FORM VIID 1.02(a)**

(Mortgage bond made by corporation, with power to confess
judgment)

**BOND[1]**

KNOW ALL MEN BY THESE PRESENTS, that I, we, Able Manufacturing, Inc., a Pennsylvania corporation having its principal place of business at 100 East Drive, Neartown, Pennsylvania (herein called the "Obligor"), are held and firmly bound unto FIRST BANK OF PITTSBURGH, a corporation organized under the laws of the United States of America, having its domicile in the City of Pittsburgh, County of Allegheny, Commonwealth of Pennsylvania, (herein called the "Obligee"), in the sum of One Hundred Thousand Dollars ($100,000) lawful money of the United States of America, to be paid to the said Obligee, its certain attorney, successors, or assigns, to which payment well and truly to be made, the said Obligor do bind myself, my heirs, executors, administrators, and assigns, and every one of them, jointly and severally, firmly by these presents. And also conditioned that anything herein provided to the contrary notwithstanding, it is expressly understood and agreed that the Obligation of this Bond shall cover, as well, any future advances that may be made by Obligee to Obligor, at any time or times hereafter, provided that at no time may the total balance due by Obligor to Obligee hereunder, whether the same represents, in whole or in part, the initial advance or any future advance or advances, exceed the sum of Fifty Thousand Dollars ($50,000), AND the said Obligor does hereby empower Peter Poe, attorney of the Court of Common Pleas at Pittsburgh, Pennsylvania, or any attorney of any Court of Record within the Commonwealth of Pennsylvania or elsewhere, to appear for me and, with or without a declaration filed, confess judgment[2] against me in favor of the Obligee, its successors, or assigns, as of any term, for the sum of One Hundred Thousand Dollars ($100,000), which sum shall include and cover all payments required to be made by the Obligor in and by the terms and conditions of this Bond as hereinafter set forth, including also an attorney's commission for collection of Five Percent (5%) of the total of all such payments, together with costs of suit; and does hereby waive stay of execution or other process on such judgment, and holding inquisition on any real estate levied on by virtue of any writ sued out on such judgment is hereby dispensed with and waived and condemnation agreed to, which real estate may be sold under any lawful writ; and all exemption of personal property from levy and sale on any execution under any law in force or hereafter passed is hereby waived, and further, I hereby waive all errors, defects, and imperfections in entering the said judgment or in any writ or process or proceeding thereon, or thereto, or in anywise touching or concerning the same, and for the confession and entry of such judgment, this shall be sufficient warrant and authority, and said Obligor, and for its successors and assigns, does hereby remise, release, and forever quitclaim to the said Obligee, its successors, and assigns, and its attorney, to confess judgment all and all manner of error, defects, and imperfections in the entering of such judgment, or any process or proceeding thereon or thereto, or anywise touching on concerning the same.

THE CONDITION OF THIS BOND IS SUCH that if the Obligor, its successors, or assigns shall well and truly pay or cause to be paid to the Obligee, its successors, or assigns, the sum of Fifty Thousand Dollars ($50,000) and all additional moneys advanced by the Obligee as herein or otherwise legally provided, lawful moneys aforesaid, with interest at the rate of Twelve Percent (12%) per annum (such interest to be computed, at the rate of one-twelfth of the above annual interest, on the unpaid balance of the loan at the beginning of each month and charged against the loan before application of the payment for the month), in monthly payments of not less than Five Hundred Dollars ($500), beginning April 1, 1983, and monthly thereafter until the loan, additional advances, interest, and other charges herein covenanted to be paid are paid in full; and shall also pay or cause to be paid unto Obligee, in addition to, and concurrently with, such monthly installments of principal and interest, a further sum equal to the total of one-twelfth of the annual taxes, and other annual charges and assessments, if any, now assessed, or from time to time to be assessed by any municipal or other public authority, against the premises described in the Mortgage securing this Obligation, one-twelfth of any annual tax hereafter levied by any duly constituted authority upon Obligee on account or measured by the amount of this mortgaged premises, and one-twelfth of the annual cost of such life insurance as to Mortgagee shall seem necessary, all insurance to be procured through insurance companies approved by the Mortgagee. Anything herein provided to the contrary notwithstanding, it is expressly understood and agreed that the Obligation of this Bond shall cover, as well, any future advances that may be made by Obligee to

Obligor, at any time or times hereafter, provided that at no time may the total balance due by Obligor to any future advance or advances exceed the sum of Fifty Thousand Dollars ($50,000), provided that nothing herein contained shall be considered as limiting the amounts that shall be secured hereby when advanced to protect the security or in accordance with covenants contained in the mortgage.

PROVIDED FURTHER, and it is expressly understood and agreed, that the monthly payments made by Obligor shall be applied first to interest on the unpaid balance of the principal sum, and the remainder thereof shall be credited on account of said sum, and (except when taxes are paid to the Obligee in monthly installments) shall also well and truly pay all taxes (which said term "taxes" shall wherever used in the Bond be taken and held to include all taxes that may hereafter be assessed, levied, or charged against the premises granted in the Mortgage accompanying this Bond as the same are or fall due, and shall on or before the first day of December of each and every year produce and deliver to the Obligee receipts for all such "taxes" for the current year assessed upon the mortgaged premises, and shall also keep and maintain at all times, in such company or companies as the Obligee shall approve, a policy or policies of insurance against loss or damage by fire, or other risk as required by the Obligee, in an amount not less than Fifty Thousand Dollars ($50,000) upon the buildings and improvements upon the said premises, and all excess of the required amount or not, shall be duly assigned as collateral security to the Obligee, and to be by said Obligee retained, and Obligor shall also pay promptly the cost and premium on said policy or policies of insurance, and shall also keep and maintain the buildings now on the mortgaged premises and any buildings erected thereon while this obligation shall be in force, in good and sufficient repair, and shall also forthwith repay unto the Obligee any sum or sums of money paid by the Obligee for or on account of any "taxes" and premiums of insurance that the Obligor has not paid and maintained as above required (which, although not so bound, the Obligee may pay and maintain without impairing any other of the rights hereunder, and, at the option of the Obligee, all such payments or advances made by the Obligee may be added to the unpaid balance of the loan).

THEN, without any fraud or further delay, this Bond shall be void.

PROVIDED, however, and it is hereby expressly agreed, that should default be made in any payment herein contracted for or any part thereof for a period of ten (10) days after the same becomes due and payable, then, in that event, Obligee shall have the right and privilege, at its option, to increase the rate of interest hereon to the maximum legal rate permitted by law, said increase to remain in effect during the continuance of the default.

PROVIDED FURTHER, however, and it is hereby expressly agreed, that if at any time default be made in payment of said monthly installments, and the total arrearages are equivalent to two (2) contracted monthly installment payments; or default be made in the payment of the monthly installment for taxes or in the payment of "taxes" when due, or the prompt and punctual maintenance of said insurance assigned as aforesaid when due, or the payment of the cost and premium thereof when due, whether purchased by the Obligor or Obligee, or of any sum or sums paid by the Obligee for or on account of any taxes or premiums of either (which payments have not, at the option of the Obligee, been added to the unpaid balance of the loan), or maintenance of said buildings in good and sufficient repair after notice from the Obligee, or in the event the building or buildings shall be changed or altered, or if the title to the mortgaged premises be transferred to anyone other than the survivor of the Obligor, without the prior written consent of the Obligee, or in case of any default under the terms hereof or the accompanying Mortgage, whereby the security of the Obligee is or shall be impaired, and such default in any of these respects exists for a period of thirty (30) days; then and in such case the unpaid balance of the loan, including additional advances and unpaid interest, shall, at the option of the Obligee, become due and payable immediately, and payment of said unpaid balance of the loan, additional advances, and all interest thereon, and other payments herein agreed to be made by the Obligor may be enforced and recovered at once, anything herein contained to the contrary notwithstanding; and a writ or writs of Fieri Facias or other lawful writ may be issued upon the judgment obtained upon this obligation by virtue of the warrant of attorney herein contained, or a complaint in an action of mortgage foreclosure may be filed upon the accompanying Mortgage and prosecuted to judgment and execution and sale to recover the unpaid balance of the loan, all additional advances made by the Obligee as herein or otherwise legally provided, all interest thereon remaining unpaid, together with all fees, costs, and expenses of collecting the same, including an attorney's commission of Five Percent (5%), anything herein contained to the contrary notwithstanding; and as a concurrent and cumulative remedy or option thereon for the benefit of the Obligee, its successors, or assigns, the said Obligor does hereby authorize and empower any attorney of any Court of Record to appear for him in any court of competent jurisdiction, to confess judgment[2] against him in favor of the Obligee, its successors, or assigns, in an amicable action of ejectment for possession of the property secured by the Mortgage accompanying this Bond.

It is further expressly understood and agreed that, if any sum or sums of money shall become payable under any policies of insurance insuring the mortgaged premises, or by virtue of any condemnation or taking of the mortgaged premises for public use, the Obligee shall have the option to receive and apply the same on account of this Obligation, or permit the Obligor to receive and use it, or any part thereof, for the purpose of repairing the mortgaged premises, or for any other purposes, without thereby waiving or impairing this Obligation, or the lien of the Mortgage securing it. The Obligor hereby expressly assigns and transfers unto the Obligee all sums of money payable under such insurance claim, condemnation proceedings, rents, rentals, royalties, or proceeds from the sale of minerals or standing timber, and does hereby irrevocably nominate, constitute, and appoint the Obligee to act for Obligor as a true and lawful attorney for the collection thereof.

It is further expressly understood and agreed that the remedies of this Obligation and the accompanying Mortgage for the enforcement of the payment of the principal sum hereby secured, together with interest thereon, and for the performance of the covenants, conditions, and agreements, matters and things herein contained are cumulative and concurrent and may be pursued singly, or succesively, or together, at the sole discretion of the Obligee, and may be exercised as often as occasion therefor shall occur.

WITNESS the hand of the duly authorized President of the Corporation and the affixing of its corporate seal this 1st day of March, 1983.

(CORPORATE SEAL)                                     ABLE MANUFACTURING, INC.

_____           By_ (Richard Able)_____
Secretary of the Corporation                             President

(Note: mortgage bond need not be acknowledged.)

[1]Compare Form VIID 1.01(a), which is a mortgage *note*.
[2]Check state statute to determine validity or enforceability of confession of judgment clause.

## FORM VIID 1.03

### (Agreement for deed having practical effect of mortgage in the state of Florida—from a business corporation [not a developer] to an individual)

### AGREEMENT FOR DEED[1]

THIS AGREEMENT FOR DEED made this 12th day of August, 1983, by and between Roe Electronics Inc., a Florida corporation having its principal place of business at 100 Main Street, Middletown, Florida 00000 (herein called "Vendor"), and John Doe, and Mary Doe, his wife, residing at 100 East Drive, Middletown, Florida 00000 (herein called "Purchaser"),

*WITNESSETH:*

1. *Description.* That if Purchaser shall first make the payments and perform the covenants herein on their part to be performed, the Vendor hereby covenants and agrees to convey to the Purchaser or their heirs, personal representatives, or assigns, and Purchasers agree to buy, the following described property in fee simple, free and clear of all incumbrances, except as stated herein, which property is located in Middle County, Florida, and described as follows:

Lot 10, Block A, PEACEFUL ACRES, according to the plat thereof recorded in Plat Book 2, Page 000, of the public records of Middle County, Florida.

TOGETHER with 1983 Super Modular Home three-bedroom, bearing Serial No. 0000: subject to the restrictions on use set forth in Rider A, attached hereto and made part hereof.

2. *Price.* The total purchase price of the above-described property shall be the sum of Thirty-three Thousand Dollars ($33,000), payable at the times and in the manner following:

(a) Purchaser is hereby given credit in the amount of Five Hundred Dollars ($500) for down payment heretofore made by Purchaser to Vendor, receipt of which is hereby acknowledged by Vendor.

(b) The balance of the purchase price, being the sum of Thirty-two Thousand Five Hundred Dollars ($32,500), to bear interest at the rate of Twelve Percent (12%) per annum, shall be paid at the rate of Three Hundred and Eighty-six and 44/100 Dollars ($386.44) per month, beginning on September 15, 1983, and on the 15th day of each and every calendar month thereafter until the sum is paid in full.

(c) Said payment shall be paid directly to Roe Developers, Inc., at the above-stated address

(d) Each of the payments shall be credited first to interest and the balance to principal.

(e) Prepayment by Purchaser shall be permitted at any time and from time to time without penalty.

3. *Delivery of Deed.*

(a) When Purchaser has completed making all payments and performs the covenants herein on their part to be performed, the Vendor shall forthwith deliver to Purchaser good and sufficient marketable title, free and clear of all incumbrances, except as stated herein, by general warranty deed of conveyance to the Purchaser.

(b) Required documentary transfer stamps shall be placed on the deed by Purchaser.

4. *Possession.* The Purchaser shall be permitted to go into possession of the property covered by this Agreement on the date of its execution, and shall assume all liability for insurance, taxes, and maintenance from and after that date. The Purchaser agrees to maintain the exterior and interior of all buildings in good condition, and to maintain fire and extended coverage insurance on the buildings in an amount of not less than the balance due Vendor under this Agreement or the maximum insurable value of the property, whichever is less, and to name the Vendor as loss payee.

5. *Default.* The time of payment shall be of the essence, and in the event of any default in payment of any part of the purchase money as and when it becomes due or in the performance of any other obligations assumed by the Purchaser in this Agreement, and in the event that the default shall continue for a period of fifteen (15) days, then the Vendor may declare the whole of the balance due under this Agreement as immediately due and payable and collectible, or the Vendor may rescind this Agreement, retaining the cash consideration paid up to the time of default as liquidated damages, and this Agreement then shall become null and void. In either event, Vendor shall notify Purchaser of its election by giving Purchaser ten (10) days' written notice by certified or registered U.S. mail to the Purchaser at the address of the above-described property, which is Star R. 1 Box 100, Middletown, Florida 00000. In the event that it is necessary for the Vendor to enforce this Agreement by foreclosure proceedings or otherwise, all costs of those proceedings, including a reasonable attorney's fee, shall be paid by the Purchaser.

6. *Benefit and liability.* The obligations and benefits under this Contract shall extend to the heirs, personal representatives, successors, and assigns of the respective parties to it.

7. *Entire agreement.* This Contract constitutes the entire agreement of the parties. No representations, oral or implied, have been made to Purchaser to induce them to enter into this Agreement, other than those expressly provided herein.

8. *Forbearance.* No waiver of any provision shall constitute a continuing waiver of such provision or of any other provision then or thereafter, unless reduced to writing and expressly made a modification of the provision.

IN WITNESS WHEREOF, the parties have duly and respectively set their hands and seals the day and year first above written.

VENDOR:
ROE ELECTRONICS, INC.

(Peter Poe)
Secretary of the Corporation

By (Richard Roe)
President

PURCHASER:

JOHN DOE

MARY DOE

(Attach Rider A setting forth any restrictions on use that are to be included in the eventual deed.)

STATE OF FLORIDA
COUNTY OF MIDDLE:

I HEREBY CERTIFY that the foregoing Agreement for Deed was acknowledged this 12th day of August, 1983, by Richard Roe, President of Roe Electronics, Inc., a Florida corporation, on behalf of the corporation.

_____
Notary Public

My commission expires:

STATE OF FLORIDA:
COUNTY OF MIDDLE

I HEREBY CERTIFY THAT the foregoing Agreement for Deed was acknowledged this 12th day of March, 1983, by John Doe and Mary Doe, his wife,

_____
Notary Public

My commission expires:

*23 Am. Jur. 2d Deeds,* paras. 4 and 5; and *55 Am. Jur. 2d Mortgages,* para. 13.

## FORM VIID 1.04

### (Deed in trust as mortgage for balance of purchase price)

### DEED IN TRUST[1]

THIS DEED made this 10th day of May, 1983, between Doe Enterprises Inc., a Virginia corporation having its principal place of business at 100 Main Street, Middletown, Virginia 00000 (herein called "Grantor"), party of the one part, and First Bank of Virginia, a Virginia banking corporation having its principal place of business at 500 East Street, Richmond, Virginia 00000 (herein called "Trustee"), party of the other part, WITNESSETH:

    1. Grantor does grant unto the Trustee the following property: (give legal description of the property as it appears on deed to Grantor):

IN TRUST to secure the payment of the balance of the purchase price of the above-described real property owed by Grantor to the Vendor, Richard Roe of 100 West Street, Middletown, Virginia 00000, balance to be secured is evidenced by a note of even date herewith in the principal amount of One Hundred Thousand Dollars ($100,000) payable on or before April 30, 1993, bearing interest at the rate of Twelve Percent (12%) per annum, payable to National Enterprises, Inc., a Delaware corporation, all terms of which note are incorporated herein by reference.

    2. Upon the full payment of the above note and the performance of all promises and covenants contained therein, and upon evidence of same being presented to the Trustee, the Trustee shall execute to Grantor a Deed of Release, reciting that the evidence of the debt marked paid has been exhibited to the Trustee.

    WITNESS the following duly authorized signatures and corporate seals of the parties the day and year above written.

(CORPORATE SEAL)            DOE ENTERPRISES, INC., Grantor

(Peter Poe)_____    By_(John Doe)_____
Secretary of the Corporation               President

(CORPORATE SEAL)            FIRST BANK OF VIRGINIA, Trustee

(Charles Coe)_____    By_(Richard Rich)_____
Secretary of the Corporation               President

[1]Used as mortgages in California, Illinois, Missouri, Virginia, and District of Columbia, inter alia. See Form VIID 1.04(a) for deed of release of deed in trust.

## FORM VIID 1.04(a)

### (Deed of release of deed in trust upon payment of the note secured by the deed in trust)

### DEED OF RELEASE[1]

THIS DEED made the 30th day of April, 1993, between First Bank of Virginia a Virginia banking corporation, party of the first part (herein called "Trustee"); and Doe Enterprises, Inc., a Virginia corporation, party of the second part; and Richard Roe of Middletown, Middle County, Virginia (herein called "Creditor"), party of the third part.

WITNESSETH THAT:

WHEREAS, the party of the second part did, by deed bearing the date 10th day of March, 1983, and recorded in the Richmond City Office of the Clerk of Circuit Court, Division II, at No. 00000, convey to First Bank of Virginia, Trustee, the following property:

(give legal description of the property as it appeared in the Deed in Trust that is being released)

in trust to secure the payment of the balance, etc.

(set forth the liability that was secured by the original Deed in Trust, using the language appearing in the Deed in Trust); and

WHEREAS, the said debt has been fully paid, as evidenced by the said note having been exhibited to the Trustee marked paid, and the said Creditor signing this deed.

NOW, THEREFORE, in consideration of the premises, and of the sum of Five Dollars ($5) to it in hand paid, the Trustee does release unto the party of the second part, his heirs, and assigns all interest, right, claim, or title that he may have in or to the above-described property, by virtue of the said Deed of Trust.

WITNESS the following signatures and seals the day and year first above written.

| | |
|---|---|
| (CORPORATE SEAL) | FIRST BANK OF VIRGINIA |
| (Charles Coe) | By (Richard Rich) |
| Secretary of the Corporation | President |
| | RICHARD ROE, CREDITOR |

COMMONWEALTH OF VIRGINIA
CITY OF RICHMOND

I, Mary Jones, a notary public in and for the state and city aforesaid, do certify that John Doe and Peter Poe and Charles Coe and Richard Rich, whose names as Presidents and Secretaries of the respective corporations, Doe Enterprises, Inc., and First Bank of Virginia, are signed to the writing above, bearing date on the 10th day of March, 1983, have acknowledged the same before me in my City aforesaid.

GIVEN under my hand and official seal this 10th day of March, 1983.

My term of offfice expires on the 1st day of January, 1984.

_____
Notary Public

(Check state statute and/or practice as to need for Creditor to join where the deed recites "that the evidence of the deed has been exhibited to the Trustee marked paid.")

COMMONWEALTH OF VIRGINIA
CITY OF RICHMOND

I, Mary Jones, a notary public in and for the state and city aforesaid, do certify that Richard Rich and Charles Coe, whose names as President and Secretary of First Bank of Virginia, are signed to the writing above, bearing date on the 30th day of April, 1993, have acknowledged the same before me in my City aforesaid.

GIVEN under my hand and official seal this 30th day of April, 1993.

My term of office expires on the 20th day of June, 1994.

_____
Notary Public

COMMONWEALTH OF VIRGINIA
COUNTY OF MIDDLE

    I, Jack Jones, a notary public for the state and county aforesaid, do certify that Richard Roe, whose name is signed to the foregoing Deed of Trust bearing date on the 30th day of April, 1993, has acknowledged the same before me in my County aforesaid.

    GIVEN under my hand and official seal this 30th day of April, 1993.

    My term of office expires on the 31st day of August, 1993.

_____

Notary Public

[1]Used to reconvey real property held under a deed in trust in California, Illinois, Missouri, Virginia, and District of Columbia, inter alia. See Form VIID 1.04 for a deed in trust.

## FORM VIID 1.05

### (Assignment by mortgagee of mortgage and bond)

### ASSIGNMENT OF MORTGAGE AND BOND[1]

    KNOW ALL MEN BY THESE PRESENTS, that the FIRST BANK OF PITTSBURGH, mortgagee in the indenture of mortgage herein described (herein called "Assignor"), for and in consideration of the sum of Twenty Thousand Dollars ($20,000), unto it paid by SECOND BANK OF PITTSBURGH, a Pennsylvania banking corporation having its principal office at P.O. Box 100, McKeesport, Pennsylvania 00000 (herein called "Assignee"), receipt whereof is hereby acknowledged, does hereby grant, bargain, sell, assign, transfer, and set over unto the Assignee, its successors, and assigns, forever, all of Assignor's right, title, and interest in that indenture of mortgage given and executed by Able Manufacturing, Inc., a Pennsylvania corporation, to Assignor on May 1, 1983, and recorded in the Office of the Recorder of Deeds of Allegheny County, Pennsylvania, in Mortgage Book 000, Page 000; and

    Also the bond received in that indenture of mortgage and all moneys, principal, and interest due and to become due on that bond, and the warrant of attorney to confess judgment contained therein; together with all rights, titles, interests, remedies, and incidents thereunto belonging;

    TO HAVE, HOLD, RECEIVE, AND TAKE, all and singular the hereditaments and premises hereby granted and assigned

    (Note: Assignee will probably want an Estoppel Certificate or a Reduction Certificate. See Forms VIB 1.07 and 1.08, or a covenant as to the amount due can be included in this assignment. See Form VD 1.06 for such a covenant in an assignment.)

    IN WITNESS WHEREOF, the Assignee to these presents has hereunto duly caused its corporate seal to be affixed and its corporate name to be signed on its behalf by its duly authorized Vice-President this 1st day of March, 1987.

(CORPORATE SEAL)                  FIRST BANK OF PITTSBURGH

(Peter Coe)_____    By_(Richard Rich)_____

Secretary of the Corporation                Vice-President

    It is hereby certified that the address of the within-named Assignee of the above mortgage indenture is P.O. Box 100, McKeesport, Pennsylvania 00000.

_____

(signature of a representative of Assignee)

COMMONWEALTH OF PENNSYLVANIA
COUNTY OF ALLEGHENY

    On the 1st day of March, 1987, before me, the undersigned officer, personally appeared Richard Rich, who acknowledged himself to be a Vice-President of First Bank of Pittsburgh, a Pennsylvania banking corporation, and that he, as such Vice-President, being authorized so to do, executed the foregoing Assignment of Bond and Mortgage for the purposes therein contained, by signing the name of the corporation by himself as Vice-President.

IN WITNESS WHEREOF, I hereunto set my hand and official seal.

_____

Notary Public

My commission expires:

[1]*55 Am. Jur. 2d Mortgages,* paras. 1269, 1273, 1277–1280, 1283, 1284, 1316–1319, 1387, 1399, and 1404. See also Form VIID 1.06, and ref. Forms VIIIB 1.07 and 1.08 for Estoppel Certificate and Reduction Certificate. Compare Form VIID 1.07 for assumption.

## FORM VIID 1.06

### (Assignment by mortgagee of mortgage securing note with covenant as to amount due on the mortgage)

### ASSIGNMENT OF MORTGAGE AND NOTE[1]

KNOW ALL MEN, that FIRST BANK OF MIDDLETOWN, Florida, a Florida banking corporation, Assignor, in consideration of One Hundred Ten Thousand Eight Hundred and Fifteen Dollars ($110,815), paid by FIRST BANK OF TAMPA, Florida, Assignee, does hereby assign to Assignee, its successors, and assigns a mortgage deed made by Doe Appliances, Inc., a Florida corporation, given to Assignor to secure a purchase money debt in the sum of One Hundred Twenty Thousand Dollars ($120,000) and interest, dated May 1, 1983, recorded on May 2, 1983, in the public records of Middle County, Florida, at O.R. 000, Page 000, covering property located in Middle County, Florida, together with the Mortgage Installment Note described in the Mortgage Deed and the money on the note with interest.

TO HAVE AND TO HOLD the same to the Assignee, its successors, and assigns forever.

AND THE ASSIGNOR hereby covenants that there is now owing upon the note secured by the mortgage, without offset or defense of any kind, the principal sum of One Hundred Ten Thousand Eight Hundred and Fifteen Dollars ($110,815), with interest at Twelve Percent (12%) per annum from May 1, 1984.

Executed in Middletown, Florida, this 1st day of June, 1984.

(CORPORATE SEAL)                 FIRST BANK OF MIDDLETOWN, FLORIDA

(Peter Poe)_____    By_(Richard Rich)_____

Secretary of the Corporation             Vice-President

STATE OF FLORIDA
COUNTY OF MIDDLE

I HEREBY CERTIFY that the foregoing Assignment of Mortgage and Note was acknowledged this 1st day of June, 1984, by Richard Rich, Vice-President of First Bank of Middletown, Florida, a Florida banking corporation, on behalf of the corporation.

_____

Notary Public

My commission expires:

[1]Ref. footnotes to Form VIID 1.05.

## FORM VIID 1.07

### (Assumption of mortgage agreement between purchaser of property from mortgagor with written consent of mortgagee)[1]

### ASSUMPTION OF MORTGAGE[1]

KNOW ALL MEN, that Roe International, Inc., a New York corporation having its principal place of business at 100 Broadway, New York, New York 00000, in consideration of One Dollar ($1)

and other good and valuable consideration, hereby assumes the payment of the debt evidenced by bond secured by a mortgage from Able Manufacturing, Inc., a Pennsylvania corporation, to FIRST BANK OF PITTSBURGH, a Pennsylvania banking corporation, dated March 1, 1983, and recorded in the office of the Recorder of Deeds of Allegheny County, Pennsylvania, in Mortgage Book, Vol. 000, Page 000, and agrees to assume payment of all sums due under said bond and the obligation of said mortgage, and to perform all covenants and promises of said bond and mortgage in accordance with the terms thereof, except as specifically modified herein.

Roe International, Inc., hereby agrees to indemnify and hold Able Manufacturing, Inc., harmless forever from all claims of FIRST BANK OF PITTSBURGH on or by reason of said bond and mortgage, including all costs and reasonable attorney's fees incurred by Able Manufacturing, Inc., in enforcing this indemnity; provided, however, that the amount presently due on the bond does not exceed Forty Thousand One Hundred and Ten Dollars ($40,110), as shown on the Mortgagee's Estoppel Certificate signed by FIRST BANK OF PITTSBURGH, which Certificate is incorporated herein by reference, together with the annexed written consent to this assumption by said mortgagee.

Executed in New York City, State of New York this 1st day of March, 1985.

(CORPORATE SEAL)                                    ROE INTERNATIONAL, INC.

(Peter Poe)                                         By  (Richard Roe)
Secretary of the Corporation                            President

## CONSENT OF MORTGAGEE

The undersigned, owner and holder of the within-described bond and mortgage, hereby consents to the foregoing assumption of mortgage by Roe International, Inc., a New York corporation, in consideration of the payment of One Dollar ($1) and the promises and covenants of Roe International, Inc., that it thereby assumes liability for the due performance of all and singular the conditions, provisions, and terms of the bond and mortgage on the part and in the stead of Able Manufacturing, Inc.

Executed in Pittsburgh, Pennsylvania, this 1st day of March, 1985.

(CORPORATE SEAL)                                    FIRST BANK OF PITTSBURGH

(Charles Coe)                                       By  (Richard Rich)
Secretary of the Corporation                            Vice-President

STATE OF NEW YORK
COUNTY OF KINGS


STATE OF NEW YORK
COUNTY OF KINGS

On the 1st day of March, 1985, before me personally came Richard Roe, to me known, who, being by me duly sworn, did depose and say that he resides at 1000 Park Ave., New York, New York; that he is the President of Roe International, Inc., the corporation described in and that executed the above instrument; that he knows the seal of said corporation; that the seal affixed to said instrument is such corporate seal; that it was so affixed by order of the Board of Directors of said corporation; and that he signed his name thereto by like order.

_____

Notary Public

My commission expires:


COMMONWEALTH OF PENNSYLVANIA
COUNTY OF ALLEGHENY

On this 1st day of March, 1985, before me, the undersigned officer, personally appeared Richard Rich, who acknowledged himself to be the Vice-President of FIRST BANK OF PITTSBURGH, a Pennsylvania banking corporation, and that he, as such Vice-President, being authorized so to do, executed the foregoing Consent of Mortgagee for the purposes therein contained, by signing the name of the corportion by himself as Vice-President.

IN WITNESS WHEREOF, I hereunto set my hand and official seal.

_____

Notary Public

My commission expires:

[1]*55 Am. Jur. 2d Mortgages,* paras. 1047–1049, 1052, 1053, and 1139. See footnotes to Form VIID 1.01(c) as to effect of a "due on sale" clause in a mortgage.

## FORM VIID 1.08

### (Partial release of mortgage by a corporation)

#### PARTIAL RELEASE[1]

KNOW ALL MEN BY THESE PRESENTS: WHEREAS, Doe Appliances, Inc., a Florida corporation, by Mortgage Deed dated the 1st day of May, A.D. 1984, and recorded in the office of the Clerk of the Circuit Court in and for the County of Middle, State of Florida, in Mortgage Book 000, Page 000, granted and conveyed unto First Bank of Middletown, Florida, its successors, and assigns, the premises therein particularly described, to secure the payment of the sum of One Hundred Sixty Thousand Dollars ($160,000), with interest as therein mentioned;

AND WHEREAS, THE SAID Doe Appliances, Inc., Mortgagor, requested the said First Bank of Middletown, Florida, Mortagee, to release the premises hereinafter described, being part of said mortgaged premises, from the lien and operation of said Mortgage;

NOW, THEREFORE, KNOW that the said First Bank of Middletown, Florida, as well in consideration of the premises as of the sum of Five Thousand Dollars ($5,000), to it in hand paid by the said Doe Appliances, Inc., at the time of the execution thereof, the receipt whereof is hereby acknowledged, does remise, release, quitclaim, exonerate, and discharge from the lien and operation of said mortgage unto the said Doe Appliances, Inc., its heirs, and assigns, all that piece, parcel, or tract of land, being a part of the premises conveyed by said mortgage, to wit:

(Give legal description of only that *part* of the entire mortgaged premises that is being released.)

TO HAVE AND TO HOLD the same, with the appurtenances, unto the said Doe Appliances, Inc., its successors, and assigns forever, freed, exonerated, and discharged of and from the lien of said mortgage, and every part thereof; provided, always, nevertheless, that nothing herein contained shall in anywise impair, alter, or diminish the effect, lien, or incumbrance of the aforesaid Mortgage on the remaining part of said mortgaged premises, not hereby released therefrom, or any of the rights and remedies of the holder thereof.

IN WITNESS WHEREOF, the said Mortgagee by its duly authorized officers had hereunto set its hand and seal this 1st day of May, 1984.

(CORPORATE SEAL)      FIRST BANK OF MIDDLETOWN, FLORIDA

(John Doe)         By_(Richard Roe)_____
Secretary of the Corporation    Vice-President

STATE OF FLORIDA
COUNTY OF MIDDLE

I, an officer authorized to take acknowledgments of deeds according to the laws of the State of Florida, duly qualified and acting, HEREBY CERTIFY that Richard Roe and John Doe respectively as Vice-President and Secretary of First Bank of Middletown, Florida, to me personally known, this day acknowledged before me that they executed the foregoing Partial Release of Mortgage as such officers of said corporation, and that they affixed thereto the official seal of said corporation, and I FURTHER CERTIFY that I know the said persons making said acknowledgments to be the individuals described in and who executed the said Partial Release of Mortgage.

IN WITNESS WHEREOF, I hereunto set my hand and official seal at said County and State, this 1st day of May, A.D. 1984.

(NOTARIAL SEAL)                    _____

                                   Notary Public

                                   My commission expires:

[1]*55 Am. Jur. 2d Mortgages,* paras. 1145–1149 and 1406–1407.

## FORM VIID 1.09

### (Satisfaction of mortgage by assignee of mortgage, sometimes called Satisfaction Piece)

### SATISFACTION OF MORTGAGE[1]

MADE this 1st day of May, 1988.
Name of mortgagor: Able Manufacturing, Inc., a Pennsylvania corporation.
Name of mortgagee: First Bank of Pittsburgh
Name of last assignee: Second Bank of Pittsburgh
Date of mortgage: March 1, 1983
Original mortgage debt: $50,000

Mortgage recorded on March 1, 1983, in the office of the Recorder of Deeds of Allegheny County, Pennsylvania, in Mortgage Book 000, Page 000, and the Last Assignment recorded on March 1, 1987, in Mortgage Book 000, Page 000, of premises known as Lots 400, 401, 403, and 405 in the City of McKeesport, County of Allegheny, Commonwealth of Pennsylvania.

The undersigned hereby certifies that the debt secured by the above-mentioned Mortgage has been fully paid or otherwise discharged, and that upon the recording hereof, said Mortgage shall be and is hereby fully and forever satisfied and discharged.

WITNESS the due execution hereof.

(CORPORATE SEAL)                    SECOND BANK OF PITTSBURGH

(Peter Coe)_____ By__(Richard Rich)_____
Secretary of the Corporation            Vice-President

COMMONWEALTH OF PENNSYLVANIA
COUNTY OF ALLEGHENY

ON this the 1st day of May, 1988, before me, the undersigned officer, personally appeared Richard Rich, who acknowledged himself to be a Vice-President of SECOND BANK OF PITTSBURGH, a Pennsylvania banking corporation, and that he, as such Vice-President, being authorized so to do, executed the foregoing instrument for the purposes therein contained, by signing the name of the corporation by himself as Vice-President.

IN WITNESS WHEREOF, I hereunto set my hand and official seal.

(NOTARIAL SEAL)                    _____

                                   Notary Public

                                   My commission expires:

[1]*55 Am. Jur. 2d Mortgages,* paras. 1127–1141 and 1399–1402, and compare para. 1387.

## FORM VIID 1.10

### (Subordination of purchase money mortgage to the lien of a construction mortgage)

### SUBORDINATION AGREEMENT[1]

AGREEMENT made this 1st day of May, 1983, between DOE DEVELOPERS, INC., owner of the property hereinafter described, and hereinafter referred to as the "Owner," and JOHN DOE and MARY DOE, his wife, holders of the Mortgage and Note hereinafter described. WITNESSETH:

WHEREAS, Owner did on March 10, 1982, execute a purchase money mortgage and note to John Doe and Mary Doe, his wife, incumbering the following described property:

(Insert legal description of the property as it appears in the purchase money mortgage.)
to secure a note in the sum of $50,000, dated March 10, 1982, in favor of those mortgages; and

WHEREAS, the Owner has executed a construction loan agreement and desires to execute a mortgage and note in the sum of $150,000, on June 11, 1982, in favor of MIDDLE COUNTY BANK, hereinafter referred to as the "Lender," payable with interest and upon the terms and conditions described therein, which mortgage is to be recorded contemporaneously herewith; and

WHEREAS, it is a condition precedent to obtaining such loan that the construction loan mortgage of the Lender shall be and remain a lien or charge upon the property hereinbefore described, prior and superior to the above-described purchase money lien or charge of the Mortgage; and

WHEREAS, the Lender is willing to make such loan, provided the Mortgage to secure the same is a lien or charge upon the above-described property prior and superior to the lien or charge of the above-described purchase money mortgage, and provided that the mortgagees will specifically and unconditionally subordinate the lien or charge of their purchase money Mortgage to the construction loan mortgage lien of the Lender,

NOW, THEREFORE, in consideration of the premises and other valuable consideration, receipt of which is hereby acknowledged, and in order to induce the Lender to make the loan above referred to, it is agreed as follows:

1. *SUBORDINATION:* The Mortgage securing the note in favor of the Lender referred to above, and any renewals or extensions of such Mortgage and the note secured thereby, shall be and remain at all times a lien or charge on the property herein described, prior and superior to the lien or charge of the purchase money Mortgage in favor of the mortgagees first above mentioned.

2. *ACKNOWLEDGMENT OF SUBORDINATION:* The purchase money mortgagees acknowledge that they hereby intentionally waive, relinquish, postpone, and subordinate the priority and superiority of the lien or charge of their purchase money Mortgage first above mentioned in favor of the lien or charge upon such land of the Mortgage in favor of the Lender, and that they understand that, in reliance upon and in consideration of this waiver, relinquishment, and subordination, specific loans and advances are being and will be made, and as part and parcel thereof, specific monetary and other obligations are being and will be entered into by third parties, which would not be made or entered into but for such reliance upon this waiver, relinquishment, and subordination. The purchase money mortgagees further acknowledge that an endorsement has been placed on the note secured by the purchase money Mortgage, and that such Mortgage has by this instrument been subordinated to the lien or charge of the Mortgage in favor of the Lender.

(Note: type Notice of this Subordination Agreement on the Purchase Money Note.)

3. *APPROVAL OF CONSTRUCTION LOAN AGREEMENT:* The purchase money mortgagees thereby declare that they have personal knowledge of and hereby approve and consent to all the provisions of the loan agreement between the Owner and the Lender for the disbursement of the proceeds of the loan of the Lender, and further acknowledge that the Lender, in making disbursement pursuant to such loan agreement, is under no obligation or duty, nor has the Lender made any representation that it will see to the application of such disbursement by the Owner, and any diversions by the Owner will not defeat this subordination agreement as to the funds so diverted.

4. *CANCELLATION OF CERTAIN PROVISIONS OF PURCHASE MONEY MORTGAGE:* The purchase money mortgagees acknowledge that this agreement shall supersede, and operate as a cancellation of those provisions, if any, in the purchase money mortgage first above mentioned that provide for the automatic superiority of the lien of the purchase money Mortgage to the lien or liens of a mortgage, or mortgages, affecting the whole or part of the above-described property.

5. *ENTIRE AGREEMENT:* This Agreement contains the whole agreement between the parties hereto as to the desired Mortgage loans, and the priority thereof as herein described, and there are no agreements, written or oral, outside or separate from this Agreement, and all prior negotiations, if any, are merged into this Agreement.

6. *BINDING EFFECT:* This Agreement shall inure to the benefit and be binding upon the legal representatives, heirs, devisees, successors, and assigns of the parties.


ATTEST:

_____     _____
WITNESS                          JOHN DOE

_____     _____
WITNESS                          MARY DOE

(CORPORATE SEAL)                                         DOE DEVELOPERS, INC.

(Mary Doe) _____       By___(John Doe)_____

Secretary of the Corporation                               President

STATE OF FLORIDA
COUNTY OF MIDDLE

I HEREBY CERTIFY that on this day personally appeared before me, an officer duly authorized to administer oaths and take acknowledgments, JOHN DOE and MARY DOE, his wife, to me known to be the persons described in and who executed the foregoing instrument, and they acknowledged before me that they executed the same.

WITNESS my hand and official seal at Middletown, County of Middle, and State of Florida, this 1st day of May, 1983.

                                          _____

                                          Notary Public

                                          My commission expires:

STATE OF FLORIDA
COUNTY OF MIDDLE

I HEREBY CERTIFY that on this day personally appeared JOHN DOE, and MARY DOE, President and Secretary respectively of DOE DEVELOPERS, INC., a corporation under the laws of the State of Florida, to me known to be the persons described in and who executed the foregoing instrument, and severally acknowledged the execution thereof to be their free act and deed as such officers, for the uses and purposes therein mentioned; and that they affixed thereto the official seal of said corporation, and the said instrument is the act and deed of said corporation.

WITNESS my hand and official seal at Middletown, County of Middle, and State of Florida, this 1st day of May, 1983.

                                          _____

                                          Notary Public

                                          My commission expires:

                *¹55 Am. Jur. 2d Mortgages, para. 341.*

## SECTION E BUILDING CONSTRUCTION FOR BUSINESS USE

The Client Questionnaire in this Section will help both the contractor and the owner of real property to avoid litigation and unnecessary delay in construction and payment if the *facts* addressed in the questionnaire are obtained and reduced to a clear and accurate writing, regardless of its formality.

Because of the unlimited forms that construction agreements[1] between the contractor and the owner take, a form for the agreement with the contractor is not included in this section.

The sample contract, Form VIIE 1.01, is a construction loan agreement. If the lender is a bank or savings and loan association or other commercial lender, it will have its own commitment form or construction loan agreement. The purpose of the form in this Section is for comparison in reviewing such a loan agreement.

---

¹*13 Am. Jur. 2d Building and Construction Contracts,* para. 31; and *55* Am. Jur. 2d Mortgages, para. 14, as to the construction loan contract with bank or other lender. See *13 Am. Jur. 2d Building and Construction Contracts,* paras. 1–7, 9, 10, and 141–143, for contract between owner and builder.

Most lenders will also want a Subordination Agreement if there is a prior mortgage on the property on which the construction is to be done. Form VIID 1.10 is a sample subordination agreement.

If the attorney is retained for drafting or reviewing the construction agreement, the plans, specifications, and drawings are a necessary part of the contract, along with the schedule of payments and completion dates. The plans and specifications must not be in disarray, as they often are when presented to the lawyer. They should be specifically recited in the contract or be incorporated by reference. Both the work to be done and the materials to be used must be clearly described.

### FORM VIIE 1.00

### CLIENT QUESTIONNAIRE FOR BUILDING CONSTRUCTION FOR BUSINESS USE

1. Names and addresses of both parties to a building construction agreement
2. If a construction loan is involved, get the name and address of the lender
3. As to the construction contract between the building contractor and the owner:
   (a) OWNER—His or its general concept
   (b) OWNER—His or its budget for the project, including amount that will be borrowed. Get commitment for loan from lender before signing construction contract, or make obtaining the loan a condition precedent to the contract
   (c) OWNER—Supply legal description of the property on which construction will take place
   (d) OWNER—Architect's plans, drawings and/or specifications, if any. If there is no architect, get a list of specifications and simple drawings. Incorporate this information in the body of the construction contract or incorporate it by reference, specifically identifying each of those contract documents
   (e) OWNER—Reevaluate plans before signing the construction contract to avoid changes that are usually expensive
   (f) OWNER—Has the contractor given a mere estimate or a firm bid? It should be a bid by the time the contract is being drafted.
   (g) CONTRACTOR—What is the value of the property? Is there a mortgage on it? If so, how much?
   (h) CONTRACTOR—Does the owner know what he or it wants? Do you know? Do you have the workmen, materials, and equipment to do the job on or before the completion dates? If not, are they available in the area?
   (i) CONTRACTOR—Firm formula for paying for changes requested by owner should be in the contract
   (j) CONTRACTOR—Does bid reflect your cost, including overhead, probable inflation, and a reasonable profit?
   (k) CONTRACTOR—Is an architect involved? Do you have a project manager on a big project? If either or both, what are their duties and responsibilities to each other and as to the project? Contract should provide for these duties and responsibilities and should make clear whose approval or certificate is necessary to get progress payments or payment on completion
   (l) CONTRACTOR—How will subcontractors be handled? Subcontractors should be required to carry their own Workers Compensation insurance before working on the project, unless contractor is willing to undertake that responsibility. Written contracts or memorandum with subcontractors should be signed by both the contractor and the subcontractor, except for minimal work
   (m) Starting date and completion date
   (n) Progress payments, if any
   (o) Payment on substantial completion (amount to be withheld)
4. As to the construction loan agreement:
   (a) Legal description of the property on which the construction will take place
   (b) Total price of construction

    (c) Total amount of loan

    (d) Copy of contract between owner and contractor

    (e) Terms for repaying the construction loan to be incorporated in the note or bond to be secured by the construction mortgage

    (f) Conditions and provisions for the lender's disbursing the construction fund as to time, person, place, and on whose approval or certificates of progress or completion disbursements are to be made.

5. As to subcontractors, is there to be a provision for reasonable approval of subcontracts by the owner or engineer or other person?

## FORM VIIE 1.01

## CONSTRUCTION LOAN AGREEMENT[1]

THIS AGREEMENT made this 1st day of May, A.D. 1983, by and between ABLE MANUFACTURING, INC., a Pennsylvania corporation (herein called "Borrower"), and FIRST BANK OF PITTSBURGH, a Pennsylvania banking corporation (herein called "Lender").

WITNESSETH: The Borrower has executed and delivered to Lender a bond payable to the order of the Lender in the principal sum of Two Hundred Thousand Dollars ($200,000), and a mortgage securing said bond, which mortgage is a first lien encumbering the following described property, to wit:

(Give legal description of the real property on which the construction is to be done.)

(herein called the "Property")

This Agreement is made to state, among other purposes, the terms and conditions of the loan evidenced by said bond and secured by said mortgage.

NOW, THEREFORE, the Borrower and the Lender, in consideration of the premises and the sum of One Dollar ($1) by each of the parties paid to the other, receipt whereof is hereby acknowledged, do hereby agree as follows:

1. *Construction fund.* The Borrower acknowledges receipt of the sum of Two Hundred Thousand Dollars ($200,000) from the Lender, all of which is to be held by the Lender as a fund (hereinafter called "Construction Fund") that shall be disbursed by the Lender to the Borrower at the times and in the manner and under the conditions set forth herein.

2. *Not a trust fund.* Nothing herein contained shall be deemed to establish any trust fund for the benefit of any person, persons, or company not a party to this Agreement.

3. *Assignability.* Lender shall have the right to assign the mortgage, provided the assignee agrees to comply with and perform the terms and conditions of this Agreement.

4. *Disbursements.*

(a) Disbursements made from the Construction Fund shall be in accordance with the payout schedule attached hereto and made a part hereof. All such disbursements shall be made to Borrower unless Borrower instructs Lender in writing to make them in another manner.

(b) Disbursements may be made, at Lender's option, in advance of any draw stage set forth in attached payout schedule and, if made, shall not be deemed an approval or acceptance by the Lender of the work theretofore done.

(c) The Borrower agrees to use all disbursements received from the Construction Fund for the payment of labor, material, and other costs in the construction of the improvements on the Property in accordance with the plans and specifications hereinafter mentioned. However, this Agreement shall in no way be construed to make Lender liable to suppliers, contractors, subcontractors, laborers, or others for materials, goods, or services delivered, performed, or rendered by them upon the Property or for debts or claims accruing to said parties against the Borrower. It is distinctly understood and agreed that there is no contractual relationship, either expressed or implied, between the Lender and any party other than the Borrower, and that relationship is strictly limited to the interim financing arrangement as provided herein.

5. *Conditions precedent.* Prior to commencement of construction on the Property, the following shall be accomplished:

(a) The mortgage hereinbefore described shall be placed of record in the office of the Recorder of Deeds of Allegheny County, Pennsylvania.

(b) Borrower shall furnish Lender with a full coverage mortgage title insurance policy in a form and from a company acceptable to the Lender, showing the mortgage to be a first and prior lien on the above-described premises, without exceptions other than those that may be approved by the Lender.

(c) A full coverage hazard insurance policy issued by a company approved by Lender shall be taken out by Borrower to cover the entire term of this Agreement in an amount no less than the amount of the mortgage, with standard loss payable clauses endorsed in favor of the Lender as such interest may appear, a copy of which shall be delivered to Lender.

(d) A survey shall be made of the Property by a licensed surveyor, and a certified copy of the map or plat thereof shall be delivered to the Lender.

(e) Borrower shall deliver to Lender a copy of the construction contract, including plans and specifications for the improvements to be made on said premises, which shall become attached hereto and made a part hereof.

6. *Representations of Borrower as to construction contract.* Construction is to be commenced within fifteen (15) days from the date hereof, and all improvements are to be completed in strict accordance with said plans, specifications, and payout schedule not later than September 30, 1983, free and clear of all claims for labor, materials, equipment, and appliances in connection therewith, and without violating or breaching any covenants, conditions, or restrictions of record, or any building or zoning ordinances of the city or county in which the Property is situated, and without encroaching upon any property, easement, or right. Extras or changes in plans or specifications are to be first approved in writing by Lender.

7. *Security interest in personal property.*

(a) All fixtures, appliances, and equipment shown in said plans and specifications and payout schedule shall constitute and become a part of the realty under the mortgage and must be paid for in full and not purchased under lease, chattel mortgage, conditional sales contract, or any other security agreement.

(b) Borrower hereby grants to Lender a security interest in all those fixtures, appliances, and equipment as they are installed.

8. *Inspection.* The Borrower hereby authorizes Lender, or Lender's authorized representative, to enter upon the Property at any time to inspect the progress of construction. All inspection and other services rendered by the Lender, or Lender's representatives, shall be performed solely for the protection and benefit of the Lender, and the Borrower shall not be entitled to claim any loss or damage against Lender for reliance on any such inspections or inspection reports or services.

9. *Default.* Any of the following shall be considered and designed as an "Act of Default" on the part of the Borrower:

(a) If Borrower, except for causes beyond its control, fails to maintain a reasonably continuous schedule of construction by which the buildings and improvements can be completed within the time herein specified; or

(b) If there shall be any changes or deviations from the plans or specifications without prior written approval from the Lender; or

(c) If the Borrower fails to pay out all amounts due for labor, materials, fixtures, appliances, equipment, or any other indebtednesses resulting from the construction and improvements, upon receipt of applicable money by the Borrower from the Construction Fund.

(d) If the Borrower fails to complete the construction and improvements within the time limit prescribed herein, or fails to comply with and perform any other of the terms and conditions herein required of Borrower.

(e) If the Borrower fails to pay said bond at date of maturity. If the mortgage provides a period of grace, then default shall occur on such grace date as provided in the mortgage.

(f) If the Borrower shall be in default, the Lender shall thereupon notify the Borrower, and any other known interested parties of such Act or Acts of Default, and may thereafter refuse to make any further disbursements from the Construction Fund until satisfied that such Act or Acts of Default are satisfactorily cured. If any such Act of Default shall occur and continue for a period of ten (10) days after written notice by Lender to Borrower, the Lender may credit any funds remaining in its hands to the indebtedness of the Borrower to the Lender and elect to declare the balance of the indebtedness of the Borrower to the Lender to be immediately due and payable, anything in said mortgage to the contrary notwithstanding, and may proceed to foreclose the said mortgage.

10. *Benefit and obligation.* The terms "Borrower" and "Lender" as used herein shall be interpreted and construed to apply to and cover their respective heirs, successors, or assigns as may be applicable.

IN WITNESS WHEREOF, we have set our hands and seals this 1st day of May, A.D. 1983.

(CORPORATE SEAL)                      ABLE MANUFACTURING, INC.

By _____

———————————————————————

Secretary of the Corporation                 President

(CORPORATE SEAL)                      FIRST BANK OF PITTSBURGH

By _____

———————————————————————

Secretary of the Corporation                 President

[1]Ref. Introduction to Chapter V E, and footnotes.

## SECTION F CONDOMINIUMS AND COOPERATIVES

The forms in this Section are used to create either condominium or cooperative ownership of real property. Many states have statutes regulating such ownership. Check the state statute before proceeding.

A sample Declaration of Condominium, often called the "Bible" for the project, would be too lengthy for inclusion in this book. Since the Declaration must be filed in the public records of the county in which the project is located, a photocopy of a Declaration filed in the county for a similar project would be the best start for drafting a Declaration.

Get the information required in the Client Questionnaire, Form VIIF 1.00, and modify the sample Declaration form accordingly.

Form VIIF 1.04(c) is a form given to a condominium purchaser that contains a list of the documents that should be prepared in addition to the Declaration in most states.

A review of the forms contained in this Section demonstrates that condominium ownership[1] is sole ownership of certain space in the condominium project and co-ownership of certain common elements, such as the land on which the project is built, the buildings' main walls, hallways, lobbies, elevators, stairways, roof, recreational, or other service facilities—all of which must be described in the Declaration of Condominium that must be filed in the public records of the county in which the land is located.

The condominium developer sells the condominium unit[2] to the purchaser. The shared condominium facilities[3] are sold and deeded by the condominium developer to the condominium owners' association.

Selling time-share condominiums is a relatively new business. The condominium documents included in this Chapter are for creating a time-sharing condominium. The forms can be adapted for creating an ordinary condominium by eliminating the time-sharing provisions.

In addition to the business of construction and sale of condominiums and time-share condominiums for residential use, ordinary condominium ownership of business properties will increase in the eighties. Shopping center condominiums where business units are owned instead of rented by the small retailers may be desirable

---

[1]*15A Am. Jur. 2d Condominiums and Cooperative Apartments, paras. 1–56. See also Appendix VIII to this book giving citations to state condominium statutes where the state has adapted the Uniform Condominium Act (1977) and (1980).*

[2]Ref. Form VIIF 1.04.

[3]Ref. Form VIIF 1.01.

as rents rise and lease taxes are imposed. Large department stores located in shopping centers typically do own their own stores.

In addition to the condominium forms included in this Section, there is a form for incorporating a cooperative and for the proprietary lease from the corporation to the tenant.

Cooperative ownership is ownership of stock in the cooperative corporation that owns the real estate, the individual units, and the common facilities. Each tenant of the building is a stockholder or member of the cooperative corporation.[4] The corporation gives the tenant a proprietary lease.[5]

## FORM VIIF 1.00

### CLIENT QUESTIONNAIRE FOR CONDOMINIUM OR COOPERATIVE[1]

1. Is the client a developer, a sole owner, or a co-owner of the land, building, or premises? Get exact names and addresses of all owners and a copy of the deed to the owner(s)
2. Is the ownership to be cooperative or condominium?
3. Is the property to be used for business or residential purposes?[2]
4. If the land is not owned by the client, is there a purchase agreement? If the land is leased by the client, what are the terms of the lease? Get a copy of the purchase agreement or the lease. *Read carefully*
5. Is there a building plan and/or survey available? If so, get a copy
6. Is there or will there be a mortgage?[3] If so, read
7. Get a description of the building(s)
    (a) Number of stories and basements
    (b) Number of units (offices or stores)
    (c) Principal construction material (brick, stone, concrete, steel)
    (d) Number and location of each unit in the building(s)
    (e) Approximate area
    (f) Number and description of immediate common areas for limited use of certain unit owners
    (g) Description of all common areas and facilities
    (h) Value of the whole property
    (i) Value of each unit (by number of the unit) and the percentage of undivided interest in the common areas and facilities
    (j) Voting rights of owner of each unit by number
    (k) Purpose of the whole development
    (l) Purpose and/or restricted use of each unit
    (m) What percentage of vote of unit owners shall be required to rebuild, repair, restore, or sell the property in the event of damage or destruction of all or part of the property?
    (n) By what method can the Declaration of Condominium be ameneded? (Note: This must be in accordance with the state condominium statute)
    (o) Who will accept service of process for the owner/developer? Get residence or business address
    (p) Look at architect's drawing(s) and construction contract(s)
8. If the ownership is to be Condominium, see Form VE 1.04(c), titled Receipt for Condominium Documents, as a checklist for documents that should be prepared if you represent the condominium developer. If you represent the purchaser, see that form to determine that your client is obtaining the necessary information in regard to the purchase
9. *If the ownership is to be Cooperative,* see Form VE 1.06 for sample articles of incorporation for the corporation that will own the project, and get the following information to be used in the articles of incorporation and in the bylaws:
    (a) Will capital stock be issued? If so, get total number of shares to be authorized; par or no-par; if residential, will there be any preferred stock to the FHA or other governmental agency?

---

[4]Ref. Form VIIF 1.06.
[5]Ref. Form VIIF 1.07.

(b) If there will be memberships instead of stock, get total number of memberships authorized; prepare membership certificates; what is the subscription price of the memberships?

(c) Since a cooperative corporation is nonprofit, include statement that no dividend will be paid

(d) Are corporate officers or directors owners of the real property to be purchased by the corporation? If so, recite the fact

(e) Can corporate officers or directors occupy or lease units? If so, provide that they can, with any limit to number of units they may acquire

(f) Other provisions required by proposed mortgagee

(g) Number of directors and titles of officers

(h) Method and time of electing directors and officers

(i) Any particular eligibility or noneligibility requirements for directors or officers

[1]*15A Am. Jur. 2d Condominiums and Cooperative Apartments*, paras. 1–56, *particularly* 9 and 13.

[2]Check your state condominium statutes for distinction, if any. For practical considerations for an office or shopping mall condominium, see Chapter V A.

[3]*15A Am. Jur. 2d Condominiums and Cooperative Apartments*, para. 45.

## FORM VIIF 1.01

(Purchase agreement between developer and the condominium association for the common elements)[1]

### ASSOCIATION PROPERTIES PURCHASE AGREEMENT
### EXHIBIT D
### TO THE DECLARATION OF CONDOMINIUM for
### HAPPY HEATH ACRES RESORT

THIS Association Properties Purchase Agreement ("Purchase Agreement") entered into by and between HAPPY HEATH DEVELOPERS, LTD., a Florida limited partnership (hereinafter called the "Grantor"), and Happy Heath Acres Condominium Association, Inc., a corporation not for profit under the laws of the State of Florida (hereinafter called "Association" and also hereinafter called "Grantee").

WITNESSETH:

1. *Agreement to Purchase and Sell.* Grantor agrees to sell to the Grantee and the Grantee agrees to purchase from the Grantor a Five Percent (5%) undivided interest in real property and improvements thereon, more particularly described in Exhibit A, attached hereto and made a part hereof, said lands lying and being in Middle County, Florida, all pursuant to the terms and provisions hereof. From time to time the Grantor, with the written consent of the Association, may convey additional real property and improvements thereon to that described in Exhibit A, pursuant to the terms and conditions of this Agreement.

2. *Determination of Purchase Price.* The agreed purchase price for the property is Ten Thousand Dollars ($10,000). The Grantor recognizes and acknowledges that the Grantee is a Condominium Association created to manage the affairs of one or more condominiums, the units of which may be committed to interval ownership. The Grantor also recognizes and acknowledges that the Association Properties (the term is synonymous with the term "Shared Facilities") is being purchased by the Association for the use and benefit of its members owning condominium units or interval weeks as described in the Declaration of Condominium for Happy Heath Acres Resort.

3. *Use of Property.* The Grantee shall have the nonexclusive right for use for its membership owning unit weeks in Happy Heath Acres Resort, and for the occupants thereof and their guests, of the property and improvements described in Exhibit A, attached hereto, together with all additions thereto, referred to as the "Association Properties" or "Shared Facilities." The parties acknowledge that the shared facilities have been designed for the nonexclusive use and occupancy of the owners, occupants, and guests of 100 condominium units, including the 50 units contained in Happy Heath Acres Resort. Therefore, it shall be necessary for Grantor and Grantee to limit the number of units entitled to the use and occupancy of the shared facilities to a total usage not in excess thereof. The right is hereby reserved for Grantor to grant a corresponding right of nonex-

clusive use and occupancy of the shared facilities to other persons; provided, that under no circumstances shall the Grantor grant a corresponding right of nonexclusive use and occupancy of the shared facilities to persons other than members of the Association whereby the total number of persons entitled to the use and occupancy of the shared facilities shall materially exceed the number for which it was initially designed.

4. *Title.* The conveyance of undivided interest in the title to the shared facilities to the Grantee shall be by fee simple deed, and shall be subject to:

(A) All rights therein reserved to the Grantor and others in the Happy Heath Acres Resort Declaration of Condominium and Exhibits attached thereto;

(B) All easements created by the Grantor, or joined in by the Grantor, for the purpose of providing for utilities, passage, or other use designed to permit the full utilization and enjoyment of the shared facilities by the Grantor and all those claiming by, through, and under the Grantor and the membership of the Grantee;

(C) Taxes and other governmental assessments and impositions;

(D) Zoning and other applicable governmental ordinances;

(E) Restrictions, limitations, reservations, reversions, easements, conditions, and agreements of record;

(F) Rights of other cotenants of the shared facilities area;

(G) Existing mortgages of record that will be satisfied in accordance with the terms thereof by Grantor.

All personal property shall be conveyed by a bill of sale as Grantor shall provide.

5. *Creation of Easements.* Grantee shall, without cost or expense to Grantor or other cotenants, join in the creation of all easements as from time to time and at any time requested by Grantor for the purpose of providing reasonable ingress, egress, and service and for other uses; provided, such other use shall not unreasonably interfere with the use of the shared facilities by the membership of the Grantee, which use is designed to permit full utilization and enjoyment of the shared facilities and adjacent properties by the Grantor, and all those claiming by, through, and under the Grantor.

6. *Condition of Property.* The property being conveyed, real and personal, is sold "as is," subject only to such warranties required by law.

7. *Management of Shared Facilities.* The Grantee has or shall enter into a Management Contract, providing for, among other things, management of the shared facilities. In order to ensure fair and equitable treatment for all cotenants of the shared facilities, the Grantee agrees, at such time as said Management Agreement shall terminate, for whatever reason, and for so long as Grantee shall own less than all of the fee simple title to the shared facilities, to join in an Agreement for management and maintenance of the shared facilities with such person or persons, natural or corporate, as shall be determined upon by those parties constituting in excess of Sixty-six Percent (66%) of the tenants in common of the said shared facilities. The said Management Agreement shall contain provisions for the maintenance and management of the shared facilities similar to those contained in the initial Management Contract above referred to, provided, however, that the management fee shall not be in excess of Ten Percent (10%) of the cost of operating and maintaining the shared facilities, including, without limitation, the costs of taxes, insurance, utilities, supplies, and other related costs; provided, however, that until such time as title to all the shared facilities shall have been delivered to the said Grantee, designation of the party with whom or with which the tenants in common shall enter into a Management Agreement pursuant to the provisions of this Paragraph, shall be subject to the approval of the Grantor.

8. *Consent and Ratification by Unit Owners.* Each and every person, whether natural or corporate, who shall acquire or take any title or interest whatsoever in or to a unit week in Happy Heath Acres Resort shall, by acceptance and/or the recordation of the deed grant, assignment, or other instrument granting, conveying, or providing for such interest, or by the exercise of the rights or uses granted therein, be deemed to have consented to and ratified the provisions of this Agreement to the same effect and extent as if such person or persons had executed the Agreement with formalities required in the deed, and shall be deemed to have acknowledged that the terms hereof are fair and reasonable to the Association.

9. *Easements.* The Grantor specifically reserves unto Happy Heath Developers, Ltd., a Florida Limited Partnership, and James Joe, Trustee, and to all those claiming by, through, and under any such party, an easement for pedestrian traffic and parking over, through, and across sidewalks, paths, walks, halls, lobbies, and other portions of the shared facilities as may be from time to time intended and is designated for such purpose and use and for vehicular and pedestrian

traffic over, through, and across such portions of the shared facilities as may from time to time be paved and intended for such purpose; provided, further, that nothing shall be construed to give or create in any person the right to park upon any portion of the shared facilities except to the extent that same may be specifically designated and assigned for parking purposes. An easement is further hereby reserved subject to such conditions as Grantor may from time to time impose, in favor of all owners of unit weeks at Happy Heath Acres Resort for all of the afore-recited uses.

10. *Rights Granted to Developer.* Until the developer shall have completed development, promotion, and sale of all unit weeks to be located at the Happy Heath Acres Resort, developer shall have the following rights with regard to the shared facilities, notwithstanding any other provisions of this Agreement to the contrary:

(A) The right to use and occupy exclusively any portion of the shared facilities designated as "offices" in the plans of the shared facilities.

(B) The right to use and occupy exclusively any portion of the shared facilities as and for a sales pavilion.

(C) The right to use, occupy, and demonstrate, on a nonexclusive basis, all of the shared facilities for the purpose of promotion and aiding in the sale or rental of the unit weeks on or to be constructed in the condominium apartment buildings. Such rights shall not be exercised in an unreasonable manner not consistent with the right of the members of the Grantee to use, occupy, and enjoy such portions of the shared facilities. Nothing herein contained shall serve in any way to reduce Grantee's obligations for the payments due under this Purchase Agreement, or for the payment of taxes, repair, and maintenance of the Property.

11. *Florida Contract.* This Contract is to be construed and enforced under the laws of the State of Florida.

12. *Guarantors.* As part of the inducement to the Grantor to make the conveyances provided for herein, the Grantee hereby designates the Grantor its attorney-in-fact.

13. *Modifications.* Except as reserved to the Grantor, neither this Agreement nor any terms hereof may be changed, waived, discharged, or terminated orally, but only by an instrument in writing signed by the party against which enforcement of the change, waiver, discharge, or termination is sought.

14. *Notice.*

(A) Grantee. Any notice, demand, or other instrument authorized by this Purchase Agreement to be served on or given to the Grantee may be served on or given to the Grantee by certified mail addressed to Happy Heath Acres Condominium Association, Inc., Star Rt. 1 Box 1, Middletown, Florida, or at such other address or addresses as may have been furnished in writing to the Grantor by the Grantee at least five (5) days prior to the mailing of such writing.

(B) Grantor. Any notice, demand, or other instrument to be served on or given to the Grantor may be served on or given to the Grantor by certified mail addressed to Happy Heath Developers, Ltd., 100 Main St., Middletown, Florida, or at such other address as may have been furnished in writing to the Grantee by the Grantor.

15. *Headings.* The headings of the sections, paragraphs, and subdivisions of this Purchase Agreement are for the convenience of reference only, and are not to be considered a part hereof, and shall not limit or otherwise effect any of the terms hereof.

16. *Invalid Provisions to Affect No Others.* In case any one or more of the convenants, agreements, terms, or provisions contained in this Purchase Agreement shall be invalid, illegal, or unenforceable in any respect, the validity of the remaining covenants, agreements, terms, or provisions contained herein shall be in no way affected, prejudiced, or disturbed thereby.

17. *Successor, Assigns Included in Parties.* Whenever in this Purchase Agreement one of the parties hereto is named or referred to, the successors and assigns of such party shall be included, and all covenants and agreements contained in this Purchase Agreement by or on behalf of the Grantee or by or on behalf of the Grantor shall bind and insure to the benefit of their respective successors and assigns, whether so expressed or not. This Purchase Agreement shall not be assigned by the Grantee without the written approval of the Grantor, but shall be freely assignable or transferable, in whole or in part, by the Grantor.

18. *Entire Agreement.* This instrument constitutes the entire agreement between the parties, and neither party has been induced by the other by representations, promises, or understandings not expressed herein, and there are no collateral agreements, stipulations, promises, or understandings whatsoever in any way touching the subject matter of this Agreement that are not expressly contained herein.

19. *Waiver of Rights.* The failure of the Grantor to enforce any covenants, obligations, or agreements of the Grantee herein contained shall not constitute a waiver of the right to do so thereafter, nor shall it constitute a waiver of the right to enforce any other convenant, obligation, or agreement herein contained.

20. *Apportionment of Maintenance and Other Costs.* During such period as the ownership of the shared facilities shall be held by tenants in common, anything contained herein or contained in any document executed pursuant to this Agreement to the contrary notwithstanding, all costs for taxes, insurance, utilities, or other shared facilities expenses as provided for in any such document shall be equitably apportioned among the tenants in common based upon the number of unit weeks the occupants and owners of which are entitled to the use and occupancy of the shared facilities by or through each such tenant in common. Such apportionment of the shared facilities expenses shall be made by the person or party responsible for the management of the shared facilities pursuant to the provisions of any then existing Management Agreement. Nothing herein shall be construed as abating, reducing, or otherwise diminishing the obligation of the Grantee, or of any tenant in common, to pay its obligations of the Grantee, or of any tenant in common to pay its obligation set forth herein, or in any document executed pursuant hereto, for maintenance and operation of the shared facilities by reason of the fact that one or more of the owners or occupants of unit weeks entitled to the use of the shared facilities shall elect not to make use thereof, or by virtue of the fact that one or more of the owners or occupants of units or unit weeks otherwise entitled to the use of the shared facilities shall be barred therefrom or prohibited the use thereof by virtue of a violation of the rules and regulations applicable to the use thereof.

21. *Title Insurance Policy.* At the time of conveyance, Grantor shall warrant its title to be conveyed thereunder to be good and marketable or insurable. Grantee shall be responsible for obtaining its own title insurance policy.

22. *Association Properties Deed.* The parties agree that the form of deed to be utilized in connection with all conveyances to be made hereunder, shall be substantially the same as the Association Properties Deed No. 1 attached hereto, except as modified in accordance with the requirements of this Association Properties Purchase Agreement and/or as required by the Grantor.

23. *Prorations.* There shall be no prorations. Grantee acknowledges that conveyance of Association Properties is being made for a nominal sum. Grantee therefore assumes liability proportionate to its undivided interest as a tenant in common for the entire expense of taxes, insurance, and other expenses usually subject to proration in the year of such conveyance.

24. *Costs.* Grantor shall pay costs of preparation of warranty deed and other instruments of conveyance. Grantee shall pay all costs of documentary stamps on the deed, and recording fees for recording the said instruments.

25. *Copies.* A copy of this Agreement shall be exhibited or delivered to each person contracting to acquire a unit week in Happy Heath Acres Resort by the Grantor for the purpose of making full disclosure of all of the terms and provisions hereof. Each such person expressly agrees and consents that minor changes, deletions, additions, and amendments may be made to this Agreement prior to the recordation thereof, and without further advice or notice to such person, for the purpose of correcting typographical errors, complying with the requirements of an institutional mortgagee, or for other reason, provided such deletion, addition, and/or amendment shall not materially adversely affect the rights of such person or the Grantee hereunder.

26. *Required Parking Spaces and Other Costs in Connection Therewith.* Applicable ordinances of Middle County, Florida, require that one and one-half (1½) paved parking spaces be provided for each condominium unit being constructed by the Grantor. Accordingly, a perpetual easement for parking, to the extent of 1½ parking spaces for each condominium unit being constructed in Happy Heath Acres Resort, is reserved and created in the real property described in Exhibit A hereto for the use and benefit of purchasers of Interval Weeks in Happy Heath Acres Resort. The provisions of this clause shall constitute a convenant running with the land and shall be binding upon the Grantor and the Grantee, their successors, and assigns, and may not be canceled or terminated except by action of the County, or its successors.

27. *Option to Purchase Additional Interests in Association Properties.* As each additional portion of Happy Heath Acres Resort is developed, the developer shall offer to sell to the Association an additional undivided Five Percent (5%) interest in the fee simple title to the Association Properties and the improvements constructed thereon, and the afore-described additional real property and improvements thereon, upon the same terms and conditions as set forth in this Purchase Agreement, provided, however, that the purchase price for such additional Five Percent

(5%) undivided interest in the Association Properties shall be that purchase price agreed upon between the Grantor and Grantee at such time.

IN WITNESS WHEREOF, the Grantor, Happy Heath Developers, Ltd., and Grantee, Happy Heath Acres Condominium Association, Inc., have caused these presents to be signed this 1st day of March, 1982. Signed, sealed, and delivered in the presence of:

HAPPY HEATH DEVELOPERS, LTD.,
a Florida limited partnership

By _____
General Partner, Richard Roe

By _____
General Partner, Peter Poe

HAPPY HEATH ACRES CONDOMINIUM ASSO-CIATION, INC., a Florida not-for-profit cor-poration

ATTEST:

(CORPORATE SEAL)

By _____
Secretary of the Corporation                President of the Corporation

[1]For Deed pursuant to this agreement, see Form VIIF 1.01(a).

## FORM VIIF 1.01(a)

### (Deed of common elements from developer to the condominium association)

### ASSOCIATION PROPERTIES DEED NO. 1[1]

Made this 1st day of September, A.D. 1982,

Between JOE JAMES, Trustee for Happy Heath Developers, Ltd., a Florida limited partnership of the County of Middle and State of Florida, party of the first part, and Happy Heath Acres Con-dominium Association, Inc., a Florida corporation not for profit of the County of Middle and State of Florida, party of the second part,

WITNESSETH, that the said party of the first part, for and in consideration of the sum of Ten Dollars ($10) and other good and valuable considerations, to him in hand paid, the receipt whereof is hereby acknowledged, has granted, bargained, sold, and transferred, and by these pre-sents does grant, bargain, sell, and transfer unto the said property of the second part all that cer-tain parcel of land lying and being in the County of Middle and State of Florida, more particularly described as follows:

An undivided Five Percent (5%) interest in that certain parcel of land lying and being in the County of Middle and State of Florida, more particularly described in Exhibit A attached hereto.

TOGETHER with all the tenements, hereditaments, and appurtenances, with every privilege, right, title, interest, and estate, dower and right of dower, reversion, remainder, and easement thereto belonging or in anywise appertaining:

TO HAVE AND TO HOLD the same in fee simple forever.

IN WITNESS WHEREOF, the said party of the first part has hereunto set his hand and seal the day and year above written. Signed, sealed, and delivered in our presence:

WITNESS

_____
Joe James, Trustee and individually

WITNESS

STATE OF FLORIDA
COUNTY OF MIDDLE

The foregoing instrument was acknowledged before me, this date, by Joe James, Trustee for Happy Heath Developers, Ltd., a Florida limited partnership, and individually.

_____
Notary Public

My commission expires:

[1]For purchase agreement leading to this deed, see Form VIIF 1.01. For purchase agreement of a condominium unit, see Form VIIF 1.04.

## FORM VIIF 1.02

### (Condominium management contract between the condominium association and a management corporation before individual units have been sold)[1]

### MANAGEMENT AGREEMENT

THIS AGREEMENT made and entered into by and between HAPPY HEATH ACRES CONDOMINIUM ASSOCIATION, INC. (hereinafter called the "Association"), and ABLE RESORT MANAGEMENT, INC., a Florida corporation (hereinafter called the "Manager").

WITNESSETH:

WHEREAS, the Association is a Florida nonprofit corporation organized for the administration and operation of the Happy Heath Acres Resort; and

WHEREAS, the Association is the Purchaser (Grantee) under the terms and provisions of the Association Properties Purchase Agreements, Association Properties Deeds, and Association Properties Notes and Mortgages, which documents shall hereinafter be collectively referred to as the "Association Properties Documents," of the Association Properties and facilities; and

WHEREAS, the size and extent of the condominiums, and each of them, and the terms and provisions of the afore-referred-to Association Properties Documents require the employment of a Manager;

NOW, THEREFORE, in consideration of the premises, and of the mutual covenants and other considerations herein contained, the parties agree as follows:

1. _Definitions._ The terms used herein shall have the meanings set forth in the Declaration of Condominium unless the context otherwise requires:

2. _Employment._ The Association does hereby employ the Manager as the exclusive manager of the condominium property and as the manager of the Association Properties to the extent that management thereof is imposed upon the Association under the terms of the afore-referred-to Association Properties Documents or the Florida Real Estate Time-Sharing Act, and the Manager hereby accepts such employment.

3. _Term._ Unless sooner terminated, as elsewhere herein provided, this Agreement shall commence on the date the Declaration of Condominium of Happy Heath Acres Resort is recorded, and shall continue thereafter for a period of three (3) years, and shall be automatically renewable every three (3) years for successive three (3)-year periods unless the unit week owners vote to discharge the manager; provided, however, that this Contract shall be subject to earlier cancellation at such time as the Developer no longer has the right to designate or elect a majority of the membership of the board of administration of the Association in the event Sixty-six Percent (66%) of the individual unit owners vote for such cancellation. This Agreement may be sooner terminated by the manager upon ninety (90) days' written notice to the Association. Termination of any of the Happy Acres Resort Condominiums or of the Association shall not terminate this Agreement, but shall operate to make each condominium unit owner a signatory to it in place and instead of the Association; provided, however, in no event shall a condominium unit owner be liable for any greater portion of the Manager's compensation than that amount for which he would have been liable in the event a condominium or the Association had not been terminated.

4. _Powers and Duties of Manager._ The Manager shall exercise on behalf of the Association all of the powers and duties of the Association as set forth in the Declaration of Condominium and in the Articles and Bylaws of the Association, excepting only such powers and duties as are specifically reserved to and required to be exercised by the directors or members of the Association.

The Manager shall further have the duty and responsibility of performing all administrative and managerial acts required to be performed by the Grantee under the terms and provisions of the Association Properties Documents. By way of illustration of the Manager's powers and duties and not in limitation thereof, the Manager shall:

(A) *Confer.* Confer freely and fully at reasonable times and upon reasonable notice with the Association's directors when so required by them in connection with the performance of its duties. The Association shall give sufficient notice of and invite the Manager to attend all of the Association's directors', members', and committee meetings; provided, however, the Manager shall not be required to attend any of such meetings.

(B) *Employees.* Select, employ, supervise, direct, and discharge, in its absolute discretion, in its name and/or in the name of the Association, as the Manager shall determine, such persons as it may require to fulfill its duties hereunder.

(C) *Collect Assessments.* Collect all regular and special assessments from the Association's members. The Association hereby authorizes the Manager to request, demand, collect, receive, and receipt for any and all assessments and charges that may be due the Association and to take such action in the name of the Association by way of making, recording, satisfying, foreclosing the Association's lien therefor, initiating legal process or taking such other action as the Manager shall deem necessary or appropriate for the collection of such assessments. The Manager shall furnish the Association with an itemized list of all delinquent accounts immediately following the 20th day of each month.

(D) *Repairs and Maintenance.* Cause the grounds, lands, appurtenances, and those portions of the common elements and limited common elements of the condominiums and of the Association Properties to be maintained and repaired in accordance with the obligations for such maintenance and repair as set forth in the Declaration of Condominium and the Association Properties Documents, including, but not limited to, landscaping, relandscaping, pool maintenance and repair, elevator maintenance, painting, roofing, cleaning, paving, road maintenance, and repair work as may be necessary; provided, however, the Manager shall not obligate the Association for any single item of repair, replacement, refurnishing, refurbishing, wherein the cost thereof would exceed Seventy-five Hundred Dollars ($7,500), without the specific approval of the board of administration of the Association, excepting only emergency repairs involving manifest danger to persons or property, or immediately necessary for the preservation and safety of the condominiums of Association Properties, or for the safety of persons, or required in order to avoid suspension of any necessary service to the condominiums, all of which may be made or authorized by the Manager, without regard to the cost thereof.

(E) *Laws.* Take such action as may be necessary to comply with all laws, statutes, ordinances, and rules of all appropriate governmental authority, and with the rules and regulations of the National Board of Fire Underwriters, or if such board shall terminate its present functions, those of any other body exercising similar functions, subject to the limitations set forth in Paragraph 4(D). The Manager, however, shall not take any action so long as the Association is contesting or has affirmed its intention to contest any such law, statute, ordinance, rule, regulation, or order, or requirements pursuant thereto.

(F) *Purchase.* Purchase equipment, tools, vehicles, appliances, goods, supplies, and materials as shall be reasonably necessary to perform its duties, including the maintenance, upkeep, repair, replacement, refurbishing, and preservation of the condominiums, the furnishings, fixtures, and appliances thereof. Purchases shall be made in the name of the Manager or, in its discretion, in the name of the Association. When making purchases, the Manager shall make a reasonable effort to obtain the best price available, all factors considered, and shall disclose to the Association all discounts, commissions, and rebates.

(G) *Insurance.* Cause to be placed or kept in force all insurance required or permitted by the Declarations of Condominium and the Association Properties Documents to be kept or placed by the Association; to act as agent for the Association, each condominium unit owner, and for each owner of any other insured interest to adjust all claims arising under insurance policies purchased by the Association; to bring suit thereon in the name of the Association and/or other insureds; to deliver releases upon payment of claims; to otherwise exercise all of the rights, powers, and privileges of the Association, and each owner of any other insured interest in the condominium property as an insured under such insurance proceeds under minor losses, payable to the Association under a Declaration of Condominium, and as Grantee under the Association Properties Documents.

(H) *Association's Records.* Maintain the Association's minute book and membership lists, give notice of membership and directors' meetings when requested to do so, and maintain all financial record books, accounts, and other records required to be kept by the Association by the Florida Condominium Act, the Florida Real Estate Time-Sharing Act, the Declarations of Condominium or its Bylaws; and issue certificates of account to members, their mortgagees, and lienors without liability for errors unless as a result of gross negligence. The Manager shall maintain a separate book of account for each of the condominiums administered by the Association. Such records shall be kept at the office of the Manager and shall be available for inspection at all reasonable times by the Association's directors, but not its membership generally, except as required by the Florida Condominium Act or the Florida Real Estate Time-Sharing Act. The Manager shall render to the Association and to each of its current members or their duly authorized representatives a statement of its receipts and accounts for each fiscal or calendar year no later than sixty (60) days following the end of the fiscal or calendar year, or annually on such date as is otherwise mutually agreed to by the parties. The Manager shall perform a continual internal audit of the Association's financial records. The Association shall be entitled to such independent audit by such auditors as it shall designate from time to time, for the purpose of verifying the same, provided the cost thereof shall be paid by, and the employment of such auditor shall be by, the Association directly and not through the Manager. Such independent audit shall be at the office of the Manager.

(I) *Manager's Records.* Maintain records sufficient to describe its services hereunder and keep financial books and records in accordance with prevailing accounting standards, sufficient to identify the sources of all funds collected and the disbursement thereof. Such records shall be kept at the office of the Manager and shall be available for reasonable inspection by the Association's directors. The Manager shall perform a continual internal audit of the Manager's financial records relative to its services as Manager for the purpose of verifying the same, but no independent or external audit shall be required of it. The Association shall have the right to an annual external independent audit, provided the cost thereof shall be paid by and the employment of such auditor shall be by the Association directly and not through the Manager, and provided that the external auditor is acceptable to the Manager, whose acceptance shall not be unreasonably withheld. Such independent audit shall be at the office of the Manager.

(J) *Apportionment.* Apportion amongst the condominiums administered by the Association costs, expenses, obligations, and income attributable to more than one condominium, such as, but not limited to, obligations imposed by the Association Properties Documents, costs of maintaining roadways and pathways throughout the Polynesian Isles Resort Condominiums, security guard service, streetlights, the expenses of maintaining an entryway, utility costs, if any, where the utility involved is shared by more than one condominium, and the like. The basis of apportioning such costs, expenses, obligations, and revenues shall be as set forth in Article 6 of the Bylaws of the Association.

(K) *Reserves.* Establish reserves, both funded and unfunded, for the payment of any and all costs and expenses of the Association to be disbursed by the Manager hereunder. Should the Association itself decide to fund special reserve accounts, the Manager shall collect and account for such funds and disburse the same on the directions of the Association.

(L) *Funds.* Deposit all funds collected from the Association's members or otherwise accruing to the Association in a special bank account or accounts, in banks and/or savings and loan associations in Osceola County, Florida.

(M) *Private Roads.* Maintain in good repair and landscape all private roads, parking areas, driveways, and landscaped areas.

(N) *Budget.* Prepare with the assistance of an accountant an operating budget setting forth an itemized statement of the anticipated receipts and disbursements for the new year, based upon the then current schedule of monthly assessments and taking into account the general condition of the Association and the condominiums, which budget shall comply with the requirements of the Bylaws. Said budget together with an explanatory statement shall be submitted to the Association in final draft at least thirty (30) days prior to the commencement of the year for which it has been made. The budget shall serve as a supporting document for the schedule of monthly assessments.

(O) *Experts.* Retain and employ attorneys-at-law, tax consultants, and other experts and professionals whose services the Manager may reasonably require to effectively perform its duties and exercise its powers hereunder. The Manager shall retain an attorney-at-law and a certified. public accountant on an annual and special fee basis, and shall retain such other professionals and experts as it may hire on such basis as it deems most beneficial. The foregoing shall not be a limitation upon the rights of the Association to employ such professionals and experts on its own account as it may desire, but the employment of the same by the Association shall in no way affect the Manager's right to employ and continue the employment of the professionals and experts that it has employed or will employ, nor shall the same in any way relieve the Association of its obligation to pay its share of the costs of professionals and experts retained by the Manager, as elsewhere herein provided. The Manager has and will continue to retain attorneys-at-law for the purpose of affording it legal counsel, advice, and representation in and about the exercise of its powers, duties, and functions hereunder.

(P) *Access.* The Manager shall have access to the common elements and limited common elements of the condominiums at all times, and further, Manager shall have access to each condominium unit during reasonable hours as may be necessary for the maintenance, repair, or replacement of any common elements or limited common element contained therein or be accessible therefrom, or for the making of emergency repairs, limited common elements, or to any other condominium unit or units.

(Q) *Transportation.* Provide for the operation, maintenance, and functioning of such transportation facilities as the Manager or the Association may elect to provide for the use of the residents of the condominiums, their guests, and invitees, and in connection therewith, to establish the rules and regulations relative thereto, and to purchase, lease, repair, and maintain motor vehicles or other modes of transportation, and to secure all appropriate insurance in connection therewith.

5. *Assessments.* Until the Association shall change or modify the same, the monthly assessments to condominium unit owners shall be as set forth in the Declarations of Condominium and Exhibits annexed thereto. The Association agrees that assessments will at all times be maintained so that the amount produced thereby shall be sufficient to provide the moneys necessary to pay all items set forth in Article 6 hereof, and to realize a sum sufficient to meet the requirements of the annual budget prepared pursuant to the provisions of Section 4(N) of this Agreement. The Manager shall not be required to pay any charges or obligations of the Association from its own funds, and shall be required to perform its services and make disbursements only to the extent that, and only so long as, revenues received from assessments or other sources on behalf of the Association shall be sufficient to pay the obligations of the Association. In the event it shall, at any time, appear to the Manager that the assessments and other revenues, if any, of the Association are insufficient to meet the obligations of the Association, the Manager shall so notify the Association, and the Association shall thereupon cause the monthly assessments of its unit owners to be increased pursuant to the provisions of the condominium instruments in an amount sufficient to enable the Association to meet its obligations, and failure on the part of the Association to adopt such an increase within a reasonable time after being notified of the necessity thereof by the Manager may, at the option of the Manager, be deemed and treated as a material breach of this Agreement.

6. *Application of Collections.* All assessments and other revenues, if any, of the Association that the Manager shall collect shall be applied as follows:

(A) *Insurance.* First, to the payment of premiums on insurance policies carried by the Association and the Manager.

(B) *Manager's.* Next, to the payment of the Manager of its fee as hereinafter set forth in Paragraph 7.

(C) *Association Properties.* Next, to the payment of taxes, insurance premiums, and other obligations imposed upon the Association as Grantee under the Association Properties Documents.

(D) *Utilities.* Next, to the payment of all utilities chargeable against the condominiums.

(E) *Balance.* The balance shall be utilized, applied, disbursed, and otherwise expended or reserved by the Manager to pay the costs and expenses of the services rendered by the Manager under this Agreement. "Costs and expenses of services" as herein used is defined to include any and all cost or expense incurred by the Manager in the performance of any of its duties or the exercise of any of its powers. By way of illustration and not of limitation, said costs and expenses of services shall include:

(1) *Association Properties.* The Association's obligations, as determined by the provisions of the Association's Properties Documents, for the upkeep, maintenance, repair, refurbishing, reconstruction, utilities, administration, programs, personnel, and operation of the Association Properties.

(2) *Condominium Lands and Buildings.* Costs attributable to the maintenance, repair, and upkeep of the condominium lands, apartment buildings, and appurtenances.

(3) *Private Roads and Landscaping.* The Association's cost of maintenance and upkeep, including repaving, landscaping, and relandscaping of any and all private roads, parking area, driveways, and planting areas.

(4) *Materials and Supplies.* The costs of all office machinery, motor vehicles, tools, equipment, goods, ware, materials, and supplies of every nature and description required by the Manager in and about the performance of its services or necessary for the utilization and enjoyment of the Association Properties.

(5) *Manager's Overhead and Expenses.* The cost of the Manager's overhead expense:

(6) *Professional Services.* Fees to accountants, attorneys, and such other professionals or experts as may be retained by the Manager pursuant to the provisions in Paragraph 4(0) of this Agreement.

7. *Manager's Compensation.* It is specifically understood and agreed that the Manager shall perform all of the services required of it hereunder at no cost or expense whatsoever to itself but solely at the cost and expense of the Association. As compensation, fee, or profit for its services hereunder, the Manager shall receive a net fee, free of all charges and expenses, of Nine Percent (9%) of assessments of every kind of the Association, except that for the purpose of computing Manager's fee, the total of such assessments shall be reduced by the fees paid to certified public accountants, attorneys-at-law, and other professional persons, to the end and extent that the Manager shall not directly or indirectly recover any compensation, fee, or profit on the charges and fees of such professionals.

8. *Condominium Units.* This Agreement contemplates the Manager's responsibility for performance of required upkeep and repair of each condominium unit. The Manager, in its absolute discretion, may perform maintenance and repair of a condominium unit as may be requested by a condominium unit owner, as an accommodation to the Association or to such condominium unit owner, and charge such unit owner who shall have requested said service of the Manager a reasonable charge in connection therewith.

9. *Office.* The Association shall provide the Manager with an office containing adequate telephone, reasonable space, air conditioning, and other facilities customarily used in the operation of hotels, including adequate provisions for registration lobby, check-in and check-out desk, bedding and linen storage.

10. *Interference.* The Association shall not interfere nor permit, allow, or cause any of its officers, directors, or members to interfere with the Manager in the performance of its duties or the exercise of any of its powers hereunder.

11. *Default.*

(A) *By the Association.* If the Association or its members shall interfere with the Manager in the performance of its duties and the exercise of its powers hereunder, or if the Association shall fail to promptly do any of the things required of it hereunder, including but not limited to, the assessment of its members of amounts sufficient to defray in full the Manager's costs and expenses as herein defined, and to otherwise pay all of the sums mentioned in Paragraph 6, then the Manager, thirty (30) days after having given written notice to the Association of said default, by delivering said notice to any officer of the Association or, in their absence, to any member of the Association, may declare this Agreement in default. Unless such default is cured by the Association within thirty (30) days after such notice, the Manager may, in addition to any other remedy given it by agreement, bring an action against the Association for damages and/or for specific performance and/or for such other right or remedy as the law may provide. All of such rights of the Manager in the event of default shall be cumulative, and the exercise of one or more remedy shall not operate to exclude or to constitute a waiver of any other additional remedy. In the event of any action at law or in equity by the Manager to enforce its rights under the provisions of this Agreement, or seeking damages by reason of any breach by the Association of its duties and obligations hereunder, the Manager shall be entitled, in the event it shall prevail in such litigation, in addition to any other relief provided by law, to the recovery of reasonable attorney's fees and court costs incurred in connection therewith.

(B) *By the Manager.* Failure by the Manager to substantially perform its duties and obligations under this Agreement for a continuous period of sixty (60) days after written notice of default from the Association, specifying the default complained of, shall be grounds for the Association's cancellation of this Agreement.

12. *Rights of Institutional First Mortgagees.*

(A) An institutional first mortgagee is defined as a bank, savings and loan association, insurance company, or trust holding a first mortgage secured by a condominium unit.

(B) The parties acknowledge and agree that the provisions of this Agreement, and the rights of the Manager hereunder, shall be subordinate to the lien of any institutional first mortgagee against a condominium unit.

(C) In the event an institutional first mortgagee shall acquire title to a condominium unit by conveyance in lieu of foreclosure, then so long as such institutional mortgagee shall continue to hold title to the said condominium unit, the compensation and fee to be paid by the Association pursuant to the terms of this Management Agreement shall be reduced by a percentage of the total management fee, the percentage being equal to the interest in the common elements and in the common surplus attributable to the condominium unit to which the institutional first mortgagee has acquired title, and such reduction in management fee shall inure to the benefit of the institutional first mortgagee acquiring title to such condominium unit by crediting the amount thereof against its share of the common expenses of the condominium. Such reduction shall continue only for such time as the institutional first mortgagee shall remain the title holder of the condominium unit, and the same shall not be occupied by a tenant or lessee holding under, by, or through the said institutional first mortgagee, and the said credit and reduction shall cease and terminate as of the date that the institutional first mortgagee conveys such condominium unit.

13. *Severability.* If any section, subsection, sentence clause, phrase, or word of this Agreement shall be for any reason held or declared to be inoperative or void, such holdings will not affect the remaining portions of this Agreement, and it shall be construed to have been the intent of the parties that the remainder of this Agreement, after the exclusion of such parts, shall be deemed and held to be as valid as if such excluded parts had never been included herein. As used in this Agreement, the term "condominium owner" or "unit owner" shall include the term "unit week owner," as appropriate.

IN WITNESS WHEREOF, the parties hereto have caused this Agreement to be executed by their duly authorized officers, and their seals affixed this 1st day of March, 1982.

ABLE RESORT MANAGEMENT, INC.

ATTEST: (CORPORATE SEAL)

_____     By _____
Secretary of the Corporation                                          President

(CORPORATE SEAL)     HAPPY HEATH ACRES CONDOMINIUM ASSO-CIATION, INC.

_____     By _____
Secretary of the Corporation                                          President

[1]*15A Am. Jur. 2d Condominiums and Cooperative Apartments,* paras. 27–29.

## FORM VIIF 1.03

(Condominium maintenance agreement between developer and the condominium association where the association is required to maintain the common elements)[1]

### MAINTENANCE AGREEMENT

AGREEMENT entered into by and between HAPPY HEATH DEVELOPERS, LTD., a Florida limited partnership (hereinafter called "Developer"), and HAPPY HEATH ACRES CONDOMINUM ASSOCIATION, a corporation not for profit under the laws of the State of Florida (hereinafter called the "Association"):

WITNESSETH :

WHEREAS, the Association has been formed to manage the HAPPY HEATH ACRES RESORT, which is to be located on the lands located in Middle County, Florida; and

WHEREAS, Developer has commenced a sales program for the sale of said condominium units to persons who will upon acquiring title become members of the Association; and

WHEREAS, an Association Properties Purchase Agreement has or shall shortly be entered into by and between the Developer, as Grantor, and the Association, as Grantee, pursuant to which an undivided Five Percent (5%) interest in the Association Properties as described therein has or shall be conveyed by Grantor to Grantee, and granting to said Association Properties for the benefit of the purchasers of condominium units at Happy Heath Acres Resort, subject to certain restrictions contained therein; and

WHEREAS, the afore-described Association Properties Purchase Agreement requires the Association to maintain the afore-described Association Properties; and

WHEREAS, the Developer has prepared and is making available to prospective purchasers of condominium units a projected operating budget that includes, among other things, the cost of operation of the said condominium and the Association Properties; and

WHEREAS, said Association Properties Purchase Agreement provides that Developer is entitled to the exclusive use and occupancy of certain improved portions of the Association Properties for sales offices and models during the time that the Developer is selling condominium units at Happy Heath Acres Resort.

NOW, THEREFORE, in consideration of the said exclusive use of a portion of the Association Properties for sales models and offices, and for other good and valuable consideration, the Developer hereby agrees to advance that portion of the cost of maintaining the common elements of Happy Heath Acres Resort and the Association Properties that is in excess of the budgeted amount thereof, as more particularly set forth in Article 1 hereof, for the period of time set forth in Article 2 hereof, all pursuant to the terms and provisions contained herein, to wit:

1. *Subsidization and Guarantee.* For the term of this Agreement, Developer shall advance to the Association, for the purpose of subsidizing the maintenance budget on behalf of Happy Heath Acres Resort Purchasers, that part of the cost of maintaining and operating the afore-described condominium and the Association Properties, exclusive of the costs of all capital improvements to the Association Properties attributable to Happy Heath Acres Resort that shall be in excess of the sum of _____ Dollars (\$) per interval week, and does hereby obligate itself to pay any amount of common expenses incurred during the period set forth in Article 2 hereof, and not produced by the maintenance fees and assessments at the aforementioned guaranteed level receivable from other unit week owners in Happy Heath Acres Resort. The Developer's obligation shall be reduced to the extent that funds shall be available to offset such common expenses and maintenance cost deficiencies respecting the common elements and Association Properties operation and maintenance deficiencies from:

(a) Revenues realized from the operation of said Association Properties;

(b) The share of the initial contribution to the Condominium Fund allocable to the maintenance and operation of the common elements and Association Properties in accordance with Articles 00 and 00 of the Declaration of Condominium of Happy Heath Acres Resort; and

(c) All other funds available to the Association for maintaining and operating the Association Properties.

2. *Guarantee Period.* The term of this Agreement shall commence upon the execution hereof and shall run until the earlier of (1) August 31, 1987, or (2) the date upon which the membership of a majority of the Association's board of administration shall first consist of persons other than designees of the Developer.

3. *Benefit.* This subsidization and guarantee is given to the Association solely for and shall inure to the benefit of purchasers of condominium units or unit weeks at Happy Heath Acres Resort.

4. *Reporting and Payment Procedures.* The obligations of the Developer pursuant to the provisions hereof shall be determined annually by an audit of the books and records of the Association by the certified public accounting firm retained by the Developer for such purpose. Such annual audit shall be prepared each fiscal or calendar year no later than sixty (60) days following the end of the fiscal or calendar year, or annually on such date as is otherwise mutually agreed to by the parties hereto.

5. *Cumulative Effects.* The Developer's obligation hereunder shall be cumulative for the terms of this Agreement and shall be adjusted at the expiration of each yearly period as set forth in Paragraph 4 above, and the completion of the afore-referred-to annual audit. In the event that the revenues derived from the monthly assessment of the sum of Fifty Dollars (\$50) per month against each purchased unit, plus the moneys derived from the other sources as set forth in Subparagraphs 1(a) through (c) above shall exceed the Association Properties' maintenance and operational costs for the common elements and Association Properties for any given year, said excess allocable to Happy Heath Acres Resort shall be applied and credited against Developer's obligations hereunder for succeeding years. It is the intent and purpose of this Agreement that funds advanced to the Association by the Developer shall constitute interest-free loans made on behalf of the Association by the Developer, to be repaid by the Association on or before the expiration of thirty (30) days from the date the final audit provided for herein is completed, but only in the event and to the extent that a surplus exists as a result of the total moneys received from

the assessment of the sum of Fifty Dollars ($50) per month for each purchased unit plus the sums realized from the sources set forth in Subparagraphs 1(a) through (c) above exceed the maintenance and operation expenses for the common elements and the Association Properties, exclusive of the cost of the Association Properties capital improvements, for each such period. In the event that no such surplus exists, or to the extent that said surplus is less than the total funds advanced by Developer to the Association, the obligation of the Association to repay said advances to Developer shall be thereby canceled and be null and void.

Should the Developer be entitled to a repayment of all or any part of the funds advanced pursuant to this Agreement, and should the Association fail to repay said amount to Developer within thirty (30) days of the completion of said final audit, then the Developer shall be entitled to collect, in addition to the amount thereof, interest thereon at a rate of Fifteen Percent (15%) per annum, together with all attorney's fees and court costs incurred in connection with the collection of such amount.

6. *Computations and Interpretations of Disputes.* All computations and interpretations required in connection with the enforcement and/or application of this Agreement shall be made by the certified public accounting firm retained by Developer to audit the affairs of the Association.

7. *Disputes.* Should any dispute arise between the Developer and the Association in connection with either the computation or interpretation of this Agreement, then such dispute shall be finally determined by the majority decision of the board of arbiters as hereinafter set forth. Should the Association dispute the findings of the certified public accounting firm retained by the Developer to audit the affairs of the Association, then the Association shall, within thirty (30) days of the Developer's mailing a copy of said annual audit to the Association by certified mail, return receipt requested, notify said Certified Public Accounting firm and the Developer in writing by certified mail, return receipt requested, indicating the nature of such dispute. Within thirty (30) days thereafter, the Association shall appoint an independent certified public accounting firm to represent the Association as an arbiter, and the Developer shall appoint a certified public accounting firm to represent the Developer as an arbiter. The two (2) arbiters so appointed shall meet with the certified public accounting firm that prepared the annual audit, and the three (3) certified public accounting firms, as arbiters, shall thereafter meet and resolve the controversy by the decision of the majority of such board of arbiters. The final determination by the board of arbiters, as afore-described, shall be final and binding upon the parties for all purposes hereof, and the entry of a final judgment based upon such finding may be entered in the Circuit Court of the State of Florida. All costs of said arbitration procedure, including reasonable fees for said arbiters, shall be paid for by the Association, provided, however, that should the Association prevail in such dispute, then said costs shall be borne equally by said parties.

8. *Amendments.* This Agreement cannot be altered or amended except pursuant to an instrument in writing signed by all of the parties hereto.

9. *Florida Law.* This Agreement shall be governed by and construed in accordance with the laws of the State of Florida.

10. *Entire Agreement.* This Agreement contains the entire agreement between the parties hereto and supersedes all prior agreements or understandings between the parties hereto relating to the subject matter hereof.

IN WITNESS WHEREOF. the parties hereto have caused this Agreement to be executed this 1st day of September, 1982.

Signed, sealed, and delivered in the presence of:    HAPPY HEATH DEVELOPERS, LTD.

By _____
WITNESS                                              General Partner

WITNESS

ATTEST:                                              HAPPY HEATH CONDOMINIUM ASSOCIATION

By _____
Secretary of the Corporation                         President

¹15A Am. Jr. 2d Condominiums and Cooperative Apartments, paras. 16 and 17.

**FORM VIIF 1.04**

(Time-sharing unit purchase agreement)

HAPPY HEATH ACRES RESORT,
an interval ownership resort

SELLER:   HAPPY HEATH DEVELOPERS, LTD.,
a Florida limited partnership

**PURCHASE AGREEMENT**[1]

Date December 10, 1982

DEED TO READ   JOHN DOE and MARY DOE, his wife

PURCHASER   John and Mary Doe

Telephone   (H)1(412)000-0000

Address   100 East Boulevard                                    (O)(412)000-0000

City   Pittsburgh

State   Pennsylvania   Zip   00000

ORAL REPRESENTATIONS CANNOT BE RELIED UPON AS CORRECTLY STATING THE REPRESENTATIONS OF THE DEVELOPER. FOR CORRECT REPRESENTATIONS, REFERENCE SHOULD BE MADE TO THIS CONTRACT AND THE DOCUMENTS REQUIRED BY SECTION 718.503, FLORIDA STATUTES, TO BE FURNISHED BY A DEVELOPER TO A BUYER OR LESSEE.

The above designated Seller agrees to sell, and the Purchaser agrees to purchase, the following described Unit Week(s) in that certain Condominium Unit committed to interval ownership in Happy Heath Acres Resort situated in Middle County, Florida, to wit:

UNIT WEEK(S) NO. *four (4)* in Condominium Unit No. *I* of Happy Heath Acres Resort, together with all the appurtenances thereto as same are set forth and defined in the "Declaration of Condominium," subject to the provisions of the aforesaid Declaration of Condominium, as recorded in Official Records Book No. *000*, at Page *000* of the Public Records of Middle County, Florida, and subject to the terms and conditions set forth hereinbelow.

1. *TERMS AND METHOD OF PAYMENT*

    STATED UNIT WEEK(S) PURCHASE PRICE                         $ _____

    (a) Initial deposit upon exe-
        cution of this Agreement:                    $ _____

    (b) Additional cash deposit due
        on or before _____:                    $ _____

    (c) Approximate principal bal-
        ance of mortgage to be ob-
        tained by Purchaser:                         $ _____

    (d) Balance of Purchase Price &
        Cost of Recording fees, Doc-
        umentary Stamps, Intangi-
        ble Taxes, Title Insurance,
        and Closing Fees to be paid
        at closing:                    $ _____      $ _____

    TOTAL PURCHASE PRICE                                      $ _____

The deposits that are required to be made, pursuant to this Contract, by the Purchaser to the Seller prior to the closing and conveyance of title shall be held in escrow by Peter Koe, Esq., of 100 Main Street, Middletown, Florida 00000.[2]

2. *DELIVERY OF DOCUMENTS.* Seller has furnished Purchaser with the following information relative to Happy Heath Acres Resort:

    (a) Copy of the Prospectus

    (b) Copy of Declaration of Condominium

    (c) Copy of the Articles of Incorporation of the Happy Heath Acres Condominium Association, Inc. (the Association)

    (d) Copy of the Bylaws of the Association

    (e) Copy of the Estimated Operating Budget for the Condominium

(f) Copy of the unit owner's percentages of ownership and share of expenses for the Condominium

(g) Copy of the floor plan of the unit in which the subject Unit Week(s) are being is (are) being purchased

(h) Copy of the plot plan showing the location of the residential buildings and the common areas of the Condominium

(i) Copy of the plot plan showing the location of the residential buildings and common areas of the contemplated related Condominiums and shared facilities within the multicondominium complex

(j) Copy of the Escrow Agreement for payments made to the Developer prior to closing

(k) Sales Brochure

The Seller reserves the right to modify or amend the foregoing documents; provided, however, that no modifications or amendments shall be permitted that would materially affect the rights of the Purchaser, or the value of the Purchaser's unit, without first obtaining the written approval of the Purchaser.

3. *APPROVAL OF PURCHASER.* The Purchaser understands and agrees that the Seller is desirous of ensuring that the Condominium is comprised of unit owners who are congenial and financially responsible, and to those ends, the Purchaser grants the Seller the right to investigate and screen the Purchaser for the purpose of obtaining sufficient assurances of the Purchaser's character and financial well-being; and the Purchaser agrees to hold the Seller harmless from all liability on account of said investigation. The Purchaser further acknowledges that the results of the aforesaid investigation may cause the Seller to arbitrarily revoke this Contract, and accordingly, the Purchaser agrees that the Seller may, in its sole discretion, rescind this Contract at any time within thirty (30) days from the date hereof, and in the event of such recision by the Seller, any sums paid to the Seller by the Purchaser shall be returned forthwith to the Purchaser, and the parties shall be relieved of all further obligations hereunder.

4. *CLOSING.* The closing of this purchase and sale transaction shall be effected in the following manner:

(a) Closing shall take place on the *10th* day of *December*, 1982, at *the office of Peter Koe, Esq., 100 Main Street, Middletown, Florida at 10:00 A.M.*

(b) The balance of the purchase price shall be paid to the Seller in currency of the United States or by a certified or cashier's check drawn on a bank or savings and loan institution authorized to do business in the State of Florida.

(c) Prorations of the following items shall be made as of the date of closing, unless possession of the unit is delivered to the Purchaser prior thereto, in which event prorations shall be made as of the date of delivery of such possession.

(i) Real estate taxes

(ii) Quarterly assessments of the Association, including, but not limited to, costs and expenses for maintenance and operation of the Condominium
(See Paragraph 4 [d] [viii], hereinbelow.)

(d) By execution of this Agreement, Purchaser acknowledges that the following closing costs and other expenses shall be paid by the Purchaser:

(i) Florida documentary stamps to be affixed to the Warranty Deed

(ii) Costs of recording the Warranty Deed

(iii) Cost of an Owner's Title Insurance Policy, which shall be provided to the Purchaser by the Seller's Attorney

(iv) Any and all costs or fees to ensure or guarantee escrow disbursement, if required or requested by the Purchaser

(v) Real Estate taxes and any other taxes assessed against the unit

(vi) Utility deposits made in respect of the unit

(vii) Purchaser's required initial capital contribution to the Association in an amount equal to One-half of One Percent (0.5%) of the purchase price of the Purchaser's Unit Week(s)

(viii) Purchaser's prorated share of the quarterly assessment for the Unit committed to Interval Ownership allocable to the Unit for the Unit Week(s) being purchased, based on the date of closing of the Condominium for the current maintenance period

(ix) All costs that any mortgagee required to be paid if Purchaser is to obtain a mortgage loan or assume a mortgage, including, but not limited to, documentary stamps and intangible taxes, charges for prepaid interest, escrow for taxes and insurance, charges for servicing of credit accounts, including cost of payment books and other service fees, abstracting, mortgagee title insurance, mortgagee attorney's fees, and all costs and fees incident to the obtaining or closing of any prior mortgage that Purchaser assumes

(x) Costs of preparing the Seller's closing statements

This agreement is subject to the terms and conditions on the reverse side hereof, which by reference is made a part hereof.

ANY PAYMENT IN EXCESS OF 10 PERCENT OF THE PURCHASE PRICE MADE TO DEVELOPER PRIOR TO CLOSING PURSUANT TO THIS CONTRACT MAY BE USED FOR CONSTRUCTION PURPOSES BY THE DEVELOPER. FLORIDA STATUTE 718.202(1) REQUIRES THAT ALL PAYMENTS UP TO 10 PERCENT OF THE SALES PRICE RECEIVED BY THE DEVELOPER FROM THE PURCHASER TOWARD THE SALES PRICE SHALL BE PAID INTO AN ESCROW ACCOUNT ESTABLISHED PURSUANT TO SAID STATUTE. IN LIEU OF THE FOREGOING, THE DIRECTOR OF THE DIVISION OF FLORIDA LAND SALES AND CONDOMINIUMS HAS THE DISCRETION TO ACCEPT OTHER ASSURANCES. THEREFORE, SALES DEPOSITS MAY BE USED FOR CONSTRUCTION PURPOSES BY THE DEVELOPER UPON APPROVAL OF ALTERNATIVE ASSURANCES BY THE DIVISION DIRECTOR.

THE UNDERSIGNED HEREBY WAIVE THE RIGHT TO RECEIVE NOTICE OF THE ANNUAL MEETING BY MAIL, WHICH MEETING IS HELD *annually on the first Wednesday in the month of January.*

TIME-SHARE ESTATES, AS DEFINED IN SECTION 718.103(19), FLORIDA STATUTES, WILL BE CREATED WITH RESPECT TO UNITS IN THIS CONDOMINIUM.

PURCHASER: _____ (SEAL)   SELLER:  Happy Heath Developers, Ltd.
        JOHN DOE

_____ (SEAL)   BY _____
MARY DOE                      President

Dated:  October 30, 1982 _____   Acceptance Date:  October 30, 1982 _____

(THIS LANGUAGE WOULD APPEAR ON THE REVERSE SIDE OF THE PURCHASE AGREEMENT WHEN IT IS PRINTED.)

1. DEPOSITS.

The initial deposit of subsequent payments made pursuant to this Agreement by Purchaser to Seller shall, prior to the closing of title, until the amount paid to the Seller equals Ten Percent (10%) of the total sales price, be held in escrow pursuant to the provisions of Section 718.202(1), Florida Statutes, by _____. All amounts paid by Purchaser to Seller in excess of Ten Percent (10%) of the total sales price shall be held in a special account by Seller or its authorized agent pursuant to the provisions of Section 718.202(2) and (3), Florida Statutes. These funds may be used prior to closing only for refund to Purchaser or in the actual construction and development of the Condominium named on the reverse side hereof; however; no part of the funds shall be used for salaries of salesmen, commissions or expenses of salesmen, or for advertising purposes. The Purchaser may obtain a receipt for his deposit upon request.

2. UNIT WEEKS.

Unit Week No. 1 for Phase I is the seven (7) days commencing on the first Sunday in each year. Unit Week No. 2 is the seven (7) days succeeding. Additional weeks up to and including Unit Week No. 51 are computed in a like manner. Unit Week No. 52 contains the seven (7) days succeeding the end of Unit Week No. 51 without regard to the month or year, plus any excess days not otherwise assigned. Unit Weeks run from noon on the first Sunday of the Unit Weeks purchased to noon on the last Sunday of said Unit Weeks. Unit Weeks for Phases II and III shall be defined in this Paragraph and in the Declaration of Condominium, except that the Unit Week shall commence on Saturday.

3. MAINTENANCE FEE.

Purchaser understands and agrees that in accordance with the Declaration of Condominium, Purchaser will be responsible for the above-described Unit Week Owner's share of Common expenses, assessments, maintenance fee, and any and all other expenses incurred in the operation of said Condominium. Seller will guarantee until August 31, 1987, that the annual maintenance fee will not exceed $00 per Unit Week for one-bedroom units and $000 per Unit Week for two-bedroom units.

4. PURCHASER'S ACKNOWLEDGMENTS.

Purchaser acknowledges by execution of this Agreement that prior to the execution of this Agreement, Purchaser received a copy of the Developer's Prospectus, and Declaration of Condominium, together with Exhibits attached thereto, which include the Bylaws and Articles of Incorporation of the Condominium Association. Additionally, Purchaser received a copy of the initial Rules and Regulations of the Condominium unit being sold hereunder and the estimated operating budget for the Condominium. Buyer further acknowledges, represents, and warrants that the purchase of the condominium unit is made for Buyer's personal use, without any representations concerning rentals, rent return, tax advantages, depreciation, or investment potential, or other monetary or financial advantage by Seller, its agents, employees, or associates. Buyer further acknowledges that the Seller is not offering and will not sponsor, arrange, or promote any program for the rental or temporary use and occupancy of apartments in the project, other than apartments owned and retained by the Seller, and that the Buyer must make any such arrangements for his own apartment, if desired, without the involvement or participation of the Seller.

5. MODIFICATIONS AND CHANGES.

The Declaration of Condominium will be recorded prior to closing. Seller reserves the right to make changes in the proposed Declaration of Condominium as provided therein, a copy of which has been delivered to the Purchaser, providing those changes do not decrease Purchaser's share in the common elements, change his voting rights, or increase Purchaser's share of the common expenses. The Condominium Unit described on the reverse side hereof and proposed improvements upon the Condominium property shall be substantially similar to drawings shown to Purchaser; however, the Seller shall have the right to make reasonable modifications to the plans and specifications as it deems advisable. Purchaser acknowledges that dimensions are approximate.

6. CONSTRUCTION OF THE CONDOMINIUM.

The Seller will construct and equip an apartment building in accordance with the plans and specifications, subject, however, to reasonable modifications approved by the Seller that do not change the size of floor plan of Purchaser's apartment, or Purchaser's interest in the common elements to the detriment of the Purchaser. Such plans and specifications are available for inspection by Purchaser at the office of Seller. The Seller agrees that any provisions of this Contract to the contrary notwithstanding, Seller is obligated to Buyer to erect (or complete the erection of), the building in which the above-described unit is located within two (2) years from the date of acceptance hereof by Seller's authorized agent. Buyer's remedy of specific enforcement of this Contract is in no wise restricted.

7. CLOSING AND TITLE.

If the Condominium Unit described on the reverse side hereof is purchased prior to or during construction, closing of purchase will be consummated no later than thirty (30) days after a Certificate of Occupancy has been issued for the building containing the Condominium Unit. If a Certificate of Occupancy has been issued for the building containing the Condominium Unit on or before the date of this Agreement, closing will be consummated no later than thirty (30) days after execution of this Agreement. If Purchaser fails to meet these requirements, this Agreement will become null and void, and, at the option of Seller, all moneys previously paid by Purchaser will be forfeited as outlined in Paragraph 14. Seller shall deliver at closing its Warranty Deed conveying fee title to the Unit Weeks to Purchaser under a plan of Interval Ownership as defined in the Declaration of Condominium, free and clear of all encumbrances, except: conditions, restrictions, reservations, limitations, zoning, and easements of record at the time of closing, terms and conditions of the Declaration of Condominium, and taxes for the then current and subsequent years. Purchaser at closing shall execute any necessary documents. All representations, duties, and obligations of the Purchaser, and the terms and conditions of this Agreement shall survive the closing. The closing will be held at the office of Peter Koe, Esq., whose address is *100 Main Street, Middletown, Florida 00000, at 10:00 A.M.*.

8. REFUND PRIVILEGE.

THIS AGREEMENT IS VOIDABLE BY BUYER BY DELIVERING WRITTEN NOTICE OF THE BUYER'S INTENTION TO CANCEL WITHIN FIFTEEN (15) DAYS AFTER THE DATE OF EXECUTION OF THIS AGREEMENT BY THE BUYER, AND RECEIPT BY BUYER OF ALL OF THE ITEMS REQUIRED TO BE DELIVERED TO HIM BY THE DEVELOPER UNDER SECTION 718.503, FLORIDA STATUTES. BUYER MAY EXTEND THE TIME FOR CLOSING FOR A PERIOD OF NOT MORE THAN FIFTEEN (15) DAYS AFTER THE BUYER HAS RECEIVED ALL OF THE ITEMS REQUIRED. BUYER'S RIGHT TO VOID THIS AGREEMENT SHALL TERMINATE AT CLOSING.

9. FURNISHINGS.

Although models and descriptive materials are for display purposes only, the Condominium Unit described on the reverside side hereof shall have furniture, appliances, equipment, and all accent furnishings substantially similar to, or of equal quality to, those shown or used in the model or descriptive materials.

10. TITLE INSURANCE AND CLOSING COSTS.

Upon closing, Seller shall cause to be issued to Purchaser an owner's title insurance policy insuring the Purchaser's title to the Condominium Unit for the Unit Week(s) purchased, subject only to the conditions of title set forth herein. If, after use of reasonable diligence to make the title insurable, Seller is unable to do so, Seller shall refund to Purchaser all moneys paid under this Agreement and shall thereupon be released from any and all obligations hereunder. Purchaser shall pay the amount of closing costs on the reverse hereof.

11. BINDING EFFECT.

This Agreement is binding upon the parties hereto and their heirs, legal representatives, successors, and assigns and may not be assigned by Purchaser without the prior written consent of Seller. This Agreement will supersede any and all understandings and agreements between the parties hereto, and it is mutually understood and agreed that this Agreement represents the entire agreement between the parties hereto, and no representations or inducements prior hereto that are not included in and embodied in this Agreement shall be of any force and effect, and this Agreement may be amended amd modified only by an instrument in writing between the parties. This Agreement shall not be recorded in the office of the Clerk in any Circuit Court of the State of Florida, and the recording of same by the Purchaser shall be considered a breach of this Agreement and shall terminate this Agreement, at Seller's option.

12. PURCHASER'S DEFAULT.

Time is of the essence, except where otherwise specifically provided for herein. Purchaser expressly waives notice of default or breach of any term or condition of this Agreement, all sums paid hereunder by Purchaser shall be retained by the Seller as liquidated and agreed damages, and the parties hereto shall be relieved from all obligations hereunder. Purchaser shall be liable for Seller's reasonable attorney's fees and costs incurred by it by virtue of any litigation as the parties' rights under this Agreement, if the Seller is the prevailing party. Purchaser covenants to defend and indemnify Seller against all claims of real estate brokers and/or salesmen due to acts of Purchaser or Purchaser's representatives other than broker or salesmen employed by Seller.

13. MORTGAGE PURCHASE.

If Purchaser desires mortgage financing, a mortgage application will be completed and submitted as part of this Agreement, in which case this Agreement is contingent upon Purchaser obtaining a first mortgage commitment for the amount specified on the reverse side of this Agreement, or upon Seller's approval of Purchaser for the mortgage requested.

14. EXCHANGE PROGRAM.

Seller has executed an agreement with DREAM RESORTS INTERNATIONAL, INC., such agreement allowing for a reciprocal exchange program for member-owners at Happy Heath Acres Resort Condominiums. Seller makes no representations as to Dream Resorts International, Inc., and all representations set forth within the brochures and literature of Dream Resorts International, Inc., are representations of Dream Resorts International, Inc. In the event the aforesaid membership agreement or any membership agreement for any other reciprocal exchange program is terminated for any reason, Buyer hereby agrees that Buyer shall have no claim or cause of action against Seller.

15. SALES AGENT.

World Marketing Realty, Inc., is the agent of the Seller, Happy Heath Developers, Ltd., with regard to the sale of the unit described on the reverse side, and will be paid a commission by the Seller upon completion of the sale.

16. MAINTENANCE FEE AND GUARANTEE.

For the purposes of being excused from the payment of shares of common expenses assessed against units unsold or otherwise retained by the Developer pursuant to the provisions of Florida Statute 718.116 (8) (b), the Developer does hereby guarantee that the assessment for common expenses of the Condominium imposed upon the Unit Owners or Unit Week Owners, as appropriate, will not increase over $*000* per unit week per year, and does hereby obligate himself to pay any amount of common expenses incurred during the period of time commencing on the date of the closing of the purchase and sale of the first Unit Week and ending on the first day of the fourth calendar month following the month in which the closing of the purchase and sale of such first Unit Week occurs, and not produced by the assessments at the aforesaid guaranteed level receivable from other Unit Owners or Unit Week Owners.

[1]*15A Am. Jur. 2d Condominiums and Cooperative Apartments* paras. 13, 18, 38–44. Check state condominium statute and federal consumer protection laws. Ref. Forms VIIF 1.04(a), (b), and (c).
[2]Ref. Form VIIIM 1.03 for irrevocable letter of credit used in this connection.

## FORM VIIF 1.04(a)

### (Disclosure statement to purchaser of time-sharing condominium unit)

### DISCLOSURE STATEMENT

The following information is furnished to the undersigned Customer by HAPPY HEATH DEVEL-OPERS, LTD., hereinafter called "Creditor," concerning a proposed mortgage loan, identified herein to be consummated hereafter.

1. Amounts to be paid by Seller,
for the account of customer, and NOT included as a Finance Charge:

| | |
|---|---|
| Mortgage Recording Fee | $ _____ |
| Deed Recording Fee | $ _____ |
| Documentary on Mortgage | $ _____ |
| Intangible | $ _____ |
| Documentary on Deed | $ _____ |
| Title Search & Owners Title Ins. Policy | $ _____ |
| Credit Reports | $ _____ |
| Other (describe) Condominium Slush Fund | $ _____ |

2. Amount to be paid to and for Customer
   (Amount of Loan)                              $ _____
3. LESS: Prepaid Finance Charge                              NONE
4. Amount Financed (2 less 3)                    $ _____
5. Finance Charge (total interest on loan)       $ _____
6. Total of Payments (sum of 4 and 5)            $ _____
7. The Finance Charge begins to accrue on the date of closing, which is estimated to be
_____ , 19____.
8. The ANNUAL PERCENTAGE RATE is _____%.
Monthly payments at $_____ per month, commencing on the _____ day of _____ , 19____, shall be made for a total of _____ months, with a final balloon payment in the amount of $ _____ on the _____ day of _____ , 19____. Total amount financed is $ _____. Total financing charge is $ _____.
A. Security interest will be granted to the Creditor in the following described property: Unit Week No./s_____ in Condominium Parcel Number _____ and/or Week No./s _____ in Condominium Parcel Number _____ of _____ , according to the Declaration of Condominium thereof, recorded in Official Records Book _____ at Page _____, in the Public Records of _____ County, Florida, and in certain other property, all as more fully described in the Mortgage to be executed by, and a copy of which has been furnished to, the Customer. Said mortgage will grant to the holders thereof a security interest in presently owned and after-acquired property therein described, and will secure other and future indebtedness of the Customer as set forth in said Mortgage.

A delinquency and collection charge may be charged on each payment that shall become and remain in default for a period of more than fifteen (15) days, in an amount equal to the highest rate allowed by law, based on the amount of the delinquent payment.

In the event of prepayment of the principal of the obligation by the Customer, a penalty charge will not be imposed. In the event the mortgage is paid in full within thirty (30) days from date hereof, all accrued interest shall be waived. No rebate upon prepayment in full. In the event the interest rate exceeds the limit of usury in the State of Florida, the legal limit shall be the maximum charged, and such excess shall be refunded.

I (we) acknowledge that I (we) received a fully completed copy hereof on December 10, 1982, before consummation of the transaction to which it relates.

_____ (SEAL)

CUSTOMER John Doe

_____ (SEAL)

CUSTOMER Mary Doe

## FORM VIIF 1.04(b)

### (Time-sharing condominium unit purchaser's acknowledgment of no oral representations)

### PURCHASER'S ACKNOWLEDGMENT

The Purchaser acknowledges that he fully understands the terms of this purchase from Happy Heath Developers, Ltd., a Florida limited partnership, and the consequences of Condominium Unit Ownership, and specifically states that in connection with the purchase of this Condominium Unit, the Purchaser is *not* relying on any representations or inducements relating to the economic benefits of unit ownership to be derived from the efforts of others, including any tax benefits, reduced cash outlay, or expectation of profits resulting from rental of his Unit. In particular, Purchaser acknowledges that his Condominium Unit has neither been offered and sold through, nor has the Purchaser relied upon any advertising, sales literature, promotional schemes, or oral representations that emphasize the economic benefits to the Purchaser to be derived from the managerial efforts of the Developer, or a third party designated or arranged for by the Developer, in renting his condominium unit.

WITNESSES:

_____

_____

PURCHASER John Doe

_____

PURCHASER Mary Doe

STATE OF FLORIDA
COUNTY OF MIDDLE

I HEREBY CERTIFY that on this day, before me, an officer duly authorized in the state and county aforesaid to take acknowledgments personally appeared *John Doe* and *Mary Doe*, to me known to be the persons described in and who executed the foregoing Purchaser's Acknowledgment, and they acknowledged before me that they executed the same.

WITNESS my hand and official seal in the county and state last aforesaid, this *10th* day of *December*, 1982.

_____

Notary Public

My commission expires:

## FORM VIIF 1.04(c)

### (Time-sharing condominium unit purchaser's receipt for required disclosure documents)

### RECEIPT FOR CONDOMINIUM DOCUMENTS

THE UNDERSIGNED acknowledges receipt of the items checked below, as required by the Condominium Act, relating to HAPPY HEATH ACRES RESORT physically located at *Highway 00 W*, *Middletown*, Florida. Place a check in the column by each item received.

If an item does not apply, place "N/A" in the column.

| *ITEM* | *RECEIVED* |
|---|---|
| Prospectus | _____ |
| Declaration of Condominium | _____ |
| Articles of Incorporation | _____ |
| By-Laws | _____ |
| Estimated Operating Budget | _____ |
| Form of Agreement for Sale or Lease | _____ |
| Rules and Regulations | _____ |
| Covenants and Restrictions | _____ |
| Ground Lease | _____ |
| Management and Maintenance Contracts | _____ |
| For more than one year | _____ |
| Renewable Management Contracts | _____ |
| Lease of Recreational and other Facilities to be used exclusively by Unit Owners of Subject Condominium | _____ |
| Form of Unit Lease if a Lease Hold | _____ |
| Declaration of Servitude | _____ |
| Sales Brochures | _____ |
| Phase Development | _____ |
| Description (see 718.503 [2] [k] and 504 [14]) | _____ |
| Lease of Recreational and Other Facilities to be used by Unit Owners with other Condominiums | _____ |
| Description of Management for single Management of Multiple Condominiums | _____ |
| Conversion Inspection Report | _____ |
| Conversion Termite Inspection | _____ |
| Plot Plan | _____ |
| Floor Plan | _____ |
| Survey of Land and Graphic Description of Improvements | _____ |
| Executed Escrow Agreement | _____ |
| Plans and Specifications | _____ |

THE PURCHASE AGREEMENT IS VOIDABLE BY BUYER BY DELIVERING WRITTEN NOTICE OF THE BUYER'S INTENTION TO CANCEL WITHIN 15 DAYS AFTER THE DATE OF EXECUTION OF THIS AGREEMENT BY THE BUYER, AND RECEIPT BY BUYER OF ALL ITEMS REQUIRED TO BE DELIVERED TO HIM BY THE DEVELOPER UNDER SECTION 718.503, FLORIDA STATUTES. BUYER MAY EXTEND THE TIME FOR CLOSING FOR A PERIOD OF NOT MORE THAN 15 DAYS AFTER THE BUYER HAS RECEIVED ALL OF THE ITEMS REQUIRED. BUYER'S RIGHT TO VOID THIS AGREE-MENT SHALL TERMINATE AT CLOSING.

ORAL REPRESENTATIONS CANNOT BE RELIED UPON AS CORRECTLY STATING THE REPRESEN-TATIONS OF THE DEVELOPER. FOR CORRECT REPRESENTATIONS, REFERENCE SHOULD BE MADE TO THIS CONTRACT AND THE DOCUMENTS REQUIRED BY SECTION 718.503, FLORIDA STATUTES, TO BE FURNISHED BY A DEVELOPER TO A BUYER OR LESSEE.

Executed this 10th day of December, 1982.

_____

PURCHASER John Doe

_____

PURCHASER Mary Doe

## FORM VIIF 1.05

### (Balloon purchase money mortgage for purchaser of time-sharing condominium unit)

THIS IS A BALLOON MORTGAGE, AND THE FINAL PAYMENT OR THE BALANCE DUE UPON MA-TURITY IS *$4,000*, TOGETHER WITH ACCRUED INTEREST, IF ANY, AND ALL ADVANCEMENTS MADE BY THE MORTGAGEE UNDER THE TERMS OF THIS MORTGAGE.

*PURCHASE MONEY MORTGAGE*

Executed the *10th* , day of *December* , 1982, by *JOHN DOE and MARY DOE, his wife*, hereinafter called the "Mortgagor," to HAPPY HEATH DEVELOPERS, LTD, a Florida limited partnership, hereinafter called the "Mortgagee":

(Wherever used herein, the terms "Mortgagor" and "Mortgagee" include all the parties to this instrument, and the heirs, legal representatives, and assigns of individuals, and the successors and assigns of corporation; and the term "note" includes all the notes herein described if more than one.)

WITNESSETH, that for good and valuable consideration, and also in consideration of the aggregate sum named in the promissory note of even date herewith, hereinafter described, the Mortgagor hereby grants, bargains, sells, aliens, remises, conveys, and confirms unto the Mortgagee all the certain land of which the Mortgagor is now seized and in possession situated in Middle County, Florida, viz:

UNIT WEEK(S) NO.(S) Four (4), of Condominium Unit Number 000, of Happy Heath Acres Resort CONDOMINIUM I, according to the Declaration thereof, recorded in Official Records Book 000, at Page 000, of the Public Records of Middle County, Florida. TOGETHER with all the improvements now or hereafter erected on the property, and all easements, rights, appurtenances, rents, royalties, mineral, oil and gas rights and profits, water, water rights, and water stock, and all fixtures, furniture, and furnishings now or hereafter in or attached to the property, all of which, including replacements and additions thereto, shall be deemed to be and remain a part of the property covered by this Mortgage:

Mortgagor agrees to promptly pay, when due, all assessments imposed by the Association that govern the Condominium, and agrees to comply with all rules, regulations, and provisions set forth in the Declaration of Condominium (and all exhibits thereto) or promulgated pursuant thereto.

Mortgagor agrees not to attempt a partition or subdivision of the Condominium, or to support any amendment that might change the percentage interest of the owners or that would affect the value of the security, without the prior written consent of Mortgagee.

If Mortgagor fails to perform any covenants or agreements of this Mortgage, or if any action is commenced that materially affects Mortgagee's interest or the value of the security, Mortgagee may, at its option, make such appearances, disburse such moneys, and take all action necessary to protect the security value, including, but not limited to, disbursing reasonable attorney's fees, paying condominium charges and assessments, making repairs, etc. Amounts disbursed, together with interest thereon at the highest legal rate, shall become an additional indebtedness secured by this Mortgage.

As additional security, Mortgagee shall be entitled to have a receiver appointed by a Court to enter upon, take possession of, and manage the property, and have the right to collect and retain rents as they become due, provided that this right shall not be utilized unless Mortgagor shall default hereunder or abandon the property.

TO HAVE AND TO HOLD the same, together with the tenements, hereditaments, and appurtenances thereto belonging, and the rents, issues, and profits thereof, unto the Mortgagee, in fee simple.

AND the Mortgagor covenants with the Mortgagee that the Mortgagor is indefeasibly seized of said land in fee simple; that the Mortgagor has good right and lawful authority to convey said land as aforesaid; that the Mortgagor will make such further assurances to perfect the fee simple title to said land in the Mortgagee as may reasonably be required; that the Mortgagor hereby fully warrants the title to said land and will defend the same against the lawful claims of all persons whomsoever; and that said land is free and clear of all encumbrances except matters set forth in the Declaration of Condominium.

PROVIDED ALWAYS, that if said Mortgagor shall pay unto said Mortgagee the certain promissory note hereinafter substantially copied or identified, and shall perform, comply with, and abide by each and every one of the agreements, stipulations, conditions, and covenants thereof, and of this Mortgage, then this Mortgage and the estate hereby created shall cease, determine, and be null and void.

AND the Mortgagor hereby further covenants and agrees to pay promptly when due the principal and interest and other sums of money provided for in said note and this mortgage, or either; to pay all and singular the taxes, assessments, levies, liabilities, obligations, and encumbrances of every nature on said property; to permit, commit, or suffer no waste, impairment, or deterioration of said land or the improvements thereon at any time; to keep the buildings now or hereafter on said land fully insured in a sum of not less than FULL INSURABLE VALUE in a company or companies acceptable to the Mortgagee, the policy or policies to be held by, and payable to, said Mortgagee, and in the event any sum of money becomes payable by virtue of such insurance, the Mortgagee shall have the right to receive and apply the same to the indebtedness hereby secured, accounting to the Mortgagor for any surplus; to pay all costs, charges, and expenses, including lawyer's fees and title searches, reasonably incurred or paid by the Mortgagee because of the failure of the Mortgagor to promptly and fully comply with the agreements, stipulations, conditions, and covenants of said note and this Mortgage, or either; to perform, comply with, and abide by each and every one of the agreements, stipulations, conditions, and covenants set forth in said note and this Mortgage, or either. In the event the Mortgagor fails to pay when due any tax, assessment, insurance premium, or other sum of money payable by virtue of said note and this mortgage, or either, the Mortgagee may pay the same, without waiving or affecting the option to foreclose or any other right hereunder, and all such payments shall bear interest from date thereof at the highest lawful rate then allowed by the laws of the State of Florida. Lawyer's fees shall include any appellate proceeding.

If any sum of money herein referred to be not promptly paid within thirty (30) days next after the same becomes due, or if each and every one of the agreements, stipulations, conditions, and covenants of said note and this Mortgage, or either, is not fully performed, complied with, and abided by, then the entire sum mentioned in said note, and this Mortgage, or the entire balance unpaid thereon, shall forthwith or thereafter, at the option of the Mortgagee, become and be due and payable, anything in said note or therein to the contrary notwithstanding. Failure by the Mortgagee to exercise any of the rights or options herein provided shall not constitute a waiver of any rights or options under said note, or this Mortgage, accrued or thereafter accruing.

IN WITNESS WHEREOF, the said Mortgagor has hereunto signed and sealed these presents the day and year first above written.
THIS IS A BALLOON MORTGAGE, AND THE FINAL PAYMENT OF THE BALANCE DUE UPON MATURITY IS $4,000, TOGETHER WITH ACCRUED INTEREST, IF ANY, AND ALL ADVANCEMENTS MADE BY THE MORTGAGEE UNDER THE TERMS OF THIS MORTGAGE.
Signed, sealed, and delivered in the presence of:

_____

WITNESS

_____          _____

WITNESS                                    JOHN DOE

_____

WITNESS

_____          _____

WITNESS                                    MARY DOE

STATE OF FLORIDA)
                )SS
COUNTY OF MIDDLE)

I HEREBY CERTIFY that on this day, before me, an officer duly authorized in the state and in the county aforesaid to take acknowledgments, personally appeared John Doe and Mary Doe, to me known to be the person(s) described in and who executed the foregoing instrument, and they acknowledged before me that they executed the same.

WITNESS my hand and official seal in the county and state last aforesaid, this 10th day of December, 1982.

My commission expires:          _____
                                 Notary Public

## FORM VIIF 1.06

### (Articles of incorporation for a cooperative office building corporation)

## ARTICLES OF INCORPORATION[1]
## OF
## MIDDLETOWN OFFICES, INC.

We, the subscribers, all natural persons of the age of eighteen years or more and citizens of the Commonwealth of Pennsylvania, acting as incorporators of a nonprofit corporation under the Pennsylvania Not-for-profit Code 15 C.P.S. 7101-8145, do hereby adopt the following Articles of Incorporation for such corporation:

### ARTICLE ONE

### NAME

The name of the corporation is Middletown Offices, Inc.

### ARTICLE TWO

### PURPOSES AND POWERS

1. The corporation is a not-for-profit corporation, and the purposes for which it is formed and the business and objects to be carried on and promoted by it shall be to construct, acquire, deal with, maintain, and operate a cooperative office building or buildings and other structures for the business use and accommodation therein of its stockholders as the occupants and users thereof, and to provide on a cooperative basis the common facilities described in Appendix A, attached hereto and made part hereof.
2. In furtherance of the corporate purpose, the corporation shall have the following powers:
    (a) To construct, maintain, operate, and improve, and to sell, convey, assign, mortgage, or otherwise encumber, or lease any real estate and any personal property necessary to the operation of such project.
    (b) To borrow money and issue evidence of indebtedness of the corporation in furtherance of any or all of the objects of the corporation's business, and to secure the same by mortgage, deed or trust, pledge, or other lien.
    (c) To enter into, perform, and carry out contracts of any kind, and to undertake and perform any other acts necessary to, or in connection with, or incidental to the accomplishment of any purpose of the corporation.
    (d) To make patronage refunds to stockholders, occupants of office units, or others as provided in the bylaws.

### ARTICLE THREE

### INITIAL PRINCIPAL ADDRESS

The street address of the initial principal office of the corporation is 100 Main Street, Middletown, Middle county, Pennsylvania.

The corporation may acquire property and conduct its business within the said county, and in any other place or places within and without the Commonwealth of Pennsylvania.

### ARTICLE FOUR

### REGISTERED AGENT

The name of the corporation's initial registered agent on whom process may be served is John Doe, whose address is that of the corporation's initial principal office.

### ARTICLE FIVE

### DIRECTORS AND OFFICERS

1. The corporation shall have five (5) directors elected by the stockholders, who shall act as directors until their successors are duly chosen and qualified, provided that the number and manner

of selection of the directors may be altered in the bylaws. Officers shall be elected as provided in the bylaws.

2. No contract or other transaction between this corporation and any other corporation or association shall in any way be affected or invalidated by virtue of the fact that any of the directors or officers of this corporation are or may be pecuniarily interested in, or are directors or officers of, such other corporation or association. Any director individually, or any firm of which any director is a member, may be a party to or pecuniarily interested in any contract or transaction of this corporation, provided that the fact of such interest of the director shall be disclosed in the minutes of this corporation; and any director of this corporation who is also a director or officer of such other corporation or association, or who is interested in such contract or transaction, may be counted in determining the existence of a quorum at any meeting of the board of directors of this corporation that shall authorize or ratify any such contract or transaction, but such director may not vote upon such contract or transaction.

Any officer, director, or stockholder of this corporation shall be fully competent and authorized to make and enter into occupancy agreements, leases, and other contracts with the corporation respecting any unit, parcel, or part of the corporate property, under the bylaws governing the same; and no infirmity or disability shall inure or attach to any such agreement, lease, or contract by reason of any such position with or interest in the corporation.

## ARTICLE SIX

### CAPITAL STOCK

The total amount of the capital stock of the corporation shall be 0000 shares of common stock, having a par value of $000 per share. No dividends shall be paid on the stock.

## ARTICLE SEVEN

### REQUIRED RESERVES

1. *Community Facility Reserve Fund.* The corporation shall at all times maintain, for replacement and repair of the community facilities of the building, the sum of Twenty-Five Thousand Dollars ($25,000), under the control of the corporation in such manner as the corporation shall prescribe.

2. *Operating Reserve Fund.* Within one (1) year of the first occupancy of any office unit, the corporation shall establish and maintain a General Operating Reserve for the office units in the sum of Twenty-Five Thousand Dollars ($25,000), under the control of the corporation for the purpose of stability during periods of special stress, and that sum may be used to meet deficiencies from time to time that results from delinquent payment by individual stockholders to provide funds for the repurchase of stock of withdrawing stockholders, or other contingencies. Reimbursements to the Operating Reserve Fund shall be made to its account upon payment of delinquencies or sale of stock for which funds were withdrawn from the reserve.

## ARTICLE EIGHT

### MAINTENANCE REQUIREMENTS

The corporation shall maintain the building and equipment appurtenant thereto and the common facilities in good repair and in such condition as will preserve the health and safety of its stockholders, except as otherwise specifically provided in proprietary leases with its stockholders.

## ARTICLE NINE

### DURATION

The existance of the corporation shall be perpetual, unless and until terminated according to the laws of the Commonwealth of Pennsylvania.

Dated this 1st day of May, 1983.

---

John Doe

---

Richard Roe

Peter Poe

Charles Coe

Mary Coe

COMMONWEALTH OF PENNSYLVANIA
COUNTY OF MIDDLE

BEFORE ME, a notary public in and for said county and state, personally appeared John Doe, Richard Roe, Peter Poe, Charles Coe, and Mary Coe, known to me and known by me to be the persons who executed the foregoing Articles of Incorporation, and they acknowledged before me that they executed the same for the purposes set forth therein.

IN WITNESS WHEREOF, I have hereunto set my hand and affixed my official seal, in the state and county aforesaid, this 1st day of May, 1983.

Notary Public

My commission expires:

[1]*15A Am. Jur. 2d Condominiums and Cooperative Apartments*, paras. 59, 62, and 84–86. For bylaws and house rules and the distinction between them, see paras. 16, 17, 65, 66, 71, and 75. See also 26 U.S.C.A. 216.

## FORM VIIF 1.06(a)

### (Providing membership instead of stock ownership in articles of incorporation for a cooperative office building corporation)[1]

### ALTERNATIVE CLAUSE

ARTICLE VI

MEMBERSHIP

The corporation is organized on a nonstock basis, and there shall be members in lieu of stockholders. Certificates of membership shall be issued to members for the sum of $000 each. No more than 000 memberships shall be issued.

[1]*15A Am. Jur. 2d Condominiums and Cooperative Apartments*, paras. 59, 63, and 78–83.

## FORM VIIF 1.07

### (Lease for cooperative apartment)

### PROPRIETARY LEASE[1]

This proprietary Lease made this 4th day of March, 1982, between H & H, Inc., a cooperative housing corporation organization and existing under the laws of the Commonwealth of Pennsylvania, with offices at 100 Forbes Avenue, City of Pittsburgh, County of Allegheny, Commonwealth of Pennsylvania (herein called "Lessor"), and John Doe and Mary Doe, his wife (herein called "Lessees").

WHEREAS, Lessor is the owner of the land and building known as Happy Towers, located at 100 Forbes Avenue, Pittsburgh, Pennsylvania (herein called the "Building"); and
WHEREAS, the legal description of the land is:

(INSERT LEGAL DESCRIPTION OF THE LAND.);

and

WHEREAS, Lessees are the joint owners of stock in a cooperative apartment corporation known as H & H Inc., and this lease is incidental to the stock ownership:

IT IS AGREED AS FOLLOWS:

1. *Premises and term.* In consideration of the following mutual covenants, and subject to the terms and conditions of this Lease, the Lessor leases to Lessees Apartment No. 5 in the Building (herein called the "Unit"), together with all fixtures and appurtenances inside and outside of the apartment that are allocated to Apartment 5, as shown in the Unit Plan attached hereto as Exhibit A, for a period of fifty (50) years, unless sooner terminated as herein provided.

2. *Rent and assessments.*

(a) During the term of this Lease, Lessees shall be jointly and severally liable for both rent and amounts proportionally assessed to Apartment No. 5 by the board of directors of Lessor in the manner provided in the bylaws of the Lessor. No deduction on account of any setoff or claim by Lessees against the Lessor shall be deducted from the rent or assessment.

(b) The rent for the Unit, Apartment No. 5, is Five Hundred Dollars ($500) per month, payable in advance on or before the fifth (5th) day of the month. No increase in rent shall be made for a period of ten (10) years from the date of this lease. Thereafter, the amount of rent may be increased only at ten (10)-year intervals, and it may be increased only if all other proprietary leases of the building are proportionally increased. No proprietary lease of an apartment in the Building shall be executed after this date for an amount of rent proportionally less than the rent provided herein.

(c) Assessments against the Unit will be made quarterly on the basis of a One Percent (1%) proportionate share of all common expenses, assessed to the Units in accordance with the provisions of the present bylaws of Lessor corporation.

3. *Repairs by Lessor.* Lessor shall at its own expense keep in good repair all of the Building, including the walls and windows of all apartment units and all gas, steam, water, or other pipes or conduits within the walls, ceilings, or floors, and all air-conditioning or heating equipment that is part of the standard Building equipment, as well as outside areas such as sidewalks, parking areas, landscaped areas on the premises, tennis courts, and swimming pools.

4. *Services by Lessor.* Lessor shall maintain and manage the Building as a first-class apartment building, and shall keep the elevators, public halls, stairways, basements, and all common areas and areas outside the partitioned apartments clean and properly lighted, cooled and heated, and shall provide the number of persons necessary, in the judgment of the directors of the corporation, for the proper care and service of the building and those appurtenances in the manner provided herein. Lessor shall provide each unit with a proper and sufficient supply of hot and cold water and with central heat and air conditioning.

5. *Damage to building or apartment.*

(a) *Insured losses.* In the event of insured loss to the building that does not make the Unit untenantable, Lessor has the duty to repair and clean in accordance with Paragraphs 3 and 4, and Lessees have the duty to repair in accordance with Paragraph 10 of this Lease.

(b) *Abatement of rent and assessments.* Rent and current assessment will proportionally abate if fire or other damage makes a unit untenantable, unless the damage was the result of an act of negligence of the Lessees, their employees, family, guests, or agents. In the case of such negligence, the rent will abate only to the extent of recovery by Lessor of any rental value insurance covering the Unit.

6. *Accounting records of Lessor available to Lessees.* Lessor shall keep full and accurate books of account in accordance with recognized accounting practice. The accounting records shall be made available to Lessees or their representatives at any reasonable time and place. Within four (4) months after the end of each fiscal year, Lessor shall deliver to Lessees an annual report of the financial affairs of the corporation, including a balance sheet and profit and loss statement prepared in accordance with recognized accounting practice.

7. *Use of premises.* Lessors shall not use the Unit or permit any part of it to be used or occupied for any purpose other than as a private dwelling. The Unit shall not be occupied by any person or persons as guest of Lessees, unless one of the Lessees is then in occupancy, for a period of longer than thirty (30) days without the written consent of the Lessor.

8. *Subletting.* Lessees shall not sublet the Unit, in whole or in part, or renew or extend any previously authorized sublease, without the written consent of the Lessor. Such consent shall not be unreasonably withheld.

9. *Assignment or other transfer of Lease.* Lessees shall not assign or otherwise transfer this Lease or their stock in the corporation without the execution of a written instrument of assignment approved, executed, and acknowledged by the Lessor, and the delivery of Lessees' stock cer-

tificates in Lessor corporation, duly endorsed in blank. Consent to assignment shall not be unreasonably withheld by Lessor.

10. *Alterations and repairs by Lessees.*

(a) Lessees shall make no alteration, enclosures, or addition to the Unit or the Building, or add or remove any fixture or appliance to the Unit or the Building without the written consent of the lessor. Such consent shall not be unreasonably withheld.

(b) Lessees shall keep the interior of the unit, including walls, floors, and ceilings, but excluding entrance doors and windows, in good repair. Lessees shall do all painting and decorating and shall be solely responsible for the maintenance, repair, and replacement of plumbing, gas, and heating fixtures and equipment used in the Unit, including the exposed gas and waste pipes attached to the fixtures and equipment as well as any special pipes or equipment that Lessees may install within the wall or ceiling or under the floor.

(c) In the event that Lessees are in default for any repairs required by this Paragraph, and Lessor incurs any expense, whether paid out or not, in performing such repairs, Lessee shall reimburse the Lessor within thirty (30) days of written demand for payment.

11. *Right of entry by Lessor.* Lessor must give reasonable notice to Lessees before its agents or authorized workman may visit, examine, or enter Apartment No. 5 at any time, except in case of emergency. In order that Lessor may at all times have access to the Unit for purposes of this Lease, Lessees shall provide Lessor with duplicate keys to the entrance door and storage rooms assigned to the apartment, including duplicates of keys to altered or changed locks.

12. *Lessor's lien for unpaid rent.* Lessor has and may enforce a lien on the Unit for any unpaid rent and/or assessment(s) and interest thereon at the legal rate in the Commonwealth of Pennsylvania. The lien shall include reasonable attorney's fees incurred by Lessor in collecting overdue rent or assessments or in successfully enforcing the lien. In any action by Lessor to enforce such lien, Lessees shall have the right to interpose any defenses, legal or equitable, that Lessees may have against Lessor under this Lease, including setoff or any other claim against Lessor arising as a result of this Lease.

13. *Termination of Lease by Lessor for Cause.* Lessor may terminate this proprietary Lease for any of the following causes, provided the Lessor gives written notice to Lessees by registered or certified mail that the term of this Lease shall expire on a date not less than ninety (90) days after the date of the notice:

(a) *Bankruptcy.* Either Lessee is adjudicated a bankrupt under the laws of the United States.

(b) *Receivership.* A receiver of all the property of either Lessee is appointed under the laws of any state or of the United States and is not vacated within sixty (60) days.

(c) *General assignment for creditors.* Either Lessee makes a general assignment for the benefit of creditors.

(d) *Unauthorized assignment of Lease.* An assignment of this Lease is made that does not comply with Paragraph 9.

(e) *Unauthorized Use.* An unauthorized use of the premises in violation of Paragraph 7, unless such use is discontinued within 30 days of written notice thereof by the Lessor.

(f) *Default in payment.* Default for a period of thirty (30) days in the payment of rent or assessment due from Lessees under this Lease.

(g) *Objectionable conduct.* Objectionable conduct by Lessees or their guests, which continues or is repeated after written notice from Lessor is mailed to Lessee addressed to Apartment No. 5, if such conduct has been determined to be objectionable by the affirmative vote of two-thirds (2/3) of the directors of the Lessor corporation at a meeting duly called for that purpose, to which meeting Lessees have been invited by ten (10) days' written notice of the meeting.

(h) *Termination of all proprietary leases.* If the Lessor corporation shareholders determine by a two-thirds vote, at a meeting duly called for the purpose of voting on termination of all proprietary leases, that all proprietary leases shall be terminated, whether or not the premises have been destroyed or damaged by fire or other cause.

(i) *Condemnation.* If at any time the Building or a substantial portion of it is taken by governmental condemnation proceedings.

14. *Rights and duties on termination.*

(a) If Lessor resumes possession of the Unit, by any legal means available to it, on expiration of the term pursuant to a notice given as provided in Paragraph 13, on the happening of any event specified in Subsections (a) to (g) inclusive of that Section, Lessees shall continue to remain liable for payment of a sum equal to the rent and assessments that would have become due hereunder, and shall pay the same in installments at the time it would be due hereunder, until the time specified in Subsection (c) of this Section. Suit brought to recover any installment of such rent or assessments shall not prejudice the right of Lessor to recover any subsequent installment.

After resuming possession, Lessor may, at its option, from time to time (1) relet the unit for its own account, or (2) relet the unit as agent of Lessees, in the name of Lessees or Lessor, for a term or terms less than, equal to, or greater than the period that would otherwise have constituted the balance of the term of this Lease, and may grant concessions or free rent in its discretion. Any reletting of the Unit shall be deemed for the account of Lessees, unless, within ten (10) days after such reletting, Lessor notifies Lessee that the premises have been relet for Lessor's own account. The fact that Lessor may have relet the Unit as agent for Lessees shall not prevent Lessor from thereafter notifying Lessees that it proposes to relet the unit for its own account. If Lessor relets the unit as agent for Lessee, it shall, after reimbursing itself for its expenses in connection therewith, including leasing commissions and a reasonable amount for attorney's fees and expenses, and decorations, alterations, and repairs in and to the unit, apply the remaining proceeds of such reletting, if any, against Lessees' continuing obligation hereunder.

(b) On termination of this Lease under the provisions of subsections (a) to (g) inclusive of Paragraph 13, Lessee will surrender to Lessor the proprietary Lease of Apartment No. 5 and stock certificate in Lessor corporation to which the Lease is an incident. Whether or not the Lease and/or certificate are surrendered, however, Lessor may issue a new proprietary lease for apartment No. 5 and a new stock certificate when a purchaser therefor is obtained, provided that the issuance of such lease of Apartment No. 5 and stock certificate to the purchaser is authorized by resolution of the directors or by a writing signed by a majority of the directors, or shareholders entitled to vote. On such issuance, the Lease of Apartment No. 5 and the stock certificate held by Lessees shall be automatically canceled and rendered null and void. Lessor shall apply the proceeds received for the issuance of the new lease toward the payment of Lessees' indebtedness hereunder, including interest, attorney's fees and other expenses incurred by Lessor. If the proceeds are sufficient to pay the same, Lessor will pay over any surplus to Lessees. If the proceeds are insufficient, Lessees shall remain liable for the balance of the indebtedness. Lessor shall not, however, be obligated to sell such membership and appurtenant lease, or otherwise make any attempt to mitigate damages.

(c) There shall be a final accounting between Lessor and Lessees on the earliest of the four following dates: (1) the date of expiration of the term of this Lease as stated in Paragraph 1: (2) the date as of which a new proprietary lease covering the Unit becomes effective; (3) the date Lessor gives written notice to Lessees that it has relet the Unit for its own account; or (4) the date on which all proprietary leases of Lessor terminate. From and after the date on which Lessor becomes obligated to account to Lessees as above provided, Lessor shall have no further duty to account to Lessees for any proceeds of reletting, and Lessees shall have no further liability for sums thereafter accruing hereunder, but such termination of Lessees' liability shall not affect any liabilities theretofore accrued.

15. *Lessor's remedies in addition to those provided in this Lease.*

In the event of a breach or threatened breach by Lessees of any provision hereof, Lessor shall have the right of injunction, and the right to invoke any remedy at law or in equity as if reentry and other remedies were not herein provided. The election of one or more remedies shall not preclude Lessor from any other remedy.

16. *Waiver.*

Failure of Lessor to insist, in any one or more instances, on strict performance of any of the provisions of this Lease, or to exercise any right or option herein contained, or to serve any notice, or to institute any action or proceeding, shall not be construed as a waiver or a relinquishment for the future of any such provisions, options, or rights. Receipts by Lessor of rent and/or assessments, with knowledge of any breach of this Lease, shall not be deemed a waiver of such breach. No waiver of any provision of this Lease shall be deemed effective unless made in a writing signed by the majority of the board of directors of the Lessor corporation.

17. *Notices.* Any and all notices given pursuant to this Lease shall be mailed by registered or certified mail to the Lessor at its office in the building or to the Lessee addressed to Apartment No. 5 in the Building, unless either party has designated a different address for notices in writing at least thirty (30) days before such notice is mailed.

18. *Effect of partial invalidity of this Lease.* If any clause or provision of this Lease is adjudged invalid or void, such adjudication shall not affect the validity of any other clauses or provision, or constitute a cause of action in favor of either party against the other.

19. *Headings.* Headings of paragraphs and subparagraphs of this lease are not to be considered a part of this Lease, and are in no way intended to limit or fully describe the contents of the paragraphs or subparagraphs they precede.

20. *Modification in writing.* This Lease may not be modified in any respect except by a writing signed by both parties.

IN WITNESS WHEREOF, the parties hereto have set their hands and seals on the above date.

H & H, Inc.

(Ruth Roe) _____          By _____

Secretary of the Corporation                          Richard Roe, President

_____

John Doe (Lessee)

_____

Mary Doe (Lessee)

## ACKNOWLEDGMENT

COMMONWEALTH OF PENNSYLVANIA
COUNTY OF ALLEGHENY

On this 4th day of March, 1982, before me, Alice Poe, the undersigned officer, personally appeared RICHARD ROE, who acknowledged himself to be the President of H & H, Inc., a corporation, and that he, as such President being authorized to do so, executed the foregoing proprietary lease for the purposes therein contained, by signing the name of the corporation by himself as President.

IN WITNESS WHEREOF, I hereunto set my hand and official seal.

(Alice Poe) _____

Notary Public

My commission expires:

COMMONWEALTH OF PENNSYLVANIA
COUNTY OF ALLEGHENY

On this 4th day of March, 1982, before me, Alice Poe, the undersigned officer, personally appeared John Doe, husband of Mary Doe, known to me to be the person whose name is subscribed to the foregoing proprietary lease, and acknowledged that he executed the same for the purposes therein contained.

IN WITNESS WHEREOF, I hereunto set my hand and official seal.

(Alice Poe) _____

Notary Public

My commission expires:

COMMONWEALTH OF PENNSYLVANIA
COUNTY OF ALLEGHENY

On this 4th day of March, 1982, before me, Alice Poe, the undersigned officer, personally appeared Mary Doe, wife of John Doe, known to me to be the person whose name is subscribed to the foregoing proprietary lease, and acknowledged that she executed the same for the purposes therein contained.

IN WITNESS WHEREOF, I hereunto set my hand and official seal.

(Alice Poe) _____

Notary public

My commission expires:

[1]15A Am. Jur. 2d Condominiums and Cooperative Apartments, paras. 59, 63, and 78–83.

**FORM VIIF 1.07(a)**

(Term of one year, with lessee option to renew proprietary lease)

**ALTERNATIVE CLAUSE**

*Premises, term and option to renew.* In consideration of the following mutual covenants and subject to the terms and conditions of this Lease, the Lessor leases to Lessees Apartment No. 5 in the Building, together with all fixtures and appurtenances inside and outside of the apartment that are allocated to Apartment 5 as shown on the Unit Plan attached hereto as Exhibit A, for a period of one (1) year, renewable for a period of fifty (50) years, at the sole and exclusive option of the Lessees, unless this Lease is terminated by the Lessor for cause. Notice of the exercise of the Lessees' option to renew shall be made, by registered or certified mail addressed to the office of the Lessor, on or before sixty (60) days from the end of each yearly term.

# PART VIII
# GENERAL AND SUPPLEMENTAL BUSINESS CONTRACT FORMS

# PART VIII

# General and Supplemental Business Contract Forms

## INTRODUCTION

This Chapter contains forms for contracts, clauses, and related documents that may be used in the various areas of contract law represented in the first seven parts of the book. One or more of these forms may be necessary or desirable for use independently or in connection with contracts that create or change corporations, partnerships, or joint ventures, or the business status of individuals. Some of them will be used in or be used to implement contracts for the sale or use of personal or real property.

The forms include acknowledgments, affidavits, and certificates, arbitration clauses in addition to those included in many of the contracts, assignments, indemnity and performance bonds, compromises and compositions, consents, escrow arrangements, extensions and renewals of contracts, guaranty agreements, indemnity agreements, letters of credit, loan agreements, powers of attorney, promissory notes, receipts, releases and satisfactions, and service contracts, arranged alphabetically.

## SECTION A    ACKNOWLEDGMENTS

Acknowledgments[1] and affidavits[2] are often confused. An acknowledgment is the act of a person who has signed a legal instrument going before a notary public or other person designated by law and stating to that authorized person that he did sign the instrument for the purpose stated in it or for the purpose of recording it in the appropriate public records.

The law of the state where the instrument is to be recorded governs the form and content of the acknowledgment of intention to record. The person authorized to accept the acknowledgment signs a certificate of acknowledgment.

Short statutory forms are provided in most states. States that have adopted the

---

[1]*1 Am. Jur. 2d Acknowledgments*, paras. 1–11.
[2]Ref. Forms VIIIB 1.00 through 1.08.

Uniform Recognition of Acknowledgments Act and/or the Uniform Acknowledgment Act, are listed in Appendixes III and IV to this book.

The state statutes providing for the use of the so-called "statutory short forms" of the Uniform Recognition of Acknowledgments Act usually provide that the provision for the short form does not preclude the use of other appropriate forms. Both long and short forms are presented in this Section.

Generally, acknowledgment of a deed or other conveyance is not necessary to pass title, but it is usually required before an instrument can be recorded.

## FORM VIIIA 1.00

### CLIENT QUESTIONNAIRE FOR PREPARING AN ACKNOWLEDGMENT[1]

1. What is the name of the person(s) who will sign the document and acknowledge it?
2. Is the document to be recorded in the public records?
3. In what capacity is the person signing: as corporate officer, partner, attorney-in-fact, trustee, or other?
4. By what authority is he signing? If there is any doubt, look at copy of corporate resolution, power of attorney, trust agreement, etc. Note date of appointment
5. Is the signer a married woman?[2]
6. Is the signer sui juris (not a minor and not adjudged incompetent)?
7. In what state and county will the acknowledgment be made? If acknowledgment will be taken outside the United States, check your state statute governing acknowledgment[3]
8. What is the title (if known) of the designated authority who will take the acknowledgment, as: (within state) notary public, clerk of a court, judge, district justice, other; or (outside U.S.A.) U.S. ambassadors, ministers plenipotentiary, consuls, commercial agents, other?
9. What is the nature of the document to be signed and acknowledged, as: deed, mortgage, lease, corporate charter or articles, etc.?

[1]Ref. Questionnaire for preparing the specific document to be acknowledged, and samples of acknowledgments included in various contract examples in this book.
[2]*1 Am. Jur. 2d Acknowledgments,* paras 31 and 35.
[3]Ref. Appendix III and Appendix IV for list of states that have adopted the Uniform Acts.

## FORM VIIIA. 1.01

### (Acknowledgment of deed made as an attorney-in-fact acting for his principal—recording of power of attorney to be simultaneous with the recording of the deed)[1]

STATE OF NEW YORK
COUNTY OF QUEENS

I HEREBY CERTIFY that on this 5th day of May, 1982, before me, a notary public, personally appeared John Doe, satisfactorily proven to me to be the individual described in and who executed the foregoing deed, and satisfactorily proven to be the attorney-in-fact of Richard Roe, the individual described in and who by his attorney-in-fact executed the foregoing deed and acknowledged that he executed said instrument as the act and deed of said Richard Roe, by virtue of a power of attorney dated May 1, 1982, to be recorded in the office of the Register of the County of Queens simultaneously with the within deed.

(SEAL)

_____
Notary Public

My commission expires:

[1]*1 Am. Jur. 2d Acknowledgments,* para. 9.

## FORM VIIIA 1.01(a)

### (Short statutory form for attorney-in-fact acting for his principal)[1]

STATE OF FLORIDA
COUNTY OF DADE

The foregoing instrument was acknowledged before me this 5th day of May, 1982 by John Doe as attorney-in-fact on behalf of Richard Roe.

(SEAL)

_____
Notary Public

My commission expires:

[1]See Appendix IV for Uniform Recognition of Acknowledgment, and related acts.

## FORM VIIIA 1.02

### (Acknowledgment of deed from corporation by corporate officer)[1]

COMMONWEALTH OF PENNSYLVANIA )
                                         SS
COUNTY OF ALLEGHENY             )

I HEREBY CERTIFY that on this 5th day of May, 1982, before me, the undersigned authority, personally appeared John Doe, who acknowledged himself to be the duly authorized President of Doe Manufacturing, Inc., a Pennsylvania corporation, and that he, as such President being duly authorized to do, executed the foregoing instrument for the purposes therein contained, by signing the name of the corporation by John Doe as President.

IN WITNESS WHEREOF, I hereunto set my hand and official seal.

My commission expires:

_____
Notary Public

(SEAL)

[1]*1 Am. Jur. 2d Acknowledgments*, para. 10.

## FORM VIIIA 1.02(a)

### (Short statutory form for corporation)[1]

COMMONWEALTH OF PENNSYLVANIA
COUNTY OF ALLEGHENY.

The foregoing instrument was acknowledged before me this 5th day of May by John Doe, President of Doe Manufacturing, Inc., a Florida corporation, on behalf of the corporation.

(SEAL)

_____
Notary Public

My commission expires:

[1]See Appendix IV for Uniform Recognition of Acknowledgments and related acts.

## FORM VIIIA 1.03

### (Husband and wife joint acknowledgment in states where there is no married woman separate or privy examination required)[1]

STATE OF OREGON
COUNTY OF MULTNOMAH

Be it remembered that on this 5th day of May, 1982, before me, the undersigned notary public in and for said county and state, personally appeared the within-named John Doe and Mary Doe, his wife, who are known to me to be the identical persons described in and who executed the within instrument and acknowledged to me that they executed the same.

(SEAL)

_____

Notary Public

My commission expires:

[1] *1 Am. Jur. 2d Acknowledgments,* paras. 7, 30, 35, and 41.

## FORM VIIIA 1.03(a)

### (Short statutory form for two (2) individuals who may be husband and wife in states where there is no married woman separate or privy examination required)[1]

STATE OF OREGON
COUNTY OF MULTNOMAH

The foregoing instrument was acknowledged before me this 5th day of May, 1982, by John Doe and Mary Doe, his wife.

(SEAL)

_____

Title or Rank
(Serial No., if any)

[1] See Appendix IV for Uniform Recognition of Acknowledgments and related acts.

## FORM VIIIA 1.03(b)

### (Wife's separate acknowledgment in state where required for renouncing dower)[1]

STATE OF SOUTH CAROLINA
COUNTY OF CHARLESTON

I, the undersigned notary public, DO HEREBY CERTIFY unto all whom it may concern that Mary Doe, wife of the within-named John Doe, did this day appear before me and, upon being privately and separately examined by me, did declare that she does freely, voluntarily, and without any compulsion, dread, or fear of any person or persons whomsoever, renounce, release, and forever relinquish unto the within-named Richard Roe, his heirs, and assigns, all her interest and estate, and also all her right and claim of dower of, in, or to all and singular the premises within mentioned and released.

_____

MARY DOE

Given under my hand and seal this 5th day of May, 1982.

_____

Notary Public

(SEAL)                                              My commission expires:

[1] Check your state statute for this requirement. See also Form VIIIA 1.03(c); and *1 Am. Jur. 2d Acknowledgments,* paras. 31 and 35.

## FORM VIIIA 1.03(c)

### (Wife's separate acknowledgment in state where required for deed relinquishing dower and homestead)[1]

STATE OF ARKNASAS
COUNTY OF LITTLE ROCK

On this day personally appeared before the undersigned notary public, within and for the county and state aforesaid, John Doe and Mary Doe, his wife, to me well known as the grantors in the foregoing deed, and stated that they had executed the same for the consideration and purposes therein mentioned and set forth.

And on the same day also voluntarily appeared before me Mary Doe, the wife of said John Doe, to me well known, and in the absence of her said husband declared that she had of her own free will executed said deed and signed and sealed the relinquishment of dower and homestead therein, for the consideration and purposes therein contained and set forth, without compulsion or undue influence of her said husband.

Witness my hand and official seal on this 5th day of May, 1982.

(SEAL)

_____
Notary Public

My commission expires:

[1]Ref. footnotes to Forms VIIIA 1.03, and 1.03(a) and (b).

## FORM VIIIA 1.04

### (Partnership acknowledgment)[1]

STATE OF NEW YORK
COUNTY OF QUEENS

I HEREBY CERTIFY that on this 5th day of May, 1982, personally appeared before me John Doe, personally known to me to be a member of the partnership of Doe and Roe, and to me known to be the person described in and who executed the foregoing instrument in the partnership name of Doe and Roe, and he acknowledged that he executed the same as the act and deed of said partnership for the purposes and uses therein mentioned.

(SEAL)

_____
Notary Public

My commission expires:

[1]*1 Am. Jur. 2d Acknowledgments*, para. 11.

## FORM VIIIA 1.04(a)

### (Statutory short form of partnership acknowledgment)[1]

STATE OF NEW YORK
COUNTY OF QUEENS

The foregoing instrument was acknowledged before me this 5th day of May, 1982, by John Doe, partner on behalf of Doe and Roe, a partnership.

(SEAL)

_____
Notary Public

My commission expires:

[1]See Appendix IV for Uniform Recognition of Acknowledgments Act and related acts.

## SECTION B    AFFIDAVITS AND CERTIFICATES OF TRUTH

An affidavit[1] is a complete written legal instrument. It is distinguished from an acknowledgment,[2] which is part of or an appendage to another legal instrument, as a deed or bill of sale.

The affidavit is sworn to by the affiant before a notary public or other officer des-

[1]*3 Am. Jur. 2d Affidavits*, paras. 12–25.
[2]Ref. Form VIIIA 1.00 through 1.04(a).

ignated to administer the oath as to the truth of the facts stated in the affidavit. It is signed by *both* the affiant and the officer taking the affidavit.

This Section gives examples of affidavits commonly used in the course of the operation of a business or consummation of a business transaction. Certificates of the truth of the taking of certain business action are included in this Section.

The certificates provided in this Section include the certificate of a corporate secretary[3] that certain action was taken or resolution made by the directors and/or stockholders of a corporation.

Also included is an "estoppel certificate,"[4] the certificate of a mortgagor as to the balance due on his mortgage, and his admission of the validity of the mortgage lien. This certificate should be prepared when the mortgage is assigned or assumed.

When real property is sold subject to a mortgage, the mortgagee should be required to give a reduction of mortgage certificate,[5] which would show the current balance.

For a debtor's affidavit included in an agreement to compromise and settle a debt, see Form VIIIG 1.04.

## FORM VIIIB 1.00

### CLIENT QUESTIONNAIRE FOR AFFIDAVITS AND CERTIFICATES[1]

1. Name, address, and telephone number of client and the affiant
2. What is the purpose of the affidavit or certificate?[2]
3. Exact name in which the affidavit or certificate will be signed
4. Capacity of the signer, as: individual, partner, agent, corporate officer, trustee, etc. Get title and evidence of authority to make a certification
5. In what state and county will the affidavit be taken or the certificate made?
6. Does affiant have actual knowledge of the facts? If not, what is the basis of his knowledge?
7. What are the facts that are to be sworn to?
8. If the document is a certificate, what facts are to be certified? Get amounts if money balance is involved.

[1]*3 Am. Jur. 2d Affidavits,* para. 19.
[2]*3 Am. Jur. 2d Affidavits,* paras. 20–25 and 29.

## FORM VIIIB 1.01

### (Affidavit of agent on behalf of his principal in the sale of used machinery—not stock in trade)[1]

### AFFIDAVIT

STATE OF FLORIDA
COUNTY OF CITRUS

John Doe, being duly sworn, deposes and says:

1. Affiant is making this affidavit on behalf of Richard Roe Company, which presently operates a construction business at Highway 00 West, Middletown, Pennsylvania.

2. Affiant resides at 100 East Street, Middletown, Middle County, Florida 00000.

3. Affiant is the duly authorized and appointed general agent of Richard Roe Company and is making this affidavit on its behalf.

4. Affiant has executed a Bill of Sale dated this 1st day of June, 1982, to Peter Poe for certain used machinery sold to him by Richard Roe Company.

5. Affiant was duly appointed general agent of Richard Roe Company and is attorney-in-fact

---

[3]Ref. Form VIIIB 1.06.
[4]Ref. Form VIIIB 1.07.
[5]Ref. Form VIIIB 1.08.

for the company, authorized to execute that Bill of Sale by an unrecorded power of attorney dated May 20, 1979, a copy of which is attached hereto and made part hereof.

6. The power of attorney described herein has not, at any time, been revoked, altered, or repudiated by Richard Roe Company, and that power of attorney remains in full force and effect.

7. The machinery described in the Bill of Sale is solely owned by Richard Roe Company, free and clear of all liens and encumbrances, except as agreed in the Bill of Sale.

8. No other person has any contract or claim for the purchase or use of the machinery being sold.

9. This affidavit is made on behalf of Richard Roe Company, for the purpose of inducing Peter Poe to purchase the machinery listed in the Bill of Sale executed by affiant by capacity of attorney-in-fact for Richard Roe Company.

---

JOHN DOE, Affiant

Sworn to and subscribed before me this 1st day of June, 1982.

---

Notary Public

My commission expires:

¹3 Am. Jur. 2d Affidavits, para. 20.

## FORM VIIIB 1.02

### (Affidavit of lost stock certificate[s])¹

STATE OF ILLINOIS
COUNTY OF COOK

John Doe, being duly sworn, deposes and says:

1. Affiant is sui juris and resides at 100 East Drive, Chicago, Cook County, Illinois.

2. Affiant is the legal and beneficial owner of One Hundred (100) shares of the common capital stock of Able Manufacturing Corporation, an Illinois corporation whose principal place of business is 100 West Street, La Grange, Illinois, which stock is represented by the certificates described as follows:

| Number of shares | Date issued | Registered Name |
|---|---|---|
| 30 | June 1, 1975 | John R. Doe |
| 70 | April 10, 1979 | John Doe |

3. Affiant and John R. Doe are one and the same person who purchased the above-described certificates.

4. Affiant purchased the certificates from Safe Securities Company of 100 Michigan Boulevard, Chicago, Illinois.

5. The above certificates were not endorsed in any manner.

6. None of the above certificates nor any of the rights of the shareholder therein have been assigned, transferred, pledged, or otherwise disposed of, in whole or part, and affiant is entitled to the full and exclusive possession of the above certificates.

7. That the certificates were lost or stolen during the move of affiants office furnishings from Suite 400 to Suite 900 in the Tall Building, Chicago, Illinois, on or about May 1, 1982, were reported lost or stolen to the Chicago police department, and have not been recovered.

8. This affidavit is made for the purpose of inducing Able Manufacturing Corporation to issue and deliver new certificates in lieu of those described above to the affiant. Affiant shall immediately surrender to Able Manufacturing Corporation the lost or stolen certificates described above in the event that they ever hereafter come into the possession of the affiant.

9. This affidavit is made for the further purpose of inducing Able Manufacturing Corporation to refuse to transfer, exchange, or make payment to any person other than the affiant on the above-described lost or stolen certificates.

10. Affiant agrees that if Able Manufacturing Corporation is subjected to any liability for failing to transfer, exchange, or pay on the above-described lost or stolen certificates, affiant shall

hold harmless and fully indemnify Able Manufacturing Corporation for any damages it sustains thereby.

11. The facts contained in this affidavit are true to the best of affiant's knowledge.

---

JOHN DOE a/k/a

John R. Doe

Sworn to and described before me this 10th day of May, 1982

---

Notary Public

My commission expires:

[1]*15 Am. Jur. 2d Commercial Code,* para. 47; and *18 Am. Jur. 2d Corporations,* paras. 270–274; 401, 402, and 445.

## FORM VIIIB 1.03

### (Affidavit of lost pawn ticket)[1]

STATE OF OKLAHOMA
COUNTY OF POTTAWATOMIE

John Doe, being duly sworn, deposes and says:

1. I reside at 1 East Street, City of Shawnee, State of Oklahoma.

2. On or about December 1981, I pawned or pledged with ROE LOANS, a licensed pawnbroker, at 100 Main Street, City of Shawnee, State of Oklahoma, a Super Swiss Calendar Watch, and received the sum of Fifty Dollars ($50) and a pawn ticket for the watch, the number of which I do not recall, which ticket evidenced the transaction.

3. The above-mentioned pawn ticket has since been lost or mislaid so that I am unable to find or produce the same.

4. I have not sold, transferred, assigned, or in any manner disposed of that pawn ticket to any person whomsoever.

5. I was the sole and lawful owner of the aforementioned property at the time I pledged or pawned it, and am still the lawful owner thereof.

6. I have not authorized any person to redeem that property or in any manner procure possession of the same.

---

JOHN DOE

Sworn to and subscribed before me this 10th day of January, 1982

---

Notary Public

My commission expires:

[1]*54 Am. Jur. 2d Moneylenders and Pawnbrokers,* para. 1 et seq.

## FORM VIIIB 1.04

### (Corporate secretary's affidavit of personal service of notice of a meeting, to be inserted in the minute book with a copy of the notice)[1]

### AFFIDAVIT

STATE OF FLORIDA
COUNTY OF CITRUS

Before me, a notary public in and for said state and county, personally appeared Richard Roe, who, being duly sworn, says:

1. That he is secretary of the XYZ corporation, a Florida corporation.

2. That, on January 4, 1983, he personally served notice of a meeting of the board of directors of the corporation, a copy of which notice is attached hereto and made part hereof, by handing a copy of the notice to each of the following directors: Richard Rich, John Doe, and Peter Poe.

_____

Richard Roe, Secretary of the Corporation

Sworn to and subscribed before me this 5th day
of January, 1983

_____

Notary Public

My commission expires:

[1] 3 _Am. Jur. 2d Affidavits,_ paras. 5 and 7. See also Part I of this book.

## FORM VIIIB 1.05

### (Affidavit of corporate officer as to his capacity to act as agent for the corporation, where such affidavit is required and agency is not inferred)[1]

STATE OF TEXAS
COUNTY OF DALLAS

Before me, a notary public in and for the above state and county, personally appeared Richard Rich, president of the Fresh Seafood Company, Inc., a Texas corporation with its principal office at 100 Market Street, Dallas, Texas, and in whose behalf affiant makes this affidavit of performance, who, being duly sworn, says:

1. Affiant is Richard Rich, who resides at 100 Circle Drive, Dallas, Texas.

2. Affiant is the President of Fresh Seafood Company, Inc., a Texas corporation, and as such is authorized by the corporation to make this affidavit on its behalf.

3., 4., etc. (State facts of which he has knowledge.)

(Richard Rich)
_____
RICHARD RICH

Sworn to and subscribed before me this 10th day
of March, 1983

_____

Notary Public

My commission expires:

[1] 3 _Am. Jur. 2d Affidavits,_ paras. 7 and 20–25. See also Part I of this book.

## FORM VIIIB 1.06

### (Certificate of corporate secretary as to vote of stockholders)

Certificate of Secretary[1]
of
TRANSLAKE CORPORATION

I, John Doe, of the city of Middletown, County of Buckeye, State of Ohio, hereby certify that I am Secretary of Translake Corporation, a corporation incorporated under the laws of the State of Ohio, having its principal office at Middletown, Ohio; that at a meeting of the shareholders of the capital stock of that corporation separately called for the purpose of considering the foregoing Agreement of Merger, held at the principal office thereof on the 20th day of May, 1983, at which meeting a majority of the voting power of the corporation was present in person or represented by proxy, the foregoing Agreement of Merger was adopted by the vote of shareholders representing at least a majority of the voting power of the corporation.

I further certify that such meeting was duly and legally called and notified in accordance with the provisions of the laws of the State of Ohio, and that the action proposed to be taken at such meeting was specified in the Notice of the meeting. Dated: May 20, 1983.

(Imprint Corporate Seal)

RUTH ROE

Secretary of the Corporation

¹See also Part I of this book.

## FORM VIIIB 1.07

### (Estoppel certificate of owner of real estate as to balance due and validity of mortgage lien)

### ESTOPPEL CERTIFICATE¹

KNOW ALL MEN BY THESE PRESENTS, that

WHEREAS, Able Manufacturing Corporation, a Pennsylvania corporation having its principal place of business at 1 Main Street, Pittsburgh, Allegheny County, Pennsylvania, is the owner in fee simple of the premises located at that address, which are more particularly described in the mortgage for the principal sum of One Hundred Thousand Dollars ($100,000), dated May 1, 1975, by it to Richard Roe recorded in the Office of the Recorder of Deeds of Allegheny County, Pennsylvania, in Mortgage Book 000, Page 000, on which mortgage and bond secured thereby there is now due the sum of Fifty Thousand Dollars ($50,000), with interest from June 1, 1982, and which mortgage is to be assigned by Richard Roe to the Acme Mortgage Corporation, a New York corporation;

THEREFORE, the ABLE MANUFACTURING CORPORATION, in consideration of the sum of One Dollar ($1) and other good and valuable consideration paid to and received by it, and to enable the assignment of the mortgage to be made, certifies as follows:

1. That the mortgage is a valid first lien on the premises for the full amount of principal and interest now due, which is Fifty Thousand Dollars ($50,000), with interest at the rate of Ten Percent (10%) per annum from June 1, 1982; and

2. That there are no defenses or offsets to the mortgage; and

3. That all of the other provisions of the bond and mortgage are in full force and effect; and

4. That the undersigned John Able has been duly authorized by Able Manufacturing Corporation to execute this certificate on its behalf.

Dated this 1st day of June 1982, in Pittsburgh, Allegheny County, Pennsylvania.

(CORPORATE SEAL)                    ABLE MANUFACTURING CORPORATION

_____     By _____
Secretary of the Corporation              JOHN ABLE, President

¹Ref. forms and footnotes in Chapter VIIC, D, and E.

## FORM VIIIB 1.08

### (Certificate by mortgagee as to reduction of mortgage)¹

### REDUCTION CERTIFICATE

KNOW ALL MEN, that the undersigned is the owner and holder of a certain indenture of mortgage and the bond or note described therein, bearing date of May 1, 1981, made and executed to the undersigned by John Doe Corporation to secure the payment of the principal sum of One Hundred Thousand Dollars ($100,000), and interest, which mortgage is recorded in the Office of the Recorder of Deeds of Allegheny County, Pennsylvania, in Mortgage Book 000, Page 000, and covers the premises situate in the City of Pittsburgh, County of Allegheny, Pennsylvania, commonly known as 100 Wood Street; and

THE UNDERSIGNED HEREBY CERTIFIES that the amount due on the bond and mortgage has been reduced by part payment, and that there is now due upon the bond and mortgage the principal sum of Sixty Thousand Dollars ($60,000), with interest at the rate of Ten Percent (10%) per annum from June 1, 1983.

Dated this 1st day of June, 1983.

_____
Charles Coe, MORTGAGEE

(Note: if the vendee of the property demands that the reduction certicate be recorded, ADD AN ACKNOWLEDGMENT.)

[1]Ref. forms and footnotes in Part VII C, D, and E.

## SECTION C     ARBITRATION CLAUSES

This Section contains some sample arbitration clauses. Others appear in the body of other contracts in the book. Consult the general index for reference to those arbitration clauses if a suitable clause is not found in this Section.

The Client Questionnaire, Form VIIIC 1.00, will aid in deciding which clause is appropriate.

Voluntary arbitration clauses in business contracts provide a practical means for moving a dispute under a business contract from the overcrowded courts to an administrative system for solving the dispute. Not all clients desire this change.

If the arbitration clause does not make arbitration "final and binding" once it is chosen, it may just create an additional step in the already prolonged judicial process, according to Chief Justice Warren Burger in his 1982 Annual Report on the State of the Judiciary, delivered to the American Bar Association. But the Chief Justice also pointed very clearly to the advantages of appropriate arbitration in large and complex commercial disputes.

If an arbitration clause is properly and appropriately drafted, it can save money and time for a small business as well as a large one. Before using an arbitration clause, the law of the state that governs the contract should be consulted.

Some states have adopted the Uniform Arbitration Act. Appendix V to this book gives the state citations to the Act.

A state arbitration act will apply as to arbitration procedure and its effect unless the contract provides for a different procedure or effect.

An arbitration clause may provide for arbitration of all disputes concerning the contract or for a particular type(s) of dispute under the contract. Consider the desire of the client before drafting the clause.

Under the Uniform Arbitration Act, the appropriate court has a certain amount of control over the arbitration procedure and its effect, such as the power to compel or stay the arbitration proceedings,[1] to vacate an award,[2] and to modify or correct an award[3] under the prescribed circumstances.

Various common law rules of arbitration and varying state statutes govern arbitration clauses in states and U.S. territories that have not adopted the Uniform Act. At this writing, those states are: Alabama, California, Hawaii, Kentucky, Mississippi, Montana, Nebraska, New Hampshire, New Jersy, North Dakota, Puerto Rico, Tennessee, Vermont, Virgin Islands, Virginia, and West Virginia.

An arbitration clause may specifically prescribe rules for arbitration and the

_____

[1]_Uniform Arbitration Act_, Section 2.
[2]_Uniform Arbitration Act_, Section 12.
[3]_Uniform Arbitration Act_, Section 13.

manner of choosing arbitrators simply and locally. Or it may provide for arbitration by the American Arbitration Association[4] or other organization or arbitration by someone else but in accordance with their rules[5].

## FORM VIIIC 1.00

### CLIENT QUESTIONNAIRE FOR ARBITRATION[1]

1. Do the parties want an arbitration clause included in the contract?
2. Should the arbitration clause apply to the whole contract or to a particular part or phase of it? If only to a part or phase, which?
3. Do the parties want a particular person(s) or association to be named in the contract as arbitrator(s)? If so, get name(s) and address(es).
4. If arbitrator(s) is not to be named, how shall the arbitrator(s) be chosen?
5. What are the notice and time limits to be involved, as: notice of demand to arbitrate, time for hearing, and decision of arbitrator(s)?
6. Is the arbitration to be final and binding or advisory only?
7. Who shall bear the expense of the arbitration, as: "equally" or "prevailing party"?

[1]*5 Am. Jur. 2d Arbitration and Award,* paras. 11–19 and 27. See Appendix V for state citations to the Uniform Arbitration Act.

## FORM VIIIC 1.01

### (General arbitration clause according to the rules of the American Arbitration Association)[1]

Any controversy or claim arising out of, or relating to, this Contract or the breach thereof shall be settled by arbitration, in accordance with the rules then obtaining, of the American Arbitration Association,[2] and judgment upon the award rendered may be entered in any court having jurisdiction of the controversy or claim.

[1]*5 Am. Jur. 2d Arbitration and Award,* paras. 27, 41, 54, 58, and 160–162.
[2]The American Arbitration Association, 140 West 51st Street, New York, N.Y. 10020.

## FORM VIIIC 1.02

### (Arbitration of employment agreement by arbitrators to be chosen by the parties as condition precedent to bringing legal action)

As an express condition precedent to any legal or equitable action or proceeding in the event of disputes or controversies as to the amount of loss or damage arising out of this Contract for employment, such disputes or controversies shall first be submitted to the arbitration[1] of two persons, one chosen by each party, who shall jointly select a third person. Each party shall pay one-half the cost of the arbitration.

[1]*5 Am. Jur. 2d Arbitration and Award,* paras. 72, 80, and 97–101.

## FORM VIIIC 1.03

### (Arbitration as to defects under construction contract by the American Arbitration Association)

Contractor shall be liable for correcting any defects in work brought to his attention by Owner and not in conformity with the terms of this Contract or the Contract plans and specifications, providing Contractor is notified of such defects in writing within ten (10) days from discovery of

---

[4]The American Arbitration Association, 140 West 51st Street, New York, N.Y. 10020.
[5]Ref. Form VIIIC 1.01.

such defects, and in any event not more than twelve (12) months from the date the work hereunder is completed. In case of any dispute regarding correction of defects or performance of the terms of this Contract, the dispute shall be subject to arbitration by and in accordance with the Arbitration Rules of the American Arbitration Association for the construction industry.

## FORM VIIIC 1.04

### (Arbitration by a single arbitrator to be mutually selected by the parties upon demand of one party)

In case of a dispute between the parties under this Agreement, the parties or their respective representatives shall meet for the purpose of mutually selecting an impartial arbitrator within ten (10) days following the mailing of a written demand for arbitration by certified mail by either of the parties.

## SECTION D   ASSIGNMENTS

The forms in this Section D are designed to assign the rights and interests in the various types of contracts discussed below.

As a general rule, *unless the contract forbids assignment,* either party may assign his beneficial rights and interest in the contract, *unless* the contract creates a personal confidential relationship (as agency or trust) or requires exceptional *personal* skill for the performance (specified actor, singer, lawyer, doctor, etc.).[1]

Even where an executory contract is not assignable, the proceeds or money to become due under the contract may be assigned *unless the contract prohibits it.*

To avoid assignment problems, every contract should, by its terms, state whether it is assignable and the conditions for assignment.

A contract for the sale of goods is assignable by either the buyer or the seller unless the parties have otherwise agreed or unless the assignment would materially change the duty of the other person, materially increase the burden or risk imposed on him by the contract, or materially impair his chance of obtaining performance by the assignee.[2]

A transfer of commercial paper, negotiable or nonnegotiable, may be made by assignment written on the document itself or by a separate paper, and the assignment may or may not effect a *negotiation* as defined in the Uniform Commercial Code.[3]

The assignee of any contract should require warranties from the assignor that the contract is "valid and enforceable, is in full force and effect, and has not been amended or breached, and that there are no setoffs or counterclaims against the assignor." For assignment of mortgage and estoppel certificate and reduction of mortgage certificate, see Part VII, Section D.

For a discussion of an assignment for benefit of creditors[4] and forms for same, see Part VIII, Section G.

---

[1] *6 Am. Jur. 2d Assignments,* paras. 9–22 and 82–101.
[2] U.C.C. 2-210(2) and U.C.C. 2-609.
[3] U.C.C. 3-201 through 207, and 3-805.
[4] *6 Am. Jur. 2d Assignment for Benefit of Creditors,* para. 32.

In drafting an assignment of a consumer sale or loan contract, the federal Truth in Lending Act,[5] the pertinent federal regulations,[6] including disclosure requirements,[7] and your state's consumer protection laws[8] should be considered.

### FORM VIIID 1.00

### CLIENT QUESTIONNAIRE FOR ASSIGNMENTS[1]

1. Get an *executed* copy of the original contract
2. Is your client to be the *assignor* or the *assignee*?
3. Names and present *notice* addresses of all parties to the original contract and of the proposed contract of assignment
4. Is there a specific provision in the original contract for or against assignability? What does it provide as to notice, consent, etc.?
5. Has client given the required notice or received the required consent? If not, prepare the notice or the written consent[2]
6. What are the terms of the assignment?
    (a) What is to be paid for the assignment, and when and how is it to be paid?
    (b) Description of the property to which the assignment relates, and description of the contract, document, or right to be assigned, giving names of parties, date and place of execution
    (c) Does assignor want to reserve any rights in the contract or right to be assigned?
    (d) Does assignor make any warranties as to the original contract? If so, what are they?
    (e) Will assignee be indemnified by assignor?
    (f) Should attorney's fees be provided?
    (g) Date assignment is to be made and date it is to become effective, if there is a difference
    (h) Was the original contract recorded? If so, get official record book and page number
    (i) Is the assignment to be recorded? If so, prepare an acknowledgment at the end of the assignment

> [1]6 *Am. Jur. 2d Assignments*, paras. 9–22.
> [2]Ref. Form VIIIH 1.01. See also Introduction and Checklist for Section VIIIH.

### FORM VIIID 1.01

### (Assignment of general contract rights without warranty or guaranty, with acceptance by assignee)[1]

### ASSIGNMENT

For value received, I, John Doe, assignor, of 100 Main Street, City of Middletown, State of Ohio, assign, transfer, and set over to Richard Roe, assignee, of 500 East Drive, City of Middletown, State of Ohio, all my right, title, and interest in and to my agreement with George Poe dated June 1, 1982, for the purchase of the tangible personal property described therein, subject to all the terms and conditions thereof, a copy of which is attached thereto and made part hereof.

I remise, release, and quitclaim to assignee all my right, title, and interest in and to the property described therein and agreed to be sold.

IN WITNESS WHEREOF, I have executed this Assignment at Middletown, Ohio, this 1st day of August, 1982.

_____

JOHN DOE, Assignor

---

> [5]15 U.S.C.A. 1601 et seq. See Appendix I in this book.
> [6]Regulations M and Z, 12 C.F.R. 213 and 12 C.F.R. 226.
> [7]12 C.F.R. 226.8(k).
> [8]See Appendixes I, IX, X, and XI for citations to state statutes which have adopted uniform acts involving consumer protection.

ACCEPTANCE OF ASSIGNMENT

I, Richard Roe, assignee, hereby accept the foregoing instrument, subject to all the terms and conditions thereof.

Dated August, _____ 1982.

_____

RICHARD ROE, Assignee

(Attach copy of contract that is being assigned. Insert an *acknowledgment of assignor*[2] before the Acceptance, if assignment is to be recorded. Send notice of assignment to George Poe, who is the other party to the original contract.)

[1] *6 Am. Jur. 2d Assignments*, paras. 9–22 and 82–101; and U.C.C. 2–210 and 2–609 as to assignment of contract for sale of goods, and 9–308 as to assignment of security agreement. Ref. Form VIIIH 1.01 for consent to assignment, and see Form VIIID 1.02 for assignment of lease. See also U.C.C. 9–106 and 9–318. See 31 U.S.C.A. 203 and 41 U.S.C.A. 15, plus filing under U.C.C. where there is an assignment of government contract rights.

[2] See Part VIII Section A for acknowledgment form, if needed.

## FORM VIIID 1.02

### (Assignment of lease from present lessee to purchaser of the lessee's business, including assumption of lease by purchaser and consent of lessor)

### ASSIGNMENT OF LEASE[1]

FOR VALUE RECEIVED, I, John Doe of 500 East Drive, Middletown, Indiana 00000, ASSIGNOR and LESSEE of premises located at 100 Main Street, Middletown, Indiana, on which the business of Doe's Appliances is presently being operated, which premises were leased to me by a lease dated May 1, 1979, hereby assign that lease to Richard Roe of 200 Oak Drive, Middletown, Indiana 00000 (herein called "ASSIGNEE").

ASSIGNEE shall pay the rent and other payments provided in that lease and shall perform all terms and conditions to be performed by the lessee, and ASSIGNEE hereby specifically assumes all rights, duties, and liabilities of the lessee under that lease, a copy of which is attached hereto and made part hereof.

PETER POE of 900 West Drive, Middletown, Indiana 00000, is lessor under that lease, and hereby accepts and consents to this assignment to ASSIGNEE, and hereby releases ASSIGNOR from all further obligations under that lease.

The assignment shall become effective on May 1, 1982.

IN WITNESS WHEREOF, the parties have executed this assignment, assumption, and consent on the 1st day of April, 1982.

_____

John Doe, ASSIGNOR

_____

Richard Roe, ASSIGNEE

_____

Peter Poe, LESSOR

[1] *49 Am. Jur. 2d Landlord and Tenant*, paras. 98, 528.

## FORM VIIID 1.03

### (General clause prohibiting assignment by either party without consent)[1]

*Assignability.* There shall be no assignment or transfer of this Contract by either party without the written consent of both parties.

[1] *6 Am. Jur. 2d Assignments*, paras. 11–18. See also U.C.C. 2–210 (2). Compare Form VIIID 1.06.

## FORM VIIID 1.04

### (General assignment of a security interest)[1]

FOR VALUE RECEIVED, the undersigned sells, assigns, and transfers to ABC Credit, Inc., its successors, or assigns, its right, title, and interest in and to the within security agreement, the property described therein, and the note thereby secured, and does hereby authorize ABC Credit, Inc., to collect the note and discharge the debtor.

Dated this 1st day of February, 1982.

Doe's Appliances, Inc.

_____

By President

[1] *69 Am. Jur. 2d Secured Transactions,* paras. 444–457. See also U.C.C. 9-405.

## FORM VIIID 1.04(a)

### (Waiver of defense by purchaser on assignment by seller to be inserted in the original security agreement)[1]

### ALTERNATIVE CLAUSE

*Waiver of defenses.* Purchaser hereby waives all rights to defend against any assignee of the Seller, in the event the Seller assigns this Contract, on any ground whatsoever; but this waiver shall in no way deprive the Purchaser of any and all of his rights to proceed against the Seller/Assignor for any reason that might constitute a legal claim or legally sufficient defense to the Contract.

[1] *6 Am. Jur. 2d Assignments,* paras. 102 and 103.

## FORM VIIID 1.05

### (Assignment of buyer rights—sale of goods where assignment not prohibited in the purchase contract)[1]

### ASSIGNMENT

FOR VALUE RECEIVED, I, John Doe of 100 Main Street, Middletown, Pennsylvania 00000, hereby assign to Richard Roe of 500 East Street, Middletown, Pennsylvania 00000, my rights to purchase five (5) 1980 Deere Tractors Model x100 for Twenty-five Thousand Dollars ($25,000) from Poe's Tractors, Inc., of 65 West Boulevard, Lancaster, Pennsylvania 00000, under a contract dated November 1, 1981, executed by me with Poe's Tractors, Inc.

I hereby warrant that the contract is valid and enforceable, is in full force and effect, is assignable, has not been amended or breached, and that there are no setoffs or counter-claims against the assignor by the seller.

Dated this 1st day of January, 1982.

_____

John Doe, ASSIGNOR

(optional)

Accepted this 1st day of January 1982 by:

_____

Richard Roe, ASSIGNEE

[1] U.C.C. 2-210(2) and 2-609.

## FORM VIIID 1.06

**(Assignment of seller rights with credit check warranty—sale of
goods where assignment not prohibited in the purchase agreement
and goods are not unique)[1]**

### ASSIGNMENT

FOR VALUE RECEIVED, we, Poe's Tractors, Inc., of 65 West Boulevard, Lancaster, Pennsylvania 00000, hereby assign to Farm Equipment Company, Inc., our rights to payment of Twenty-five Thousand Dollars ($25,000) from John Doe of 100 Main Street, Middletown, Pennsylvania 00000, upon delivery to Doe of the five (5) 1980 Deere Tractors Model x100, in accordance with the terms of the sale agreement dated November 1, 1981, executed by us with John Doe.

We hereby warrant that we have done our usual credit investigation of the Buyer and have found the Buyer's credit to be satisfactory under our usual business credit standards; and we know of no fact that would impair the ability of the Buyer to pay for the goods in accordance with the terms of the contract hereby assigned.

Dated this 1st day of January, 1982.

POE'S TRACTORS, INC.    _____

By _____
President

[1]U.C.C. 2–210(2). See also U.C.C. 9–101 and 9–104(f) if a sale of accounts is involved.

## SECTION E    BONDS (BY INDIVIDUAL SURETY)[1]

The forms in this Section are for use when an individual is the surety.

A surety bond is a written instrument guaranting performance of something or payment of money under certain conditions. The principal under the bond is the person whose performance or whose payment is guaranteed. The surety is the guarantor. The beneficiary or obligee of the bond is the person or persons who can demand payment from the surety if the principal does not perform or pay.

Where "bond with sufficient surety" is required by a state statute, a surety and guaranty corporation duly authorized to do business in the state is considered sufficient by statute in most states.

Where a corporate surety is not required by statute, any sui juris individual can execute a valid surety bond for a principal, whether or not the principal is sui juris. At common law, a married woman could not be a surety, but, in most states, statutes have removed that disability.

A private indemnity bond is a guaranty against loss from the failure of the principal to perform for or pay the beneficiary or obligee up to the amount of the bond, and is to be distinguished from a statutory bond.[2] It is also to be distinguished from a contract of guaranty.[3]

For forms where a corporation is the surety, see Part VIII, Section F.

---

[1]*12 Am. Jur. 2d Bonds,* paras. 25 and 32; and *41 Am. Jur. 2d Indemnity,* paras 4 and 29.
[2]See Introduction to Part VIIIF and footnotes to Form VIIIF 1.01.
[3]Ref. Part VIIIK and Forms VIIIK 1.01 through 1.04.

## FORM VIIIE 1.00

### CLIENT QUESTIONNAIRE FOR INDIVIDUAL SURETY BOND[1]

1. Is your client the principal, surety, or beneficiary?[2]
2. Is the surety sui juris?
3. Will the bond guarantee performance or payment? Get copy of the contract being bonded
4. What is the amount of the bond?
5. Is the obligee or beneficiary to be named, or will the bond cover unnamed third-party beneficiaries?[3]
6. What is the time limit on the bond?
7. What notice to the surety of nonperformance or nonpayment is required? Must the notice be written? If so, when, where, and how shall it be delivered?
8. Does the surety own real property? If so, get copy of deed and appropriate affidavits[4] as to liens, encumbrances, etc., to protect the obligee or beneficiary(ies)
9. Get other appropriate information and balance sheet[5] of the surety to protect the obligee or beneficiary(ies)

[1] *12 Am. Jur. 2d Bonds,* paras. 25 and 32.
[2] Ref. Introduction to Part VIIIE.
[3] Ref. Introduction to Part VIIIF and Form VIIIF 1.02.
[4] Ref. Forms VIIIB 1.07.
[5] Ref. Form IA 2.09.

## FORM VIIIE 1.01

### (Indemnity bond by individual against damage from lease of banquet room to amateur theater group)[1]

### INDEMNITY BOND

KNOW ALL MEN, that we, Middletown Little Theater Association, an unincorporated association that produces and presents amateur theatricals in Middle County, Pennsylvania (herein called "Principal"), and Richard Rich, an individual residing at 100 Oak Drive, Middletown, Pennsylvania 00000 (herein called "Surety"), are held and firmly bound to John Doe, an individual doing business as the Middletown Inn at 100 Main Street, Middletown, Middle County, Pennsylvania (herein called "Obligee"), in the sum of One Thousand Dollars ($1,000), for which payment the Surety and the Principal bind ourselves, our successors, heirs, and assigns, jointly and severally, intending to be legally bound hereby, by these presents,

SIGNED, sealed, and dated on September 1, 1982.

WHEREAS, the Principal desires to lease the second floor banquet hall in the Middletown Inn from the Obligee for three days beginning at 9:00 A.M. on November 16, 1982, and ending at midnight on November 18, 1982, for the purpose of presenting a theatrical production called *The Little Ones;* and

WHEREAS, the Obligee is willing to rent the banquet hall to the Principal for that purpose, only upon condition that he shall receive a bond indemnifying him, his heirs, successors, and assigns, from and against all loss and damage to the premises known as the Middletown Inn located in Middletown, Pennsylvania, suffered as a result of the aforesaid rental agreement, within the period of three (3) months from this date, then this obligation shall be null and void; otherwise, it shall remain in full force and effect:

PROVIDED, HOWEVER, and this bond is executed upon the following express conditions:

1. *Notice.* That the Obligee shall promptly notify the Surety, in writing, of any loss or damage that is suffered within four (4) months from this date, or this obligation shall become null and void.

2. *Election to repair.* That the Surety shall have the right, at his own expense, to cause the damage to be repaired.

3. *Personal injury nonliability.* That the Surety shall not be liable for damages to the person of anyone, under or by authority of any statutory provision for damages or compensation to any employee or otherwise; and

4. *Limitation of action.* That no action, suit, or proceeding, at law or in equity, shall be had or maintained against the Principal or Surety, their heirs, successors, or assigns, unless the same shall be commenced and process served within three (3) months after loss or damage shall have been sustained by the Obligee, and in no event after one (1) year from this date.

MIDDLETOWN LITTLE THEATER ASSOCIATION

BY _____ (L.S.)

Mary Roe, Chairman

_____ (L.S.)

Richard Rich, SURETY

(Attach copy of the rental agreement.)

[1] *12 Am. Jur. 2d Bonds,* paras. 25, 32; and *41 Am. Jur. 2d Indemnity,* paras. 4 and 29. Compare statutory bonds in *12 Am. Jur. 2d Bonds,* paras. 26, 27, and 38.

## SECTION F     BONDS (BY CORPORATE SURETY)[1]

The forms in this Section are for bonds where a corporation is the surety.

Where "bond with sufficient surety" is required by a state or federal statute, a corporation with surety and guaranty powers that is duly authorized to do business in the state is considered "sufficient" in most states. Contracts for United States government buildings and other public works prescribe the necessary bond for the contractor.[2] Most states and local governments have similar statutes and requirements for bonding their public works.

The general practitioner is not generally called upon to draft a corporate surety bond or provisions for it unless he represents the surety and guarantee company. The bonding company has its printed form, and the lawyer usually accepts it without question. Obviously, the attorney should quickly distinguish between a performance bond[3] and a payment bond[4] when he approves a bond on behalf of a property owner or a fidelity bond for employees. He should be familiar with the general purpose and the specific conditions of all bonds he approves, including the statutory requirements and provisions for required notice *to the surety.*

Bail bonds for accused criminal defendants, corporate and government bonds issued as securities for investment are not treated in this book.

For forms where an individual is the surety, see Part VIII, Section E.

## FORM VIIIF 1.00

## CLIENT QUESTIONNAIRE FOR CORPORATE SURETY BOND[1]

1. Is your client the principal or the obligee? Get names and addresses of both
2. What is the name and address of the surety company and the name and address of its local agent with whom you are dealing? What is the "rating" of the company, and is it registered with the Insurance Department or Commissioner of your state?

---

[1] *12 Am. Jur. 2d Bonds,* paras. 26, 27, and 38.
[2] See footnotes to Form VIF 1.01.
[3] Ref. Form VIIIF 1.01.
[4] Ref. Form VIIIF 1.02.

3. What is the purpose of the bond, as: a contractor's performance bond, payment bond, fidelity bond, or other?
4. Get a copy of the printed bond form that will be used from the agent for the surety company, unless you are familiar with it. If you are to draft the bond, see Forms VIF 1.01 and 1.02 for general contractor's bonds, or use the surety company's appropriate printed form as a starting point
5. Get a copy of any contract that is being bonded
6. What is the amount of the bond?
7. What are the conditions of the bond as to notices, completion, and subrogation rights in a contractor's performance bond, excuse for nonperformance, personal liability exceptions, or other?
8. If architect or other person or company prepared the plans and specifications for the contract, get his or its name and address

¹See footnotes to Form VIIIF 1.01.

## FORM VIIIF 1.01

### (General contractor's performance bond)

### PERFORMANCE BOND¹

KNOW ALL MEN, that Super Construction Company, Inc., a Florida corporation having its principal place of business at Highway 26 East, Middletown, Florida 00000 (herein called "Principal"), and Valley Surety and Guaranty Corporation, a Pennsylvania corporation duly authorized to do business in the state of Florida, having its principal place of business at 100 West Street, Middletown, Pennsylvania 00000 (herein called "Surety"), are held and firmly bound unto Doe Development Corporation, a Florida corporation having its principal place of business at 100 New Boulevard, Tampa, Florida 00000 (herein called "Obligee"), in the sum of Five Hundred Thousand Dollars ($500,000), to the payment of which sum the Principal and the Surety bind themselves, their successors, and assigns, jointly and severally, firmly by these presents.

Signed, sealed, and dated this 5th day of March, 1982.

WHEREAS, the Principal has entered into written agreement with the Obligee dated March 5, 1982, for the erection and completion of a condominium office building, in accordance with the terms, covenants, and conditions of the agreement, and the plans and specifications prepared by John Smith of 100 Central Avenue, St. Petersburg, Florida 00000, all of which are made a part of this Bond by reference (herein called "Contract"):

NOW, THEREFORE, THE CONDITION OF THE FOREGOING OBLIGATION is that if the Principal shall save harmless the Obligee from any pecuniary loss resulting from the breach of any of the terms, covenants, and conditions of the Contract on the part of the Principal to be performed, then this obligation shall be void, otherwise it shall remain in full force and effect;

PROVIDED, HOWEVER, that this Bond is issued subject to the following conditions and privileges:

1. *Notice to Surety by Obligee.* In the event of any default by Principal in the performance of any of the terms, covenants, and conditions of the Contract, no liability shall attach to the Surety unless the Obligee shall promptly, and in any event not later than thirty (30) days after knowledge of such default, deliver written notice to the Surety at its above address of that default, which notice shall contain a statement of the principal facts showing that default to the date of the notice. Upon sending that notice of default to the Surety, the Obligee shall not pay the final payment provided in the Contract to the Principal without the written consent of the Surety.

2. *Completion and subrogation rights.* In case of any default by the Principal, the Surety shall have the right, at its sole option, to assume and complete or procure the completion of the Contract; and, in case of any default by the Principal, the Surety shall be subrogated to all of the rights and properties of the Principal arising out of the Contract and otherwise, including all securities and indemnities previously received by the Obligee, and all deferred payments, retained percentages, and credits due the Principal at the time of such default, or to become due by the terms and dates of the Contract.

3. *Liability limit.* In no event shall the Surety be liable for a greater sum than the penalty of this Bond.

4. *Limitation of action.* In no event shall the Surety be subject to any suit, action, or other legal proceeding that may be instituted later than March 5, 1984.

5. *Excuse for nonperformance.* In no event shall the Surety be liable for any damage resulting from or for the failure of Principal to perform resulting from any act of God or the public enemy, or labor strikes, mobs, riots, or civil commotion.

6. *Personal injury nonliability.* The Surety shall not be liable for damages to the person of anyone under or by the authority of any statutory provision for damages or compensation to any employee or otherwise.

Signed, sealed, and delivered this 5th day of March, 1982.

(CORPORATE SEAL)           SUPER CONSTRUCTION COMPANY, INC.

By _____

_____
Secretary of the Corporation          President or other title

(CORPORATE SEAL)           VALLEY SURETY AND GUARANTY CORPORATION

By _____

_____
Secretary of the Corporation          President or other title

(Obligee [owner] should attach the executed bond to an *executed* copy of the contract, plans, and specifications.)

> [1]Compare language in this bond to language in Form VIIIF 1.02, which is a payment bond. *17 Am. Jur. 2d Contractors Bonds,* paras. 1–42 and 43–118. See also state Public Works Statutes for contractor's bond requirements. For federal buildings and public works, see *Miller Act,* 40 U.S.C.A. 270(a)–270(e), as amended.

## FORM VIIIF 1.02

### (General contractor's labor and material payment bond)

#### PAYMENT BOND[1]

KNOW ALL MEN, that Super Construction Company, Inc., a Florida corporation having its principal place of business at Highway 26 East, Middletown, Florida 00000 (herein called "Principal"), and Valley Surety and Guaranty Corporation, a Pennsylvania corporation duly authorized to do business in the state of Florida, having its principal place of business at 100 West Street, Middletown, Pennsylvania 00000 (herein called "Surety"), are held and firmly bound unto Doe Development Corporation, a Florida corporation having its principal place of business at 100 New Boulevard, Tampa, Florida 00000, the owner of the construction site (herein called "Obligee"), in the sum of Five Hundred Thousand Dollars ($500,000) for the use and benefit of claimants as defined herein, for the payment of which Principal and Surety bind themselves, their successors, and assigns, jointly and severally, firmly by these presents.

Signed, sealed, and dated this 5th day of March, 1982.

WHEREAS, the Principal has entered into a written agreement with the Obligee dated March 1, 1982, for the erection and completion of a condominium office building, in accordance with the terms, covenants, and conditions of the agreement, and the plans and specifications prepared by John Smith of 100 Central Avenue, St. Petersburg, Florida 00000, all of which are made a part of this Bond by reference (herein called "Contract"):

NOW, THEREFORE, THE CONDITION OF THE FOREGOING OBLIGATION is that, if Principal shall promptly make payment to all claimants as defined herein, for all labor and material used or reasonably required for use in the performance of the Contract, then this obligation shall be void; otherwise it shall remain in full force and effect, SUBJECT TO THE FOLLOWING CONDITIONS:

1. *Definition of claimant.* A claimant is a person or other legal entity having a direct contract with the Principal or with a subcontractor of the Principal for labor, material, or both, used or reasonably required for use in the performance of the Contract. Labor and material shall include that part of water, gas, power, light, heat, oil, gasoline, telephone service, security service, or rental of equipment, which service rental is directly applicable to the Contract.

2. *Attorney's fees for suit on bond for use of claimant.* The Principal and Surety, jointly and severally, agree with the Obligee, as owner of the construction site, that the Obligee may sue the Principal and Surety, or either of them, on this Bond for the use of every claimant, as defined herein, who has not been paid in full before the expiration of a period of ninety (90) days after the date of which the last of such claimant's work or labor was done or performed or materials were furnished, and the Obligee may prosecute the suit to final judgment for such sum or sums as may be justly due claimant and have execution. Furthermore, the Obligee shall not be liable for the payment of any costs or expenses of any such suit, and the costs and reasonable expenses, including reasonable attorney's fees for services rendered to the Obligee in connection with such suit, shall be included in any judgment against the Principal and Surety or either of them.

3. *Notice by subcontractors.* Unless the claimant, as defined herein, other than one having a direct contract with the Principal, shall have given notice in the following manner, no suit or action shall be commenced by that claimant or for his use by the Obligee. Written notice shall be given by that claimant to any two of the following: the Principal, the owner Obligee, or the Surety. The notice shall be given within ninety (90) days after such claimant performed the last of the work or labor or furnished the last of the materials for which the claim is made, stating with substantial accuracy the amount claimed and the name of the party for whom the work was done or to whom materials were furnished. The notice shall be mailed by registered or certified mail, postage prepaid, to the Principal, Obligee, or Surety at their respective address shown above, or to any office that is regularly maintained for the transaction of their respective business, or the notice may be served in any manner in which legal process may be served in the State of Florida, except that such service need not be made by a public officer.

4. *Limitation of action.* Unless this limitation is prohibited by law in the State of Florida, no suit or action shall be commenced by any claimant or for his use after the expiration of one (1) year following the date on which Principal ceased work on the contract.

5. *Venue.* No suit or action by any claimant or for his use shall be commenced in any court other than in a state court of competent jurisdiction in and for the county in which the construction site is situated, or the United States District Court for the district in which the construction site is situated.

6. *Bond reduction by payments.* The amount of this Bond shall be reduced by and to the extent of any payment or payments made in good faith, including payment by Surety of mechanic's liens that may be duly filed against the construction property, whether or not a claim for the amount of such lien be presented under and against this Bond.

Signed, sealed, and delivered this 5th day of March, 1982.

|                       |                                        |
|-----------------------|----------------------------------------|
| (CORPORATE SEAL)      | SUPER CONSTRUCTION COMPANY, INC.       |
|                       | By _____ |
| _____ |                                      |
| Secretary of the Corporation | President or other title           |
| (CORPORATE SEAL)      | VALLEY SURETY AND GUARANTY CORPORATION |
|                       | By _____ |
| _____ |                                      |
| Secretary of the Corporation | President or other title           |

(Obligee [owner] should attach the executed bond to an executed copy of the contract, plans, and specifications.)

¹Ref. footnotes to Form VIIIF 1.01.


## SECTION G     COMPROMISES AND COMPOSITIONS

The forms in this Section are diverse and are distinguished by reference to particular forms contained in this Section as their legal nature is discussed below.

An agreement by the parties to a contract to *compromise or settle*[1] a claim under

---

[1] *17 Am. Jur. 2d Compromise and Settlement,* paras. 461–466. See also Chapter VIIIS, Release and Satisfactions.

the contract is described by the legal term "accord." The payment of the "accord" is called a "satisfaction" and satisfies the original contract claim in full by paying the agreed lesser amount of money or performing differently (usually less valuably). In a lawsuit, an accord and satisfaction is an affirmative defense to a claim for payment or performance of the full consideration for the original contract.

There are certain federal tax implications where a claim for breach of contract or a debt is compromised.[2]

The compromise of the amount of indebtedness by a solvent debtor[3] with one or more creditors is not a "composition with creditors."[4] Both a "compromise" and a "composition with creditors" are to be distinguished from an "assignment for the benefit of creditors."[5] An "assignment for the benefit of creditors" is a transfer of the debtor's *property* in trust to a trustee who will apply the property to the debts of the assignor.[6] It is not an agreement of the creditors to have their debts discharged by payment of any amount less than the original debt. A "composition with creditors"[7] is the latter. It is an arranged agreement between an insolvent debtor and his creditors whereby all or substantially all the creditors of the debtor agree to accept less than the amounts owed them, and the debtor is allowed to retain his assets upon the condition of his making the payments to the creditors as agreed. Upon making the agreed payments, the full original amount of the debts is discharged. It has an effect similar to an "accord and satisfaction" and is an affirmative defense to any of the original claims, unless the debtor fails to perform in accordance with the terms of the "composition" or gets involved in a federal bankruptcy proceeding.[8]

In addition to the formal agreements in this Section, there is a compromise and settlement of a debt by letter, Forms VIIIG 1.01, and a letter offering settlement with a check enclosed, Forms VIIIG 1.02 and 1.02(a).

A debtor's affidavit is included in Form VIIIG 1.04. Such an affidavit may be prepared for use in connection with any form of compromise and settlement.

## FORM VIIIG 1.00

### CLIENT QUESTIONNAIRE FOR COMPROMISES AND COMPOSITIONS[1]

1. Is your client the debtor or the creditor?
2. Does client want a "compromise"[2] or a "composition with creditors"?[3]
3. Name and address of debtor and creditor(s)
4. If there is more than one creditor, debtor's solvency must be considered
5. Is client solvent or insolvent by the standards of the insolvency laws of your state or the federal bankruptcy law? He may not know unless you explain
6. Is the creditor's claim based on a writing? If so, get a copy of the letter, the contract, or the last statement sent if the claim is an "account stated"
7. What is the amount of the original claim? If it is not a claim for money, what performance is claimed?
8. What reduced amount is the debtor to pay, or what difference or change in performance of the original contract is to be made?

---

[2]Ref. Forms VIIIG 1.01 through 1.04. See 26 U.S.C.A. 166.

[3]*15 Am. Jur. 2d Compromise and Settlement*, paras. 11 and 19. Ref. Forms VIIIG 1.01 through 1.04.

[4]*15 Am. Jur. 2d Composition with Creditors*, para. 1 et seq. Ref. Form VIIIG 1.06.

[5]*6 Am. Jur. 2d Assignment for Benefit of Creditors*, para. 32.

[6]See your state insolvency laws, and compare Federal Bankruptcy Law.

[7]Ref. Form VIIIG 1.05 and 1.06.

[8]11 U.S.C.A. 101 et seq.; particularly para. 301 for "voluntary" and para. 303 for "involuntary." See also paras. 343 and 521 and the Bankruptcy Rules.

9. How long is the offer of compromise or composition open?
10. Has the client negotiated the compromise or composition, or does he want you to do the negotiating as well as drafting the agreement?
11. Will the creditor(s) want any affidavits from the debtor?[4]
12. Does client want a formal contract[5] drawn, or an offer in letter form,[6] or a notice[7] to the other party?
13. If a "composition of creditors" is being considered, is voluntary bankruptcy[6] or a proceeding under your state insolvency laws a viable or necessary alternative?

[1]See Introduction to Section VIIIG.
[2]Ref. Form VIIIG 1.01–1.04.
[3]Ref. Form VIIIG 1.05–1.07.
[4]Ref. Form VIIIG 1.04.
[5]Ref. Forms VIIIG 1.04 and 1.05.
[6]Ref. Form VIIIG 1.01.
[7]Ref. Form VIIIG 1.02 and 1.02(a).
[8]26 U.S.C.A. 301.

## FORM VIIIG 1.01

### (Compromise and settlement letter from creditor, and acceptance by debtor)[1]

ABLE MANUFACTURING CORPORATION
100 EAST DRIVE
CLEVELAND, OHIO 00000

June 1, 1982

John Doe, President
Doe Appliances, Inc.
100 Main Street
Middletown, Pennsylvania 00000

Re: Account # 3896

Dear Mr. Doe:

We regret the misunderstanding between our people in regard to your account.

Pursuant to our telephone conversation on May 25, 1982, in which we discussed your reasons for delaying payment on the above account, I have had our sales and billing departments check the orders, deliveries, and balance due on the account. We do not find any discrepancies in our records, but we do value your business and friendship and your usual prompt payment of invoice, and desire to avoid litigation.

We agree to accept as full settlement of the above account to this date the sum of Four Thousand Sixty-eight Dollars ($4,068) payable on or before July 1, 1982, instead of the Five Thousand Sixty-eight Dollars ($5,068) shown on our records.

On payment of that sum, your company shall stand fully released and discharged from all claims and demands that we have against you on the above account.

It is understood, however, that if the above amount is not paid in full by July 1, 1982, then we shall be discharged of this agreement to accept Four Thousand Sixty-eight Dollars ($4,068) in compromise and settlement of our claim for money due on the above account, and you will not be entitled to raise this compromise and settlement as a defense if we find it necessary to institute suit for the full amount we contend is due us.

This letter is being sent to you in duplicate, both being signed by me. Please sign both at the places indicated and return one to me.

Cordially,

Richard Roe, President

I hereby agree and bind Doe Appliances, Inc., to perform and carry out the above compromise and agreement in accordance with the provisions thereof.

DOE APPLIANCES, INC.

By _____
John Doe, President

[1] *15A Am. Jur. 2d Compromise and Settlement*, paras. 15, 24, and 25; and *1 Am. Jur. 2d Accord and Satisfaction*, paras. 47 and 51. Compare formal agreement in Form VIIIG 1.03.

## FORM VIIIG 1.02

### (Notice of offer by debtor to creditor to compromise and settle for a lesser amount—accompanied by a check)[1]

DOE APPLIANCES, INC.
100 MAIN STREET
MIDDLETOWN, PENNSYLVANIA 00000

June 1, 1982

Richard Roe, President
Able Manufacturing Corporation
100 East Drive
Cleveland, Ohio 00000

NOTICE—your account # 3896

Dear Mr. Roe:

This is to notify you that we hereby offer to compromise and settle our account with you to date for the sum of Four Thousand Sixty-eight Dollars ($4,068) in full payments for all claims against us for money due you on that account.

Our check for that amount is enclosed. Your cashing the enclosed check shall constitute your acceptance of this offer of compromise and settlement and shall not be considered as a payment "on account."

Very truly yours,

Richard Roe, President

(See Form VIIIG 1.02(a) for form of endorsement on the enclosed check.)

[1] *1 Am. Jur. 2d Accord and Satisfaction*, paras. 18–23.

## FORM VIIIG 1.02(a)

### (Form of endorsement to be written on back of check offered for compromise and settlement of debt)[1]

In full compromise and settlement of debt claimed on Account No. 3896, pursuant to Notice dated June 4, 1982.
ABLE MANUFACTURING CORPORATION

By _____
AGENT

[1] *1 Am. Jur. 2d Accord and Satisfaction*, paras. 18–23.

## FORM VIIIG 1.03

(Agreement to compromise and settle claim for damages for breach
of contract for sale of goods)

### COMPROMISE AND SETTLEMENT[1]

AGREEMENT made this 1st day of May, 1982, between DOE NOVELTIES, INC., a New York corporation (herein called "Claimant"), and NOVELTY IMPORT CORPORATION, a California corporation (herein called "Distributor"), WITNESSETH:

WHEREAS, Claimant asserts a disputed claim against Distributor based on the fact the Distributor failed to deliver certain goods pursuant to a contract between the parties dated August 10, 1981, under which Distributor was required to deliver One Thousand (1,000) Squiggle Toys (herein called "Toys") to Claimant on or before September 30, 1981, for resale by Claimant during the 1981 holiday season, and Distributor delivered only Five Hundred (500) of the Toys to Claimant by that date; and

WHEREAS, by reason of Distributor's failure to deliver the Toys purchased, Claimant has suffered loss of profit estimated by him to exceed Fifteen Hundred Dollars ($1,500), and Claimant believes in good faith that Distributor is liable to it for that amount, and is entitled to refuse Distributor's present offer to deliver the additional Five Hundred (500) Toys, as Claimant asserts that time was of the essence of the contract; the parties hereby compromise and settle Claimant's claim for damages and agree to terminate further obligations of both parties under the contract in consideration of the following mutual covenants:

1. On or before June 1, 1982, defendant shall reimburse Claimant for its claimed loss of profit by shipping five hundred (500) Toys to Claimant, freight prepaid, invoiced "no charge," to Claimant at 100 Fifth Avenue, New York, New York 00000.

2. Upon delivery by Distributor of the goods without charges to Claimant, all contracts, claims, rights, duties, obligations, and liabilities arising out of the sale contract dated August 10, 1981, existing between the parties prior to or at the time of the execution of this agreement are satisfied, discharged and terminated.

Dated this 1st day of May, 1982.

DOE NOVELTIES, INC.

By _____
(title of person who signed sale contract)

NOVELTY IMPORT CORPORATION

By _____
(title of person who signed sale contract)

[1]15A Am. Jur. 2d Compromise and Settlement, paras. 15, 24, and 25; and 1 Am. Jur. 2d Accord and Satisfaction, paras. 47 and 51. Compare informal letter, Form VIIIG 1.01.

## FORM VIIIG 1.04

(Agreement to compromise and settle a debt, with affidavit of
debtor's financial status)[1]

### COMPROMISE AND SETTLEMENT

AGREEMENT made June 1, 1982, between John Doe, of 100 Main Street, Providence, Rhode Island 00000 (herein called "Claimant"), and Peter Poe, of 200 East Street, Middletown, Rhode Island (herein called "Debtor").

1. Claimant asserts a claim against Debtor d/b/a Pete's Garage in the sum of One Thousand Dollars ($1,000), plus interest at the rate of Six Percent (6%) per annum from June 1, 1981, for money loaned to Debtor for the operation of his garage business.

2. Debtor acknowledges the existance of an indebtedness to Claimant, but disputes the amount of such indebtedness.

3. A compromise and settlement of the indebtedness has been negotiated between the parties, under the terms of which Debtor is to pay the sum of Six Hundred Fifty Dollars ($650) in full settlement and satisfaction thereof.

4. In agreeing to that amount, Claimant is relying on Debtor's statement to him that Debtor has no attachable assets of any kind or character, which statement is reflected in the attached affidavit of Debtor.

Debtor understands and agrees that Claimant shall be bound by this Agreement only on the condition that the statements made by Debtor as to his personal responsibility and as to his assets are true.

Debtor further agrees that in the event of a recision of this Agreement, Claimant may retain the sum received hereunder and apply that sum toward satisfaction of the original obligation. In such event, Debtor also waives the right to plead any statute of limitations as a defense to any action on the original obligation.

IN WITNESS WHEREOF, the parties have executed this Agreement at Middletown, Rhode Island, the day and year first above written.

_____
JOHN DOE

_____
PETER POE

STATE OF RHODE ISLAND
COUNTY OF KENT

Before me, a notary public in and for the above state, personally appeared Peter Poe of 200 East Street, Middletown, Kent County, Rhode Island, who, being duly sworn, deposes and says:

1. That he has no property or assets of any kind or nature; no money due him from any person; no real property; no stocks, bonds, or funds in any bank; no credits due him; no beneficial interest in any property held by any other person for him; and no property standing in the name of assignees, trustees, or any other persons for him and for his benefit, with the following exceptions only:

(a) Personal property consisting of wearing apparel and household furniture valued at Eight Thousand Dollars ($8,000), and Five Thousand Dollars ($5,000) proceeds of an accident policy, some or all of which is exempt from attachment or levy as provided in R.I. Gen. Laws, 1956 9-26-4, and 27-18-24.

_____
Peter Poe, AFFIANT

Sworn to and subscribed before me this 1st day
of June, 1982

_____
Notary Public

My commission expires:

[1]15A Am. Jur. 2d Compromise and Settlement, para. 19. See also U.S.C.A. 113(b)(3), for tax consequences of compromises and settlement of a debt.

## FORM VIIIG 1.05

### (Composition with creditors where contractor is the debtor and subcontractors are the creditors)

### COMPOSITION AGREEMENT[1]

AGREEMENT made this 1st day of June, 1982, between John Doe d/b/a Middle County Building Contractors at State Rt. 1, Box 123, Middletown, Arizona 00000 (herein called "Contractor"), and the undersigned parties, who are subcontractor-creditors of Contractor who, by signing this Agreement, severally become parties to it (herein called "Subcontractors"), recite and agree as follows:

1. Contractor has contracted with ROE DEVELOPMENT CORPORATION to erect certain buildings at 100 South Drive, Middletown, Arizona (herein called "Contract"), and has subcontracted part of the Contract work to the Subcontractor.

2. Contractor is having financial difficulty in completing the project described in the Contract as agreed, and hereby notifies the Subcontractor of that fact.

3. The Subcontractors have agreed to furnish or have furnished certain labor, material, or both as set forth in Schedule A, attached hereto and made part hereof, which labor and/or materials have been used or are to be used by Contractor in the completion of the Contract.

4. In order to realize a part of the money due them from Contractor, and to enable Contractor to continue with the project described in the Contract, the Subcontractors hereby agree to the following plan for carrying the work of the project to completion, and for the payment of their accounts by Contractor.

COMPOSITION PLAN

A. *Appointment of disbursing agent.* First Bank of Middletown (herein called "Bank") shall be appointed disbursing agent for Contractor, with power to receive all payments hereafter required to be made by Roe Development Corporation (herein called "Roe") under its contract dated January 1, 1982, with Contractor for the construction of the project.

B. *Disbursements before completion.* The payments required of Roe under the Contract are to be made to Contractor on the architect's certificates duly issued to Contractor pursuant to the Contract. Contractor hereby agrees to immediately endorse all future payments received from Roe to the Bank. The Bank, on receipt of those payments, shall disburse the same to the several undersigned Subcontractors for work performed or materials supplied prior to June 1, 1982, in an amount equal to Fifty Percent (50%) of the payment received by disbursing agent in the proportions that each Subcontractor's prior claim, as set forth below, bears to the prior claims of the other undersigned Subcontractor as set forth below. One Percent (1%) of each payment shall be retained by the Bank in full payment for its services as disbursing agent, and the other Forty-nine Percent (49%) of the payment shall be paid to new claimants, as defined in Section C of this plan, in full for new work, and the balance, if any, shall be paid to Contractor on or before thirty (30) days after receipt of the payment by the Bank.

C. *Definition of new claimants.* Certain of the undersigned Subcontractors have agreed to furnish labor and material in excess of that already supplied, and they will fulfill such agreements promptly and in a workmanlike manner. Contractor may be required, in the interest of completion of the project, to hire additional subcontractors from time to time. Pursuant to Section D, the Contractor shall notify disbursing agent of all additional labor and material. Both the undersigned who do additional work, to the extent of the additional work, and other required new subcontractors shall be considered new claimants in determining priority and payment under Section B.

D. *Notice of additional work.* Contractor shall notify the disbursing agent and the architects, in writing, immediately after making contracts for or purchasing such additional labor and material as may be necessary for the completion of the work, and that is not already contracted for, stating the amount of such contracts or purchases, and that payments for such work shall be made from time to time by the disbursing agent in the manner specified.

E. *Disbursement upon completion.* No claim will be made for further payment on labor and materials furnished to Contractor for use in this project prior to June 1, 1982, until such time as work under the Contract is entirely completed, at which time the disbursing agent shall pay to the undersigned Subcontractors, pro rata, from the full amount received by Contractor from Roe as final and full payment under the construction contract. Each Subcontractor shall receive a sum representing the proportion that his full claim bears to the total amount paid to Contractor under the construction contract, up to the full amount of his claim. If any balance remains after all creditors on this work are paid in full, such balance is to be paid to Contractor.

IN WITNESS WHEREOF, the parties to this Agreement have hereunto duly set their hands and seals on the day and year above written.

JOHN DOE d/b/a Middle County Building Contractors
_____

ABC CEMENT PRODUCTS, INC.
_____

By _____
   President

POE LUMBER COMPANY, INC.

By _____
   General Manager

John Jones d/b/a Jones Masonry
_____

Peter Poe d/b/a Ace Electric Contractors
_____

Jack Smith d/b/a A-1 Plumbing
_____

Accepted by:
FIRST BANK OF MIDDLETOWN
By _____
   Vice-President

(Note: Prepare and attach Schedule A to the agreement.)

| NAME AND ADDRESS OF SUBCONTRACTOR | TOTAL AMOUNT OF SUBCONTRACT | SUBCONTRACT WORK COMPLETED PRIOR TO June 1, 1982. |
|---|---|---|
| _____ | $ _____ | $ _____ |

(Prepare sufficient lines to list all subscribing subcontractors.)

¹*15A Am. Jur. 2d Composition with Creditors*, paras. 1–10. Compare Form VIIIG 1.06

### FORM VIIIG 1.06

(Composition agreement between creditors and a debtor corporation and its stockholders, by which the corporation will continue its business subject to certain powers in a creditors' committee)

### COMPOSITION AGREEMENT[1]

AGREEMENT made this 1st day of June, 1982, by and among the several undersigned CREDITORS (herein individually called "Creditor" and collectively called "Creditors"); DOE MANUFACTURING CORPORATION, a Pennsylvania corporation having its principal place of business at 537 Wood Street, Pittsburgh, Pennsylvania 00000 (herein called "Debtor Corporation"); John Doe, Peter Poe, and Richard Roe, stockholders of the Debtor Corporation (herein called "Stockholders"); and John Jones, Richard Rich, and James George, members of creditors' committee (herein collectively called the "Committee"), WITNESSETH:

WHEREAS, Debtor Corporation is indebted to Creditors in the amounts set opposite their names in Schedule A, which is attached hereto and made part hereof; and

WHEREAS, Debtor Corporation is presently unable to pay those debts in full because of unforeseen financial difficulties; and

WHEREAS, Debtor Corporation has submitted to Creditors a balance sheet[2] and income statement,[3] and Creditors have agreed among themselves and with Debtor Corporation that it will be in the best interest of all the parties that the business of the Debtor Corporation be continued or sold as a going concern, but under the direction of the Committee; and

WHEREAS, Debtor Corporation and the Stockholders have represented to Creditors that Debtor Corporation has made no preferential payment(s) of debts to any of its creditors, whether or not such creditors are parties hereto, and have further represented that the Debtor Corporation desires to make pro rata payments out of its assets and property to creditors who join this Agreement; and

WHEREAS, the capital stock of the Debtor Corporation consists of One Hundred (100) shares of common stock, all of which has been issued and is outstanding as follows:

| *Name and address* | *Number of shares* |
|---|---|
| John Doe<br>100 East Avenue<br>Pittsburgh, Pa. 00000 | 35 |
| Peter Poe<br>100 Main Street<br>Middletown, Pa. 00000 | 35 |
| Richard Roe<br>100 West Street<br>Pittsburgh, Pa. 00000 | 30 |

WHEREAS, the directors and officers of the Debtor Corporation are:

Directors: John Doe, Peter Poe, and Richard Roe
President: John Doe
Treasurer: Peter Poe
Secretary: Richard Roe

NOW, THEREFORE, IT IS AGREED:

1. *Transfer of stock.* Each Stockholder shall immediately assign and transfer to the Committee all his shares of stock in the Debtor Corporation, to be held by the Committee in trust for the purposes expressed in this Agreement.

2. *Resignations and election.* Peter Poe and Richard Roe shall immediately deliver to the Committee their written resignation as directors and Treasurer and Secretary, respectively, of the Debtor Corporation. Before such resignations, all the directors and executive officers of Debtor Corporation shall cooperate in calling such stockholder and board meetings as may be necessary in accordance with the Articles of Incorporation and Bylaws of the Debtor Corporation, and at the time requested by the Committee, and to elect at such meeting or by written consent in lieu thereof the following:

| | |
|---|---|
| John Doe | Director and President |
| John Jones | Director and Vice-President |
| James George | Director and Secretary-Treasurer |

3. *Delivery of corporate records.* Each Stockholder, in his capacity as director and/or executive officer of Debtor Corporation, shall, upon the execution of this Agreement, make available to the Committee all books, papers, documents, records, reports, and accounts of the Debtor Corporation that are in his possession or control; and each Stockholder shall cooperate to the best of his ability with the Committee in advancing the interests and profitability of the Debtor Corporation.

4. *Duration and conditions of this Agreement.* Conditioned upon the performance of the above Agreement of the Stockholders, Creditors hereby give and grant to Debtor Corporation full liberty and license to conduct its business of manufacturing steel products and to convert into money any or all of its stock in trade, assets, and property for a period of two (2) years from the date of this Agreement. The undersigned Creditors, or any of them, will not institute or maintain any actions, suits, or legal proceedings of any kind against the Debtor Corporation or its business, assets, and property or against any of the Stockholders, officers, or directors, past or present, or the property or assets of the Stockholders.

5. *Appointment of Committee.* The following persons are hereby appointed as the Committee to represent the undersigned Creditors in accordance with the terms and covenants of this Agreement:

John Jones
Richard Rich
James George

If a member of the Committee should die, resign, or become otherwise incapacitated, his successor shall be selected by the remaining members of the Committee. If all members of the Committee should die, resign, or become otherwise incapacitated at the same time, their successors shall be selected by the Creditors, whose action may be taken at a meeting called for that purpose, after notice to all Creditors or by ballot of all Creditors by mail. All successor members of the Committee shall have the same powers, authority, and rights as the members of the Committee appointed herein.

6. *Tenure and compensation of present executive officers of Debtor Corporation.* John Doe is hereby authorized to continue as a director and President of Debtor Corporation, but his compensation and the duration of his tenure as an executive officer shall be determined by the Committee and approved by the board of directors of the Debtor Corporation. Peter Poe and Richard Roe may continue as employees of the Debtor Corporation, but their compensation and tenure as employees shall be determined by the Committee and approved by the board of directors of the Debtor Corporation.

7. *Powers and duties of the Committee.* The Committee shall have the following powers and duties:

(a) *Member's powers.* Members of the Committee may become directors or executive officers of the Debtor Corporation, and the Committee may exercise its voting power of all shares of stock held in trust by the Committee in favor of the election of themselves or any of them or others as directors. A member of the Committee may do or perform any other act or thing that is authorized or permitted by this Agreement, but he shall not incur any debts or liabilities on behalf of any creditor, or charge or pledge the credit of any creditor in any manner, and no such authority shall be implied by any other provisions of this Agreement.

(b) *Operation of Debtor Corporation's business by Committee.* The business of the Debtor Corporation is to be continued for such period of time as the Committee, in its discretion, may deem to be in the best interest of the undersigned Creditors. Members of the Committee, in their capacity as directors or executive officers, as the authority may be, shall select present or future officers and employees, determine their number and compensation, duration of employment, and benefits, and shall determine the need for and amount of any other expense of operating the Debtor Corporation. If, at any time during the period provided in Paragraph 4 or any extension thereof as provided herein, the Committee determines that it is in the best interest of the Creditors that the business of the Debtor Corporation be discontinued or be sold as a going enterprise, then the Committee is hereby authorized to take such action with respect thereto as Committee, in its sole discretion, is deemed advisable. The Committee is hereby expressly authorized to implement such determination by exercising the voting power of the shares of stock transferred to it by this Agreement in favor of a sale of the business of the Corporation, all, but not part of, its stock, or the liquidation of all or any part of the assets of the Debtor Corporation.

8. *Application of moneys by the Committee.* From moneys realized from the operation of the business of the Debtor Corporation and/or received from the sale of Debtor Corporation's property and collection of receivables, the Committee shall first pay all taxes of the Debtor Corporation and the costs of operating the business, including payment for goods purchased to replenish manufacturing materials, and thereafter shall pay present small debts of Debtor Corporation that do not exceed the sum of Five Hundred Dollars ($500) each. After the payment of the foregoing, if, from time to time, there is a sufficient sum on hand to pay an amount equal to Fifty Percent (50%) of that sum to the Creditors, the Committee shall cause that sum to be distributed and paid to the Creditors as a creditor's dividend, pro rata, as to amounts shown in Schedule A.

9. *Compensation of the Committee.* As compensation for their services as members of the Committee, each member shall be entitled to the sum of Two Hundred Dollars ($200) for each full month he has served, in addition to any compensation he may earn as an officer or employer of the Debtor Corporation. If the debts due Creditors are paid in full in the manner herein provided, such compensation of Committee members shall be paid from surplus over and above the amount of debts. If the assets and property of Debtor Corporation are insufficient to pay all debts, then this compensation of Committee members shall be deducted from the dividends payable to Creditors as provided in Paragraph 8.

10. *Termination and reassignment of stock.* After payment of all debts, taxes, expenses, costs, and compensation of Committee as provided above, Committee members shall assign and transfer the shares of stock in Debtor Corporation held by them hereunder to, or on the written order of, the Stockholders from whom they received such shares, and at the same time shall deliver their signed resignations as directors and executive officers of Debtor Corporation.

11. *Extension.* If, at the expiration of the period of two (2) years from the date of this Agreement, all of the debts owing to Creditors are not paid in full, the Committee is authorized and empowered, in its discretion, without any further authroity from the parties, to extend the above period for a further term or period of six (6) months by endorsement on this Agreement.

12. *Acceptance of appointment as Committee members.* Members of the Committee appointed herein have executed this Agreement to evidence their acceptance of the appointment.

13. *Persons bound by this Agreement.* This Agreement shall inure to the benefit of and be binding on each of the parties hereto, their personal representatives, successors, and assigns.

IN WITNESS WHEREOF, the parties and the initial members of the Committee have duly executed this Agreement at Pittsburgh, Pennsylvania, on the day and year above written.

(CORPORATE SEAL)                              DOE MANUFACTURING CORPORATION

————————————————                      By ————————————————
Secretary of the Corporation                        President

                                              STOCKHOLDERS:

                                              ————————————————
                                              JOHN DOE

                                              ————————————————
                                              PETER POE

                                              ————————————————
                                              RICHARD ROE

                                              MEMBERS OF CREDITORS' COMMITTEE:

                                              ————————————————
                                              JOHN JONES

                                              ————————————————
                                              RICHARD RICH

                                              ————————————————
                                              JAMES GEORGE

(CORPORATE SEAL)                              CREDITORS:
                                              ACE STEEL CORPORATION

————————————————                      By ————————————————
Secretary of the Corporation                        President

(CORPORATE SEAL)                              FABRICATION EQUIPMENT, INC.

————————————————                      By ————————————————
Secretary of the Corporation                        President

(CORPORATE SEAL)                              ELI TRUCKING CORPORATION

————————————————                      By ————————————————
Secretary of the Corporation                        President

(CORPORATE SEAL)                              FIRST BANK OF ALLEGHENY

————————————————                      By ————————————————
Secretary of the Corporation                        President

                                              JONES & JONES, a partnership

                                              By ————————————————
                                                    Partner

                                              Albert Able d/b/a ABLE SUPPLIES

                                              By ————————————————
                                                    Albert Able

(Attach Schedule A listing subscribing creditors' names and addresses, nature of each debt, and amount of each debt.)

[1]*15A Am. Jur. 2d Composition with Creditors*, paras. 1–10. Compare Form VIIIG 1.05.
[2]Ref. Form IA 2.09.
[3]Ref. Form IA 2.08.

## SECTION H    CONSENTS

The forms in this Section are simple consent forms. In drafting a "consent," one should consider whether it is a mere formality required or allowed by the original contract or whether the "consent" is a modification, extension, or substitution,[1] a "compromise and settlement"[2] that may create an "accord and satisfaction" or a "novation" or an express "account stated."

The parties to a contract may change it any time by mutual agreement, but the later agreement must also have consideration if it is to modify or replace an original contract, and it should be executed with the same formality if the original contract was required by statute to be in writing.

Whether or not a simple consent is required by the contract to be in writing or a modification of a contract is required by statute to be in writing, the safest course is to put either in writing.

If there are any conditions to a simple consent, the consentor should sign the consent, and the other party should accept the consent as shown in Forms VIIIH 1.01 and 1.02.

### FORM VIIIH 1.00

### CLIENT QUESTIONNAIRE FOR USE AND DRAFTING CONSENT[1]

1. Names and addresses of parties involved
2. Is there a written original contract? If so, get copy
3. Is the consent to be between the parties to the original contract, or is it a consent to the assignment of the contract?
4. If it is a consent to assignment, has the assignment been drawn, and what are its terms? If not drawn, does client want you to prepare the assignment *and* the consent?
5. Will the assignment and/or consent be typed or attached to the original contract? If so, they will be prepared and signed *in duplicate* even though the consent is required of and signed by just one party
6. Are there any conditions to the Consent? If so, what are they? (other party should sign "acceptance" on the "consent instrument" if there are conditions)

[1]Ref. Introduction to Chapter VIIIH.

### FORM VIIIH 1.01

(Consent to assignment of the contract providing that both assignor
and assignee be liable)

### CONSENT TO ASSIGNMENT[1]

In consideration of One Dollar ($1) paid by John Doe, the undersigned, being the duly authorized agent of Able Manufacturing, Inc., an Ohio corporation, hereby consents on behalf of the Corporation to the foregoing assignment of the sale contract dated May 1, 1982, between the Corporation as seller and John Doe, an individual d/b/a Doe Appliances, as buyer to Doe Appliances Inc.,

[1]Ref. Part VIII, and Forms VIIIJ 1.01 and 1.02.
[2]Ref. Forms VIIIG 1.01 through 1.03.

a Pennsylvania corporation, upon the condition that the Assignor shall continue to be liable and that the Assignee shall assume liability for the due performance of the sale contract.

ABLE MANUFACTURING, INC.

By _____

Vice-President

ACCEPTED:
DOE APPLIANCES, INC.

By _____

President

[1]*6 Am Jur. 2d Assignments,* para. 21. Ref. Form VIIA 1.09 and 1.09(a) for sale and assignment of a business lease that includes the consent in the agreement. Ref. Section VIIID for assignments.

## FORM VIIIH 1.02

### (Lessor's conditional consent to improve or alter leased premises accepted by lessee)

### CONSENT TO ALTERATIONS[1]

The undersigned, John Doe, owner and lessee of the premises located in Middletown, Middle County, Florida, and more particularly described in a lease from the undersigned to Super Chain, Inc., dated May 1, 1980, in consideration hereby consents to the remodeling and alteration of the premises in accordance with the plan and specifications prepared by Smith's Building Designs, Inc., dated August 4, 1981, a copy of which is attached hereto and made part hereof.

In consideration of this Consent being given, it is understood and agreed that the remodeling and alteration described herein shall be done at the sole expense of the lessee and shall become the sole and exclusive property of the undersigned at the termination of the lease for any cause.

In consideration of the increased use of lessor's property, all covenants and undertakings of the lessee set forth in the lease, including, but not limited to, care, use, and insurance of the premises shall apply to the remodeled and altered premises, and lessee shall hold lessor harmless from any liens, encumbrances, or damages of any kind whatsoever, including reasonable attorney's fees, arising out of the remodeling or alteration hereunder.

Signed this 1st day of September, 1981, in Middletown, Florida.

_____
John Doe, OWNER/LESSEE

ACCEPTED:
SUPER CHAIN, INC.

By _____
(Title)

[1]*49 Am. Jur. 2d Landlord and Tenant,* para. 249.

## SECTION I     ESCROW

At common law, the term "escrow" applied only to the holding of legal instruments conveying land, but today the term applies to holding any instrument or money for parties until certain agreed conditions between the parties are met. The escrow agent is usually a bank or an attorney-at-law, but any sui juris person who is willing can act as an escrow agent.

In the absence of an escrow contract[1] among the party delivering the instrument or money, the party entitled to the instrument or money when the conditions are met, and the escrow agent, a delivery of the money or instrument to the proposed escrow agent is merely an offer, and it may be withdrawn at any time before the other party has performed.

An escrow agreement may be a separate contract[2] signed by the three parties, or it may be incorporated in the original agreement between the parties with a later written acceptance by the escrow agent. The sample agreement in this Section incorporates the escrow agreement in an underlying agreement.[3]

The use of an escrow arrangement in completing a particular business transaction may have important federal tax consequences that should be carefully considered in the preparation of the escrow agreement.[4]

In addition to the escrow agreement in this Section, there are supplemental forms to be used with any escrow agreement. They are the acceptance by the escrow agent and his receipt for the documents, amendment to his instructions, notice to defaulting party of cancellation of the escrow, and notice of cancellation to the escrow agent by mutual consent of the buyer and seller.

## FORM VIII I 1.00

### CLIENT QUESTIONNAIRE FOR ESCROW AGREEMENT[1]

1. Names and addresses of the parties to the underlying agreement and the proposed escrow agent
2. Is the escrow arrangement to be included in an original contract? If so, see client questionnaires for the particular type of agreement
3. To prepare a separate escrow agreement or to draft the escrow provisions in the original contract, get the following information:
    (a) What is the underlying agreement, and what is the purpose of the escrow arrangement?
    (b) Is the proposed escrow agent willing to act? If not, get name and address of a willing escrow agent or get specified date for selecting the escrow agent
    (c) What is to be delivered to the escrow agent? Make a list
    (d) When is it to be delivered? Have all items on list (c) at the closing
    (e) What are the escrow agent's *duties* (the conditions of the escrow)?
    (f) Who will give the escrow agent his instructions if they are not to be spelled out in the agreement, as: mutual instructions to be signed by both parties, or separate instructions to be signed by a designated party?
    (g) How, when, and in what amount will the escrow agent be compensated for his services?
    (h) Who will bear the expense of the escrow?
    (i) Who will bear any loss from a default by the escrow agent?
    (j) What is the time limit for the escrow agreement?
    (k) On what conditions can the escrow agreement be terminated before that time?
    (l) If the escrow involves a "bulk transfer," check bulk transfer compliance[1]
    (m) *How*, where, and when small notices between the parties be given? Be specific

[1]See also Form VIIIR 1.05 for receipt for return of documents by escrow agent.

---

[1]*28 Am. Jur. 2d Escrow*, para. 4.
[2]Ref. Form IA 2.05(a).
[3]Ref. Form VIIII 1.01.
[4]*Am. Jur. 2d Federal Tax Guide to Legal Forms*, para. 2170.

### FORM VIII I 1.01

(Escrow agreement incorporated in underlying agreement for sale
of an office building, with instructions to and acceptance by the
escrow agent)[1]

### AGREEMENT

THIS AGREEMENT made March 4, 1982, among John Doe of 100 East Avenue, Pittsburgh, Pennsylvania 00000 (herein called "Seller"); Rich Realty, Inc., a Pennsylvania corporation having its principal place of business at 500 Main Boulevard, Philadelphia, Pennsylvania 00000 (herein called "Buyer"); and Midtown Mortgage Corporation, a Pennsylvania corporation having its principal place of business at Suite #100, Town Building, Pittsburgh, Pennsylvania 00000 (herein called "Escrow Agent"), WITNESSETH:

WHEREAS, Seller owns the office building (known as the Doe Building) that is located at 537 Wood Street, Pittsburgh, Pennsylvania, and Buyer desires to purchase that building; and

WHEREAS, Seller and Buyer desire to have the sale closed by the Escrow Agent; and

WHEREAS, Escrow Agent is willing to act as escrow agent to effect the closing of that sale in accordance with this Agreement; IT IS AGREED as follows:

1. *Description of property and price.* Seller agrees to sell, and Buyer agrees to buy, the real property known as the Doe Building located in Pittsburgh, Allegheny County, Pennsylvania, and more particularly described as follows:

(insert legal description)

for the sum of Five Hundred Thousand Dollars ($500,000) on or before June 4, 1982, free and clear of all encumbrances, except as set forth in the escrow instructions attached hereto and made part hereof (herein called the "Instructions").

(Prepare and attach list of encumbrances and present leases, concessions, and/or licenses, and detailed instructions to Escrow Agent in regard to each, as well as general closing instructions. HAVE ALL PARTIES SIGN OR INITIAL the Instructions.)

2. *Appointment of Escrow Agent.* Seller and Buyer hereby appoint and employ Escrow Agent to effect the closing of the sale in accordance with this Agreement, and each agrees to deliver to the Escrow Agent all instruments, forms, and moneys necessary to comply with this Agreement and the instructions incorporated herein on or before May 4, 1982, including an unexecuted general warranty deed from Seller to Buyer.

3. *Duties of Escrow Agent.* Upon receipt of all documents and money required herein, Escrow Agent shall prepare a closing statement and notify Seller and Buyer in writing of the time of closing, which shall be held at the offices of the Escrow Agent, no later than June 4, 1982, without the written consent of the Buyer and Seller. The Seller shall execute the general warranty deed at the closing. The Escrow Agent shall file the deed in the office of the Recorder of Deeds of Allegheny County, Pennsylvania, instructing the Recorder of Deeds to mail the deed to the Buyer at the address shown above.

4. *Compensation and liability of Escrow Agent.* Buyer and Seller agree that Escrow Agent assumes no liability, other than the exercise of good faith, for its reception, retention, or delivery of documents or money hereunder of for any other action in connection with the performance of its duties hereunder. Escrow Agent is hereby authorized to deduct and withhold from the payment due the Seller the amount of One-half of One Percent (0.5%) of the purchase price, and all fees, costs, and expenses incurred by reason of its appointment and performance hereunder.

IN WITNESS WHEREOF, the parties have signed and accepted this Agreement on the day and year first above written.

<table>
<tr>
<td>(CORPORATE SEAL)</td>
<td>John Doe, SELLER<br>RICH REALTY, INC.</td>
</tr>
<tr>
<td>_____<br>Secretary of the Corporation<br>ACCEPTED:<br>MIDTOWN MORTAGE CORPORATION</td>
<td>By _____<br>         President<br><br>(CORPORATE SEAL)</td>
</tr>
<tr>
<td>By _____<br>      (Title)</td>
<td>_____<br>Secretary of the Corporation</td>
</tr>
</table>

[1]*28 Am. Jur. 2d Escrow,* paras. 1–10, particularly 4. See Form IA 2.05 for separate escrow agreement, and Form VIIN 1.01 for pledge of stock in escrow.

## FORM VIII I 1.02

### (Acceptance by escrow agent and receipt of documents)

### ACCEPTANCE AND RECEIPT[1]

The undersigned escrow holder, Richard Roe, attorney-at-law, with offices in Suite 100, Tower Building, Des Moines, Iowa 00000, hereby acknowledges receipt of the following:

1. General warranty deed executed and acknowledged June 1, 1982, from Seller, John Doe of 100 East Drive, Des Moines, Iowa 00000, to Buyer, Roe Industries, Inc., an Iowa corporation having its principal place of business at 500 Industrial Drive, Des Moines, Iowa 00000.

2. Escrow Instructions dated June 1, 1982, signed by Buyer and Seller.

The undersigned agrees with the Buyer and Seller to hold the deed in escrow and to deliver it to the Buyer or his assigns or legal representatives on the payment of all the moneys provided to be paid by Buyer as the purchase price for the land in accordance with the Escrow Instructions.

In the event that the Buyer does not perform in accordance with the Escrow Instructions on or before September 1, 1982, the undersigned agrees to redeliver the deed to the Seller forthwith upon demand by the Seller.

Dated this 15th day of June, 1982.

_____
Richard Roe, ESCROW HOLDER

[1] *28 Am. Jur. 2d Escrow*, paras. 1, 10, 16, and 17.

## FORM VIII I 1.03

### (Amendment of instructions to escrow agent, to be signed by the supplier of the original instructions as authorized in the contract)[1]

### AMENDMENT OF ESCROW INSTRUCTIONS

ESCROW ACCOUNT NO. 1043
June 1, 1982
To:  First National Bank of Middletown
     100 Main Street
     Middletown, Tennessee 00000

The undersigned herewith submit the following amendments to the Escrow Instructions on the above Escrow Account dated May 1, 1982, submitted to you by the undersigned, which amendments supersede contrary provisions in those Instructions:

1. No satisfaction of mortgage for the mortgage from John Doe to Richard Roe, recorded in Deed Book Vol. 000, Page 000, shall be required before delivery of the deed, as the same has been assumed by the Buyer.

2. The closing date shall be on or before June 16, 1982.

Dated this June 1, 1982.

(CORPORATE SEAL)

Peter Poe, SELLER
Rich Manufacturing Corp., BUYER

By _____

_____
Secretary of the Corporation          President

[1] *28 Am. Jur. 2d Escrow*, paras. 7 and 8.

**FORM VIII I 1.04**

(Notice to defaulting party of cancellation of escrow agreement)[1]

### NOTICE OF CANCELLATION

To:  JOHN DOE
     100 Main Street
     Middletown, Florida 00000

Due to your failure to secure a partial release of mortgage on or before May 31, 1982, on the premises to be purchased by the undersigned pursuant to our agreement dated January 30, 1982, you are hereby notified that the undersigned hereby elects to and does hereby cancel and rescind that agreement for the purchase of the property, and shall demand from the Escrow Agent the return to the undersigned of any and all moneys paid and any and all papers executed by it pursuant to such agreement, including Escrow Instructions dated January 30, 1982.

Dated this 1st day of June, 1982.

ABLE MANUFACTURING, INC.

By _____
                    President

[1]*17 Am. Jur. 2d Contracts,* paras. 509 and 510.

**FORM VIII I 1.05**

(Notice of cancellation to escrow agent by mutual consent of buyer
and seller)[1]

ESCROW ACCOUNT NO. 1043
June 1, 1982
To:  First National Bank of Middletown
     100 Main Street
     Middletown, Florida 00000

Referring to the Escrow Instructions dated May 1, 1982, executed by the undersigned for the above Escrow Account, you are hereby notified that such instructions are cancelled by the mutual consent of the parties. We hereby request that you return and deliver all money and papers delivered to you for the above Escrow Account in the following manner:

1. General warranty deed executed by Seller—to the Seller, upon his payment to you of one-half (½) of your total escrow fee of One Hundred Dollars ($100) to date.
2. Ten Thousand Dollars ($10,000) earnest money paid by Buyer—to Buyer, less one-half (½) of your total escrow fee of One Hundred Dollars ($100) to date.

Dated this June 1, 1982.

_____
Peter Poe, SELLER

Rich Manufacturing Corp., BUYER

By _____
                    President

(CORPORATE SEAL)

_____
Secretary of the Corporation

[1]*28 Am. Jur. 2d Escrow,* paras. 5 and 8.

## SECTION J    EXTENSIONS AND MODIFICATIONS OF CONTRACTS[1]

The parties to a contract, may, by later agreement, change it at any time. It may be altered or modified[2] in any respect, supplemented, rescinded in whole or in part,

---

[1]*17 Am. Jur. 2d Contracts,* paras. 458–464.
[2]U.C.C. 2-209 and 9-318.

or another contract may be substituted. Under the common law, the modified or new agreement, including an extension of time for performance, must be based upon a new consideration. *Under the Uniform Commercial Code, a modified commercial contract governed by the Code may be enforced without consideration.*[3]

A novation[4] extinguishes one obligation or contract by the substitution of a new contract, and frequently by the substitution of new parties. The U.C.C. makes no reference to a novation, but under certain conditions it may be advisable as where an assignment with the consent of the parties is to be made, and the assignor wants to be sure that he is relieved of any obligation under the contract being assigned.[5]

## FORM VIIIJ 1.00

### CLIENT QUESTIONNAIRE FOR EXTENSION OR MODIFICATION OF CONTRACT[1]

1. Names and addresses of parties to original contract
2. Get copy of original contract or writings that constituted offer and acceptance[2]
3. Was the original contract a common law contract or a commercial contract governed by the U.C.C.?[3] If commercial, was it a sale of goods,[4] or the creation of a security interest,[5] or both?
4. Has there been any course of dealing or is there any usage of trade that affects the original contract or its modification if it is a commercial contract governed by the U.C.C.? If so, what is it?
5. What modification of the contract is desired?[6]
6. If the contract to be modified is not a commercial contract governed by the U.C.C., what is the consideration for the extension or other modification?[7]

[1]*17 Am. Jur. 2d Contracts*, paras. 458–481; and *68 Am. Jur. 2d Secured Transactions*, para.71.
[2]U.C.C. 2-202, 205, 206, 207.
[3]U.C.C. 2-104.
[4]U.C.C. 2-201 et seq.
[5]U.C.C. 9-901 et seq.
[6]Ref. Forms VIIIJ 1.01 and J 1.02.
[7]Ref. Introduction to Section J above.

## FORM VIIIJ 1.01

### (Modification of sale contract by extension of time for delivery and definition of f.o.b. term—to be signed by buyer and seller)[1]

ABLE MANUFACTURING, INC.
500 Industrial Park
Middletown, Virginia 00000

June 4, 1982

MODIFICATION MEMORANDUM

It is agreed that the contract of sale between us dated May 4, 1982, for the delivery of 1,000 50-lb. cartons Model X cane chairs be modified as follows:

1. Paragraph 4 relating to the time of delivery is changed to read:

The goods shall be delivered to Buyer at 100 Main Street, Middletown, Virginia, no later than August 10, 1982.

2. Paragraph 7 relating to delivery is changed to read:

The goods shall be shipped by the Seller f.o.b. the Buyer at 100 Main Street, Middletown, Virginia. This term is a price term only. The risk of loss shall be on the Buyer after delivery is made by the Seller to the carrier of goods conforming to the contract.

[3]Ref. U.C.C. 2-209, 2-210, and 9-318.
[4]Ref. Form VIIIJ 1.02.
[5]Ref. Part VIIID.

The contract dated May 4, 1982, is confirmed by us in all other respects.
ACCEPTED:
DOE APPLIANCES, INC.                                ACE MANUFACTURING, INC.

By _____         By _____
      President                                           President

            [1]*17 Am. Jur. 2d Contracts*, paras. 471–481; and *68 Am. Jur. 2d Secured Transactions*, para.
71; U.C.C. 2-207, 2-209, 2-210, 2-319, 2-609, and 9-318.

---

### FORM VIIIJ 1.02

(Novation agreement among buyer, seller, and a delegate who
undertakes to perform the original contract and relieve the original
seller of his duty to supply the goods)[1]

### NOVATION AGREEMENT

    THIS AGREEMENT is entered into on June 1, 1982, among UNIQUE INDUSTRIES, INC., of 100
Highway 26 South, Middletown, Kentucky 00000 (herein called "Seller"); DOE'S CRAFTS, INC., of
000 Fifth Avenue, New York, New York 00000 (herein called "Buyer"); and COUNTRY ARTS, INC.,
of 500 Main Street, Weston, Kentucky 00000 (herein called "Delegate").

    The parties agree as follows:

    1. The Seller and Buyer executed a written contract dated May 4, 1981, for the purchase and
sale of local handmade items, a copy of which is attached hereto and made part hereof.

    2. It is agreed among the Seller, the Buyer, and the Delegate that the Delegate shall perform
all obligations of the Seller under that contract and shall be entitled to all the rights of the Seller
thereunder, except as otherwise modified herein, and that the Seller shall not be liable in any way
to the Buyer for the performance or nonperformance by the Delegate of that contract or that contract as modified herein by the Delegate and the Buyer.

    3. The Buyer and Delegate agree that the contract is herein modified only as to the duration
of the contract, which is hereby extended to May 4, 1984.

              UNIQUE INDUSTRIES, INC., SELLER

              By _____
                   (title)

              DOE'S CRAFTS, INC., Buyer

              By _____
                   (title)

              COUNTRY ARTS, INC., Delegate

              By _____
                   (title)

      [1]*17 Am. Jur. 2d Contracts*, paras. 458–464; U.C.C. 2-209, 2-210, and 9-318.

---

### SECTION K   GUARANTY AGREEMENTS[1]

    This Section includes a guaranty as part of a note or purchase contract, a sep-
arate guaranty agreement[1], and a conditional guaranty agreement.

    The Statute of Frauds[2] requires that a guaranty agreement be in writing. A
guaranty is the result of a person's guaranteeing payment or other performance of a
third person.

---

[1]*38 Am. Jur. 2d Guaranty*, paras. 12–22.
[2]See state version of Statute of Frauds.

The guaranty agreement may be written as part of the original agreement, in which case the guarantor should be a party or should sign an acceptance of the terms of the contract.

The guaranty may be drafted as a separate agreement or added to the agreement, performance of which is being guaranteed.[3]

A bond is a separate contract of guaranty.[4] A letter of credit is also a guaranty agreement.[5] Guaranty agreements are usually between a promisor (guarantor) and a creditor and debtor. The guaranty may be absolute or conditional.[6] Compare indemnity agreements in Part VIII L.[7]

## FORM VIIIK 1.00

### CLIENT QUESTIONNAIRE FOR GUARANTY AGREEMENTS[1]

1. Names and addresses of the parties to the written contract, note, mortgage, or other instruments, or oral agreement creating the debt that is to be guaranteed
2. Get a copy of that instrument, or details of the oral agreement if there is no writing
3. Is the guaranty to be absolute or conditional?
4. If conditional, what are the conditions?
5. If the client is the "guarantor," what demand or notice does he want if the debtor defaults?
6. What is the maximum amount to be guaranteed?
7. Is there a time limit on the duration of the guaranty—for performance by guarantor or for limitation of action on the guaranty?
8. If the client is the "creditor," does he want costs and attorney's fees included in the guaranteed amount?

[1]See Introduction to Section VIII K above.

## FORM VIIIK 1.01

### (Guaranty of payment of note, costs, and attorney's fees—written on the note after the maker's signature)[1]

For Value Received, the undersigned, residing at 100 Main Street, Middletown, Ohio, unconditionally guarantees payment of the within note in all its terms, and agrees that if an attorney is used from time to time to enforce any of the rights granted to the payee bank or to obtain payment of the sums as provided in the note, whether by proceedings at law or in equity, or by any other means whatever, an attorney's fee of Fifteen Percent (15%) of the amount due, including principal and interest, shall be added to the amount due and hereby guaranteed.

Dated June 1, 1982.

_____

John Doe, GUARANTOR

[1]U.C.C. 3-106; and *38 Am. Jur. 2d Guaranty*, paras. 17–18, 21.

## FORM VIIIK 1.02

### (Guaranty of payment of an account—separate agreement)

### GUARANTY AGREEMENT[1]

In consideration of the making of a contract in writing on this date between John Doe and Country Gas Company for the supply of natural gas by the Company to John Doe, and for value

---

[3]Ref. Form VIIIK 1.01.
[4]Ref. Part VIIIE and F.
[5]Ref. Form VIIIM.
[6]Ref. Form VIIIK 1.03
[7]For federal tax implications regarding choice of indemnity over guaranty or suretyship agreements, see *Am. Jur. 2d Federal Tax Guide to Legal Forms, Guaranty, Indemnity and Suretyship*, para. 2540.

received, I, Richard Rich, residing at 100 East Drive, Middletown, Pennsylvania 00000, guarantee to the Country Gas Company the payment of the account of Richard Roe from time to time for the period of three (3) years, and I waive notice of any nonpayment of the account by John Doe, and further waive failure of attempt by the Company to collect the same, except by sending monthly statements.

Dated May 1, 1982.

Attest:

_____

WITNESS

_____     _____

WITNESS                              Richard Rich, GUARANTOR

[1] *38 Am. Jur. 2d Guaranty*, paras. 17–18, 21.

## FORM VIIIK 1.03

(Conditional guaranty by stockholders to bank of loans and advances to their corporation—limited in amount and subject to demand)[1]

### GUARANTY AGREEMENT

In consideration of the granting of certain future loans and advances and other pecuniary considerations by the First Bank of Middletown, New York (herein called the "Bank"), to be made to Doe Corporation, a New York corporation having its principal place of business at 100 Main Street, Middletown, New York 00000 (herein called "Corporation",) and for value received in assurances that otherwise unsecured loans of a minimum of Twenty-five Thousand Dollars ($25,000) will be granted to the Corporation, this day, the undersigned, being all the stockholders of the Corporation, do hereby, jointly and severally and for ourselves and each of our heirs, executors, and administrators, guaranty and warrant to the First Bank of Middletown, New York, its successors, and assigns the prompt payment at maturity of each and all notes, checks, drafts, bills of exchange, trade acceptance, and other obligations in writing of every kind that are signed, drawn, accepted, or endorsed by the Corporation that the Bank now has or may later have, hold, purchase, or obtain within one (1) year from this date; provided, however, that this Guaranty does not and shall not exceed the total sum of Twenty-five Thousand Dollars ($25,000), including interest and any other charges or expenses pertaining to or arising out of such writings.

In case of default by the Corporation in the payment of any or all of the above obligations of the Corporation, we jointly and severally covenant, promise, and agree to pay the amount due the Bank, up to the total amount of Twenty-five Thousand Dollars ($25,000), upon written demand served upon us by certified U.S. mail directed to the addresses indicated under our signatures below.

This is a continuing guaranty for the period of one (1) year from the date hereof, to the extent of a total of Twenty-five Thousand Dollars ($25,000).

Dated this 1st day of March, 1982.

ATTEST:

_____

WITNESS

_____     _____

WITNESS                              John Doe, Stockholder

_____

WITNESS

_____     _____

WITNESS                              Mary Doe, Stockholder

_____

WITNESS

---

WITNESS

---

WITNESS

---

WITNESS

---

Richard Roe, Stockholder

---

Peter Poe, Stockholder

*38 Am. Jur. 2d Guaranty,* paras. 12–18, 21, and 22. For release of guarantor, see *38 Am. Jur. Guaranty,* para. 80; and for notice of default to guarantor see *38 Am. Jur. 2d Guaranty,* paras. 103–107. See Section VIIIS for other releases and satisfactions.

### FORM VIIIK 1.04

### (Guaranty of payment of price by an assignor of a purchase contract—usually printed on back of a purchase money security agreement)[1]

*Guaranty.* In consideration of the execution of the foregoing security agreement, we jointly and severally guarantee to any holder the payment promptly when due of every installment thereunder and the payment on demand of the entire unpaid balance if customer defaults in payment of any installment at its due date or in any other manner, without first requiring holder to proceed against customer. We waive notice of acceptance hereof and default thereunder and consent that holder may, without affecting our liability, release any rights against and grant extensions of time of payment to customer and other obligors.

[1]See Form VI C 1.04 for purchase money security agreement providing for assignment by Seller.

### SECTION L INDEMNITY AGREEMENTS

Indemnity agreements and alternative clauses are included in this Section.

An indemnity agreement[1] is an agreement whereby a party agrees to make good any loss or damage suffered by another party or parties. The indemnitor(s) obligates himself to pay damages for loss or injury or to hold indemnitee harmless from liability.

Casualty and liability insurance, including professional malpractice insurance, are indemnity agreements. A corporation may agree to indemnify its directors and officers for any loss or expense to them suffered as a result of the performance of their corporate duties (limited in most states by statute to losses that were not caused by their own negligence or crime).

A person whose debt or performance under a contract has been guaranteed[2] may execute an indemnity agreement to indemnify his guarantor from loss on the guaranty.

### FORM VIII L 1.00

### CLIENT QUESTIONNAIRE FOR INDEMNITY AGREEMENT[1]

1. Names and addresses of parties and their status as indemnitor(s) or indemnitee(s)
2. What is the reason (consideration) for the indemnity?
3. What type of indemnity will be given, as:
    (a) Against *loss or injury* to the person of or the property owned or controlled by the indemnitee only

---

[1]*41 Am. Jur. 2d Indemnity,* paras. 6–41.
[2]Ref. Part VIII, Section K.

    (b) Against *liability* of the indemnitee to others for loss or damage, whether or not due to indemnitee's negligence

    (c) Against both *loss* and *liability*

4. Maximum amount to be indemnified, if any[2]

5. During what time period is the indemnitee to be indemnified?

6. Is there to be a time limitation (less than statute of limitations) for bringing action on the claim for indemnity? If so, what limit?

7. Will indemnitor pay indemnitee interest before judgment on loss indemnified against? If so, what percentage?[3]

8. Will attorney's fees be included in costs for enforcing the indemnity agreement?[4]

9. *When* and *how* shall the indemnitee give the indemnitor notice of any loss and/or claim of liability? Be specific as to notice for each type[5] if both *loss* and *liability* are involved

10. Shall the indemnitor have the duty to defend claims? If so, which shall be the final judge of the acceptability of an offer to compromise or settle the claim?[6]

11. Who shall have the right to choose the attorney who will defend a claim against the indemnitee, if any?

[1]See Introduction to Part VIII L.
[2]*41 Am. Jur. 2d Indemnity,* paras. 35, 36.
[3]*41 Am. Jur. 2nd Indemnity,* para. 36.
[4]*41 Am. Jur. 2d Indemnity,* para. 36.
[5]*41 Am. Jur. 2d Indemnity,* para. 40.
[6]*41 Am. Jur. 2d Indemnity,* paras. 40, 41.

## FORM VIII L 1.01

**(Indemnity agreement to indemnify seller of building leased as a department store against liability for security deposit of tenant, including attorney's fee)**

### INDEMNITY AGREEMENT[1]

    AGEEEMENT made June 1, 1982, between Commercial Realty, Inc., a Pennsylvania corporation having its principal place of business at 537 Wood Street, Pittsburgh, Pennsylvania 00000 (herein called "Indemnitor"), and Richard Roe of 100 East Street, Pittsburgh, Pennsylvania 00000 (herein called "Indemnitee"), in consideration of the sum of One Dollar ($1) and other good and valuable consideration, is as follows:

    1. *Subject of Indemnity.* Indemnitor, purchaser of the within-described premises, undertakes to indemnify and hold Indemnitee harmless from any and all liability, loss, or damage that Indemnitee may suffer as a result of claims, demands, costs including attorney's fees, or judgments or other action against him for the return of a security deposit of Five Thousand Dollars ($5,000) heretofore paid to Indemnitee by Doe Department Store, Inc., as security for the performance of the lease dated May 1, 1979, between Indemnitee and Doe of the office building located at 100 Penn Avenue, Pittsburgh, Pennsylvania.

    2. *Consideration.* This indemnity is given as consideration for the Indemnitee's turning over to Indemnitor at the time of the execution of this Agreement the above-described Five-Thousand-Dollar ($5,000) security deposit, receipt whereof is hereby acknowledged; which sum the Indemnitor agrees to pay to Doe Department Store, Inc., as tenant under the lease, when and to the extent that it becomes returnable under the terms and conditions of the above-described lease or any renewal thereof.

    3. *Duration.* Indemnity under this Agreement shall commence on the date of this Agreement and shall continue in full force and effect until the return of the security deposit under the terms of the above-described lease or any renewal thereof.

    4. *Notice to Indemnitor.* Indemnitee agrees to notify Indemnitor in writing within thirty (30) days, by registered or certified mail at Indemnitor's address as stated above, of any claim made against Indemnitee of the obligations herein indemnified.

IN WITNESS WHEREOF, the parties have duly executed this Agreement at Pittsburgh, Pennsylvania, on the day and year first above written.

(CORPORATE SEAL)                                    COMMERCIAL REALTY, INC., Indemnitor

                                                    By _____
_____
Secretary of the Corporation                            President

                                                    _____
                                                    RICHARD ROE, Indemnitee

[1] *41 Am. Jur. 2d Indemnity*, paras. 1, 4, 6–12, 28, 29–31. Ref. Form IA 2.07(b) for an indemnity clause in a stock purchase agreement.

## FORM VIII L 1.01(a)

### (Interest on indemnity claim prior to judgment)

### ALTERNATIVE CLAUSE

*Interest prior to judgment.*[1] Indemnitor agrees to pay Indemnitee interest at the rate of Ten Percent (10%) per annum on the amount of the loss indemnified against, from the date of the loss until such amount, plus interest, is paid to Indemnitee. Further, Indemnitor agrees to pay Indemnitee interest at the same rate on any sums Indemnitee is obligated to pay, either in the enforcement of this Indemnity Agreement, including attorney's fee for enforcement, or any other payment of the loss indemnified against until such sums, including interest, are paid to the Indemnitee.

[1] *41 Am. Jur. 2d Indemnity*, para. 36.

## FORM VIII L 1.02

### (Notice from seller to carrier indemnifying carrier—to stop goods in transit when buyer is in default)

### NOTICE[1]

TO:  Super Truck Lines, Inc.
     100 Main Street
     Chicago, Illinois

The undersigned, on behalf of Ace Manufacturing, Inc., as an unpaid Seller, hereby gives you notice to withhold delivery of the goods hereinafter described, consigned by the Corporation, through you, to Doe's Appliances at 500 Industrial Drive, Middletown, Pennsylvania 00000. We hereby agree to pay all lawful charges for storage and reshipment of the goods. *This notice is sent pursuant to the right of stoppage in transit vested in us by law.*[2] The goods were shipped under Bill of Lading No. X43679 o, which is hereby surrendered to you, and consists of the following:

     50 ABC stereo systems 1981 Model 643

We hereby agree to hold harmless and indemnify you, and each of you, against all claims and demands that may be made against you by any person or persons for or in respect of the goods or the nondelivery thereof, and also against all loss, expense, costs, and attorney's fees that may be incurred by you by reason of this notice, and we further agree, so long as the goods are in our possession or under our control, to deliver the same to you, if you are compelled to deliver the same to the consignee.

Dated this 1st day of June, 1982
ACE MANUFACTURING, INC.

By _____
     (Title)

                          (Enclose bill of lading. Send copy of notice to Buyer.)

[1] U.C.C. 2-705; and see footnotes to Form VIII L 1.01.
[2] U.C.C. 2-705(3)(a).

## SECTION M     LETTERS OF CREDIT

Before using the forms in this Section, the drafter must be familiar with the legal rules and usages discussed below as they relate to the forms discussed below.

Until the Uniform Commercial Code was adopted by all the states, the principal sources of rules governing the use of letters of credit[1] in the United States or other parts of the world were the Uniform Customs and Practice for Documentary Credits and the American Foreign Trade Definitions promulgated by the United States Chamber of Commerce, as interpreted by the various courts of the states and the federal courts. Article 5 of the U.C.C. now specifically relates to and governs letters of credit. Many of the contractual guidelines of the U.C. and P. have been written into Article 5 to resolve doubts and to settle conflicts of judicial authorities.

Article 5 cannot be and is not comprehensive. Terms of the letter of credit itself, custom, and judicial precedent must be considered in drafting or interpreting a letter of credit. A copy of the latest revision of the Uniform Customs and Practice for Documentary Credits is availale from The ICC Publishing Corporation, Inc., 801 Second Avenue, Suite 1204, New York, N.Y. 10017,[2] and is a helpful checklist for preparing bank letters of credit, as United States banks have agreed to adhere to them, and under the Uniform Commercial Code they would be considered as accepted "custom and usage." That publisher also has a 1980 edition of ICC INCO TERMS[3] (printed in both French and English), which terms most organizations concerned with international trade, including banks, have approved and recommended to replace the former American Foreign Trade Definitions.

Simply defined, a letter of credit[4] is a writing by a bank or other person or company committing itself to honor drafts or other demands for payment by creditors of the person who requested and obtained the letter of credit, upon compliance with the conditions specified in the letter of credit.[5] A "traveler's check" is a form of letter of credit.

A commercial letter of credit[6] is employed to facilitate the purchase of goods, either foreign or domestic. It usually provides that drafts drawn pursuant to it shall be accompanied by certain specified documents assuring that, upon payment, the issuer will have documents of title.

A letter of credit[7] addressed to a particular person or company is said to be a "special letter of credit"[8] rather than a "general letter of credit." Any letter of credit may be revocable or irrevocable. If it is to be revocable, that should be stated in the letter, or it will be presumed to be irrevocable in some states.[9]

A letter of credit may also be a security agreement[10] and subject to Article 9 of the Uniform Commercial Code as well as to Article 5.

Standard forms[11] for issuing documentary credits pursuant to the U.C. and P

---

[1]Article 5 U.C.C.
[2]In 1981—No. 290, price $3.50.
[3]In 1981—No. 350, price $6.00.
[4]*50 Am. Jur. 2d Letters of Credit and Credit Cards*, para. 1 et seq.
[5]U.C.C. 5–103(1)(a).
[6]Ref. Forms VIIIM 1.02, 1.02(a).
[7]*50 Am. Jur. 2d Letters of Credit and Credit Cards*, para. 10.
[8]Ref. Form VIIIM 1.02 and 1.03.
[9]See Appendix for your state version of U.C.C. 5-103.
[10]*68 Am. Jur. 2d Secured Transactions*, para. 11.
[11]U.C.C. 5-102 and 5-104.

and using INCO TERMS are available in a booklet[12] printed by the ICC Publishing Corporation, Inc., supra.

The beneficiary of a letter of credit is the person (creditor of the applicant)[13] who will be paid by the issuer of the letter of credit upon compliance with its conditions. Banks usually supply their own forms for applications for and letters of credit.

## FORM VIIIM 1.00

### CLIENT QUESTIONNAIRE FOR LETTER OF CREDIT[1]

1. Names and addresses of the applicant and the issuer of the letter of credit *and* the proposed creditor(s), unless it is a general letter of credit, *as the names and addresses will appear on all documents (shipping, insurance, invoices, etc.)*
2. Is a foreign bank or company involved (as in case of an export letter of credit)?[2]
3. If foreign, is it confirmed by a prime American bank?
4. What is the amount of credit desired or the maximum allowed? Has the client included cost of goods plus profit, all transportation, forwarding fees, insurance, inspection, consular fees, and inland transportation for export goods, and/or any foreseeable miscellaneous charges? If client is uncertain about the amount, add the word "about" or "approximately" or "not exceeding."
5. For a commerical letter of credit: *correct* description of the merchandise, quantity to be shipped, and basis of delivery, as f.o.b., c.f., etc.
6. Shipping dates and time limits
7. To get the information for 4 through 6, it is best to compare the letter of credit terms with the corresponding contract of sale. Get copy of contract from client if he is the applicant, or have issuer (bank) get it from the applicant if the bank is your client
8. Is the letter of credit to be revocable or irrevocable?[3]

[1]U.C.C. 5-102.
[2]Ref. Introduction to Part VIIIM; and United States Chamber of Commerce brochures referred to in the Introduction footnotes.
[3]U.C.C. 5-103.

## FORM VIIIM 1.01

### (Application by letter to bank for an irrevocable letter of credit)[1]

### ABLE MANUFACTURING CORPORATION

June 1, 1982

First National Bank of Pittsburgh
100 Smithfield Street
Pittsburgh, Pa. 00000

Gentlemen:

Please issue by U.S. mail your irrevocable commercial letter of credit on the conditions below, for which we will duly sign your standard form of letter of credit agreement:

1. In favor of Coe Chemical Corporation, 100 Main Street, Middletown, Delaware 00000.
2. Available by drafts First National Bank of Pittsburgh.
3. For account of Able Manufacturing Corporation.
4. For not exceeding One Hundred Thousand Dollars ($100,000).
5. Drawn at sight.
6. Against shipment of One Thousand (1,000) tons of A grade X18 chemical compound powder.
7. Shipment from Middletown, Delaware, to our plant at 100 Highway 14 South, Middletown, Pennsylvania, by rail.

[12]In 1981—No. 323, price $7.50.
[13]Ref. Form VIIIM 1.01.

8. Bill of lading to be dated not later than September 1, 1982 (add all other conditions of the purchase agreement, as: insurance forwarding agent, or other)
9. Documents to accompany the drafts shall be: (specify and list documents, as: invoice in triplicate, bill of lading, weight certificates, government certificates, etc.).
10. Drafts are to be drawn prior to November 1, 1982. We appreciate your prompt attention to this matter.

Cordially, _____

JOHN DOE, President

  [1]*50 Am. Jur. 2d Letters of Credit and Credit Cards*, para. 10; and *68 Am. Jur. 2d Secured Transactions*, para. 11.

### FORM VIIIM 1.02

#### (Commercial letter of credit—special)[1]

FIRST NATIONAL BANK OF PITTSBURGH
100 Smithfield Street
Pittsburgh, Pennsylvania 00000

June 10, 1982

Coe Chemical Corporation
100 Main Street
Middletown, Delaware 00000

Our Credit No. 12345

Gentlemen:

In accordance with instructions received from Able Manufacturing Corporation of this city, we issue an irrevocable credit in your favor for account of Able in an amount not to exceed One Hundred Thousand Dollars ($100,000), covering the shipment of One Thousand (1,000) tons of X18 chemical compound powder to Able Manufacturing Corporation at their plant at 100 Highway 14 South, Middletown, Pennsylvania, by rail on the following conditions:
  (repeat the conditions stated by applicant for the letter of credit)
Drafts under this credit are to be drawn at sight on this bank and are to be accompanied under one cover by the following documents:
  Commericial invoice in triplicate
  Weight certificate
  (government safety certificate, if required)
  Bill of lading (or other order carrying with it control of the contents of the shipment)
This is an irrevocable credit and will remain in force to and including November 1, 1982, subject to the conditions contained herein.
When drawing drafts under this credit, drafts shall be clearly marked as follows:
  "Drawn under authorization of the First National Bank of Pittsburgh Credit No. 12345"[2]
Very truly yours,

Richard Roe
(title)

  [1]*50 Am. Jur. 2d Letters of Credit and Credit Cards*, paras. 3–10, 12–17; and U.C.C. 5-102 and 5-104.
  [2]*50 Am. Jur. 2d Letters of Credit and Credit Cards*, para. 21.

### FORM VIIIM 1.02(a)

#### (When applicable)

#### ALTERNATIVE CLAUSE

*Confirmation.* This credit is to be confirmed by a correspondent bank (name it).

## FORM VIIIM 1.03

(Irrevocable letter of credit to return condominium sales deposits)[1]

### IRREVOCABLE LETTER OF CREDIT

DATE: September 1, 1982
TO: Peter Roe, Esq. ("Escrow Agent"), and
  DIVISION OF FLORIDA LAND SALES AND CONDOMINIUMS ("Division")
RE: Letter of Credit #*J1234*
Dear Ladies and Gentlemen:
We hereby open our clean irrevocable letter of credit for the purpose of securing sales deposits pursuant to the foregoing Escrow Agreement to which this letter of credit is attached. The letter is in your favor in the amount of United States *Five Hundred Thousand Dollars ($500,000)*, effective as of this date and expiring at our office at the close of business on: August 31, 1984.

Funds under this Letter of Credit are available to the Division or Escrow Agent, as payee, in an aggregate amount not to exceed the amount stated above, upon presentation to us of a signed statement by the Division or Escrow Agent to the effect that the sums required are due as part of the obligations of Happy Heath Developers, Inc., under any of its contracts with purchasers of condominium parcels at Happy Heath Acres, Highway 00, West Middletown, Florida, pursuant to that certain Escrow Agreement attached hereto and made a part hereof. Funds under this Letter Of Credit are available to the Division as payee, within thirty (30) days of this Letter's expiration, absent renewal or extension of this Letter, or issuance of a new letter in the place of this Letter, upon representation of a signed statement calling the funds by the Division. This Letter of Credit sets forth in full terms our undertaking, and such undertaking shall not in any way be modified, amended, or amplified except by written agreement among all parties hereto. This Letter of Credit is given to assure condominium sales deposits of $500,000 that would otherwise be deposited in escrow in accordance with Section 718.202 (1), F.S.

If we receive your sight draft and statement as mentioned above at our office at Middletown, Florida, on or prior to the expiration date hereof, we will give notice to and honor such draft within fifteen (15) days from receipt thereof. All drafts drawn under this Letter of Credit must be marked: "Drawn under _____

_____, Letter of Credit No. 1234 dated
September 1, 1982."
Sincerely,
FIRST BANK OF MIDDLETOWN
By: _____      ATTEST _____
    President                                   Secretary

[1]Ref. Form VIIF 1.01 and VIIF 1.04 for purchase agreement for condominium units.

## SECTION N      LOANS (SECURED)

The forms in this Section are used where the collateral is delivered to the lender. Chapter VI F contains a sample security agreement and note for the purchase price of consumer goods.[1] That Section also has a sample security agreement where business personal property is the security for a loan of operating capital.[2] In those cases, the goods are in the possession of the debtor, and the security interest must be "perfected"[3] by filing in the appropriate public records, unless the collateral is exempt from filing. See also Promissory Notes in Chapter VIP.

Where collateral for a second loan is a negotiable instrument(s), as stock, bonds, etc., as distinguished from a document (of title), the security interest in those in-

[1]Ref. Form IVF 1.01.
[2]Ref. Form IVF 1.02.
[3]U.C.C. 9-303.

struments can be perfected only through possession,[4] except as provided under U.C.C. 9-304 (4) and (5). The possession may be by the secured party or by an escrow agent for the secured party. Form VIIIN 1.01 is an example of the latter form. It is followed by a basic form for a collateral note pledging securities where the lender will take possession of the collateral under the terms of the note itself.[5]

Form VIIIN 1.02 is a supplemental form for a corporate resolution to authorize a pledge of its property to secure a loan.

Promissory note forms appear in Part VIII, Section P as well as supplements to other contracts in this book. Check the bank Index for particular note forms if the appropriate form is not included in this Section.

## FORM VIIIN 1.00

### CLIENT QUESTIONNAIRE FOR SECURED LOAN BY PLEDGE[1]

1. Names and addresses of borrower and lender
2. Amount of the loan
3. What are the terms to be included in the note evidencing the loan? See Client Questionnaire Form VIP 1.00.
4. Nature of the collateral: tangible personal property; documents of title to personal property, as motor vehicle title or warehouse receipt; or negotiable instruments, as stocks or bonds?
5. Description of the collateral
    (a) Get brand name, model, manufacturer's identification serial numbers of personal property that does not require title documents
    (b) Get the document itself where the collateral is a document of title instead of the personal property itself
    (c) Get name of issuer, certificate number, number and type of shares, and/or face amount of bond if the collateral is securities
6. Is possession of the collateral to be delivered to the lender[2] or to an agent[3] for the lender?
7. If an escrow agent is to hold the collateral, get the agent's name and address and his agreement to act as the escrow,[4] and the terms of the escrow[6]
8. What use can debtor make of tangible personal property, and *where* must it be kept?
9. If collateral is document of title or is securities, get necessary blank assignment(s) from debtor
10. Who is to get the income or increase from collateral that is being pledged?
11. Can secured party demand additional collateral? If so, under what conditions?

> [1]See footnotes to Form VIIIN 1.01, and compare security interest in personal property Part VI Section F.
> [2]Ref. Form VIIIN 1.01(a).
> [3]U.C.C. 9-304 and 9-305.
> [4]Ref. Form VIIIN 1.01.
> [5]Chapter VIII I for escrow generally.

## FORM VIIIN 1.01

### (Pledge in escrow of stock and bonds to secure a business loan to a corporation from an individual, including indemnification of escrow agent)

### COLLATERAL PLEDGE AGREEMENT[1]

THIS AGREEMENT is made among John Doe of 100 Main Street, Middletown, Pennsylvania 00000 (herein called "Secured Party"); Able Manufacturing, Inc., a Pennsylvania corporation hav-

---

[4]U.C.C. 9-305.
[5]Ref. Form VIN 1.01(a).

ing its principal place of business at 100 East Street, Pittsburgh, Pennsylvania 00000 (herein called "Debtor"); and Poe & Coe, Attorneys-at-law, of Suite 500, Big Building, Pittsburgh, Pennsylvania 00000 (herein called "Escrow Agent"); in consideration of the sum of One Dollar ($1) and the mutual covenants and agreements made as follows:

1. *Debt.* Debtor is indebted to the Secured Party in accordance with the terms of a promissory note dated June 1, 1982, in the amount of Ten Thousand Dollars ($10,000) payable in ninety (90) days.

2. *Description of collateral.* Simultaneously with the execution of that note and this Pledge Agreement, the Debtor delivers 100 shares of the common capital stock of Super Corporation represented by Certificate No. 3 for 50 shares and Certificate No. 5 for 50 shares, and a $5,000 R.T. Company, Inc., first mortgage 7% serial bond No. B-4963, together with separate assignments in blank[2] to secure the payment of that note.

3. *Appointment of Escrow Agent.* The Debtor and the Secured Party do hereby appoint the Escrow Agent to accept possession of that pledged property and to hold it for the purposes and under the conditions set forth herein.

4. *Acceptance by Escrow Agent.* The Escrow Agent hereby acknowledges receipt of that pledged property, which shall be held, kept, and preserved by it in its possession until the payment in full of the promissory note; or until the Debtor defaults in the payment of the note or in any of the Debtor's undertakings thereunder.

5. *Return of property on performance.* When the note is paid in full according to its terms, the Escrow Agent shall return the pledged property and the written assignments to the Debtor, upon the written demand of the Debtor and the Secured Party and the receipt of the Debtor.

6. *Return of property on nonperformance.* If the Debtor defaults in the payment of the note or in any of the Debtor's undertakings thereunder, the Escrow Agent shall, upon written demand and receipt by Secured Party, deliver the pledged property and the written assignments to the Secured Party to be dealt with by the Secured Party in accordance with the terms of the promissory note.

7. *Dividends on stock.* So long as the Debtor is not in default in the payment of the note or in any of the Debtor's undertakings thereunder, the Debtor shall have the right to receive all ordinary dividends, excepting any liquidating dividend, on the pledged stock and shall have the right to vote the shares of stock at all meetings of the corporation, except that he shall not vote the shares of stock for changing the present authorized capital stock of the corporation or for consolidation, merger, liquidation, or dissolution of the corporation without the prior written consent of the Secured Party.

8. *Interest on bond.* So long as the Debtor is not in default in the payment of the note or in any of the Debtor's undertakings thereunder, the interest on the pledged bond shall be paid to Debtor at his above address or at such other address as it may designate to the Escrow Agent in writing. Any payment of principal on the bond shall be paid by the Escrow Agent to the Secured Party, and that payment shall be applied by the Secured Party to reduce the principal sum secured by the promissory note.

9. *Indeminification of Escrow Agent.* The Debtor and the Secured Party do hereby release the Escrow Agent from, and agree to jointly and severally indemnify it against, any liability whatsoever arising out of this Agreement.

Dated this 1st day of June, 1982.

ABLE MANUFACTURING, INC.,
Debtor

_____     By _____
John Doe, SECURED PARTY                    President
            Poe & Coe, Attorneys-at-law

            By _____
                Peter Poe, Partner

[1]U.C.C. 9-304(4) and (5). See also U.C.C. 305, 306, 309, and 315. For exemptions from U.C.C., see 9-104. See also *10 Am. Jur. 2d Banks,* paras. 683 and 686; *68 Am. Jur. 2d Secured Transactions,* paras. 48–81; and *11 Am. Jur. 2d Bills and Notes,* paras. 294–296. Ref. Form VIF 1.02 for loan secured by business personal property as collateral.

[2] See Form IA 2.18 and 2.18(a).

## FORM VIIIN 1.01(a)

(Collateral note pledging securities to lender for a loan, interest
deducted in advance)

## ALTERNATIVE FORM

## PROMISSORY COLLATERAL NOTE[1]

$10,000                                                                            June 1, 1982

Ninety (90) days after date, for value received, the undersigned promises to pay to John Doe
or his order at 100 Main Street, Middletown, Pennsylvania 00000, the sum of Ten Thousand Dollars ($10,000) and interest at the rate of Twelve Percent (12%) per annum for such further time
as the principal sum or any part shall remain unpaid, we having deposited with the payee of this
obligation as collateral security: 100 shares of the common capital stock of Super Corporation represented by Certificate No. 3 for 50 shares and Certificate No. 5 for 50 shares, and a $5,000 R.T.
Company, Inc. first mortgage 7% serial bond No. B-4968, with authority in the holder hereof to
sell the same without notice, at either public or private sale, or otherwise, at the option of the
holder or holders hereof, in the event of nonperformance of this promise, the undersigned to receive any balance of the net proceeds of sale remaining, after paying all sums due from us to the
holder or holders hereof, who may purchase all or part of the collateral at the sale.

ABLE MANUFACTURING, INC.

By _____

Richard Roe, President of the Corporation

(Have payee give maker a written receipt for the collateral, including certificate numbers, at the
time the maker signs the note and delivers the collateral.)

[1]Compare Form VIF 1.02 for loan secured by business personal property instead of
securities.

## FORM VIIIN 1.02

(Resolution by corporation shareholders authorizing general
borrowing on authority of directors, and resolution by directors
authorizing a loan secured by a pledge)

(a) STOCKHOLDERS GENERAL AUTHORIZATION TO BOARD TO BORROW.[1] RESOLVED, that
the Board of Directors of this Corporation is hereby authorized to borrow from time to time such
sums of money as it may deem advisable, upon the notes of this corporation, and for that purpose
to pledge or assign any or all bills and accounts receivable or any other available assets of the
Corporation to secure such notes.

(b) DIRECTORS AUTHORIZATION OF OFFICERS TO BORROW. RESOLVED, that the officers of
this Corporation are hereby authorized and directed, for the purposes of the Corporation, to borrow
a sum, not exceed in the aggregate Ten Thousand Dollars ($10,000) for such time and upon such
terms as they may deem proper, and for that purpose to pledge and assign as security for the
payment thereof the whole or any part of this Corporation's holdings of the capital stock of Super
Corporation and the bonds of R.T. Company, Inc., and to do and perform all other things and acts
necessary and proper to carry out the provisions of this Resolution.

(These resolutions are typed in the minutes of the respective meetings. For alternative procedure, see Form VIN 1.02[a].)

[1]For use with Form VIIIN 1.01. Compare alternative Form VIIIN 1.02(a).

**FORM VIIIN 1.02(a)**

(Closed corporation action in lieu of shareholders' *and* directors'
meetings to authorize a loan secured by a pledge, including
evidence of corporate authority to execute note and pledge
agreement)[1]

**ALTERNATIVE FORM**

WRITTEN ACTION BY STOCKHOLDERS AND DIRECTORS
OF
ABLE MANUFACTURING, INC.

The undersigned, being all the stockholders and directors of ABLE MANUFACTURING INC., a Pennsylvania corporation, hereby take the following action:

1. We hereby approve a ninety (90)-day loan to this Corporation by John Doe of 100 Main Street, Middletown, Pennsylvania 00000, in the amount of Ten Thousand Dollars ($10,000) and hereby authorize the execution of a note of this Corporation and the pledge of One Hundred (100) shares of stock in Super Corporation owned by this Corporation, together with the pledge of a $5,000 R.T. Company, Inc., first mortgage 7% Serial Bond No. 4963 to secure payment of the note on such further terms and conditions and in such manner as is approved by the officers of the Corporation.

2. Richard Roe is the President of this Corporation.

3. Mary Roe is the Secretary of the Corporation.

Dated: November 17, 1982

*SHAREHOLDERS*                                   *DIRECTORS*

_____         _____

_____         _____

_____         _____

[1]For use with Form VIIIN 1.01. Compare alternative Form VIIIN 1.02

## SECTION O     LOANS (UNSECURED)

The forms in this Section are for use where there is no collateral for a loan.

An unsecured loan agreement is merely a contract for the repayment of money. For secured loans, see Chapter VIII N and the security interest section, Chapter VI F. Compare promissory notes in Chapter VIII P.

In most states, the borrowers cannot waive their statutory exemptions as judgment debtors, so a waiver of such exemptions in the agreement would be unenforceable. A usurious agreement may be void in its entirety or void as to the excess interest, depending on the state.

Although the *Truth in Lending Act,* 15 U.S.C.A. 1601–1665 and its Regulation Z, 12 C.F.R. 226 regulate *consumer* loans and do not apply to business and commercial loans, the Uniform Commercial Code makes an "unconscionable" contract voidable.[1] For that reason, the provisions and disclosures required for consumer loans should not be completely ignored in drafting a business loan agreement or note.[2]

_____

[1]U.C.C. 2-302.

[2]See Appendixes I, IX, X, and XI for Consumer Credit Protection Laws.

Small loan businesses and their loan contracts, and pawnbrokers are governed by state statutes.[3]

## FORM VIIIO 1.00

### CLIENT QUESTIONNAIRE FOR UNSECURED LOAN

1. Name and address of lender and borrower
2. Purpose of the loan. Is the loan a consumer loan?[1]
3. Amount of the loan
4. Rate of interest
5. Manner and time of repayment
6. Are there any penalties as for late charges or prepayment?
7. Will loan balance be accelerated on default? If so, what notice of default and acceleration shall be required?
8. Is the note assignable? If not, by whom and what consents, if any, shall be required to assign rights under the agreement?
9. Is a promissory note evidencing the loan to be prepared?[2]
10. If either party is a corporation, get evidence of authorization to make or take the loan.

[1]15 U.S.C.A. 1601 et seq.; Regulation Z, 12 C.F.R. 226, and Regulation B, 12 C.F.R. 202.
See also Appendix I for other Consumer Credit Protection Law.
[2]Ref. Chapter VIIIP, and compare Part VIIIN.

## FORM VIIIO 1.01

### (Unsecured installment loan agreement between a close corporation and its stockholders, and individual lender for money to operate the corporation business)

### LOAN AGREEMENT[1]

THIS AGREEMENT made June 1, 1982, between John Doe of 100 Main Street, Middletown, Pennsylvania 00000 (herein called "Lender"), and Roe Industries, Inc., a Pennsylvania corporation having its principal place of business at 100 East Avenue, Middletown, Pennsylvania 00000, and Peter Poe and Mary Poe of 100 West Street, Middletown, Pennsylvania 00000 (herein collectively called the "Borrowers"), is as follows:

1. *Consideration.* In consideration of the promises and covenants contained herein, the Lender agrees to loan to the Borrowers, jointly and severally, the sum of Ten Thousand Dollars ($10,000) by delivering a check drawn to the joint order of the Borrowers at the time of the execution of this Agreement, the receipt whereof is hereby acknowledged by the Borrowers.

2. *Repayment of loan.* The Borrowers, jointly and severally, agree to repay the loan to the Lender at the above address of the Lender or at any other address designated in writing by the Lender as follows:

(a) *Monthly installments.* On July 1, 1982, the sum of Two Hundred Fifty Dollars ($250) on account of principal shall be paid, and a like amount shall be paid monthly from that date, on or before the 5th day of each month, until the balance of the loan is paid. Interest shall be paid as provided in (c) below.

(b) *Prepayment.* If payments on principal and interest are current, the Borrowers may pay, on account of the unpaid principal of the loan, on any day fixed for payment of any installment of principal, an additional amount, not less than Five Hundred Dollars ($500), as they may elect, without penalty of any nature.

(c) *Interest.* In addition to the above payments on principal, the Borrowers shall pay interest on the unpaid balance of principal monthly, on or before the 5th day of each month, beginning July 1, 1982, at the ANNUAL PERCENTAGE RATE of Twelve Percent (12%) per annum, and continuing until the full sum of the Ten-Thousand-Dollar ($10,000) principal has been paid, the total FINANCE CHARGE for this loan being the total of the interest to be paid hereunder.

---

[3]*54 Am. Jur. 2d Moneylenders and Pawnbrokers*, paras. 7–17. See Form VIIIB 1.03 for Affidavit of Lost Pawn Ticket.

3. *Acceleration.* In the event of any default in the payment of any installment of principal or interest hereunder, the Lender may give to the Borrowers written notice of such default and demand that it be cured within (10) days of the mailing of the notice. If the default is not cured within (10) days, the entire sum remaining unpaid, together with interest thereon from the date of default, shall become immediately due and payable without further notice.

4. *Notice.* All notice given by the Lender to the Borrowers shall be given by registered or certified mail addressed to the corporation borrower and to the individual borrowers at the above-stated addresses, or to such other addresses as each or any of them may, respectively, designate in writing at least five (5) days before the mailing of such notice.

5. *Assignability.* Neither this Agreement nor any rights under it may be assigned, pledged, hypothecated, or otherwise aliened by either of the parties, without the written consent of all other parties to this Agreement.

6. *Joint and several liability.* The liability of the Borrowers shall be both joint and several.

7. *Benefit.* This Agreement shall be binding upon and inure to the benefit of the parties, their respective heirs, executors, administrators, and assigns.

Executed and delivered in Middletown, Pennsylvania, this June 1, 1982.
ATTEST:

_____

WITNESS

_____

Witness

(CORPORATE SEAL)

_____

Secretary of the Corporation

_____

Witness

_____

Witness

_____

Witness

_____

Witness

_____

John Doe, LENDER

ROE INDUSTRIES, INC., Borrower

By _____

_____

Peter Poe, BORROWER

_____

Mary Poe, BORROWER

[1]Ref. footnotes to Form VIIIN 1.01. For drafting a form to be printed for consumer loan note, see Appendix I Consumer Credit Protection Laws.

## SECTION P    NOTES (PROMISSORY)

In addition to the note forms in this Section, check the book Index for notes particularly appropriate to specific contracts, which notes appear as supplemental forms in other parts of the book.

A negotiable promissory note (U.C.C. "note")[1] is an unconditional promise in writing made by one person to another engaging to pay, on demand or at a fixed or determinable future time, a sum certain in money to order or to bearer. A note is distinguishable from a draft or check (bills of exchange) in that the note is a promise or undertaking by the maker himself, while a draft or check is an order to another.[2]

The U.C.C. Article 3[3] governing Commercial Paper must be interpreted in con-

_____

[1]U.C.C. 3-104 through 3-119.
[2]U.C.C. 3-104; *11 Am. Jur. 2d Bills and Notes,* paras. 21, 22, 42, 48, 54–58, 70–72.
[3]See Appendix VI for state citations to the U.C.C.

junction with the general Article 1 of the Code in drafting, negotiating, or enforcing any promissory note.

If the note is secured, Article 9 of the U.C.C. Secured Transactions must also be considered.

If the note is for a consumer loan, federal credit protection laws will apply.[4] State usury laws will also affect the enforceability of a promissory note.[5] A cognovit note, one containing a confession of judgment clause, is illegal or unenforceable in some states, but its legal inclusion does not affect the negotiability of the note.[6] Merely adding the word "SEAL" or the abbreviation "L.S." to a signature line in a note does not make it a sealed instrument, if the instrument itself does not contain an acknowledgment in its body that it is a sealed instrument.[7]

The Uniform Commercial Code provides certain construction rules[8] in addition to or in lieu of general contract rules that otherwise do apply.

See Form VIIIP 1.04 for forms for endorsements of notes.

## FORM VIIIP 1.00

### CLIENT QUESTIONNAIRE FOR PROMISSORY NOTE[1]

1. Names and addresses of maker(s) and payee(s). If there is more than one maker, are they jointly or jointly and severally liable? Is it a retail consumer note?[2]
2. Amount of note (are any charges to be added to the amount of the actual loan, as: credit investigation, filing fees, etc.?)
3. Amount of monthly or other periodic payments, if it is to be an installment note
4. Date of maturity (fixed or determinable future time), giving date of first payment and times for making future payment on an installment note
5. Address at which note is to be paid
6. Rate of interest (what is the consideration for the note, if it is non–interest bearing, is there a concern about IRS tax considerations?)
7. Is there to be a difference in times when principal and interest are to be paid? Will you prepare or obtain an amortization statement?
8. Are there to be late-charge payments, increased interest in case of default, attorney's fees in case of default, or other charges?
9. Will payment of the note be accelerated on default? What notice of default is required?
10. Will there be a prepayment penalty or prepayment conditions as to amounts or times of prepayment, or other?
11. Is the maker a corporation? If so, get evidence of authority for the person signing to bind the corporation, and indicate the signer's title as well as the exact corporate name to be shown above his signature line
12. Is there a mortgage[3] or other security agreement[4] to be prepared in conjunction with the note? If so, get that information

[1]U.C.C. 3-104 through 3-119; *11 Am. Jur. 2d Bills and Notes*, paras. 21, 22, 42, 48, 54–58, 70–72; and Introduction to Part VIIIP.
[2]See Appendix I for Consumer Credit Protection Laws.
[3]Ref. Part VD.
[4]Ref. Part IVF.

---

[4]Ref. Appendixes I, IX, X, and XI for Consumer Credit Protection laws.
[5]Ref. Introduction to Part VIII.
[6]U.C.C. 3-112.
[7]U.C.C. 3-113.
[8]U.C.C. 3-118.

## FORM VIIIP 1.01

### (Unsecured promissory note made by an individual to pay for professional or business services—one payment)

#### NOTE

$1,000
Middletown, Florida
June 1, 1982

Ninety (90) days after date, FOR VALUE RECEIVED, I promise to pay to Doe & Roe, P.A., at 100 Main Street, Middletown, Florida, the sum of One Thousand Dollars ($1,000), with no interest to that due date, but with interest of Twelve percent (12%) per annum thereafter until paid, if the principal of this Note is not paid on or before that due date.

In the event suit is commenced to enforce payment of this Note or any part hereof, I agree to pay such attorney's fees as the court in such action may adjudge reasonable.

_____
Peter Poe

[1]*11 Am. Jur. 2d Bills and Notes,* para. 21.

## FORM VIIIP 1.02

### (Unsecured promissory note made by a corporation to another corporation to pay for professional or business services rendered to the maker—one payment)

#### NOTE[1]

$2,000
Middletown, Florida
June 1, 1982

Six (6) months after date, FOR VALUE RECEIVED, Jones Construction Corporation, a Florida corporation having its principal place of business at 100 Highway 00 West, Middletown, Florida 00000, promises to pay to Concrete Supply, Inc., at P.O. Box 55, Eastown, Florida 00000, the sum of Two Thousand Dollars ($2,000), with interest from this date at the rate of Twelve Percent (12%) per annum thereafter.

In the event that suit is commenced to enforce payment of this Note or any part hereof, we agree to pay such attorney's fees as the court in such action may adjudge reasonable.

The Jones Construction Corporation has caused this Note to be executed on its behalf by its undersigned duly authorized officers.

JONES CONSTRUCTION CORPORATION

By _____
President of the Corporation

(CORPORATE SEAL)
optional

By _____
Secretary of the Corporation

[1]*11 Am. Jur. 2d Bills and Notes,* paras. 569–584. See also paras. 530–549; and U.C.C. 3-415(5). Compare Form VIIIO 1.01.

## FORM VIIIP 1.02(a)

### (Confession of judgment clause where a cognovit note is allowed by state law)[1]

#### ALTERNATIVE CLAUSE

*Confession of judgment on default.* The undersigned hereby authorizes any attorney-at-law to appear in any court of record in the Commonwealth of Pennsylvania, or any other state in the United States, on default in the payment of any installment due on the above obligation, and waives the issuance and service of process, and confess a judgment against the undersigned in favor of the holder hereof for the amount of the note, together with the costs of suit and attorneys' fees of Fifteen Percent (15%), and to release all errors and waive all right of appeal.

[1]U.C.C. 3-112; *11 Am. Jur. 2nd Bills and Notes,* para. 199. Also check state statute for validity and enforceability of confession of judgment clause.

## FORM VIIIP 1.02(b)

### (Waiver of defense of statute of limitations)[1]

### ALTERNATIVE CLAUSE

It is expressly agreed that suit may be maintained to enforce collection of any and all payments due on this Note at any time within five (5) years after maturity of this Note. The right to plead any and all statutes of limitations as a defense to any demand under this note during that time period is hereby waived.

[1]*51 Am. Jur. 2d Limitations of Actions,* paras. 426–430. Check your state statute on limitations of actions.

## FORM VIIIP 1.03

### (Secured promissory installment note made by a corporation to another corporation to pay for business equipment purchased from the other—payable in installments)

### INSTALLMENT NOTE[1]

$12,000

Middletown, Florida
June 1, 1982

FOR VALUE RECEIVED, Jones Construction Corporation, a Florida corporation, promises to pay to Doe Equipment, Inc., a Georgia corporation, at 100 Peach Street, Atlanta, Georgia, the sum of Twelve Thousand Dollars ($12,000), with interest thereon at the rate of Ten Percent (10%) per year from date hereof, in installments as follows: Eleven Hundred Dollars ($1,100) on July 1, 1982, and the balance of Twelve Thousand One Hundred Dollars ($12,100) in equal monthly installments of Eleven Hundred Dollars ($1,100) each on or before the 5th day of each month thereafter, being a TOTAL PAYMENT of Thirteen Thousand Two Hundred Dollars ($13,200), including interest at the ANNUAL PERCENTAGE RATE of Ten Percent (10%).

In the event of default in the payment of any of the installments provided herein, time being of the essence, the holder of this Note may, at its option, without notice or demand, declare the entire unpaid balance of principal and interest thereon due and payable immediately.

In the event that suit is commenced to enforce payment of this Note or any part hereof, we agree to pay such attorney's fees as the court in such action may adjudge reasonable.

THIS NOTE IS SECURED by a purchase money security agreement[2] executed simultaneously herewith by the undersigned, as debtor, and Doe Equipment, Inc., as secured party, which security provisions are incorporated herein by reference.

The Jones Construction Corporation has caused this note to be executed on its behalf by its undersigned duly authorized officers.

JONES CONSTRUCTION CORPORATION

(CORPORATE SEAL)
(optional)

By _____
President of the Corporation

By _____
Secretary of the Corporation

[1]U.C.C. 3-104.
[2]U.C.C. 3-105(1)(e). Ref. Form VIIIP 1.03(a); *11 Am. Jur. 2d Bills and Notes,* para. 202. Compare Form VIIIO 1.01.

## FORM VIIIP 1.03(a)

### (Where business loan note is made payable to a bank, and bank is to have a continuing lien on maker's money and securities that are in the bank's possession)

### ALTERNATIVE CLAUSE

*Continuing lien.*[1] In addition to any other collateral security, the Bank is hereby given a continuing lien for the amount of the obligations evidenced by this Note on any and all money, securities, and other property of the undersigned and the proceeds thereof, now or hereafter actually or constructively held or received by, or in transit in any manner, to the Bank, its correspondents, or its agents, from or for the undersigned, whether for safekeeping, custody, pledge, transmission, collection, or otherwise, or coming into the Bank's possession in any way, and also on any and all deposits, general or special, and credits of the undersigned with the Bank, and any and all claims of the undersigned against the Bank existing at any time. The Bank shall have the right at any time, without prior notice, to withhold payment of any general or special deposits or credits of the undersigned with or claims of the undersigned against the Bank and to apply them against any obligations of the undersigned to the Bank, although contingent or unmatured.

[1]*10 Am. Jur. 2d Banks,* paras. 660 et seq.

## FORM VIIIP 1.03(b)

### (Discount for early payment in *full*)[2]

### ALTERNATIVE CLAUSE

*Allocation of payments.* All payments shall be first applied to accrued interest and then to principal. A discount of Two Percent (2%) of the face amount of this Note shall be allowed if this Note is paid in full within sixty (60) days from date of this Note.

[2]*11 Am. Jur. 2d Bills and Notes,* para. 162.

## FORM VIIIP 1.04

### (Endorsements of notes payable to John Doe to be written on reverse side of note for negotiation)[1]

Blank endorsement:[2]
John Doe

Qualified endorsement:[3]
Pay to Doe Manufacturing, Inc., without recourse
John Doe

Restrictive endorsement:[4]
Pay to Doe Manufacturing, Inc., for collection
John Doe

Special endorsement:[5]
Pay to the order of Doe Manufacturing, Inc.
John Doe

Successive endorsements:[6]
Pay to the order of Peter Poe
John Doe
Pay to the order of ABC CORPORATION
Peter Poe

[1]See Appendix VI for state citations, which may vary from U.C.C.
[2]U.C.C. 3-204, 3-402, 3-414, and 3-417.
[3]U.C.C. 3-402, 3-413, 3-414, and 3-417.
[4]U.C.C. 3-205, 3-206, 3-402, 3-414, and 3-417.
[5]U.C.C. 3-204, 3-402, 3-414, and 3-417.
[6]U.C.C. 3-201, 3-302, 3-402, 3-414, and 3-417.

## SECTION Q     POWER OF ATTORNEY

A power of attorney creates an agent or agents to act for the principal(s) under the terms of the power of attorney. If the power is given to two or more persons, the law presumes that they are to act jointly unless the instrument clearly shows the intent that they may act severally.[1]

A power of attorney may be general[2] or special.[3] A general power of attorney should not be lightly given. Some states provide for a "durable family power of attorney."[4]

If a power of attorney is to be recorded in the public records, it must be acknowledged.[5] A power of attorney to deal with real estate should be recorded. It must be written. A power of attorney to perform services or to deal with personal property need not be recorded, but it *may* be recorded if acknowledged.

Various government agencies require a power of attorney to be filed with the agency if a person is acting for a principal in dealing with the agency.[6]

If a power of attorney has been recorded or is recordable, any revocation[7] or modification by the principal should also be recorded. A renunciation or termination *by the attorney-in-fact* to the principal, whether recorded or recordable, can be accomplished by a *notice to the principal*[8] without recording the same.

---

[1]*3 Am. Jur. 2d Agency,* para. 196.
[2]*3 Am. Jur. 2d Agency,* para. 31; and ref. Forms 1.01, 1.01(a) and 1.01(b).
[3]Ref. Forms VIIIQ 1.02, 1.03.
[4]See your state statute. The Uniform Durable Power of Attorney Act is contained in the Uniform Probate Code 1979 amendment.
[5]Ref. Part VIII A.
[6]Ref. Form VIIIQ 1.03.
[7]Ref. Form VIIIQ 1.05.
[8]Ref. Form VIIIQ 1.04.

## FORM VIIIQ 1.00

## CLIENT QUESTIONNAIRE FOR POWER OF ATTORNEY

1. Names and addresses of both the principal(s) and the agent(s)
2. Is there more than one agent? If so, may the agents act separately?
3. Is the power of attorney to be general[1] or special[2]?
4. If special, what is the specific purpose of the power of attorney? What ancillary powers should be included?
5. Does the power involve dealing with real estate? If so, it should be recorded in the public records, and the principal must acknowledge it for recording.
6. Does the power involve dealing with a government agency on behalf of the principal as an accountant, a lawyer, an officer of a corporation? If so, the agency may have its own form that should be completed from the information obtained from the client
7. If a corporation is giving the power of attorney, get evidence of corporate authority for the appointment
8. If client is the agent and wants to renounce[3] the power of attorney, the principal should be notified, and the renunciation should be recorded if the power of attorney was recordable or recorded (consider any contract that requires performance)
9. If client is the principal and wants to revoke, the agent should be notified (consider whether the power of attorney is revocable, etc.), and the revocation should be recorded if the power of attorney was recordable or recorded[4]

[1]*3 Am. Jur. 2d Agency,* para. 20.
[2]*3 Am. Jur. 2d Agency,* paras. 26, 27, 93–142.
[3]Ref. Form VIQ 1.04.
[4]Ref. Form VIQ 1.05.

## FORM VIIIQ 1.01

### (General power of attorney to one person for a limited time, with acknowledgment for recording)[1]

### POWER OF ATTORNEY

KNOW ALL MEN BY THESE PRESENTS, that I, John Doe, of 100 Main Street, Middletown, Cuyahoga County, Ohio, hereby make, constitute, and appoint Richard Roe of 500 East Street, Middletown, Cuyahoga County, Ohio my true and lawful attorney-in-fact for me and in my name, place, and stead, giving and granting to Richard Roe full power and authority to do and perform all and every act and thing that I may legally do through an attorney-in-fact, and every proper power necessary to carry out those acts and things, with full power of substitution and revocation, hereby ratifying and affirming that which Richard Roe or his substitute shall lawfully do or cause to be done by virtue of this power.

This power shall end on June 1, 1983.

IN WITNESS WHEREOF, I have hereunto set my hand and seal this 1st day of June, 1982. Sealed and delivered in the presence of:

_____

Witness

_____                    _____

Witness                                      JOHN DOE

STATE OF OHIO
COUNTY OF CUYAHOGA

BEFORE ME, a notary public in and for said county, personally appeared the above-named John Doe, who acknowledged that he did sign the foregoing Power of Attorney, and that the same is his free act and deed.

IN TESTIMONY WHEREOF, I have hereunto subscribed my name at Middletown, Cuyahoga County, Ohio, this 1st day of June, 1982.
(NOTARIAL SEAL)                              _____

                                             Notary Public

                                             My commission expires:

[1]3 *Am. Jur. 2d Agency,* paras. 20, 26, 27, 30, 31, 80, and 84. See also special powers of attorney in this Section, and compare stock proxy in Forms IA 2.01, 2.01(a), and (b).

## FORM VIIIQ 1.01(a)

### (Power of attorney to two persons with power to act jointly or severally)[1]

### ALTERNATIVE CLAUSE

..... and my attorneys-in-fact, Richard Roe and Peter Poe, are empowered to act either jointly or severally hereunder for and in my name, place, and stead.

[1]3 *Am. Jur. 2d Agency,* para. 196.

## FORM VIIIQ 1.01 (b)

### (Power of attorney to be exercised jointly only)[2]

### ALTERNATIVE CLAUSE

..... and my attorneys-in-fact, Richard Roe and Peter Poe, are enpowered to act jointly, but not severally, hereunder for and in my name, place, and stead.

[2]3 *Am. Jur. 2d Agency,* para. 196.

## FORM VIIIQ 1.02

### (Special power of attorney by one corporation to a realty corporation to sell, convey, and receive the purchase price for particular real estate)[1]

## POWER OF ATTORNEY

KNOW ALL MEN BY THESE PRESENTS, that DOE DEVELOPMENT, INC., an Ohio corporation having its principal place of business at 100 Main Street, Cleveland, Ohio 00000, does hereby constitute and appoint ROE REALTY CORPORATION, and Arizona corporation having its principal place of business at 100 Main Street, Middletown, Middle County, Arizonta, its true and lawful attorney-in-fact for it and in its name, place, and stead, to grant, bargain, sell, convey, and contract for the sale and conveyance of the following described property owned by it:

(Insert legal description, including book, map, and parcel number.)

The attorney-in-fact appointed hereby is authorized to grant, bargain, convey, sell, or to contract for the sale and conveyance of any or all of the above-described property to any person for such price or prices, and on such terms and conditions, as said attorney-in-fact may deem proper, and in our name to make, execute, acknowledge, and deliver a good and sufficient deed or deeds of conveyance, or other instrument or instruments, necessary to effect such sale, conveyance, or agreement, including, but not limited to, recording the power of attorney in Middle County, Arizona, and making affidavit of value required by the State of Arizona; to request, demand, sue for, collect, recover, and receive all moneys that may become due and owing to us by reason of such sale and conveyance; and to do every proper thing or act necessary to carry out those powers, with full power of substitution and revocation.

Any and all powers of attorney heretofore made by us authorizing any person(s) to do any of the enumerated acts relative to the above-described real property are hereby revoked.

IN WITNESS WHEREOF, the duly authorized officers of the Corporation have caused the corporate name and seal of the Corporation to be hereunto signed and affixed, respectively, this 1st day of June, 1982.

(CORPORATE SEAL)                                    DOE DEVELOPMENT, INC.

Mary Poe                                           By John Doe
_____                    _____
Secretary of the Corporation                       President

STATE OF OHIO
COUNTY OF CUYAHOGA

BEFORE ME, a notary public in and for said county, personally appeared John Doe and Mary Poe, known to me to be the persons who, as President and Secretary, respectively, of Doe Development, Inc., the corporation that executed the foregoing Power of Attorney, signed the same, and acknowledged to me that they did so sign said instrument in the name and upon behalf of said corporation as such officers, respectively; that the same is their free act and deed as such officers, respectively, and the free and corporate act and deed of said corporation; that they were duly authorized thereunto by its board of directors; and that the seal affixed to said instrument is the corporate seal of said corporation.

IN TESTIMONY WHEREOF, I have hereunto subscribed my name and affixed my official seal at Cleveland, Ohio, this 1st day of June, 1982.

(NOTARIAL SEAL)                                    _____

                                                   Notary Public

                                                   My commission expires:

(Note:  Since both Arizona and Ohio have adopted the Uniform Recognition of Acknowledgments Act, an authentication certificate of the notary's power would not be required. If the state where the power of attorney concerning land is to be used may require an authentication, check the acknowledgment statutes of both states for requirement and method of obtaining.)

[1] *3 Am. Jur. 2d Agency*, paras. 26, 27, 30–31, and 117–142; *77 Am. Jur. 2d Vendor and Purchaser*, para. 9; and *71 Am. Jur. 2d Specific Performance*, para. 34. For power to sell personal property, see *3 Am. Jur. 2d Agency*, paras. 93–116.

## FORM VIIIQ 1.03

### (Power of attorney to accounting firm to represent a corporate taxpayer before the U.S. Treasury Department)[1]

### POWER OF ATTORNEY

KNOW ALL MEN BY THESE PRESENTS:

That ABC Homes, Inc., a corporation duly organized and existing under the laws of the State of Florida, with its principal office at 100 Main Street, in the City of Middletown, County of Orange, State of Florida, does hereby constitute and appoint the accounting firm of Richard Roe, P.A., of 500 East Street, City of Middletown, County of Orange, State of Florida, and each member of the firm, its several, true, and lawful attorneys-in-fact, to appear before the Treasury Department of the United States or any bureau or official thereof, and to represent the Corporation in all matters pertaining to its federal tax returns.

Said attorneys-in-fact are hereby granted the right to examine all documents and data in the possession of the Treasury Department with respect to any federal tax liability of the Corporation, and to secure from the Treasury Department any information relative thereto for all taxable years to the date of this Power.

The Corporation gives and grants to each of its attorneys in fact full power and authority to do and perform every act and thing necessary to be done in this matter, as fully as the Corporation might or could do for itself, with full powers of substitution and revocation, and hereby ratifies and confirms all that said attorneys-in-fact or any substitute appointed by any of them shall lawfully do or cause to be done by virtue hereof.

All prior powers of attorney filed by this taxpayer corporation are hereby revoked and canceled.

The Treasury Department is hereby requested to furnish copies of all communications addressed to this corporate taxpayer to the accounting firm at the above-stated address until this power shall be revoked or canceled in writing directed to the Department.

IN WITNESS WHEREOF, the duly authorized officers of the taxpayer corporation have caused the corporate name and seal to be affixed.

Dated May 1, 1983.

(CORPORATE SEAL)                                    ABC HOMES, INC.

                                                    By _____

_____                       John Doe, President
Secretary of the Corporation

STATE OF FLORIDA
COUNTY OF ORANGE

The foregoing Power of Attorney was acknowledged before me this 1st day of May, 1983, by John Doe, President of ABC Homes, Inc., a Florida corporation, on behalf of the corporation.

(NOTARIAL SEAL)                          _____
                                                    Notary Public

                                         My commission expires:
                                         FEE STATEMENT[2]

This is to certify that neither Richard Roe, P.A., nor any of its officers, members, or employees, including those mentioned in this power of attorney, have executed a contingent or partially contingent fee arrangement for the representation of the above-named taxpayer before the Treasury Department.

Dated May 1, 1983.

                                         RICHARD ROE, P.A.

                                         By _____
                                                    Richard Roe

[1] 3 *Am. Jur. 2d Agency,* paras. 20, 22, 25, and 79; and 1 *Am. Jur. 2d Accountants,* paras. 9, 12, and 18.

[2] Check state statute as to accountant's right to a professional lien for services.

## FORM VIIIQ 1.04

### (Renunciation and termination by attorney-in-fact of power of attorney contained in agency agreement for purchase of personal property for a principal)[1]

TO:  Ace Equipment Corporation
     100 Main Street
     Middletown, New York 00000

Pursuant to the terms of our agency agreement dated March 22, 1982, wherein you appointed the undersigned attorney-in-fact to purchase certain personal property described therein for you, the undersigned hereby renounces and terminates said appointment, the same to be effective May 30, 1982.

Dated April 22, 1982.

_____
John Doe

[1] *3 Am. Jur. 2d Agency*, paras. 40–43. Compare revocation by principal in Form VIIIQ 1.05.

## FORM VIIIQ 1.05

### (Revocation by principal of recorded power of attorney)[1]

### REVOCATION OF POWER OF ATTORNEY

KNOW ALL MEN BY THESE PRESENTS, that I, John Doe, d/b/a Doe Real Estate Development Company, 5 Circle Drive, City of Middletown, County of Orange, State of Florida, hereby revoke the written power of attorney dated June 1, 1981, that made and appointed Richard Roe, of 100 Main Street, City of Middletown, County of Orange, State of Florida, my true and lawful attorney-in-fact for the purposes and with the powers therein set forth, which power is recorded in the public records of Orange County, Florida, in O.R. 383, Page 151.

IN WITNESS WHEREOF, I have signed this revocation the 5th day of February, 1983.

_____
JOHN DOE

STATE OF FLORIDA
COUNTY OF ORANGE

Before me, a notary public in and for the above county and state, personally appeared John Doe, known to me to be the person described in and who acknowledged the foregoing Revocation of Power of Attorney and acknowledged before me that he executed the same.

Sworn to and subscribed before me this 5th day of February, 1983.

(NOTARIAL SEAL)                        _____
                                       Notary Public

                                       My commission expires:

(Record the Revocation of the original power of attorney was recorded.)

[1] *3 Am. Jur. 2d Agency*, paras. 37–39, 42–45, and 48. Compare renunciation by agent in Form VIIIQ 1.04.

## SECTION R    RECEIPTS

The forms in this Section are to be used in conjunction with the discussion below. See the Table of Contents for Chapter VIII, Section R for a quick view of the receipts included in this Section. A written receipt is documentary evidence that money or other tangible or intangible property or documents have been delivered. The receipt may contain conditions or acknowledgments. Everyone knows that, but many persons, including lawyers and businessmen, often overlook the importance of both *giving* and *getting* a receipt in everyday transactions. Many people do not read the receipt except as to the amount involved.

Receipts, as trust receipts[1] and warehouse receipts,[2] are contracts with conditions. Rent receipts or other money receipts prove performance of contracts to pay money.

Receipts for documents or the return of documents from attorneys and other fiduciaries or custodians[3] are necessary to protect the person who delivers, and are a reminder of the whereabouts of the items described in the receipt to the person who receives.

If property is itemized in a receipt, it should be reasonably described. Receipts for documents should include names, dates, and general subject matter or nature of the document to avoid misunderstandings.

Receipts may or may not constitute a release or satisfaction,[4] depending on the terms or conditions stated in the receipt. If a receipt covers a deposit that is refundable, it should state the refund conditions to avoid misunderstanding and/or litigation.[5]

## FORM VIIIR 1.00

### CLIENT QUESTIONNAIRE FOR RECEIPTS

1. Name(s) and address(es) of the person(s) who are to deliver and who are to receive the money or items
2. Description of items: year, model, serial numbers, etc., of tangible personal property; if receipt is for money, the amount of money and reasonable identification of the debt that it pays; nature of document and certificate and other identifying numbers of intangible personal property
3. Purpose of the receipt
4. *Conditions of the receipt* (as to warranties, inspection, storage, insurance, risk of loss, charges, etc.)[1]

> [1]Appropriate sections of the U.C.C. apply if receipt involves a sale of goods, or a banking or a commercial transaction.

## FORM VIIIR 1.01

### (Receipt for refundable deposit on proposed lease)[1]

### RECEIPT

Middletown, Pennsylvania
February 1, 1982

RECEIVED from Doe Appliances, Inc., a Pennsylvania corporation, the sum of Three Hundred Dollars ($300) as a deposit for the first month's rent of a retail storeroom located at 100 East Street, Middletown, Pennsylvania, owned by the undersigned, the rent of which shall be Three Hundred Dollars ($300) per month for a period of five (5) years beginning May 1, 1982, subject to the following conditions:

1. The undersigned shall, at his own expense, contract for and cause the remodeling of the storeroom, in accordance with the drawing and specifications attached hereto, to be done by April 1, 1982.

2. In the event that the remodeling is not accomplished to the reasonable satisfaction of the

[1]*68 Am. Jr. 2d Sales*, paras. 431–433; and U.C.C. 2-513, 2-601 through 2-607.
[2]*15 Am. Jur. 2d Commercial Code*, para. 14; and U.C.C. 7-202, 7-204, and 7-403.
[3]Ref. Form VIIIR 1.05.
[4]Ref. Chapter VIIIS and Form VIIIR 1.04.
[5]Ref. Form VIIIR 1.01.

proposed tenant on or before April 1, 1982, the deposit shall be refunded to him and all liability under this Agreement shall end.

3. If the remodeling is accomplished to the reasonable satisfaction of the proposed tenant on or before April 1, 1982, the owner shall tender to the proposed tenant a lease of the premises on the above terms, which the proposed tenant shall forthwith execute and return to the owner, with an additional sum of Three Hundred Dollars ($300) to be applied to the last month's rent.

4. Upon failure of the proposed tenant to execute the lease forthwith and pay the additional sum, all rights of the proposed tenant shall cease, and the owner shall retain the deposit for which this receipt is given as liquidated damages for the proposed tenant's breach of this Agreement to Lease.

_____
Richard Roe, Owner

Accepted:
DOE APPLIANCES, INC.

By _____
President

[1]For right to refund on statutory recission of consumer contract, see Appendix I for Consumer Credit Protection Laws.

## FORM VIIIR 1.02

### (Receipt for payment of goods in which buyer acknowledges inspection)[1]

INVOICE NO. . . . .

DOE FURNITURE MART
100 Industrial Park
Atlanta, Georgia 00000

TO:  ROE'S HOME FURNISHINGS
500 Main Street
Middletown, Florida

_____
_____
_____
_____

PAYMENT RECEIVED                    RECEIVED above-described order:
Doe Furniture Mart

By _____    _____
Driver                              BUYER'S SIGNATURE

WHEN SIGNED BY BUYER, this receipt acknowledges inspection by the Buyer and acceptance of the goods described above.

[1]U.C.C. 2-513, and 2-601 through 2-607; 67 Am. Jur. 2d Sales, paras. 431–433.

## FORM VIIIR 1.03

### (Receipt of personal property for specific use)[1]

#### RECEIPT

RECEIVED from Able Manufacturing Corporation of 100 Industrial Park, Cleveland, Ohio 00000, one (1) model Kitchen Kit for use in promoting and advertising kitchen appliances manufactured by Able and sold by us at our retail store located at 100 Main Street, Pittsburgh, Pennsylvania 00000, which Kit we agree to use for that purpose and to return to Able upon thirty (30) days' written demand from Able in as good condition, reasonable wear, tear, and damage excepted, as the Kit was in when delivered to us for the above purpose.

The agreed value of the Kit at the time of this delivery is Two Hundred and Fifty Dollars ($250).

Dated: March 1, 1983

DOE APPLIANCES, INC.

By _____

General Manager

[1] *8 Am. Jur. 2d Bailments,* paras. 139–155; and 66 *Am. Jur. 2d Release,* para. 1. See also Part VIA for bailments generally.

## FORM VIIIR 1.04

### (Receipt for payment by promissory note)[1]

### RECEIPT

RECEIVED from Doe Appliances, Inc., of 100 Main Street, Pittsburgh, Pennsylvania 00000, its promissory note to my order for One Thousand Dollars ($1,000), payable ninety (90) days after this date, with Ten Percent (10%) interest. It is understood and agreed that, if the note is paid in full on or before its due date, it shall constitute payment in full of the purchase price of Two Hundred (200) Super Radios in cartons billed to the maker by our Invoice No. 3842, dated April 2, 1982. If the note is not paid, then this receipt shall be of no force and effect, and we shall have the right, at our option, to take legal action against the maker and to recover for the full amount owed on the Invoice No. 3842.

Dated April 2, 1982.

ABLE MANUFACTURING CORPORATION

By _____

(title)

[1] For forms and use of promissory notes, see Part VIII P.

## FORM VIIIR 1.05

### (Receipt for return of documents by escrow agent)[1]

### RECEIPT

The undersigned, on behalf of Able Manufacturing Corporation, a Pennsylvania corporation, hereby accepts and acknowledges receipt of all moneys and documents deposited under the escrow agreement with Richard Roe, P.A. dated May 1, 1982, which are as follows:

(List checks, giving maker, payee/drawee names and amounts; stock certificates by name of issuing corporation, and name of stockholder, number of certificate(s), and number of shares represented by each; and reasonably describe other property being returned.)

and Richard Roe, P.A., the Escrow Agent, is hereby relieved of any liability for the custody of the above-described property as of this date:

Dated: May 1, 1982

ABLE MANUFACTURING CORPORATION

By _____

(Title or designation and the name of recipient, as recipient's signature is often illegible.)

[1] *28 Am. Jur. 2d Escrow,* para. 17. See also Part VIII Section I for Escrow.

## SECTION S     RELEASES AND SATISFACTIONS

This Section contains forms for use in connection with both real and personal property. The Table of Contents for Part VIII, Section S, should be consulted for a quick list of the subjects covered in this Section.

A release may be general[1] or specific.[2] It may also include a particularized receipt.[3]

Consideration for the release may be satisfaction of the full claim,[4] or it may be an accord and satisfaction.[5]

Before drafting a release, one should get the *facts* concerning the purpose and scope of the release to be sure that the release is truly effective against all parties[6] who may be involved.

For partial release of mortgage on real estate, see Part VII, Form VIID 1.08.

For mortgage satisfaction, see Part VII, Form VIID 1.09.

## FORM VIIIS 1.00

### CLIENT QUESTIONNAIRE FOR RELEASE OR SATISFACTION OF CLAIM

1. Name(s) and address(es) of releasor(s) and releasee(s)
2. Purpose of the release
3. Consideration for the release
4. Is the claim being released a *recorded* claim? If so, the release should be acknowledged[1] and also recorded[2]
5. Does the release include a receipt? If so, in what amount or description of property?[3]
6. Is the releasor a corporation? If so, what is the title of the person who will sign? What evidence is there of his authority to sign?
7. Are *all* parties who may have a claim releasing their claims? If not, why not?[4]
8. Is the release to include unknown claims?[5]
9. Is the release a mutual release?[6]

[1]See Chapter VIIIA.
[2]*46 Am. Jur. 2d Judgments,* para. 237 et seq.
[3]See Chapter VIIIR.
[4]*47 Am. Jur. 2d, Judgments,* para. 989; and *66 Am. Jur. 2d Release,* para. 35 et seq.
[5]*66 Am. Jur. 2d Release,* para. 32. See your state statute as to validity and waiver of the statute.
[6]Ref. Forms VIIIS 1.07 and 1.08.

## FORM VIIIS 1.01

(General release—could be given by creditor to debtor, releasing joint debtors)[1]

### GENERAL RELEASE

The undersigned, ABLE MANUFACTURING CORPORATION, an Ohio corporation having its principal place of business at 100 Main Street, Middletown, Ohio 00000, for and in consideration of the sum of Five Hundred Dollars ($500), received from or on behalf of DOE APPLIANCES, INC., a Pennsylvania corporation having its principal place of business at 100 East Street, Pittsburgh, Pennsylvania, and assigns of individuals, and the successors and assigns of corporations, wherever the context so admits or requires.

HEREBY remises, releases, acquits, satisfies, and forever discharges[2] the said second party of and from all, and all manner of, action and actions, cause and causes of action, suits, debts, dues,

[1]Ref. Form VIIIS 1.01.
[2]Ref. Form VIIIS 1.02 through 1.08.
[3]Ref. Form VIIIS 1.05, 1.07, and 1.08.
[4]Ref. Form VIIIS 1.05 and 1.08.
[5]For Accord and Satisfaction, see Part VIIIG, Compromise and Compositions.
[6]*47 Am. Jur. 2d Judgments,* para. 989; and *66 Am. Jur. 2d Release,* paras. 35 et seq.

sums of money, accounts, reckonings, notes, bonds, bills, specialties, covenants, contracts, controversies, agreements, promises, variances, trespasses, damages, judgments, executions, claims, and demands whatsoever, in law or in equity, that said releasor ever had, now has, or that any personal representative, successor, heir, or assign of releasor hereafter can, shall, or may have, against releasee, for, upon, or by reason of any matter, cause, or thing whatsoever, up to and including the date of this Release.

We hereby waive any claim or right to assert any claim whatsoever, known or unknown, that has been, through oversight or error, intentionally or unintentionally, omitted from this Release.[3]

This Release shall be binding on all individual parties, their heirs, executors, administrators, and assigns, and all corporate parties, their predecessors, successors, subsidiaries, parents, and assigns.

This Release expressly includes all persons and legal entities who are or may be liable to the undersigned releasor as joint debtors or the releasee.[4]

Dated this 1st day of June, 1982.

Signed and delivered in presence of:

ABLE MANUFACTURING CORPORATION

_____

WITNESS

_____  By _____

WITNESS  (Title)[5]

(If a general release is to be recorded, add an acknowledgment. Ref. Chapter VI A.)

[1]*66 Am. Jur. 2d Release*, paras. 1, 2, 4–7, 28–34, and 43. See also *37 Am. Jur. 2d Fraudulent Conveyances*, para. 71. Compare *special* release Forms VIS 1.02–1.08.

[2]See U.C.C. 1-107 and 1-203 if release is for a transaction covered by the U.C.C.

[3]*66 Am. Jur. 2d Release*, para. 32; and statutes in Calif., Mont., S.Dak., and N.Dak. where release of unknown claims are exempt from general release.

[4]*66 Am. Jur. 2d Release*, paras. 35–38.

[5]For release by an agent, see *66 Am. Jur. 2d Release*, para. 27; and *3 Am. Jur. 2d Agency*, para. 91.

## FORM VIIIS 1.02

### (Mutual special releases by parties who are mutually rescinding a contract)[1]

### RELEASE

AGREEMENT made this 1st day of August, 1982, by and between Richard Roe of 100 East Street, Middletown, New York 00000, and Doe Discount, Inc., a New York corporation having its principal place of business at 100 East Parkway, Buffalo, New York 00000, WITNESSETH

WHEREAS, the parties had a written Agreement dated June 1, 1982, to lease certain premises owned by Richard Roe and located at 100 Main Street, Middletown, New York, upon certain conditions; and

WHEREAS, the parties hereto being the parties to that Agreement to Lease mutually desire to rescind that Agreement;

IT IS AGREED AS FOLLOWS:

1. *Rescision.* The parties hereto mutually rescind the above-described Agreement to Lease dated June 1, 1982.

2. *Releases.* The parties hereto mutually remise, release, acquit, satisfy, and forever discharge each other of and from all and all manner of action and actions, cause and causes of action, suits, debts, dues, sums of money, accounts, reckonings, bonds, bills, specialties, covenants, contracts, controversies, agreements, promises, variances, trespasses, damages, judgments, executions, claims, and demands whatsoever, at law or in equity, that either of the parties hereto ever had, now has, or hereafter can or shall have against the other party hereto for, upon, or by reason of any matter, cause, or thing whatsoever, concerned with or arising out of the above-described Agreement to Lease, from the beginning of time to the date of this Rescision and Release.

3. *Persons bound and benefited.* This Rescision and Release shall bind and inure to the ben-

efit of the parties and their respective heirs, personal representatives, and assigns or their predecessors, successors, subsidiaries, parents, and assigns.

Dated this 1st day of August, 1982.

_____

RICHARD ROE

DOE DISCOUNT, INC.

By _____
        (Title)[2]

[1]*17 Am. Jur. 2d Contracts,* paras. 490, 491, and 517; and *49 Am. Jur. 2d Landlord and Tenant,* paras. 990 and 991.

[2]For release by an agent, see *66 Am. Jur. 2d Release,* para. 27; and *3 Am. Jur. 2d Agency,* para. 91.

## FORM VIIIS 1.03

### (Release by landlord of claims against tenant under lease)[1]

### RELEASE

In consideration of One Dollar ($1) and other good and valuable consideration paid to him by Doe Appliances Inc., a Pennsylvania corporation, Richard Roe does hereby release and forever discharge said Doe Appliances, Inc., from any and all demands of the undersigned, his heirs, executors, administrators, and assigns from any and all claims of any nature whatsoever that he ever had, now has, or they can, shall, or may have against Doe Appliances, Inc., concerning or arising out of the lease dated June 1, 1980, for premises located at 100 Main Street, Middletown, Pennsylvania, by the undersigned to the Releasee.

Dated October 1, 1982.

_____

Richard Roe, Lessor

[1]*49 Am. Jur. 2d Landlord and Tenant,* paras. 166–174. Compare Consent in Part VIII, Section H and Assignment of lease in Form VIIID 1.03.

## FORM VIIIS 1.04

### (Release of corporation including its subsidiaries and officers, etc., individually)[1]

### RELEASE

. . . . . . . up to and including the dates of this Release.

The undersigned releasor intends that this Release shall apply to all subsidiary corporations of ABLE MANUFACTURING, INC., and to its and their respective predecessors, successors, and assigns, and to all of its and their past, present, and future officers, directors, agents, and employees, and their respective heirs and legal representatives.

[1]*66 Am. Jur. 2d Release,* paras. 35 and 36. For employee's release of claims against employer, see *66 Am. Jur. 2d Release,* paras. 24 and 26. Ref. other forms in this Section for appropriate preliminary paragraphs for a release.

## FORM VIIIS 1.05

### (Release of full judgment lien against real estate, to be filed in county where the real estate is located and judgment from another county has been recorded)[1]

### RELEASE OF JUDGMENT LIEN

In consideration of Five Thousand Six Hundred and Thirty Dollars ($5,630) paid to it by Doe Development Corporation, a Florida corporation, receipt whereof is hereby acknowledged, Super

Manufacturing, Inc., a Florida corporation, hereby releases real property located in Orange County, Florida, more particularly described as follows:

(Insert legal description and official record book and page number to deed to Doe Development Corporation.)

from all claim and interest in the same, or any part thereof, it may have by reason of the judgment rendered in the Circuit Court for the 0th Judicial Circuit, Middle County, Florida, on April 10, 1979, at case No. C–00000 against Doe Development Corporation for the sum of Five Thousand Dollars ($5,000), plus costs of Eighty-seven Dollars ($87), and attorney's fees of Five Hundred Dollars ($500), and interest in the amount of Fifty Dollars ($50), being a total of Five Thousand Six Hundred and Thirty-seven Dollars ($5,637), and from all liens and encumbrances that have attached to the real property described herein by reason of the recovery of the judgement, as free and clear in all respects as though the judgment had not been rendered.

Dated March 12, 1982.

(CORPORATE SEAL)                              SUPER MANUFACTURING, INC.

(Peter Poe) _____          By (Richard Roe) _____

Secretary of the Corporation                 President

STATE OF FLORIDA
COUNTY OF MIDDLE                             (State and county where executed may differ from place where release is filed or judgment was obtained.)

The foregoing Release of Judgment Lien was acknowledged before me this 12th day of March, 1982, by Richard Roe, President, and Peter Poe, Secretary, of Super Manufacturing, Inc., a Florida corporation, respectively, on behalf of the corporation.

_____

Notary Public

My commission expires:

(File in the county where the real property is located, and where a judgment from another county or federal court district was filed.)

[1]46 *Am. Jur. 2d Judgments,* paras. 237, 246, and 256.

## FORM VIIIS 1.06

### (Release and waiver of all mechanic's liens by contractor and materialmen)[1]

### RELEASE OF LIEN

We, the undersigned, of New Port Richie, Florida, in consideration of One Dollar ($1) severally received, to our full satisfaction, from John Doe of New Port Richie, Florida, do hereby waive and relinquish all liens and claims of liens that we now have, or that we may hereafter have, upon that certain tract of land, and all the buildings thereon, situated in New Port Richie, and more particularly bounded and described as follows:

(Insert legal description. Give official record Plat Book No. if the property has been platted.)

for work performed and materials furnished for the construction and erection of the said buildings or any of them.

Dated this 12th day of August, 1982.

Richard Roe d/b/a ROE CONSTRUCTION

By _____
    RICHARD ROE, Proprietor
    Peter Poe d/b/a M & M MASONRY

By _____
    Peter Poe
    EL-RIGHT ELECTRIC, INC., a Florida corporation

By _____
    Charles Coe, President

STATE OF FLORIDA[2]
COUNTY OF PASCO

The foregoing instrument was acknowledged before me this 12th day of August, 1982, by Richard Roe d/b/a Roe Construction and Peter Poe d/b/a M & M Masonry.

(NOTARIAL SEAL)            _____

                                     Notary Public

                                     My commission expires:

STATE OF FLORIDA
COUNTY OF PASCO

The foregoing instrument was acknowledged before me this 12th day of August, 1982, by Charles Coe, President of El-Right Electric, Inc., a Florida corporation, on behalf of the corporation.

(NOTARIAL SEAL)            _____

                                     Notary Public

                                     My commission expires:

[1]*53 Am. Jur. 2d Mechanic's Liens,* paras. 294, 296–302, 315, and 325–333. See also U.C.C. 9-104 and 9-310, and your state mechanic's lien statute. Standard printed forms are usually available at a local legal printing office.

    [2]Statutory short form of acknowledgment. See Appendix III and Appendix IV.

## FORM VIIIS 1.07

### (Mutual releases and division of jointly owned real and personal property)

### AGREEMENT AND MUTUAL RELEASES

AGREEMENT made October 1, 1982, among John Doe, Mary Doe, Richard Roe, Peter Poe, and George Coe, all of Middletown, Middle County, Pennsylvania, WITNESSETH:

WHEREAS, the parties to this Agreement desire to divide certain real and personal property interests acquired by the parties through the past years (herein collectively called the "Properties"); and

WHEREAS, the Properties are the following: (List properties and all liens and encumbrances: giving legal description of real estate; usual identification names and numbers of tangible and intangible personal property; specific identification of other interest or rights in property, as beneficiaries of trust, etc.) AND IT IS AGREED:

1. *Transfer of property.* Within thirty (30) days from the date of the execution of this Agreement, the parties shall duly execute, acknowledge, and deliver to each other all documents or instruments necessary to transfer their interests in the Properties to each other in accordance with Paragraph 2 of this Agreement, including, but not limited to, such instruments as may be required by the laws of any jurisdiction now in effect or that may become effective before the actual transfer that may affect the property rights of the parties as between themselves or with others.

2. *Division of Property.* The parties shall receive the following Properties as identified by Item No. opposite their respective names:

| | |
|---|---|
| John Doe | Items 3, 6, and 14 |
| Mary Doe | Items 2, 5, and 8 |
| Richard Roe | Items 1, 4, 7, 12, and 13 |
| George Coe | Items 9, 10, 11, 14, and 15 |

3. *Representations.* No representations are made by any of the parties as to the present value or condition of any of the property transferred by him pursuant to this Agreement unless same are included in the description of Properties given herein, nor are any representations as to liens and encumbrances made unless same are included in the description of Properties given herein.

4. *Consideration.* The consideration for the division of Properties provided herein is the subjective desire of each party to own the Property transferred to him pursuant to this Agreement, and the mutual releases and the mutual promises contained herein.

5. *Mutual Releases.* Upon the execution, acknowledgment, and delivery of the instruments and documents of transfer described herein, the parties mutually remise, release, acquit, satisfy, and forever discharge each other of and from all and all manner of action and actions, cause and causes of action, suits, debts, dues, sums of money, accounts, reckonings, bonds, bills, specialties, covenants, contracts. controversies, agreements, promises, variances, trespasses, damages, judgments, executions, claims, and demands whatsoever, at law or in equity that each or any of the parties hereto ever had, now had, or that any personal representative, successor, heir, or assign of any party hereto hereafter can, shall, or may have against any other party hereto, for, upon, or by reason of any matter, cause, or thing whatsoever, from the beginning of the world to the day of these presents concerning any of the Properties to be transferred pursuant to this Agreement and Mutual Releases.

6. *Completeness.* This Agreement and Mutual Releases contains the entire understanding of the parties.

7. *Persons Bound and Benefited.* This Agreement and Mutual Releases shall bind and inure to the benefit of the parties and their respective heirs, executors, administrators, successors, and assigns.

IN WITNESS WHEREOF, the parties have signed, sealed, and acknowledged this Agreement and Mutual Releases.

```
_____ (SEAL)
   JOHN DOE

_____ (SEAL)
   MARY DOE

_____ (SEAL)
   RICHARD ROE

_____ (SEAL)
   PETER POE

_____ (SEAL)
   GEORGE COE
```

STATE OF PENNSYLVANIA
COUNTY OF ALLEGHENY

I hereby certify that on this day before me, a notary public, personally appeared John Doe, Mary Doe, Richard Roe, Peter Poe, and George Coe, to me known to be the persons described in and who executed the foregoing Agreement and Mutual Releases, and acknowledged before me that they executed the same for the purposes stated therein.
SWORN TO AND SUBSCRIBED BEFORE ME
this 9th day of May, 1982.

_____

Notary Public

My commission expires:

## FORM VIIIS 1.08

### (Mutual special release of officers and directors, and receipt for assets transferred to stockholders on liquidation of corporation)

### RELEASE

We, the undersigned, being all the stockholders of J.M. Doe Company, Inc., a Pennsylvania corporation, in consideration of the delivery to us severally of the assets of the Corporation in full liquidation thereof, as more particularly shown in Schedule A, attached hereto and made part hereof, do hereby mutually remise, release, acquit, satisfy, and forever discharge each other of and from all and all manner of action, suits, debts, dues, sums of money, accounts, reckonings, bonds, bills, specialties, covenants, contracts, controversies, agreements, promises, variances, tres-passes, damages, judgments, executions, claims, and demands whatsoever, at law or in equity, that any of the parties hereto ever had, now have, or hereafter can or shall have against any other party hereto for, upon or by reason of any matter, cause, or thing whatsoever, concerned with or arising out of the formation, operation, or liquidation of J.M. Doe Company, Inc., a Pennsylvania corporation, from the beginning of time to the date of this Release.

Dated this 10th day of June, 1982.

ATTEST:

_____

WITNESS

_____          _____

WITNESS                                     JOHN DOE

_____

WITNESS

_____          _____

WITNESS                                     MARY DOE

_____

WITNESS

_____          _____

WITNESS                                     PETER POE

_____

WITNESS

_____          _____

WITNESS                                     CHARLES DOE

(Attach Schedule A.)

## SECTION T    SALE OF "SERVICES" CONTRACTS

The forms in this Section are contracts dealing primarily with the sale and purchase of services[1] rather than of goods. As we know, a contract for unique services, as for the services of an entertainer or perhaps a super chef, is not assignable. Other commercial service contracts may be assignable, but it is best to be specific in the contract about the right to assign the contract or to delegate the service.[2]

The Uniform Commercial Code deals specifically with "goods,"[3] not "services."[4] A contract that involves both goods and services would be governed by the Code in connection with the goods.[5]

In the case of commercial bailments, there is some divergence of opinion as to the practical application of the Code to particular fact situations where the goods are merely incidental to the services.

Federal consumer protection laws[6] and your state consumer protection laws[7]

_____

[1] *17 Am. Jur. 2d Contracts*, paras. 4–8, 14, 39–40, 76. Ref. and compare Parts V, VI, and VII of this book.

[2] Ref. Part VIIID.

[3] U.S.S. 2-105.

[4] *67 Am. Jur. 2d Sales*, para. 33.

[5] U.C.C. 2-104(1) and (3).

[6] See Appendixes I, IX, X, and XI for Basic Federal Consumer Credit Protection laws.

[7] See your state unfair trade practice and deceptive advertising statutes.

should be considered in reviewing or drafting "commercial" service contracts as well as contracts for the sale of goods.

Where the services are to be performed on the purchaser's premises or on the purchaser's goods, by an independent service contractor, provision should be made for insurance and indemnification for loss and damage and/or liability[8] as to both parties.

Modern consumer service contracts[9] for automobiles, televisions, and household appliances are becoming quite common. These contracts are to be distinguished from a "warranty" contract to provide certain services "free" for a certain period of time after purchase. Some questions to be considered by the purchaser, reviewer, or drafter of a "service contract" are:

1. What parts are covered—all major systems and all parts of those systems *or* just certain systems and parts of systems?
2. Are incidental damages covered, as: towing or pickup and delivery, and/or use of substitute car or appliance while service is being performed?
3. Replacement provisions
4. Time, place, and manner of making payment for work not covered by the service contract
5. Is there a contract limit of the amount of service that is covered by the service contract? If so, what is it?
6. Where can you get the service? One location only, or in what geographical area?

If you are drafting a consumer service contract,[10] be sure to comply with state unfair trade practices and deceptive advertising statutes in making proper disclosure.

A service contract may make the provider of service an agent of the purchaser or an independent contractor.[11] It may create a bailment employment contract.[12]

### FORM VIII T 1.00

### CLIENT QUESTIONNAIRE FOR SALE OF "SERVICES"[1] CONTRACT

1. Names and addresses of the parties
2. What is the service to be performed?
3. Is the service delegable, or is the contract assignable by *either* party? If so, which, and under what conditions?
4. Description of services
5. Time, place, and manner of performances (include standards for judging performance, if necessary). Who is to control the time, place, and manner of performance?
6. Are the services professional services, as: medical, legal, dental, architectural, engineering, etc.? Consider the professional and statutory regulations of the profession involved
7. Are the services regulated by any state or federal statute or regulation, as: laundries and dry cleaners, carriers of hazardous materials, operators of amusements and exhibitions, etc.?[2]
8. Is the service contract with a "consumer,"[3] or is it "between merchants"?[4]
9. Time service is to begin and to end. What termination rights in case of default?
10. Time, manner, and place of payment

---

[8]*41 Am. Jur. 2d Independent Contractors*, paras. 1–4, 18, 21, 48–50. Ref. also Part VIII, Section L.
[9]For practical information, bulletins and brochures are issued by Bureau of Consumer Protection, Office of Consumer Education, Washington, D.C. 20580.
[10]Ref. Part VI, Section A.
[11]Compare Form VIIIT 1.01 with Form VIIIT 1.04, and ref. Part V, Section B.
[12]Ref. Form IVA 1.01.

11. Liability
    (a) For personal injury or property damage
    (b) Faulty materials or equipment
    (c) Indemnification of one party by the other? To what extent?
    (d) Insurance or bond

> [1] *17 Am. Jur. 2d Contracts,* paras. 4–8, 14, 39–40, 76; and *67 Am. Jur. 2d Sales,* para. 33. Ref. also Parts IV, V and VI of this book.
> [2] Ref. Forms VIII T 1.03 and VIII T 1.04. See your state statutes, regulating these services.
> [3] See Appendix I for Basic Federal Consumer Credit Protection Laws and Appendixes IX, X and XI to this book for your state unfair trade practices and deceptive advertising statutes.
> [4] U.C.C. 2-104(1) and (3).

## FORM VIII T 1.01

### (Cleaning service agreement for office building)

#### SERVICE CONTRACT[1]

CONTRACT made December 1, 1982, between John Doe of 100 Graham Street, Pittsburgh, Pennsylvania (herein called "Owner"), and Commercial Cleaning Services, Inc., a Pennsylvania Corporation having its principal place of business at 100 East Street, Pittsburgh, Pennsylvania 00000 (herein called "Contractor"), WITNESSETH:

WHEREAS, Owner owns and leases to others an office building located at 100 Wood Street, Pittsburgh, Pennsylvania, and Owner desires to have the following services performed by Contractor at that building; and

WHEREAS, Contractor agrees to perform these services for Owner under the terms and conditions set forth in this Contract;

NOW THEREFORE, in consideration of the mutual promises set forth herein, it is agreed by and between Owner and Contractor as follows:

1. *Description of work.* The work to be performed by Contractor includes all services generally performed by Contractor in his usual office building cleaning service business, including, but not limited to, the daily, weekly and bimonthly services enumerated in Schedule A, attached hereto and made part hereof.

2. *Payment.*[2] Owner will pay Contractor the total sum of Twenty-four Thousand Dollars ($24,000) for the work to be performed under this Contract, payable Two Thousand Dollars ($2,000) per month on or before the 15th day of each month.

3. *Control and rights of parties.*[3]
    (a) *Independent contractor status.* The parties to this Contract intend that the relation between them created by this Contract is that of Owner–independent contractor. No agent, employee, or servant of Contractor shall be or shall be deemed to be the employee, agent, or servant of Owner. Owner is interested only in the results obtained under this Contract; the manner and means of conducting the work are under the sole control of Contractor. None of the benefits provided by Owner to his employees, including, but not limited to, compensation insurance and unemployment insurance, are available from Owner to the employees, agents, or servants of Contractor. Contractor will be solely and entirely responsible for his acts and for the acts of his agents, employees, servants, and subcontractors during the performance of this Contract.
    (b) *Control of work and workmen by Contractor.* Contractor shall have sole control of the manner and means of performing this Contract, and he shall complete it according to his own means and methods of work. He shall direct the performance of all workmen and subcontractors.
    (c) *Supervision by Contractor or his representative.* Contractor will be responsible for and will superintend the execution of all work covered by this Agreement, either personally or through a representative. If Contractor uses a representative, Contractor agrees that the representative shall be competent and qualified and with full power to act for Contractor in all matters pertaining to this Contract.
    (d) *Employment of workers by Contractor.* Contractor shall furnish duly qualified and experienced cleaning personnel, artisans, workmen, foremen, and supervisors to carry out the services to be provided under this Contract; and shall, at all times, enforce strict discipline

and maintain good order among the workers performing the work, and shall cause the workers to observe all reasonable fire prevention, safety, and health regulations in force at the Owner's building. Workers used by Contractor in performing this Contract shall be his employees or subcontractors. Contractor shall pay all of his own employees, and each employee or subcontractor of the Contractor who works in the Owner's building shall be covered by a fidelity bond to protect the property of occupants of the Owner's building.

(e) *Contractor to furnish materials.* Contractor shall furnish, at its own expense, all labor, materials, equipment, and other items necessary to carry out the terms of this service Contract.

(f) *Contractor's responsibility for use of Owner's tools and equipment, if any.*[4] Owner shall not be held liable for any injury or damage to person or property resulting from the use, misuse or failure of any equipment used by Contractor or any of its employees or subcontractors, even if such property or equipment is furnished, rented, or loaned to Contractor by Owner. The acceptance or use of any such property or equipment by Contractor or any of his employees or subcontractors shall be held to mean that Contractor has duly inspected said property or equipment before using it and accepts full responsibility for its uses, and Contractor agrees to indemnify and hold harmless the Owner against any and all loss or liability whatsoever to any person or persons resulting from the use, misuse, or failure of said property or equipment.

4. *Indemnification of Owner.*[5] The work to be performed under this Contract will be performed entirely at Contractor's risk. Contractor will carry, for the duration of this Contract, public liability insurance in an amount acceptable to Owner and will cause fidelity bonds to be secured for all its employees and subcontractors who work in Owner's building to secure the property of occupants of the building. Contractor agrees to indemnify Owner for any and all liability or loss arising in any way out of the performance of this Contract.

5. *Duration and termination.* Either party may cancel this Contract on _____ 18 _____ day's written notice; otherwise, the contract shall remain in force for a term of _____ 19 ____ from date.

IN WITNESS WHEREOF, the parties have executed this Agreement at Pittsburgh, Pennsylvania.

_____

JOHN DOE, Owner

COMMERCIAL CLEANING SERVICES, INC.

By _____
General Manager

[1]*53 Am. Jur. 2d Master and Servant,* paras. 14 and 41; *41 Am. Jur. 2d Independent Contractors,* paras. 1, 3, 5–23. Compare management contract for condominium, Form VIIF 1.02.
[2]*41 Am. Jur. 2d Independent Contractors,* para. 14.
[3]*41 Am. Jur. 2d Independent Contractors,* paras. 6–9, 12, 13, and 17.
[4]*41 Am. Jur. 2d Independent Contractors,* para. 48.
[5]*41 Am. Jur. 2d Independent Contractors,* para. 21.

## FORM VIII T 1.02

### (Linen supply agreement for hotel, restaurant, barber, beauty shop business)[1]

CONTRACT made December 1, 1982, between Doe Linen Supply, Inc., a Florida corporation having its principal office at 100 West Street, Miami, Florida 00000 (herein called the "Company"), and Oceanview Motels, Inc., a Florida corporation operating a motel and restaurant at 79000 Collins Avenue, Miami Beach, Florida (herein called the "Customer"), is as follows:

1. *Agreement to supply.*

(a) Customer shall rent from Company all the linen supplies used in Customer's business, and Company shall use diligence to provide an uninterrupted supply of linen sufficient to meet customer's requirements, subject to the provisions of Paragraph 15.

(b) Customer shall rent a minimum of linen so that the service charge under this Contract shall amount to at least Five Hundred Dollars ($500) per month for the duration of this Agreement.

2. *Property rights in linen.*

All linen supplies are furnished on a rental basis only, and remain the property of Company. Customer shall not remove any of the supplies from its place of business and, except for ordinary wear, shall be liable to Company for the cost value of any furnished supplies that are lost or damaged.

3. *Legal seizure of linen.*

If any of Company's linen supplies are seized by the use of any legal process, Customer shall immediately notify Company of such seizure. Customer shall also notify the person(s) making such seizure of Company's ownership of the linen supplies.

4. *Laundering of Company's linen.*

Customer shall not launder, or give to be laundered, to anyone other than Company any of the linen supplies furnished by Company. If Customer violates the terms of this Section, Customer shall be liable to Company for five (5) times the rental value of all of the linen laundered by someone other than Company.

5. *Company's access to Customer's property.*

Company shall have access to Customer's business premises to check all of its property in the possession of Customer at any time during Customer's normal business hours.

6. *Sale of Customer's business.*

If Customer sells his business or any portion thereof, Customer shall immediately notify Company. Customer shall be liable to company for all supplies furnished until such notice is given to Company.

7. *Duration and termination.*

This Agreement shall become effective on January 1, 1983. Either party may terminate this Agreement by giving the other party ten (10) days' written notice. If Customer terminates this Agreement without cause, before January 1, 1984, Customer shall pay Company a service charge of Five Hundred Dollars ($500) at the time of termination stated in that notice, and shall simultaneously return all Company's property to the Company.

8. *Governmental regulation.*

This Agreement may be changed to comply with any law or governmental regulation that affects the validity of the Agreement.

9. *Proof of amount of linen service provided.*

Company's pickup and delivery tags shall be conclusive proof of the amount of linen service furnished to Customer, unless Customer shall give written notice of any discrepancy in the service provided within five (5) days after the delivery of such service.

10. *Attorney's fees and costs.*

The prevailing party shall pay all costs, including reasonable attorney's fees, incurred by either party in enforcing any of the terms of this agreement.

11. *Assignment.*

This Agreement shall be binding on the successors and assigns of the parties.

12. *Entire agreement.*

This Contract contains the entire agreement between the parties, and neither party has relied on any prior or contemporaneous representations, either oral or written, that are not set forth herein.

13. *Delivery schedule.*

Company shall pick up dirty linen and deliver a supply of clean linen to Customer every weekday, Monday through Friday.

14. *Time of payment.*

Customer shall pay the charges listed below for the service utilized by him for each week, on the last day of each week thereafter, until service is discontinued and all of Company's property has been returned.

15. *Prices for services to be provided.*

The services and the prices at which such services are to be provided for the duration of this Agreement are shown in Schedule A, attached hereto and made part hereof, and the number of items to be delivered can be changed only by a written notice given by Customer twenty-four (24) hours before a scheduled delivery.

(Attach Schedule showing items to be supplied, the number of each, and the total price of each.)

Dated this 1st day of December, 1982.

OCEANVIEW MOTELS, INC.

By _____
   Manager
DOE LINEN SUPPLY, INC.

By _____
   General Manager

[1]Ref. footnotes to other service contracts in this Section, and see *50 Am. Jur. 2d Laundries, Dyers and Drycleaners,* para. 1 et seq.

## FORM VIII T 1.03

### (Contract for promotion and production of annual corporated sales meeting)[1]

## CONTRACT

CONTRACT made February 1, 1982, between Doe Promotions, Inc., a New York corporation having its principal place of business at Suite 100, Big Building, New York, New York 00000 (herein called "Producer"), and Able Manufacturing, Inc., an Ohio corporation having its principal place of business at 100 Industrial Drive, Middletown, Ohio 00000 (herein called "Company").

### RECITALS

(a) The Company intends to hold its biannual companywide sales meeting in Chicago, Illinois, for three days beginning July 22, 1982 (herein called the "Meeting").

(b) Producer is in the business of promoting, organizing, producing, and supervising programs for sales and other industrial meetings throughout the United States, and employs approximately One Hundred (100) capable persons for performing that service.

(c) Producer agrees to promote, organize, produce, and supervise Company's biannual companywide sales meeting in Chicago, under the terms and conditions set forth in this Contract as follows:

### DESCRIPTION OF SERVICES

(a) *Time of essence.* Company has submitted to Producer a proposed general agenda for the Meeting and a budget for the Meeting, as more particularly outlined in Schedule A, attached hereto and made part hereof. It is estimated that Two Hundred Fifty (250) employees of Company will attend the Meeting, which Producer shall organize, produce, and supervise in accordance with a detailed written plan and agenda to be submitted by Producer to Company's Vice-President in charge of sales on or before March 15, 1982. The Company shall give its written approval or disapproval of the plan to Producer on or before March 31, 1982, or this Agreement shall become null and void and of no effect. Time is of the essence of this Contract. Each party shall bear its own expense of preliminary planning in the event that either party fails to act in accordance with this Paragraph.

(b) *Producer's Plan.* The Producer's Plan (herein called the "Plan") shall include:

   (1) Suggestions for one or more promotional themes for the Meeting that is (are) designed to motivate Company's sales employees.

   (2) Description and prices of proposed sales prizes, as: trips, jewelry, furs, other.

   (3) Description and names of speakers, entertainers, amusements, or exhibitions proposed for the meeting, and fees for same.

   (4) List of available hotels and rates as meeting headquarters, and description of accommodations and rates available for Two Hundred Fifty (250) persons and appropriate meeting room(s).

   (5) Estimate of cost and plan, including refreshments, for welcome party for salesmen and their wives.

   (6) Estimate of cost and plan, including menus, for closing-night banquet for salesman and their wives.

   (7) Estimate and plan for theater, sight-seeing, or shopping tour during one day of meeting for wives.

   (8) List of supplies, signs, decorations, and equipment to be used at meeting, including cost or rental fee.

(9) Agenda for meeting, incorporating the business agenda attached hereto in Schedule A and the social agenda of the Plan.

(10) The Producer's service fee for implementing the Plan as provided herein.

(c) *Service and supervision by Producer.*

(1) Producer shall contract in its own name, as agent for the Company, for the items, persons, and services provided in the Plan when it is accepted and approved by the Company pursuant to (a) above.

(2) Before or at the Meeting, Producer shall arrange for delivery and acceptance of all items at the Meeting hotel, and shall install and place them safely and appropriately for use in accordance with the Plan.

(3) During the Meeting, Producer shall have at least one (1) of its duly authorized representatives present in the Meeting hotel at all reasonable times, available for consultation with the Company's representatives. Producer shall have as many additional representatives present at the Meeting hotel and in the Meeting as are reasonably necessary to perform its services hereunder.

### COORDINATION OF APPROVED PLAN

When the Plan is accepted by the Company as provided herein, each party to this Agreement shall designate, in writing, to the other its Plan Coordinator, and shall give the names, titles, addresses, and telephone numbers of the Plan Coordinator and an alternate Plan Coordinator.

### PAYMENT

(a) When the plan is accepted by the Company, the Company shall pay the Producer one-third (1/3) of the Producer's service fee. One-third (1/3) shall be paid on or before ten (10) days after the Meeting.

(b) On or before thirty (30) days after receipt thereof by the Company, it shall pay all statements, invoices, and bills for the Meeting that have been authorized by Company in approving the Plan and that have been approved in writing after receipt by the Producer.

(c) Upon receipt of written certification by the Producer that all statements, invoices, and bills for the Meeting have been received and submitted to the Company, the Company shall pay the balance of Producer's fee in full.

Dated this 1st day of February, 1982.

DOE PROMOTIONS, INC.

By _____
　　　　(title)

ABLE MANUFACTURING, INC.

By _____
　　　　(title)

[1] *17 Am. Jur. 2d Contracts, paras. 4–8, 39, 40, and 76; 4 Am. Jur. 2d Amusements and Exhibitions, paras. 1 et seq.*

## FORM VIII T 1.04

### (Service contract to keep a consumer-purchased item in repair)[1]

## SUPER DEPARTMENT STORES, INC.
## STAR SERVICE CONTRACT

IN CONSIDERATION of the payment of Fifty-three Dollars ($53) by John Doe of 100 Main Street, Middletown, Pennsylvania 00000 (herein called "Buyer"), to Super Department Stores, Inc. (herein called "Seller").

SELLER shall keep the Super Television Model No. 123, Serial No. 891012A (herein called the "Purchase"), purchased by Buyer on June 1, 1982, in good order and repair, and shall, at Seller's expense, furnish all material, parts, and labor necessary for that purpose, and replace the Purchase or any part thereof that is found by Seller to be defective, for a period of one (1) year from the date of delivery of the Purchase. The service shall be performed at Buyer's premises unless, in the sole discretion of Seller, it is necessary to remove the Purchase or any part thereof to the Seller's premises for proper service and repair.

THIS CONTRACT shall not cover the making of any repairs, the performance of any labor, or the furnishing of any parts for the repair or replacement of the Purchase or any part thereof where the need for such repair or replacement is caused by the negligence or want of care of the Buyer in maintaining the Purchase or by any wrongful use thereof.

DATED June 1, 1982.

SUPER DEPARTMENT STORES, INC.

By _____        _____
       (Title)                                 JOHN DOE

[1] *17 Am. Jur. 2d Contracts,* paras. 413–415 and 487; *67 Am. Jur. 2d Sales,* paras. 33 and 464; *72 Am. Jur. 2d Statute of Frauds,* para. 140. Ref. Forms IVA 1.02 and IVC 1.03. Compare Form IIIB 1.01.

# APPENDIX I
## CONSUMER CREDIT PROTECTION LAWS[1]
### (by popular names)

| | |
|---|---|
| *Electronic Fund Transfer Act* | 15 U.S.C.A. 1601, 1693–1693r |
| *Equal Credit Opportunity Act* | 15 U.S.C.A. 1601, 1691b–1691f |
| *Fair Credit Billing Act* | 15 U.S.C.A. 1601, 1602, 1610, 1631, 1632, 1637, 1666–1666j |
| *Fair Credit Reporting Act* | 15 U.S.C.A. 1601, 1681–1681t |
| *Fair Debt Collection Practice Act* | 15 U.S.C.A. 1601, 1692–1692o |
| *Truth in Leasing Act* | 15 U.S.C.A. 1601, 1640, 1667–1667e |
| *Truth in Lending Act* | 15 U.S.C.A. 1601–1614, 1631–1646, 1661–1667e, 1691f |

For REGULATION Z, see 12 C.F.R. 226, and for reprint of the new Regulation Z, effective April 1, 1981, with compliance optional until October 1, 1982, see reprint of the new regulation in 15 U.S.C.A. foll. 1700. For REGULATION M for Consumer Leasing, see 12 C.F.R. 213.

For the UNIFORM CONSUMER CREDIT CODE, adopted by some states, see Appendix IX. Check your state statutes for other consumer credit protection laws if your state has not adopted the Uniform Consumer Credit Code. See also Appendix X for the UNIFORM CONSUMER SALES PRACTICES ACT and Appendix XI for the UNIFORM DECEPTIVE TRADE PRACTICES ACT.

---

[1]*Consumer Handbook to Credit Protection Laws* (5th Printing, 1982) is prepared in layman's language and without legal citations, by the Board of Governors of the Federal Reserve System, and may be obtained by writing to the Federal Trade Commission, Legal and Public Records, Room 180, Washington, D.C. 20580.

# APPENDIX II

# ERISA

*Employment Retirement Income Security Act of 1974, as amended September 26, 1980*— 29 U.S.C.A. 1001 et. seq. For Regulations, see 29 C.F.R. 2509.75–2673.4

*Multiemployer Pension Plan Amendments Act of 1980*—29 U.S.C.A. 1322a, 1322b, and 1323

For interrelated IRS participation, see also 26 U.S.C.A. 401,[1] 402,[2] 404, 410,[3] 418–418e, and 3304

*OUTLINE OF ERISA, as amended September 26, 1980*

SUBCHAPTER I   29 U.S.C.A. 1001–1145
Subtitle A   General provisions 29 U.S.C.A. 1001–1003
Subtitle B   Regulatory provisions to protect employee benefit rights,[4] as: reporting and disclosure, participation and vesting, funding, fiduciary responsibility, administration and enforcement 29 U.S.C.A. 1021–1145

SUBCHAPTER II   29 U.S.C.A. 1201–1242
Subtitle A   Jurisdiction, administration, and enforcement by IRS, and coordination between Department of the Treasury and Department of Labor 29 U.S.C.A. 1201–1204
Subtitle B   Joint task force and studies 29 U.S.C.A. 1221–1232
Subtitle C   Enrollment of actuaries 29 U.S.C.A. 1241 and 1242

SUBCHAPTER III   29 U.S.C.A. 1301–1461
Subtitle A   Creation of Pension Benefit Guaranty Corporation (PBGC),[5] establishment of funds and portability assistance[6] 29 U.S.C.A. 1301–1309
Subtitle B   Coverage, aggregate limit on benefits and plan fiduciaries 29 U.S.C.A. 1321–1323
Subtitle C   Terminations 29 U.S.C.A. 1341–1348
Subtitle D   Liability of employer and of PBGC and lien for liability of employer 29 U.S.C.A. 1361–1368
Subtitle E   Special provisions for Multiemployer Plans,[7] including rules for employer withdrawals and for merger or transfer of plan assets or liabilities or reorganization, financial assistance, and benefits after termination 29 U.S.C.A. 1381–1453
Subtitle F   Effective dates as to various types of plans from 1974 to September 26, 1983 29 U.S.C.A. 1461

---

[1]Nondiscriminatory rule for tax-free trust status 26 U.S.C.A. 401(a)(5).
[2]Rollovers 26 U.S.C.A. 402(a)(5)(B)(i)(ii).
[3]Percentage coverage rule for tax-free trust status 26 U.S.C.A. (b)(1).
[4]Participation 29 U.S.C.A. 1052.
 Year of service 29 U.S.C.A. 1053(b).
 10-year vesting 29 U.S.C.A. 1053(a)(2)(A).
 15-year graded vesting (25% partial vesting in 5 years) 29 U.S.C.A. 1053(a)(2)(B).
 "Rule of 45 Formula" 29 U.S.C.A. 1053(a)(2)(C).
 Accrual of benefits 29 U.S.C.A. 1054.
[5]Address of Pension Guaranty Corporation is: 2020 K Street N.W., Washington, D.C. 20006, Telephone (202) 254-4817.
[6]Portability assistance 29 U.S.C.A. 1309.
[7]New multiemployer plan benefits guaranteed 29 U.S.C.A. 1322a. See also 29 U.S.C.A. 1341a and 1381 et seq.

ERISA PROCEDURE 75-1

This is the exemption procedure under Section 408(a) of ERISA and Section 4975(c) of the IRC. This joint procedure is to grant exemptions from "prohibited transactions" imposed by Sections 406(a) and 407(a) of ERISA. Ref. TIR-1367 issued by IRS on April 25, 1975

Information and/or publications explaining the benefits and requirements of ERISA plans are available from:

> Office of Communications and Public Services
> Pension and Welfare Benefit Programs
> Labor-Management Services Administration
> 200 Constitution Avenue
> Washington D.C. 20216

or from the following Labor Management Services Administration (LMSA) area offices:

Atlanta, GA 30309
1365 Peachtree Street, NE
Tel: (404) 881-4090

Boston, MA 02108
110 Tremont Street
Tel: (617) 223-6736

Buffalo, NY 14202
111 W. Huron Street
Tel: (716) 846-4861

Chicago, IL 60604
175 W. Jackson Boulevard
Tel: (312) 353-7264

Cleveland, OH 44199
1240 E. Ninth Street
Tel: (216) 522-3855

Dallas, TX 75202
Griffin & Young Streets
Tel: (214) 767-6831

Denver, CO 80294
1961 Stout Street
Tel: (303) 837-5061

Detroit, MI 48226
231 W. Lafayette Street
Tel: (313) 226-6200

Honolulu, HI 96850
300 Ala Moana
Tel: (808) 546-8984

Kansas City, MO 64106
911 Walnut Street
Tel: (816) 374-5261

Los Angeles, CA 90012
300 N. Los Angeles Street
Tel: (213) 688-4975

Miami, FL 33169
111 NW 183rd Street
Tel: (305) 350-4611

Minneapolis, MN 55403
100 N. Sixth Street
Tel: (612) 725-2292

Nashville, TN 37203
1808 West End Building
Tel: (615) 251-5906

East Orange, NJ 07018
576 Central Avenue
Tel (201) 645-3712

New Orleans, LA 70130
600 South Street
Tel: (504) 589-6173

New York NY 10007
26 Federal Plaza
Tel: (212) 264-1980

Philadelphia, PA 19106
601 Market Street
Tel: (215) 597-4961

Pittsburgh, PA 15222
1000 Liberty Avenue
Tel: (412) 644-2925

St. Louis, MO 63101
210 N. Twelfth Boulevard
Tel: (314) 425–4691

San Francisco, CA 94105
211 Main Street
Tel: (415) 556-2030

Hato Rey, PR 00918
Rm. 650, Federal Office Bldg.
Carlos Chardon Street
Tel: (809) 753-4441

Seattle, WA 98174
909 First Avenue
Tel: (206) 442-5216

Washington, DC 20036
1111 20th Street, NW
Tel: (202) 254-6510

# APPENDIX III

**UNIFORM ACKNOWLEDGMENT ACT (which supersedes the Uniform Acknowledgments Act). See also APPENDIX IV for the UNIFORM RECOGNITION OF ACKNOWLEDGMENTS ACT**

| *STATE* | *CITATION* |
|---------|------------|
| Arizona | A.R.A. 33-511 to 33-513 |
| Arkansas | Ark. Stats. 49-101 to 49-114 |
| Connecticut | C.G.S.A. 1-28 to 2-41 |
| Hawaii | HRS 502-41 et seq. |
| Idaho | I.C. 55-701 et seq. |
| Maryland | Maryland Code 1957, art. 18, 1 to 16 |
| Massachusetts | M.G.L.A. c. 183-30, 31, 33, 41 and 42; c. 183 App. Forms 13 to 16; c. 222-11 |
| Montana | MCA 1-5-101 et seq. |
| New Hampshire | RSA 456:1 to 456:15 |
| New Mexico | NMSA 1978, 14-13-4 et seq. |
| North Dakota | NDCC 47-19-13 et seq. |
| Pennsylvania | 21 P.S. 291.1 to 291.13 |
| South Dakota | SDCL 18-5-1 to 18-5-18 |
| Utah | U.C.A. 1953, 57-2-1 to 57-2-17 |
| Virgin Islands | 28 V.I.C. 81 to 93 |
| Wisconsin | W.S.A. 706.07 |
| Wyoming | W.S. 1977, 34-2-114 to 34-2-118 |

# APPENDIX IV

# UNIFORM RECOGNITION OF ACKNOWLEDGMENTS ACT[1]
## (See also APPENDIX III for Uniform Acknowledgment Act)

| STATE | CITATION |
|---|---|
| Arizona | A.R.S. 33-501 to 33-508 |
| Colorado | C.R.S. 1973, 12-55-201 to 12-55-210 |
| Connecticut | C.G.S.A. 1-57 to 1-65 |
| Delaware | 29 Del. C. 4321 to 4328 |
| Illinois | S.H.A. ch. 30, 221-230 |
| Kansas | K.S.A. 53-301 to 53-309 |
| Kentucky | KRS 423.110 to 423.190 |
| Maine | 4 M.R.S.A. 1011-1019 |
| Michigan | M.C.L.A. 565.261 to 565.270 |
| Minnesota | M.S.A. 358.32 to 358.40 |
| Nebraska | R.R.S. 1943, 64-201 to 64-211 |
| New Hampshire | RSA 456-A:1 to 456-A:9 |
| North Dakota | NDCC 47-19-14.1 to 47-19-14.8 |
| Ohio | R.C. 147.51 to 147.58 |
| Oklahoma | 49 Okl. St. Ann. 101 to 109 |
| Oregon | ORS 194.500 to 194.580 |
| South Carolina | So. Carolina Code 1976, 26-3-10 to 26-3-90 |
| Virginia | Virginia Code 1950, 55-118.1 to 55-118.9 |
| West Virginia | West Virginia Code 39-1A-1 to 39-1A-9 |
| Wisconsin | W.S.A. 706.065 |

---

[1]There is a new *Uniform Law on Notarial Acts*, which was adopted by the National Conference of Commissioners on Uniform State Laws in 1982. The new uniform law will replace both this Act and the Uniform Acknowledgment Act when it is adopted by the states. The new Act covers other notarial acts in addition to "acknowledgments," and consolidates the provisions of the present two Acts.

# APPENDIX V
# UNIFORM ARBITRATION ACT

| *STATE* | *CITATION* |
|---|---|
| Alaska | AS 09.43.010 to 09.43.180 |
| Arizona | A.R.S. 12-1501 to 12-1518 |
| Arkansas | Ark. Stats. 34-511 to 34-532 |
| Colorado | C.R.S. 1973, 13-22-201 to 13-22-223 |
| Delaware | 10 Del. C 5701 to 5725 |
| District of Columbia | D.C. Code 1981, 16-4301 to 16-4319 |
| Idaho | I.C. 7-901 to 7-922 |
| Illinois | S.H.A. ch. 10, 101 to 123 |
| Indiana | A.I.C. (West) 34-4-2-1 to 34-4-2-22 |
| Kansas | K.S.A. 5-401 to 5-422 |
| Maine | 14 M.R.S.A. 5927 to 5949 |
| Maryland | Maryland Code, Courts and Jud. P. 3-201 to 3-234 |
| Massachusetts | M.G.L.A., c. 251, 1-19 |
| Michigan | M.C.L.A. 600.5001 to 600.5035 |
| Minnesota | M.S.A. 572.08 to 572.30 |
| Missouri | V.A.M.S. 435.350 to 435.470 |
| Nevada | N.R.S. 38.015 to 38.205 |
| New Mexico | NMSA 1978, 44-7-1 to 44-7-22 |
| North Carolina | G.S. 1-567.1 to 1-567.20 |
| Oklahoma | 15 Okl. St. Ann. 801 to 818 |
| Pennsylvania | 42 Pa. C.S.A. 7301 to 7320 |
| South Carolina | So. Carolina Code 1976, 15-48-10 to 15-48-240 |
| South Dakota | SDCL 21-25A-1 to 21-25A-38 |
| Texas | Vernon's Ann. Civ. St., 224 to 238-6 |
| Wyoming | W.S. 1977, 1-36-101 to 1-36-119 |

# APPENDIX VI
## UNIFORM COMMERCIAL CODE[1]

| STATE | CITATION |
|---|---|
| Alabama | Alabama Code 1975, 7-1-101 to 7-11-108 |
| Alaska | AS 45.01.101 to 45.09.507 |
| Arizona | A.R.S. 44-2201 to 44-3307 |
| Arkansas | Ark. Stats. 85-1-101 to 85-9-507 |
| California | Ann. Cal. Com. Code (West) 1101 to 1109 |
| Colorado | C.R.S. 1973, 4-1-101 to 4-11-102 |
| Connecticut | C.G.S.A. 42a-1-101 to 42a-10-109 |
| Delaware | 6 Del. C. 1-101 to 10-104 |
| District of Columbia | D.C. Code 1981, 28:1-101 to 28:11-108 |
| Florida | F.S.A. (West) 671.101 to 680.111 |
| Georgia | O.C.G.A. 11-1-101 to 11-11-104 |
| Guam | 13 G.C.A. 1101 to 11104 |
| Hawaii | HRS 490:1-101 to 490:11-108 |
| Idaho | I.C. 28-1-101 to 28-10-104 |
| Illinois | S.H.A. ch. 26, 1-101 to 11-108 |
| Indiana | A.I.C. (West) 26-1-1-101 to 26-1-9-507 |
| Iowa | I.C.A. 554.1101 to 554.11109 |
| Kansas | K.S.A. 84-1-101 to 84-10-102 |
| Kentucky | KRS 355.1-101 to 355.10-102 |
| Louisiana (Articles 2, 6, & 9 excluded) | LSA-R.S. 10:1-101 to 10.5-117; 10.7-101 to 10.7-701; and 10:8-101 to 10:8-501 |
| Maine | 11 M.R.S.A. 1-101 to 10-108 |
| Maryland | Maryland Code, Commercial Law 1-101 to 10-112 |
| Massachusetts | M.G.L.A. 106, 1-101 to 9-507 |
| Michigan | M.C.L.A. 440.1101 to 440.11102 |
| Minnesota | M.S.A. 336.1-101 to 336.11-108 |
| Mississippi | Miss. Code 1972, 75-1-101 to 75-11-108 |
| Missouri | V.A.M.S. 400.1-101 to 400.10-102 |
| Montana | MCA 30-1-101 to 30-9-511 |
| Nebraska | Neb. U.C.C. 1-101 to 10-104 |
| Nevada | N.R.S. 104.1101 to 104.9507 |
| New Hampshire | RSA 382-A:1-101 to 382-A:9-507 |
| New Jersey | N.J.S.A. 12A:1-101 to 12A:11-108 |
| New Mexico | NMSA 1978, 55-1-101 to 55-9-507 |
| New York | McKinney's Uniform Commercial Code 1-101 to 13-105 |
| North Carolina | G.S. 25-1-101 to 25-11-108 |
| North Dakota | NDCC 41-01-02 to 41-09-53 |
| Ohio | R.C. 1301.01 to 1309.50 |
| Oklahoma | 12A Okl. St. Ann. 1-101 to 11-107 |
| Oregon | ORS 71.1010 to 79.5070 |
| Pennsylvania | 13 Pa. C.S.A. 1101 to 9507 |

---

[1]All states except Louisiana have adopted the Uniform Commercial Code, some with slight variations. Louisiana adopted Articles 1, 3, 4, 5, 7, and 8. The territories except Puerto Rico have adopted it. The Puerto Rico Code of Commerce covers most business contract topics. For example, see Title 10 LPRA 1701 and 31 LPRA 3751 et seq. for Sales and Title 19 LPRA 1 et seq. for commercial paper.

| *STATE* | *CITATION* |
|---------|------------|
| Rhode Island | Gen. Laws 1956, 6A-1-101 to 6A-9-507 |
| South Carolina | So. Carolina Code 1976, 36-1-101 to 36-10-103 |
| South Dakota | SDCL 57A-1-101 to 57A-11-108 |
| Tennessee | T.C.A. 47-1-101 to 47-9-507 |
| Texas | V.T.C.A., Bus. & Com. 1.101 to 11.108 |
| Utah | U.C.A. 1953, 70A-1-1-1 to 70A-11-108 |
| Vermont | 9A V.S.A. 1-101 to 9-507 |
| Virgin Islands | 11A V.I.C. 1-101 to 9-507 |
| Virginia | Virginia Code 1950, 8.1-101 to 8.11-108 |
| Washington | RCWA (West) 62A:1-101 to 62A:11-109 |
| West Virginia | West Virginia Code 46-1-101 to 46-11-108 |
| Wisconsin | W.S.A. 401.101 to 409.905 |
| Wyoming | W.S. 1977, 34-21-101 to 34-21-1002 |

# APPENDIX VII

## UNIFORM COMMERCIAL CODE DEFINITIONS
### (general definitions U.C.C. 1-201)

**– A –**

ACCELERATION (of payment or performance) U.C.C. 2-610 and 2-611. See also WHEN HE DEEMS HIMSELF INSECURE
ACCEPTANCE: U.C.C. 2-102, 2-106, 2-606, 2-607, 2-608, 3-410. See also AT WILL
ACCOMMODATION PARTY: U.C.C. 3-415
AGREEMENT: U.C.C. 1-201(3). Compare CONTRACT
AIRBILL: U.C.C. 1-201(6)
ALLOCATION OR DIVISION OF RISK: U.C.C. 2-303, 2-509, 2-510
ALTERATION (of commercial paper): U.C.C. 3-407. See also UNAUTHORIZED SIGNATURE
AT WILL (option to accelerate payment or performance): 1-208. See also WHEN HE DEEMS HIMSELF INSECURE
AUCTION SALE: U.C.C. 2-328

**– B –**

BAILEE: U.C.C. 7-102
BANKS: U.C.C. 1-201(4) and 4-101 et seq.
BANKERS' CREDIT: U.C.C. 2-325. See also LETTER OF CREDIT and CONFIRMED CREDIT
BANKING: U.C.C. 4-104
BEARER: U.C.C. 1-201(5) and 8-102(1)(e)
BETWEEN MERCHANTS: U.C.C. 2-104(3). See also MERCHANT
BILL OF LADING: U.C.C. 1-201(6), 2-323, and 7-301 through 7-309, 7-401 et seq.
BONA FIDE PURCHASER: U.C.C. 8-302
BRANCH BANK: U.C.C. 1-201(7)
BULK TRANSFERS (definitions and documents required in addition to the contract of sale or transfer): U.C.C. 6-101 et seq.
BURDEN OF ESTABLISHING: U.C.C. 1-201(8)
BUYER: U.C.C. 2-103(a)
BUYER IN ORDINARY COURSE OF BUSINESS: U.C.C. 1-201(9)

**– C –**

C & F or C.F.: U.C.C. 2-320, 2-321
CIF.: U.C.C. 2-320
CANCELLATION: U.C.C. 2-106(4)
CERTIFICATE OF DEPOSIT: U.C.C. 3-104
CERTIFICATION: U.C.C. 3-411
CERTIFICATED SECURITY: U.C.C. 8-102(1)(a), (c), (d), and 8-105
CHECK: U.C.C. 3-104
CLEARING CORPORATION: U.C.C. 8-102(3)
COMMERCIAL PAPER (general definitions and exceptions): U.C.C. 3-102, 3-103
COMMERICAL UNIT: U.C.C. 2-105(6)
CONFIRMED CREDIT: U.C.C. 2-325. See also BANKER'S CREDIT and LETTER OF CREDIT
CONFORMING TO CONTRACT: U.C.C. 2-106
CONSIGNMENT: U.C.C. 2-326(3), 7-102, 9-114
CONSPICUOUS (in reference to appearance of a term or clause in a commercial instrument): U.C.C. 1-201(10)
CONSUMER GOODS: U.C.C. 9-109
CONTRACT: U.C.C. 1-201(11) and 2-106. Compare AGREEMENT
CONTRACT FOR SALE U.C.C. 2-106(1)
COURSE OF DEALING: U.C.C. 1-205. Compare USAGE OF TRADE

C (continued)

COVER: U.C.C. 2-711 and 2-712
CREDITOR: U.C.C. 1-201(12)

**— D —**

DAMAGES FOR BREACH OF CONTRACT FOR SALE OF GOODS: U.C.C. 2-702 et seq.
DAMAGES FROM BANKS: U.C.C. 4-103 et seq.
DEFINITE TIME: U.C.C. 3-109
DELIVERY: U.C.C. 1-201(14), 2-308, 2-309, 2-503, 2-505, 2-507, 2-614, 2-615, 2-616
DISHONOR: U.C.C. 3-507, 3-508
DOCUMENT OF TITLE: U.C.C. 1.201(15) and 7-101 et seq., 9-105(b)
DRAFT: U.C.C. 3-104 and 3-801 E
DULY NEGOTIATE: U.C.C. 7-501

**— E —**

ENDORSEMENTS: See INDORSEMENTS
ENTRUSTING: U.C.C. 2-403
EXCLUSIVE DEALING: U.C.C. 2-306
EX-SHIP: U.C.C. 2-322

**— F —**

F.A.S.: U.C.C. 2-319
FAULT: U.C.C. 1-201(16)
FINANCING AGENCY: U.C.C. 2-104(2) and 2-506
F.O.B.: U.C.C. 2-319
FORGERY: See UNAUTHORIZED SIGNATURE OR INDORSEMENT
FUNGIBLE: U.C.C. 1-201(17)
FUTURE GOODS: U.C.C. 2-105

**— G —**

GENUINE (as to legal instruments regulated by the U.C.C.): U.C.C. 1-201(18)
GOOD FAITH: U.C.C. 1-201(19), 2-103(b), 2-403, and 7-404
GOODS: U.C.C. 2-102, 2-105, 7-102. See also FUTURE GOODS
GUARANTOR: See SURETY

**— H —**

HOLDER: U.C.C. 1-201(20)
HOLDER IN DUE COURSE: U.C.C. 3-302
HONOR: U.C.C. 1-201(21)

**— I —**

IDENTIFICATION OF GOODS: U.C.C. 2-501 and 2-613. See also GOODS and INSURABLE
  INTEREST
INSPECTION: U.C.C. 2-512 and 2-513
INSOLVENCY PROCEEDINGS: U.C.C. 1-201(22)
INDORSEMENTS: U.C.C. 3-204, 3-205, 3-206, and 3-208. See also UNAUTHORIZED
  SIGNATURE
INSOLVENT: U.C.C. 1-201(23) and 2-502
INSTALLMENT CONTRACT: U.C.C. 2-612
INSURABLE INTEREST IN GOODS: U.C.C. 2-501. See also GOODS and IDENTIFICATION OF
  GOODS
INVESTMENT SECURITIES (general definitions): U.C.C. 8-102
ISSUE (of commercial paper): U.C.C. 3-102(a), 7-102, and 8-201

**— J —**

JOINT PAYEES: U.C.C. 3-116(b)
JUDGMENT (power to confess in commercial paper): U.C.C. 3-112

**– K –**

KNOWLEDGE: U.C.C. 1-201(25)

**– L –**

LETTER OF ADVICE: U.C.C. 3-701
LETTER OF CREDIT: U.C.C. 2-325, 5-101 et seq. See also BANKERS' CREDIT and CON-
FIRMED CREDIT
LOT: U.C.C. 2-105(5) and 2-307

**– M –**

MERCHANT: U.C.C. 2-104. See also BETWEEN MERCHANTS

**– N –**

NEGOTIABLE INSTRUMENT: U.C.C. 3-104
NEGOTIATION: U.C.C. 3-202, 3-207, 7-501
NO ARRIVAL, NO SALE: U.C.C. 2-324
NOTE: U.C.C. 3-104
NOTICE: U.C.C. 1-201(25), (26), (27), 3-803. See also SEND and TELEGRAM

**– O –**

ON DEMAND: U.C.C. 3-108
ORDER (in commercial paper): U.C.C. 3-102(b)
ORGANIZATION: U.C.C. 1-201(28)
OUTPUT OF SELLER: U.C.C. 2-306
OVERISSUE (of a security): U.C.C. 8-104
OVERSEAS: U.C.C. 2-323

**– P –**

PARTY: U.C.C. 1-201(29)
PAYMENT (of commercial paper): U.C.C. 3-603 and 3-604
PERSON: U.C.C. 1-201(30) and 2-707
PERSON IN POSITION OF SELLER: U.C.C. 2-707. See also PERSON
PRESENT SALE: U.C.C. 2-106(1). See also SALE
PRESENTMENT (of commercial paper): U.C.C. 3-504
PRESUMPTION or PRESUMED: U.C.C. 1-201(31)
PRICE: U.C.C. 2-304, 2-305, 2-511, and 2-709
PROMISE: U.C.C. 3-102(c) and 3-105
PROTEST (of commercial paper): U.C.C. 3-509
PURCHASE and PURCHASER: U.C.C. 1-201(31) and (32)

**– R –**

REASONABLE TIME: U.C.C. 1-204
RECEIPT OF GOODS: U.C.C. 2-103(c)
REGISTERED (form of certificated security): U.C.C. 8-102(1)(d)
REJECTION OF GOODS: U.C.C. 2-602 through 2-605
REMEDY: U.C.C. 1-201(34) and 2-702 et seq. See also RIGHTS
RENUNCIATION (of rights in commercial paper): U.C.C. 3-605
REPRESENTATIVE: U.C.C. 1-201(35)
REQUIREMENTS OF BUYER: U.C.C. 2-306
RIGHTS: U.C.C. 1-201(36). See also REMEDY and RENUNCIATION

**– S –**

SALE (generally): U.C.C. definitions in 2-104, 2-105, and 2-106
SALE ON APPROVAL: U.C.C. 2-326(1)(a) and 2-327. Compare CONSIGNMENT and SALE OR
RETURN
SALE OR RETURN: U.C.C. 2-326(1)(b) and 2-327. Compare CONSIGNMENT and SALE ON
APPROVAL
SEASONABLY: U.C.C. 1-204(3)

S (continued)

SECONDARY PARTY (commercial paper): U.C.C. 3-102(d)
SECURED PARTY: U.C.C. 9-105(1)(m)
SECURITY AGREEMENT: U.C.C. 9-105(1)(1)
SECURITY INTEREST (general definitions): U.C.C. 9-105
SECURITY INTERESTS EXCEPTED: U.C.C. 9-104
SELLER: U.C.C. 2-103(d)
SEND: U.C.C. 1-201(38)
SIGNATURE: U.C.C. 3-401 through 3-406. See also ALTERATION and UNAUTHORIZED
   SIGNATURE
SIGNED: U.C.C. 1-201(39)
SUBSEQUENT PURCHASER (of investment security): U.C.C. 8-102(2)
SUM CERTAIN: U.C.C. 3-106
SURETY: U.C.C. 1-201(40)

## — T —

TELEGRAM: U.C.C. 1-201(41)
TERM: U.C.C. 1-201(42). See also AGREEMENT
TERMINATION: U.C.C. 2-106
THIRD PARTY (commercial paper): U.C.C. 1-202, 3-803
TITLE TO GOODS SOLD: U.C.C. 2-401

## — U —

UNAUTHORIZED SIGNATURE: U.C.C. 1-201(43). See also FORGERY and ALTERATION
UNDERLYING OBLIGATION (commercial paper): U.C.C. 3-802
UNDER PROTEST: U.C.C. 1-207. See also WITHOUT PREJUDICE
UNLIKE GOODS (treated as like): U.C.C. 1-201(17)
USAGE OF TRADE: U.C.C. 1-205. Compare COURSE OF DEALING

## — V —

VALUE: U.C.C. 1-201(44)

## — W —

WAREHOUSE RECEIPT: U.C.C. 1-201(45), 7-201 through 210, and 7-401 et seq.
WARRANTIES (sale of goods): U.C.C. 2-312, 2-313, 2-314, 2-315, 2-316, 2-317, and 2-318
WHEN HE DEEMS HIMSELF INSECURE: U.C.C. 1-208. See also AT WILL
WITHOUT PREJUDICE: U.C.C. 1-207. See also UNDER PROTEST and ACCELERATION
WRITTEN OR WRITING: U.C.C. 1-201(46)

# APPENDIX VIII

## UNIFORM CONDOMINIUM ACT (1977) and (1980)
## or VARIATIONS REGULATING CONDOMINIUM OWNERSHIP[1]

| *STATE* | *CITATION* |
|---------|-----------|
| Florida | F.S.A. (West) 718.101 to 718.622 |
| Illinois | Ill. Rev. Stat. (1979) 30-301 et seq. |
| Maine | 33 M.R.S.A. 560-587 |
| Minnesota | M.S.A. 515A.1-101 to 515A.4-117 |
| New Mexico | NMSA 1978 47-7-1 et seq. |
| Ohio | R.C. 5311.01 et seq. |
| Oregon | ORS 91.500-671 and 91.990 |
| Pennsylvania | 68 Pa. C.S.A. 3101 to 3414 |
| South Carolina | So. Carolina Code 27-31-10 |
| Virginia[2] | Virginia Code 55-79.39 to 55-79.103 |
| West Virginia | West Virginia Code 36B-1-101 to 36B-4-115 |

---

[1]The above citations include citations to state statutes that adopted either the original or amended uniform act, or that contain some of the same or similar provisions. The list is not exhaustive. Check your state condominium statutes before preparing condominium or condominium time-sharing documents.

[2]*The Model Real Estate Time Share Act (1980) and (1982)* has also been enacted in the State of Virginia.

# APPENDIX IX
## UNIFORM CONSUMER CREDIT CODE (U.C.C.C.)[1]

| *STATE* | *CITATION* |
|---|---|
| Colorado | C.R.S. 1973, 5-1-101 to 5-9-103 |
| Guam | 14 G.C.A. 1101 to 8103 |
| Idaho | I.C. 28-31-101 to 28-39-108 |
| Indiana | A.I.C. (West) 24-4.5-1-101 to 24-4.5-6-203 |
| Iowa | I.C.A. 537 |
| Kansas | K.S.A. 16a-1-101 et seq. |
| Maine | 9A M.R.S.A. 1.101-6.415 |
| Oklahoma | 14A Okl. St. Ann. 1-101 to 9-101 |
| South Carolina | So. Carolina Code 1976 37-1-101 to 37-9-102 |
| Utah | U.C.A. 1953, 70B-1-101 to 70B-11-105 |
| Wisconsin | W.S.A. 421.101 to 427.105 |
| Wyoming | W.S. 1977, 40-14-101 to 40-14-702 |

---

[1]See Appendix I for citations to Federal Credit Protection Laws.

# APPENDIX X
## UNIFORM CONSUMER SALES PRACTICES ACT[1]

| STATE | CITATION |
|-------|----------|
| Kansas | K.S.A. 50-623 to 50-643 |
| Ohio | R.C. 1345.01 to 1345.13 |
| Oklahoma | 15 Okl. Stat. 721, 722 and 753 |
| Utah | U.C.A. 1953, 13-11-1 to 13-11-23 |

---

[1]See also Appendix I for Federal Consumer Protection Laws; Appendix VIII for Uniform Consumer Credit Code; and Appendix XI for Uniform Deceptive Trade Practices Act. Many states combine the provisions of these Codes and Acts as their "consumer protection laws." Check your state statutes. For example, see the *South Carolina Consumer Protection Code* 37-1-101 to 37-9-102, and the Puerto Rican consumer protection laws administered by the Puerto Rico Department of Consumer Affairs, as they appear in 3 LPRA 341 et seq.

# APPENDIX XI
# UNIFORM DECEPTIVE TRADE PRACTICES ACT

| *STATE* | *CITATION* |
|---------|------------|
| Colorado | C.R.S. 1973, 6-1-101 to 6-1-114 |
| Delaware | 6 Del. C. 2531 et seq. |
| Georgia | O.C.G.A. 10-1-370 to 10-1-375 |
| Hawaii | HRS 481A-1 to 481A-5 |
| Illinois | 38IRS 121½-311-317 |
| Maine | 10 M.R.S.A. 1211-1216 |
| Minnesota | M.S.A. 3250.43 to 3250.48 |
| Nebraska | N.R.S. 1943, 87-301 to 87-306 |
| New Mexico | NMSA 1978, 57-12-1 to 57-12-16 |
| Ohio | R.C. 4165.01 to 4165.04 |
| Oklahoma | 15 Okl. Stat. 751-765 |
| Oregon | ORS 646.605 to 646.656 |

# APPENDIX XII

## UNIFORM FRAUDULENT CONVEYANCE ACT

| STATE | CITATION |
|---|---|
| Arizona | A.R.S. 44-1001 to 44-1013 |
| California | Cal. Civ. Code (West) 3439 to 3439.12 |
| Delaware | 6 Del. C. 1301 to 1312 |
| Idaho | I.C. 55-910 to 55-922 |
| Maryland | Maryland Code, Comm. Law, 15-201 to 15-214 |
| Massachusetts | M.G.L.A. c. 109A, 1-13 |
| Michigan | M.C.L.A. 566.11 to 566.23 |
| Minnesota | M.S.A. 513.20 to 513.32 |
| Montana | MCA 31-2-301 to 31-2-325 |
| Nebraska | R.R.S. 1943, 36-601 to 36-613 |
| Nevada | N.R.S. 112.010 to 112.130 |
| New Hampshire | RSA 545.1 to 545.12 |
| New Jersey | N.J.S.A. 25:2-7 to 25:2-19 |
| New Mexico | NMSA 1978, 56-10-1 to 56-10-13 |
| New York | McKinney's Debtor and Creditor Law, 270 to 281 |
| North Dakota | NDCC 13-02-01 to 13-02-11 |
| Ohio | R.C. 1336.01 to 1336.12 |
| Oklahoma | 24 Okl. Stat. Ann. 101 to 111 |
| Pennsylvania | 39 P.S. 351 to 363 |
| South Dakota | SDCL 54-8-5 to 54-8-19 |
| Tennessee | T.C.A. 64-308 to 64-321 |
| Utah | U.C.A. 1953, 25-1-1 to 25-1-16 |
| Virgin Islands | 28 V.I.C. 201-212 |
| Washington | RCWA (West) 19.40.010 to 19.40.130 |
| Wisconsin | W.S.A. 242.01 to 242.13 |
| Wyoming | W.S. 1977, 34-14-101 to 34-14-113 |

# APPENDIX XIII

## UNIFORM LIMITED PARTNERSHIP ACT (1916)
## and REVISED UNIFORM PARTNERSHIP ACT (1976)[1]

| STATE | CITATION |
|---|---|
| Alabama | Ala. Code 1975, 10-9-1 to 10-9-91 |
| Alaska | AS 32.10.010 to 32.10.290 |
| Arizona (1976) | A.R.S. 29-301 to 29-363 |
| Arkansas (1976) | Ark. Stats. 65-501 to 65-566 |
| California (1976) | Cal. Corp. Code Ann. (West) 15511 to 15623 |
| Colorado (1976) | C.R.S. 1973, 7-62-101 to 7-62-1201 |
| Connecticut (1976) | C.G.S.A. 34-9 to 34-38n |
| Delaware (1976) | 6 Del. C. 17-101 to 17-1107 |
| District of Columbia | D.C. Code 1981, 41-201 to 41-229 |
| Florida | F.S.A. (West) 620.01 to 620.32 |
| Georgia | O.C.G.A. 14-9-1 to 14-9-91 |
| Hawaii | HRS 425-21 to 425-52 |
| Idaho (1976) | I.C. 53-201 to 53-267 |
| Illinois | S.H.A. c. 106½, 44-73 |
| Indiana | A.I.C. (West) 23-4-2-1 to 23-4-2-30 |
| Iowa (1976) | I.C.A. 545.101 to 545.1106 |
| Kansas | K.S.A. 56-122 to 56-151 |
| Kentucky | KRS 362.410 to 362.700 |
| Maine | 31 M.R.S.A. 151 to 181 |
| Maryland (1976) | Maryland Code, Corps. and Ass'ns, 10-101 to 10-1104 |
| Massachusetts (1976) | M.G.L.A. c. 109, 1 to 62 |
| Michigan (1976) | M.C.L.A. 449.1101 to 449.2108 |
| Minnesota (1976) | M.S.A. 322A.01 to 322A.87 |
| Mississippi | Miss. Code 1972, 79-13-1 to 79-13-57 |
| Missouri | V.A.M.S. 359.010 to 359.290 |
| Montana (1976) | MCA 35-12-501 to 35-12-1404 |
| Nebraska (1976) | R.R.S. 1943, 67-233 to 67-297 |
| Nevada | N.R.S. 88.010 to 88.310 |
| New Hampshire | RSA 305:1 to 305:30 |
| New Jersey | N.J.S.A. 42:2-1 to 42:2-30 |
| New Mexico | NMSA 1978, 54-2-1 to 54-2-30 |
| New York | McKinney's Partnership Law, 90 to 120 |
| North Carolina | G.S. 59-1 to 59-30 |
| North Dakota | NDCC 45-10-01 to 45-12-04 |
| Ohio | R.C. 1781.01 to 1781.27 |
| Oklahoma | 54 Okl. St. Ann. 141 to 171 |
| Oregon | ORS 69.150 to 69.530 |
| Pennsylvania | 59 Pa. C.S.A 501 to 545 |
| Rhode Island | Gen. Laws 1956, 7-13-1 to 7-13-31 |
| South Carolina | So. Carolina Code 1976, 33-43-10 to 33-43-300 |

---

[1]All states except Louisiana have adopted one or the other version of the Uniform Limited Partnership Act. Of the territories, the Virgin Islands has adopted the Limited Partnership Act. To compare general partnership regulation see the Uniform Partnership Act, in Appendix XIV.

| *STATE* | *CITATION* |
|---|---|
| South Dakota | SDCL 48-6-1 to 48-6-64 |
| Tennessee | T.C.A. 61-2-101 to 61-2-130 |
| Texas | Vernon's Ann. Civ. St. art 6132a |
| Utah | U.S.A. 1953, 48-2-1 to 48-2-27 |
| Vermont | 11 V.S.A. 1391 to 1419 |
| Virgin Islands | 26 V.I.C. 201 to 228 |
| Virginia | Virginia Code 1950, 50-44 to 50-73 |
| Washington (1976) | RCWA (West) 25.10.010 to 25.10.690 |
| West Virginia (1976) | W. Virginia Code, 47-9-1 to 47-9-63 |
| Wisconsin | W.S.A. 179.01 to 179.30 |
| Wyoming (1976) | W.S. 1977, 17-14-201 to 17-14-1104 |

# APPENDIX XIV

# UNIFORM PARTNERSHIP (GENERAL) ACT[1]

| STATE | CITATION |
|---|---|
| Alabama | Ala. Code 1975, 1-8-1 to 10-8-103 |
| Alaska | AS 32.05.010 to 32.05.430 |
| Arizona | A.R.S. 29-201 to 29-244 |
| Arkansas | Ark. Stats. 65-101 to 65-143 |
| California | Ann. Cal. Corp. Code (West) 15001 to 15045 |
| Colorado | C.R.S. 1973, 7-60-101 to 7-60-143 |
| Connecticut | C.G.S.A. 34-39 to 34-82 |
| Delaware | 6 Del. C. 1501 to 1543 |
| District of Columbia | D.C. Code 1981, 41-101 to 41-142 |
| Florida | F.S.A. (West) 620.56 to 620.77 |
| Guam | G.C.C. 2395 to 2472 |
| Hawaii | HRS 425-101 to 425-143 |
| Idaho | I.C. 53-301 to 53-343 |
| Illinois | S.H.A. ch. 106½, 1-43 |
| Indiana | A.I.C. (West) 23-4-1-1 to 23-4-1-43 |
| Iowa | I.C.A. 544.1 to 544.43 |
| Kansas | K.S.A. 56-301 to 56-343 |
| Kentucky | KRS 362.150 to 362.360 |
| Maine | 31 M.R.S.A. 281-323 |
| Maryland | Maryland Code, Corps. and Ass'ns, 9-101 to 9-703 |
| Massachusetts | M.G.L.A. c. 108A, 1 to 44 |
| Michigan | M.C.L.A. 449.1 to 449.43n |
| Minnesota | M.S.A. 323.01 to 323.43 |
| Mississippi | Miss. Code 1972, 79-12-1 to 79-12-85 |
| Missouri | V.A.M.S. 358.010 to 358.430 |
| Montana | MCA 35-10-101 to 35-10-615 |
| Nebraska | R.R.S. 1943, 67-301 to 67-343 |
| Nevada | N.R.S. 87.010 to 87.430 |
| New Hampshire | RSA 304-A:1 to 304-A:43 |
| New Jersey | N.J.S.A. 42:1-1 to 42:1-43 |
| New Mexico | NMSA 1978, 54-1-1 to 54-1-43 |
| New York | McKinney's Partnership Law, 1 to 74 |
| North Carolina | G.S. 59-31 to 59-73 |
| North Dakota | NDCC 45-05-01 to 45-09-15 |
| Ohio | R.C. 1775.01 to 1775.42 |
| Oklahoma | 54 Okl. St. Ann. 201 to 244 |
| Oregon | ORS 68.010 to 68.650 |
| Pennsylvania | 59 Pa. C.S.A. 301 to 365 |
| Rhode Island | Gen. Laws 1956, 7-12-12 to 7-12-55 |
| South Carolina | So. Carolina Code 1976, 33-41-10 to 33-41-1090 |
| South Dakota | SDCL 48-1-1 to 48-5-56 |
| Tennessee | T.C.A. 61-1-101 to 61-1-142 |
| Texas | Vernon's Ann. Civ. St. art. 6132b |

---

[1]All states except Georgia and Louisiana have adopted the Uniform Partnership Act. The territories, except Puerto Rico, have adopted the Act. For the Uniform Limited Partnership Act, see Appendix XIII.

| *STATE* | *CITATION* |
|---|---|
| Utah | U.C.A. 1953, 48-1-1 to 48-1-40 |
| Vermont | 11 V.S.A. 1121 to 1335 |
| Virgin Islands | 26 V.I.C. 1 to 135 |
| Virginia | Virginia Code 1950, 50-1 to 50-43 |
| Washington | RCWA (West) 25.04.010 to 25.04.430 |
| West Virginia | West Virginia Code, 47-8A-1 to 47-8A-45 |
| Wisconsin | W.S.A. 178.01 to 178.39 |
| Wyoming | W.S. 1977, 17-13-101 to 17-13-615 |

# Index